ATLAS

OF THE

IRISH
RURAL
LANDSCAPE

Edited by
F. H. A. Aalen,
Kevin Whelan
and
Matthew Stout

University of Toronto Press
Toronto   Buffalo

Published in Ireland, UK and Europe by
Cork University Press
University College, Cork, Ireland

Published in North America in 1997 by
University of Toronto Press Incorporated

ISBN 0 8020 4294 5

Canadian Cataloguing in Publication Data

Main entry under title:

Atlas of the Irish Rural Landscape

Includes bibliographical references and index.
ISBN 0-8020-4294-5

1. Landscape changes - Ireland - Maps. 2. Man - Influence
on nature - Ireland - Maps. 3. Land use, Rural - Ireland -
History - Maps. 4. Ireland - Geography. I. Aalen, F. H. A.
II. Whelan, Kevin. III. Stout, Matthew.

G1831.G4A84 1997 333.76'09415'022 C97-930818-6

Colour Reproduction by Phototype-Set Ltd., Dublin
Printed in China through Phoenix Offset.

CONTENTS

THE CHALLENGE OF CHANGE

REGIONAL CASE STUDIES

LIST OF CONTRIBUTORS

Professor F. H. A. Aalen, lectures in cultural geography, landscape history and planning in the Department of Geography, Trinity College, Dublin. His publications include *Man and the landscape in Ireland* (1978), *The future of the Irish landscape* (ed.) (1985) and *Landscape study and management* (ed.) (1996).

Dr Gillian Barrett is Senior Lecturer in Geography at the University of Wolverhampton. Since 1989 her research has concentrated on aerial survey and photography in Ireland, designed to record cropmark images and also to monitor the scale and implications of landscape change.

Üte Bohnsack was educated at the University of Hanover, Germany and in UCD. She now lives in Kilfenora, county Clare and works as a freelance environmental consultant and REPS planner.

Professor R. H. Buchanan formerly lectured in the Geography Department, The Queen's University of Belfast, and was Director of the Institute of Irish Studies in the university. He is presently chairman of the National Trust in Northern Ireland. Publications include *Man and his habitat* (ed. with E. Jones and D. McCourt) (1971) and *Province, city and people - Belfast and its region* (ed. with B. Walker) (1987).

Billy Colfer is a school teacher and local historian, resident in the Hook peninsula, county Wexford. He has written about various aspects of Wexford's history and heritage. Publications include 'Anglo-Norman settlement in county Wexford' in *Wexford. History and society* (1987) and *Historic Hook Head* (1992).

Dr David Drew is Senior Lecturer in the Department of Geography, Trinity College, Dublin with a particular interest in the hydrology and landforms of karstic regions of Ireland. Publications include *Man-Environment processes* (1983) and *Groundwater and karstification in mid-Galway, south Mayo and north Clare* (with D. Daly) (1993).

Professor P. J. Duffy, a graduate of UCD, lectures in the Department of Geography, St Patrick's College, Maynooth. His interests are rural and historical geography. Publications include *Landscapes of South Ulster - a parish atlas of the diocese of Clogher* (1993).

Dr John Feehan lectures in the Resource and Environment Policy Centre, University College, Dublin. His publications include *The landscape of Slieve Bloom* (Dublin, 1979), *Environment and development in Ireland* (Dublin, 1992) and *The bogs of Ireland* (with G. O'Donovan) (Dublin, 1996).

Dr Fred Hamond, a graduate in archaeology of Cambridge University, lives in Belfast where he has been a freelance industrial archaeologist since 1987. He has worked on a number of mill restoration projects throughout Ireland and co-edited *Landscape archaeology in Ireland* (1983).

Dr Eilis Kennedy studied environmental science at the Dublin Institute of Technology and the University of Ulster. Her major research interests are in the rural environment and she is presently employed in an environmental consultancy in Dublin.

Dr James Killen is Senior Lecturer in the Department of Geography, Trinity College, Dublin. His major research interest is transport in Dublin and Ireland, past and present. Among his publications is *Mathematical programming methods for geographers and planners* (1983) and 'Transport in Dublin: past, present and future' in *Dublin city and county* (1992).

Sadhbh McElveen is a graduate of the National College of Art and Design in Dublin with a diploma in Wildlife Illustration from Carmarthen College in Wales. She works freelance in Dunsany, county Meath, painting mainly in wash and watercolour.

Professor G. F. Mitchell is Fellow Emeritus, Trinity College, Dublin, and former President of the Royal Irish Academy. His numerous writings cover Irish Quaternary history, archaeology and environmental issues and include *Shell guide to reading the Irish landscape* (1986) and *Man and environment in Valencia Island* (1989).

Terence Reeves-Smyth is an archaeologist and architectural historian working in the Environment and Heritage Service (Northern Ireland). He has published books on gardens, architecture and archaeology and was co-editor of *Landscape archaeology in Ireland* (1983).

Tim Robinson was born in England, studied mathematics at Cambridge and worked as a visual artist before moving to the Aran Islands, and later to Connemara. His publications include maps of Aran, the Burren and Connemara, a two-volume study, *Stones of Aran* (1993) and *Setting foot on the shores of Connemara* (1996).

Dr Colin Rynne is a Cork-based archaeologist and curator of the Cork Butter Museum. His research interests focus on early medieval Ireland, especially on mills and milling. His publications include *The archaeology of Cork city and harbour* (Cork, 1993).

Dr Andrew Stott was formerly Landscape Assessment Officer at the Countryside and Wildlife Branch, DoE NI, helping to promote and designate Areas of Outstanding Natural Beauty in Northern Ireland, and is now responsible for strategic research and monitoring at the Wildlife and Countryside Directorate of DoE in Bristol.

Geraldine Stout is an archaeologist with the Archaeological Survey of Ireland and formerly co-director of its Sites and Monuments Record Office. Her publications include *Archaeological survey of the barony of Ikerrin* (1984) and articles on the Boyne Valley and other parts of Ireland.

Dr Matthew Stout is cartographer, Department of Geography, Trinity College, Dublin. His main research interests are in early medieval Irish settlement and his publications include articles and *The Irish ringfort* (1997).

Dr Roy Tomlinson is Senior Lecturer and head of the Department of Geography, School of Geosciences, The Queen's University of Belfast where his teaching specialisms are biogeography and remote sensing. He has long-standing research interests in Irish peatlands and woodlands and was closely involved with the CORINE land cover mapping of Ireland.

Professor Kevin Whelan, geographer and historian and former Royal Irish Academy Fellow, is currently visiting Professor in the Department of History, University of Notre Dame, Indiana. Among his publications are *Wexford: history and society* (ed.) (1987), *Common ground* (ed. with W. Smyth) (1988), *Dublin city and county* (ed. with F. Aalen) (1992) and *Tree of liberty* (1996).

PREFACE AND ACKNOWLEDGEMENTS

This atlas seeks to increase appreciation of the Irish rural landscape as a central element of national heritage, to demonstrate its relevance in education and public policies, and to inspire fresh approaches to landscape study and management. The work explores the physical and human elements which give the landscape its distinctive character, emphasising the human elements such as settlements, fields, buildings, demesnes, archaeological and historical monuments, woodlands and bogs. The whole island is covered, with contributors from north and south.

Drawing on numerous disciplines, the atlas shows how the landscape was moulded by human activities from prehistoric times and how it is currently managed. The immense ecological, educational, aesthetic and economic significance of the landscape is stressed. In drawing attention to contemporary forces of change, the atlas underscores the need for more informed care of our landscape and the promotion of a modern way of life in rural areas which understands and respects landscape heritage, enriching rather than diminishing it.

This atlas complements the general Atlas of Ireland published by the Royal Irish Academy in 1979 and the Academy's Irish Historic Towns Atlas produced since 1986 as a series of fascicles. The project was initiated with a pilot study carried out in 1992/3 under the auspices of the Academy. An advisory committee was established by the Academy which helped to determine the general structure of the atlas and consisted of the editors, the Honorary Secretary of the Irish National Committee for Geography (Royal Irish Academy), Professor R. Buchanan and Dr R. Tomlinson of Queen's University, Belfast, Professor W. Smyth of University College, Cork and Professor Anngret Simms of University College, Dublin. The National Committee for Geography has provided sustained encouragement to the editors in completing the atlas.

Generous financial support, absolutely crucial to the production of the atlas, was given by the National Heritage Council, Department of Arts, Culture and the Gaeltacht. The editors are deeply grateful for this assistance and for the kind involvement of Lord Killanin, the chairman of the Council, who officially launched the pilot study. Funding was also received from the Office of Public Works, the Northern Ireland Department of Education, Bord Failte, Coillte and the Trinity College Dublin Trust; we express our sincere thanks to each for their interest and generosity.

The editors wish to thank the many individuals and organisations who have assisted them. First and foremost, we are grateful to the contributors, whose time and expertise were readily given without remuneration. We applaud them for their commitment and patience during a convoluted editing process. Matthew Stout, in addition to wider editorial duties, was responsible for the cartography and for laying out the pages and arranging the text and figures. Brian MacDonald assisted enthusiastically with the administration and cartography from 1994 to 1995 and was succeeded by Miriam Crowley who efficiently coordinated and brought the project to completion. Eileen Russell, Terence Dunne, Richard Haworth and Sheila McMorrow of the Department of Geography in Trinity College have been unfailingly helpful even in the midst of other onerous duties. Sadhbh McElveen, Maura Shaffrey and Daphne Levinge have made attractive artistic contributions and Caroline Moloney gave expert advice on the format of the atlas.

As well as financial support, the Office of Public Works provided numerous excellent photographs and other materials, and access to the Sites and Monuments Record allowed the production of new and more complete distribution maps of archaeological sites. In this context, we are particularly indebted to the constant support of Eugene Keane (Assistant Principal Officer), and for the assistance of David Sweetman (Chief Archaeologist), Victor Buckley (Senior Archaeologist), Edward Bourke (Archaeologist), Geraldine Stout (Archaeologist), Muiris de Buitleir and Sharon McMenamin of the GIS Section and Con Brogan, John Scarry and Anthony Roche of the Photographic Section. The Environment and Heritage Service in Northern Ireland has also been supportive and we are especially grateful to Brian Williams, Claire Foley and Gail Pollock who obtained vital photographs and archaeological data which made it possible to compile distribution maps for the whole island.

We make grateful individual acknowledgement for an abundance of high quality photographs. Our major debt to the impressive photography of Daphne Pochin Mould, Gillian Barrett and Michael Diggin will be readily apparent; each showed an informed interest in the atlas, for which we are deeply appreciative. Aerofilms Ltd, Walter Pfeiffer Studios Ltd and the Ordnance Survey of Ireland were also productive sources of high quality photographs. Barry O'Reilly, Brian MacDonald, Maura Shaffrey, Terence Dunne and Brian Redmond donated numerous fine photographs, many taken specifically for the atlas. Photographs by Mark Costello, Edward Culleton, Elizabeth FitzPatrick, Grafton Architects, Mark Hennessey, David Hickie, John Ironside, Alan Johnston, McAdam Design, Theresa McDonald, Conleth Manning, Mansil Miller, Noel Mitchel, Patrick Nolan, Margaret O'Flanagan, Niell Warner, A. and J. Wejchart and many others are incorporated in the atlas

Numerous institutions and individuals deserve recognition for their assistance. The institutions include the National Library; National Museum; National Archives; Map Library, Manuscripts Department, Department of History of Art, Geography Department, and Geology Department, Trinity College, Dublin; Library, Royal Irish Academy; Department of Folklife, University College, Dublin; Department of Agriculture, Food and Forestry, Dublin; Department of Transport, Energy and Communications, Dublin; Bord na Mona; Geological Survey of Ireland; Ordnance Survey Office, Dublin; Electricity Supply Board; Cork County Council; Waterford Corporation; Irish Co-operative Organisation Society Ltd; Monaghan County Museum; Asahi Chemical Industry (Ireland); Cement Roadstone Holdings; B9 Energy Systems; Ulster Folk and Transport Museum; Ulster Museum; Institute of Irish Studies, Queen's University, Belfast; Public Records Office, Northern Ireland; Northern Ireland Tourist Board; British Library; English Countryside Commission; Welsh Folk Museum and the Heritage Committee, Council of Europe. We wish to acknowledge the help and advice of the following individuals; John Andrews, Jack Burtchaell, Mary Davies, Edward Farrell, Rachel Finnegan, Michael Gibbons, the Knight of Glin, Arnold Horner, Mary Kelly-Quinn, John Lee, Rolf Loeber, Liam Lyons, Niall McCullough, Paul Mills, Austin O'Sullivan, Adrian Phillips, the Earl of Roden, Noel Ross, Michael Ryan, Charles Shier, Christopher Stillman, Leo Swan, Mary Tubridy and Peter Woodman. Finally, we record our gratitude for the efficiency and flexibility of Cork University Press and Phototype-Set Ltd., Dublin.

In a composite work of this kind, detailed referencing of sources is impracticable. Each chapter has a short bibliography containing a selection of key sources. Photographs are individually acknowledged, but to avoid cluttering of the text, the sources of maps and diagrams and any technical aspects of their compilation are detailed in an appendix to the atlas. Ordnance Survey extracts have been reproduced by permission of the government (permit no. 6395). The geographical location of photographs and maps is shown with a colour-coded bullet on the small maps of Ireland at the bottom of the page. There has been no insistence on any rigid structure for individual contributions. In order to unify the volume, the editors have written a brief introduction to each section.

Anseo, foscailte os mo chomhair
go díreach mar bheadh leabhar ann
tá an taobh tíre seo anois
ó Dhoire Chonaire go Prochlais.
Thíos agus thuas tím na gabháltais
a briseadh as béal an fhiántais.
Seo duanaire mo mhuintire;
an lámhscríbhinn a shaothraigh siad go teann
le dúch a gcuid allais.
Anseo tá achan chuibhreann mar bheadh rann ann
i mórdhán an mhíntíreachais.
Léim anois eipic seo na díograise
i gcanuint ghlas na ngabháltas

Here the prospect opens
like a book before me
from Doire Chonaire to Prochlais.
I survey the meagre farms, up and down
snatched from the maw of the wild.
Here is gathered the anthology of my community
the texts inscribed through their inky sweat.
Now, each enclosure like a verse records
their supreme achievement in claiming the land.
I can now read this epic of endurance
in the green dialect of the crofts.
And it hits home that I am only sealing a covenant
When I also undertake to tackle the void

Extract from *Anseo ag Staisiun Chaiseal na cGorr*,
by Cathal Ó Searcaigh
Translated by Kevin Whelan

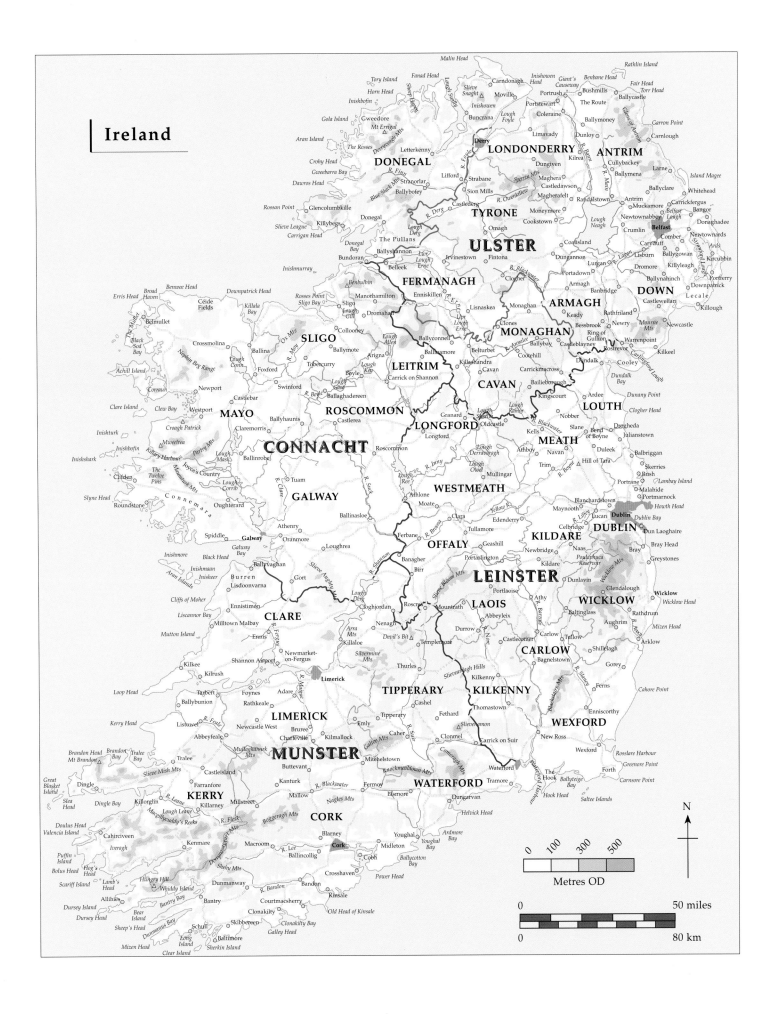

Ireland

Deserted settlements, county Galway

THE MAKING

OF THE

IRISH LANDSCAPE

THE MAKING
OF THE
IRISH LANDSCAPE

THE IRISH RURAL LANDSCAPE: SYNTHESIS OF HABITAT AND HISTORY

The famous French geographer Vidal de la Blache once observed that 'man and his environment are more intimate than a snail and his shell' while the great British geographer Sir Halford Mackinder, using even quainter imagery, remarked that 'man is part of his own environment, as cheese mites are part of the cheese'; that reciprocal relationship between culture and nature is worked out and embodied in the landscape. Human interaction with the environment of Ireland has produced a wide range of characteristic landscape features and a rich variety of distinctive rural landscapes, reflecting both the cultural complexity and natural diversity of the country. This atlas explores those features which give the Irish rural landscape its distinctive character, especially the cultural elements such as field and settlement patterns, buildings, archaeological and historical monuments, demesnes, woodlands, bogs, communications, mines and factories. Moulded over long periods of time, Ireland's remarkable landscape legacy is now threatened by potent forces of change. The atlas seeks to increase awareness of the landscape as an important element of national heritage; it emphasises too, the need for a wide range of rural activities, public and private, to be decisively tempered by concern for landscape qualities, and for necessary change to be carried out in sympathy with inherited landscape features.

DAPHNE POCHIN-MOULD

●Fig. 1 Hungry Hill in county Cork. Human endeavour transforms the natural world to form the cultural landscape.

CULTURAL LANDSCAPES

The physical and biotic world has been so strongly modified by human agency that the resulting landscape is a synthesis of natural and cultural elements; natural landscapes, the product of geological, climatic and biological processes unaffected by humans, are already rare, perhaps non-existent. In long and closely settled areas such as Ireland, the human impress is so pervasive that it is appropriate to speak of a cultural landscape. Here, the profusion of human features coalesce and form a virtually continuous layer. This cultural landscape is our major and most productive creation; it is both an artefact, based on foundations of geology and climate, and a narrative, layer upon layer of our history and nature's history intertwined.

In increasingly urbanised societies, there is a misplaced view of the countryside as 'natural'. Like cities, the rural landscape is artificial, skilfully contrived through time to meet social and economic ends. Thus, for example, Irish grasslands, seemingly so obvious a natural product, are in fact a cultural artefact, painstakingly created and maintained by many generations of farming people. A rigid distinction between natural and cultural landscapes is, however, misleading, since natural processes operate in both: in a cultural landscape, humans simply channel

Fig. 2 Diverse landscapes. ●A) The Nore valley in county Kilkenny. One of the major rivers of south-east Ireland, the Nore winds through undulating lowlands between bare hill ranges. The drift-covered and bog-free lowland is characterised by prosperous mixed farming (meadow, pasture and arable), carefully tended land and medium sized dispersed farms. Although generally rectangular, the hedged fields show little evidence of regulated layout. Coniferous plantations are few while deciduous woodland occurs mainly in demesnes and on the steep river banks. ●B) In the drumlin belt, moving ice has moulded the surface into innumerable elongated hillocks and ridges. In north-west Cavan, the drumlins have seriously disorganised the drainage and the River Erne seeps into a complex series of lakes and channels between the drumlins. Although densely settled, the area clearly provides obstacles to communication and farming. Each drumlin possesses varied soils; cultivation possibilities are dependent on steepness and the land is best used as pasture or meadow. Field patterns are closely adjusted to the terrain with the main boundaries running across the drumlins. This is a fragmented, introverted landscape favouring small territorial units, townlands and farms. ●C) Beauparc, county Meath. The Boyne here flows over a gently undulating drift surface in the north-east of the central lowlands. This is a stable, pastoral landscape of large farms and large, orderly fields, celebrated for its fine grass pastures. Portions of the obsolete Boyne canal can be seen. ●D) Inis Meáin (Inishmaan) is one of the Aran islands stretching across the mouth of Galway Bay. Seemingly inhospitable, the island has supported a community since prehistoric times. The limited stony soils have been extended and fertilised by sand, seaweed and manure to support crops of potatoes and rye, but most of the land is grazing for cattle and sheep. The bare limestone surface is intricately divided by dry-stone walls, reflecting the dense settlement which characterised the island down to recent decades.

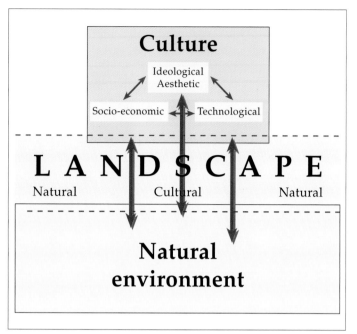

Fig. 3 The cultural landscape is the product of a dynamic interaction between cultural components (social organisation, technology, ideology) and the natural environment (bedrock, relief, climate, soils and vegetation).

natural processes towards a preferred outcome. Agriculture, of which much of our rural cultural landscape is largely a by-product, remains inescapably dependent on the natural world – on photosynthesis, biochemical cycles and non-human organisms, for example. It does not override but simply rearranges ecological processes: like many land-use systems, it may not be stable or sustainable in the long run. These considerations are equally important in understanding agrarian and landscape history and for contemporary landscape management.

A deep time perspective is required to understand fully the significance of modern landscape features. Landscape is not static but the dynamic product of a complex interaction between human society and its habitat: if either society or habitat changes, so inevitably must the landscape. A continuous process of landscape transformation results: cultural and technological developments alter the relationships between humans and their environment, while the natural environment itself is continually changing, usually slowly but occasionally abruptly and conspicuously. Concentrated periods of transformation can be recognised, certainly in post-medieval Ireland, but most landscape change was gradual and partial. The elaborate social organisation and complicated technology necessary to restructure human ecological relationships developed slowly and the inherited fabric of fields and farms remained intact, unless subjected to severe social or environmental pressures. Our landscapes therefore are not the product of contemporary activities alone: they have matured over

lengthy periods of prehistoric and historic time. While present land uses modify the cultural landscape, it is essentially a legacy from the past. Its evolution can be reconstructed, permitting an understanding of the historical and ecological significance of its present-day components as well as insights into long-term human/environment interactions. This evolutionary interpretation is helpful to landscape management, the past being necessary not only to understand the present but to evaluate the outcome of modern trends.

Territorial frameworks have been created at many different periods to impose an overall lay-out on the rural landscape, ranging from medieval manors to plantation seigniories, from landed estates to the Congested Districts Board and the Land Commission. However, planning was rarely thoroughgoing within these structures. Until recent centuries, there were few concerted attempts to create harmonious, aesthetic or functional landscapes based on ideal concepts; even when such attempts were then made, the effects were confined to miniature setpieces such as demesnes. An informal, vernacular landscape evolved organically at the level of farm and field, to provide shelter and livelihood, using local skills, materials and traditions. Until very recently, rural landscapes remained those of necessity; they were the products of rural communities adjusting to their intimate habitat and adapting it to their needs. The identity, harmony and therefore beauty of these landscapes does not derive from unity of design, but rather from a sensitive adaptation to the land, dictated by technological and social constraints on environmental change. The resulting 'sense of place' is organic, produced by the balance between natural background and overlying cultural features. This balance generated enduring elements, emanating from the practical needs of a specific people in a specific place: successful adaptations, such as vernacular building styles, field patterns and land-use, were transmitted by tradition. Hence, as the American folklorist Henry Glassie intimates, the search for pattern in abiding vernacular features yields 'regions', whereas a search for pattern outside the vernacular realm, subject to fashion and restless style, yields 'periods'.

While a landscape constantly changes, its regional identity is enhanced as long as the need to work within the limits of local environment and society exists. In the industrial era, and especially in the post-industrial era of recent decades, the inherited character and diversity of landscape has been damaged, primarily because new technology and a global economic system have decisively breached the environmental and cultural limits that formerly conferred uniqueness and sustainability on places. These new penetrative forces

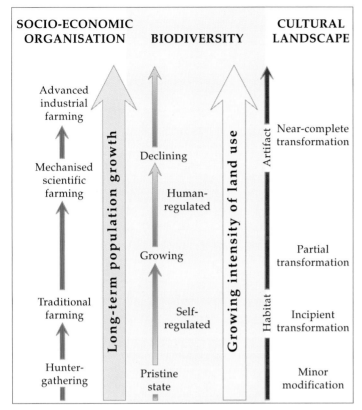

Fig. 4 The long-term human impact on environment and landscape change.

have an invasive reach of unprecedented power, far beyond anything experienced in the past. Landscape quality can only be restored and preserved by conscious design and comprehensive and sustained action.

Because it is the dynamic interface between natural and cultural systems, our landscape is immensely complex and no single academic discipline can usurp its understanding. Many can contribute, including ecology, palaeoecology, archaeology, historical and cultural geography, architecture and anthropology; their approaches are inevitably disparate, with the result that there is no agreed theory or methodology for landscape study. However, a suitable starting point for integrated research should be the landscape itself. As a direct object of study, as a metaphor for our complex society, and for its capacity to unify research projects and to focus environmental policies, the landscape should be at the core of environmental debate, at the cutting edge of the serious dialogue between scientists and humanists which is necessary to solve fundamental environmental problems.

Amongst others, this atlas draws together physical and human geographers, archaeologists, palaeobotanists, local historians and landscape ecologists to explore the major components of our landscapes and to emphasise their immense ecological, economic, educational and aesthetic richness. By so doing, the work encourages a more attentive appreciation of the landscape, while providing the necessary context within which conservation policies can be designed and implemented. A particular aim is to stimulate the interest of rural communities in their historic landscapes. Our landscapes cannot be satisfactorily protected solely by a managerial élite; more vital is the informed stewardship of local communities whose heritage they are. There should be clearer recognition of the connections and interdependence of rural people and of safeguarding the rural heritage, and a growing emphasis on the involvement of local communities, whose characteristic long-term self interest and place-specific knowledge need to be supplemented by an enhanced self-awareness and deeper environmental understanding. By increasing the legibility of our landscapes, this atlas will contribute to an emerging Irish environmental ethic, with community responsibility at its centre.

PHYSICAL ENVIRONMENT
Geology and relief
The cultural landscape of Ireland has developed on a background of ancient rocks, much influenced by the folding and faulting of the Caledonian and Armorican mountain building phases which formed the structural framework of north-western Europe. Owing to prolonged denudation, the country is now mainly lowland: three-quarters lies below 150m and only five per cent above 300m. Relief variations are related more to the differing resistance of rock types to denudation than to tectonic forces. However, there is a discernible north-east to south-west grain in the relief of the north and west of Ireland and in the Leinster mountains which is a legacy of Caledonian folding. Armorican folding is responsible for the conspicuous east-west orientation of the parallel ridges and valleys of Munster. Ireland also possesses the largest continuous stretch of carboniferous limestone in Europe; underlying the Central Lowland, it nourishes rich, bone-building pastures, the luxuriant carpet of grass which gives Ireland its popular epithet 'the emerald isle' and its high repute as a horse-breeding country.

Glaciation Although the rocks are generally extremely old, the surface landforms have been moulded by recent geological events and particularly by recurrent glaciations. When the ice finally melted some 12,000 years ago, it left the surface relief much as it now is, except that coastlines have been significantly altered by a subsequent rise of the sea-level caused by the melting of the ice. This rise finally severed the land link with Britain and the continent.

On lowland areas, the dominant action of ice was the deposition of drift sheets on which the productive soils of

Geology

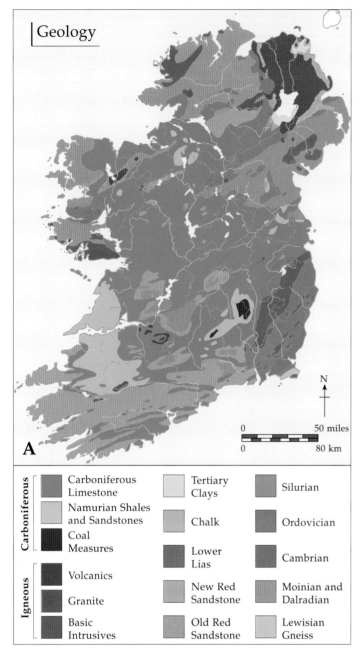

A

0   50 miles

0   80 km

Carboniferous	
■ Carboniferous Limestone	
■ Namurian Shales and Sandstones	
■ Coal Measures	

Igneous	
■ Volcanics	
■ Granite	
■ Basic Intrusives	

■ Tertiary Clays

■ Chalk

■ Lower Lias

■ New Red Sandstone

■ Old Red Sandstone

■ Silurian

■ Ordovician

■ Cambrian

■ Moinian and Dalradian

■ Lewisian Gneiss

Relief

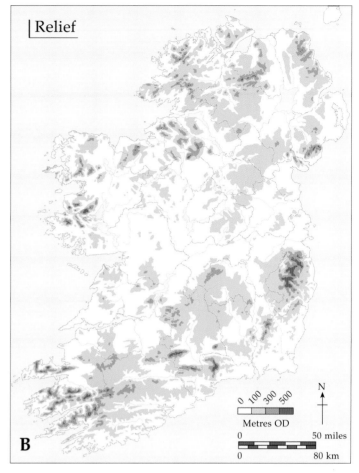

B

0 100 300 500

Metres OD

0   50 miles

0   80 km

Fig. 5 Geology (A) and relief (B). Denudation has removed many rock formations including most of the coal measures; the remaining rocks are generally very old and relief differences are mainly attributable to differential resistance to erosion and weathering. The vast extent of level Lower Carboniferous strata (over 20,000 km^2) is most striking, underlying the central lowlands with older rocks outcropping on the lowland edges where they form detached and generally inhospitable upland masses. Ireland has close geological and scenic relationships with Scotland and Wales; the relationships with England are more distant and the differences underpin historical contrasts. Plentiful coal measures, for example, gave England a major advantage over Ireland during the industrial revolution. The easily worked Mesozoic limestones and sandstones of lowland England sustained a rich vernacular building tradition; in Ireland, hard limestones and tough granites were less permissive.

the country have mainly developed. The distribution, composition and surface morphology of the drift have had a marked influence on landscape and land use. Although generally reflecting the character of the rocks over which the ice sheets moved, the drift cover is variable, ranging from irregular deposits of boulder clay to water-sorted sands and gravel. Moreover, it is smeared unevenly, varying in thickness and continuity, and has been moulded into a wide variety of landforms. While level or gently undulating surfaces can occur, as for example in the Dublin region, the surface is generally highly irregular. Meltwater deposits constitute the numerous sinuous eskers in the Midlands where they provide routeways through the confused lowland bogs and the watery Shannon callows.

In some areas, there is a jumble of hummocky kame, meltwater channels and retreat moraines.

On the northern and western edges of the Central Lowlands, the drift is frequently moulded into a tightly packed mass of rounded hillocks, called drumlins, interspersed with a multitude of diminutive lakes and bog patches. This distinctive drumlin topography is best developed in a broad swathe across the country from Strangford Lough in north-eastern Ireland to Sligo and Donegal bays on the Atlantic coast. Owing to its irregular terrain and poor drainage, as, for example, in the archipelagic confusion of the Erne basin, the drumlin belt has been a barrier to communication and a cultural divide in the country since prehistoric times.

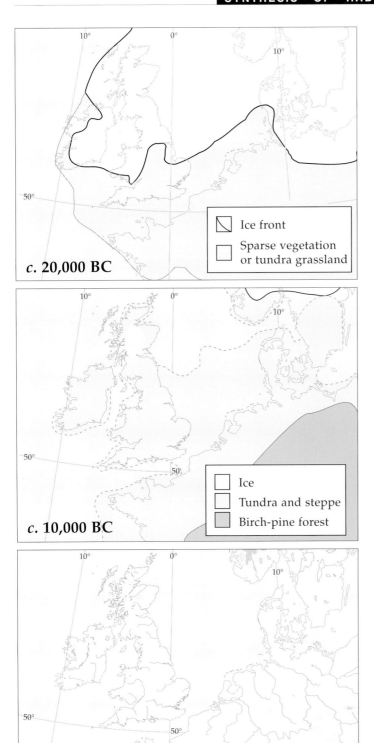

c. **20,000 BC**

● Fig. 7 Donegal Bay. Tightly packed drumlins are here the dominant feature. Their alignment marshals the pattern of roads, fields and farms.

Given Ireland's moist climate, low relief and sticky soils, drainage is generally poor. Streams are devious and ill-defined. Numerous lakes occur, the remnants of larger water bodies progressively shrunk by fen and bog encroachment. Waterlogging has encouraged extensive peat bogs. The midlands in general are lake-littered and bog-pocked. Sand and gravel sheets, originating as glacial outwash features or deltaic deposits, are more freely drained than the areas of boulder clay, providing fertile islands of grazing and arable land amid bog. The Curragh of Kildare is the classic example.

Glacial action has generally accentuated the contrasts between uplands and lowlands. Erosion stripped the uplands, scouring out spectacular relief features such as corries and deep valleys but stripping the rock surfaces of soil. In lowlands, the deposition of soil-forming tills and the mantling of inhospitable bedrock have been among the major consequences. Tongues of drift extend up many glaciated valleys but rarely above 240m; their upper boundary often forms a striking divide, determining the

● Fig. 8 Carrauntuathail ridge in the MacGillicuddy's Reeks in county Kerry, rises to 1041m, the highest ground in Ireland. Formed from Old Red Sandstone layers of grits and shale, the ridge bears the sharp imprint of local mountain glaciers in its numerous corrie basins and ice-fretted crags.

Fig. 6 Glaciation: Ireland and Europe. At the peak of the last glaciation (20,000 BC), Ireland and much of north-western Europe were covered by ice. Maritime influences limited the grip of the ice in the south-west of Ireland where an ice-free zone existed. Sea levels were lower than at present and a landbridge connected Ireland to Britain. The environment and the coastal outlines of Ireland changed substantially as the ice sheets retreated (10,000 BC). Tundra grasslands developed on the lowlands and rising sea levels eventually severed the country from Britain and Britain from Europe. The first colonists in Ireland (*c.* 7000 BC) made the journey by sea, presumably making their initial landfalls on the north-east coast.

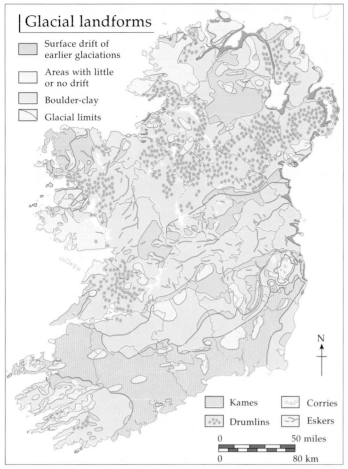

Glacial landforms

- Surface drift of earlier glaciations
- Areas with little or no drift
- Boulder-clay
- Glacial limits

N

- Kames
- Corries
- Drumlins
- Eskers

0   50 miles
0   80 km

Fig. 9 Glacial landforms. The erosional and depositional effects of the successive ice ages in Ireland were profound, more so than in Britain. Glaciers transported eroded material to the lowlands where it forms the widespread glacial drifts. These determine the surface topography and soils to which successive Irish societies have had to adapt. Long terminal moraines mark retreat stages of the last ice sheet. Also conspicuous are the extensive drumlin swarms and eskers which originated under the ice; the Irish terms for these glacial landforms have been adopted internationally. The drumlin symbols represent the prevailing alignment in each area and not individual drumlins.

DAPHNE POCHIN-MOULD

●Fig. 10 Meltwater channels formed by drainage escaping from ice-impounded lakes are impressive features of the Irish landscape. The Pass of Keimaneigh with its vertical rock walls slices through the Shehy mountains for over three kilometres and is utilised by the spectacular road from Bantry Bay to the upper Lee valley.

altitudinal limits of farming and improved land. Where limestone-based, the drift is friendly, permitting small farming communities to nestle high on the mountain slopes.

Landscape and substrate

Despite its small size (83,000 km^2), the narrow ground of Ireland is variegated internally, each land type evoking unique human responses. The country consists of a broad central lowland, interrupted by a number of detached hill and mountain blocks and ringed by a broken rim of distinctive upland areas. Only in the east between Dundalk and Dublin is the upland perimeter completely absent and here the lowlands reach the sea. Elsewhere, easy communication to the coast is provided by corridors between the upland areas. The valleys of the Bann, the Erne and the Moy and the lowlands behind Galway Bay and Clew Bay,

for example, are Atlantic avenues: the Slaney, Barrow, Nore and Suir valleys are strategic corridors to the south coast, slicing dramatically through the circling mountains.

The Central Lowland   Lying for the most part between 60m and 120m, this region is underlain mainly by Carboniferous limestone, entirely concealed by a mantle of recent glacial deposits and sometimes an additional soggy coat of peat bogs. The Shannon, more than 320 km long, dominates the drainage system. The great but sluggish river sometimes braids into multiple channels as it seeps through drumlin swarms: lower down, it swells into the midland lakes of Lough Allen, Lough Ree and Lough Derg. Extensive seasonal flooding of the surrounding shallow lowlands is frequent. The Central Lowland is internally divided, owing to the varied nature of its superficial deposits and the presence of sharply defined upland

● Fig. 11   The highland masses on the borders of counties Galway and Mayo are dissected by a network of glaciated valleys. The deepest of these valleys has been flooded by the sea to form the long fjord-like inlet of Killary Harbour. Settlement and improved land on the steep sides of the inlet coincide with the presence of glacial drift.

areas. Three segments can be distinguished, north, central and south.

The **central** segment, in which the lowland is best developed and most continuous, lies north of a line roughly from Galway Bay to Dublin and south of the drumlin belt. Glacial drift thickens to over 60m in the east but thins markedly west of the Shannon into a threadbare blanket.

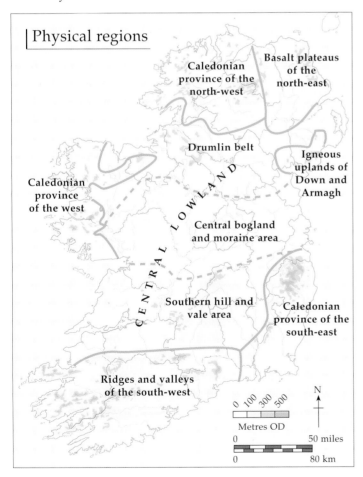

● Fig. 13   The Shannon is the major drainage channel of the Central Lowlands with a catchment area covering fifteen per cent of the area of the Republic. Over much of its course, the river has no recognisable valley and penetrates drumlin swarms and expands into lakes. Extensive winter flooding is still common on the 'callows', or flanking water meadows. A) The normal width of the river at Banagher, county Offaly and B) the extensive floods in 1970.

Here sporadic outcrops of bare limestone occur, on which the dominant landforms have been produced by solution of the rocks and distinctive karstic landscapes, such as the Burren, have developed. The large lakes of Corrib and Mask occupy solution hollows, probably enlarged by ice erosion. Their limestone base is friendly to fish and insect life, and these two lakes have an international reputation as fly-fishing venues.

In the **northern** and **southern** segments, the lowland relief is frequently interrupted by two types of upland. First are residual plateaux of Upper Carboniferous shales, grits and thin coal seams which are younger than the limestones. These include the bleak Castlecomer plateau and Slieve Ardagh escarpment in county Kilkenny, whose

Physical regions

Caledonian province of the north-west

Basalt plateaus of the north-east

Drumlin belt

Igneous uplands of Down and Armagh

Caledonian province of the west

CENTRAL LOWLAND

Central bogland and moraine area

Southern hill and vale area

Caledonian province of the south-east

Ridges and valleys of the south-west

0 100 300 500

Metres OD

N

0   50 miles

0   80 km

Fig. 12 (left) Physical regions: landscape and substrate. Solid geology, relief and superficial glacial deposits combine to produce a diversity of physical landscapes, with a general east to west zonation. These provide a useful framework for the study of settlement and agrarian history. However, in response to climate, soils and historical forces, the physical zones have been differentiated internally into eastern and western regions (see fig. 33).

E. CULLETON

• Fig. 14 This cliff on the shores of south-east county Wexford displays the depth of the limestone till cover in eastern Ireland. The even surface of the till is attractive to agriculture and facilitates easy expansion of settlements.

DAPHNE POCHIN-MOULD

• Fig. 16 The thin drift cover on the lowlands of east county Galway is clearly evident at Coole Lough with its rocky islands. The bare karstic landscape of the Burren rises in the background.

poorly drained surfaces rise to over 300m, the more subdued but scenically similar plateau surfaces around the Shannon estuary, and the angular plateaux of Leitrim, Sligo and Fermanagh, dissected into spectacular steep-sided blocks like Ben Bulben with flat, bog-covered summits lying between 460m and 610m. The second upland type are the isolated mountain ranges formed on anticlinal inliers of the resistant Old Red Sandstone and Silurian slates and shales which underlie the Carboniferous limestone. Slieve Bloom, Slieve Aughty, Slieve Bernagh, Devilsbit, Silvermine and Galtee mountains are examples. More numerous in the southern segment, they provide the most prominent landscape elements, rising abruptly from lowlands to over 300m and in some cases 600m.

Between these various uplands are broad valleys, well-drained and relatively bog-free, diversified by sinuous end-moraine deposits: these green valleys nourish the richest pasturelands of Ireland, especially in the Golden Vale of

south Tipperary and east Limerick. In the northern segment of the Central Lowlands, the drumlin collar is a conspicuous feature, a distinctive environment of lasting difficulty. The poor farmland is confined to scraggy patches of stoney-grey soil on the better-drained flanks of the drumlins. Here, amidst the confusion of small hills, chaotic watersheds and sodden hollows, an intimate landscape of limited views has developed with a distinctive small-farm lifestyle. In Northern Ireland, the drumlin belt extends off the Carboniferous limestone to the north-east; owing to a higher sand content and lower rainfall, the soils here are more easily worked for arable crops, especially on the fat drumlins of north Down.

Peripheral to the central lowlands are upland areas which can be divided into four broad regions, distinguished by age, structure and relief. With the exception of the north-east basaltic province, they are formed of very ancient, pre-Carboniferous rocks.

DAPHNE POCHIN-MOULD

• Fig. 15 Ben Bulben (527m), county Sligo, is a flat-topped plateau, its cliffs formed from limestones, the lower scree-covered slopes from shales. The boggy plateau surface has traditionally been used for peat cutting and rough grazing.

DAPHNE POCHIN-MOULD

• Fig. 17 Lough Gur lies in the lowlands at the western end of the Golden Vale, south of Limerick city. There is a strong emphasis on cattle rearing and milk production for creameries and virtually all improved land is given to hay and pasture. Prehistoric sites are numerous around the lake shores.

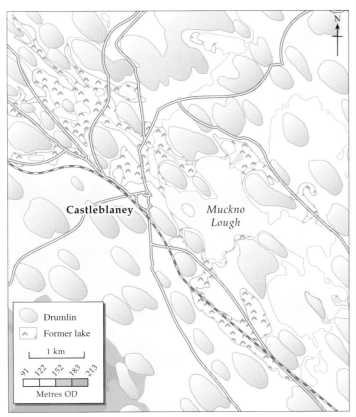

DAPHNE POCHIN-MOULD

●Fig. 18 The numerous drumlins around the Castleblaney area in county Monaghan are orientated in the direction of the ice flow. Former lakes and damp hollows between the drumlins have been widely drained.

The Caledonian North-West This region, underlain by pre-Cambrian rocks, falls into two parts, west Connacht and Donegal; although separated by Carboniferous rocks around Donegal Bay, they possess striking similarities. While Caledonian folding is evident in the south-west/north-east trend of the valleys, the major relief features are correlated with rock character and resistance to erosive forces. Metamorphic rocks and granites form the upland areas, with stark quartzitic peaks, like the Twelve

●Fig. 19 Errigal mountain (752m), county Donegal, is an isolated cone of quartzite with scree-covered slopes, a landmark in an ice-moulded lowland covered by blanket bog.

MICHAEL DIGGIN

●Fig. 20 Magheraroarty bay, county Donegal. The landforms of the Donegal coast are varied. The numerous bays and inlets which lie between the rocky headlands are often closed at their entrances by sandy spits and tombolos, formed from morainic and glacio-fluvial material refashioned by Atlantic wind and waves. This is well demonstrated at Magheraroarty. In the foreground is a small coastal clachan, or farm cluster, its miniature fields lying across a subdued drumlin ridge.

Pins of Galway, Croagh Patrick in Mayo and Mount Errigal in Donegal. The lowlands and valleys are developed on softer rocks, such as schists, and along faults. The dramatic Atlantic coastline has steep cliffs and fiordic inlets, alternating with coastal lowlands fringed by sandy bays and offshore islands. Heavily glaciated, even the low-lying portions are stripped of soil and the barren rock surfaces are festooned with innumerable small lakes and bog patches. As exemplified in inner Connemara, human settlement hugs the coasts and the interiors are almost desolate.

Drift conceals the ancient rocks in the Foyle lowlands but they outcrop again along the Tyrone-Derry border. Here, the rounded, bog-coated Sperrins form a barrier between the eastern and western lowlands of Ulster, the former centred on Lough Neagh and the latter on the Foyle basin. The Sperrins uplands have been neatly described by John Montague as a landscape of

> *merging low hills and gravel streams,*
> *oozing blackness of peat-banks, pale upland grass.*

The Caledonian South-East In the south-east, the Leinster mountain chain with its north-east to south-west orientation also shows the influence of Caledonian folding. The mountains are developed on a granite mass originally intruded into overlying Ordovician strata. Denudation has subsequently unroofed the granite which now forms the most extensive continuous tract of high ground in the country, extending from Dublin Bay almost to the Barrow estuary in county Waterford. The Slaney valley marks the only lowland route through the mountains, squeezing

AEROFILMS

● Fig. 21 Glenmalure in county Wicklow is the longest of the Wicklow glens. A straight glaciated valley, the glen has been partially filled by alluvial materials which form level land used for pasture and cultivation; small farms are strewn along the junction of the sediments and the rocky sides of the glen on which coniferous plantations have been widely established. The surrounding open moorland is used for sheep grazing and game.

DAPHNE POCHIN-MOULD

● Fig. 22 A continuous sheet of nutrient-rich glacial till covers the landscape of south-east Wexford, levelling the uneven bedrock topography to form a flat to undulating lowland with well drained, highly productive soils. The entire area is evenly settled and intensively farmed, with dispersed steadings and small hedged fields. Farm production is mixed, with more arable than is normal in Ireland. Tacumshin lake in the foreground is a shallow bay which has been closed off by sand bars.

between the Blackstairs and the Wicklow mountain ranges before flowing through farmland to the sea at Wexford.

The Wicklow end of the Leinster Chain is a rolling, drift-free upland, much of it over 300m high, difficult of access and suitable only for sheep because of its extensive covering of blanket bog. While there are extensive level surfaces within the Wicklow Mountains, they are also gashed by seven glaciated glens and some precipitous corrie basins. On either side of the Wicklow uplands, Ordovician shales and slates form a jagged edge to the rounded granite, promoting topographic diversity and creating the magnificent scenery of east Wicklow, notably in Powerscourt, Glendalough and Glenmalure.

In county Wexford, Ordovician and other rocks underlie a fertile lowland, long renowned for high quality farming. Drift covered, this area is greatly diversified by a scatter of volcanic and quartzitic hills aligned parallel to the Blackstairs Mountains, including Vinegar Hill outside Enniscorthy. Well-drained and almost bog-free, Wexford's long-standing arable traditions are in strong contrast to the pastoralism of the Leinster Mountains.

Munster; Ridge and Valley A third major upland occurs in Munster. Parallel ridges and valleys here display the Armorican east-west grain with text-book clarity. However, it is differential erosion rather than the

Armorican folding itself which has produced the present relief features. Carboniferous limestone floors the valleys while the resistant ridges are of Old Red Sandstones; the soft Carboniferous cover has been removed, exposing the tougher sandstones which remain upstanding. In the east, the valleys are broad and the ridges narrow. There are peaks of over 600m in the Comeraghs and Knockmealdowns but level surfaces are also extensively developed in southern county Cork and county Waterford. Westwards, in Kerry and west Cork, the uplands become broader and higher, while dramatic glacial features accentuate the spectacular topography. Towards the Atlantic, the limestone valleys are invaded by the sea to form deep rias, like Bantry Bay, separated by bony, mountainous peninsulas. The Munster rivers flow eastwards before characteristically

DAPHNE POCHIN-MOULD

● Fig. 23 Imposing mountains which rise abruptly from the lowlands are features of the landscapes of south and central Ireland. The Knockmealdowns (795m) are separated from the Galtee range (920m) to the north by a wide, fertile plain.

MICHAEL DIGGIN

• Fig. 24 The mountainous Iveragh peninsula in county Kerry is predominantly moorland and bog with a closely settled coastal fringe seen here on Valencia Island. The equally mountainous Dingle peninsula and the Blasket Islands are on the horizon.

turning abruptly southwards to reach the sea; submergence of their lower valleys has produced long estuaries, as along the Lee and Blackwater. In Munster too, there has been an enduring human contrast between the 'mountainy men' and the comfortable lowland farmers, the ridge and valley topography underpinning the rough and smooth of life experiences. Edmund Spenser, very familiar with this type of region between the Ballyhoura and the Nagles mountains, encapsulates the surrounding landscape contrasts as the 'breathing fields and mountains hore' in *The Faerie Queene*.

The North-East   Two contrasting upland areas occur in north-east Ireland. The first occupies the eastern borderlands of Ulster and Leinster around the deep fiordic inlet of Carlingford Lough, where complex igneous intrusions have formed four distinct mountain masses – Slieve Gullion, the Carlingford peninsula, the Mournes and Slieve Croob. Strongly affected by ice erosion, their unimproved flanks, ice-scoured and largely drift-free, overlook tightly

DAPHNE POCHIN-MOULD

• Fig. 25 The Blackwater estuary in county Waterford, looking upriver to the distant Knockmealdowns. The farmland here is diversified by attractive demesne woodlands.

MICHAEL DIGGIN

• Fig 26 On the eastern edge of the Antrim Plateau, the thick Tertiary basaltic sheets terminate abruptly in steep cliffs, deeply dissected in the seaward facing Glens of Antrim. At Glenariff, the sombre moorland above the scarps contrasts sharply with the sheltered and well settled landscape of the glen.

settled lowlands, thickly blanketed with morainic material. Slieve Gullion (575m), the highest mass, is an intrusion of gabbro, enclosed by a remarkably complete doleritic ring-dyke, forming a circle of lower, barren hills. In the Carlingford Mountains, igneous rocks form rugged peaks and a broken ring-dyke appears in the gabbro hills of Slieve Foye. Slieve Croob is formed of granite and its elevated moorlands merge to the south with the Mourne foothills. The Mournes themselves are more recent granite domes, diversified by glacial corries, constituting a splendid scenic panorama as they sweep down to the Irish sea.

In the north-eastern corner of Ulster, the dreary surface of the Antrim plateau is developed on Tertiary basalt sheets which rise above 360m over wide areas. These are the eroded remnants of much more extensive lava flows. The highest areas overlook the north-eastern coast where these flows terminate in an abrupt escarpment of black basalt on white chalk, deeply dissected into the seaward-facing nine Glens of Antrim. To the west, the basalt is downwarped beneath Lough Neagh (the largest freshwater body in Britain and Ireland) and the drift-filled valley of the Bann, but it surfaces in Derry as a topographical continuation of the Sperrins.

Climate, soil and vegetation

Ireland's diverse morphological regions underpin major scenic contrasts as well as varied settlement patterns, economic activity and cultural landscape features. But, owing to the drift-smothered geology, the stony roots of Ireland seldom break the surface and variations in rock

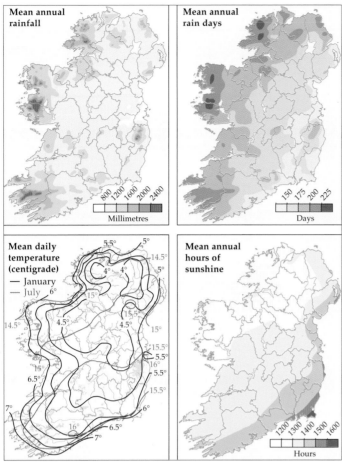

Fig. 27 The west averages 1000 to 1500mm of rain annually while the eastern half of the country has 750 to 1000mm with sharp rises in mountainous areas. It is not, however, the absolute value but the frequency and persistence of rain which is critical; combined with high humidity and feeble evapotranspiration, this ensures the all-encompassing wetness of the environment.

type often have only a muted expression in the landscape. Ireland's cultural landscape is not ultimately dependent on geological variations; it is more heavily influenced by other factors, such as climate, drainage, soils and history. The uniqueness of the Burren, for example, is largely because it is one of the few places in Ireland where the rock skeleton is not clothed by a skin of soil. Here, green and brown abdicate to grey, and soft outlines and masked horizons are replaced by an abstract geometry of clean, hard lines, unusual in the Irish landscape.

The prevalent, moist westerly winds from the warm waters of the North Atlantic ensure that Ireland has a markedly oceanic climate with frequent rain and low annual temperature ranges. Temperature extremes and harsh frosts are rare. Rainfall is higher in the west and even over low ground, totals decline from west to east. The eastern coastlands between Dublin and Drogheda are the driest parts of the country, which has helped their evolution as a geopolitical focus since the time of the Boyne valley tombs and Tara onwards. Effectively, this dry, bog-

free lowland, close to Britain, has functioned as the 'centre' of the country, usurping the midlands, whose bogs have stultified the advantages of a heartland location.

The character and hues of the landscape are constantly affected by the variable weather: the same places never look exactly the same. The hazy humid atmosphere mutes colours, producing a subtle spectrum of green, brown and blue. In the relentless rain of winter, the landscape sinks into a sodden gloom, as the country cowers under the wind-driven Atlantic rain or is wrapped in a shroud of clinging mist. But in the sunshine and showers of spring and summer, kaleidoscopic colour changes occur as light is filtered through moving banks of cloud or sporadic rain; with clear air and direct sunlight, the lush grass and foliage spring into vivid almost lurid colours. In the west of Ireland, the open vistas, theatrical cumulus mushrooms and melodramatic sunsets generate a dynamic quality of light, addictive to the romantic artist, photographer and film maker.

Irish soils are a sensitive response to parent materials, local relief and, most important, climatic conditions. Their extreme moistness is crucial, resulting from the cloudiness and low summer temperatures, which check evaporation rates, as well as from persistent rainfall, impeded drainage, and the impermeable materials from which the soil cover is derived. The precipitation-evaporation ratio generally favours precipitation and leaching is the dominant soil-forming process, leading to widespread podsolisation, hard-pan development and soil acidity. Under intense leaching, podsols are developed freely on lime-deficient parent materials such as granites. They are widespread in

Fig. 28 Paul Henry's well-known landscape paintings of the west of Ireland are based mainly on Achill in county Mayo, where he painted for a number of years. Dramatic clouds and blue mountains are recurrent features in his work, elements of an enduring romantic image of the west which he helped to create and which persists in tourism publicity.

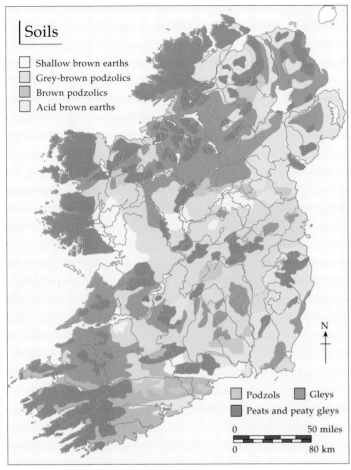

Fig. 29 The generalised distribution of major soil types. Poorly drained peats and gleys, best suited to grazing and forestry, predominate in the north and west. The more fertile soils, with wider land-use capability, occur mainly in the south-east.

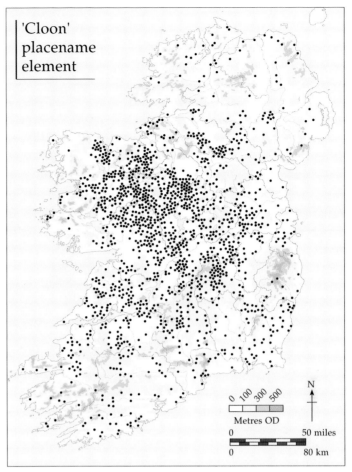

Fig. 30 The common placename elements 'clon' and 'cloon' (cluain) connote a meadow or a dry site. They are abundant in wet or boggy regions where dry meadow land was a valued resource; cloon place-names abound, for example, on the esker ridges of the boggy central lowlands and across the drumlin belt.

the west and the peripheral uplands, where the coarse grass and heather growing on the impoverished soils are suitable only for extensive rough grazing. Peaty soils are especially characteristic of mountain areas on the western seaboard. The problems of wet soils have generated an extensive vocabulary in the Irish language to describe them, and placenames also resonate with drainage conditions.

On lowland drifts, grey brown and brown podsols are more widespread than pure podsols, covering a quarter of the country; variable in quality, they include the most fertile soils. However, gleying increases towards the rainier north and west. In favourable locations, these soil types grade into brown earths of still higher fertility. Brown earths and brown podsolic soils are more frequently found in the drier conditions and better drained subsoils of the south and east of Ireland. They possess a wider land use capability and will support good grassland as well as arable. Flexible crop rotations are thus possible and farmers can change production easily in response to changing market demands. Everywhere in Ireland, the dominant farm economy is livestock production based on permanent

● Fig. 31 This portrayal of bogs in west county Roscommon is characteristic of the meticulous work of the Commissioners for Bogs in the early nineteenth century. Bog patches and small loughs are scattered in hollows between the numerous north-west/south-east trending esker ridges with their concentrations of 'cloon' placenames indicative of drier conditions.

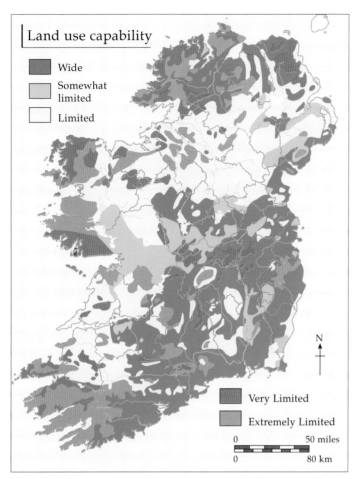

Fig. 32 Land use capability. The map shows, in a highly generalised way, the varying strength of the limitations on farming imposed by a combination of physical factors, including soil character, slope, rock outcrop and drainage conditions.

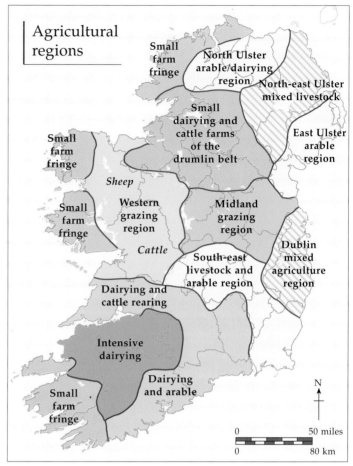

Fig. 33 Four-fifths of Irish land is devoted to agriculture. Livestock production based on permanent grassland is dominant everywhere and a major component in the appearance of the landscape. The pattern of farming is mixed. Variations in the relative importance of individual agricultural enterprises, such as dairying, beef or crop production, provide a basis for dividing the country into agricultural regions but these are superimposed on a common pastoral basis. Tillage occurs mainly in the drier eastern areas, livestock specialisation dominates in the north central lowlands and intensive dairying is marked in the south-west and north-west.

grassland; of various differences superimposed on this common pastoral basis, tillage in south-east Leinster is the most notable. Even there, tillage rarely exceeds one-third of the total farmed area, but ploughed fields and crops significantly diversify the rural scene and more care is lavished on the land.

Soils as well as vegetation have been considerably altered from their natural state by long periods of human interaction. The soil cover developed originally under forest vegetation before the advent of farming. With the removal of trees, the soils were more exposed to leaching and degradation and the spread of peat was facilitated. Cattle grazing affected the surface layers of soil, and cultivation disturbed the natural profiles. New materials and fertilisers have also been applied over long periods, including sand and seaweed to coastal soils and lime to counteract upland acidity. As a result, notably on the coastal rim of the west of Ireland, many soils are effectively *plaggen* – man-made soils accumulated through generations of intensive spade labour and continuous applications of sod, seaweed, sand, soot, turf, farm refuse

and decayed thatch. Bog clearance and land drainage have long been underway, especially in the east where the intensity of land improvement has reinforced the natural superiority of the soils.

Within Ireland, broad regional contrasts in environmental conditions have had a formative influence upon historic settlement and cultural landscapes. The fundamental contrast is between the poorer western and north-western parts, with their wide extents of wet upland, blanket bogs and ill-drained, acid soils, and the more accessible, physically well-endowed south and east of the country, with their drier climate and extensive drift-covered lowlands. The east has had closer cultural and commercial links to Britain and Europe. In the historic period, it has attracted a succession of invading groups, notably the Normans and New English; diverse ethnic and settlement traditions have thus further differentiated the region. The recurrent particularist tendency of the north of the island has resulted

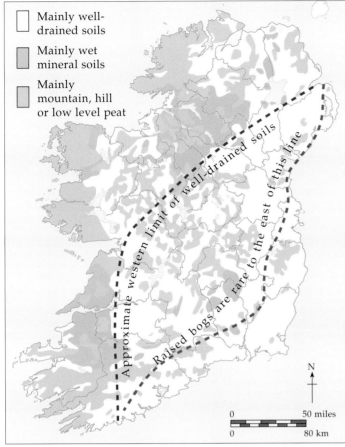

Fig. 34 The major environmental contrast within the country has influenced human settlement and land use throughout history. The west and north-west is generally inhospitable, wet, mountainous and boggy. The east and south-east is more congenial with extensive lowlands, drier climate and fewer bogs.

largely from the region's cultural bonds with adjacent Scotland and the relative isolation from the rest of Ireland produced by the drumlin belt, mountains and lakes. The regional break is pronounced along the southern edge of the drumlin belt. As an Ulster proverb expressed it:

> Ta cúige Uladh síos is cúig mhíle croc ina lár
> is condae na Mídhe ina suídhe chomh chomthrom le clár
> [Ulster sits in the middle of five thousand hills,
> But the county of Meath lies level as a board]

THE CULTURAL IMPRINT

Ireland provides an ideal island laboratory for the study of landscape history. The country combines a varied ecology with a long history of human settlement, a well preserved archaeological record of all major periods, and the persistent presence of traditional life-styles. Archaeological and palynological research is well developed. Fossil pollen, sealed in the widespread bogs, provides valuable evidence for prehistoric environmental history, demonstrating regional trends in the origin, composition and evolution of vegetation, and permitting calibration of human impacts.

Although an island on the rim of the continent, Ireland has been continuously influenced by European culture - in language, architecture, religious traditions, art, industry and landscape. More specifically, Ireland shares ecological and cultural parallels with Atlantic Europe, the fringe of peninsulas and islands stretching from Galicia through Brittany, Cornwall and Wales to Highland Scotland and Norway. Here, for example, the predominant pastoralism, dispersed settlement, infield-outfield cultivation and long-house traditions may be adaptations to the oceanic environment or legacies of ancient cultural unity derived (with the exception of Norway) partly from Celtic roots and preserved by long-standing coastwise interaction.

Intense relations between Ireland and its larger island neighbour have been inescapable; while marked by periods of conflict, they more generally involved mutual interchange of people and ideas, including the frequent transmission of European influences through Britain to Ireland. In the early modern period, Ireland was forcibly incorporated into an aggressively expanding English state and simultaneously reorientated towards the emerging colonial Atlantic world. In the early twentieth century, it entered on the painful search for political independence, with one unintended by-product being partition of the island between two states. Since 1973, Ireland has been an enthusiastic member of the European Community. Thus, from earliest times, this dialogue between insularity and continentalism, between indigenous and exogenous forces, has been a defining element in the Irish experience, finding varied expression in the landscape. While this expression is sometimes explicit, it is more often implicit, involving subtle gradations, blurred mosaics and inextricably hybrid forms of settlement, agrarian organisation and popular tradition. In this sense, the cultural landscape is a profoundly pluralist entity.

Perspectives of space and time

Irish prehistory exhibits a broad succession of cultural stages, comparable to the European experience. Considerable indigenous cultural development was enriched by a varied succession of immigrant groups. Cultural changes, however initiated, altered assessments of environmental resources while increasing the ability to modify the natural environment. Mesolithic hunting groups pioneered and settled the land about 9000 years ago. Foraging widely, they focussed on sea, lake and river shores with their rich renewable resources and there was no significant interference with the natural forest ecosystem. By the fourth millennium BC, a farming economy

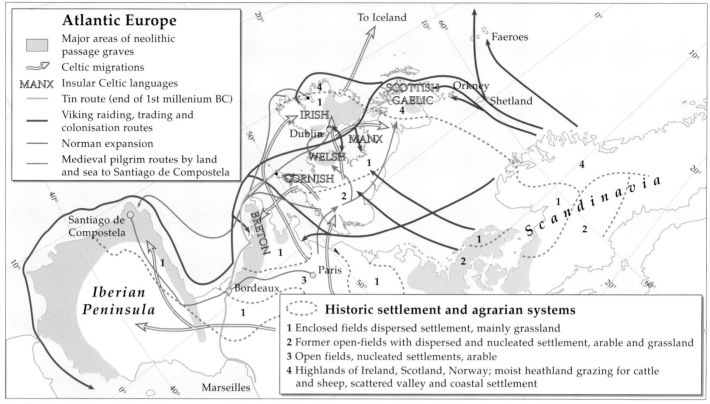

Atlantic Europe

- Major areas of neolithic passage graves
- Celtic migrations
- MANX Insular Celtic languages
- Tin route (end of 1st millenium BC)
- Viking raiding, trading and colonisation routes
- Norman expansion
- Medieval pilgrim routes by land and sea to Santiago de Compostela

Historic settlement and agrarian systems

1 Enclosed fields dispersed settlement, mainly grassland
2 Former open-fields with dispersed and nucleated settlement, arable and grassland
3 Open fields, nucleated settlements, arable
4 Highlands of Ireland, Scotland, Norway; moist heathland grazing for cattle and sheep, scattered valley and coastal settlement

Fig. 35 Atlantic Europe. Ireland shares many ecological and cultural characteristics with the islands and peninsulas of western Europe which have been linked throughout history by migrations, trade and cultural contacts.

was developing, probably introduced by immigrant neolithic groups, and forest clearance began in earnest. Thereafter, the archaeological and pollen records demonstrate an increasingly settled and ordered landscape with livestock and cereal production and some fixed field boundaries. The numerous massive stone tombs used for collective burial in the Neolithic period are a testament to the enduring links between local communities and their territories. Regional variations in tomb styles imply gradual differentiation of societies and landscape. At Céide fields in county Mayo, an extensive neolithic farm landscape has been fossilised under the bog, with a strong emphasis on pastoralism, dependent on the year-round grazing then available.

Early farmers spread throughout Ireland but, because of their elementary technology, they preferred lighter soils and upland margins where woodland cover was thinner and the soils free-draining. Extensive agricultural use of the productive though heavy soils of the ill-drained Central Lowlands was restricted, with the notable exception of the Boyne valley. However, Bronze and Iron Age farmers, with their improved equipment, made some headway and by the Early Christian period, Irish lowlands as a whole were well-settled, an ecological adjustment that has persisted to modern times. In the Bronze Age, the uplands in general and seaboard lowlands in the north

and west declined as areas of settlement, experiencing ecological deterioration partly induced by human interference. The forests, extensively cleared, never regained their former dominance, giving way to rough pasture, heath and blanket bog used by transhumant herders; woodland regeneration, however weak, was constantly checked by persistent grazing and burning.

With cultural advance and population growth, the natural forest cover was progressively removed for

● Fig. 36 Spring burning of rough grazing land in the Wicklow mountains. Fire was used to clear the natural vegetation cover in prehistoric times and is still widely used by farmers in hill areas to check colonisation by scrub and eventually woodland. Old heather is burnt off during dry spells in spring and early summer to produce a mixed growth of fresh palatable heather and grass.

AEROFILMS

● Fig. 37 These two ringforts near Athenry in county Galway are the settlement sites of substantial farmers of the Early Christian period. The circular banks mark the boundaries of farmyards and not the foundations of buildings; each ringfort originally contained several small structures of which little trace remains. The ringforts are removed from present-day settlement which lies along the road. Slight traces have survived of the irregular fields belonging to the ringforts but show no relationship to the modern pattern of rectangular fields. Enclosure on the thin drift soils of east Galway is mainly by stone walls and sheep rearing is the primary farm activity.

cultivation while livestock grazing and the cultural landscape became ever more extensive and all embracing. However, landscape transformation was not an even development. The pollen record indicates cyclical waves of clearance, agricultural usage, and reversion to woodland, often over several centuries in duration, before extensive clearances became permanent. These cycles probably reflect local usage of the land in ways which were not sustainable. Lengthy, marked and general vicissitudes are also discernible. The close of the Bronze Age and succeeding Iron Age in particular were marked by woodland regeneration, spread of bogs, and suggestions of declining cultivation and strengthening pastoralism. These developments were accompanied and perhaps partly initiated by cooler, wetter conditions, as well as by soil misuse and degradation. They reflect the difficulties encountered by early farmers in achieving a stable adjustment to the unstable Irish environment.

Human relationships with the environment during these early stages of settlement cannot be divorced from a succession of natural changes in the environment itself, especially those induced by secular climatic change. Efforts to disentangle climatic causes from human impacts

have only equivocal success because human-mediated deforestation has altered regional vegetation in ways that mimic climatic shifts; at some stages, humans may have been accentuating natural changes but in others were actively working against them. From the earliest period, the Irish environment has been the product of a dynamic interaction between culture and nature. There is no simple narrative of a pristine environment progressively degraded by human interference, no Edenic garden of Ireland to which we could all revert if only we behaved more sensibly. Many of the most distinctive features of the Irish landscape – from bogs to beech trees, from rabbits to donkeys,

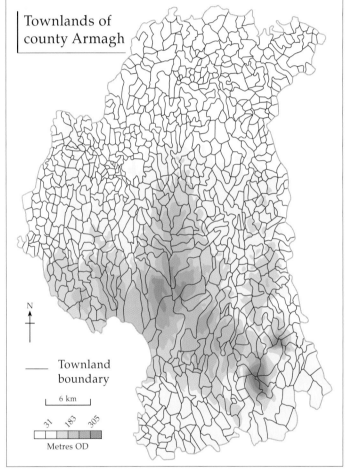

Townlands of
county Armagh

N

—— Townland
boundary

6 km

Metres OD

● Fig. 38 Since at least the medieval period, every county and parish has been divided into small land units known generally as townlands. These units were formerly called by a variety of local and regional names, such as 'balliboes' in parts of Ulster, 'tates' in Fermanagh and Monaghan and ploughlands in some southern counties. Despite frequent enlargement and division, the basic townland pattern has survived to the present day. Of varying area, townlands average 1.3 km², large enough to contain a number of farms whose owners were kin and traditionally co-operated in various ways. Townland boundaries are often marked by streams or deep ditches, banks and old hedges. Numbering over 60,000, the townlands no longer have significance as units of social and agrarian life, but in a country of dispersed rural settlement where farms lack individual names, the ancient units still have use for conveying topographical information and for postal addresses. County Armagh shows a complex pattern of townlands, which are characteristically larger and elongated in elevated areas but dense on the lowlands, with a recognisable north to south orientation reflecting that of the drumlin swarms.

Fig. 39 Rural settlement patterns. ●A) Scattered dwellings near Caherdaniel, county Kerry. Dispersed farms are the most characteristic settlement in rural Ireland, often densest in the poorer coastal areas of the west. ●B) Farm clusters occur in scattered localities and until the nineteenth century were much more widespread particularly in the north and west. This cluster lies in the hills behind Killybegs in south Donegal.

from potatoes to pheasants – are in fact surprisingly recent human imports.

The Early Christian period (*c.* 500-1000 AD) witnessed a profound transformation in Ireland, associated with a new religious culture and new technologies. Ireland evolved a close-knit but decentralised society, in which cultural unity co-existed with political fragmentation. Marked economic and social revival characterises the Early Christian period; woodland clearance is renewed and grassland expands. Numbering over 45,000, the ring-forts (raths and cashels) of the period, accompanied by their small patches of irregular fields, reflect a rural economy focused on the lowlands with a decided preference for stock-raising over tillage. Ringforts occur throughout the country, indicating the strong cultural unity of the period. The plenitude of Early Christian earth-works in the present landscape is remarkable, reflecting their original abundance and subsequent preservation on grasslands little disturbed by ploughing. A millennium-old settlement pattern has survived in a state of complete-ness unique in Europe, and constitutes one of the richest layers in the Irish landscape, from a period when the cultural record elsewhere in Europe is less assured.

Despite the suggestive similarity between the lowland distribution and dispersed pattern of ringforts and present-day farmsteads and their common pastoral economy, long-running continuities in the landscape should not be over-emphasised. The enduring townland system did originate late in the Early Christian period but a succession of settle-ment and landscape changes intervened between Early Christian and modern times, with a constantly changing balance between settlement nucleation and dispersal. In many areas today, the dispersed farms are of recent origin. In the late eighteenth and early nineteenth centuries, for

example, nucleated settlements and open-field organisation prevailed over much of the west of Ireland.

Internal and intrusive forces have moulded the land-scape during historic times. Invaders tended to influence particular regions and to modify rather than overwhelm the resilient indigenous culture. Vikings strengthened urban life and commercial traditions, reorienting the insular culture with its network of proto-urban monastic centres towards the coasts before eventually gelling into a Hiberno-Norse hybrid. The Normans established manorial villages and towns mainly in the south and east. Their towns were enduring but many rural settlements were destroyed or decayed; at some sites the decay was complete, but at others, ruined fragments remain. The Normans were neither the first nor the last invaders to achieve the half-conquest of the island. Their descendants – the Old English – were eventually transformed by cultural

●Fig. 40 Buolick, county Tipperary, is the site of a medieval rural borough, of which the only visible traces are a deserted parish church and a towerhouse with subdued earthworks between them. The landscape is now entirely pastoral; nothing survives of the arable open fields. The field wall on the site contrasts with the earthen field banks elsewhere and was probably constructed with stones from earlier buildings.

F.H.A. AALEN

● Fig. 41 This substantial late medieval towerhouse at Castle Hacket, county Galway, was inhabited until the early seventeenth century. It is still well preserved and possesses part of its original courtyard or bawn.

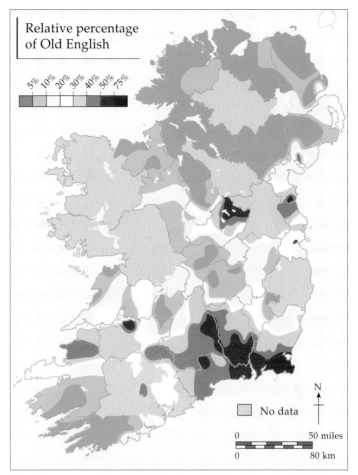

Relative percentage of Old English

5% 10% 20% 30% 40% 50% 75%

No data

N

0   50 miles
0   80 km

Fig. 42 The relative distribution of Old English as returned in 1660 poll-tax abstracts. W.J. Smyth's map shows that the distribution of family names in 1660 reflects entrenched regionalisms. High concentrations of Old English names correspond to the original areas of dense Anglo-Norman colonisation in the south-east lowlands and the hinterlands of major ports. The old Pale area is still recognisable to the north of Dublin. The north and west is overwhelmingly Gaelic and there are still strong Gaelic communities in the midlands.

fusion into a rich hybrid culture, most visibly reflected in the numerous late medieval towerhouses.

State organised plantation schemes in the sixteenth and seventeenth centuries brought over 100,000 English and Scottish settlers into Ireland, the biggest internal contemporary movement of population within Europe and commensurate with the total number of Spaniards settling in Latin America. By 1660, almost one-fifth of the island's population was immigrant (of which 45% was in Ulster, and only 5% in Connacht). The massive influx of Scottish settlers created a dynamically expanding settlement frontier down the Bann valley, in the Foyle basin, and around Lough Swilly in Donegal. It left a permanent imprint on east Down and south Antrim in cultural landscape, language, religion and politics. Most plantation schemes were failures. Vast areas of Irish land were transferred to the settlers but only in east Ulster was the plantation sufficiently large-scale and socially varied to produce viable communities as

opposed to a sparse landlordry. Because the plantations were associated both with the widespread religious wars of the period, and with the colonising project of the newly centralising English state, they introduced divisive rifts into the island which have never been properly closed.

The seventeenth century also saw the emergence of the estate system. Agrarian improvements and town building, often sponsored by major landlords, influenced the more prosperous agricultural regions of Ireland in the eighteenth and nineteenth centuries and had a decisive role in forming the modern landscape. A reorganised pattern of farms, fields and roads was introduced and the large residences of the landowning class, each surrounded by a landscaped park, became a principal feature of the landscape. In poorer districts, however, there is often little trace of estate organisation in the settlement pattern.

Rapid population growth (from 1.5 million in 1600, to 3 million in 1700 and 8.5 million in 1840) led to urgent

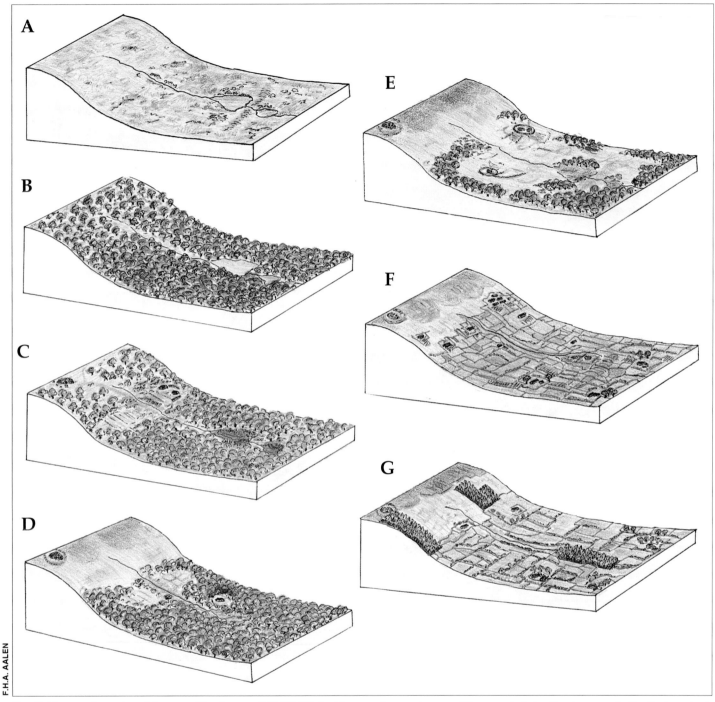

F.H.A. AALEN

Fig. 43 The transformation of the natural landscape. A) 10,000 BC. At this stage, the country was still unpeopled. As climate warmed after the ice retreat, boggy grassland and bushes invaded the lowlands but there was little vegetation on hill slopes. Lakes were still large and numerous, often ponded by terminal moraines. B) 6,000 BC. With post-glacial warming, the entire landscape, save for river and lake shores, was eventually covered by deciduous woodland, thinning out only on higher ground. Mesolithic hunters may have formed small clearings along lakes, rivers and the sea-shore for their camps. C) 2,500 BC. Neolithic farmers made clearances in the woods for grazing and cultivation, especially on the hill flanks where woodland was thinner and the soils free-draining. Upland areas were used for rough grazing and large burial cairns were built on the summits. Lake basins and ill-drained hollows on the lowlands were progressively filled by natural peat growth. D) 500 BC. By the end of the Bronze Age, largely owing to burning and grazing pressures, the hill areas had been completely cleared, and on the summits blanket bogs replaced the woodland. On lowlands, clearance for cattle-grazing continued; forest regrowth was vigorous and cultivation receded owing to climatic deterioration. E) 800 AD. In the Early Christian Period, population growth and expansion of farming led to widespread environmental change. New settlements were created, chiefly in ringforts surrounded by small fields with extensive open grazing in woodland clearances. Use of the lowland bogs and surviving woodland was controlled by the local community. The uplands remained open and bog strewn, serving primarily for summer grazing. F) 1840. Immediately before the Great Famine, the lowlands were densely settled and the farmland sub-divided by regular, enclosed fields; woodland was extremely sparse. Small farms were multiplying on the hill slopes and bogs. Livestock remained the basic pursuit but potatoes and grain were widely grown for subsistence and commercial purposes. G) Contemporary landscape. Sustained depopulation has reduced rural population densities, many smallholdings have disappeared and the remaining farms and fields have been enlarged. Grassland is emphatically the dominant land use. The lowland and upland bogs have been reduced in size and their boundaries straightened by cutting for fuel. New coniferous forests have been established on abandoned hill farms and lowland bogs.

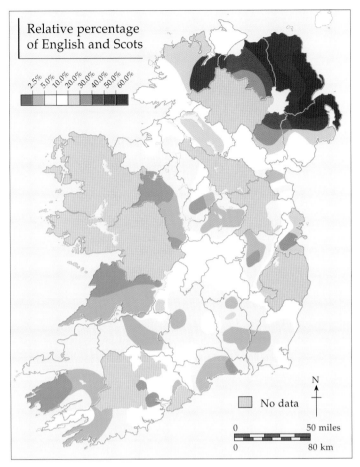

Fig. 44 The distribution of 'English and Scots' in 1660. Planter settlement is most concentrated in east Ulster and thins out to the west and south. A clear core exists in the old Pale around Dublin and settlement is strengthening in Laois and Offaly. In the south, planter settlement is associated with Cork and the Munster Plantation.

●Fig. 45 Bellamont Forest, a fine mansion built in the late 1720s for the Coote family and designed by Sir Edward Lovett Pearce, surveyor general for Ireland and the foremost exponent of Palladian architecture in Ireland. The demesne with its ornamental parkland, lake and substantial court-yard farm separated from the house is set in the drumlins along the border of counties Monaghan and Cavan.

settlement expansion and intensified use of farmland. In south Ulster and north Connacht, the spread of domestic spinning and weaving on the small farms facilitated the minute subdivision of holdings and exceptionally dense rural populations. The rapid advance and equally rapid retreat of settlement, aided by the potato's capacity to flourish in wet, acid soils, was especially pronounced in the west of Ireland, encouraging exuberant colonisation of hill margins, bogs and offshore islands. The Great Famine of the 1840s caused a traumatic check on this process. Subsequent population decline over the last century and a half has reduced population pressure and led to considerable abandonment of fields and farms, especially in upland areas and the poorer parts of Connacht and west Ulster. The population collapse is mirrored in the stricken ruins and swathes of lazy beds which festoon the deserted hill and bog edges - 'like shards of a lost culture, the whole landscape a manuscript we have lost the skill to read, a part of our past disinherited' (John Montague).

Legislation from the 1880s began the complete dismantling of the estate system. A change of proprietorship was introduced rather than major land redistribution. Tenants were converted into proprietors on their existing holdings, a change which had little immediate effect on the landscape, save in the Congested Districts where consolidation often accompanied land purchase. By 1921, two-thirds of the tenants had acquired their holdings and Ireland, unlike Britain, became essentially a nation of small farm proprietors. The demesnes were not directly affected by the land legislation, but landlordism was fatally weakened and the demesnes were increasingly abandoned by their owners, suffering general neglect and sometimes destruction.

The layering of the Irish landscape has been superimposed on an enduring environmental base. However, as this brief survey shows, the cultural formations of Ireland are as stratified and faulted as its geology. The regional diversity of the island is more intensely rooted in culture than nature; more than rocks or rain, it is people who have made the differences.

Shaping the land

As the Irish forests dwindled, they were gradually replaced by farmland (mainly improved grassland with patches of cultivation) on the better lowland soils, by moorland on the uplands, and by bogs which flourish both in lowland and upland conditions. These three basic types of vegetation have dominated the landscape in historic times. Fragments

TERENCE DUNNE

● Fig. 46 Cattle drinking on the Shannon callows. Cattle feature prominently in the earliest literature of Ireland; they have remained central to
rural life and a formative influence on the landscape. Their grazing kept
the woodland at bay and the enclosed permanent pastures of modern
times are a reflection of their pivotal importance in farming.

of natural or semi-natural woodland survived only in a
precious handful of tiny places unsuited to farming.
Ireland is markedly less wooded than most European
countries and lacks their heavily forested regions; Irish
woodland occurs characteristically in small, scattered and
ecologically isolated patches. Contrasts between hill areas
are particularly striking. From prehistory down to very
recent years, most Irish uplands have been open treeless
expanses of heather and peat while many continental hill
areas, such as the Vosges, Pyrenees and Carpathians,
remained well wooded throughout historic times. Irish
woodland was scattered and more characteristic of
lowlands than of uplands. Mountain ground in Ireland was
used primarily for pasturing cattle and sheep. As a result,
Irish hill nomenclature is remarkably rich and mountains
like Slievenamon, the Mournes and Croagh Patrick figure
prominently in place consciousness. Similarly, Irish myths
are based in the fields rather than threatening forests,
around bulls and cattle, not wolves and bears. Modern
state afforestation has transformed many hill areas and
lowland bogs, introducing markedly rectilinear patterns of
coniferous plantations.

The mild, moist Irish climate has favoured a luxuriant
vegetation growth, extensive peat bogs, and soils generally
impoverished by leaching. Many long-standing features of
Irish society are adaptations to this oceanic environment.
Once cleared of deciduous woodland, the land was best
suited to pastoralism rather than crop growth which,
although always necessary, was hindered by high rainfall.
Plentiful grass and mild winters permit livestock to graze
throughout the year; sheds and byres were superfluous
and cows were traditionally milked in the fields. Early

medieval and early modern Irish society was preoccupied
with cattle, especially cows, and milk and its products
accounted for a large part of the national diet. Cattle
became of decisive importance in the rural economy, in the
total ecology of the countryside and in the evolution of the
cultural landscape. Forest was cleared deliberately for
crops by felling and burning, but also inadvertently by
livestock grazing the patches temporarily cleared for cultivation and checking the rate of forest regeneration. Cattle
reduced the forest cover but by recycling minerals to the
soil as urine and dung they were an effective replacement
for the forest's role in restoring fertility to cleared areas.
The cattle economy and the permanent grasslands were
thus interdependent and the progressive opening of the
landscape by cattle was a self-reinforcing trend. Even
today, where grazing pressure is removed, untended land
soon reverts to its natural condition of deciduous forest.

Tenacious pastoralist traditions encouraged the
dispersed pattern of settlement evident in many periods,
for example the ringforts of the Early Christian period, the
late medieval towerhouses and, to some degree, the
dispersed farmsteads of the present-day landscape.
Pastoral proclivities may also have retarded an early emergence of urban life, favouring instead the peripatetic and
ephemeral urbanism of the fair. The rarity of medieval
lynchets and ridge-and-furrow in Ireland suggests that the
extent and duration of open-field tillage was insufficient to
allow their gestation. This negative evidence (compare, for
example, the English midlands) emphasises the strength of
the Irish pastoral tradition.

Transhumance, or booleying, was a deeply rooted
feature of the rural economy, involving the movement of
livestock to upland pastures in the summer months
accompanied by herders and their families who lived in
temporary dwellings while producing milk and dairy
products. Because it required extensive areas of rough
grazing, booleying preserved the open character of the
hills; it also removed animals from unenclosed infields
around the permanent settlements while crops were in the
ground and conserved the home pastures for winter
feeding. In the sixteenth and seventeenth centuries,
booleying was sometimes confused by outside observers
with nomadism. The custom remained vital until the
seventeenth century but thereafter declined, surviving
only in a vestigial form in some remote areas until the
nineteenth and early twentieth century.

The Irish folk-life scholar A.T. Lucas observed that, until
very recently, cattle 'touched the lives of everyone from
sunrise to sunset and from birth to death'; a corpus of ritual
and magic existed to promote their fertility and milk yield;

they had a status virtually as members of society. The cow was the measure of most things, the unit of value; in many parts of the country, a 'cow's grass' was traditionally the effective unit of land measurement, its size varying with grazing quality. From the seventeenth century, with the growth of the estate system and commercial farming, dry stock gained in economic importance over milch cows, and the substantial growth of rural population in the eighteenth and early nineteenth centuries favoured the spread of the potato as a major foodstuff replacing traditional milk products. Nevertheless, cattle remain the chief preoccupation of Irish farming and permanent grassland is still emphatically the major land use.

Like many parts of Atlantic Europe but in contrast to the immense zone of open-field villages on the plains of western, central and northern Europe, Irish farmed areas now possess a much enclosed or *bocage* landscape. The widespread pattern of rectilinear fields, enclosed by banks, hedges and walls, has developed mainly since the seventeenth century to facilitate improved farming with more intensive livestock rearing, crop rotations and individual management of consolidated holdings; often it replaced and was influenced by older systems of open-field organisation with intermixed strip holdings but it was also established *de novo*, especially on newly reclaimed hillsides and bogs. The typical rural settlement pattern of single dispersed farms is generally envisaged as emerging along with the *bocage* in recent centuries, displacing nucleated settlement and open-fields. Enclosed fields are now the most ubiquitous and conspicuous element of the cultural landscape. Their size, shape and construction contribute much to the distinctive character of regional landscapes.

The tendency in lowland areas for the banks, trees and hedges to conceal the dispersed farms and give the countryside an empty appearance has often been noted. Elizabeth Bowen in *Bowen's Court* writes perceptively:

> The country is not as empty as it appears. Roads and boreens between high hedges, sunk rivers, farms deep in squares of sheltering trees all combine by their disappearance to trick the eye. Only mountainy farmhouses, gleaming white on their fields reclaimed from the bog and facades of chapels on hills or hillocks, show. The country conceals its pattern of life, which can only wholly be seen from an aeroplane. This is really country to fly over – its apparent empty smoothness is full of dips and creases. From the air, you discover unknown reaches of river, chapels, schools, bridges, forlorn graveyards, interknit by a complex of untravelled roads.

● Fig. 47 *Bocage* landscape, east county Kerry.

Boglands have strongly influenced rural settlement distribution and communications but are themselves deeply humanised landscapes, originating and evolving in close association with land use systems. While in part natural, the initiation of blanket bog at some sites is attributable to human removal of the forest cover for farming. Blanket bogs in upland and western lowland areas are frequently developed over tree stumps. Charcoal layers in the peat suggest that burning of surface vegetation was a factor in bog development; even more telling, bogs have sometimes submerged ancient settlements and fields. As their rounded outlines indicate, raised bogs typically originated in damp lowland hollows, uninfluenced by human agency. Like blanket bogs, their area has been greatly reduced since prehistoric times through hand cutting for fuel. Boglands are also a unique form of natural diary,

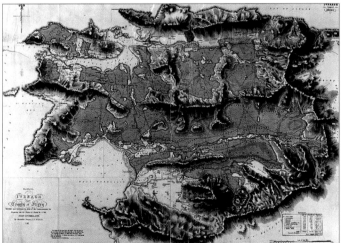

● Fig. 48 Extensive blanket bog covers most of the Iveragh peninsula in county Kerry. This superb map of bog distribution was prepared for the Bog Commissioners by Alexander Nimmo in 1811.

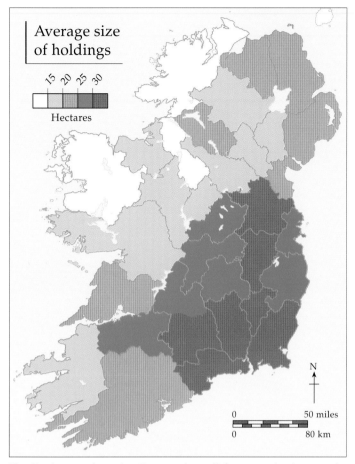

Fig. 49 Average farm size. In general, small farms are dominant to the north of a line drawn approximately from Galway to Dundalk, and holdings increase in size towards the south-east. The smallest holdings are in the poorest areas of the north-west. In the richer agricultural areas of the south and east, there are many small farms but large farms occupy a greater area of the total farmed land.

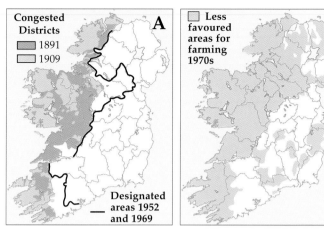

Fig. 50 The physical and economic problems of the west have long been recognised in government planning. A) The Congested Districts Board was established in 1891 to relieve western poverty by developing industries, improving agriculture and fishing, and reforming land tenure. Congested districts were usually but not necessarily densely populated: they were not congested as regards quantity, but rather the quality of the land, being districts where rateable valuation divided by population fell below a critical threshold. In 1909, the definition of the congested districts was considerably widened to include most of the territory of western seaboard counties, embracing a third of the country and a quarter of the population. The Underdeveloped Areas Act 1952 was the first instrument of regional development policy in the new southern state; it was designed specifically to aid development in areas similar to the congested districts, which were still characterised by rural decline, weak industrial development and heavy emigration. The Industrial Development Act of 1969 defined Designated Areas as the congested areas recognised in the Underdeveloped Areas Act, and new industrial projects there were given significantly higher grants than elsewhere in the country. B) Less favoured areas for farming as defined for the purpose of EC directives in the 1970s corresponded with the north western areas of poorly-drained soils, limited land-use capability and small farms.

soaking up the annual pollen rain and preserving it in layers which are especially conducive to palynological techniques. Thus, the detailed narrative of vegetation change, and consequently of climatic change, in the post-glacial period can be recovered with great precision from Irish bogs, and they are among the richest world sites for environmental archaeometry.

Historically, boglands have been a dynamic interface between the natural world and the forces of human history and economy. Over the centuries, a complex management system for boglands emerged, designed to maintain ecological equilibrium while maximising bogland utilisation. This equilibrium depended on recognition within farm communities of the limited carrying capacity and fragile ecosystems of the bog, recognition enshrined in customary practices such as stinting, commonage, collop and turbary rights. Such intimate local adjustments were reflected in a rich complex of behaviour. In the Irish language, there are 130 words specific to bogland – testimony to the sophisticated knowledge accumulated from the symbiosis.

In the eighteenth and nineteenth centuries, bogs were frequently seen by landlords and government agencies as negative features, as an endless brooding expanse beyond farming, useless unless drained and 'improved' to provide agricultural land. In the twentieth century, interest turned to large-scale, mechanised exploitation for fuel. Today, after much depletion, bogs are increasingly perceived as assets to be conserved for their scientific, educational, amenity and landscape qualities. Bogland is an important aesthetic, spiritual and cultural resource. In a country denuded of forest, the bog is *par excellence* the Irish venue for experiencing the natural world with the greatest intensity – a place of exploration and discovery, where an environmental ethic can be inculcated. Bogs have inspired a wide range of artistic endeavour in Ireland – Seamus Heaney's poems, John McGahern's novels, the paintings of Paul Henry, Maurice MacGonigal and Colin Midleton, and an evocative repertoire of songs and tunes in Irish traditional music.

The force of environmental influences on the cultural landscape should not be overemphasised. Prevailing regional differences in rural population density, farm size, settlement and field patterns are equally a response to historical and socio-economic as well as to strictly environmental factors. The concentration of small farms on the poorer lands of the north-west and of larger farms in the south-east, for example, has complex causation involving historical, economic and demographic factors, notably land inheritance and subdivision practices. The striking differences in Ulster's cultural landscapes cannot be explained without reference to the plantations and the pattern of 'catholic' uplands and 'protestant' lowlands. Moreover, the character and regional distribution of agricultural production has varied considerably, suggesting the permissiveness of the physical environment. In the Late Medieval period, for example, a decline of cultivation and probably of population occurred in the Norman area, followed by a reversion to pastoralism. Crop production increased substantially in the west and east during the Napoleonic wars, while in the past century and a half, the area of arable crops has halved and the number of cattle doubled. In the last decade, EU policy has promoted a surge in the number of sheep. Economic and social forces continue to modify the rural landscape in various ways, some of which give rise to considerable concern among ecologists and those concerned with landscape heritage.

FUTURE ORIENTATION

Throughout Europe, there is presently a marked growth of public and political concern for landscapes, prompted particularly by a sense that the quality and diversity of the continent's rich landscape legacy have been diminished in the post-war period by many forces, especially more mechanised and intensive farming and forestry and a general standardisation of culture. Further changes in the landscape are imminent, although the patterns of future change cannot be predicted precisely.

There is growing awareness that landscapes are important cultural, ecological and economic assets which should be managed in the interests of social well-being. The concern has emphatically widened from the traditional protection of sites and of exceptional landscapes to the management of all landscapes, since these form the daily surroundings of society. Within the Council of Europe and elsewhere, it is now being argued that the benefits derived from landscape are so substantial that peoples and governments must make deliberate efforts to protect and enhance landscape qualities by modifying where necessary the processes of change. The campaign for Europe's landscapes is an heroic endeavour, as is the search for appropriate policies and means of landscape management. Problems and policies will vary from country to country and between regions but clearly Ireland must be involved because of the oustanding quality of its landscapes: despite persistent

abuse by private and public activities, they are still of immense cultural and economic significance to the nation.

Landscape conservation and diversity should be given prominence in overall rural development policies. Landscape quality and socio-economic progress are mutually supportive, not competitive considerations. Policies are needed which ensure that, as the landscape evolves, its beauty and diversity are retained and wherever possible enhanced. Necessary changes need to be harmonised with the totality of landscape features, respecting, for example, the lay-out of historic settlements and working with the grain of inherited field and farm patterns, developing traditional building forms and using local building materials and skills. New developments should be permitted only if they make a positive contribution to the rural scene.

Protection of the Irish landscape has been a low priority; there is still widespread insensitivity to landscape deterioration and spineless acquiescence in brutal acts of spoliation. Although public concern for the landscape is growing, it remains too diffuse to influence sufficiently the agencies and individuals responsible for change. Certain features of landscape change, such as the uncontrolled proliferation of dispersed bungalows, the destruction of bog environments which are rare elsewhere in Europe, and the general weakness of nature conservation policies, have been repeatedly condemned by conservationists within and outside Ireland. In the Republic, there is no clear landscape policy; no central authority exists to develop integrated conservation policies for landscape, nature and historic heritage, and the planning system remains too weak to implement any. There is not even a centralised landscape advisory body for use by local authorities and other government departments. Conservation policies in Northern Ireland are generally more effective and voluntary bodies stronger, but, nevertheless, achievements are patchy and there have been conspicuous shortcomings.

There are diverse reasons for the low priority given to landscape protection. In a lightly urbanised country, the very extent of the countryside encourages an uncaring and irresponsible attitude, while the pace of rural change is not sufficiently calamitous to induce concerted reactions. Farmers refuse to romanticise the landscape and agricultural practices have rarely been tempered by considerations such as the visual effects of innovations. Recent political and social history has also encouraged negative attitudes to conservation. There has been hostility to features associated with the old ascendancy but also little regard for vernacular landscape features, such as traditional rural buildings and field patterns, in a society anxious to distance itself as rapidly as possible from all associations with an impoverished rural past. Both sets of attitudes have vitiated conservation endeavours in general and compromised their public acceptability. Attitudes are now changing and more informed perspectives are apparent but a predatory exploitation of the rural landscape and resources is still rampant, notably the selfish development of individual features and sites without due regard for the wider landscape context. House building, farming, forestry, industry, tourism and recreation are all implicated here.

National attitudes to the landscape are seldom explored in Irish literature. Séan Ó Faoláin, however, made an arresting observation in his book *An Irish Journey*. Writing of the site of the Battle of Kinsale, Ó Faoláin describes its 'suffusion of association with things past' but remarks that this is rare in Ireland. He asserts:

> *Our history has seemed to fade from the land like old writing from parchment. Traditional memory is broken. Our monuments are finest when oldest: but then so old that their echoes have died away. The pietas which is so cherished and nourished in other countries has here an inadequate number of actual moulds to hold it. National emotion is a wild sea spray that evaporates like a religion without a ritual. We are moved by ghosts. Something powerful and precious hangs in the air that holds us like a succubus; but what it is we can hardly define because we have so few concrete things that express it.*

Has there been a collective subconscious breaking with the past, a feeling that the rural landscape is not a genuinely Irish thing but something irredeemably tainted by impoverishment, with colonial dispossession and landlord oppression; 'a data bank of humiliation'? Does this help to explain the massive destruction of features such as demesnes, boreens and bogs and the energetic creation of new landscape elements such as bungalows, pubs, churches and pine forests, which have no sense of context or continuity and display only a rootless, commonplace modernity?

Whatever the nature and origin of landscape perceptions, deeper understanding of the Irish landscape contradicts the idea that rural communities are living in places which are not their own, in landscapes shaped for them but not by them. As well as sharp ruptures in landscape evolution, there are strong continuities and much of the landscape is truly vernacular, the product of evolving hybrid cultures coaxed or disciplined by the environment into recognisably Irish moulds.

The cultural landscape thus offers both identity and continuity – the living past in tangible form. Cultural landscapes are a communal creation: they are the cumulative result of countless generations of people living in a specific place, the sedimentation of cultural forms from the stream of time. Paul Vidal de la Blache showed that landscapes are 'medals struck in the image of their people'. They are thus precious components of a nation's identity, demanding the same respect and care as the more obvious expressions of that identity, like art and literature. As such, they can nourish fundamental social and psychological needs by providing a sense of continuity for modern people. They remain too, an enduring source of spiritual and artistic inspiration, stimulating creativity in our best artists and writers. Because successful solutions to living in a particular environment are embodied in their structures, cultural landscapes also conserve the wisdom of human experience. They provide a font of ideas on how we can best use our land, consistent with the wider search for ecological sustainability and socio-economic well-being.

BIBLIOGRAPHY

F. Aalen, *Man and the landscape in Ireland* (London, 1978).

F. Aalen (ed.), *Landscape study and management* (Dublin, 1996).

G. Cooney and E.Grogan, *Irish prehistory: a social perspective* (Dublin, 1994).

E. Evans, *Irish folk ways* (London, 1957).

E. Evans, *The personality of Ireland* (Belfast, 1981).

E. Evans, *Ireland and the Atlantic heritage: selected writings* (Dublin, 1996).

A. Fenton and D. Gillmor (ed.), *Rural land use on the Atlantic periphery of Europe: Scotland and Ireland* (Dublin, 1994).

T. Freeman, *Ireland. A general and regional geography* (London, 1969).

D. Gillmor (ed.), *The Irish countryside* (Dublin, 1989).

B. Graham and L. Proudfoot (ed.), *An historical geography of Ireland* (London, 1993).

G. Herries Davies and N. Stephens, *Ireland* (London, 1978).

J. Johnson, *Ireland. A human geography* (London, 1994).

A. Lucas, *Cattle in ancient Ireland* (Kilkenny, 1989).

F. Mitchell, *The Shell guide to reading the Irish landscape* (Dublin, 1986).

A. Orme, *Ireland* (London, 1970).

S. Ó Faoláin, *An Irish journey* (London, 1941).

P. Robinson, *The plantation of Ulster* (Dublin, 1984).

T. Reeves-Smyth and F. Hamond (ed.), *Landscape archaeology in Ireland* (Oxford, 1983).

W. Smyth and K. Whelan (ed.), *Common Ground. Essays on the historical geography of Ireland* (Cork, 1986).

EARLY LANDSCAPES: FROM PREHISTORY TO PLANTATION

The Irish countryside is steeped in the physical remains of nine millennia of human occupation. Over 136,000 archaeological sites and monuments, dating before 1700 AD, have been recorded by archaeological surveys; this massive corpus provides extensive material for analysis and interpretation. Monuments range from the fragile remains of stone tool working sites of mesolithic (Middle Stone Age) date, to elaborate deserted villages of the medieval period, to plantation-era castles. In some areas, monuments are sufficiently numerous and visible to lend a special flavour to the landscape. Striking concentrations of particular categories of monuments, such as tower-houses in east Limerick and cashels on the Aran Islands, contribute to a distinctive regional landscape character.

These archaeological monuments are increasingly valued as an integral cultural element of Irish life: there has accordingly been a renewed emphasis on their public presentation. With a base-line archaeological survey recently completed for the whole island, archaeologists, geographers and landscape historians are in an unique position to assess the frequency of different monument types and also to interpret the patterns which are now emerging in space and through time. In many areas, there is now sufficient archaeological evidence to allow study of past socio-cultural patterning on a more meaningful scale than is possible from investigation of individual sites. Increasingly, the landscape region rather than specific sites will be the analytical unit for understanding past human societies.

However, each site is potentially significant in building up the larger scale picture of the evolution of Irish settlement and of the interaction between natural and human processes which have shaped our immensely varied modern landscape. Preservation of all surviving monuments must be the ultimate goal of island-wide planning legislation.

DEPARTMENT OF ARTS, CULTURE AND THE GAELTACHT

• Fig. 1 Photographed in 1913, this impressive stone row, known locally as the 'Finger Stones', is at at Garranes, county Cork. Stone alignments and isolated standing stones are probably connected with late prehistoric ritual but are difficult to date precisely.

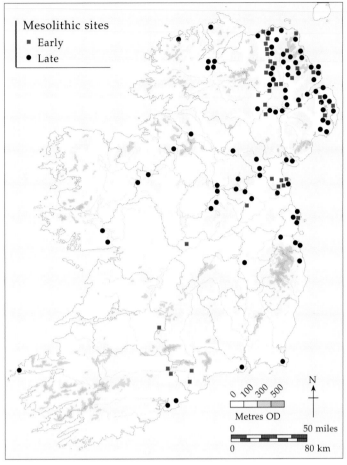

Fig. 2 Mesolithic material shows a marked concentration in north-east Ireland, but systematic field research in the south and south-east is starting to alter this picture which may simply reflect the intensity of research in the north-east.

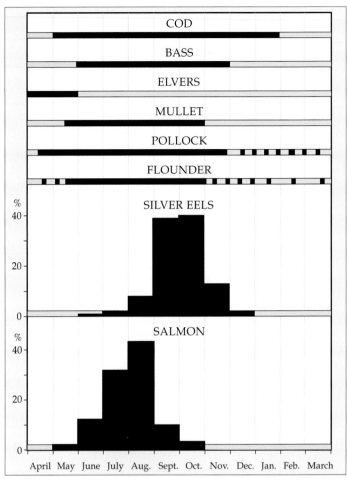

● Fig. 4 Fish from the River Bann, a major component in the diet of the mesolithic community at Mount Sandel, could be exploited for much of the year.

THE MESOLITHIC PERIOD

Ireland was first settled 9000 years ago. In the context of western Europe, this relative lateness may be explained by Ireland's geographical isolation and the limited resources available for human survival. The first settlers were mesolithic hunters, fishers and gatherers. They encountered a heavily wooded landscape of hazel scrub, overshadowed by oak, ash, elm and pine, and relieved only by an expanse of lakes and large bodies of shallow open water in the midlands and the flood plains of the Shannon. Very few large mammals (red deer and wild pig) roamed these woodlands, making fish and game birds (woodpigeon, woodcock and gooseshank) significant elements in the mesolithic diet.

In general, the only surviving indication of mesolithic habitation is a scatter of stone tools or a midden of occupation debris consisting largely of shells, usually found exposed on a river bank or sea shore. However, excavated sites have provided a greater insight into the working of

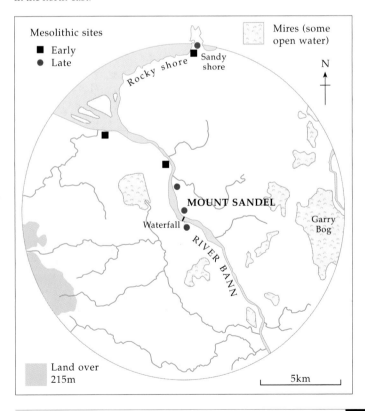

● Fig. 3 (left) A variety of habitats and mesolithic settlements existed within a 10km radius of Mount Sandel, county Londonderry at 7000-6000 BC.

these pioneering communities, such as those at Lough Boora in county Offaly and Mount Sandel in county Derry. In the 1970s, the earliest known mesolithic 'base camp' was excavated at Mount Sandel, overlooking the estuary of the Lower Bann. Traces of timber huts were uncovered adjacent to an area where stone tools were manufactured. The plant food and bone remains showed that these people could live off the immediate wood and estuarine resources for most of the year, exploiting migratory fish such as salmon and eels, hunting wild boar and collecting fruit and nuts. This relatively settled picture of life from the Mount Sandel investigations runs contrary to earlier impressions of a highly mobile society prior to the introduction of agriculture.

The discovery of mesolithic settlements by river banks, lake margins, islands and coasts highlights the intimate relationship of these communities with their immediate food supply. As new information emerges, it is clear that these settlements eventually spread throughout the entire island. The marked concentration of mesolithic sites in the north-east of Ireland was explained in the past by the availability of good flint supplies. However, at Lough Boora and a late mesolithic site at Ferriter's cove, county Kerry, chert and rhyolite were used in tool production where flint was not available locally. The discovery of mesolithic assemblages from the Blackwater valley in county Cork and from Ballylough in east county Waterford indicates the potential of a more strategic programme of field search and excavation in the future.

The Neolithic Period

The gradual spread of farming throughout Europe brought with it the custom of communal burial in great stone structures known as megalithic tombs. Traditionally, the beginning of the Neolithic in Ireland has been associated with the appearance of these tomb-builders around 4000 BC. However, there is now considerable evidence for individual burials of Early Neolithic date. These discoveries suggest that communities in the south-east and in Munster were practising a simpler 'Linkardstown type' burial tradition. The site at Linkardstown, county Carlow, comprised a cist (stone box) of megalithic proportions, containing the disarticulated remains of an adult woman, accompanied by a polished stone axe and decorated necked bowl, under a low mound of layered construction. These individual burials are sited on glacial gravels in relatively low-lying situations (usually close to streams or rivers) and have been casually discovered as a result of gravel extraction or land clearance. The number of recorded individual burials is still relatively small but may indicate an incipient stage of colonisation in the south-east.

The communal megalithic tombs, however, form the most coherent and distinctive groups in the Irish Neolithic. With almost 1500 tombs recorded, the first farmers left behind impressive remains, still prominent in the landscape. Only in the Midlands and parts of Munster are tombs largely absent. These megaliths have been intimately associated with Irish mythology, with topographical names such as the 'Giant's Grave' and 'Dermot and Grainne's Bed' testifying to the way subsequent generations incorporated these enigmatic remains into their mental landscapes.

Four types of megalithic tombs have been identified on the basis of architecture, excavation artifacts and distribution patterns: court, portal, passage and wedge. These various tomb types have been interpreted as a chronological sequence, starting with the court tomb builders and ending with wedge tombs. However, the extensive range of recent C14 dates provides evidence for considerable overlap. Their differing distributions may represent territorial divisions between diverse religious/political groups.

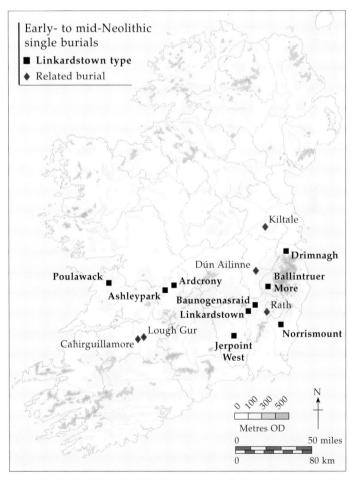

Early- to mid-Neolithic single burials
■ **Linkardstown type**
♦ Related burial

Fig. 5 Early Neolithic individual burials (named after a site excavated at Linkardstown, county Carlow in the 1940s) have been discovered in Leinster and Munster. The burials comprise an adult inhumation accompanied by a characteristic necked vessel in a stone chamber under a circular earthen mound.

Court tombs

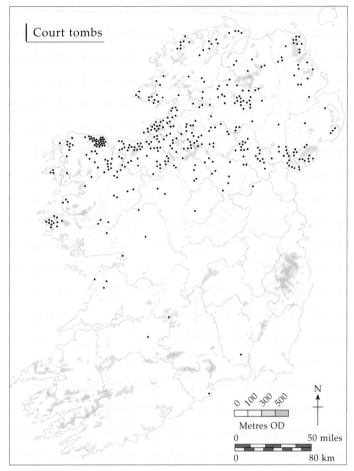

Fig. 6 Court tombs are concentrated in the northern part of the country, with only seven tombs occurring south of a line from Dundalk Bay to Clifden. Irish court tombs are part of a larger group of neolithic sites in northern and western Europe. These include the unchambered or wooden chambered long barrows, the chambered tombs of the Severn-Cotswold area, the Clyde cairns of Scotland and Irish portal tombs.

DEPARTMENT OF ARTS, CULTURE AND THE GAELTACHT

•Fig. 7 A court tomb at Deerpark, overlooking Lough Gill in the Sligo uplands. An encroaching forestry plantation has robbed this site of its landscape context. Court tombs consist of an orthostatically defined court, giving access to a long, segmented stone burial chamber with an overlying elongated cairn. They are often in upland locations, near the limits of present-day cultivation.

ENVIRONMENTAL SERVICE, DOE (NI)

•Fig. 8 A fine portal tomb at Glenroan, county Tyrone. Portal tombs consist of a chamber with an imposing entry formed of two large portal stones and covered by an enormous capstone sloping down to the rear of the chamber.

Portal tombs

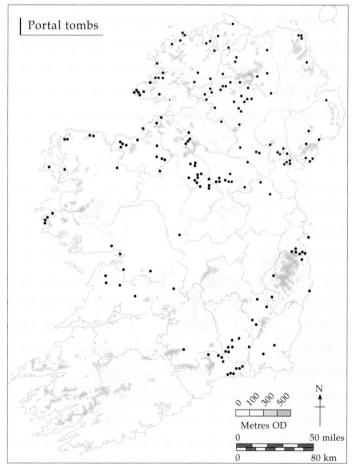

Fig. 9 Portal tombs occur largely in the north but they are also found in Cork, Clare, south Galway and the south-east. Similarities in distribution and morphology have been used to argue that portal tombs developed from court tombs, probably in the mid-Ulster area, and later spread southwards. The extensive gap between the Ulster and Leinster groupings suggests a sea-borne expansion.

● Fig. 10 Passage tomb cemetery at Carrowkeel, county Sligo. In passage graves, the burial chamber is approached by a long passage and the whole monument is covered by a circular cairn. Clusters of tombs often occur on mountain summits. This cemetery is in the Bricklieve mountains overlooking Lough Arrow.

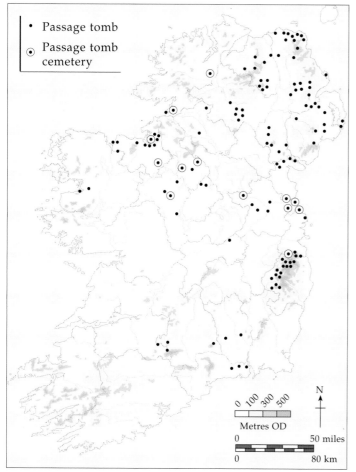

Fig. 11 Passage tombs are known from the north and east, with a few outliers in Munster. They often occur in cemeteries which vary from clusters of fifty to sixty sites (as at Carrowmore, county Sligo) to groups of three or four tombs. A conspicuous belt of cemeteries lies across the northern edge of the Central Lowlands; a second major concentration of tombs lies along the western shoulders of the Wicklow Mountains.

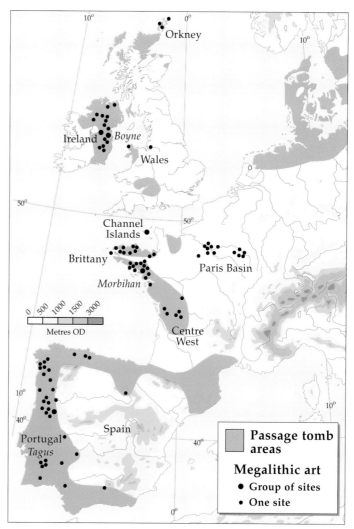

Fig. 12 Western European megalithic art is found on passage graves in Iberia, western France, Ireland and Britain. Passage grave art can be found on tomb orthostats, lintels and kerbstones.

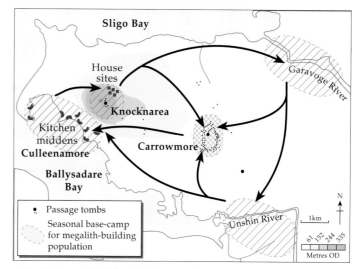

● Fig. 13 A model of the circulation and seasonal utilisation by the megalith-builders of the coastal and inland food resources of Knocknarea peninsula, county Sligo. Irish passage tomb cemeteries show recurring patterns of tomb siting which indicate that they evolved in a deliberately chosen way. Tombs are grouped into clusters, normally with a number of smaller tombs around a larger site, such as the central part of Carrowmore.

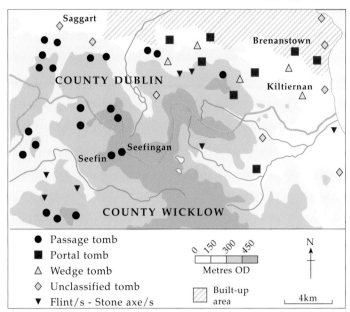

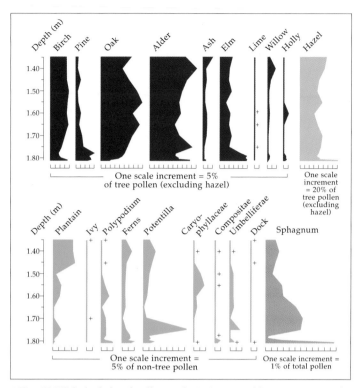

• Fig. 14 Within the south Dublin/north Wicklow uplands, the various megalithic tomb types form distinct patterns which may indicate the existence of different tomb-building communities. Passage tombs crown the western and northern summits of the mountains; portal tombs lie further to the east and down-slope, extending into the lowlands at Brenanstown and Kiltiernan; wedge tombs overlap portal tombs but tend to be upslope and in proximity to one another.

This 'tomb-led' approach to the study of early farming communities has recently been challenged by archaeologists attempting to fill the geographic gaps in early settlement patterns through systematic field collecting and excavation. In 1983, a regional programme of field survey and excavation was initiated to investigate neolithic settlement around Waterford Harbour, the magnificent estuary of the rivers Barrow and Suir. The results from this 'Ballylough Project' have been startling; over 400 locations have been identified, indicating extensive penetration of a countryside almost devoid of upstanding evidence for neolithic settlement. These range from habitations or camp sites for tool-making to scatters of stone artifacts. In addition to field survey and surface collecting, excavations were carried out at six sites, one of which produced charred plant remains, including cultivated barley, vetch, goosefoot and knotgrass. Neolithic pottery sherds were found at another site. A definite preference for locating settlements along the coast and estuary was noted.

County Kildare, in particular the Barrow basin, has also produced a significant concentration of stone axe finds. Although in use since the mesolithic period, the axe is a diagnostic tool of the Neolithic, essential to large scale forest clearance during this period; therefore, the discovery

• Fig. 16 (right) At Behy and Glenulra, county Mayo, Séamus Caulfield has discovered a well-organised, preshistoric field system (Céide Fields) under the bog in association with neolithic remains; it comprises parallel walls of stone running inland from the coast for at least 800m, with cross-walls dividing the strips. Farming took place here between 3710-3220 BC.

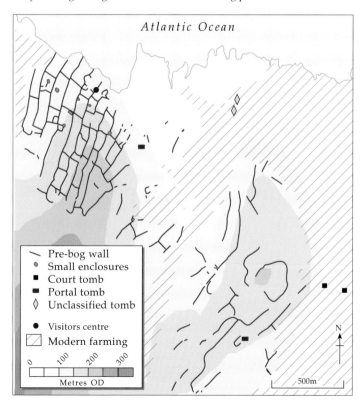

• Fig. 15 With the help of pollen analysis, it is possible to reconstruct the prehistoric environment of neolithic communities and the large scale vegetational changes introduced by farming. This pollen diagram is drawn from a sample taken from a blanket bog within the Wicklow granite area on a saddle of land between Seefin and Seefingan; both these peaks are crowned by impressive passage tombs. At the base of the sample, typical *landnam,* or clearance, features were identified; a decline in elm and pine occurs, associated with the appearance of plantain which is an agricultural indicator. This phase was followed by the spread of blanket bog, which began as a heath. Scientists ascribe this spread to the negative impact of early farming on vegetation and soils over a long period.

Wedge tombs

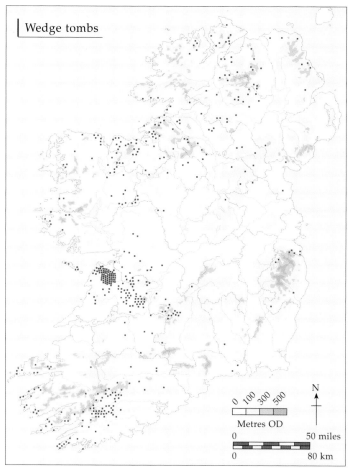

Fig. 17 Wedge tombs are the most numerous category of megalithic tomb and exhibit a marked territorial exclusiveness. The distribution is essentially western, with 120 sites in Clare and about the same number in the rest of Munster. Beaker pottery as well as barbed and tanged arrowheads in several wedge tombs indicate a date in the mid-third millennium BC, placing them at the end of the tomb building period. Bronze implements occur in the tombs and the concentrations in Kerry and Cork may reflect nearby copper deposits. The conspicuous tomb cluster on the Burren in county Clare is difficult to explain but may reflect the valuable grazing resources, especially in winter.

of stone axes in an area is an indication of early settlement. Mapping their distribution in Ireland provides a clearer view of the true extent of neolithic settlement, confirming major concentrations in the north-east, where there were prehistoric axe factories, and high densities coinciding with field monuments in the Boyne valley, county Meath and Lough Gur, county Limerick. Again, there are considerable gaps in Munster.

Tomb-building communities had a dramatic impact on the landscape, identifiable in both pollen and faunal records. The introduction of domestic cattle and sheep dramatically increased the number and range of mammals in Ireland. A mixed farming economy required field boundaries to keep cattle out of the crops. In north Mayo, Valencia Island and elsewhere, these prehistoric field systems survive under bogs. On the other hand, areas of contemporary rich agricultural land exist where tombs are

ENVIRONMENTAL SERVICE, DOE (NI)

• Fig. 18 Wedge tomb at Tireighter, county Londonderry. The narrowing of the stone chambers of these tombs at one end produces a diagnostic wedge shape.

Early Bronze Age cist graves

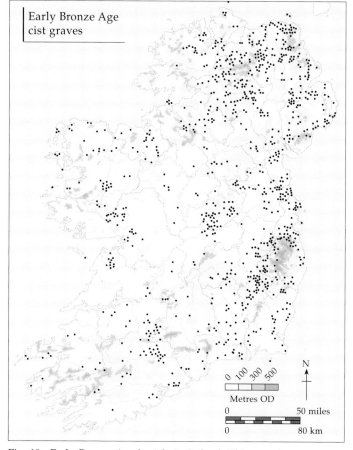

Fig. 19 Early Bronze Age burials in Ireland. This map incorporates a variety of funerary rituals dating from 2000-1500 BC; unburnt burials, cremated burials, cist graves, pit graves, tumuli and flat graves. Pottery, often placed in these burials, comprises bowl and vase food vessels, enlarged food vessels and collared urns. Burials are sometimes accompanied by stone, metal and bone artifacts.

present but where landscape evidence for the early phases of agriculture has been lost, the Boyne valley being a good example. Faunal assemblages from the excavation at Newgrange, and pollen and seed analysis from Knowth

and Newgrange suggest an enclosed neolithic landscape in the Boyne valley.

THE BRONZE AGE

In the Bronze Age, settlement expanded in lowland areas. This trend is highlighted in the distribution of graves dating from the period which reveals an eastern, lowland bias. Their tendency to cluster where glacial sands and gravels are abundant may reflect the pattern of grave discovery which often occurs during sand and gravel extraction activities. Taking this bias into account, such a strong body of evidence indicates a major growth of population in the lowlands during the Bronze Age.

The nature of burial was simpler and certainly did not involve the major construction feats of the previous era. Burials were in pits or cists, sometimes in cemeteries or under mounds. The communal tomb tradition persisted in the western half of Ireland with the construction of wedge tombs. Greater emphasis was placed on worship for the living; ceremonial circles built of earth, free-standing megalithic stones, or timber posts were being erected in particular regions throughout Ireland.

● Fig. 21 The 'Giant's Ring', a massive henge or ceremonial embanked enclosure at Ballynahatty, county Down, measures 225m in diameter. As in the Boyne valley, where the main concentration of this site type is found, the enclosure is associated with an earlier megalithic tomb.

Within the lowland river valleys of county Meath, including the famous passage tomb heartland of the 'Bend of the Boyne', there is another major regional group of circles built of earth and one timber example. These monuments are among the six most remarkable concentrations of 'henge' monuments (ceremonial circles) in Britain and Ireland. The main characteristic of these 'Boyne-type' enclosures is their flat-topped earthen bank, which encloses a circular to oval space with a domed or hollowed interior, generally breached by a single entrance. There is no evidence for a construction ditch as the enclosing bank was created from material scarped from the interior.

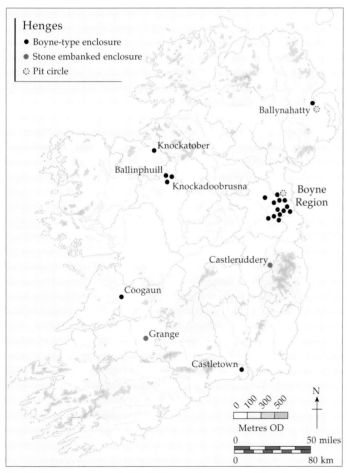

Henges
● Boyne-type enclosure
● Stone embanked enclosure
○ Pit circle

Ballynahatty ○

Knockatober ●

Ballinphuill ●

Knockadoobrusna ●

Boyne Region

Castleruddery ●

Coogaun ●

Grange ●

Castletown ●

N

0 100 300 500

Metres OD

0   50 miles

0   80 km

Fig. 20 Henge monuments (Early Bronze Age ceremonial enclosures). The builders of these enclosures occupied the farmed lands of the passage tomb societies, as in the Boyne valley.

● Fig. 22 This ring barrow is enclosed within the hillfort at Clogher, county Tyrone. The practice of constructing earthen mounds over human cremations was widespread in Ireland from the Bronze Age to the Iron Age, with the possibility of overlap with Early Christian burial rites. These small earthworks come in a wide range of types; most examples are merely ring ditches, but more elaborate barrows have multiple banks and ditches, and raised interiors resembling upturned saucers.

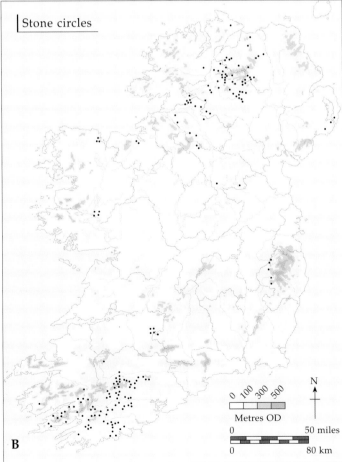

Fig. 23 Stone circles were primarily ritual monuments. They occur in regional groups, in both Britain and Ireland. A) In England and Wales, the distribution is essentially western with notable clusters in Devon and Cornwall. Sites are plentiful in Scotland, especially in the north-east and the southern uplands. B) The largest Irish groupings are in Cork and Kerry (in Munster) and Fermanagh and Tyrone (in Ulster).

Henges sometimes incorporate earlier burial mounds. Ring ditches within their interiors have been identified from aerial photographs. Excavation of an embanked enclosure at Monknewtown revealed a pit cemetery, a habitation site and a ring ditch dating from circa 1860 BC. However, the large pit circle or 'woodhenge' south of the Newgrange passage tomb produced Beaker and Grooved Ware pottery, suggesting an earlier date of 2000 BC for the building of large ritual circles in the Boyne valley. This renewed phase of monument building coincides with an apparent decline in the fabric of the passage tombs, resulting in cairn collapse at Newgrange. It is also associated with the adoption of new pottery-styles and a simpler burial practice. Similar changes affected neighbouring Britain and have been interpreted as evidence of a more stratified society with a focus on individual burial rather than on communal tombs.

Towards the end of the Bronze Age (or even later), another type of ceremonial monument – the stone circle – was constructed in great numbers throughout Britain and Ireland. In Ireland, there are two major stone circle complexes, a south Munster series occupying large areas of Cork and parts of south-west Kerry, and a mid-Ulster series in Tyrone, Derry and east Fermanagh. The circles and associated stone rows in the Ulster group are very different from those in south Munster. They are more irregular in plan and composed of smaller stones with the rows usually set tangentially to them. The most famous site is at

DEPARTMENT OF ARTS, CULTURE AND THE GAELTACHT

● Fig. 24 A stone circle, Bohonagh, county Cork. Recent radiocarbon dating has challenged the traditional interpretation that these monuments date only from the Bronze Age: some appear to date from the Iron Age.

Beaghmore in county Tyrone. Associated with the south Munster circles are stone rows, monoliths and boulder burials. In the south-west of Ireland, the building impetus for these ritual monuments arose from the rich mining wealth of the south-west peninsulas, heavily exploited between 2000 BC and 1500 BC. These mine workings are still visible today along the south Cork coastline from Clonakilty to Mizen Head.

Reliance on the funerary and ritual evidence for this period stems from a dearth of settlement sites of Bronze Age date. However, the discovery of ancient cooking sites or fulachta fiadh, and their narrow dating to between 1900 BC and 1400 BC, is helping to fill the vacuum. One of the least well known of Irish monument types, they are found throughout northern Europe and Britain, where they are referred to as 'burnt mounds'. The method of cooking involved lighting a fire in which stones were heated and then dropped into a trough filled with water until it was brought to the boil when the parcel of food was added to cook. The shattered stones were thrown into a pile surrounding the trough on three sides. Over time, this developed into the diagnostic horseshoe-shaped mound which is often present today. In some cases, huts have been found close by as at Ballyvourney, county Cork and Ballycroghan, county Down. Because these cooking sites were marked only on the OS maps in counties Cork, Wexford and Kilkenny, their distribution was thought to have been predominantly in the southern half of Ireland, particularly in county Cork where a recent estimate puts their number at 2000. However the picture is changing fast. As fieldworkers become more familiar with these monuments, they are being found in their hundreds in county Mayo, around the margins of bogland in the midlands, and in the drumlin zone in county Fermanagh, where recent fieldwork has uncovered fulachta fiadh buried under hillwash deposits.

LATE BRONZE AGE/EARLY IRON AGE

While deposition of hoards was a feature of the Early Bronze Age, this happened more frequently and with a larger array of items in the final stages of the Bronze Age. The reason is difficult to determine. Throughout the Bronze Age, hoards were deposited either for safety or as votive offerings. In large areas of Europe where grave goods and graves are lacking for this period, hoards are vital in shedding light on the technological achievements of the contemporary communities. The general absence of Irish burials from this period suggests that these hoards could represent votive deposits associated with a burial ritual. Certainly the contents are often of a personal nature. On the other hand, palaeobotanical evidence indicates a

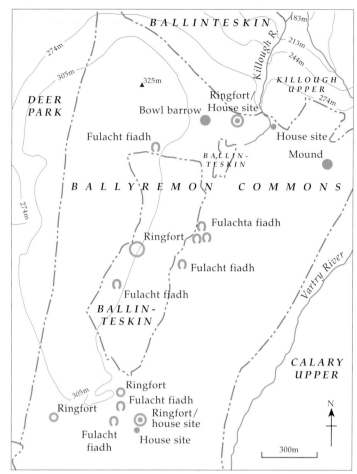

● Fig. 25 Ballyremon Commons on the western foothills of the Sugarloaf mountain near the village of Kilmacanoge contains the most extensive group of fulachta fiadh in county Wicklow. Eight sites have been identified in association with a bowl barrow, a possible burial mound, hut sites and enclosures. In 1983, one of the fulachta fiadh was excavated. The investigations exposed a clay-lined pit into which axe sharpened stakes had been placed at an angle, indicating that a wooden tripod was erected above the pit. A C14 sample dated the site to the middle of the second millennium BC. Ringforts indicate that the area remained occupied in the Early Christian period.

● Fig. 26 A fulacht fiadh or ancient cooking place at Rathlogan, county Kilkenny. The location on marshy ground is typical of these sites.

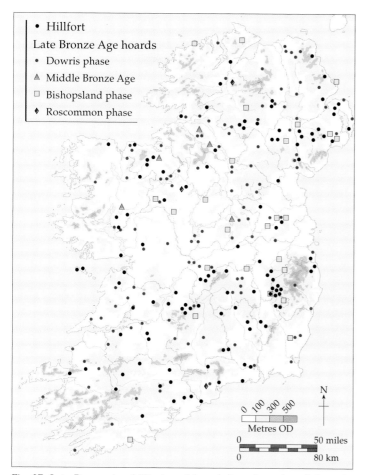

- Hillfort

Late Bronze Age hoards
- • Dowris phase
- ▲ Middle Bronze Age
- ☐ Bishopsland phase
- ◆ Roscommon phase

Metres OD
0   100   300   500

N

0   50 miles
0   80 km

Fig. 27   Late Bronze Age hillforts and hoards have been found throughout Ireland. Nearly half of the hoards had been deposited in 'wet' sites such as bogs, marsh and lake shores.

climatic deterioration in the latter half of the second millennium BC which may have led to general famine and fear of a future calamity, triggering the impulse to hoard valuables. Farming during this period is believed to be partially responsible for the spread of upland bog; tree regeneration was hampered by farming and resulted in soils becoming wetter and poorly drained. Hoards have been found almost nationwide, mainly in bogs and along lake shores. The political turbulence of this period is also suggested by the occurrence of spearheads and swords which now enter the archaeological record. Hilltops were starting to be defended; at Rathgall, county Wicklow, excavations have exposed considerable evidence for the industrial manufacturing of weapons in the Later Bronze Age.

By the middle of the second millennium BC, knowledge of iron working had come to central Europe. The material culture of these early iron-using peoples is given the name Halstatt, after a site in Austria. From the mid fifth century, a Celtic Iron Age civilisation emerged in Europe which extended from the Atlantic to the Black Sea. This La Tène culture, so named after the site of a diagnostic votive deposit on Lake Neuchatel in Switzerland,

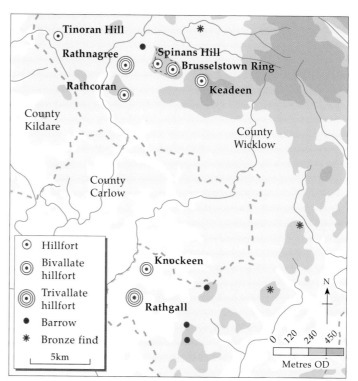

Tinoran Hill

Rathnagree   Spinans Hill

Brusselstown Ring

Rathcoran   Keadeen

County Kildare

County Wicklow

County Carlow

Knockeen

☉ Hillfort
◉ Bivallate hillfort
◎ Trivallate hillfort
● Barrow
✳ Bronze find

5km

Rathgall

N

0   120   240   450
Metres OD

● Fig. 28   The greatest concentration of hillforts in the country is found on the high ground north of Rathgall and east of Baltinglass in west Wicklow. They include univallate, bivallate and multivallate types. Rathgall is the only excavated site. Its ramparts enclose over seven hectares; the site was used in the Late Bronze Age and the Iron Age and again during the thirteenth and fourteenth centuries. There is evidence for the manufacture of bronze weaponry on the site during the seventh and sixth centuries BC.

TOM CONDIT

● Fig. 29   The spectacular hillfort known as Brusselstown Ring, county Wicklow, is linked to a remarkable (possibly contemporary) stone rampart surrounding Spinans Hill and enclosing an area of over 130ha. The essential feature of hillforts is the enclosure of extensive hill-top areas or other defensible natural positions by roughly circular ramparts of earth or stone. A number of sites are distinguished by burial mounds, probably older than the enclosures themselves; otherwise, apart from ramparts, they generally lack surface structures or evidence of habitation and their purpose remains obscure. They may have served as ritual centres or temporary refuges for the local population and have held few permanent inhabitants.

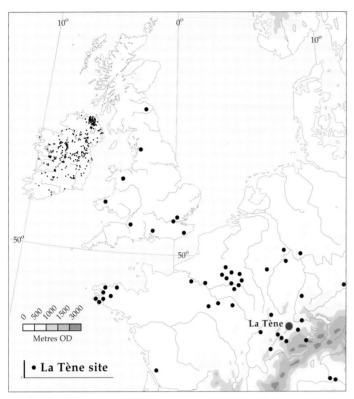

Fig. 30 Major La Tène material and monuments in north-western Europe. Around 400 BC, Ireland became part of an Iron Age culture that stretched from the Atlantic to the Baltic Sea. La Tène artifacts are characterised by distinctive curvilinear designs.

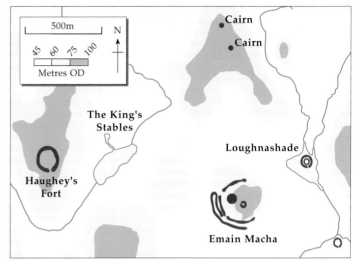

● Fig. 32 The environs of Emain Macha, county Armagh, became a focus for ritual activity in the Late Bronze Age/Iron Age. To the east lies the sacred lake of Loughnashade where bronze trumpets were deposited in the Iron Age; to the west of Emain Macha is the King's Stables, another ritual lake dug in the Late Bronze Age; further west is 'Haughey's Fort', an Iron Age hillfort.

dominated Europe until it eventually succumbed to the Roman empire. Unconquered by Rome, the 'insular Celts' survived in Ireland and parts of Britain for many centuries longer. Ireland felt the influence of La Tène culture around the third century BC. Evidence for this contact is mainly artifactual in nature, based on a limited range of weapons, highly decorated horse trappings and armour. There are also some carved heads and decorated standing stones, such as that at Turoe in county Galway, which provide insight into the cult activities of these Celtic people. La Tène material and monuments are concentrated in two principal regions; east Ulster and a broad band stretching from Meath to Galway. This pattern contrasts so sharply with the distribution of hillforts, which continued to be used in Ireland, that the theory has been advanced that two distinct cultural groups lived in the country during the Iron Age.

● Fig. 31 A royal ceremonial enclosure at Dún Ailinne, county Kildare. This site was used in the Late Bronze Age, Iron Age and into the Middle Ages, presumably for periodic meetings and ritual purposes; there is no evidence of continuous settlement or proto-urban functions.

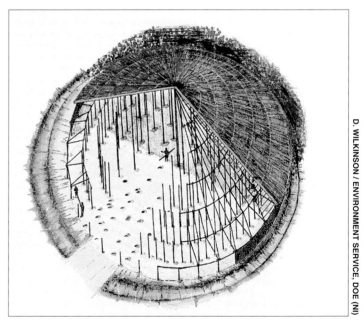

● Fig. 33 In 94 BC, the people of Emain Macha erected an enormous wooden building with four rings of regularly placed upright posts. This was used for ceremonial gatherings by the surrounding communities. Remains of a Barbary ape (an exotic gift?) were found in this structure.

Fig. 34 Coastal promontory forts have an almost entirely western European distribution, suggesting a separate building tradition and not an adaptation of the local brand of hillfort to a coastal site. Promontory forts in county Dublin have produced evidence for sustained contact between Ireland and the Roman world.

● Fig. 35 One of the largest coastal promontory forts, Loughshinny, county Dublin. A substantial earthwork protects the promontory on the landward side. Roman and Celtic artifacts have been found here in recent years.

This period witnessed the emergence of kingdoms and the consolidation of territories defended by hilltop fortifications and linear earthworks. The linear earthworks are defensive banks and ditches which stretch discontinuously for miles across the countryside. The best known examples, the 'Black Pig's Dyke' in counties Armagh, Monaghan and Donegal, and the 'Dorsey' in south Armagh, are the visible defences of ancient Ulster. Other linear earthworks have been identified in counties Kerry, Waterford, Kilkenny and Louth. The 'Doon of Drumsna' in north-east Roscommon served as a major defensive line, guarding an extensive fordable stretch of the Shannon and forming part of the northern frontier of Connacht, thereby protecting its capital at Cruachain.

Within these miniature Iron Age kingdoms, works on a grand scale were built during the latter half of the second century BC. This period witnessed the creation of many of Ireland's finest archaeological landscapes; Cruachain in Roscommon, Tara in Meath, Emain Macha in south Armagh, and Dún Ailinne in Kildare. These feature earthworks of varying types, burial mounds and enclosures.

The Irish Sea was certainly a unifying factor towards the end of the Iron Age; it was a much travelled highway over which there were continuing and intimate contacts between communities on both sides. Coastal promontory forts belong to this cultural zone. Many of them developed as trading centres during the Roman period. The Roman historian Tacitus wrote of Ireland at the end of the first century AD: 'the interior parts are little known, but through commercial intercourse and the merchants there is better knowledge of the harbours and approaches'. In the mid-second century AD, Claudius Ptolemaius from Alexandria undertook a survey of the known world and a map of Ireland has been reconstructed from coordinates given in his work. Many of the places identified on this map along the east coast of Ireland are sites of promontory forts which have produced evidence for Roman contacts. There are, for instance, sherds of Samian ware from Loughshinny, county Dublin and first-century AD Roman period burials from Lambay Island. Ogham stones may be another element reflecting this cultural contact around the Irish Sea.

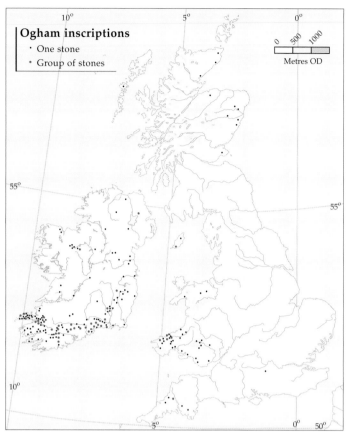

Fig. 36 The earliest writing in Ireland dates from *c.* 300 AD, inscribed on standing stones in the alphabet know as ogham; the script continued in use for several centuries. Ogham inscriptions are densest in Munster and south Wales, indicating intimate contacts between communities on both sides of the Irish Sea.

EARLY CHRISTIAN SETTLEMENT

Although we do not as yet fully understand the processes at work, Ireland underwent radical change from the fifth century. The pollen record testifies to a huge upsurge in grasses and weeds associated with pasture and arable farming. This upsurge is the more pronounced due to a preceding prolonged period of relative inactivity, described in recent palaeobotanical research as the 'Late Iron Age Lull'. A combination of factors led to a revolution in the landscape.

Foremost among these changes was the introduction of Christianity early in the fifth century. Its arrival is also indicative of closer contacts with the Roman world, which facilitated the spread of technological advances. A new type of plough and the horizontal mill were two innovations which must have improved Irish agriculture and food production, permitting population increase. Economic and demographic expansion led to the construction of tens of thousands of ringforts (or raths). Ringforts vary in size but most are small circular enclosures, some 30m in diameter, usually consisting of an earthen bank and an outer fosse which was the source of the bank material. In areas of

Fig. 37 A group of five ringforts near Ardfert, county Kerry. Each site enclosed a family farm whose main economic activity was the exploitation of milch cows.

shallow soil, the banks are constructed of stone and these enclosures are known as cashels. Ringforts are the most common archaeological sites in the modern rural landscape; the banks mark the perimeter of farmyards not of fortresses and would have enclosed a house and farm buildings. However, internal structures were made of perishable materials such as wood and straw and have left few surface traces. Over 18,000 ringforts have been positively identified while a further 28,000 have been identified from cartographic sources and aerial photography – as crop marks and much denuded earthworks. A few upland enclosures contain numerous hut sites and may represent transhumant or temporary summer quarters.

The impressive number of ringforts in Ireland, combined with early misinterpretations of archaeological findings, made many researchers conclude that these sites

Fig. 38 Cathair Murphy, a stone ringfort (cashel) at Fahan, county Kerry. The circular structures in the interior are clocháin which may also date from the Early Christian period.

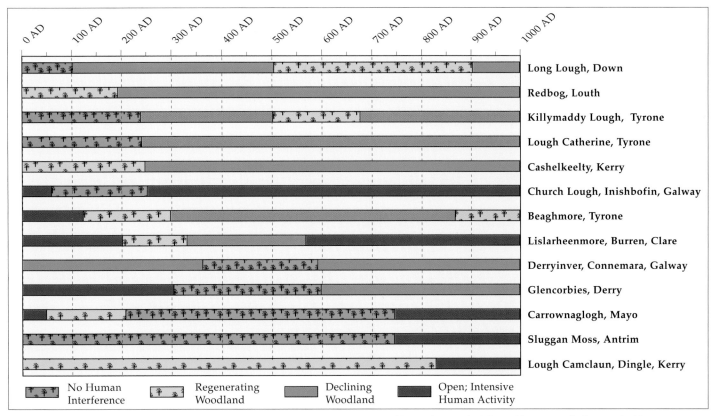

Fig. 39 This summary of thirteen pollen diagrams shows how the 'Late Iron Age Lull' was frequently followed by a period of intensified human activity from 250 AD. Agricultural improvements and population growth left many of the sampled sites clear of woodland during the Early Christian period.

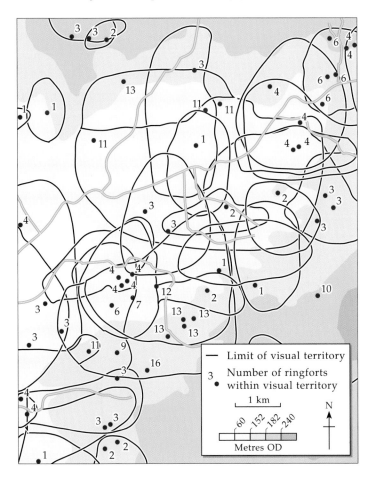

represented a form of domestic habitation dating from the Neolithic to the seventeenth century AD. This interpretation masked the sharp discontinuity represented by the Early Christian period in Ireland. Modern techniques, especially dendrochronology and carbon dating, have placed ringforts within a narrow range of dates between the fifth and tenth centuries AD. As a result, recent research has analysed Early Christian distributions based on the underlying assumption that ringforts are roughly contemporaneous. The focus is now placed on the pattern of differing classes of ringfort (univallate/bivallate, large/small) and the relationship between these domestic enclosures and Early Christian ecclesiastical centres.

Characteristic patterns of settlement are evident. Firstly, ringforts enclosed single farmsteads involved in a predominantly pastoral economy. Some crop growth occurred and irregular field boundaries can sometimes be faintly discerned around ringforts and cashels, preserved best in hilly or stony terrain where later agriculture has had little impact. Ringfort dwellers had a decided preference for sloping sites within lowland areas where there was access to better-drained soils and visibility over the

● Fig. 40 The overlapping 'visual territories' of ringforts in the Braid valley, county Antrim as mapped by Linda Black. Although ringforts are a form of dispersed settlement, their intervisibility afforded additional security beyond that provided by defensive banks and ditches.

Ringforts

N

| 0 | 100 | 300 | 500 |
Metres OD

0   50 miles

0   80 km

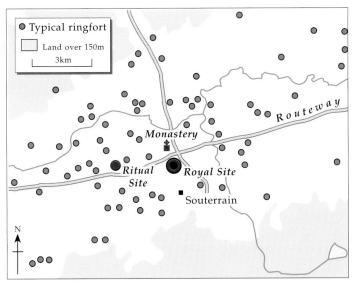

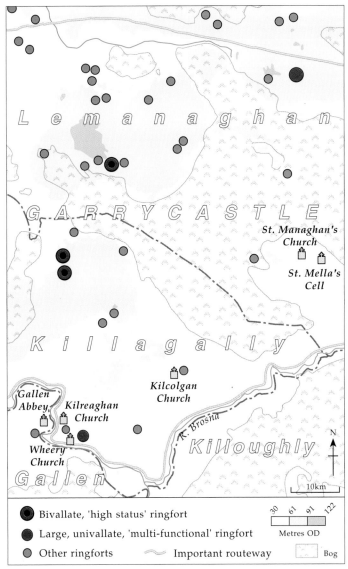

• Fig. 42 At Clogher, county Tyrone, a royal ringfort is associated with a major routeway, an Early Christian monastic site, a ritual mound and a dense pattern of surrounding ringforts.

surrounding landscape afforded some warning of imminent attack. This locational preference may partially explain why some of the most fertile low-lying areas in Ireland today have low ringfort densities. Lowlands, owing to their forest cover and poor drainage, were initially harder to settle than free-draining hill flanks, but when eventually reclaimed and developed, they could become the most populous and productive areas. Larger, more important ringforts, which may have accommodated the

• Fig. 43 Tillage farming and road construction have left untouched this ringfort at Rathroe near Ramsgrange in county Wexford. Roads and field boundaries often respect ringforts, especially in eastern Ireland where roads and enclosures were formed early and organically rather than through comprehensive planning.

• Fig. 44 The distribution of Early Christian sites in county Offaly highlights the relationship between lay and ecclesiastical elements of society. Ringforts occupy the better-drained hill slopes, with church sites located in the river valleys near important arteries of communication. 'High-status' ringforts are at some distance from both roadways and church sites. Large 'multi-functional' ringforts are in strategic locations.

highest grades of society, often act as foci for smaller sites, the pattern perhaps representing a 'defence in depth' strategy for mutual protection. It may also reflect the inferior status of the occupants of the smaller ringforts; their proximity to major sites could stem from large landowners letting holdings to landless tenants.

Broadly contemporary with the ringfort, comparable in size and roughly circular in shape was the crannóg (so named because of the large quantities of wood used in its construction – crann being the Irish for tree) or lake

Fig. 41 (left) Over 45,000 ringforts are found throughout Ireland, avoiding only bogland and land above 335m. They are densest in north Connacht (counties Sligo and Roscommon) and north Munster (counties Clare and Limerick), regions which were also densely settled during the prehistoric period. Another zone of dense ringfort settlement stretches from the eastern shores of Lough Neagh to north Galway. Leinster is the only area of good soils which has low ringfort numbers. As this ringfort-free zone coincides with the area of heaviest Norman occupation, it is possible that centuries of ringfort destruction by tillage farming accounts for the anomaly. An alternative settlement form of unenclosed dispersed farms which relied on underground chambers (souterrains) for protection may partly explain low ringfort densities outside the sphere of Norman influence, for example in county Antrim and north Louth.

SADHBH MCELVEEN

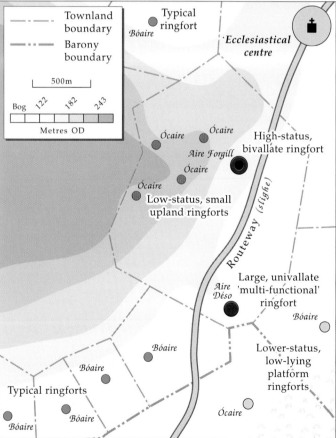

— · — · —	Townland boundary
— · · — · · —	Barony boundary

500m

Bog 122 182 243

Metres OD

Typical ringfort
Bóaire

✝ *Ecclesiastical centre*

Ócaire Ócaire

Aire Forgill High-status, bivallate ringfort

Ócaire

Ócaire

Low-status, small upland ringforts

Routeway *(slighe)*

Aire Déso Large, univallate 'multi-functional' ringfort

Bóaire

Bóaire Lower-status, low-lying platform ringforts

Typical ringforts

Bóaire *Bóaire*

Bóaire Ócaire

● Fig. 45 Artist's impression of the Early Christian landscape based on the findings described in the figure to the left. The large ringfort in the centre of the painting is occupied by a lord (aire forgill) who may have rented much of his 80ha of land to landless freemen. These ócaire occupied small, upland ringforts on 14ha holdings. At the bottom of the illustration is a large ringfort near a tribal (túath) boundary which would have been occupied by a prominent individual (aire déso) with responsibility for inter-territorial issues, along with farming a 40ha holding. An ecclesiastical centre can be seen to the right. The landscape is largely unenclosed and contains considerable areas of woodland which were important to the rural economy.

dwelling. They were sited on semi-artificial islands for security and made with timber, sods and stones. Crannóga are still conspicuous in lake-strewn areas such as Fermanagh, as neat, round and scrub-covered islets. Unlike ringforts, a crannóg absorbed a great deal of labour and material and it is consequently thought that they accommodated high-status or royal individuals. A ring of close-set piles was pounded into the lake bed or in a

● Fig. 46 This model of ringfort distribution summarises the results of detailed spatial analysis in the south-west midlands. A 'high-status' ringfort (occupied by an aire forgill) is found in close proximity to a group of smaller upland sites (occupied by ócaire). The 'high-status' site is located near a routeway to an ecclesiastical enclosure which would have enhanced the value of the associated land. This 'high-status' site also affords protection to the less significant upland enclosures. Downslope, a large 'multi-functional' ringfort (occupied by an aire déso) is located at the edge of the townland/barony boundary. Segregated from the larger ringforts, but in close proximity to one another, are four typical sites (occupied by bóaire). These are strung out along the 122m contour on good land that is less strategically placed. Two isolated platform ringforts (occupied by either ócaire or bóaire) are located in a level, low-lying position.

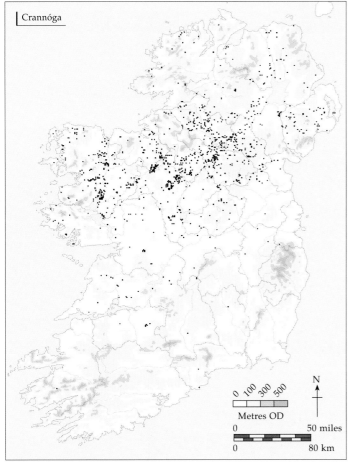

Crannóga

Fig. 47 There are nearly one thousand crannóga in Ireland. Predictably, these are most commonly sited in the shallow inter-drumlin lakes found in Ireland north of the central plain. Some are known from contemporary documents to be royal sites.

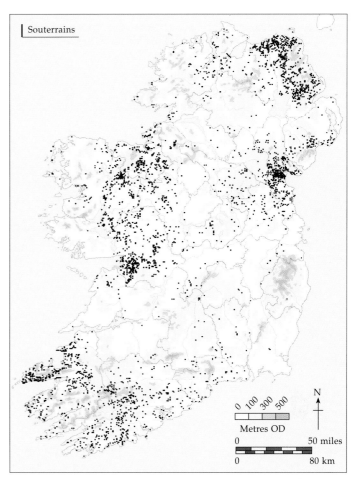

Souterrains

Fig. 48 Souterrains are a hidden, underground component of the Early Christian landscape. Over 3,500 sites are known and these are located in four main groupings; in counties Antrim and Louth, central Connacht and south-west Munster. This puzzling pattern remains to be explained.

marshy area at the margins of a bog. This kept in place great quantities of stones, gravel, domestic rubbish, peat and brushwood which were laid down in alternating layers until a dry habitable platform was achieved. Timbers from crannóga, which survive due to the water-logged nature of their deposits, have yielded precise dendrochronological dates, suggesting that they were constructed during two short and intense phases; 424 AD to 648 AD and 722 AD to 926 AD.

Towards the end of the first millennium, ringforts and crannóga fell out of use. The reasons for this is uncertain but the abandonment of these widespread settlement forms is probably associated with the ever increasing powers of over-kings, paralleling European-wide trends towards feudalisation. Some scholars have also suggested that the arrival of the Vikings led to an intensification of warfare which rendered ringfort defences obsolescent.

As ringfort use declined, a further innovation in defensive architecture became widespread. Souterrains, artificial underground structures, were built in large numbers; some are within pre-existing ringforts but many are unassociated with enclosing features. Souterrains are, most commonly, built of dry-stone walling within an open topped trench which is filled in after the structure is completed. A tunnelled example from the royal ringfort at Rathmore, county Antrim is 130m long. Because of the large number of inbuilt defensive features, it is thought that these underground structures were built mainly for use as places of refuge not as storage areas. As ringforts are linked to a pastoral economy, the inverse is also possibly true, namely that unenclosed settlement is associated with an economy dominated by tillage. In county Louth and north county Meath, souterrains are common but are not associated with ringforts. It is therefore possible that an alternative, unenclosed settlement form was dominant in the tillage areas of the eastern midlands as the protection of grain stores, not being as portable as beef on the hoof, did not require defending banks.

Ecclesiastical sites are the second major component of Early Christian settlement. The new religion was readily accepted – there were no Irish martyrs – and it spread throughout the island in the fifth and sixth centuries.

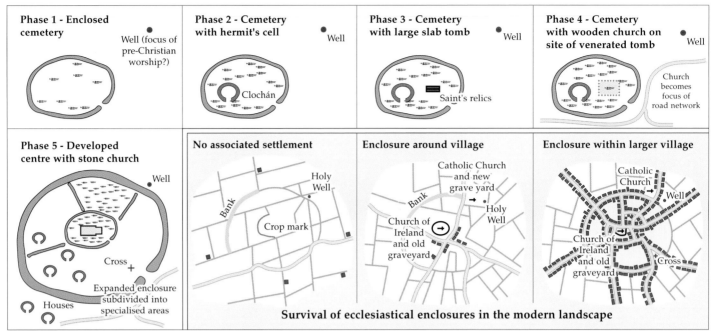

Phase 1 - Enclosed cemetery

Well (focus of pre-Christian worship?)

Phase 2 - Cemetery with hermit's cell

Well

Clochán

Phase 3 - Cemetery with large slab tomb

Well

Saint's relics

Phase 4 - Cemetery with wooden church on site of venerated tomb

Well

Church becomes focus of road network

Phase 5 - Developed centre with stone church

Well

Cross +

Houses

Expanded enclosure subdivided into specialised areas

No associated settlement

Holy Well

Bank

Crop mark

Enclosure around village

Catholic Church and new grave yard

Bank

Holy Well

Church of Ireland and old graveyard

Enclosure within larger village

Catholic Church

Well

Church of Ireland and old graveyard

Cross

Survival of ecclesiastical enclosures in the modern landscape

Fig. 49 Evolution of ecclesiastical enclosures as envisioned by F. Aalen. Circular or oval ecclesiastical enclosures of earth or stone are numerous in the landscape; most date from the first millennium AD and are characteristically associated with churches, existing or disused burial grounds and holy wells. Placename elements such as 'kil' and 'disert' also connect these enclosures with the early church. Small, enclosed graveyards, similar in size to ringforts, are particularly numerous and probably the oldest forms; some of these subsequently developed through acquiring the tomb of a revered holy person (phase 3) and eventually a small church, first of wood, later of stone (phase 4). Some favoured sites developed further into monasteries and proto-urban centres with an enlarged outer enclosure (phase 5). There are large enclosures within and around villages and towns and also in the open countryside, which are comparable in scale to hillforts. Often the enclosures are only partially preserved and the complete form is detectable only as crop marks.

Religious enclosures survive in large numbers in the landscape; they are of earth or stone and of varying size, some little larger than an average ringfort while other imposing examples have diameters over 300m. The enclosing earthworks are usually much reduced, surviving merely as a degraded bank or ditch, field boundary or laneway and sometimes traceable only on aerial photographs. A number of sites developed into full-scale monasteries and major foci of social organisation; where towns or villages later grew on these sites, the old circular plan might be incorporated into the street pattern, but some small settlements are located entirely within enclosures. Many of the enclosures were abandoned, while others continued simply as isolated church and graveyard sites through the Middle Ages and even into the modern period. A number of abandoned sites were reused as burial grounds (cillíní or cellúracha) in recent centuries, often for unbaptised children. However, the isolated rural graveyard, sometimes far from contemporary settlement or church, is a widespread feature and does not necessarily have Early Christian origins.

Ecclesiastical centres were often sited in the low-lying areas, perhaps in locations dictated by lay authority, and many of the major centres developed in the poorly drained midlands. A number of ecclesiastical centres grew more powerful and by the eighth or ninth century had evolved into monasteries which were effectively proto-urban

centres involved in specialised activities, including small industries, arts and crafts, education, commerce, and providing depositories for lay and ecclesiastical wealth. The expanding monasteries dispensed patronage for a growing number of artists and masons. Masons produced grave markers, which were now being used in burial grounds. At first these were single stone slabs with inscribed Christian symbols laid on the graves. Later the slabs recorded the dead person's name. Notable developments in stone

● Fig. 50 Derrynaflan, county Tipperary where a famous hoard of altar plate was discovered in 1980. The ecclesiastical enclosure lies on a low morainic 'island' in extensive bog, typical of Early Christian monasteries in the midlands.

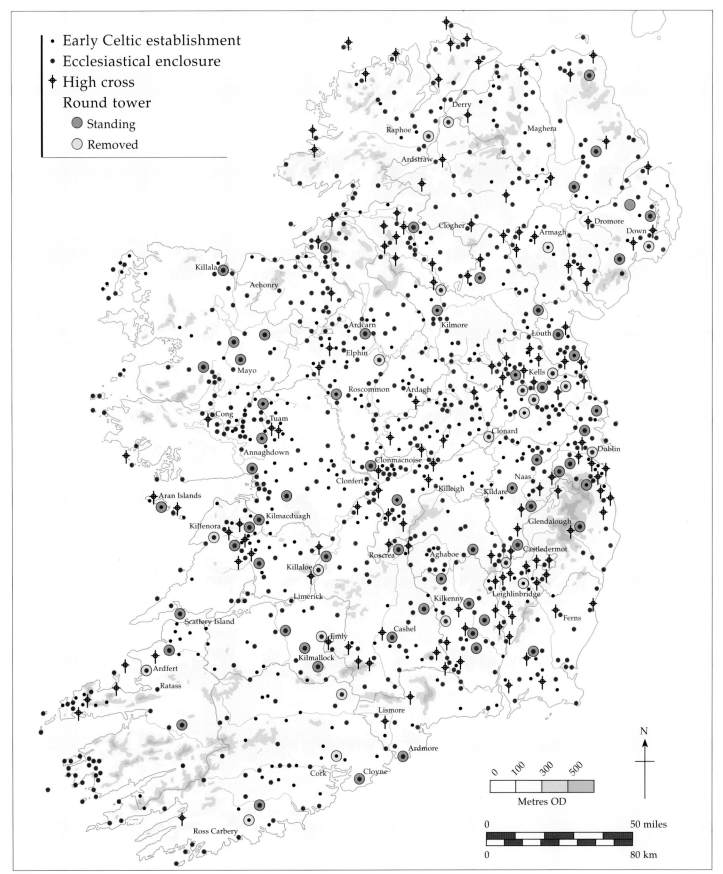

- • Early Celtic establishment
- • Ecclesiastical enclosure
- ✦ High cross
- Round tower
  - Standing
  - Removed

Fig. 51 Early Christian ecclesiastical sites, enclosures, round towers and high crosses. The Christian church spread throughout Ireland during the fifth and sixth centuries, developing a distinctively monastic character in contrast to the diocesan-based European model. Notable concentrations of more important monasteries (as indicated by round towers and high crosses) occur in Meath, west Offaly and west of the Leinster mountains from Dublin to south Kilkenny.

LEO SWAN

ENVIRONMENT SERVICE, DOE (NI)

●Fig. 52 The ecclesiastical enclosure at Lusk, county Dublin, is preserved in the street plan and property boundaries. The round tower marks the centre of this Early Christian settlement. Fairs, recorded in Lusk from 739 AD, enhanced the economic significance of the Early Christian church.

●Fig. 54 The tenth-century monastery of Nendrum, county Down. Located on an island in Strangford Lough, the remains include concentric enclosures, the stump of a round tower, a church, cells and cross slabs, and workshops. In medieval times, the site was occupied by the Benedictines.

carving took place at the end of the seventh century. It had been customary among the Irish monasteries to set up a wooden cross as a symbol of Christianity in the central enclosure of the monastery, at the cardinal points, or at the entrances to the monastery. In the eighth century, this tradition was translated into stone. Crosses such as those at Ahenny, county Tipperary, were divided up into panels containing geometrical motifs similar to the Book of Kells; others contained scenes from the Old Testament and had a teaching function for a largely illiterate population. The distribution pattern of these crosses suggests the existence of particular schools of excellence. Crosses of a particular

style occur regionally, such as the granite crosses of Kildare and Kilkenny. Within the European context, the high cross form is peculiar to Ireland and Britain but there is a resemblance between the subject matter of continental frescoes and the figured panels on Irish high crosses.

Monastic wealth attracted the predatory interest of the Vikings. The frequency and danger of Viking raids recorded

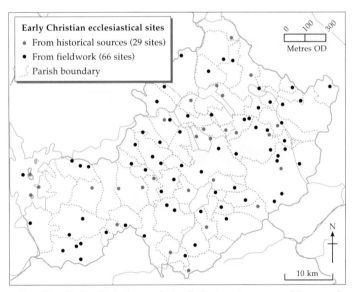

●Fig. 53 Early Christian ecclesiastical sites in county Westmeath. Detailed fieldwork can triple the number of sites identified from historical sources alone. Half of Westmeath's parishes have one early church site, which suggests that parish boundaries have their origins in the Early Christian period.

Fig. 55 Many Irish monasteries grew from humble origins as isolated monastic cells to proto-urban centres with considerable power. Their influence was felt throughout continental Europe where monasteries were founded by distinguished Irish churchmen.

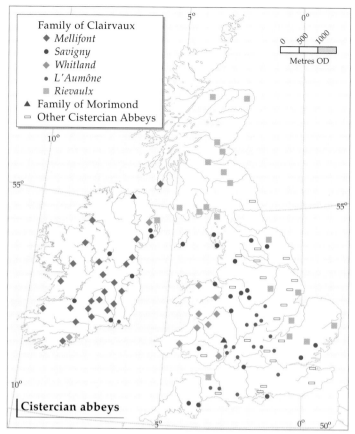

Fig. 56   Between 1142 and 1230 AD, thirty-three successful Cistercian monasteries were founded throughout Ireland. These were part of Cistercian monastic 'families' which maintained strong links between Britain, Ireland and the continent.

● Fig. 57   The Cistercian Abbey at Boyle in county Roscommon, founded in 1161, was a daughter house of Mellifont.

DEPARTMENT OF ARTS, CULTURE AND THE GAELTACHT

in the Annals coincided with the construction of round towers over much of Ireland, serving predominantly as campaniles, status symbols and anti-theft devices. The monastic cores have survived in the landscape, containing perhaps the stump of a round tower and church foundations within an enclosing earthwork. However, they were often ignored as locations for the monasteries of continental orders established from the twelfth century onwards.

In the twelfth century, the Church experienced a revolution throughout Europe, resulting in the foundation of many new religious orders. The Cistercians were the first of these continental orders to come to Ireland, settling by the Mattock river at Mellifont, county Louth in 1142. Such was the popularity of this order that thirty-three monasteries had been established by 1230 AD. They now constitute some of the most picturesque ruins in this island. The ordered layout of their buildings, arranged around a square or quadrangle, contrasts sharply with the informal arrangement within the earlier Celtic monasteries. Cistercian buildings had considerable impact in Ireland and influenced styles in church building outside the order.

This new approach was also evident in land management. The Cistercians played a major role in agricultural development, including the creation of internal and external markets for selling cattle, horses and wool. Because the order depended on its own labour, it created the institution of the lay brother for the provision of agricultural labour; monastic lands were divided into farms or 'granges', each with its own buildings which accommodated these lay brothers. The location of granges can often only be identified now by placename evidence.

Within Ireland, Cistercian abbeys were located in relatively isolated positions but near good supplies of water and with access to better land. They undertook considerable reclamation of wetlands and woodlands. Overall, the monasteries show a south-eastern bias, favouring the richer, freely drained soils which were ideal for cultivation. This settlement bias was to continue throughout the Norman period.

THE MEDIEVAL PERIOD

The introduction of continental-style monasteries coincided with a period of political unrest initiated by the power vacuum which followed the death in 1014 of Brian Borúmha. Diarmáit MacMurchadha, deposed king of Leinster, sought the support of mercenaries from England, Wales and Flanders to assist him in his challenge for the kingship. Norman involvement in Ireland began in May 1169 when Richard de Clare and his followers landed in Wexford to support MacMurchadha. Two years later, Richard de Clare – alias 'Strongbow' – inherited the kingdom of Leinster. By the end of the twelfth century, Normans had succeeded in conquering much of the country.

Land occupation was carried out according to the customs of Norman feudalism. A military establishment was needed to maintain a hold over such an extensive territory.

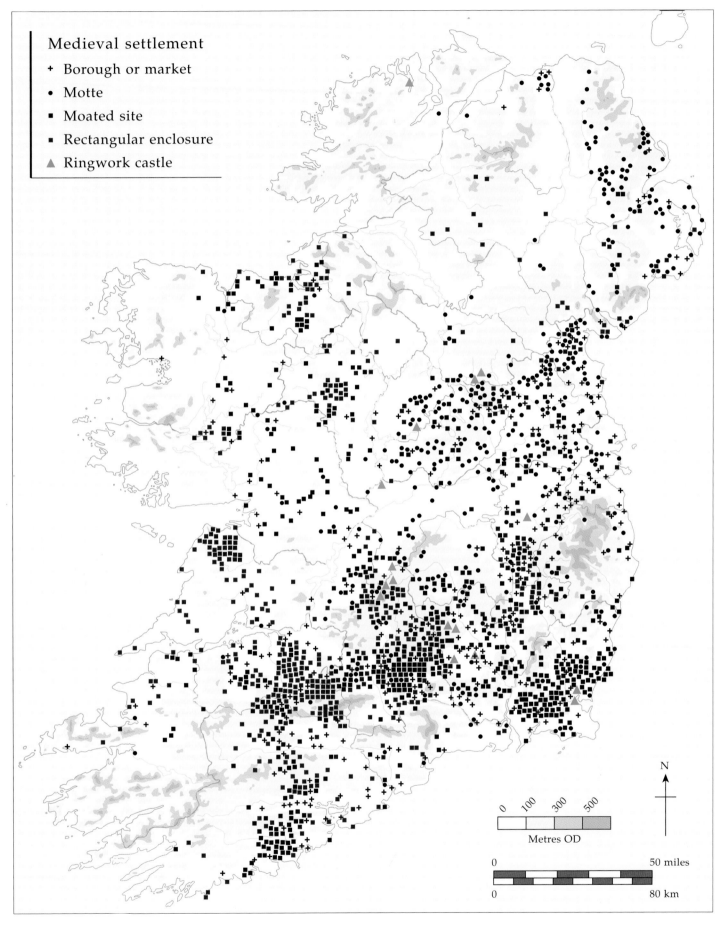

Medieval settlement

+ Borough or market
● Motte
■ Moated site
■ Rectangular enclosure
▲ Ringwork castle

0 100 300 500
Metres OD

N

0   50 miles

0   80 km

● Fig. 59 An illustration from the early fifteenth-century text written by Jean Creton, who travelled to Ireland with Richard II in 1399. It depicts a meeting between Art Macmurchadha Caomhánach and a party of heavily armoured English knights near Arklow, county Wicklow. This contemporary illustration shows how the 'colonists', most at home on the fertile plains, perceived the Gaelic-held woods and uplands.

The colony was divided on the basis of knight's fees and these were further sub-infeudated, resulting in the distribution of land to sub-tenants. Newly created manors and villages with open-field systems were occupied by colonists from England and Wales, encouraged by favourable tenurial terms. A network of towns, castles and roads made settlers more secure and wealthy. Between 1170 and 1350, the Norman influence was stamped on the landscape, especially in the south-eastern quadrant of the country.

The initial stage of the invasion was marked by the construction of defensive earthworks, referred to as mottes. These are flat-topped earthen mounds, often surrounded by a fosse. Some mottes have an attached enclosure or 'bailey' but these are rare in Ulster. A timber tower and palisade would have been erected on the summit of the mound. At Lismahon, county Down, a platform ringfort was converted into a motte around 1200. Excavations uncovered the remains of a house with a timber tower. Another wooden tower surrounded by a palisade and a timber and earthen breastwork was excavated at Lurgankeel, county Louth. Mottes were built to form a defensive screen along settlement borders. In county Wexford, for instance, they were built in two continuous lines, running from south-west to north-east

Fig. 58 (left) Norman settlement. The greatest density of mottes, probably constructed between 1170 to 1230 in the initial phase of the Norman invasion, is found in the eastern half of Ireland. These fortifications were built at strategic locations to consolidate the position of the invaders. A conspicuous line of mottes protected Leinster from unconquered Ulster, north of the drumlin belt. The Normans also built ringworks for defensive purposes, formed by a palisade bank and ditch with a fortified gate tower. Ringworks were a common earthwork of the medieval period in both Normandy and Britain. Moated sites occur at the margins of the colony where the settlers were often under pressure from the Gaelic population, anxious to repossess their lands. The Norman farmers needed the water-filled moats and earthen banks topped by a palisade to protect themselves and their goods. These sites were occupied during the twelfth and thirteenth centuries. The rectangular enclosures in Clare may be small post-medieval fields and sheep-folds rather than defensive settlements. The Normans established a network of towns throughout Ireland, except for the west and north which remained largely under Gaelic control. Many of these are identified as medieval boroughs from their charters and the presence of impressive architectural remains. The greatest concentration of Norman settlement is found in two fertile zones – one arcing from south Wexford to east Limerick, the other south of the drumlin belt from Louth to east Longford. This distribution is comparable to that of the later towerhouses.

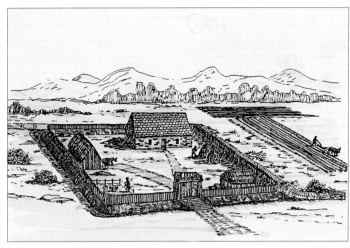

• Fig. 60 A superbly sited and once substantial medieval castle on the rock of Dunamase, county Laois, the site of an earlier Iron Age fortification. During the medieval period, the castle frequently changed hands in conflicts between the English and the Irish O'Mores; it fell into decay in the Cromwellian period.

Fig. 62 Artist's impression of an occupied moated site. These were well defended farmsteads usually on the margins of Norman territory.

along the frontier between the well colonised south and thinly penetrated north.

Mottes have not been found in all the counties where there is documented evidence for Norman activity. However, within the gaps of motte distribution, another

type of defensive site, the 'ringwork castle', was often built. The main defensive element of this monument was the peripheral palisade, bank and ditch and fortified gate. These monuments are common from the early medieval period in Normandy, Britain and in particular Wales whence came many of the Irish colonists. Forty-five examples have been identified and their distribution extends further west into

• Fig. 61 The medieval church at St Mullins, county Carlow lies on the site of an Early Christian monastery; nearby is a Norman motte overlooking the River Barrow. The Normans often constructed their primary defenses at pre-existing centres of native Irish population. These then developed into parish or manorial centres. A 'pattern' is still held annually at St Mullins, indicating the enduring veneration for these early monastic sites.

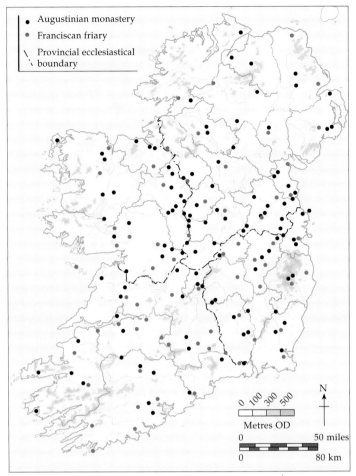

Fig. 63 While Augustinian monasteries were present in Ireland prior to the coming of the Normans, foundations accelerated under Norman patronage up to the fourteenth century. Many had strategic boundary locations. Franciscan friaries had a greater impact on religious life in the west of Ireland.

Legend:
● Augustinian monastery
● Franciscan friary
\ Provincial ecclesiastical boundary

N

0 100 300 500
Metres OD
0   50 miles
0   80 km

DEPARTMENT OF ARTS, CULTURE AND THE GAELTACHT

● Fig. 64 The Franciscan friary on Sherkin Island, county Cork, was founded in the latter half of the fifteenth century by local Gaelic lords.

Mayo and Sligo where large numbers of moated sites have also recently been identified.

Once the Normans consolidated their military position, they erected permanent fortifications at strategic settlement centres. This great castle-building period extended from the end of the twelfth century for at least 130 years. The large military castles, dominant in the countryside prior to the advent of siege ordnance, were built at this time. Castles built prior to the mid-thirteenth century have a great tower or 'keep' as their main feature, either incorporated into the outer defences or isolated within the walls. Carrickfergus and Trim Castles are the finest examples of this type. In the second half of the thirteenth century, there was a shift away from the isolated keep towards strong curtain walls: the domestic buildings were now insulated within protective perimeter walls.

Moated sites or rectangular earthen enclosures were built as part of the secondary sub-infeudation of Norman areas which took place after the original fiefs were granted and the parochial system was established. Excavated moated sites show evidence for occupation at the end of the thirteenth century, lasting until the first half of the fourteenth century. They have a peripheral distribution, concentrated along the marches of Norman territories.

The Norman invasion also provided a further impetus to the change that was taking place in the Irish church, speeding its re-organisation on a parochial basis. New parish churches were built throughout the country. The church grew wealthy under the patronage of Norman families. Many parish churches from this period are plain in plan with internal divisions between nave and chancel. The main focus for ornamentation is the windows and doors. Mouldings, window tracery and shape of doorways are often the only indication of probable date.

The foundation of Continental monastic orders, initiated by the Cistercians, continued apace during the medieval period. Augustinian, Dominican and Franciscan houses were founded throughout Ireland until the economic decline of the mid-fourteenth century. The 'Gaelic revival' of the fifteenth century inaugurated a new phase of church building dominated by the Franciscans. Ninety new houses, including sixty-seven Franciscan houses, were founded between 1400 and 1508, mainly in Gaelic-held Connacht and Ulster. Only four of these were located in Leinster, indicating the link between these new foundations and the indigenous culture. Many of the early monastic houses were also enlarged: the tall belfry towers built during this period form distinctive landmarks in the countryside.

In Ireland, the late fourteenth/fifteenth century was a period of general unrest and economic decline. A combination of factors – the Bruce Invasion, Black Death, climatic deterioration, Gaelic resurgence – pressurised the Norman lordship. By 1515, apart from the walled towns, the remain-

ing territory under English control had shrunk to an eastern coastal strip, incorporating counties Dublin, Louth, Meath and parts of Kildare. This enclave was protected by a series of linear earthworks known as the Pale, fragments of which can still be traced. In both Norman and Gaelic areas, the towerhouse became a familiar feature during the fifteenth and sixteenth centuries. Symptomatic of the unrest and insecurity of the time, they are small stone castles or keeps, three or four stories in height linked to walled enclosures or bawns. Towerhouses occur in medieval towns and villages – for example in Carrickfergus, Carlingford and Newcastle Lyons – but the bulk are dispersed rural dwellings built to accommodate upper-class landowners. Several thousand towerhouses, mostly in decay, still survive in the Irish countryside, especially in the south-west and west where they are testimony to the strength of Gaelic lords prior to the Tudor conquests. Towerhouses are characteristic too of Scotland and the Anglo-Scottish border, areas which, like Ireland, continued to experience an absence of centralised authority through

●Fig. 66 This strategic crossing of the River Barrow at Leighlinbridge in county Carlow, is guarded by a sixteenth-century towerhouse.

the Middle Ages. In most of England and Wales, towerhouses are rare, a reflection of the greater political stability of these countries and the precocious existence of strong centralised government.

●Fig. 65 Towerhouse at Rockstown, county Limerick. Towerhouses were equally the dwellings of prominent Gaelic landholders and 'Old English' (descendants of medieval colonists loyal to the English crown) landholders. They form a striking vertical presence in the Irish landscape.

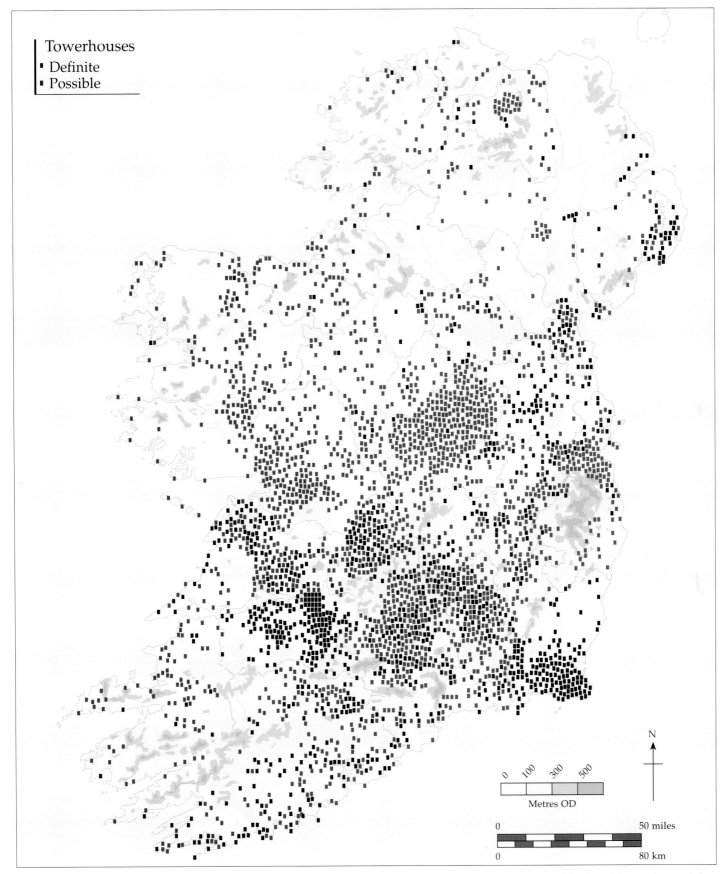

Towerhouses
■ Definite
▪ Possible

Fig. 67 Although towerhouses have a Norman origin, they became very popular in Gaelic-held areas in the Later Middle Ages. More widespread than the earlier Norman fortifications, they are densest in the Earldom of Ormond (modern counties Tipperary and Kilkenny), in county Westmeath on the Old English/Gaelic marchlands, and in the matrix of Old English and Gaelic lordships in south Galway, east Clare and east Limerick.

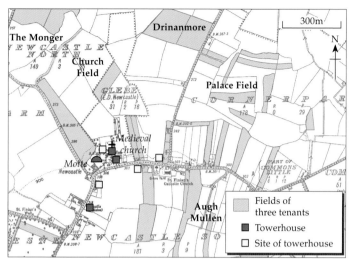

● Fig. 68 Newcastle Lyons, county Dublin, retains many features of a medieval village. As late as 1765, the remnants of a three-field system could be detected in the scattered ownership of long strip fields and the existence of commons.

The persistence of a Gaelic polity in the late medieval period is indicated by the presence of over fifty inauguration sites, known from contemporary sources, tradition and placename evidence. Inauguration ceremonies of local Gaelic kings were recorded by English administrators in the late sixteenth century as an expression of their concern over the persistence of outlawed Gaelic laws and life-styles. The sites themselves are situated on low hills in association with a wide range of monuments and features, including mounds, ringforts, flagstones, stone chairs and sacred trees. While many inaugurations suggest continuous ceremonies at one location, others rotated, their locations reflecting the expansion and contraction of territorial boundaries in different periods and displacement during times of upheaval.

THE PLANTATION PERIOD

Between 1534 and 1609, the English government gradually regained control of Ireland through its military-based administration in Dublin. Immigration of British settlers took place at an accelerated pace as government control expanded. In some regions, state-organised schemes of large-scale colonisation (plantation) were introduced, but with varying degrees of long-term success. During the seventeenth century, ownership of land throughout Ireland was ruthlessly transferred to an immigrant landlord class, mainly protestant, and of English or Scots origin. In most areas, however, the native Irish remained undisturbed as a tenantry on the land.

Military and civil settlements resulting from this invigorated colonial policy in the sixteenth century quickly made an impression on the landscape. Numerous settlements containing a fort or manor house were established to serve

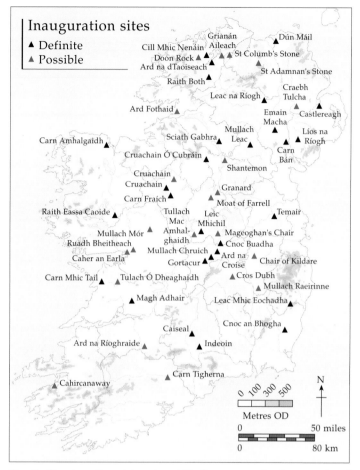

Fig. 69 The strength and tenacity of Gaelic customs, despite centuries of colonial intrusion, is apparent from the large number of inauguration sites recorded on the eve of the Tudor conquest. Elizabeth FitzPatrick's research shows that most of these sites are on low, unassuming hills (60m-150m), but whose summits afford an unexpected panorama of the regal territory.

as markets and centres for the enforcement of laws through a court leet and a court baron. Communications were improved by cutting passes through woods and the building of bridges. In order to improve government control on the frontiers of the Pale, fortified garrisons, called Fort

● Fig. 70 Cnoc Buadha, the Mag Eochagáin inauguration site at Rahugh, county Westmeath.

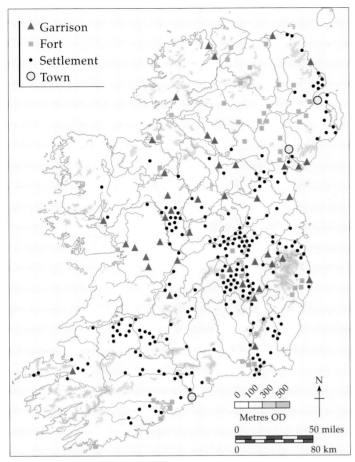

Fig. 71   Between 1534 and 1609, the English government – radiating outwards from the Pale – regained control of Ireland. Settlements which followed the conquest left a permanent impression on the landscape.

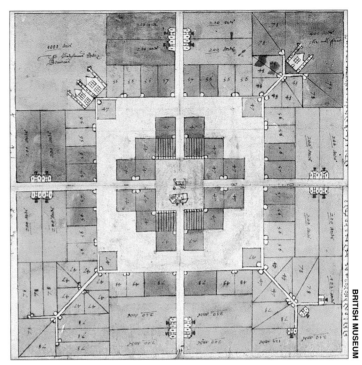

Fig. 73   A contemporary schematic layout for settling a seigniory in Munster, 1586. This plantation blue-print envisaged a 6.8ha square, which would double as manor and parish, and whose central elements would be a parish church with four roads radiating from it. Farmhouses were to be located on their own compact land, beside a road or lane, in clusters of two to six houses. The smallest units were located near the centre and these would form a green village where agricultural labourers and crafts-men could be accommodated. There is no clear evidence that ordered settlement schemes of this kind ever materialised. In reality, plantations conformed to the long established townland template, just as the earlier Norman colonisation was forced to do.

Governor (later Philipstown and now Daingean) and Fort Protector (later Maryborough and now Portlaoise) were built in 1546-48 to provide additional protection for the settlers of the Laois and Offaly Plantation.

After the failure of their rebellion in Munster (1579-83), the confiscated lands of the Earl of Desmond and his followers amounted to 230,000ha, scattered across the province. Plantation strategy in Munster was to attract

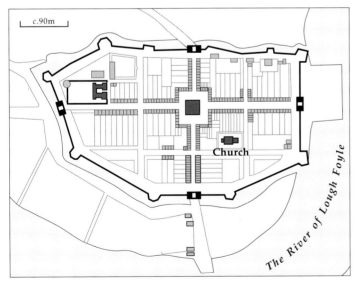

● Fig. 72   The plantation town of Londonderry, established in the early seventeenth century, with its impressive defences and regular street plan converging on a central square.

● Fig. 74   Plantation castle at Tully, county Fermanagh. Built by Sir John Hume in 1618, it is indicative of the insecurity of early seventeenth-century planters in Ulster. The isolated castle and bawn were seized and burnt by the Maguires in 1641 and have remained a spectacular ruin.

DEPARTMENT OF ARTS, CULTURE AND THE GAELTACHT

● Fig. 75 A star-shaped fort at James Fort, county Cork built in 1602. With Charles Fort (built in 1677), this massive fortification protected the entrance to Kinsale Harbour. Numerous forts were established by the English as military and administrative centres during the late sixteenth and seventeenth centuries. They were built in conformance with state-of-the-art Italian prototypes. Their polygonal plans and strong bastioned walls are a response to the advent of artillery warfare.

colonists from England headed by a group of powerful landlords who each received one seigniory, amounting to 5,000ha. These undertakers were required to settle ninety families who had to live close to each other. Owing to unrest and insecurity, systematic planning was frustrated and plantation developments were scattered and piecemeal. A number of towns were built, but in many areas, the enduring features were stone manor houses of the Tudor style built by major planter families and often connected to ruined towerhouses of dispossessed landowners. In some places, however, towerhouses themselves were occupied and refurbished.

The military conquest of Ulster, much of which remained independent and outside the sphere of English influence, commenced at the end of the sixteenth century. Conquest was followed by plantation, more ambitious, thoroughgoing and successful than in Munster or elsewhere. Thousands of Protestant settlers drawn mainly from western Scotland were settled in the countryside and newly-built towns. While many Irish were expelled, most were permitted to stay, mainly as tenants. Forests were reclaimed by the planters and arable farming increased in importance, contrasting with the traditional pastoral economy of the Irish. The planned establishment of towns and villages was an outstanding feature of the Plantation. A castle and bawn typically formed the nucleus of settlements, around which, in time, a church, session house, prison, mills and houses were usually built. Urban growth rarely exceeded thirty to forty houses which were often timber-framed dwellings similar in style to English houses. Londonderry, the last great *bastide* built in western Europe,

was the most impressive of the plantation towns, but the term 'town' was applied to many settlements no larger than average villages with populations of less than two hundred. The plantation plan prescribed a settlement pattern based on town and landlord villages, but the resulting rural settlement pattern was usually a compromise between small villages and dispersed settlement.

Massive land confiscations and plantations in the seventeenth century were accompanied by major mapping enterprises, such as the surveys by Francis Jobson in Munster and Bartlett and Bodley in Ulster. The Down Survey, implemented in the 1650s under William Petty, covered most parts of Ulster, Leinster and Munster parish by parish and was the first cadastral survey of Ireland comprehensive enough to serve as a basis for an improved small-scale map of the whole country. Concerned mainly with property boundaries, these early maps are disappointing as sources of information about the landscape. However, there was a surge in topographical writings in the seventeenth century, demonstrated in works by Petty, Gerard Boate, William Molyneux, Roderick O'Flaherty and Henry Piers.

After the definitive defeat of Catholic forces in the Williamite Wars (1689-91), Ireland, under a firmly entrenched Anglican landlordry, experienced a prolonged period of relative stability and economic development. A new era of landscape change was instigated, much of it centred on the demesne and estate village and influenced by widely prevalent ideas of 'agricultural improvement' which emphasised a new, commercialised and scientific pattern of farming, operating within a reformed and rationalised field system. The essential elements of the present-day rural landscape, the enclosed fields and

ORDNANCE SURVEY

● Fig. 76 Throughout Ireland, the distribution of different monument types shows how the landscape was utilised by various populations and testifies to centuries of human occupation and the struggle for control of the land. At Shanid, in county Limerick, a ringfort of the first millennium stands cheek by jowl with a later Norman motte topped by a stone castle, evidence of the need for a prolonged security presence.

dispersed farms on consolidated holdings, demesnes, and many of the villages and small rural towns, are expressions of these new forces and ideas.

Nonetheless, as the landscape was gradually modernised and transformed during the last three centuries, the evidence of thousands of years of prior human occupation persisted. Certain monuments were protected by local respect and by the limits of technology. In recent decades, however, with the implementation of state and European policies of agricultural development, there has been an accelerated rate of destruction; in some parts of Ireland, one-third of all earthworks marked on the Ordnance Survey maps of the mid-nineteenth century have disappeared. An increased awareness of Ireland's surviving field monuments will help guarantee the preservation of this extraordinary landscape legacy.

BIBLIOGRAPHY

F. Aalen, *Man and the landscape in Ireland* (London, 1978).

G. Barrett, 'Recovering the hidden archaeology of Ireland: the impact of aerial survey in the river Barrow valley 1989-91' in *Forschungen zur Archäologie im Land Brandenburg*, iii (1995), pp 45-60.

L. Barrow, *The round towers of Ireland* (Dublin, 1979).

T. Barry, *The archaeology of medieval Ireland* (London, 1987).

V. Buckley (ed.), *Burnt offerings: international contributions to burnt mound archaeology* (Dublin, 1991).

A. Burl, *The stone circles of the British Isles* (London, 1976).

G. Burenhault, *The archaeology of Carrowmore: environmental archaeology and the megalithic tradition at Carrowmore, county Sligo* (Stockholm, 1984).

B. Colfer, 'Anglo-Norman settlement in county Wexford' in K. Whelan (ed.), *Wexford: history and society* (Dublin, 1987), pp 65-101.

G. Cooney, 'Irish neolithic landscapes and land use systems: the implications of field systems' in *Rural History*, ii (1991), pp 123-9.

G. Cooney and E. Grogan, 'A preliminary distribution map of stone axes in Ireland' in *Antiquity*, lxiv (1990), pp 559-61.

G. Cooney and E. Grogan, *A social prehistory of Ireland* (Dublin 1995).

M. de Paor and L. de Paor, *Early Christian Ireland* (London, 1961).

R. de Valera, 'The court cairns of Ireland' in *R.I.A. Proc.*, lx (1960), C, pp 9-140.

N. Edwards, *The archaeology of early medieval Ireland* (London, 1990).

G. Eogan, *Hoards of the Irish later bronze age* (Dublin, 1983).

P. Harbison, *Guide to national and historic monuments of Ireland* (Dublin, 1992).

P. Harbison, *The high crosses of Ireland*, 3 vols. (Bonn, 1992).

M. Herity, *Irish passage graves* (Dublin, 1974).

HMSO, *Historic monuments of Northern Ireland: an introduction and guide* (Belfast, 1983).

R. Lamb, *Iron age promontory forts in the British Isles* (Oxford, 1980).

H. Leask, *Irish churches and monastic buildings*, 3 vols. (Dundalk, 1955-1971).

H. Leask, *Irish castles and castellated houses* (Dundalk, 1973).

R. Loeber, *The geography and practice of English colonisation in Ireland 1534-1609* (Athlone, 1991).

F. Mitchell, *The Shell guide to reading the Irish landscape* (Dublin, 1986).

K. Molloy and M. O'Connell, 'Palaeoecological investigations towards the reconstruction of environment and land-use changes during prehistory at Céide Fields, western Ireland' in *Probleme der Küstenforschung im südlichen Nordseegebiet*, xxiii (1995), pp 187-225.

H. Mytum, *The origins of Early Christian Ireland* (London, 1992).

E. Norman and K. St Joseph, *The early development of Irish society* (Cambridge, 1969).

S. Ó Nualláin, 'The stone circle complex of Cork and Kerry' in *R.S.A.I. Jn.*, cv (1975), pp 83-131.

S. Ó Nualláin, 'Irish portal tombs: topography, siting and distribution' in *R.S.A.I. Jn.*, cxiii (1983), pp 75-105.

S. Ó Nualláin, *Survey of the megalithic tombs of Ireland, V: county Sligo* (Dublin, 1989).

S. Ó Riordáin, *Antiquities of the Irish countryside*, fifth ed., revised by R. de Valera (London, 1979).

B. Raftery, 'Irish hillforts' in C. Thomas (ed.), *The iron age in the Irish Sea province* (London, 1972), pp 37-58.

B. Raftery, 'Iron age burials in Ireland' in D. Ó Corráin (ed.), *Irish antiquity* (Cork, 1981), pp 175-204.

B. Raftery, *La Tène in Ireland: problems of origin and chronology* (Marburg, 1984).

B. Raftery, *Pagan celtic Ireland: the enigma of the Irish iron age* (London, 1994).

E. Shee-Twohig, *Irish megalithic tombs* (Buckinghamshire, 1990).

R. Stalley, *The Cistercian monasteries of Ireland* (New Haven, 1987).

G. Stout, 'The embanked enclosures of the Boyne region' in *R.I.A. Proc.*, xci (1991), C, pp 245-84.

M. Stout, 'Ringforts in the south-west midlands of Ireland' in *R.I.A. Proc.*, xci (1991), C, pp 201-43.

M. Stout, *The Irish ringfort* (Dublin, 1997).

L. Swan, 'Enclosed ecclesiastical sites and their relevance to settlement patterns of the first millennium A.D.' in T. Reeves-Smyth and F. Hamond (ed.), *Landscape archaeology in Ireland* (Oxford, 1983), pp 269-94.

J. Waddell, *Irish bronze age burials* (Galway, 1990).

R. Warner, 'The archaeology of early historic Irish kingship' in S. Driscoll and M. Nieke (ed.), *Power and politics in early medieval Britain and Ireland* (Edinburgh, 1988), pp 47-68.

P. Woodman, *Excavations at Mount Sandel 1973-1977* (Belfast, 1985).

P. Woodman, 'Problems in the colonisation of Ireland' in *Ulster Jn. Arch.*, il (1986), pp 7-17.

P. Woodman, 'Filling in the spaces in Irish prehistory' in *Antiquity*, lxvi (1992), pp 259-314.

M. Zvelibil and S. Green, 'Looking at the stone age in south-east Ireland' in *Arch. Ir.*, vi (1992), pp 20-3.

Recovering the hidden landscape

The stony terrain of the west of Ireland, and many upland and pastoral environments, can be considered as 'zones of archaeological survival' with a rich array of monuments recorded on the first edition Ordnance Survey maps of the 1830s and 1840s, and also incorporated within the modern landscape. By contrast, in the more fertile arable zones of the south and east, successive phases of occupation and more intensive agricultural systems have modified the earlier horizons of settlement and land use. In these 'zones of archaeological destruction', the pattern of land-scape evidence is more fragmented. Many archaeological monuments were erased at ground level before the middle of the nineteenth century, and were therefore not recorded on the first edition maps. However, traces of early landscapes often remain buried beneath the ground surface and are revealed on aerial photography as subtle colour and height variations in the crops growing above sub-surface archaeological remains. From a light plane, travelling at a height of about 365m, these transient cropmark images can be identified and recorded with a camera.

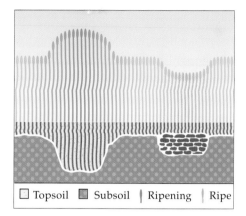

| ☐ Topsoil | ■ Subsoil | ▮ Ripening | ▮ Ripe |

Fig. B The formation of cropmarks. Positive crop-marks form where buried ditches lie hidden beneath the ground surface. The extra depth of soil, with its increased moisture and nutrient content, enhances crop growth. The taller, more luxuriant plants remain green for a longer period, while the remainder of the crop ripens. Negative cropmarks develop where stony deposits remain beneath the ground surface; plant growth is stunted and the crop ripens early. Although colour and height differences are sometimes evident at ground level, their location and significance is usually only apparent from the air.

The potential of an aerial survey as a technique of archaeological discovery in Ireland was first demonstrated in the pioneer photography of J. K. S. St Joseph in the 1960s and 1970s. Since 1989, systematic programmes of aerial reconnaissance by Gillian Barrett in the south-east of Ireland have revealed extensive cropmark sequences throughout the arable zone. These discoveries yield a wide range of previously unrecorded archaeological features, comprising burial sites, settlement enclosures and field systems, ranging in date from the prehistoric to the medieval period. Each successive year of aerial survey generates a cumulative pattern of discovery, providing a rapidly expanding source of data for archaeologists, geographers and historians in their studies of the formation of the Irish landscape.

INFILLING THE ARCHAEOLOGICAL LANDSCAPE AT DUNMANOGE, COUNTY KILDARE

The contribution of aerial survey is best appreciated at local level, where cropmark

GILLIAN BARRETT

Fig. A Positive cropmarks within a ripening cereal crop, near Ardfinnan, county Tipperary reveal earlier horizons of landscape development and provide a window on a past landscape. Ground survey and excavation are required to clarify the precise function and dating of these newly identified archaeological features.

evidence discovered through aerial reconnaissance can be integrated with archaeological data from other sources.

The Dunmanoge area on the east bank of the Barrow in county Kildare

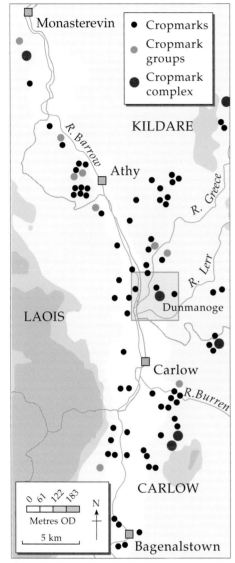

Fig. C The Barrow valley is a rich zone of aerial discovery. Between Monasterevin and Bagenalstown, the River Barrow flows through some of the most fertile land in Ireland. With a high level of tillage in the eighteenth and nineteenth centuries, the Barrow valley can be seen as a 'zone of destruction' in which the archaeological record has been substantially modified through agricultural activity. However, the light, well-drained soils and extensive cereal cultivation also provide responsive conditions for the formation of cropmarks and the detection of the sub-surface archaeology. In July 1989, low rainfall and soil moisture deficits exceeding 100mm generated large numbers of cropmarks of great clarity. In six hours of aerial reconnaissance, spread over three days, 137 cropmarks were recorded, 106 being newly identified archaeological features. One new site was thus located and recorded every three minutes, making aerial survey a very cost-effective technique of archaeological prospecting.

illustrates the fragmented nature of archaeological survival within a fertile arable region, the process of archaeological discovery over time, and the contribution of aerial survey in augmenting the archaeological record.

The study area of 16 km² incorporates a limited 'visible' archaeology, with only three sites recorded on the first edition Ordnance Survey map of 1837, including an Early Christian ringfort, a medieval moated homestead and the early church at Dunmanoge, which is the only monument now surviving in the modern

landscape. However, aerial survey has revealed an extensive 'hidden' landscape, consisting of fourteen archaeological sites recorded as cropmarks, including five enclosures recorded by St Joseph on a single flight in 1971, and a further nine sites identified in a renewed programme of aerial reconnaissance between 1989 and 1991. The cropmark evidence indicates a far more complex pattern of early settlement on the east bank of the Barrow than is reflected in the area's field archaeology or from chance finds.

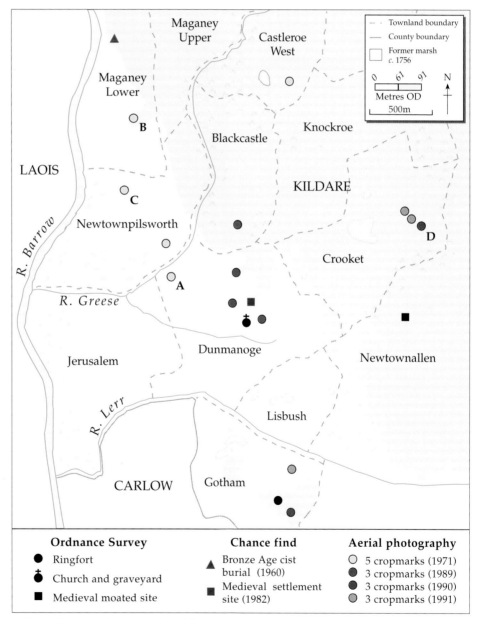

Fig. D The cumulative impact of aerial discovery between 1971 and 1991 has transformed the archaeological record at Dunmanoge, county Kildare.

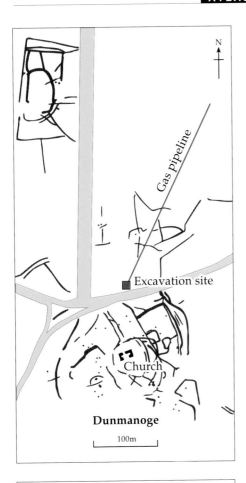

Dunmanoge

L___100m___l

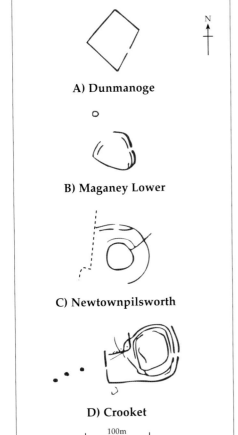

A) Dunmanoge

B) Maganey Lower

C) Newtownpilsworth

D) Crooket

L___100m___l

Fig. E (left) Reconstructing the early landscape at Dunmanoge. A sequence of aerial photographs taken between 1989 and 1991 has been used to reconstruct the cropmark landscape surrounding the church at Dunmanoge. Individual photographs, taken in different seasons, with contrasting weather and crop conditions, each provide extra detail, permitting the compilation of a composite map of the 'hidden' landscape. A computerised mapping system has been employed to correct the tilt distortion of the oblique aerial view. An accurate plan is then produced, integrating the cropmark evidence discovered and recorded over the three-year period.

GILLIAN BARRETT

Fig. G 'Visible' and 'invisible' components of the landscape at Dunmanoge, county Kildare. The isolated, ruined church and graveyard contrast with the extensive cropmark landscape recorded in 1989, indicating an ecclesiastical centre of considerable scale and complexity. Aerial photographs require careful interpretation since cropmark sequences record not only the archaeological horizons, but also more recent facets of landscape change, for example farm drainage schemes (far right) and gas pipelines (diagonal line, centre).

Fig. F (left) The cropmark enclosures discovered through aerial survey vary from the simple to the complex. These cropmarks, recorded in adjacent townlands, may not be contemporaneous, but probably represent settlements of contrasting social status and function in the Early Christian and medieval periods.

THE MODERN LANDSCAPE: FROM PLANTATION TO PRESENT

At the beginning of the seventeenth century, Ireland was a lightly settled, overwhelmingly pastoral, well wooded country. The economy, with its weak urbanism and technological archaisms, was characterised by the unprocessed nature of its exports – hides, fish and timber – and by a low population of about one million. By the end of the century, the most rapid transformation in any European seventeenth-century economy, society and culture had been effected. Two processes were central to this process; the initial subjugation, subsequent colonisation and final integration of Ireland into the expanding English state, and the concurrent enhancement of Ireland's location within the North Atlantic commercial world. After 1685, that Atlantic world was increasingly an English one, and the fusion of the two processes accelerated the remaking of Ireland. From being an island behind an island on the rainy rim of Western Europe, Ireland now became the last European stepping-stone to America, tightly tied to Britain and its Atlantic colonies.

These close encounters with the emerging world economic system led to abrupt transformations in regional economies, the agrarian order and the landscape itself. This rapid transition to comparative modernity, without the long conditioning of other societies, was not achieved without severe social and cultural trauma, including the decline of the national language and the intrusion of deep cultural and economic fissures. The native élite was largely obliterated, elbowed aside by a new, Protestant and British landed class. Given the changing economic climate, this landed class was able to play a pivotal role in the economic, political and social life of the country over the next two centuries. Later, political developments in the early twentieth century saw the creation of two separate states on the island with divergent rural and environmental policies, while entry to the European Community and modernisation from the 1960s onwards have profoundly affected the whole island, reflected in convergence in their landscapes.

AEROFILMS

Fig. 1 Until the conquest of the Atlantic Ocean, Ireland was a wallflower in Europe, remote from its warm Mediterranean heart. With the 'discovery' of America, the centre of gravity of Europe shifted dramatically towards its north Atlantic shores, relocating Ireland as strategically vital and also sucking it into the orbit of a rapidly expanding English economy and polity.

THE LANDLORD AND THE LANDSCAPE

The ubiquity and strength of the landed estate in Ireland from the 1660s onwards is remarkable. The older mosaic of lordships with their protective canopy of kinship was shattered by the centralising state, to be reconstituted as a commercial system of landed estates. This seventeenth-century transition also witnessed a complete reorganisation of the landowning élite and a consequent restructuring of rural settlement and society around the new principal components of the estates. The detailed mapping of the Irish countryside emerges precisely at this moment of geopolitical relocation and landscape transformation.

Powered by the imperial impulse, the new estate system generated market momentum; a universally applied leasing system became the pacemaker for agricultural production to become price-responsive, and therefore flexible in meeting external demand. As a result, Irish agriculture, and with it rural settlement and society, was reorientated to suit a commodity-based economy, increasingly integrated by fairs and markets, and by the newly created villages which proliferated in the period. In these ways, the landed estate became the principal engine of growth in the eighteenth-century Irish economy, fuelled by a rent-paying tenantry.

These dramatic changes ushered in a rapid phase of house, demesne and village building, of agricultural and infrastructural development, and of sweeping settlement reorganisation. The landlords became the main agents of

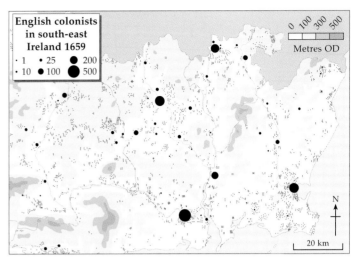

Fig. 3 Colonists in south-east Ireland, c. 1660. The first half of the seventeenth century was a period of intensive colonisation. In the south-east, the larger towns (Waterford, New Ross, Wexford, Kilkenny and Carlow) were major magnets for settlers; smaller centres like Tullow, Callan and Thurles were also significant seed-beds. The newcomers fanned out along the fertile river valleys of the Slaney, Barrow, Nore and Suir and inserted themselves in well-settled lowland areas like south-east Wexford, north Carlow, mid Kilkenny and mid Tipperary. They avoided wooded, upland or strongly gaelicised regions such as west Wexford, south Carlow and north Kilkenny. The influence of individual landowners who strongly encouraged immigrant tenants is responsible for obvious concentrations.

the Age of Improvement. The agricultural revolution was enthusiastically introduced with new crops (rape and hemp), vegetables (potato, artichoke and asparagus), deciduous trees (lime and chestnut), rotations (clover and turnips replacing fallow) and improved breeds (sheep and fat cattle). There was also an insistent emphasis on technological innovations in farming practices – liming, draining, enclosure, the provision of outhouses, large-scale reclamation projects on bogs and mountains. An associated market revolution was facilitated by increased accessibility through road and canal building. The cumulative result was impressive productivity and export growth, intense market penetration and a surging demographic profile. Rents rose ten-fold between 1660 and 1800 and the surplus income permitted an architectural revolution in Ireland.

The pivotal transition was in the 1730s, when the first post-Boyne generation of landowners came to power. These developments marked the maturing of a specifically Irish identity, linked to a novel sense of security in the countryside. With this, the older military/plantation ethos of imposing 'pacification' and 'civilisation' could metamorphose into a milder enlightenment ethos of order, progress and rationality. This was also a period when rentals began to rise, as favourable leases granted to tenants in the cash-starved 1690s expired.

The self-confidence of the landed class, with its assured political position and flourishing rentals, initiated a sustained period of house building. The embattled vertical

BRITISH LIBRARY

Fig. 2 This late sixteenth-century portrait of Queen Elizabeth I celebrates the incipient imperial moment of England. The defeat of the Spanish Armada ensured English control of the Atlantic and dominance of its emerging economy, symbolised by the firm royal hand on the globe. This confident, centralising, aggressively imperial England would no longer tolerate the ambiguous situation of its neighbouring island; the Elizabethan period was marked by determined efforts to extend the half-conquest of Ireland by military subjugation and plantation.

towerhouse gave way to the confident horizontality of Georgian architecture – portcullis yielded to portico, battlement to pediment, loophole to sash window, bawn to walled garden. The zest for lavish houses was at once utilitarian and symbolic – a reassuring landscape expression of a stable, anglicised, Protestant society. Between the 1600s and 1740s in county Cork alone, the number of big houses shot up from 25 to 200 but every Irish county saw a similar spate of building.

Palladian neo-classicism was a common Enlightenment style, well suited to the gentry's view of their own cardinal position in a balanced hierarchical society. The great houses of this period all serve an exemplary function, asserting in their cosmopolitan styles a pan-European sense of a landed gentry. These grand houses set the tone for a century of building. Similar concerns were exhibited in their demesnes, gardens and associated villages, based on principles of rationality and control, manipulating landscape as a decorous adjunct to power. While demesne creation was an exercise in image building, in creating exemplary landscapes, it was also designed to stimulate a mimetic response in smaller fry, thereby acting as an agency for diffusing 'taste'.

Once the 'natural' style of demesne replaced the earlier formal designs, the sites of big houses shifted decisively to

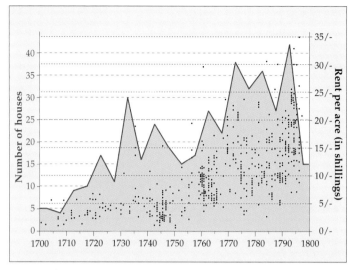

● Fig. 5 The construction dates of over 300 'Big Houses' between 1700 and 1800 show the importance of the 1730s before the downturn induced by the 1740-41 famine. The sustained rental increases from the 1740s financed building among the lesser gentry, rising to a peak in the early 1770s, when the Irish landed world stood at the apex of its wealth, power and influence. House building remained buoyant in the 1780s, before the changing political circumstances of the 1790s punctured self-confidence. When the building data is superimposed on a chart showing rental movements (county Wexford data) over a similar period, the correlation between increasing rental income and investment in housing is particularly clear.

slopes and river valleys. Favoured locations became nests of big houses – as along the Blackwater, Slaney and Suir, or in the environs of solid towns like Mallow, Youghal, Birr or Clonmel. The Liffey and the Boyne particularly threaded through demesnes, subdued versions of the Thames above London, or the lower Loire in France.

Despite the sweeping changes, areas of continuity in estate ownership (and of settlement) from before the mid

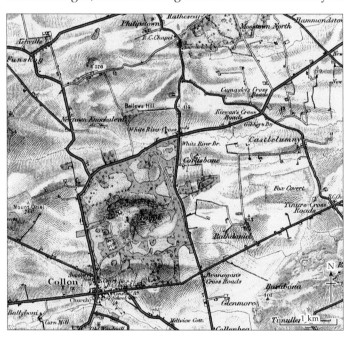

● Fig. 4 From the mid eighteenth century, the Fosters (first Anthony and then John) had ambitiously developed their new estate on the Collon hills in mid Louth. A grid of roads was pushed through the hills, establishing a template for the formation of new farms through intensive drainage, liming, reclamation and enclosure. Collon village was established alongside the impressive demesne and big house, using a colony of northern linen weavers to stimulate proto-industry. As an aspiring politician and an economic expert, it was important for John Foster that his estate should become a model. The modern landscape around Collon is still essentially that laid out in this period.

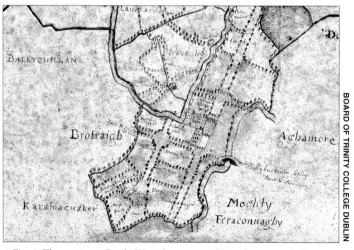

● Fig. 6 The estate at Castle Waterhouse near Lisnaskea, county Fermanagh had been extensively developed by the late seventeenth century. The big house was framed by a geometric grid of formalised planting, enclosing a network of regular, symmetrical fields, bearing resonantly English names. Mills and meadows lined the river, which was already bridged on the then Dublin to Lisnaskea road. The overall impression is of a determined effort to introduce fashionable European designs into the Ulster countryside, with the landlord inhabiting an exemplary landscape around his big house.

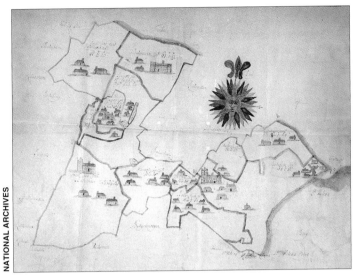

● Fig. 7 This 1727 map of the Ballyhire estate near Rosslare, county Wexford depicts an area which had been intensively settled by the Normans and was already well-developed by the late medieval period. The estate system here had a subdued influence. Continuity is indicated by the three new houses added to the existing towerhouses (including that at Ballyhire itself). A cabin cluster is still intact around the medieval church at Churchtown. The windmill on the coast indicates intensive tillage, while an evolved social structure can be inferred from the diversity of house types, ranging from one-room cabins to substantial two-storeyed farmhouses.

seventeenth-century upheavals through to the nineteenth century are much greater in extent than was previously assumed and striking variations can be shown between 'old' and 'new' estates. Almost one-fifth of the island remained in relatively undisturbed ownership and experienced only modest reorganisation; even more importantly, these undisturbed estates were concentrated heavily in

● Fig. 8 Newbridge demesne in north county Dublin. Demesnes were frequently designed as set pieces. The cocooning effect of the boundary planting, the focus on the big house and the manicured landscape all reflect precise planning, creating an island effect within the more organically evolved surrounding countryside.

certain regions – notably the Pale, the Galway-Clare-Mayo area, and south Leinster.

Besides location and ownership continuity, the size of estates also determined their settlement and landscape impact. Smaller estates, unable to finance large-scale social or landscape engineering projects, tended to conserve older settlement forms. Such small estates were often contiguous in areas where fragmented medieval landowning patterns were inherited directly. Settlement here was insulated from radical transformation, because they tended to be already well developed. With (by seventeenth-century standards) heavy population densities, enclosures and agricultural improvements, they were shielded from the radical changes on estates in more marginal regions.

PRE-FAMINE REGIONAL SETTLEMENT PATTERNS

The island possessed a variegated set of environments and an inherited web of culturally diverse regions. The landscape impact, therefore, of modernisation evolved out of the complex interplay between environment, history, economy, society and settlement. Five major regions can be

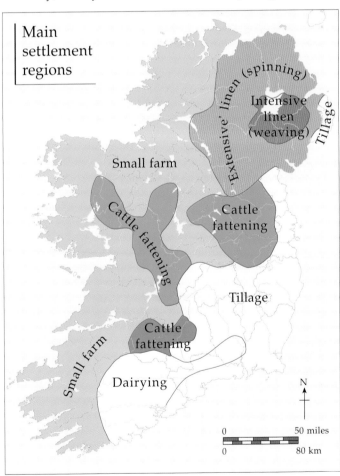

Main settlement regions

Fig. 9 The main eighteenth-century regions had well defined cores and more ambiguous edges, where one activity competed with another.

identified: dairying, cattle-fattening, commercial tillage, proto-industrial and small farming. Distinctive landscape features emerged in each region which have decisively influenced the landscapes of today.

Dairying

In south Munster and especially in the hinterland of Cork city, the eighteenth century was the crucial period in laying the framework of the modern landscape. The rapid rise in external demand led to the equally rapid rise of a market-oriented agriculture, with an especially buoyant period between 1740 and 1815. There was an abrupt transition from unprocessed primary products to processed beef and butter. These changes were facilitated by the estate system, by a dietary revolution which saw the potato eclipse 'whitemeats' (milk products), and by the commercialisation of agricultural production. In particular, butter, previously consumed as a food, was now released to the market, being substituted in the diet by the potato. Cork city became the most significant centre for commercial butter production in the Atlantic world as its grass-rich hinterland with its old dairying tradition became an intensive butter-producing region.

From the 1690s onwards, dairying ousted extensive sheep and bullock-fattening. In the mid-Munster countryside, the dairyman system dominated, especially in the Lee and Blackwater valleys. This system revolved around the great dairy master. Like the grazier, he was usually a townland tenant and a big one could own 1000 cattle (fear míle bó). He leased 20-40 cows to a dairyman in return for a butter rent. The dairyman disposed of the calves, kept the buttermilk and was given a cabin and potato ground.

Fig. 10 This Van Keulenboech engraving of the early eighteenth century depicts the Munster dairying industry. The indigenous 'black' or 'Kerry' cow is milked into a wooden pail by a woman in the fields. The milk is then churned by the woman and the butter is carried in flat wooden containers (lossets) to the custom-built water-tight barrels (firkins). Using wooden mallets, it is packed tightly into the firkins which are being inspected by the local butter factor and a Dutch merchant.

Fig. 11 Dinely's seventeenth-century drawing emphasises the dominance of women in dairying work. The 'Kerry' cow is lightly spancelled with straw (sugán) ropes to prevent her kicking. The woman, warmly dressed in her cloak-like mantle, milks the cow in the open air into a wooden keeler.

Dairy houses were also supplied, with a room for milk and the necessary utensils. The herd size did not exceed forty, which was the maximum that could be milked by hand by a single family.

Given the region's mild winters and soft summers, and consequent all-year-round grazing, there was no need for custom-built byres; cows were driven morning and evening to the bawn (bó-dhún), a sheltered milking place near the dwelling house. Its tolerance of outdoor wintering, disease resistance and high milk yield guaranteed the pre-eminence of the 'black' or Kerry cow – the indigenous genetic variety – in dairying. Hay was necessary for winter feeding and meadow grounds were in jealous demand; their absence militated against dairying in upland areas, concentrating intensive dairying in the limestone valleys.

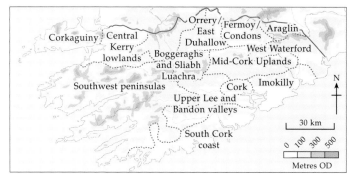

Fig. 12 South Munster farming regions in the eighteenth century, as identified by David Dickson, based on soil type, relief, market and fertiliser access, land use and history.

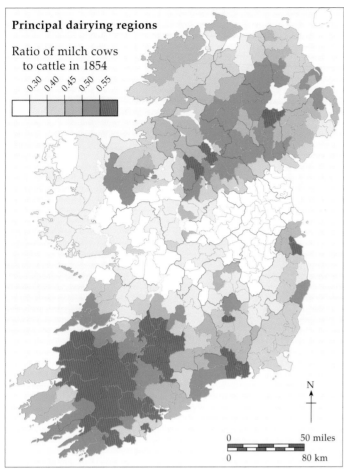

Principal dairying regions

Ratio of milch cows
to cattle in 1854

0.30 0.40 0.45 0.50 0.55

N

| 0 | 50 miles |
| 0 | 80 km |

Fig. 13 The ratio of cow to cattle numbers in 1854 when the first detailed agricultural statistics became available. The west Munster bias of dairying is apparent, dominating a broad swathe of territory from north Kerry to Cork city, with an outlier in south-west Tipperary. A less intensive zone stretches through the south Ulster drumlin belt, from north Armagh to Longford. Restricted dairying zones appear around the bigger cities – Waterford, Dublin, Kilkenny, Limerick and Belfast.

As fattening proceeded, cattle were moved from west to east, and from upland to lowland; Kerry calves became Cork heifers on their rite of passage from coarse mountain grazing to lush limestone valleys.

From the mid-1760s onwards, as farmers' conditions improved due to the sustained rise in the prices of butter, cheese and calves, the butter rent gave way to a cash equivalent and small independent dairy farmers emerged, leasing land for cash. In the process, the dairy masters reverted to being plain middlemen. The influence of dairying peaked between 1750 and 1770, losing ground thereafter to commercial tillage farming. However, it did create a solid farming class in the more accessible lowland regions of mid-Munster and its influence reached back into the poorer hills of west Munster.

The rapid expansion of dairying had pronounced landscape effects. It led to clearance of furze and heath scrub, as enclosure crept up the 'coarse' mountains; it saw permanent settlement colonise the old buaile summer pastures; it

WATERFORD CORPORATION

●Fig. 14 Eighteenth-century Waterford was a major port, with extensive trading links from Iberia to Newfoundland. It commanded a versatile agricultural hinterland, based on the river valleys of the 'Three Sisters' – the Barrow, Nore and Suir. Van der Hagen's 1730 painting emphasises the city's main asset – its long, deep and sheltered inland port. The river is alive with shipping and the cramped city crouches towards the water, fronted by a tall array of arcaded mercantile buildings. The backdrop depicts a well-enclosed *bocage* landscape, typical of the south-east.

led to the making of sheltering hedges and ditches in smaller fields and a spate of marling, liming and draining to sweeten the sour hill pastures, especially adjacent to Cork city. And as dairying became ever more closely integrated into mixed small farm systems, it led to a drop in average farm size, a rise in population, and a consequent compacting of the landscape.

Cattle fattening

The pastoral tradition in Ireland was overwhelmingly weighted towards cattle although sheep were locally and periodically important. Favoured by a climate so mild that winter housing was unnecessary, blessed with rich pasture-lands on a healthy limestone base, and with low production and labour costs, Ireland could produce cattle more cheaply to a higher quality than any of its European competitors. Ireland was also ideally placed between the English and American markets. Its provisions trade fed the many extra mouths generated by the industrialising British economy, and the still not self-sufficient Caribbean and American colonies.

Permanent pasture in Ireland remained tightly anchored to its limestone-based cores in north-east Leinster, north Munster (especially east Limerick and west Tipperary), and inner Connacht (east Mayo, east Galway and the celebrated plains of Boyle in mid-Roscommon). Between these cores, cattle-fattening oscillated in response to price fluctuations, notably where good and badlands alternated promiscuously in the confused bogs and meadows of Offaly, Longford and Westmeath. Cattle fattening was very responsive to market fluctuations

CUCAP

● Fig. 15 At Colliesduff in south Mayo, an eighteenth-century pattern of regular fields for cattle grazing is superimposed on an earlier rundale system. The site is called Sean-Bhaile (old settlement), indicating the existence of a tillage-based small-farm cluster which had been ousted by the spread of commercialised cattle rearing.

within the hinterlands of the great cities. East Limerick and the Golden Vale in particular shifted from store cattle to dairying in the nineteenth century.

This flourishing export market had a number of impacts on cattle production. Specialised breeding and finishing areas developed and cattle were moved from west to east as they got older, from the rearing lands in the hills and bogs, to the fattening lands on the sleek pastures of north Leinster and mid-Munster. Cattle were bought to be sold, and sold to buy others; cattle dealing became the most vital skill of the farmer, and cattle became the primary exchange currency of the Irish countryside. Fairs mushroomed in the hothouse export economy, from 700 in the 1600s to 3000 in the 1770s to 5000 in 1845. So dense was the fair network that no drove roads emerged, unlike contemporary Scotland, Denmark and Hungary.

If the cow supplied all this prosperity, there was an inevitable downside. Beef cattle production swallowed up pasture land – squeezing out small farmers from the good lands, forcing them to the hills and bogs unfit for fat cattle, while bullocks roamed on the best land. The bullock spread desolation across the territories it colonised, accentuating the dislocation already inflicted by the seventeenth-century transition in land ownership. In settlement terms, the pastoral expansion accentuated erosive effects on older tillage-based 'village'

communities, especially in Roscommon, Westmeath, Tipperary, east Clare, east Galway, east Limerick and north Cork. Much of the 'village' desertion in Ireland may thus have been in the seventeenth century rather than in the late medieval period.

In cattle-fattening areas, grazier holdings became the cornerstone of leasing policy and of settlement patterns. Given its extensive mode of land use, the grazier economy created a barren landscape with an attenuated social structure and only rudimentary settlement forms, where the lonely box-Georgian graziers' houses were juxtaposed with the crude cabins of the herds. The large silent fields of grazing bullocks were anomalous in an Irish world which elsewhere was so noisy, crowded and complex. In counties Meath and Kildare, it was common in the late eighteenth century for 400 or 600 hectares to be in the hands of a single grazier. In the grazing baronies of Carra, Kilmaine and Clanmaurice in Mayo, the average field size on grazier holdings in 1800 was forty hectares.

In the eighteenth century, sheep farming was largely confined to the limestone lowlands. Sheepwalks – large twenty hectare fields, with tightly cropped grass and flimsy enclosures, where sheep were fattened – were found on some of the driest limestone soils in Ireland, in south Tipperary, mid Carlow, Roscommon and east Galway. Unlike its nineteenth-century equivalent, sheep farming was not associated with hill pastures at this stage, with the exception of the Burren and the Joyce Country in Galway which mainly produced lambs to be fattened on the adjacent lowland sheepwalks.

Tillage

The third main agricultural region was based on tillage, essentially mixed farming but with a specialisation in intensive commercial tillage. Built out of the environmentally favoured Norman coastlands, the tillage zone waxed strongly in the second half of the eighteenth century, boosted by bounties on the transport of flour to Dublin (from 1758) and then accelerating as European demand peaked in the Napoleonic period. By the late eighteenth century, the commercial tillage zone was concentrated in the south-eastern third of the country, largely within a quadrangle linking Cork, Dundalk, Strangford and Wexford.

By 1770, no fewer than fifteen counties (even as far away as Cork and Galway) were supplying flour to Dublin. This induced a transport revolution, as the new commodities being transported – corn, flour, lime – all had a low specific value. Only heavier loads were therefore economical; four-wheeled 'scotch' carts replaced the old

two-wheeled 'truckle' carts, and carried twice the load. Between 1700 and 1850, the road mileage for wheels doubled, and much of this was added in the tillage boom. Tillage created an almost frenzied demand for lime and marl to sweeten acid soils, and lime kilns proliferated. The spread of commercial tillage had another effect. It generated heavy investment in processing facilities – mills, malt houses, breweries and distilleries, especially in towns commanding navigable waters and good hinterlands. Fermoy, Clonmel, Kilkenny, Carlow, Athy, Enniscorthy and Navan all prospered in this phase.

The commercialisation of the tillage economy was accompanied by a dramatic increase in the number of agricultural labourers. Many of these were accommodated as cottiers – labourers who were given a one-roomed cabin and a manured potato plot (up to 0.4 ha in size) in return for unpaid labour for as much as two-thirds of the year. Tillage farmers favoured this arrangement as it guaranteed a cheap and disciplined labour force, while the intensively cultivated potato was an ideal precursor to the following

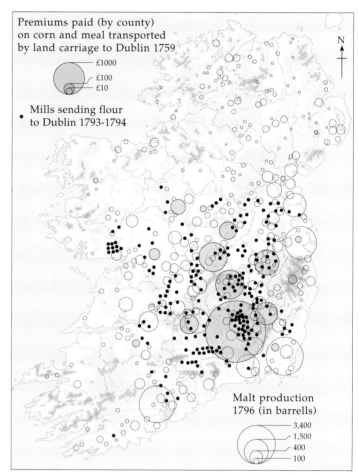

Fig. 17 The regional character of Irish commercial tillage had changed markedly throughout the eighteenth century. Until mid-century, Dublin had its own tillage zone in close proximity, in north Dublin, south Meath and north Kildare, essentially within the old Pale. In the eighteenth century, tillage expanded appreciably, especially in Kildare, Laois, Offaly, Carlow, Kilkenny and Tipperary. The widening of Dublin's hinterland also generated modernisation and mechanisation in the Irish flour-milling industry from the 1760s, initially in mid Kilkenny and south Tipperary. The valleys of the Kings River, the Nore and the Suir acted as cradles of innovation. At the height of its capacity in 1796, the malting industry had been established in every town and to a surprising extent through the countryside as well. Its most intensive development was closely linked to the tillage region. Wexford town was the biggest centre nationally, followed by Cork, Dublin and Drogheda. Notable concentrations appear in the coastal corridor from Dublin to Dundalk, in mid Kilkenny/north Carlow, and in north Tipperary/south Offaly.

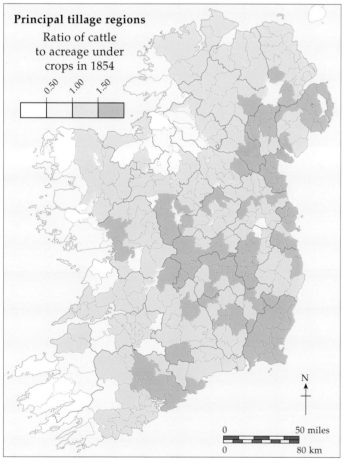

Fig. 16 An intensive tillage zone was concentrated in the eastern third of the country. The environmental advantage of this area included lower rainfall, well drained lighter soils and good access to rivers and harbours for cheap transportation. Many of the corn producing districts (the Ards, Lecale, Cooley, Fingal, Forth and Bargy, Imokilly) had been long-established tillage areas, with a tradition stretching back into the medieval period.

cereal crop. Expansion in the tilled area was achieved by the simple expedient of increasing the number of cottiers. On large commercial tillage farms, the dependent cottier population could run to double figures. Their notoriously impoverished housing was located in straggles of roadside cabins, in dishevelled cross-roads clusters, in shanties on the edge of towns, piled up in their dilapidated back lanes and alleys, or squeezed onto commonages.

The existence of independent labourers' houses was strikingly different from Britain, where the dominant mode of controlling agricultural labour was through the unmarried live-in servant or later the tied cottage. The prolific potato and the prevalence of turf achieved a greater

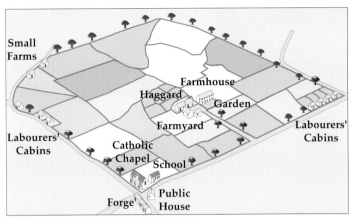

Fig. 18 A tillage farm and its cottiers *c.*1800. Cottiers were accommodated in a necklace of cabins strung loosely around the farm fringe, the social dichotomy mirrored in the micro-segregation. The farmhouse itself was often discreetly distanced from its perimeter of poverty, down a lane (bóithrín). In the south-east, these big farms had sometimes evolved out of earlier towerhouses; occupied by Catholics with wealth, local stature and inherited leadership roles, the farms also frequently hosted Catholic chapels which, in turn, generated embryonic chapel villages.

NATIONAL LIBRARY

Fig. 20 In the 1770s, Arthur Young first drew international attention to the plight of the Irish labourers, described by the great agriculturalist as the most impoverished class that he had yet seen in Europe. His illustration depicts their squalid one-roomed cabins, windowless and chimneyless, with light coming from the open door and turf smoke issuing through the dishevelled thatch. The background shows the essential lazy-beds and their precious potatoes.

freedom for the Irish agricultural labourer, reflected in the ease with which they could set up separate households. Their independence was purchased at the expense of depressed living standards as they were paid essentially a potato wage. However, the cottier system became one of the principal demographic dynamos in the Irish countryside.

The hiving-off of farmers and labourers into distinct settlement forms was an eighteenth-century phenomenon. On the mid seventeenth-century Down Survey maps, the cabin cluster around the towerhouse was the settlement expression of a society where the classes shared a site, and where even relatively substantial farmers were living in the traditional cabin. As agricultural modernisation progressed, capitalist penetration prised these elements

apart; the labourers were dispersed to the farm fringes, where roads performed a fly-catcher function. By the eve of the Famine, at least half of the population in tillage areas were farm labourers, a new social class generated by economic growth. This stratification of farmer and labourer was the most obvious social dimension of tillage areas.

The field-pattern in tillage areas was much tighter than in the dairying and especially cattle-fattening regions. The average field size was smaller and the land under 150m in a tillage area was well enclosed, generally in a framework of low earthen banks with hawthorn or furze hedges. Farms also had a more extensive array of buildings, often neatly disposed around a courtyard. Towns and villages were more frequent, and there was a busy artisan element,

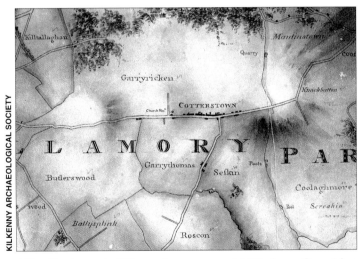

KILKENNY ARCHAEOLOGICAL SOCIETY

● Fig. 19 A county Kilkenny barony map of 1817 shows Garryricken House near Callan, and Cotterstown, its associated settlement of agricultural labourers. Typically, the cottier cabins line the roadside. Within a generation, Cottierstown had disappeared, the flimsy mud-walled cabins dissolving into the earth, leaving scarcely a landscape trace.

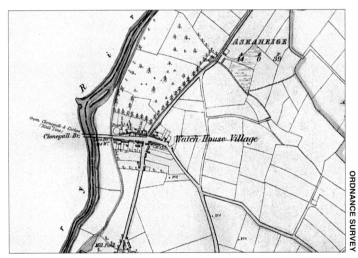

ORDNANCE SURVEY

● Fig. 21 Watch House 'village' adjoining Clonegal on the Wexford-Carlow border was a crossroads accumulation of labourers' houses, typical of the south-east tillage belt. While some worked seasonally in the nearby mill or in the village, the labourers mostly depended on the local big farmers for employment.

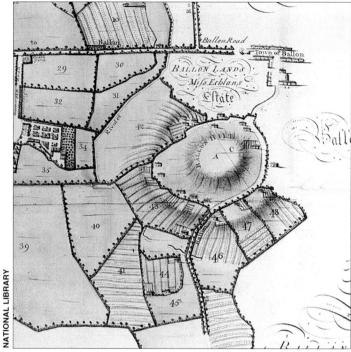

NATIONAL LIBRARY

● Fig. 22 Estate maps were both a valuable estate management tool, and aesthetic objects in themselves. 'A map of the townland of Ballykealey' by Francis Matthews dates from 1787 and shows the Lecky estate in county Carlow. Ballon Hill is ringed by cottier settlers and lazy-bed cultivation, while an early T-plan thatched chapel is shown in the village. Ballykealey House is depicted in profile; its formal garden and well developed hedgerows show the landscape influence of an 'improving' landlord.

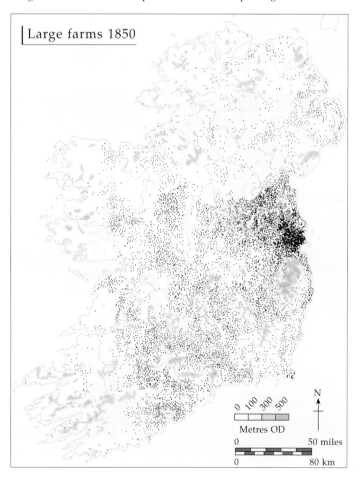

Large farms 1850

N

0 100 300 500

Metres OD

0   50 miles

0   80 km

especially blacksmiths. Tillage areas were bustling, strongly committed to agricultural improvement, and noticeably greater care was lavished on the land. It was in this period, for example, that Wexford acquired the nickname 'the model county', from its commitment to improved tillage.

Proto-Industrialisation

With beef and butter, linen was the third great Irish export product. The growth of the linen industry in Ulster to one of the world's leading half-dozen industries by the end of the eighteenth century is intimately related to the evolving world economic system. Linen production in Ireland became possible for four reasons: Ulster landlords encouraged their tenants to diversify into linen production, to keep rentals buoyant on poor land, especially in a period of population growth; Ireland (unlike Scotland) could grow its own flax; landlords supervised the rapid development of a marketing system, which allowed independent farmers/weavers to evolve; Irish linens were cheaper to produce in a low labour-cost environment. Thus, linen production rose phenomenally: exports rose from one and a half million yards in 1712, to 17 million yards in 1760, and 46 million yards in 1796.

This expansion was sustained by technical innovation, via the application of chemicals and water power, especially in bleaching. Because water power was widely distributed, so were beetling mills, but there was a concentration of these mills and associated bleach yards where a steady supply of water was guaranteed. These positive factors generated intense proto-industrialisation. As elsewhere in Europe, this was accommodated by subdivision of lease holdings, population growth, and the incorporation of women and children into the workforce. Thus, the Ulster countryside was festooned with a myriad of small weaver/farmer holdings. The cradle of linen weaving was north Armagh, initially around the Brownlow estate at Lurgan. By 1729, Antrim, Armagh, Down, Derry and Tyrone were described as counties fully embarked upon linen manufacture, while Donegal, Monaghan and Cavan were involved in spinning.

The distinctive weaver's house could be identified by its length, as it incorporated an extra room for the tall, heavy looms. Towns were vibrant, especially on market days and

Fig. 23 Large farms (valued at over £100), c. 1850 as mapped by T. Jones Hughes. The strong-farm world of eighteenth and nineteenth-century Ireland was drawn from the tillage, dairying and cattle fattening regions. Big farmers were preferred tenants, possessing the necessary capital and entrepreneurial drive to effect landscape improvements. Most notably, they would construct two-storeyed, slated, stone-walled houses; plant orchards and trees; lime and drain; rotate crops and reclaim land. The distribution of 7,200 of these units demonstrates that the environmentally-favoured areas of Leinster and Munster were the territorial base of large farms. These areas were also sufficiently resilient culturally to adapt to commercialising forces.

PRONI

●Fig. 24 A linen draper's residence in Lurgan, county Armagh in the early nineteenth century. The long, low thatched house is typical of the region; the additional bay accommodated looms, while the tall windows ensured adequate light for skilled weavers. In the centre, the new factory building of the early nineteenth century shows the advent of industrial production, while the buildings to the right house the carts and provide the storage space necessary for a busy draper.

there was a dense network of roads which carried a lively trade. In summer, the countryside flushed blue, as the flax flowered. The intensive proto-industrial area, especially the famous linen triangle between Dungannon, Lisburn and Armagh, created a prosperous aureole of agricultural production (yarn, oats, potatoes, turf) in the surrounding region arcing from north Connacht to north Leinster.

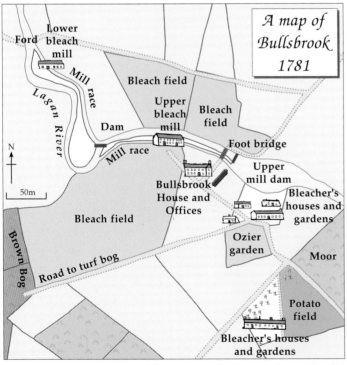

PRONI

●Fig. 25   Rivers were valuable assets in the linen industry. In this example from Bullsbrook on the Bann in 1781, the river zips together a proto-industrial landscape of bleachyards, beetling mills, weavers' houses and mercantile villas.

MONAGHAN COUNTY MUSEUM

●Fig. 26 The linen industry was intensively commercialised and provided a fillip to town life in Ulster. Independent weavers brought their webs to be bought by drapers in weekly open-air linen markets, as in this example from Monaghan, painted by Henry MacManus in 1830. Tight supervision of quality, pricing and measuring ensured the success of this system, organised by the Linen Board.

Intensification of agricultural production via tiny family farms triggered demographic growth. By 1770, there were 42,000 weavers in Ulster: by 1820 when the proto-industrialisation phase was at its height, there were 70,000. The vast majority of these were never organised on a putting-out (*verslegen*) system, but were independent farmer/weavers who sold their webs of cloth in the many provincial towns with linen markets fostered by landlords eager to cash-in on the trade.

Linen production was specially suited to regions of inferior land such as the difficult drumlin country of south Ulster; this adaptation to coarse land is illustrated by the inability of the proto-industrial economy to make any

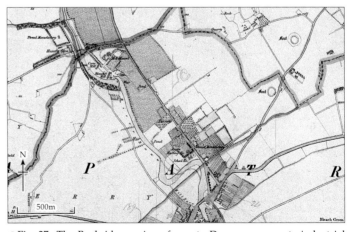

Fig. 27 The Banbridge region of county Down was a proto-industrial area, as depicted on the first edition O.S. map.

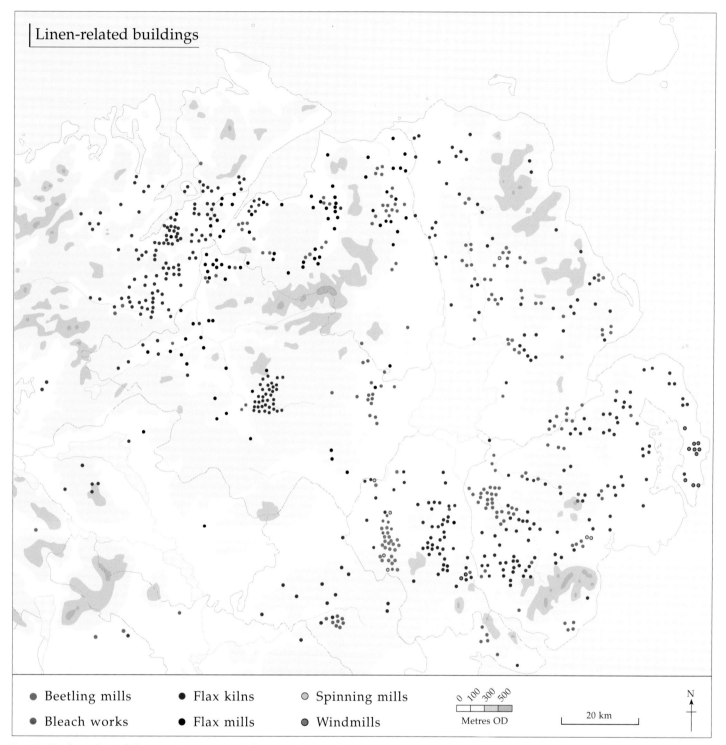

Linen-related buildings

- ● Beetling mills
- ● Bleach works
- ● Flax kilns
- ● Flax mills
- ○ Spinning mills
- ● Windmills

0 100 300 500
Metres OD

20 km

N

Fig. 28 The first edition O.S. maps depict an extraordinary profusion of linen-related buildings across the Ulster countryside – mills, bleachworks, kilns. Activity is heaviest in west Antrim, mid Armagh and mid Down. Beetling mills and associated bleach yards were concentrated where a good supply of water was available – as on the Lagan between Belfast and Lisburn, the upper Bann, the Callan in Armagh and on the streams cascading off the Antrim plateau. Flax kilns occur in tight clusters in mid Tyrone and east Armagh: they were necessary where open air drying alone was insufficient to dry flax fibres after retting. Some areas – the Glens of Antrim, south Down, Lecale, the Ards, south Derry and all of Fermanagh – were only lightly affected by proto-industrialisation, remaining committed to agricultural production.

impression on the fertile fattening lands of north Leinster. Indeed, there was a crisp interface between the two economies, fundamentally dictated by the underlying environmental constraints. This in turn underpinned the association of good lands and low population densities which became an increasingly pronounced feature of the Irish scene. By the middle of the nineteenth century, county Armagh had population densities in excess of 190 per square kilometre – among the heaviest concentrations of rural population anywhere in contemporary Europe.

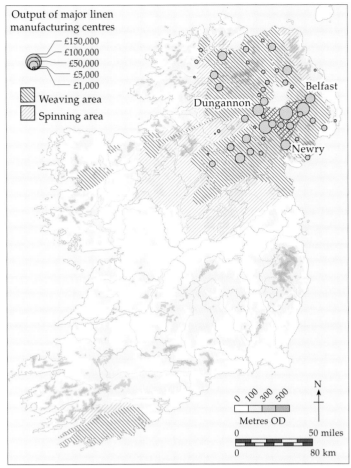

Output of major linen
manufacturing centres

£150,000
£100,000
£50,000
£5,000
£1,000

▨ Weaving area

▦ Spinning area

Dungannon

Belfast

Newry

N

0 100 300 500
Metres OD

0   50 miles
0   80 km

Fig. 29 In 1783, the leading brown linen markets were Lurgan, Lisburn, Armagh, Dungannon, Ballymena, Belfast, Derry, Newry and Cootehill. The commercialisation of the linen industry was most intense in the fine weaving areas, especially in the linen triangle between Dungannon, Lisburn and Armagh. By 1810, just before the advent of full-scale industrialisation, the linen industry reached its maximum extent. The initial core in the Lough Neagh crescent between Antrim, Down and Armagh had spread to the adjacent counties of west and south Ulster. This weaving area was fringed by a less extensive spinning zone (dominated by women), which arced from east Donegal through Fermanagh and Leitrim, around to Westmeath and north Meath. Two outliers existed — a triangle at the head of Clew Bay and a coastal strip in west Cork.

ULSTER FOLK AND TRANSPORT MUSEUM

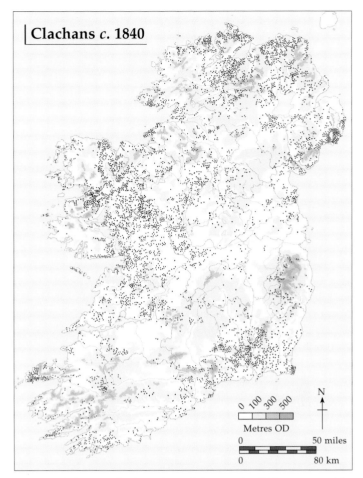

Clachans *c.* 1840

N

0 100 300 500
Metres OD

0   50 miles
0   80 km

Fig. 31 Clachans on the first edition O.S. maps (*c.* 1840), as mapped by Desmond McCourt. The concentration west of the Shannon, especially in inner Connacht, is remarkable. There is also a noticeable thickening adjacent to the Atlantic coastline, with the peninsulas (Inishowen, Fanad, the Mullet, Loop Head, Corca Dhuibhne, Caha and Beara) especially prominent. A different tradition of clustered settlement is evident in south Leinster, where farm villages have medieval antecedents.

Small Farming

The areas of commercialised farming or proto-industrialisation can be contrasted with those areas where small family farms dominated, especially on the Atlantic littoral. The western small farm fringe was a novel phenomenon, in part responsive to, in part creating, the surging population of Ireland, which expanded from three to eight and a half million between 1700 and 1845. This explosion generated intensive reclamation, subdivision and expansion into previously unsettled areas, aided by the potato's ability to flourish in wet, thin, nutrient-poor soils. Much of Ireland's Atlantic region was only heavily settled as an outreach product of massive population growth. Therefore, one of

Fig. 30 William Hinck's magnificent series of engravings (1783) depict the Ulster linen industry in loving detail. This print emphasises the role of women and children in the production process. To the left and right of the fire, the flax is being spun into thread by two women using spinning wheels, while the seated boy feeds the flax fibres to them. To the right, the thread is reeled by another woman into neat rolls, ready for the weaver. The playful kittens, cheerful fire and light-filled window add an optimistic glow to this benign interpretation of domestic industry.

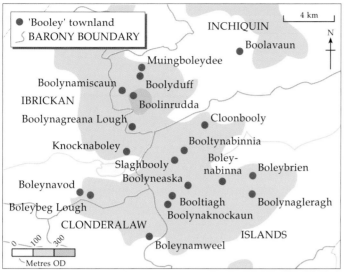

• Fig. 32 The gritstone upland of south-west Clare, with its moor and bog covering, is surrounded by lowlands sloping towards the Atlantic. Nineteen buaile ('booley') placenames are concentrated on this upland region, indicating that it was an active transhumance site prior to the eighteenth century. Its comparative accessibility from all sides encouraged a gradual encroachment of settlement, accompanied by the laying out of new townlands, intensive reclamation and enclosure, and the establishment of small farms.

the major changes in the nature of the Irish landscape after 1700 was the transformation of the west of Ireland into a thickly-settled small farm area.

A principal determinant of the west of Ireland settlement pattern was the rundale and clachan system. A clachan (or baile or 'village') was a nucleated group of farmhouses, where land-holding was organised communally, frequently on a townland basis, and often with considerable ties of kinship between the families involved. Although the misleading English word 'village' was used to describe the baile, these clusters of farm houses were not classic villages, in that they lacked the service functions of church, pub, school or shop. While the houses might have adjacent individual vegetable gardens (garraí), they were surrounded, on the best available patch of land, by a permanently cultivated infield; a large open-field, without enclosures, with a multiplicity of 'strips' separated by sods or stones, in which oats or potatoes were grown. Each family used a variety of strips, periodically redistributed, to ensure a fair division of all types of soil – deep, shallow, sandy, boggy, dry. Outside the infield, and generally separated from it by a sturdy wall, was the outfield – poorer, more marginal, hilly or boggy ground where an occasional reclamation might be made for the purpose of growing potatoes. The rest of the townland (or lease holding) was treated as a commonage; grazing was organised communally using the old Gaelic qualitative measure (the 'collop' or 'sum') to define the amount of stock each family was allowed to have on the pasturage so as not to overstock it.

Occasionally, if the outfield spread into high mountain pastures, cattle might be moved there in the summer, attended by young boys or girls who lived in temporary huts. This was called the buaile and was especially important for butter-making.

The periodic redistribution of strips in the infield guaranteed an environmental egalitarianism. This system as a whole was called 'rundale' (based on a Scottish word) by contemporaries and was practically universal on the poorer lands of the west of Ireland in the pre-Famine period. Rundale was a viable functional adaptation to a specific set of ecological and demographic circumstances. These ecological settings were overwhelmingly marginal – on mountainous, hilly, or boggy areas. The glacially-scoured environment of the west of Ireland gave access to only a limited amount of arable land with a wet climate, stone-infested thin drift, impeded drainage, high wind exposure

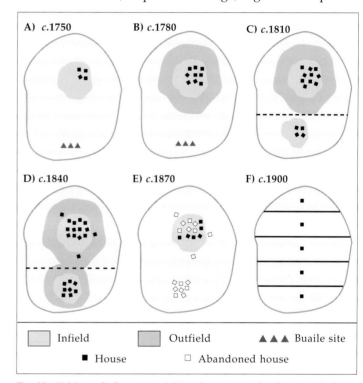

Fig. 33 A) Many clachans were initiated as partnership leases on hitherto unsettled townlands in the eighteenth century. These were organised on the rundale system and incorporated buaile ground. B) As population grew in the second half of the century, shares in the system were subdivided, leading to the rapid expansion of the clachan. C) In the first half of the nineteenth century, as population pressure intensified, new nuclei were created, often through permanently occupying the buaile site and dividing the townland into two or more rundale systems. D) Despite the fragile environmental base, these systems continued to expand up to the eve of the Famine, as a result of the partible inheritance pattern, which continued to divide shares. E) Many collapsed under the weight of population pressure, a process horribly accentuated during the Famine. The secondary settlements on the more marginal land were gradually abandoned then, and the primary clachan contracted in size due to death and emigration. F) Eventually the tenants themselves, the landlords or, later in the nineteenth century, the Congested Districts Board broke up the shrunken clachans, reallocating the rundale land into individual, dispersed and frequently 'ladder' farms.

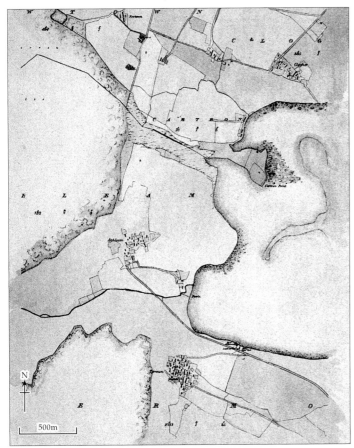

● Fig. 34 The western peninsulas, close to the renewable resources of seaweed fertiliser, tended to develop large clachans on their coastal fringes. The first edition O.S. maps show Aghleam and Termon, two typical examples on the Mullet peninsula in county Mayo. The tight packing and common orientation of houses to minimise western storm damage are typical, as are the unenclosed infields on the sandy portion of the peninsula.

and excessive leaching. The use of a permanently cultivated infield can be seen as an intelligent response to these ecological conditions, where tiny patches of glacial drift were smeared on a waste of bog or mountain. Collective use of the infield maximised utilisation of the limited amount of arable land provided by those precious drift pockets. Because it was permanently cultivated, the infield was nurtured by drawing on the non-arable sector for resources – manure, sand, peat, sods and seaweed – which established a balanced nutrient flow and maintained the fertility of the infield. Cattle were central to the ecology, as manure was the single most significant infield input. The amount of cattle that one could graze accordingly determined the size of one's infield holding.

The demand for manure intensified as the population grew, leading to a frantic search for alternative fertiliser sources – including lime and seaweed whose use escalated throughout the eighteenth century. Yet organic fertilisers remained pre-eminent. The dung heap beside the door was not, as casual observers all too frequently asserted, a symbol of indolent slatternliness, but of persevering

industry. In the absence of artificial fertilisers, natural ones were valuable. As a seasonally renewable resource, seaweed was especially prized; within five miles of the coast, rundale villages were noticeably swollen and more frequent, and the cearta trá (seaweed collection rights) were immensely important, so much so that a farmer was described as a 'fear talamh is trá' – 'a man of land and strand'. The rocky reticulations of the Atlantic shoreline were ideal for seaweed and its abundance was one of the main reasons for the surge in population, once it was realised that the potato crop thrived on seaweed. Bogs also exerted a gravitational pull on settlement, given their treasure trove of turf - the poor man's fuel.

Rundale systems were not the degraded relics of an archaic aboriginal settlement form, practising primitive agriculture in 'refuge' areas. They were instead a sophisticated response to specific ecological and social problems, which maximised the carrying capacity of a meagre environment in an expanding demographic regime. They were well judged adaptations to the interface between limited arable and extensive non-arable land. Co-operative management, agreed land use and a joint labour system for complex tasks were a necessary ecological adjustment to using a fragile environment, where technology and capital

● Fig. 35 This recent aerial photograph depicts a rare surviving infield on remote Tory Island off the north-west coast of Donegal. Note the parquet-floor arrangement of unenclosed strips in the fan-shaped infield, the enclosed garraí (vegetable gardens) close to the clustered dwelling houses, the head wall around the infield and the degraded commonage (the cumulative result of despoliation of sods to replenish the infield).

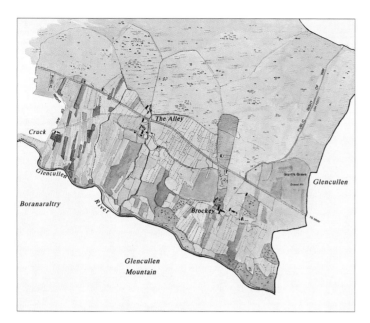

DEPARTMENT OF IRISH FOLKLORE, UCD

● Fig. 36 While rundale-and-clachan was most in evidence in the western half of the island, the practice also developed on mountainous areas elsewhere, which can be seen as 'eastern' extensions of marginal 'western' conditions. On the doorstep of Dublin city, on the Glencullen flank of the Wicklow mountains, a late nineteenth-century estate map depicts an intact rundale system around Brockey and The Alley clachans. The unenclosed infield, divided into a myriad of tillage strips, was located between the riverine meadows of the lower slope and the rough grazing commonage of the more exposed mountain side. To illustrate the intricacies of landholding in such a system, the properties of two farmers – one in each clachan – are highlighted.

With the potato and turf, there was ready access to cheap food and fuel; housing could also be provided cheaply using local materials – stones for walls, tempered clay for floors, 'wreck' timber for rafters, oats, bent grass or reed for thatch. With restrained material expectations, there were few formal barriers to early marriage and family formation. As the Irish proverb expressed it: 'Dá mbéadh prátaí is móin againn, bhéadh an saol ar a thóin againn' (If we had potatoes and turf, we could take life easy).

were limited but labour was unrestricted. Hand tool cultivation (spade, sickle and scythe) and the garden-like technique of iomairí (lazy beds) were universal.

Taken together, the potato, lazy bed and rundale had a striking long-term settlement impact. They facilitated the shift in population density from east to west, from good

● Fig. 37 The proliferation of population and settlement expansion in the west of Ireland were driven in part by off-farm income from fishing, proto-industry and kelping. This nineteenth-century painting by Samuel Lover shows kelp being manufactured in Connemara. The rods of the prolific seaweed, *Fucus vesiculosus*, were gathered, dried and burned in custom-built kilns. Iodine could then be extracted. The system was extensively organised by Scottish merchants, especially from Glasgow, along the north-western coastal fringe.

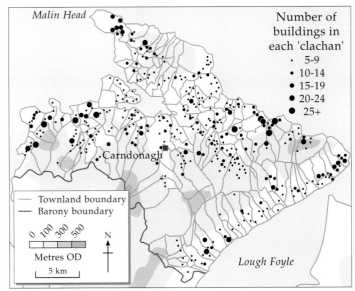

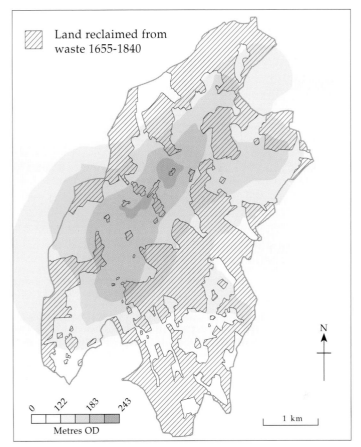

● Fig. 38 By 1850, there were 400 'clachans' on the great north-western peninsula of Inishowen, exhibiting the characteristic Atlantic pattern of a densely populated perimeter fringing desolate, bog-blanketed uplands. The clachans evolved within the master framework of thin tapering townlands – the structural resource unit, mediating between rough mountain, arable lowland and the foreshore. Within the townlands, the primary lowland clusters are centrally located, on the junction between the arable infield and the mountain commonage. This location safeguarded the fundamental rundale principle of equal access to all land types – a stabilising balance between social solidarity and environmental endowment. There is a secondary pattern of more subdued reclamation or 'overspill' clachans upslope - very clearly displayed on the Foyle-side coast between Derry and Greencastle. The variation in size and incidence of clusters is determined by the interplay between soil quality, tenurial arrangements and estate management practices.

● Fig. 39 Between 1650 and 1840, settlement limits rose from 150m to 250m – an important expansion in the Irish context of fragmented (and therefore accessible) uplands. The ragged reclamation pattern can clearly be seen on the commons of Forth Mountain, near Wexford town.

land to poor land, from port hinterlands and valleys to bogs and mountains. It was the potato, not Cromwell, which peopled the west of Ireland. With the exception of some favoured locations (notably Corca Dhuibhne [Dingle peninsula] and the Burren), the west of Ireland was generally an area of new, not of old settlement; it was a modern rather than an archaic cultural landscape. New settlement gravitated to the Atlantic littoral, to the soggy Connacht interior, and to mountain slopes everywhere. Such poor land was simply repulsive to large commercial farmers and nurtured a potato-dependent rundale system because no one else wanted to do anything with it. Landlords tolerated it as a means of extracting maximum rent from marginal land.

If one adds the benefits of proto-industrialisation to the prolific potato, the ubiquitous presence of friendly turf, a mild climate, and the cheap cost of housing, the west of

Ireland at this time must have appeared a poor man's paradise, where plenty of niches were available to make the small farmer independent, if not comfortable.

Only partially a subsistence economy, the region was integrated into the more commercialised world at many points. Noticeable among these was the sale of young cattle

● Fig. 40 (right) Stages in making lazy beds in county Leitrim, as sketched by Estyn Evans. Using súgán (straw) ropes, the line of the initial bed is pegged out and manure is then laid along it. Sods from either side of the bed are then lapped over the manure, leaving a trench on either side. With their grassy side downwards, the sods create a flat-topped manure sandwich. A thin-bladed spade (the loy) is used to construct the bed. Dibbing sticks (stíbhín, cípín) are used by the planter (gogaire) to set the seed potatoes into the ridges. The completed ridges and furrows are of equal width. In the following year, the furrows are dug in the middle of the old ridges.

EMYR ESTYN EVANS

NATIONAL LIBRARY

● Fig. 41 The lazy bed was environmentally perfectly adapted to harsh Atlantic conditions. It was constructed by slicing through and then inverting sods, which made it easy to deal with scutch grass while killing weeds efficiently. A drainage channel was also created in this way while raising the seedbed above any surface water contamination. The geometry of the bed itself ensured maximum exposure to the sun for growing potatoes, while the continuous moulding (the shovelling of soil from the trenches onto the beds) added minerals to the roots, breaking the iron pan in a soil structure prone to leaching. The lazy bed also generated its own microclimate; air flowing from the top to the bottom of the ridges reduced frost susceptibility, especially on bogland. This depiction of lazy-beds at Dugort (Achill) in 1855 is the first photographic illustration of potato growing in Ireland.

to the graziers further east, the supply of oats to the northern weaving areas, the successful prosecution of the fishing industry (especially herring), kelp making, seasonal migration, and involvement in the linen industry (flax growing and spinning) in Sligo, Mayo and Galway. The first half of the nineteenth century also saw continuous expansion of the road network in the west of Ireland. In Mayo, for example, in the decade prior to 1845, over two hundred miles of new road and 150 new bridges had been constructed, while the amount of roads maintained or improved had increased ten-fold. Settlement spread in their wake from the previously more accessible coast into the interior. Once roads opened up the bogs and hills, settlers quickly followed: first, they established a small sod cabin; then a potato garden, very rough in its first year, but gradually ameliorating as ashes and manure were spread on it: and finally a tiny farm with stone fences and oats patches amongst the potato ridges.

Small farm communities also developed on the mountain slopes above the 150m contour. The seventeenth-century privatisation of what had been communal mountain pastures freed an ecological niche to be colonised by small farmers. Using intensive spade cultivation, relying on the excellence of the potato as a reclamation crop and maximising environmental resources through the rundale system, a small farm tier developed high above the commercialised lowland big farms. Whether on the western slopes of the Wicklows, on the sunny southern and eastern

● Fig. 42 Bog edges were scalloped by myriad small-scale reclamations, especially at the height of population pressure in the mid nineteenth century. This example is at Derrycrib, on the eastern edge of the Bog of Allen in Kildare, as surveyed on the first edition O.S. map.

edges of the Blackstairs and the Slieve Blooms, perched on the Munster ridges or pushing up the Mourne Mountains, almost every upland area attracted this small farm fringe; the height to which it climbed was dependent on the presence of glacial drift, especially if limestone-based, and on the availability of turf. Where mountain commonages existed, the population pile-up was accentuated as on Forth Mountain in Wexford, Sliabh Grine on the Drum hills in west Waterford and Hungry Hill in west Cork.

Between 1770 and 1840, rural dwellings increased five times as fast on uplands (over 150m) as on lowlands, and despite poorer fertility, the density of dwelling sites on uplands in 1841 was nearly twice that on lowlands. Good farmland was much more stable demographically than the hills and bogs which so often encircled it. Pre-Famine population grew fastest where there was land available for it to grow and where institutional and social controls were weakest. It was poor land that developed heavy population pressure, and it was small, not big farms, that were sub-divided.

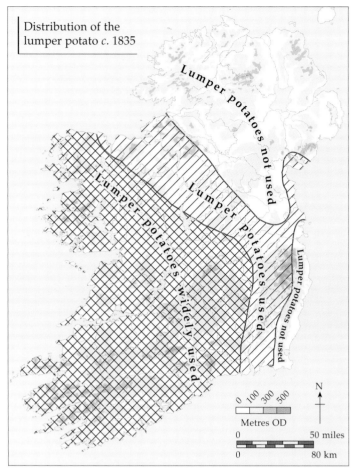

Distribution of the lumper potato *c.* 1835

Fig. 43 After 1810, there was a consistent decline in potato varieties in favour of the Lumper - a high bulk variety which could tolerate poorer soils and required little manure. The Lumper quickly became ubiquitous over Munster and Connacht and by the 1830s it was pushing into Leinster. It made little inroads into the 'oatmeal' zone of Ulster.

History of the Potato
(after Bourke)

ORIGINS	1590-1675	Supplementary food and famine stand-by; concentration in south Munster; garden crop; no serious disease.
SPREAD	1675-1750	Winter (September-March) food of poor and supplementary diet of all classes; early planting; field crop; 'black' potato since *c.*1715; spread into Connacht and Leinster; widespread adoption of lazy bed; one meal a day.
ZENITH	1750-1810	Staple all-year diet of poor (labourers and small farmers): accelerated genetic evolution and hence adaptability; Apple (*c.*1760) and Cup (*c.*1800); spectacular expansion; clearing crop in tillage rotation and rise of cottier system: later planting; use as reclamation agent; dominance in south and west; two meals a day.
DECLINE	1810-1845	Increasing monocultural dependence; adoption of inferior varieties especially Lumper *c.*1810; degeneration of existing varieties; elimination of oats and milk out of diet of poor except in northeast; spread into high mountain and wet bog; increasing susceptibility to disease; three meals a day; Blight 1845.

The small farm lifestyle of the west of Ireland, in particular, has permitted the prevalent perception of pre-Famine Irish society as a socially homogeneous, impoverished and archaic 'peasant' culture. Yet, while small farms festooned the ragged Atlantic edge and the difficult drumlin belt, their overall extent was restricted. Even at their maximum development in the mid nineteenth-century, they were never the dominant settlement type nationally. Their importance was in allowing massive colonisation of marginal areas and the concurrent paradox of Irish population density: the poorer the soil, the denser the population (or as the Irish aphorism expressed it, 'ganntanas talaimh, tiubh na daoine').

The importance of the potato The potato had a number of advantages which made it an attractive proposition in Irish circumstances. It was well adapted to a wet, dull climate and to sour acidic soils, especially when it had a long growing season in a temperate climate: the potato's principal enemy was frost rather than rain. Unlike grain, the potato required no processing to make it edible; its producers therefore retained direct control over their means of subsistence. The potato was nutritious: with milk added, it formed a balanced diet, containing adequate amounts of protein, carbohydrates and minerals. Its high energy value and low fat content made it a healthy food source. In agricultural terms, the potato remained relatively disease-resistant in the Irish context. It also replicated the vaunted turnip; it was a root crop which replaced fallow, a winter crop for livestock, and a valuable reclaiming agent in previously untilled ground. In this sense, the prosaic potato did everything and more in Irish agriculture than did the much-touted turnip.

There were two problems with the potato. One was that it could not be stored for more than three-quarters of a year: this made the summer months between the end of the

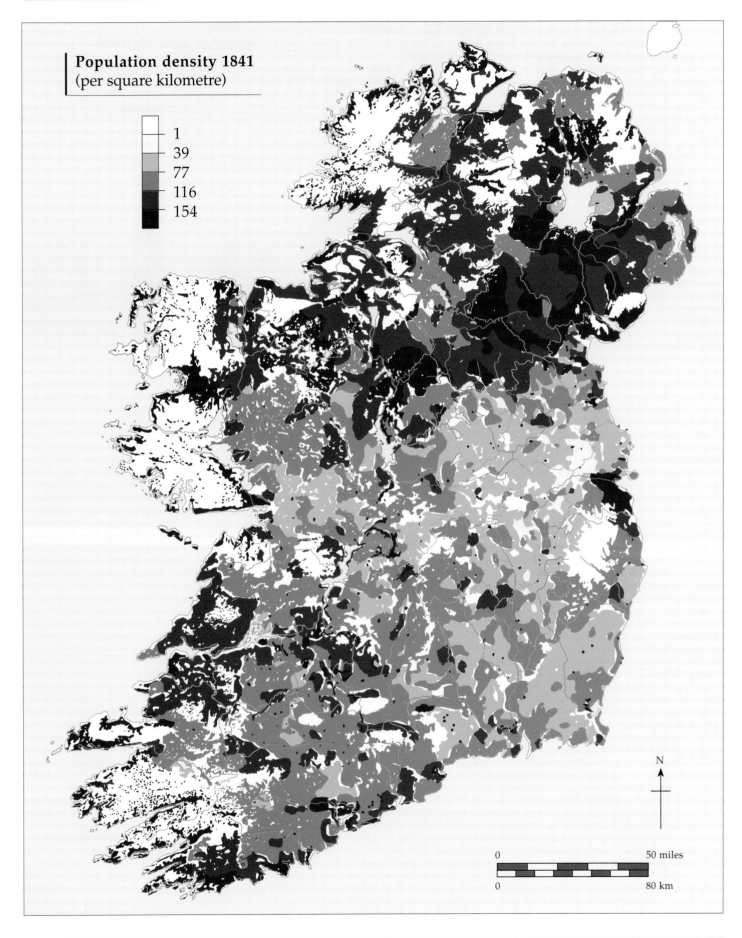

Population density 1841
(per square kilometre)

1
39
77
116
154

N

| 0 | 50 miles |
| 0 | 80 km |

old season's crop and the beginning of the new crop very difficult, with dependence on the green crops, the 'July na gCabáiste' of the folk tradition. The problem of storage was partially solved by the pig – an efficient ecological hoover, who consumed surplus, waste, small and damaged potatoes and their skins, and which thereby functioned as a mobile potato store. The second problem was that the potato was difficult and expensive to transport. This militated against regional specialisation in potato production, and explains why the potato became so widely diffused in Ireland. With the exception of some highly favoured coastal areas which serviced the Dublin markets – Carbery in Cork, the Dungarvan area in Waterford, east Wicklow, Lecale and the Kingdom of Mourne in Down – commercial potato production never prospered.

The spread of the potato   The rapidity of the potato's spread should be linked to the sheer scale of social and cultural dislocation in Ireland in the seventeenth century. Diet is normally stable and resistant to change: the potato advanced so rapidly because of the space cleared for it by unprecedented upheaval. Initially a garden crop for the gentry, the potato quickly jumped the garden wall and gained the freedom of the fields. It began its Irish career along the Cork and Waterford coastline in the late seventeenth-century. This area had the benefits of a mild and frost-free climate, as well as a rapidly expanding dairy economy; given the potato's lack of storability, it made sense to substitute it for dairy products, and release the cash crops (initially butter, later oats) onto the market. The potato spread rapidly in Munster as the winter food of the rural poor in the first half of the eighteenth century. The Cork-Waterford coast became famous for early potatoes grown on its sandy soil; this area pioneered the use of seaweed as a fertiliser and already by the 1720s it was shipping potatoes to the Dublin market.

Acclimatised and acculturated, the potato then began its long march out of south Munster towards Connacht and Leinster. As it did so, it squeezed out two earlier diet-traditions – the whitemeats (butter, milk and cheese) of the gaelicised south and west, and the pulses and cereals (especially oats) of the normanised east. And in these regions, it exhibited new virtues – as an incomparable reclamation crop, and as a cleansing rotation in tillage

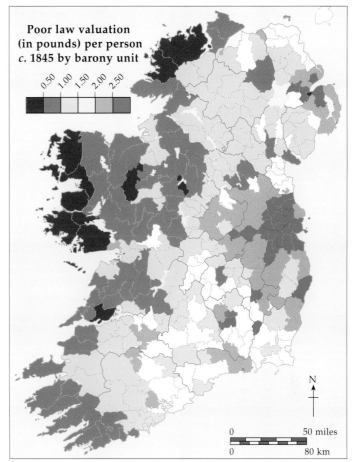

Fig. 45 Land valuation in 1845. The pronounced regional divides within the country are clearly depicted here: the wealthy core encompassing Dublin city and the Pale, a similar but restricted belt in east Ulster, the sharp south-east/north-west gradient, with a dividing line running from Dundalk to Limerick to Cork city, the poorer regions of west Munster, Connacht and west Ulster, and the impoverished Atlantic fringe, especially from Connemara to west Donegal.

areas. Its rapid expansion outside its Munster heartland was also facilitated by the genetic evolution, and hence adaptability, of potato varieties. The Apple, edible all year round, allowed the potato to evolve from being a winter food of the poor to being an annual staple (with winter cabbage and summer herring) in the second half of the eighteenth century. Because surplus potatoes were a good animal food, the potato enhanced the production of pigs and bacon. From the 1760s onwards, as cereal cultivation expanded in response to growing British markets, the development of Ulster as a food-deficit region, and the continuing growth of Dublin's population, the potato-based cottier system also surged. Economic development

Fig. 44 (left) Population density in 1841 as mapped by T.W. Freeman. Densities of over 150 per square kilometre were especially apparent in the south Ulster/north midlands proto-industrial belt and along the far western fringe. The rapid decline in both farm size and age of marriage within the proto-industrial zone, the constant reclamation, intense subdivision of shares within the rundale system and exuberant expansion into previously unsettled areas drove the astonishing demographic profile of post-plantation Ireland: its population rose from one million to eight and a half million between 1600 and 1845, with four million being added between 1780 and 1845 alone. Population growth was focused on land previously considered too poor to be permanently settled, thus creating the paradox of population density being greatest on the more marginal land. Pressure was easier in the environmentally richer big-farm areas of Leinster and Munster, where commercial agriculture and social controls both worked to contain it. Although Ireland's population has been markedly reduced by emigration since the mid nineteenth century, the rural landscape still bears the clear imprint of pre-famine demographic pressures.

and the evolution of Ireland as the larder of the Industrial Revolution brought with it a permanent, proliferating and potato-dependent underclass. Heavy potato consumption among the impoverished Irish labourers had as its ultimate beneficiaries the British urban consumer, recipient of the island's cereal and bacon exports.

The potato ultimately deranged the balance between tillage and pasture in environmentally frail areas. Traditionally, land use had been regulated not by permanent possession of a precise piece of land but by abstract rights – the cuibhreadh or share, which was determined by a balance between kinship affiliations, lease obligations and environmental constraints. These were dictated by the qualitative estimation of the carrying capacity for livestock, 'the cow's grass' which then allowed for the precise quantification of grazing rights (sums and collops). These in turn defined tillage rights in the infield, on the basis that manure was the key to the sustainability of the system. The balance of pasture and tillage was determined traditionally, by that blend of necessity and experience which embodied the legacy of accumulated environmental experience. The equilibrium of land use prior to the potato emphasised pastoralism at the expense of tillage. In the west of Ireland, the Lumper intensified the imbalance between tillage and pasture which the swollen clachans caused.

By the early nineteenth century, the diet of the labouring poor had become ever more potato-dependent; as oats became a cash crop and as cows were increasingly beyond their capacity, their diet was stripped of oatmeal and milk. This pushed them into a monocultural dependence on the potato, notably on the Lumper, a coarse variety which required little manure. By the 1830s, one-third of the population (three million people) relied on potatoes for over 90% of their calorie intake. Only in the north-eastern oatmeal zone did the potato not triumph utterly.

The lazy bed   From the Neolithic period onwards, as we know from the evidence buried under bogs, ridges (lazy beds) had been used to grow grain crops in Ireland. In the seventeenth and early eighteenth centuries, it was discovered that the lazy bed was especially suited to potato cultivation. Nourished by seaweed manure in these beds, the potato flourished in the wet western soils. All that was required was the high labour inputs required to construct and maintain the ridges during the growing season – essentially, hand cultivation based on the spade. There was five times as much labour expended in digging rather than ploughing an equivalent area, and twenty times as much as was expended in stock raising. The considerable energy costs necessitated by spade cultivation of marginal land

Fig. 46   For two and a half centuries, the potato had been a remarkably reliable crop. The advent of the blight in 1845 (only identified as *Phytophtora infestans* two decades later) was as stunning as it was unprecedented, inflicting gothic horrors on a devastated countryside. Daniel MacDonald's painting captures contemporary incomprehension of this 'visitation of God' and its doom-laden portents for the Irish people.

DEPARTMENT OF IRISH FOLKLORE, UCD

were absorbed by population growth. In a sense, then, as in Highland Scotland, increased population became its own resource. Together, the potato (tolerant, prolific and nutritious) and the lazy bed (adaptable, effective and productive) maximised the resource potential of marginal land.

The ridges ensured that there was no waste of soil or space by minute adjustment to soil type, slope conditions and rockiness. And lazy bed cultivation was efficient: its potato yield was three times higher than in horse-ploughed drills. It was an ingenious method of absorbing both an unrestricted labour supply and non-infield resources. At its pre-Famine zenith, much of the cultivated land of the west of Ireland was composed of man-made soils, laboriously created in this fashion. By the constant addition of sand, seaweed and manure, repeated over decades, the infields eventually were composed of carefully maintained artificial soils. Thus, the pre-Famine landscape of Ireland was the creation of a labour-rich society, a landscape where demography triumphed, temporarily, over determinism.

PROLOGUE TO THE FAMINE

Cheap food, fuel and housing had permitted the population to expand prodigiously between 1760 and 1815, which in retrospect was the golden age of both the potato and the Irish poor. That golden age ended in the aftermath of the Napoleonic wars, when a sharp depression bit into the area. Agricultural prices halved, the fickle herring deserted the west coast (where they had been abundant between 1780 and 1810), the linen industry was dislocated by factory-based spinning and weaving – a succession of hammer blows, accentuated by a series of wet summers and bad harvests. The combination of a distressed proto-industrial sector and a volatile agricultural situation swelled a shifting underclass in Irish society in the immediate pre-famine years. This period witnessed the explosive expansion of cabin shanties on the edge of towns, bogside squatter colonies like the Erris 'troglodytes' or the wretched settlers oozing onto the wet deserts of the Bog of Allen, voracious assaults on commonages, and on the limits of cultivation. The bogland fringe became the locus of the dispossessed, eking out a living on the existential and environmental margins of the society from which they had been extruded in a relentless modernising process.

The cumulative impact of these changes strengthened dangerous tendencies within the society. Firstly, in the pre-Famine period, the more solvent tenants tended to emigrate, thereby simplifying and weakening the social structure. Secondly, the prolonged depression drained existing capital resources and damaged resilience in the face of crisis years. Thirdly, the weakening of other cash inputs forced tenants to sell all their oats production, and dragged them increasingly towards dependence on the inferior Lumper. The ecological knife-edge was constantly sharpening, pushing those communities ever closer to the potato precipice.

The dependence on the potato was deepening, as the emaciated economy was squeezed by a seemingly inexorable demographic regime. In these circumstances, the advent of the unprecedented potato blight was utterly devastating. One million died and two million emigrated in the next two decades, cruelly paralleling the three million 'potato people' who were totally dependent on the now fickle tuber in the immediate pre-Famine period. These deaths were disproportionately concentrated in the areas of new settlement dominated by rundale and clachan, and by the Lumper.

A dominant official response to the Famine was to see it as an opportunity to replace the backward, degenerate potato as a food-source by a 'higher' form, like grain, which would forcibly elevate the feckless Irish up the ladder of civilisation. By linking food, race and religion (the Potato, Paddy and Popery) in a stadial view of civilisation, the famine could then be interpreted benevolently as an accelerator effect.

These attitudes influenced the decision to import maize (Indian corn) as the preferred relief food. Maize could not be grown in Ireland and therefore would be a purchased food. This by itself would eliminate the potato wage which underpinned the cottier system, utilised by farmers as a source of cheap labour and acting as a brake on agrarian

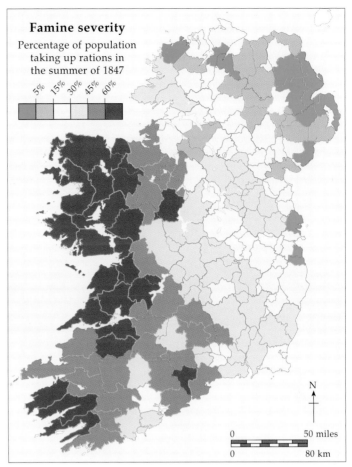

Famine severity
Percentage of population taking up rations in the summer of 1847

5% 15% 30% 45% 60%

Fig. 47 The Famine's impact fell disproportionately on the areas dominated by clachans, where contagious diseases were rampant in the dense huddles of housing. Connacht (where 25% of the population died) and west Munster were worst affected. Leinster and especially Ulster escaped more lightly. The least affected areas were in the immediate hinterlands of Belfast and Dublin and there is a general north-east to south-west gradient in the intensity of distress.

modernisation. Labourers would have to be then paid in cash rather than in kind (potatoes); this would force farmers to become more efficient. Eliminating the potato would also liquidate the western micro-farmer, alleged source of endemic poverty and overpopulation. The result would be a modern Irish agricultural sector, with large-scale farmers and a wage-earning sector – a lumpen rather than a lumper proletariat. These changes would generate a healthier social structure, more closely approximating the English and Scottish model. The Famine's long-term effect, then, would be as an accelerator of agrarian anglicisation in Ireland, thereby copper-fastening the Union. The promotion of social engineering of this type determined the British administrative and political response to the Famine. The assault on the potato as a food source was also made by landlords and agents, who welcomed the Famine as an inducement to agrarian modernisation, ridding their estates of a pauper tenantry whose tenacious grip on the land was providentially loosened by the blight.

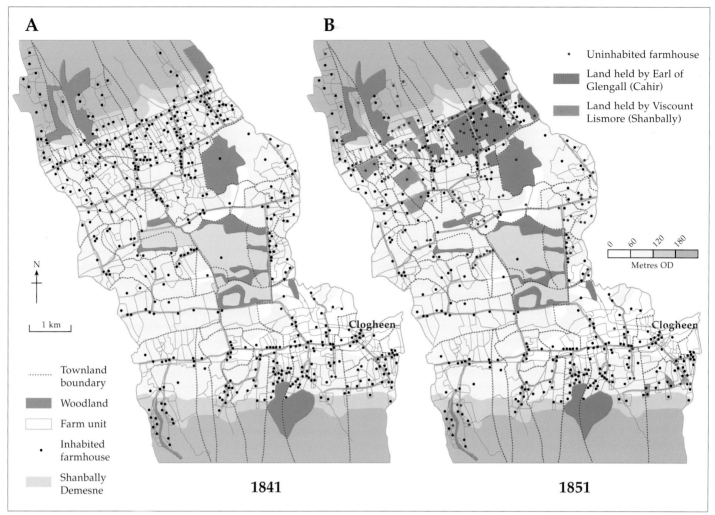

● Fig. 48 These maps depict pre- and post-Famine landscape change in the parish of Clogheen-Burncourt in environmentally complex and socially stratified south Tipperary. A fertile limestone corridor ran between sandstone mountain walls – the Galtees to the north, the Knockmealdowns to the south. A) By 1840, the crowded landscape reflected the culmination of an explosive phase of demographic growth and settlement expansion after 1760, with a trebling of population. On the long-settled valley floor, a new landlord demesne had been carved out and the commercialisation of the pastoral economy consolidated substantial grazier farms. The mountain slopes attracted intensive potato-based colonisation, followed by subdivision to create an intricate web of small farms. In this way, population pressure was deflected away from the lowlands, with the exception of the proliferation of landless cottiers along its roadsides and back lanes. B) By 1851, the shattering impact of the Famine had exposed the fragility of these small farm and landless families. The collapse was especially precipitous on the northern Galtee slopes, where there was ruthless landlord clearance of crowded middleman tenancies. Lowland big farms ingested their small farm neighbours by encroachment up the slopes. The more diversified small farm zone to the south on the Knockmealdowns survived better, but it too would succumb to slow attrition over the next half century. The landless class was decimated by the Famine and emigration, leaving an empty lowland, but with its big farm structure intact and strengthened.

POST-FAMINE LANDSCAPE CHANGE

Behind these conceptions of cultural inferiority lay the utopian ideal of *tabula rasa* – a clean Irish slate on which the new English values could be legibly inscribed, deleting the chaotic scrawl which the Irish had scribbled all over their dishevelled landscape. That whole agrarian mess should now be swept away as so much accumulated junk, the visible embodiment of the arrears column in the double entry bookkeeping practised in the landlords' rentals. The policy arms to this scenario were the £4 rating clause (which made landlords responsible for the rates on all holdings valued at under £4 - effectively most western small holdings), and the Gregory quarter-acre clause, which refused relief to anyone holding more than that

amount. Small farmers were legally rendered a parasitic encumbrance on landlord property; these two clauses became a clearance charter, encouraging massive eviction, especially in the poorest rundale counties of Mayo, Galway and Clare. As many as half a million people were evicted in the entire Famine period.

The failure of the potato as a food source was accompanied by an onslaught on the rundale and clachan system, in the belief that only individual farms would encourage initiative and self-reliance. The clachans needed to be dispersed to break the cultural moulds which sustained mutual aid (comhar na gcomharsain) and thereby fostered a debilitating dependency. The linearisation of landscape spread ladder farms over the west of Ireland, obliterating

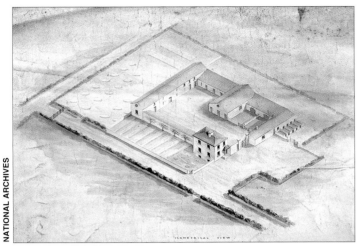

NATIONAL ARCHIVES

● Fig. 49 Post-Famine legislation envisioned a radical reorganisation of the Irish countryside to bring it closer to the English model. However, the Encumbered Estates and Land Improvement Acts had only a tenuous landscape impact. This farmyard scheme at Newstone in Meath was submitted in 1852 for a land improvement grant by a prominent lawyer: it reflects the desired landscape change which would be facilitated by the Famine.

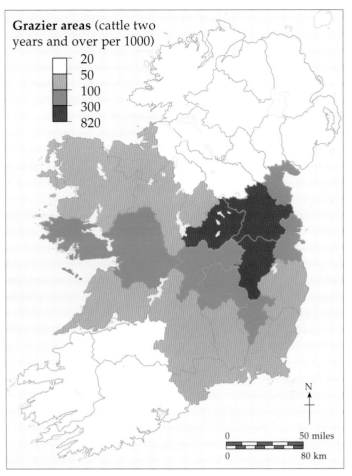

Grazier areas (cattle two years and over per 1000)

- 20
- 50
- 100
- 300
- 820

N

| 0 | 50 miles |
| 0 | 80 km |

Fig. 50 Post-Famine Ireland witnessed the intensification of store cattle production for the British market. A specialised grazier core emerged in the south Meath/north Kildare area. In Meath alone, cattle numbers doubled between 1850 and 1890. These finishing areas required young cattle, which came from the west. By 1900, Galway and Roscommon were the two premier 'young' cattle counties, while Kildare, Meath, Westmeath, Offaly and Dublin were the leading store cattle counties.

the earlier informal networks of the rundale system. The cottier system also disappeared in the post-Famine decades. From being thirty per cent of all houses in 1841, the one-roomed cabin dropped to ten per cent by 1861, and had virtually disappeared (at one per cent) by 1911. Small farmers also came under pressure. Across Ireland in the aftermath of the Famine, strong farmers and graziers increased their holdings at the expense of their weaker neighbours.

In the long term, the strong farmer became the (unintended) beneficiary of the Famine, in that it simultaneously removed the vexatious cottier class, while weakening the landlord's moral and political authority. The relatively untroubled transition to peasant proprietorship which ensued could not have occurred without the smoothing effect of the Famine and large-scale emigration. In retrospect, it was the quietness of the social revolution in nineteenth-century Ireland which was astonishing. The Land War cost remarkably little in lives or property (compare, for example, the turmoil in the later rural revolutions of eastern Europe).

In the landscape itself, one could also see the consequences of long-term changes. One was the eclipse of the arable by the pastoral sector: 1.8 million hectares under arable in 1851 halved to 0.9 million by 1911. Simultaneously, live cattle exports rose dramatically, helped by the advent of railways and steamships and by a growing English market. From 50,000 in the 1820s, exports quadrupled to 200,000 in the 1840s, doubled by the 1860s and doubled again to reach 800,000 by the 1900s. This surge was accompanied by an emerging regional specialisation in cattle fattening around Dublin. Tillage had weakened inexorably, as the Irish

farmer was exposed to increased competition from distant areas with significant advantages in production costs. By 1908, the hen and the duck were more important in the agrarian economy than wheat and oats together.

A principal beneficiary of all these changes was the grazier or large-scale cattle rancher. As landlords set their faces against rundale and clachan, and against the partnership leases which underpinned it, the grazier tenant became a preferred option. By the end of the century, of 70,000 hectares in Connemara, one-third were held by ninety graziers. Across Connacht as a whole, the graziers leased the level limestone lowlands, while the rundale farmers were tolerated only on the bog and mountain fringes. The glaring environmental and social asymmetries were to be a powerful stimulus to the Land League, and later to the anti-grazier United Irish League.

In the post-Famine period, Ireland effectively de-industrialised, with the prominent exception of the Belfast region. Railway and steamship communication intensified

● Fig. 51 Dooagh village, Achill *c.* 1900, photographed by William Lawrence. This is one of the finest visual records of an intact clachan.

British penetration of Irish markets, squeezing out indigenous industry. The country as a whole was far more monolithically agricultural in 1900 than in 1800. Only the linen industry made a successful transition to factory production and consequently, Ulster generated a series of mill villages – like Bessbrook, Darkley, Sion Mills and Donaghcloney.

With the exception of gaunt institutional buildings like workhouses, asylums, railway stations and prisons, and assertive Catholic churches, post-Famine Ireland saw little new building. Emigration quickened appreciably, leading to the retreat from the poorer hill and bog areas that had been so assiduously colonised in the pre-Famine period. The settlement tide ebbed down the hillsides, leaving only the tell-tale pattern of forlorn lazy-beds, quilted under bracken and gorse, and morbid cabin ruins. The small farm areas were worst affected, especially those inland from the coast in inner Connacht and south Ulster. The littoral fringe endured stubbornly until the 1880s, albeit increasingly recognised as a problem region.

● Fig. 53 By the late nineteenth century, many scholars shared a perception of the west of Ireland as an archaic, pristine rural culture, preserved in the amber of European isolation. The famous anthropologists A.C. Haddon (known as 'Haddon the Headhunter' from his Melanesian work) and C.R. Browne conducted extensive fieldwork along the west coast in the 1890s. Here, a seated Haddon is shown at work on the Aran Islands, recording cephalic indices.

THE CONGESTED DISTRICTS BOARD

The second half of the nineteenth century witnessed the emerging identification of the west of Ireland as a problem region, equivalent to the Highlands and Islands of Scotland. 1859-64 were renewed crisis years, with blight, animal deaths and severe hardship, a scenario replicated between 1879-84, which precipitated the Land League crisis. After 1880, the imperative of state intervention gathered momentum, as a means of ensuring long-term reorganisation rather than charitable palliatives. The impact of the Land League, the advocacy of the influential philanthropist James Hack Tuke (who popularised the word 'congestion') and the cumulative evidence of four government commissions – Richmond (1881), Bessborough (1881), Technical Instruction (1884) and Industries (1885) – all prepared the

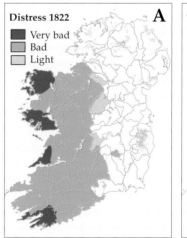

A — Distress 1822
■ Very bad
■ Bad
□ Light

B — Distressed Poor Law Unions 1847-8

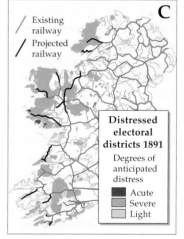

C
／ Existing railway
／ Projected railway

Distressed electoral districts 1891
Degrees of anticipated distress
■ Acute
■ Severe
□ Light

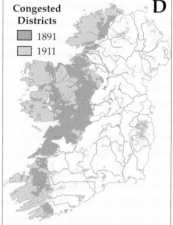

D — Congested Districts
■ 1891
□ 1911

Fig. 52 The west of Ireland as a problem region: A) As early as the crisis of 1822, the ten worst affected counties were in the west. B) The Famine of the 1840s devastated the region, requiring special treatment for its poor law unions. C) Renewed distress in 1891 led to careful delimitation of areas likely to suffer from distress, as well as railway relief works. D) Out of these concerns for the west as a rural slum emerged the Congested Districts Board of the 1890s, with its exclusively western remit.

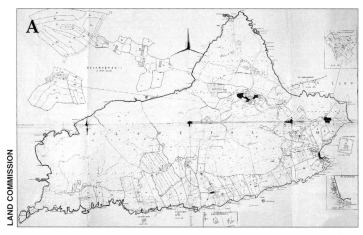

● Fig. 54 Clare Island still retained a functioning rundale system in the late nineteenth century, carefully maintained within the townland structure. Each townland had an intact clachan, unenclosed infield and separate mountain commonages. Settlement closely hugged the south and east facing slopes of the island, creating a thickly settled strip between the shore and the open upper mountain slopes (A). The island was completely remodelled by the Congested Districts Board when they acquired it from the insolvent O'Donnell estate in 1895. This map of August 1897 was the legally-binding document memorialising the agreement between the Board and the island's 79 tenants. An elaborate series of individual holdings was created, ingeniously deploying the ladder farm model, which retained the older rundale principle of access to a variety of environmental resources, from seashore to mountain grazing. The Board oversaw the construction of a massive stone wall separating the new farms from the mountain commonages. It also reached an agreement with its tenants strictly delimiting the individual grazing rights on the reassigned mountain commonages. The older rundale arrangement retains a spectral presence in the newly rationalised landscape (B).

● Fig. 55 This *c.* 1960 photograph of Clare Island shows the regimented CDB ladder farms superimposed on the preceding, more informal rundale network. The coastal strip is corrugated by lazy-beds, the ground 'pleated like a piece of paper that cannot be smoothed out' (Brian Lynch).

way for a dramatic policy change, presaging far-reaching state intervention in rural society comparable to that accomplished in the later Russian Revolution. The Tories, under pressure to prove that the Union worked, developed the policy of 'constructive Unionism' or 'killing Home Rule with kindness'; remedial reforms would be an effective antidote to nationalism, strengthening the imperial impulse in Ireland. A sequence of highly publicised bad years, culminating in near-famine in the west in 1889-90, led to the setting up of the Congested Districts Board, brainchild of Tuke and the old Irish political hand, Arthur Balfour.

The Congested Districts were defined by land quality (acreable valuation divided by population); with their extension in 1909, they covered 1.4 million hectares of the western littoral from Donegal to west Cork, about one-third of the country. To initiate long-term improvement, the board encouraged infrastructural development (roads, railways, piers and harbours); agricultural improvement (new breeds of cattle, sheep, pigs, asses and poultry); domestic industry (Donegal tweeds, woollens, lace and carpets); co-operatives; life-style improvements (itinerant nurses, domestic economy and hygiene) and fishing (new boats, twenty fish curing stations). The Board popularised the 'Zulu' and 'noddy' boat types, introduced 1,600 cocks and promoted bee-keeping and the Spanish jackass (the famous 'congisted ass'), the Indian runner duck and potato spraying. With capable, sympathetic and locally knowledgeable administrators, it was able to promote far-reaching changes.

While initially strongly focused on the coastline, avoiding land purchase as being too expensive, the Board's policies were gradually redefined by insistent political pressures. John Dillon and William O'Brien spearheaded an advanced social agenda within Irish nationalism, which led to the anti-grazier 'ranch-war' of the early twentieth century, especially in Connacht and the Midlands. Irish MPs and populist opinion forced the purchase and redistributive option on a reluctant imperial parliament. To assuage land agitation and to detach agrarian from political issues, the CDB brief was eventually expanded to

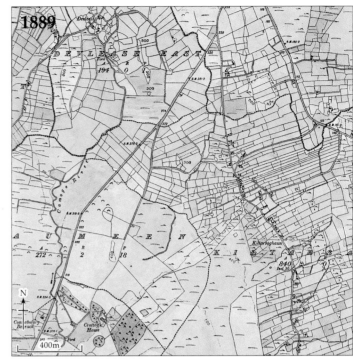

● Fig. 56 Large areas of the west of Ireland landscape were reorganised in the late nineteenth century, changes which become immediately obvious when various editions of O. S. maps are compared. In Kiltarsaghaun townland in county Mayo, the clachan-and-rundale of 1840 has been obliterated by the wholesale striping depicted in 1899. Across much of the west, the cultural landscape has been remodelled so thoroughly and so recently that the pre-Famine landscape can now be recovered only by archaeological or historical means, not by direct inspection.

encompass compulsory acquisition from graziers for sub-division; in so doing, its emphasis inevitably shifted from the coast to inland areas (especially after 1909, in its expanded regional coverage).

The Board completely remodelled whole landscapes, on showpieces like Clare Island, the French estate at Ballygar (Galway), the Digby estate in Erris and the 32,000 hectare Dillon estate at Ballaghadereen on the Mayo-Roscommon border. When the Board was dissolved in 1923, one thousand estates had been purchased for £10.4 million, containing almost 60,000 holdings of which half had been restructured: 300,000 hectares had been distributed for the relief of congestion. Total expenditure on the improvement of holdings was £2.25 million, half on houses and half on drainage, fencing and road making. The CDB had striking landscape impacts. It encouraged dispersion of farms, rather than the clachan system; on hygiene grounds, it insisted on the removal of the dung-heap from the door and the provision of byres and stables. Continuing an existing tradition of landlord reform, the clustered farm settlements and rundale holdings were reorganised over extensive areas into consolidated striped holdings in which new farmhouses were located along replanned roads. A modern landscape of regular enclosed fields and compact dispersed farms was superimposed on the earlier system.

Land reorganisation could not be accomplished without the relocation of tenants and the CDB was obliged to provide new dwellings for them. Housing thus became a major item of board planning and expenditure. The Board devised a meticulously planned and costed sequence of house plans (from £82 to £152), notable for their insistence on slate or tiles rather than thatch and a liking for two-storeyed plans. Over 6,000 houses and 4,000 outbuildings were built or substantially improved and a further 3,350 houses improved by tenants at the Board's expense. The standardised CDB housing is still a distinctive ingredient of the west of Ireland areas that it remodelled.

The Congested Districts Board was part of the great Victorian wave of social reform. In Britain, this had a mainly urban focus, but in Ireland it acquired an uniquely rural emphasis, with the west of Ireland being treated essentially as a rural slum. The CDB was highly innovative – in its socio-economic planning (the 'baseline reports'), in its parish committees, in its regional emphasis, and in its inclusive, non party-political composition. In effect, the CDB became the earliest clear example of rural regional planning in Europe.

THE END OF LANDLORDISM

The legislative euthanasia of the Irish gentry was a remarkable feature of the late nineteenth century. The Irish landed class had generally forfeited British sympathy during the Famine, when they were blamed for having recklessly allowed huge pauper populations to pile up on their

NATIONAL LIBRARY

● Fig. 57 By the second half of the nineteenth century, the Irish landed gentry were widely blamed in British and Irish political circles for exacerbating Irish problems. During the Land War of the 1880s, evictions became the resonant symbol of landlord iniquities, a symbol brilliantly deployed through the new technique of photography in this image of an evicted family and their scanty possessions outside Lord Lucan's gate at Castlebar, county Mayo.

estates, irresponsibly swelling their rentals. They also stood indicted of abdicating their social and political responsibilities, having failed to domesticate British rule in Ireland. At both an economic and political level, they were therefore dispensable, and this encouraged the British government in endorsing unusually broad state intervention in the rights of private property. The remorseless shift towards 'peasant proprietorship' began as early as 1869, when the Church Disestablishment Act indicated that the writing was already on the demesne walls. It accelerated in the wake of

MICHAEL DIGGIN

● Fig. 58 As the landed gentry were stripped of their political and economic functions through the changing political climate and the Land Acts, many abandoned their Irish homes for British or other colonial settings. In post-partition Ireland, these desolate houses, as here at Killarney Castle in county Kerry, were striking landscape icons — for most, welcome signs of the destruction of an exploitative and ultimately decadent colonial minority, for some, evidence of a narrow bitterness in the emerging Free State, and an assault on a cultured class.

the novel and potent combination of agrarian and nationalist issues in Parnellite politics. The Gladstone (1881), Ashbourne (1885), Balfour (1891) and the generous Wyndham (1903) and Birrell (1909) Acts all encouraged Irish landlords to divest themselves of their lands. Almost four and a half million hectares were transferred to tenants who purchased 316,000 holdings. By the beginning of World War I, two-thirds of Irish tenants owned their land and a remarkable social revolution had been effected.

Because tenants purchased their existing holdings without large-scale reorganisation (except in the congested districts), the landscape impact of this momentous change was limited. Big houses and demesnes, shorn of their supporting broad acres, were abandoned by the newly marginalised gentry and sank into dishevelled husks of their former selves. These mouldering piles, where ivy rooted in profusion, with their decaying families in adverse political and economic circumstances provided an ideal backdrop for the 'Protestant Gothic' in Irish fiction, with such memorable déclassé landlords as Melmoth the Wanderer and Dracula, the ultimate in soil-starved landlordism.

A further innovation of constructive unionism was the public provision of housing for the rural poor. The Land Acts were seen to have benefited the farmer but not the agricultural labourer. Still dependent on conacre, living in squalid cabins, and under threat from farm mechanisation, the labourers' plight was obvious. From 1883 onwards, Poor Law Unions (and after 1898 Rural Districts) were enabled to build cottages for them. By 1914, 50,000 had been built to varying designs, using half-acre sites dispersed in small roadside groupings. This first public housing initiative in Britain and Ireland was inspired by 'constructive unionism' but it also had the covert aim of stabilising the Irish rural poor at home, and thereby preventing their drift to English slums. These simple, practical cottages were most in evidence in the big farm zones of Munster and Leinster, especially in tillage areas.

THE LAND COMMISSION

Given the intimate relationship between land and colonisation, the agrarian and national questions were inextricably linked at the end of the colonial phase. By 1922, much of the road to the achievement of full owner-occupancy had already been travelled. In the Free State, a Land Commission, formed from the older CDB, was given powers to complete the final transfer to owner-occupancy. It continued the work of the CDB in reshaping the chaotic fragmentation of the west, while also assuming the wider role of reorganising the structure of agriculture throughout

the Free State. The comparable work of farm consolidation and land redistribution was undertaken in Northern Ireland by the Land Purchase Commission, but in a much more subdued fashion.

In the Free State, the Land Commission attempted to create small, family-farm units, making intensive use of the land and with 'frugal comfort' as the economic standard. A cohesive, classless society could be created in this way. Large holdings were deemed to be immoral, because they deprived people of the opportunity of owning their own holding. The success of the Land Commission depended on its ability to acquire and distribute land, and a ready supply existed in the large grazier farms, especially in inner Connacht, where these farms predominated. A convenient scapegoat was thus available - 'the bullock for the road and the land for the people'. Economically, such units were not an attractive proposition in the depressed 1930s and 1940s. Their owners were also likely, in many cases, to see little future for themselves in the emerging post-colonial state.

The Land Commission was able to tackle problems which had defeated the improving landlord, because it had a corporate as opposed to a personal identity, adequate finance, strong government backing and a large field-staff which was in close contact with the intimate realities at local level. The work of the Land Commission was concentrated in three directions. Firstly, they were responsible for the transfer of ownership from landlord to tenant in those cases where this had not been completed. Secondly, they

DUBLIN OPINION

Fig. 60 'Dividing up the estate or the Land Commission goes crazy'. Under the sternly small-farm imperatives of Éamon de Valera and Fianna Fáil, the Land Commission ruthlessly acquired and divided surviving estates and grazier holdings. Even at the time, their activities were sometimes considered over-zealous, as this cartoon shows.

assumed the role of the CDB in the west of Ireland's most congested areas, continuing to break up the cramped clusters, and rationalising the agricultural structure. Thirdly, they were responsible for acquiring and distributing land in other locations where it was deemed advisable. The policy of 'transplanting' from the west to the midlands and east was one expression of these goals, resulting in the remarkable Irish-speaking colony of Rath Cairn in county Meath.

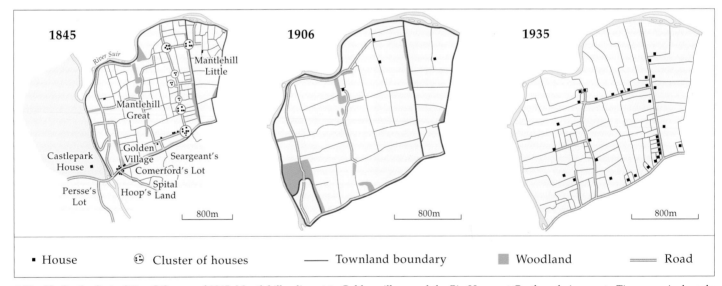

• House   ⊕ Cluster of houses   —— Townland boundary   ■ Woodland   ══ Road

• Fig. 59 On the first edition O.S. map of 1845, Mantlehill, adjacent to Golden village and the Big House at Castlepark, in county Tipperary, is densely settled. A straggling settlement is strung out along the Cashel road east of the village, while cabin clusters and tiny plots mark concentrations of agricultural labourers. By 1906, following multiple evictions in the 1870s, the townland has been cleared, creating a new pattern of large regular fields around a single substantial grazier farmhouse. In 1933, the 273 ha townland was acquired by the Land Commission. Twenty-five new holdings, averaging eleven hectares, were established on a pattern perpendicular to the River Suir to ensure water access. The end product was an egalitarian landscape of small houses, fields and farms. The beneficiaries were landless men from the hill country around Donohill and Upperchurch, including many members of the Third Tipperary Brigade, I.R.A. This was Dan Breen territory. Breen, as a celebrated I.R.A. veteran and then parliamentary representative, had the reputation and political influence to secure the farms for his colleagues and neighbours.

Their activities in the west were responsible for the radical transformation of the landscape and society, but most especially in grazier areas like mid Roscommon where large swathes of holdings were broken up.

The Land Commission followed a crude form of environmental determinism: the provision of eight-to-twelve hectare holdings would inevitably convert their holders into the ideal 'Irishmen' envisaged by Éamon de Valera, embodying the best qualities of the Irish people. However, the result was inefficient farm units; instead of solving the structural problem in Irish agriculture, the Land Commission exacerbated it. Eight or twelve hectares may have seemed an ideal farm size in the 1930s, but it was in the long-run pitifully inadequate, except in the drumlin region where intensive forms of agricultural production – pigs, poultry and mushrooms – underpinned it.

The Land Commission was generally effective only in areas where the agricultural system was weak. In other regions, such as the big-farm, tillage and dairying areas, and the drumlin belt, its efforts were mainly cosmetic, involving the transfer of land-ownership from landlord to tenant. It was in the far west and inner west that its work has been most far-reaching, building on the prior activities of the CDB.

PARTITION AND THE NEW STATES

In Northern Ireland, the difficult inter-war period brought general economic decline but agriculture revived with World War II. Supported by subsidies and an inflated British wartime market, farming entered a period of unprecedented prosperity and rural incomes were decidedly higher than in the south. In the post-war period, old problems reasserted themselves, of declining rural population and static commercial life in the villages and rural towns. Through these vicissitudes, the historic framework of small fields, scattered farms and rural lifestyles remained surprisingly intact.

In Southern Ireland, the economic stance of the 1920s and 30s was national self-sufficiency. Because of the difficulties of providing industrial jobs for displaced agricultural workers, efforts were made to retain the rural population on the small farms and the countryside suffered from deep inertia. At mid-century, agriculture still dominated the Republic's economy; Ireland seemed destined by nature or providence to an agricultural way of life. There was little to suggest that the country was on the verge of a rapid transition to a modern industrial society.

By comparison with the actual ownership of land, the use made of it was of secondary importance; the symbolic rather than the use value of the land counted. Hardly any

DUBLIN OPINION

Fig. 61 'Happiness'. A *Dublin Opinion* cartoon of 1949 bathes Irish rural life in an idyllic summer glow. The jagged edge between soft-focus de Valeran rhetoric and the hard reality of emigration, stagnation and deprivation is carefully erased.

land passed onto the market; there was little or no rationalisation. The actual land-structure pertaining at the time of the transfer to owner occupancy was fossilised. This rigidity in the farming system made it chronically unable to respond to market conditions. The mechanics of the family-farm system stressed impartible inheritance. However, the continuity of farm and family was achieved only at the expense of dispensing with the non-inheriting family members. The result, in a weak economic system, was massive emigration.

A shrinking rural population and a frozen land-owning structure occupied a landscape whose fundamental character had been set in the crowded pre-Famine years. With the exception of the precipitate decline of the 'Big House', the activities of the Land Commission and the moves by Bord na Móna to mechanise peat production, post-independence Ireland saw remarkably little landscape change. The small-scale mixed-farming bias was intensified by the introspective influence of both the Economic War of the 1930s and neutrality in World War II.

The dominant class of owner-occupiers moulded the tone and ethos of the Irish Free State. A powerful rural-

ASAHI CHEMICAL INDUSTRY (IRELAND) LTD

● Fig. 62 The Asahi factory near Killala, county Mayo, established in 1978. The rural location of this giant Japanese-owned chemical factory is testament to the policy of industrial dispersion favoured in Ireland. Factory employment has helped to stabilise the small-farm rural population in its hinterland, with many of its workforce being part-time farmers.

fundamentalist strain emerged, an Irish version of Jeffersonian republicanism, erected behind an economic green curtain. The quintessential Irish civilisation was deemed to be rooted in the soil; the true genius of the Irish character could be developed only in a life lived close to nature. This life offered a fuller, deeper existence, which was more harmonious and fulfiling than life in the deracinated city. The Catholic church similarly stressed the sanctity and value of rural life. Fianna Fáil gave these rural-fundamentalist principles political expression, from the 1930s onwards. Two of its central tenets were the development of a social system in which 'as far as possible equal opportunity would be afforded to every Irish citizen to live a whole and a useful Christian life' and 'the distribution of the land of Ireland in order to get the greatest possible number of Irish families rooted in the soil of Ireland'. Rural fundamentalism was thereby assigned a primary importance in the formulation of ideas of cultural identity in the new Irish state.

The cumulative impact of these processes was to install conservatism at the heart of the farming system, a conservatism which deemed the maintenance of the existing situation as the primary aim, and which was ill-equipped or inclined to make radical changes to accommodate to the changing circumstances of the second half of the twentieth century. There was a shocking disparity between rhetoric and reality and the rural young voted with their feet by emigrating in shoals, contributing to a pervasive gloom in the countryside.

THE IMPACT OF THE EUROPEAN COMMUNITY

By the 1950s, with emigration rampant and a stagnant economy, it was obvious that sweeping changes were

necessary. Rural electrification produced major social and landscape changes in both states in the mid twentieth century. Apart from the visual impact of poles and cables, the schemes launched since the 1950s by the E.S.B. and N.I.E. have radically altered life for Irish rural communities. Rural group water schemes have had a similar social impact in more recent times. Mechanisation, including the widespread introduction of tractors and other farm machinery, also heralded profound changes and undoubtedly accelerated the flight from the land by displaced agricultural labourers and their families.

In 1958, the first programme of economic development, masterminded by T. K. Whitaker, was launched, opening the Republic to multinational companies (MNCs). This coincided with the global boom of the 1960s and the advent of the consumer society, and culminated in EEC entry in 1973, vociferously supported by modernising influences within Irish society and strongly advocated by the big-farm lobby, anxious to gain entry to the advantages of the Common Agricultural Policy.

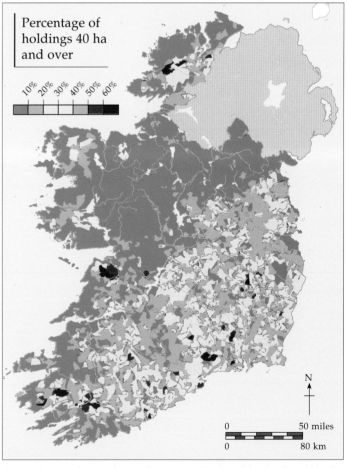

Percentage of holdings 40 ha and over

10% 20% 30% 40% 50% 60%

N

0   50 miles

0   80 km

Fig. 63 Farms of more than 40 hectares in the Republic. By the 1980s, the Irish farm system – and the landscape with it – had developed sharper divisions beween big and small farm sectors. The demarcation was especially crisp along a frontier between Dundalk and Limerick: Leinster and Munster had successful large-farms based on tillage, dairying and cattle; Connacht and the border regions had struggling small farms.

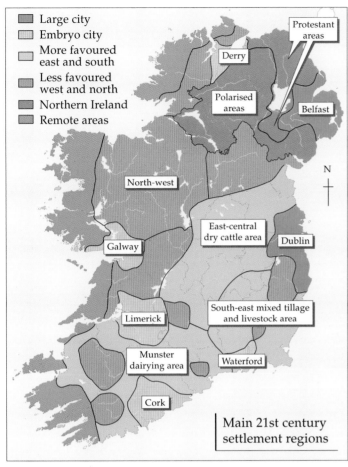

Large city
Embryo city
More favoured
east and south
Less favoured
west and north
Northern Ireland
Remote areas

Protestant
areas

Derry

Polarised
areas

Belfast

N

North-west

East-central
dry cattle area

Dublin

Galway

Limerick

South-east mixed tillage
and livestock area

Munster
dairying area

Waterford

Cork

Main 21st century
settlement regions

Fig. 64 Major contemporary regions as identified by Arnold Horner.

Despite rapid changes, a rural emphasis continued to influence southern policy. A striking result was the deliberate scattering of MNC branch plants promiscuously across the regions, often in totally rural locations. Simultaneously, Irish farming broke out of its organic mould of 'mixed' farming, through the triple impact of cheap artificial fertilisers, machinery and specialised production methods. Waving these technological wands over the countryside transformed agricultural production from small-scale, balanced and sustainable ecological systems to intensive, large-scale and essentially industrial production processes. Added to the tendency of the CAP to favour the bigger farmer, the EEC accelerated class transformation in Irish rural society. In the tillage and dairying areas particularly, access to European markets and finance supports favoured the prosperous big-farm class, able to modernise rapidly around larger farm sizes, new machinery and competitive production systems. The grant system to farms rather than farmers disproportionately favoured those bigger units. Farmyards were ruthlessly reconstructed to facilitate heavier machinery; silage pits, milking parlours, slatted sheds and larger barns were added. Intensive land reclamation and drainage schemes were undertaken and field boundaries were altered to accommodate heavy machinery, notably in the tillage region.

By contrast, small farmers did poorly under the CAP, and the small-farm region continued to disintegrate apace, especially in the more peripheral and ecologically disadvantaged areas like the north-west and the border region. Agricultural policy was biased heavily towards 'vanguard' farmers, the agrarian entrepreneurs, at the expense of the wide range of small, diversified, transitional and traditional farmers. On west of Ireland small farms, income support was more important than price supports and capital grants. Here, off-farm employment became crucial to the maintenance of the small-farm sector, but these part-time farmers found great difficulty in obtaining grants and assistance from Europe, the Irish advisory bodies and the banks. Because they were small-scale and family run, these farms could only shed labour slowly and were therefore disadvantaged in the race towards increased productivity. In the more peripheral areas, small farms collapsed and emigration tightened its grip on rural communities through the distressed 1980s. A vicious spiral existed, whereby population loss led to the elimination of pivotal elements in the infrastructure of local communities – schools, post-offices, shops – which, in turn, fed further emigration. The maintenance of a viable population base, services and infrastructure became increasingly difficult in these small-farm zones.

LAND USE AND LANDSCAPE CHANGE NORTH AND SOUTH

There has been considerable stability in the overall pattern of land use in the twentieth century. The predominantly pastoral nature of land use has strengthened; over 90% of the land area is now accounted for by improved and rough grazing. Continuing an inexorable post-Famine trend, tillage has declined in relation to grassland. The trend was interrupted only briefly during the two world wars as a result of government inducements. Since World War II, the decline of tillage has been marked, north and south. Yet, agricultural output has increased substantially, albeit without enlarging the productive acreage. Both states have experienced comparable patterns of agricultural and landscape change, although different administrative regimes have led to some differentiation.

In the North, agriculture has been more heavily subsidised than in the Republic. After World War II, the UK continued policies of guaranteed prices and subsidies along with schemes for farm improvements by capital grants. Thus pump-primed, farming in Northern Ireland remained ahead of the Republic. However, convergence occurred with impressive rapidity after agricultural

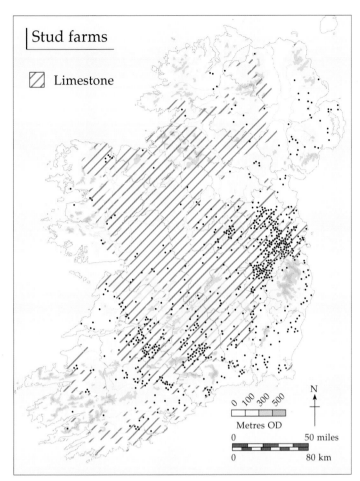

Fig. 65 Stud farms in Ireland in 1976. The intense concentration in the Pale (Kildare, Dublin, Meath) and a lesser concentration across the Golden Vale (south Tipperary, east Limerick, north-east Cork) is noticeable. The stud farms generally locate on the richest limestone-based pastures.

● Fig. 66 The Irish bloodstock industry has been very successful since the 1960s and the richer pasturelands, especially those close to Dublin, have many stud farms. This is Vincent O'Brien's stud farm at Coolmore near Fethard in county Tipperary, with 800 boxes and 800 hectares.

modernisation began in the Republic in the 1960s. After 1973, when both the UK and the Republic joined the European Community, both states have been increasingly influenced by, and subject to, European policy and funding, especially through the application of the CAP. Its impact was decisive in creating rapid and widespread change.

Agricultural productivity rose most strikingly in the dairying sector, with a pronounced growth in both the number of cows and their milk yields from the 1950s onwards. Sensitive to policy and grant aid, sheep numbers soared dramatically in the 1980s, especially in the west, leading to severe problems of environmental degradation on vulnerable hill and bog grazing. The general intensification of agriculture affected the landscape in many ways: field drainage, hedgerow removal (especially in tillage areas), new outbuildings, and farmhouses, the adoption of silage in place of hay making. It also witnessed less visible but equally profound changes - for example in the application of fertilisers, the pollution of watercourses, overstocking and soil erosion. The connection between an expansionary agricultural policy and the quality of the rural environment was only slowly recognised. Farm modernisation took precedence over wider considerations such as the ecological and visual effect of innovations. Short-term economic gains were seen to override long-term environmental losses, in an economy ravaged by unemployment. By the mid 1980s, a growing consensus emerged that the diversity, quality and aesthetic appeal of the Irish rural landscape had declined appreciably - a consensus vocally expressed in debate over the destruction of archaeological monuments and valued wildlife habitats. This debate culminated in the 1990s in the shrill public controversy over the proposed interpretative centre at Mullaghmore in the Burren, which crystallised in a peculiarly stark way the battle between economic and environmental interests.

Under CAP reforms initiated in the 1980s, agricultural over-production is now being discouraged by, for example, Set-Aside and Environmentally Sensitive Areas schemes. At least implicitly, there is an emphasis instead on the promotion of farming in harmony with the inherited landscape, and of stewardship of the wider environment. Conservation schemes include the Rural Environmental Protection Scheme (REPS) in the Republic and the Sub-Programme for Agriculture and Rural Development (SPARD) in Northern Ireland. Both schemes support environmental and conservation work on farms, including the maintenance of traditional field boundaries. In the Republic, the REPS scheme subsumed the earlier discredited ESA schemes, but the ESAs have been relatively effective in Northern Ireland,

CON BROGAN

● Fig. 67 The Slieve Russell hotel in small-farm west Cavan near the village of Ballyconnell. Built in the late 1980s, this massive facility is in open country-side, with all the trappings of a country club – golf course, swimming pool and conference centre.

where they cover one-fifth of the agricultural land area, correlating roughly with the designated Areas of Outstanding Natural Beauty (AONB). Nevertheless, repairing the extensive landscape damage inflicted by earlier governmental and EC-supported programmes presents a daunting challenge. The present commitment (especially financial) to conservation schemes is inadequate to staunch the gaping holes ripped in the fabric of the rural landscape by prior vandalising policies. In particular, the repair schemes are limited by their voluntary nature, and are therefore patchy or of limited spatial extent.

By the 1980s, the split into big and small farm sectors had deepened. The only truly viable small farms were those which embraced intensive processing – notably in the mushroom, pig and poultry units of the drumlin belt. They had, however, serious environmental consequences; slurry run-off, for example, has led to severe eutrophication in the

KEVIN WHELAN

● Fig. 68 Farm modernisation has brought great changes to the Irish countryside. At Kilcarry near Clonegal, county Carlow, this 120 hectare farm was acquired by new owners in the late 1970s, who then cleared it completely of its field boundaries and coppices, leaving one huge field which has subsequently been in continuous tillage.

MICHAEL DIGGIN

● Fig. 69 The proliferation of silage has released farmers from their bondage to Ireland's fickle summers. The gleaming black silage bales, with their lurid markings to deter birds, are a distinctive feature of modern techno-farming. After use, the plastic containers are often carelessly discarded and the ragged remnants litter the countryside. These silage bales are on the Sheeps Head peninsula in county Cork.

rivers and lakes in the region and fish-kills became commonplace. Another solution was for small farmers to become part-time, a process aided by the policy of industrial dispersal and the inexorable spread of tourism. The advent of women in the workforce helped greatly: many western small farms remained viable only through income from bed-and-breakfast, seasonal tourism employment, or a factory job. The spread of the car, freeing ties between workplace and living-space, spawned extensive commuter belts around regional centres. Small farms survive best in the shadow of these labour catchments as, for example, around Tralee, Ennis, Galway, Sligo and Letterkenny.

The rise of the commuter had one other striking effect – the spread of the ubiquitous bungalow which has increasingly given an incongruously suburban look to the roadside swathes of the countryside. Indeed, this 'bungalowisation' is the single biggest change in the Irish landscape in the recent past. The absence of effective long-term planning control in a situation where short-term economic targets assumed overwhelming precedency, the fact that the Irish housing stock had been largely stagnant since the 1840s and was completely modernised in the decades from 1960, when architectural respect for traditional buildings was at a low ebb, the assertion of new city-led usages for the countryside, the ability of the car to divorce workplace and living place and the consequent fundamental change in the occupational profile of rural dwellers, the permeability of the planning process to political manipulation – all these fed the bungalow phenomenon. The result has been a

linearisation of landscape, bungalows strung in repetitive beads along the roads, insulated from any engagement with a broader landscape context.

The other major recent change in the Irish landscape has been the revival of forestry through state initiatives. The current low level of forest cover – 7% as against a European average of 35% – derived from three features: the widespread availability of turf as an alternative to wood as fuel, the enormous land hunger of the nineteenth century, and the twentieth-century presumption that forest should only be a last resort user of soils too poor to sustain any form of agriculture. The result was to confine Irish forests to the hills and bogs.

Due to the difficulty of acquiring land and the lack of a national land-use policy, Irish forests remain exceptionally fragmented by European standards. The only exceptions are in county Wicklow with its 18% cover, the Slieve Blooms and the Slieve Aughtys. Irish forests are extremely young, mostly planted in the last two decades. The story of twentieth-century Irish forestry revolves around the success story of two north American coniferous imports – the Sitka spruce and, to a lesser extent, the Douglas fir: both were highly productive species, superbly adapted to environmental conditions and to market requirements. The outstanding feature of Irish forests is the dominance of Sitka spruce: it occupies 85% of the total area in the Republic, where the commercial success of the conifer has meant that only 4% of planting is broadleaf. Both north and south, the emphasis has recently been shifting to private

DAVID HICKIE

● Fig. 70 Soil erosion due to overgrazing has reached a crisis on the uplands of the western seaboard. Headage and ewe premium grants have encouraged overstocking. Where the plant cover is destroyed by the grazing and trampling of sheep, the thin peaty soils are loosened and easily washed away, exposing areas of bare rock. The effects are evident on this hill slope at Lough Feeagh in county Mayo.

forests on improved farmland. The trend for conversion of farmland to forest is intensifying: following the European pattern, it will be one of the driving forces in future landscape change.

Like forestry, tourism has flourished in the two most recent decades. This has resulted in infrastructural developments, as for example, the controversial interpretative centres, golf and country clubs, and in a proliferating informal bed-and-breakfast sector whose effects are markedly coastal. However, perhaps due to the highly publicised 'Troubles', the Irish countryside has not had a major influx of retirement or second-home dwellers, with the exception of small pockets in west Cork, west Kerry and Connemara. This is now a marked difference between the rural communities of Ireland and those of Scotland and Wales. The 'Troubles' had other landscape effects – the creation of an intensely fortified frontier, with extensive military installations, surveillance towers and sealed-off unapproved crossings, and a blighted shadow on either side of it.

CONCLUSION

If, as is commonly argued, two million European farmers could produce food sufficient for the continent's needs, then a very large portion of the European landscape could be withdrawn from agricultural production. The question of what to do with that vast freed landscape and how to absorb the seven million farmers displaced in the process

has scarcely been broached. In a *laissez-faire* situation, immense social dislocation and the desertification of large swathes of some of Europe's most valued landscapes would result. This would be a quantum leap, a revolution equivalent to that in the Neolithic, in the eighteenth and nineteenth-century improvement phase and in the twentieth-century mechanisation, intensification and chemicalisation of agriculture. In the absence of intervention, the European and Irish farm structure would continue its bifurcation. One component would be intensive, competitive and technologically driven; the other would be extensive, uncompetitive and ecologically friendly.

The result would be the continuing transformation of the traditional territorial, settlement and social structures of the Irish countryside. Increased mobility would also permit the functional – and at times morphological – blending of town and country. A key change would be the breakdown of the old easy equation between 'rural' and 'agricultural'; already in Ireland, almost half of country dwellers have no direct contact with the land. In the midst of these changes, the landscape itself is changing at an unprecedented rate, through the impact of an increasingly invasive global economy on a pressurised environment. But also to an unprecedented degree, landscape change is responsive to policy measures. That very fact dictates the requirement for an informed policy, as the Irish landscape itself undergoes accelerating change.

BIBLIOGRAPHY

F. Aalen, 'Constructive unionism and the shaping of modern Ireland' in *Rural History*, iv (1993), pp 137-64.

J. Andrews, 'Land and people *c.* 1780' in *A new history of Ireland*, iv (Oxford, 1986) pp 236-64.

J. Andrews, *Interpreting the Irish landscape: explorations in settlement history* (Dublin, 1997).

B. Brunt, *The Republic of Ireland* (London, 1988).

W. Crawford, *The handloom weavers and the Ulster linen industry* (Belfast, 1994).

L. Cullen, *The emergence of modern Ireland 1600-1900* (London, 1981).

D. Dickson, An economic history of the Cork region in the eighteenth century, unpublished Ph.D. thesis (Trinity College Dublin, 1977).

J. Feehan (ed.), *Environment and development in Ireland* (Dublin, 1992).

L. Gibbons, *Transformations in Irish culture* (Cork, 1996).

A. Horner, 'Dividing Ireland into geographical regions' in *Geog. Viewpoint*, xxi (1993), pp 5-24.

N. Johnson, 'Building a nation: an examination of the Irish Gaeltacht Commission report of 1926' in *Jn. Hist. Geog.*, xix (1993), pp 157-68.

T. Jones Hughes, 'The large farm in nineteenth-century Ireland' in A. Gailey and D. Ó hÓgáin (ed.), *Gold under the furze* (Dublin, 1982), pp 93-100.

C. Ó Gráda, *Ireland: a new economic history 1780 - 1939* (Oxford, 1994).

W. Smyth, 'Society and settlement in seventeenth-century Ireland: the evidence of the 1659 census' in W. Smyth and K. Whelan (ed.), *Common ground: essays on the historical geography of Ireland* (Cork, 1987), pp 55-83.

W. Smyth, 'Landholding changes, kinship networks and class transformation in rural Ireland: a case study from county Tipperary' in *Ir. Geog.*, xvi (1983), pp 17-36.

W. Smyth, 'The making of Ireland: agendas and perspectives in cultural geography' in B. Graham and L. Proudfoot (ed.) *An historical geography of Ireland* (London, 1993), pp 399-438.

K. Whelan, 'Ireland in the world system 1600-1800' in H. Nitz (ed.), *The early modern world system in geographic perspective* (Stuttgart, 1993), pp 204-18.

K. Whelan, 'Settlement and society in eighteenth-century Ireland' in G. Dawe and J. Wilson (ed.), *The poet's place* (Belfast, 1991), pp 45-62.

K. Whelan, 'Settlement patterns in the west of Ireland in the pre-famine period' in T. Collins (ed.), *Decoding the landscape* (Galway, 1994), pp 60-78.

Clonmacnoise, county Offaly

COMPONENTS

OF THE

IRISH LANDSCAPE

COMPONENTS
OF THE
IRISH LANDSCAPE

BOGS

Despite centuries of sustained cutting for fuel, bogs are among the most characteristic landscape features in Ireland, covering one-sixth (1.34 million ha) of the total land area, a higher proportion than in any other European country except Finland. With bog depletion elsewhere in western Europe, Irish bog landscapes have increasing value as scientific, cultural and aesthetic resources of international significance. The extent of bog varies greatly, with major concentrations in the midlands and west; only 3% of county Wexford is bog covered but 62% of west Donegal. Whilst boglands have strongly influenced rural economy and culture, settlement distribution and communications, they are themselves deeply humanised landscapes which have evolved, indeed sometimes originated, in close association with land use systems. The bog has been etched as deeply into the human as into

the physical record in Ireland, to an extent unrivalled elsewhere in Europe.

The distinction between major types of bog (raised bogs, upland and lowland blanket bogs) is based on their precise mode of formation. Although their vegetation and morphology may appear very similar, there are essential differences which arise from contrasts in location, extent and altitude, as well as from varying patterns of actual and potential land use. Blanket bogs, in both their upland and Atlantic lowland varieties, provide vast, relatively flat vistas, treeless and dominated by the peat layer itself. Scattered over the central lowlands, raised bogs are usually smaller: their open character and natural vegetation contrast markedly with the surrounding farmed land. They are more attractive for large-scale, commercial turf production.

MICHAEL DIGGIN

● Fig. 1 Blanket bog near Glencar, county Kerry. The MacGillycuddy Reeks are in the background. The sods are being wind-dried in small stooks.

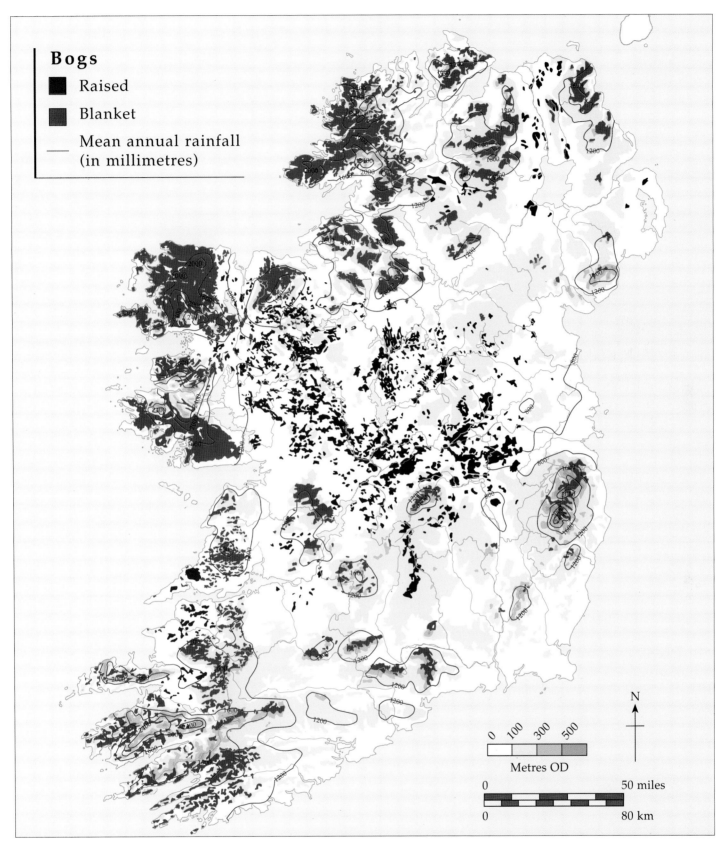

Bogs

- ■ Raised
- ■ Blanket
- — Mean annual rainfall (in millimetres)

Fig. 2 The distribution of bogs types in Ireland. Blanket bogs grow more extensively in western and northern areas with high rainfall and waterlogged, acid parent soil. Unlike raised bogs, they occur in elevated positions as well as lowlands and are found on major mountain masses throughout the country. Blanket bogs have developed primarily as a response to climate but in many places their formation was encouraged by human activities. Raised bogs, or lowland bogs, form in areas of lower rainfall and flourish principally in the Central Lowlands where they originated in damp hollows but have frequently grown upwards above the level of their surroundings and expanded onto the adjoining terrain. Transitional bogs are found in the wetter, western parts of the Central Lowlands.

RAISED BOGS

Raised bogs, so-called because of their elevated centres, occur widely across northern Europe and Asia, northern Japan and North America. In Ireland, they cover 314,000 ha, approaching one-quarter of the peat-covered area. They are found mainly in the central lowlands and towards the east of the country. While bog distribution is multi-causal, different kinds are associated with different rainfall regimes. Irish raised bogs are found in areas where yearly rainfall is between 800 and 1100 mm. The blanket bogs are associated with higher rainfall, and/or lower evapotranspiration and a higher number of rain days per year.

Irish raised bogs vary in thickness from three to over twelve metres with an average depth of seven metres. Their characteristic domed profiles are produced by continued upward growth through accumulation of undecayed mosses and other plant remains. This eventually elevates the bog surface slightly above the level of the surrounding countryside. The dome of the bog is flat and very wet; pools of standing water alternate with drier cushions and hummocks. Towards the margins, the bog slopes quite steeply (called the rand), is drier and has different plant assemblages, sometimes including sweet gale. At the very edge, where there is more movement of groundwater, a belt of marginal fen or lagg may be formed. Centuries of exploitation , especially cutting, have modified the edges of most bogs and the rand and lagg are seldom seen intact today.

Raised bogs have accumulated during most of post-glacial time, originating in lakes or low-lying hollows in the early post-glacial landscape. Here, drainage was obstructed by irregular glacial deposits. High water tables resulted in widespread flooding, particularly in the broad, shallow basins of the Shannon and Erne systems. As water table and lake levels fell, reed swamps developed and peat accumulated. Eventually, the peat and its perched water table was elevated above the surrounding land so that no mineral water was entering the bog; the vegetation changed to species tolerant of low nutrient conditions and associated with bogs fed only by rainwater – particularly the *Sphagnum* mosses (bog mosses). The peat continued to grow upward, taking the water table with it, and the acidic raised bogs were produced. Open lakes and reed swamps of the post-glacial period began to give way to fen vegetation around 9000 years ago, and raised bog had overgrown most fens about 7000 years ago.

Raised bogs are thus characterised by a basal layer of fen peat overlain by bog moss or *Sphagnum* peat. The rate of accumulation and character of the peat were greatly influenced by fluctuations in climate. Peat originating

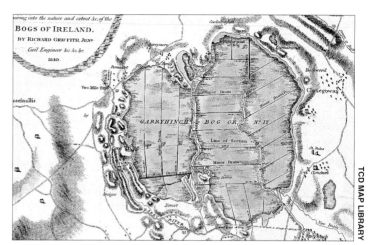

● Fig. 3 The Bog Commissioners reports contain the earliest detailed bog-land maps for most of the country. They were completed in the early nineteenth century, when the bogs were still relatively undisturbed and near their maximum extent. This map by Richard Griffith in 1810 shows the raised bog at Garryhinch in county Offaly, located in a basin bounded by morainic ridges. Drainage channels for the proposed improvement of the bog are marked.

during drier intervals has a higher proportion of heather and cotton grass, and less *Sphagnum*. When the climate was especially dry, pine could invade the bog surface and these periods are marked by the occurrence of trees in the peat profile, sometimes at several levels. Wetter and cooler conditions after 500 BC resulted in increased *Sphagnum* growth, and the contrast between a lower level of highly humified peat and a poorly humified upper level is well marked in most raised-bogs.

The growing bogs initially were confined within lake basins. As the climate became wetter, they extended laterally, swamping woods which grew on the margins of the ancient lakes and fens. Two processes, terrestrialisation and paludification, are involved therefore in the formation of these bogs. Terrestrialisation is the sequence by which shallow lakes go through a process of ecological succession that ends with the development of a bog. Paludification is the process by which restricted drainage at the margins allows a bog to encroach over adjacent mineral soil. Areas of raised bogs which have swollen out beyond the boundaries of their original lake basins are called intermediate. They occur in areas where precipitation is between 1000 and 1300 mm. Intermediate bogs are really raised-bogs which, because of higher rainfall and humidity, extended out of the depressions in which they initially formed. Although the distinction is based on their flora, these bogs are also intermediate in their geographical distribution, occurring primarily in central county Galway and central Mayo.

From the botanical viewpoint, there are two sorts of raised bogs in Ireland – the Midland and the Transitional. The true Midland sub-type is characterised by cranberry

● Fig. 4 Clongowny-Derrinlough raised bog, county Offaly, depicted on an estate map from the 1840s. Owing to population increase, land reclamation was particularly marked in the decades before and after the Great Famine. Numerous detailed surveys were undertaken on major estates with a view to more intense development including the reclamation of bogland.

and bog rosemary, but to the west, as climate becomes wetter, there is a subtle change in the composition of the plant communities towards those characteristic of blanket bog. Beyond the 1000 mm isohyet, there is a distinct change. The indicator species of the Midland sub-type are no longer prominent: their place is taken by the indicator species of the Transitional sub-type of raised-bog, the liverwort *Pleurozia purpurea* and the moss *Campylopus artovirens*.

SURVEY AND MAPPING

Implemented in 1810-14 under the direction of the government-appointed Commissioners for Bogs, the first comprehensive survey of Ireland's bogs estimated the total area at 1.2 million ha. About half was upland bog; the remainder was raised bog (296,000 ha) and low-level blanket bog (344,500 ha). As this survey was carried out with large-scale reclamation for agriculture in mind, it did not pay much attention to bogs less than 200 ha in extent.

Bogs were mapped more systematically during the course of the primary Geological Survey of the country between 1845 and 1887, and the one-inch maps published by the Geological Survey (and the six-inch sheets upon which they are based) are the most detailed systematic maps of Ireland's bogs ever produced; the accompanying memoirs also contain valuable notes on the bogs in each district. In 1920, the Geological Survey published a coloured peat map of Ireland based on its survey work. A comprehensive government survey of Ireland's peatlands was carried out by An Foras Talúntais in the 1970s, resulting in the publication in 1979 of a monograph on the peatlands and the first map (at a scale of 1:575,000) to show different classes of bogs. The most recent comprehensive map of the bogs is provided by the European Community's CORINE land cover project, compiled from satellite imagery of 1989-90.

UTILISATION

Camp sites around the pre-bog lake at Boora in county Offaly indicate that the raised-bog area of central Ireland had been settled in mesolithic times. Subsequent patterns of settlement distribution and social evolution have been much influenced by the evolution and spread of the peatlands. As early as the Neolithic, trackways were constructed across the bogs to connect areas of farmland. During the Bronze Age, the expanding bogs began to encroach on farmland. Bog pools and lakes then were regarded with veneration and votive offerings deposited in their mysterious depths accumulated to form the celebrated bog hoards of archaeology. The widespread occurrence of fulachta fiadh along the fringing fen aureole (lagg) which surrounded intact bog is indicative of the water supply it provided in the Bronze Age. Seepage deposits of ochre were exploited as a significant source of iron ore during the Iron Age.

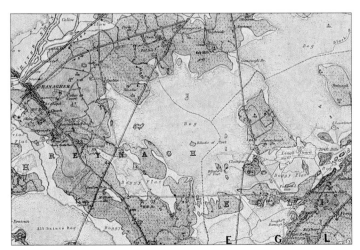

● Fig. 5 Geological Survey map (published in 1870) showing the Clongowny-Derrinlough bog in county Offaly.

● Fig. 6 The distinctive cone of the ESB sod-peat burning electricity station near Portarlington, county Laois. The station, commissioned in 1950 and closed in 1988, is now scheduled for dismantling.

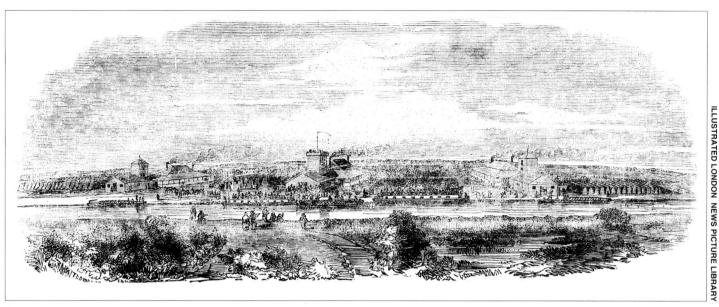

• Fig. 7 Derrymullen peat charcoal works, near Robertstown in county Kildare, 1850. This early attempt at the industrial development of peat resources was initiated in the Bog of Allen by the Irish Amelioration Society. The turf was dried on frames over the retorts and then converted into charcoal which was conveyed to market by barges on the Grand Canal. The society's unrealized ambition was to establish two hundred such stations to provide fuel and to reclaim the bogs for agricultural use.

• Fig. 8 Bord na Móna milled peat harvesters in operation near Edgeworthstown, county Longford. They collect sun dried milled peat, which has been laid out in linear ridges. The harvesting process involves transferring the peat ridges into one massive longitudinal stockpile where it is stored until required for briquette manufacture or for burning in peat-fired power stations.

Peat has long formed the chief fuel of a large part of the population. 'Saving' of turf from the edge of bogs by hand-cutting, using the traditional north European peat spade known in Ireland as a sleán, was a feature of the rural economy by the medieval period. Extensive bog reclamation for agriculture only began with the rapid rise of population following the seventeenth century. Interest initially focused on the creation of new farmland by direct conversion of the bog following drainage and nutrient input. Drainage invariably changes bog ecosystems. Arterial and field drainage in the nineteenth and twentieth centuries have affected raised-bogs by lowering water tables, depleting their floristic diversity; many bogs survive in a degraded form as a result.

Major developments in bog exploitation only commenced with the setting up of the Turf Development Board by the Irish Free State in 1934. Extraction of fuel peat under this board necessitated widespread compulsory land purchase. There was limited use of mechanical means of extraction until World War II, after which there was a rapid acceleration. Estimates as to how much bogland has been cut away over the centuries range from around 300,000 ha to twice that figure. By the time Bord na Móna, a semi-state body, was established in 1946, nearly half of the total area of large Midland raised-bogs recorded in 1814 had been cut away by hand. This was equivalent to some 800 ha a year; at one thousand tons of fuel to the acre, this involved a total of two million tons of turf. Calculations in 1969 showed that there were then just over 100,000 ha of raised-bog in the Midlands, of which Bord na Móna owned around 45,000 ha. Most of the larger bogs worked by the Bord will be exhausted before the middle of the twenty-first century. Development of smaller bogs using more compact machines could continue for much longer; already, more sod peat is harvested each year by these small machines than by the massive ones operated by Bord na Móna.

CONSERVATION AND THE FUTURE

Although no entirely natural raised bogs survive, they remain a characteristic landform, and conservation is desirable for ecological, scientific, archaeological and cultural reasons and for the maintenance of landscape diversity. Conservation policies are emerging in both jurisdictions. In the Republic, government objectives are for the conservation of at least 10,000 ha of raised bog and 40,000 ha of blanket bog; these are modest targets, given the international significance of Irish boglands. In Northern Ireland, it is intended that all remaining areas of lowland bog will be declared ASSI where they meet the minimum scientific criteria along with four extensive areas of blanket bog on Garron plateau, Pettigo plateau, Cuilcagh and Slieve Beagh.

The cutting away of the large raised bogs will result in the creation of one the most extensive new cultural landscapes which Ireland has witnessed for a century. Increasing attention is being paid to future land use. In the context of EU farm over-production, conversion of much cutaway to agricultural use is less attractive, and much of the cutover is unsuitable for forestry. Hence, more attention is now being given to the restoration and enhancement of the natural and cultural diversity of cutover, and the exploration of new economic contexts in which other land uses may be developed for recreation and tourism.

● Fig. 9 New landscape are being produced by mechanised peat cutting. Tractor driven, lightweight fuel peat machines (compact harvesters) have come to dominate domestic fuel peat extraction. Peat is extruded onto the surface in 'sausages' taken from near-vertical slits in the ground by either a disc or a chain-saw. In years of good weather, the peat is soon dry and gathered; in wet years, it may never be collected and smothers the vegetation, already damaged directly by the tractor or indirectly through compaction under its weight. More than one cut may be taken each year; in those circumstances, there can be an almost complete loss of vegetation and the expanse of dark, bare peat remains until cutting stops. Recovery appears to be slow with no immediate return to the species composition which existed before cutting. One of the first colonisers is bog cotton and square patches of its white heads in summer often indicate the sites of former machine cutting.

Ardee Bog, county Louth

The Great Bog of Ardee is one of the most easterly raised bogs in Ireland. Following the retreat of the last ice sheet, an extensive lake occupied the site, its irregular shoreline reflecting a series of north-east to south-west trending morainic ridges scattered over the limestone bedrock. This lake was slowly silted up and fen peat accumulated. From around 7000 BC, a carpet of mosses began to form over the fen peat, characterised by a chain of peat domes which slowly extended onto the moraine slopes to the north. Extensive fen remained in the southern half of the area, fed by lime-rich spring water.

Although surrounded by productive farmland and used for many centuries as a source of peat fuel, the bog-fen complex was little altered by humans until the nineteenth century. Turf cutting uncovered ancient trackways, or tochair, across the bog but drainage was limited and haphazard. The area remained impassable to wheeled traffic; a ring of roads encircled it with dead-end lanes extending to the bog edge. The entire bog was transformed in the 1840s by large-scale drainage schemes undertaken by the Board of Works. The southern fen area was changed into pastureland, while drying out of the raised bog to the north made it much more accessible to turf cutting.

After World War II, cutting on the bog declined as electricity and oil became more generally available, and the bog reverted to wilderness. The situation was reversed abruptly in the 1980s with the introduction of mechanised cutting with tractor-mounted turf diggers. Extraction was vigorously renewed and the wilderness has been destroyed; 'black devastation' is widespread and biodiversity reduced. Additionally, the trailers which carry loads of peat off the bog have been used to dump vast quantities of domestic and farm rubbish onto the bog.

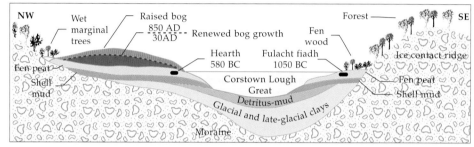

Fig. B Diagrammatic section of bog deposits at Corstown Lough Great. Late Bronze Age occupation has been identified in peat deposits at the margins of the lake.

•Fig. A Towards the end of the last Ice Age around 11,000 years ago, glacial deposits impeded drainage and a large lake formed. The Irish giant deer grazed at the margins of this lake until they died out prior to 8000 BC.

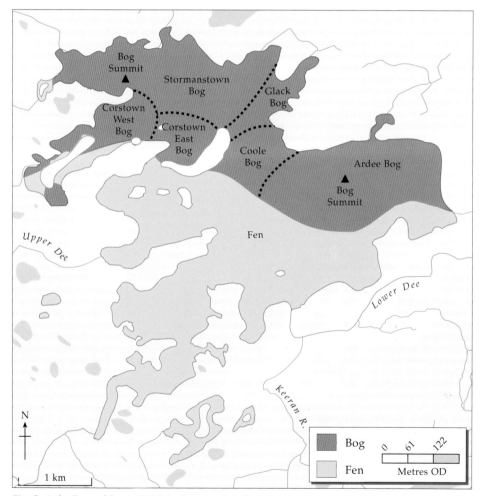

Fig. C Ardee Bog and fen c. 1000 BC. Deposits of shell-mud at the margins of the lake supported plant life and open water gradually gave way to an accumulation of fen-peat. As the fen-peat thickened, mosses grew over the fen. Raised bog growth then took place in the northern half of the lake.

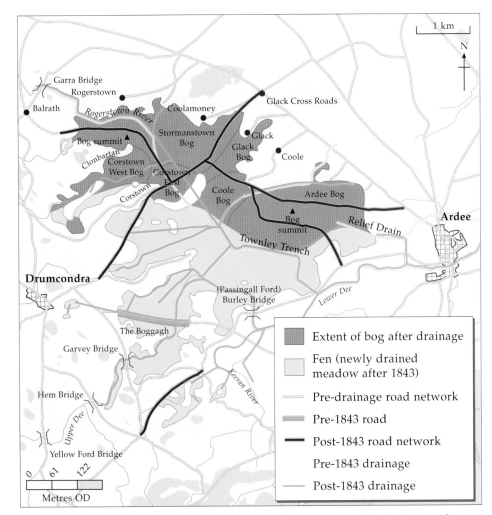

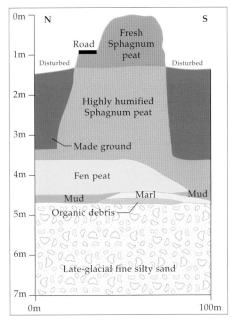

Fig. F Section of Ardee Bog.

Fig. D Ardee Bog underwent dramatic changes from the eighteenth century. Early drainage trenches were financed by the landlord between 1766 and 1778 but most drainage work was carried out by the Board of Works in the mid-nineteenth century. These drainage works facilitated the construction of new roads and peat harvesting. The former fen-peat was converted into farmland.

Fig. G Occupation of Ardee Bog continued into this century, often in conditions of unimaginable poverty.

Fig. H The moulding of mud-turf was recorded at Ardee Bog in 1652. The practice continues to this day, albeit on a smaller scale.

Fig. E Aerial photograph of the western section of the Ardee Bog complex from the south-east.

The changing use of raised bogs: prehistory to the present

Fig. A Following the Ice Age 10,000 years ago, mesolithic communities settled along the shores of the lakes which preceded the raised bogs, making their living by fishing in the productive waters, hunting animals such as hare, deer and waterfowl, and gathering wild plants. Human impact on the wider landscape was still limited. Hazel dominated the wooded landscape of esker and moraine which surrounded the bogs, and pine was still abundant. The scene depicted here reconstructs the type of settlement uncovered by Michael Ryan beneath Boora Bog in county Offaly.

Fig. B Over a period of thousands of years, the open water receded gradually, replaced successively by reed-swamp, fen and finally bog. By the middle Bronze Age, only small fen-fringed lakes remained. These pools were sacred places. Sometimes, votive offerings of weapons and ornaments were deposited in them, perhaps at special times of the year; this type of ceremony would have accompanied the deposition of the Dowris Hoard. Humans were clearly interested in the bogs despite their limited economic potential. By this time, the natural woodland cover of oak, ash, and elm on the eskers was partly replaced by farmland, giving trees like hawthorn a new prominence in the vegetation.

SADHBH MCELVEEN

SADHBH MCELVEEN

Fig. C Towards the end of the Bronze Age, the bogs, though actively growing, were considerably drier than in later times, with abundant heather and fringes of birchwood. With the onset of wetter conditions after 500 BC Sphagnum mosses became more dominant. Agricultural settlement often focussed on the edges of these drier bogs, which would have provided useful spring grazing, and where the reliable water supply was exploited for domestic purposes through the construction of fulachta fiadh.

Fig. D The raised bogs were at their most active phase of growth during the Celtic Iron Age. The surrounding landscape was now widely settled and small enclosed fields were spreading. Human activities extended from the bog edges over the bog surfaces. Wooden trackways (tochair) were constructed across the bog to connect separated areas of farmland, and sometimes to provide access to the deposits of ochre which occurred at seepage areas in the bog. These ore deposits were smelted to produce the iron which was so vital to the economy, possibly using charcoal made from turf, which was already in use as a fuel at this time. Later, during the Early Christian period, isolated bog margins were settled by early ecclesiastics as expressed in a contemporary poem:

> I wish . . . for a hidden little hut in the wilderness that it might be my dwelling, all-grey shallow water beside it (St Manchán's Wish).

SADHBH MCELVEEN

Fig. E Widespread exploitation of the raised bogs for fuel accompanied the rapid rise in population after the seventeenth century, by which time woodland had virtually disappeared from the landscape. Almost all of this was cut and saved by hand, although mechanical harvesting of peat was undertaken by a number of short-lived ventures in the nineteenth and early twentieth centuries. There was also considerable reclamation both of cutover and uncut bog for agriculture, primarily grassland with remnants of naturally colonising birch or willow forming intermittent hedges along field boundaries. Handcutover areas usually suffer the limitation of poor drainage and are frequently abandoned and undergo natural recolonisation. The bogland edge attracted settlements of marginal people, as turf was the poor man's fuel. In bogs close to towns or navigation systems, commercial cutting took place, but most exploitation was at the level of the individual small-farm family. 'Saving the turf' became a much enjoyed annual ritual, occupying a prominent part in the rhythm of the agricultural year. Access to peat resources was highly prized and enhanced the value of holdings. Until recent decades it was difficult to escape the sight or scent of turf in the Irish countryside.

SADHBH MCELVEEN

Fig. F Extensive mechanical exploitation of peat for fuel and horticultural use by Bord na Móna commenced after World War II. Until very recently, bogs were ruthlessly exploited as a 'free' resource and little or no consideration was given to conservation or to future land use. Growing awareness of the precious ecological value of Ireland's boglands, largely generated by foreign interest, has caused a welcome rethink and bogs now occupy a much more prominent role in environmental debates. All of the larger raised bogs will be cut away before the middle of the next century. Some cutaway will be suitable for farming or forestry or developed as amenity wetland and woodland, but much will be allowed to regenerate a complex mosaic of semi-natural ecosystems: fen, grassland, birchwood, heath and (where hydrological conditions are favourable) new bogland. Even small areas of cutaway can be of a complex nature and unsuitable for any one use. Eventual land use patterns cannot be foreseen, much depending on the structure of ownership. A few exceptional bogs are being preserved, such as Clara and Mongan bogs in county Offaly.

BLANKET BOGS

The blanket bogs of western and northern Ireland and on the mountains of Scotland, Wales and south-west England, form a distinctive rural landscape in Europe. Blanket bog is so-called because of its appearance; closely following the topography, peat mantles all but the steepest slopes. It is a harsh landscape, difficult for people to live in. Viewed differently through time, it was until recently considered wasteland, suitable only for use as a source of fuel or for sheep grazing; it is now increasingly regarded as an important recreational and tourism resource. One of the few remaining types of country in Europe that is wild and open, it is valued as a rare ecosystem by a population that is becoming more environmentally sophisticated.

Unlike raised bogs, which began their growth without appreciable human interference and in some cases before the arrival of man, blanket bogs developed after millennia of settlement and are essentially post-neolithic. Although following a complex regional and local pattern, their initiation and spread in the first and second millennium BC were probably stimulated by deteriorating climate, combined with substantial woodland clearance by farmers. Human activities were especially influential in the growth of lowland blanket bog in western Ireland, where the acidic rocks provided favourable circumstances for peat development. Many western bogs developed on soils previously used by neolithic farmers, as is classically demonstrated at Céide fields, county Mayo.

There is an approximate correspondence between the distribution of blanket peat and areas with over 1250mm precipitation per annum, but the balance between precipitation and evaporation is equally significant. In uplands, precipitation is increased while evaporation and temperatures are reduced by altitude. Lowland or Atlantic blanket bog has high precipitation and low evapotranspiration as a

ORDNANCE SURVEY

● Fig. 11 Blanket bog near the Sally Gap in the Wicklow mountains. The central parts of the mountains consist of rounded granite uplands with numerous summits rising to over 600m. High precipitation and acid rocks have encouraged extensive peat growth, typically clothing all but the steepest slopes. Heather dominates the slopes with wetter blanket bog widespread on flatter summits. Peatland is only interrupted on the highest summits, on the steep slopes of glaciated glens and corrie crags. Erosion of the peat cover is evident, perhaps owing to natural wasting but also induced by cutting (which produces channels which accelerate run-off and allow gullies to develop), burning of heather by sheep farmers, and heavy sheep grazing. At the Sally Gap, peat removal has revealed pre-bog features.

consequence of position relative to the prevailing moist westerly air flow. There are species differences between these two types of blanket bog. For example, Atlantic bogs are often dominated by black bog rush and purple moor grass, the former species restricted largely to the western seaboard. Their sedge and grass dominated vegetation contrasts with the greater cover of ling, other heathers and bog mosses found in many of the upland blanket bogs. The difference is not related entirely to natural factors but is also a response to greater intensity of burning and grazing in the Atlantic blanket bogs.

In addition to plant species differences, micro-features add interest to what is too easily dismissed as a monotonous landscape. In areas of deep blanket bog, pools and hummocks can be found formed over basins and the bog may assume convex profiles similar to those of raised bogs. Elsewhere, in Mayo and Connemara, large pools and lakes punctuate the bog. In these lakes, islands free from grazing, with well grown heathers, crowberry and juniper, attest to the influence of sheep and burning in significantly reducing the vegetation of the surrounding Atlantic bogs.

R. TOMLINSON

● Fig. 10 An area of dense, hand-cut plots in north-west county Donegal. Heather-covered banks separate the individual turbary plots.

Fig. 12 The human role in blanket bog evolution. A) About 5000 years ago, all but the highest parts of the uplands had a woodland cover of pine and birch on a freely-draining mineral soil. Some of the rainfall intercepted by this vegetation was evaporated so that percolation down the soil profile was reduced. B) At various periods during the last two millennia BC, peat was initiated, possibly extending out from basins on the upland slopes as a result of climatic deterioration and the lower interception caused by people clearing trees for farming. With increased percolation, plant nutrients and clay particles were washed down the soil profile, leaving behind a progressively more acid soil; an impervious hard-pan sometimes formed at a depth in the soil, impeding drainage and encouraging waterlogging. C) As soil became more acidic, so plants adapted to this environment - heathers, sedges, rushes - increased and their remains accumulated as acid humus in the cool, damp conditions. Biological breakdown of plant remains was slow because of the plant species found and because of the harsh environment. As bog mosses invaded, so the soil became increasingly waterlogged and remaining trees were killed. D) In the waterlogged, anaerobic conditions, peat accumulated because of the lack of biological breakdown of plant material. Tree stumps, and sometimes man-made features such as field walls, were buried by the peat which in flatter areas or in basins reaches depths of three metres or more.

Intact peatland, not affected by past or present extraction, forest planting or erosion, is relatively rare and of declining extent in Ireland. Human activity has both reduced and fragmented the blanket peat landscapes. In the Republic of Ireland, an estimated fifteen per cent of blanket peatland has been cut away and in Northern Ireland almost a half has been cut at some time in the past. Forestry occupies large areas of the remaining blanket peatland, and reclamation for agriculture has reduced the original area by a considerable amount. On intact peatland, overgrazing by sheep is leading to serious erosion in many places.

Cutting by spade (hand cutting) is less common in blanket peatland than formerly, except in some limited areas where land ownership, turbary rights or local attitudes have prevented the widespread adoption of machines. In these areas, the distinctive vertical faces of peat may still be seen as they eat into the turbary plot. Sometimes, where the cutting is less intense, the face is into intact peatland. In other areas, turbary plots are so dense and so heavily used that they form a pattern of dark, square depressions separated by banks on which there is a profuse growth of heather.

R. TOMLINSON

● Fig. 13 Pool and hummock complexes occur in the blanket bogs, often, as here on the Antrim Plateau, over deep peat-filled basins. Indeed, these sites could be classified as raised bog within the expanse of blanket peat.

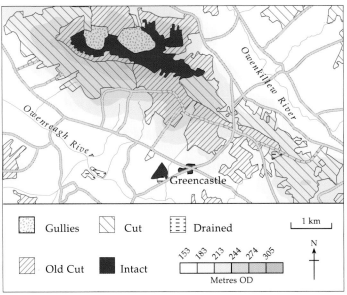

| | Gullies | | Cut | | Drained | 1 km |
| | Old Cut | ■ | Intact | | | |

153 183 213 244 274 305

Metres OD

N

● Fig. 14 The impact of peat cutting and reclamation on blanket bog landscape, low Sperrin mountains, county Tyrone. Reaching summit heights of 330m, the ridge between the Owenkillew and Owenragh rivers is generally gently sloping and rounded with peat extending down to about 200m. The lower limit of the peat is not a smooth one but has been affected by reclamation; hence the map shows a zig-zag boundary where ladder-like fields have extended up-slope and into peatland. Gentle slopes have allowed easy access, so that not only are there roads along the lower flanks of the ridge, but others which cross it and some roads and tracks which merely extend into the hillside. This network facilitated peat cutting; indeed, some of the tracks were specifically built for turbary. Intact peatland, unaffected by cutting, remains only on the most inaccessible part of the ridge and is surrounded by an extensive stretch of cut-over peatland. The sharp limits of the intact peat are again angular and indicate the way in which peat banks have eaten back into the bog. The cut-over area is now of relatively shallow peat, dominated by coarse grasses, sedges and heather, which has facilitated reclamation for agriculture.

In the last fifteen years, cutting of peat for fuel has revived in many areas, with the development of lightweight, tractor-driven 'sausage' machines which can extract the year's demand for household fuel in a few hours and without the hard labour involved in spade cutting. In Northern Ireland in 1991, for example, there were approximately 420 hand cutting incidences but 1020 sites of machine

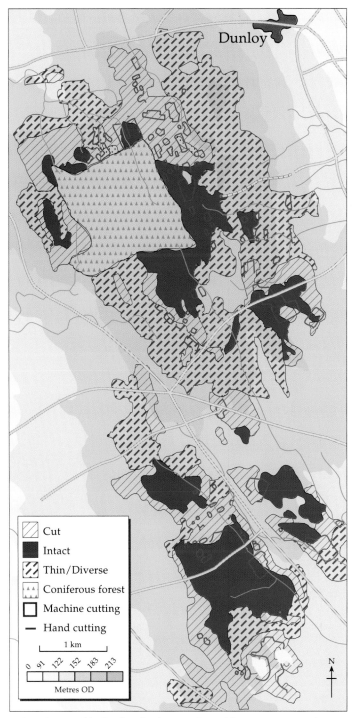

Dunloy

	Cut
■	Intact
	Thin/Diverse
▲	Coniferous forest
□	Machine cutting
—	Hand cutting

1 km

0 91 122 152 183 213

Metres OD

N

● Fig. 15 New blanket bog landscapes, Long Mountain, county Antrim. Although not so numerically preponderant as in some other areas, a large number of small plots of mechanised peat extraction occur mainly on formerly hand-cut areas, whereas the larger sites are on, or extend onto, areas of intact peat.

cutting which accounted for 3769 ha of blanket peatland. In contrast, hand cutting has virtually no areal extent in any one year, perhaps only eating about half a metre into the bog. Machine cutting is on a fundamentally different scale to traditional hand winning and is creating a new blanket peat landscape characterised by horizontal expanses of exposed peat rather than the traditional vertical face.

●Fig. 16 Peat winning by traditional methods; cutting, drying and transport on the MacGillycuddy Reeks, county Kerry. Bog conditions, and hence methods of working, varied considerably from place to place. A) Peat is generally cut by a special spade (sleán) from a neat vertical bank often almost down to the underlying mineral soil. Before cutting, the thin top layer of tough, fibrous sod, which makes poor fuel, is skimmed off, and may be spread below the bank for dry footing. In time, the pared sods consolidate so that rough grazing can redevelop on the cut-away at a lower level. B) The wet sods are wind-dried in small stooks on the pared surface and shrink considerably. C) They are then moved into progressively larger piles by barrow or, if the ground is wet and soft, by slipe, or sledge. D) Finally they are transferred from the bog and stacked in or near the farmsteads. A donkey with creels (strong baskets made with willow, or 'sally' rods) was the most dexterous means of transport on an irregular bog surface. A wooden sled, or slipe, was sometimes used to move the turf over wet bog surfaces. Larger conveyances on rollers also were used.

Mechanised cutting is widespread but sites tend to be concentrated in the most accessible areas, near to roads and tracks and on past-cut peat; their visual impact is therefore greater than their overall extent (in Northern Ireland, for example, about three per cent of the blanket peatland in 1990). Size and distributional patterns are related to turbary. The mechanised cutting in most cases merely replaces hand cutting on turbary plots in cut-over peatland. In Northern Ireland in 1990, 77% by area of machine cutting was on past-cut peatland, 64% of sites were less than one hectare and only 6% were above 31 ha. Many

larger cuttings tend to extend onto, or be developed on, intact peatland, possibly because high dividing banks within cut-over areas make extensive mechanised extraction difficult. This is not always the case, however, since large cuttings are produced by amalgamation of individual plots. The peat is cut as one operation on behalf of individual turbary holders in that area. Large-scale commercial extraction for horticulture or fuel is relatively rare in blanket peatland, in contrast to the raised bogs.

Expanses of bare peat are not restricted to areas of extraction. At higher altitudes, natural erosion leaves

behind small islands of peat capped by living vegetation (haggs), surrounded by extensive, quite friable peat which, especially when dry, may be eroded further and loosened by frost, wind and water action. Erosion on flatter uplands of deep peat often assumes a random network of channels but on slopes may consist of parallel to sub-parallel gullies.

CONSERVATION AND THE FUTURE

Less rewarding than raised bogs for large-scale commercial turf production and located in lightly populated upland and western areas, the blanket bogs have generally escaped acute land-use pressures. They are used for a range of activities; afforestation and reclamation for grass-land have made significant inroads and in recent years the peat has been affected by renewed erosion, attributable in part to intensified grazing and burning. Withdrawal of improvement grants and cutting back of agricultural production should reduce further 'improvement' of bog areas and increase forestry opportunities on lower, more fertile ground. However, small-scale harvesting with privately owned equipment is leading to more vigorous extraction of peat than ever before. While protection is required urgently for highly valued sites, a more fundamental need is for management strategies for bog landscapes as a whole. These should aim for a combination of land uses sympathetic to the landscape and compatible with the ecology of the bogs.

R. TOMLINSON

● Fig. 17 Branching channels on the high, flat summit of Sawel, Sperrin mountains, county Londonderry, with small islands (haggs) of peat left between.

BIBLIOGRAPHY

J. Cross, *Peatlands: wasteland or heritage?* (Dublin, 1989).

M. Cruickshank, R. Tomlinson, et. al., 'A peatland database for Northern Ireland: methodology and potential resource' in *Biology and Environment*, xcii (1993), B, pp 13-24.

G. Doyle (ed.), *Ecology and conservation of Irish peatland* (Dublin, 1990).

J. Feehan and G. O'Donovan, *The bogs of Ireland. An introduction to the natural, cultural and industrial heritage of Irish peatland* (Dublin, 1996).

P. Foss (ed.), *Irish peatlands. The critical decade* (Dublin, 1991).

P. Foss and C. O'Connell, *Irish peatland conservation plan 2000* (Dublin, 1996).

R. Hammond, *The peatlands of Ireland* (Dublin 1979).

F. Mitchell and B. Tuite, *The great bog of Ardee* (Dundalk, 1995).

R. Tomlinson, 'The erosion of peat in the uplands of Northern Ireland', in *Ir. Geog.*, xiv (1981), pp. 51-64.

H. Van Eck, *Irish bogs. A case for planning* (Nijmegen, 1984).

FORESTS AND WOODLANDS

The Irish countryside presents a deceptive impression of being well-wooded, since many trees are in overgrown hedgerows around small fields, in patches of scrub on steep slopes, or on land otherwise unsuitable for agriculture. Together, private woodland and state forests account for only 7% of the land area of Ireland, one of the lowest percentages in Europe. The vast majority is in conifers; broadleaved woodland constitutes less than 1% of the land area. These figures hide variation in the distribution of broadleaved woodlands, coniferous plantations, mixed woodlands and total wooded area. Satellite imagery now provides an all-Ireland cover, not easily obtained previously for woodlands outside forests because most surveys of private woodlands were by sampling or in specific areas.

Since the seventeenth-century despoliations, there has been an enduring perception of the bareness of the Irish landscape. The great gaelic lament poem *Cill Chais* used the cutting of the woodland in south Tipperary as a symbol for the destruction of the whole social order.

Cad a dhéanfaimid feasta gan adhmad
Tá deireadh na gcoillte ar lár
[What shall we do without timber
The last of our woods is gone]

Ireland's remarkable demographic and settlement history ensured that by the mid nineteenth century, it was among the countries most denuded of timber in all of Europe. Since then, only a gentle recovery has taken place.

The understanding of current resources in historical and ecological terms is crucial to the formulation of woodland policy. This is all the more pressing since EU agricultural policies and technical advances will ensure that large areas of farmland will be surplus to food production needs in the coming decades. Woodland is the main alternative, given Ireland's congeniality to specific conifer types, and given Europe's deficiency in timber resources. Accommodating these new and numerous forest developments, while meeting environmental, visual and social needs, is a major challenge for positive landscape planning.

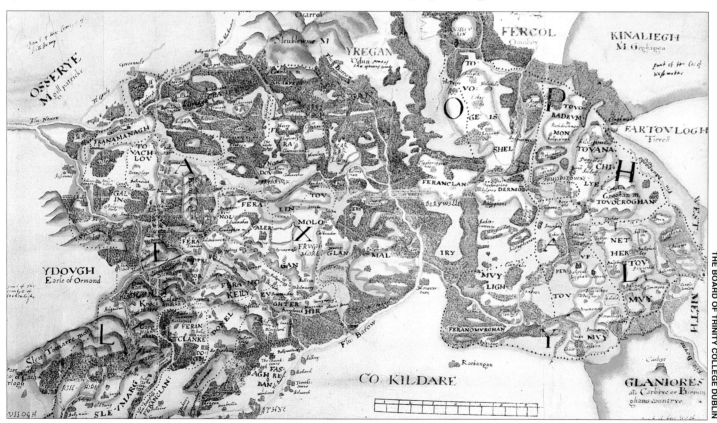

Fig. 1 Laois and Offaly *c*. 1562. This early map is exceptionally thorough and accurate in its depiction of the environment. At a scale of approximately 1:125,000 (half an inch to the mile), and with north to the right, it shows a typical tract of midlands landscape between the Barrow and Slieve Bloom. Colours are deployed with great vividness – green for woods (along with penned tree symbols), grey for bog, brown for upland. The distinctive esker ridges of the region are carefully shown, as are the woods, bogs and passes which loomed so large in Elizabethan English perceptions of the Irish midlands. The extent of surviving woodland is very high, especially in the foothills of the Slieve Blooms and in the river valleys. Note how woodland rings the bogs – a patterning which undoubtedly heightened perceptions of its pre-eminence in the landscape.

BROADLEAVED WOODLAND

ORIGIN

Broadleaved woodland is comparatively rare in Ireland. From *c.* 7500 BC onwards, the vegetation cover gradually developed from open grassland into woodland. Around 4500 BC, this 'wildwood' can be grouped into botanical provinces. Ireland was mainly in the hazel-elm zone: in the south-west and west, this yielded to oak-hazel and in the Galway and Mayo mountains to an outlier of the pine prevalent in the eastern Scottish highlands. The landscape was not continuous woodland, since raised bogs developed over basins left after the ice-sheets retreated. Mesolithic peoples had a minimal effect on this woodland, but a long period of clearance followed in the Neolithic, and from the Bronze Age the poorly wooded character of Ireland began to be established. Clearance accelerated in the Early Christian and medieval periods and estimates of the extent of woodland at the beginning of the seventeenth century vary from one-eighth of the whole country to only two per cent.

The date of 1600 AD is significant not only because of the imminent Plantation of Ulster and its associated woodland clearance, but because it is taken technically as the division between 'ancient' and 'recent' woodland, contemporary maps are first available and plantations (even-aged stands of trees usually of one or few species) become important. All primary woodland ('wildwood') is ancient, but more significantly, any secondary woodland (developed on land that was completely clear of trees at some time) present by 1600 has had time to acquire sufficient species and structures to render them indistinguishable from primary woodland. They can therefore also be regarded as ancient.

The survival, species content and structure of ancient woodlands depend not only on soils, slope and climate, but also on management techniques. Woodland existed in the past as wood-pasture, coppice-with-standards and coppice, amongst others, and tree management included coppicing and pollarding. Remaining ancient woodlands therefore vary in form and species content, in addition to differing from recent woodlands.

Investigations of specific woods in Ireland are few, but from at least the Early Christian period, there is evidence of coppicing. The extensive use of wattle for building in Hiberno-Norse Dublin and Cork implies this kind of woodland management and the Civil Survey (1654-6) records 'pasturable wood', 'woody pasture', 'underwood' and 'copps' which indicate that woodmanship or wood management continued at least into the seventeenth century. Thereafter, these skills declined in importance,

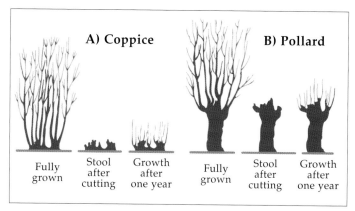

Fig. 2 Traditional methods of managing wood producing trees. A) Coppicing is the periodic cutting of trees at the base to produce many shoots rather than one main trunk. This gave a constant supply of wood – hazel and willow for wattle and basketry, oak and ash for fuel in ore-smelting furnaces. Formerly a widespread system of woodland management, coppicing results in even-aged stands, detectable hundreds of years later. B) Pollarding is simply coppicing at a height, to protect the shoots against grazing animals.

adding to the failure of many ancient woodlands to survive. However, some coppice and coppice-with-standards was present in the eighteenth and nineteenth centuries in Killarney and coppice wood management continued on the Fitzwilliam estate in south county Wicklow in the eighteenth century. Generally, Irish landowners adopted plantations earlier and more completely than in England, thereby replacing areas of traditional woodland management. Small patches of ancient woodland possibly linger within such plantations; their identification requires intensive fieldwork and documentary study.

While the loss of woodmanship, which maintained tree vigour, contributed to the decline of ancient woodlands, the main reason for their reduction was felling. Much wood was used for cooperage and iron smelting but the major pressure for clearance since 1600 AD was the growing demand for farm land. Only around ten per cent of woodland present in the mid-1600s remained at the time of the first edition of the Ordnance Survey (1830-44); most had been converted into farmland in a phase of unprecedented population expansion and land hunger. In 1850, Thomas Carlyle described Ireland as 'one of the barest, raggedest countries now known; far too ragged a country, with patches of beautiful park and fine cultivation, like shreds of bright scarlet on a beggar's clouted coat'.

TYPES OF BROADLEAVED WOODLAND

Oak woodlands on mainly base-poor soils

The ancient woodlands of Killarney around Lough Leane and Muckross Lake suffered considerable clearance and modification between the seventeenth and nineteenth centuries. This included coppicing and large-scale planting

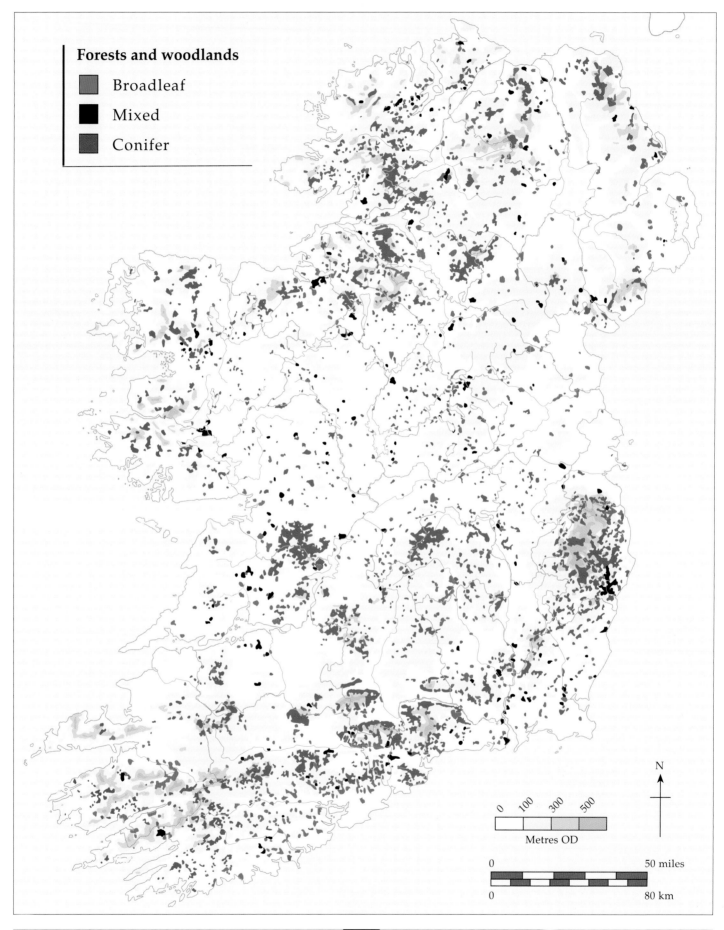

Forests and woodlands

- Broadleaf
- Mixed
- Conifer

0 100 300 500

Metres OD

N

0   50 miles

0   80 km

programmes following substantial felling between 1800 and 1810. Oak was the main species planted but Scots pine, ash, sycamore, larch, beech and more exotic conifers were included. Despite these modifications, large areas of the woods have developed to their present seemingly natural state as a result of the dual protection of estate management and the agriculturally useless steep slopes. The term 'ancient woodland' does not imply an absence of felling – simply that regeneration takes place without intervening use as pasture or tillage. Whereas the Killarney tree layers resemble ancient woodland, the field layer is poor because deer and sheep grazing has been at high levels for the past two centuries. Saplings are rare because of browsing.

The Killarney woodlands are not all of the same type. The most extensive (1200 ha) are of sessile oak, forming almost pure stands of high forest (stands of continuous mature trees) with few clearings. The trees are between thirteen and twenty metres in height and have an understorey of holly. Birch and rowan are frequent and the famed Mediterranean element, the strawberry tree, is common at lower woodland margins. Ground flora is dominated by mosses and lichens and, where present, the field layer – bent grass, hard fern, wood-rush, wood sorrel, bracken and bilberry – reflects the acid soils of Devonian sandstone. The extreme western location and the oceanic environment ensure that the Killarney oakwoods support rich epiphytic communities of mosses, liverworts and lichens and are a type example of western oakwoods.

Reenadinna Wood on the Muckross peninsula occupies 25 ha and is developed on limestone pavement and reef; the wood is of yew with some hazel and holly. This is one of the rarest woodland types in Ireland, although the trees are under pressure from deer stripping the bark. The limestone pavement is covered by mosses and liverworts. Another woodland type, carr or swamp, occurs at the edge of Muckross lake. It is mainly of alder and is amongst the largest of its type in Ireland.

The extent of the Killarney woods is exceptional: other ancient or relict woodlands are smaller and protected by locations unfavourable to agriculture. (The term 'relict' woodland is used for sites where survival from primary woodland is indicated but whose history is obscure.) Shannawoneen Wood (c. 34 ha) is located two kilometres north of Spiddal, county Galway and possibly represents the only surviving native (primary) woodland in coastal

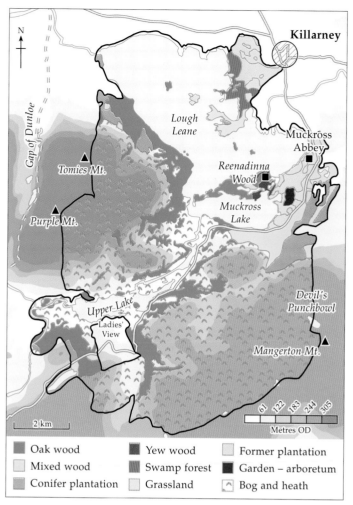

● Fig. 4 Killarney National Park, county Kerry, and its woodlands. The famous landscape of Killarney contain glaciated lakes set amid heathery mountains with luxuriant evergreen woodland vegetation on the lower slopes. Sheltered by the high sandstone mass of the MacGillycuddy Reeks, the area has a markedly mild, equable climate. The Upper Lake lies within the northern, ice-scoured slopes of the Reeks; Lough Leane lies below it on drift-covered carboniferous limestone.

southern Connemara, escaping clearance because of its boulder-strewn floor. The dominant species is sessile oak, forming an almost complete canopy six to twelve metres high in the western part of the wood. Although the woodland has extended in some parts since the 1830s, its main outline seems remarkably constant.

Derryclare, another small but ancient Connemara woodland, is managed as a nature reserve. It has survived partly because of the rocky surface and through a ditch and peat bank constructed in the nineteenth century which has restricted grazing. The woodland is of several parts: on steep, lime-free slopes, oak is dominant, whereas on carbon-

Fig. 3 (left) Wooded areas 1990. Broadleaved woodland has a scattered and patchy distribution, associated mainly with demesnes. There are areas of greater concentration, notably the Killarney woodlands, and a belt through Cork, Waterford and Kilkenny. In the north, there are relatively extensive woodlands around Upper and Lower Lough Erne. Large parts of the country, however, are devoid of broadleaved woodland because altitude or peat cover prevent tree growth. The scattered distribution of mixed woodland is related mainly to demesnes; for example, the area inland of Arklow which stretches through the Vale of Avoca northward is demesne-studded. Coniferous forests show an apparently random pattern of many small patches with larger forests in the south-east and south (Wicklow, Wexford, south Kilkenny, Waterford, south Tipperary, Cork), in the west and north-west (Galway, Mayo, Leitrim, Fermanagh, Donegal, Londonderry and north Antrim) and in central Ireland, where Slieve Bloom and Slieve Aughty have striking concentrations.

In county Down, Rostrevor oakwood, on steep slopes overlooking the town, is almost pure oak 'high forest' with a holly understorey. The present woodland is possibly derived from regeneration following felling in the 1730s. No period of tillage or pasture is thought to have intervened between felling and regrowth, so that this wood too may be regarded as ancient.

Woodlands on base-rich soils

Oak woodlands, or often oak-ash woodlands, also occur on base-rich parent materials, but in many cases these have been planted and managed to produce 'high forest' with little undergrowth. For example, oak and ash woodlands are present at Charleville (county Cork) and Abbeyleix (county Laois) where both species can attain heights of over twenty-five metres. Some trees at Charleville have been dated to between 350 and 450 years old and could be successors of the wildwood.

Relict woodlands on limestone soils, as with oak woodlands on base-poor materials, are found most often where land is unsuitable for agriculture – on limestone pavement or steep rocky slopes. Much present limestone woodland is really hazel-dominated scrub whose structure depends on exposure to prevailing winds. In the western Burren in county Clare, hazel scrub may be only one and a half metres in height on more exposed pavement but it reaches to eight metres in sheltered valleys and hollows. In the eastern Burren, low forest up to eleven metres high may be found, although this is thought to be largely secondary.

Well-developed hazel woodland can be seen in parts of the glens of Antrim, particularly on the western slopes of Glenariff where basalt gives way to chalky drift. Here, hazel forms over half of the canopy, which averages nine metres in height, and has intermixed hawthorn, birch, willow and mountain ash. There are a few emergent ash, but also sycamore, wych elm and occasional beech and larch.

Marble Arch Nature Reserve, in the limestone country of Fermanagh, is an example of ash woodland, although it may be divided into three zones. In the north and northwest, ash is dominant with little oak or beech. Birch, willow, wych elm, alder, rowan and hawthorn are frequent and there is an understorey of hazel. On the west side of the gorge, there is a zone of beech-with-oak, while an ash-oak zone occurs in the east and south.

Woodlands of wetter areas

In wetter areas, woodland composition depends partly on the acidity/alkalinity of the water. Carr woodland, like that at Killarney, can be found in the Gearagh, in the Lee valley near Macroom, county Cork. Here on drier islands between

ROY TOMLINSON

Fig 5 Breen Wood, county Antrim. This wood, with its high epiphytic moss and lichen communities, is typical of a western oakwood. The field layer is poor; following fencing to prevent grazing, it has become dominated by wood-rush.

ate-rich areas with deep, free-draining soils, hazel and ash proliferate. However, the two areas are not sharply delineated so that much of the site is in transitional woodland. Localised areas of waterlogging also vary in their cover depending on alkalinity. There is a well-developed lichen flora and the species richness may indicate an ancient status.

Breen Wood, seven kilometres south of Ballycastle in county Antrim, occupies marginal meltwater channels whose precipitous sides ensured its survival. Managed as a National Nature Reserve, it is regarded as a relict oakwood. The oaks have been coppiced in the past and are intermixed with birch which becomes dominant on the wetter plateau between the meltwater channels. The wood has undergone periods of clearance, the last dated to around 500 AD. Regrowth occurred around 1350 AD, well before the threshold date of 1600 AD for recognition as ancient.

DAPHNE POCHIN-MOULD

Fig. 6 The Gearagh, near Macroom, county Cork. This semi-natural woodland flourishes, beyond the reach of livestock, in the wet environment of the Lee valley where the river flows in numerous narrow channels. Willow and alder dominate the wettest parts, with oak, ash and birch on the drier islands.

Species sponsored by the Dublin Society

By 1744	**In 1760s**
Oak	Silver fir
Ash	Norway spruce
Elm	Scots pine
Beech	Weymouth pine
Walnut	Larch
Chestnut	Norway maple
	Sweet chestnut
	Black cherries

In 1780s	
Purple beech	Black oak
Copper beech	White oak
Scarlet maple	Lebanese cedar
American elm	Tulip tree
American birch	Athenian poplar
Scarlet oak	Black larch
Turkey oak	Whole-leaf ash
Prickly oak	Cembo pine
Turner oak	Swamp pine
Lucombe oak	Newfoundland spruce
American swamp oak	Hemlock
Champagne oak	Two thorned acacia

the braided channels, the woodland is of oak, ash, and downy birch with an understorey of hazel and hawthorn. In wetter depressions and on stream sides, the trees are mainly willows and alder; the wood margins have spindle, guelder rose and cherry. There is a rich field layer with many spring- flowering plants.

Whereas in many parts of lowland Ireland, bogs have disappeared completely, there are frequent cut-over bogs which have become drier and colonised by trees. In some areas, these newly wooded bogs make a significant contribution to the woodland total and to the landscape; in south Armagh, they account for one-quarter of the woodland area.

MIXED WOODLAND

ORIGIN

Although woodland loss was considerable from the seventeenth century onwards, there was some planting. Initially, this was in shelter belts around new farm houses and in avenues leading to big houses; it consisted of recently introduced exotic species such as sycamore, beech, walnut, lime and horse-chestnut. Planting in blocks began in the early 1700s and was encouraged by the Dublin Society from 1740 onwards. The Society awarded prizes for planting and nominated suitable species. These lists influenced fashions in planting and may account for some of the present content of demesne woodlands.

During the eighteenth century, an estimated 53,500 ha was planted in private woodlands. Of this, almost a quarter was broadleaved, a very small area coniferous and three-quarters mixed. An emphasis on oaks is notable, since they comprised one-fifth of these plantings. The

fashion was to create a park which appeared 'natural'. By 1841, there were almost 140,000 ha of plantation but conifers now represented seven per cent of trees planted and mixed plantings four-fifths. Broadleaves were down to twelve per cent with oaks at nine per cent. Throughout the Victorian era, plant collectors scoured the world and fashions changed to conifers, and in particular to those from western North America which included Douglas and Noble firs, Sitka spruce and Lodgepole pine. These plantations further diminished ancient woodland as indigenous tree species were replaced with more desirable exotic ones. In this century, demesne woods have been extended or replanted with conifers.

EXAMPLES OF MIXED AND PLANTED WOODLANDS

The woods of Mourne Park, county Down are typical of a demesne and show how planting fashions changed over time. An important focus in the landscape, they form one of the most significant areas of woodland on the south side of the Mournes. There was established woodland around the house in the late eighteenth century, some of which may be original and not the planting of landscape improvers. Presently, the park consists of several named woodlands which can be traced through various Ordnance Survey editions. Most woodland was established by the middle of the nineteenth century and the park escaped large-scale conifer planting.

Nearby Ballyedmond is more clearly divisible into distinct areas. The 1834 Ordnance Survey map shows the

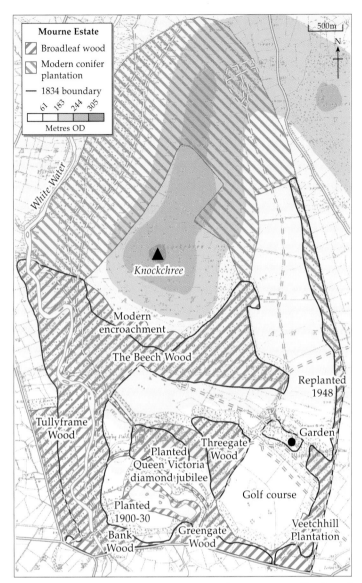

Fig 7. Mourne Park, south county Down. The various woodlands and periods of planting are shown. Despite its name, Beech Wood has a range of species including oaks, sweet chestnut, ash, Scots pine and Grand fir. While beech comprised only one-third of trees sampled in 1985, their impact is dominant when viewed from a distance because they were planted in groups. The composition of Threegate Wood illustrates the use of different species at various times. Whereas the pre-1834 woodland has pedunculate oak, sweet chestnut, beech, horse-chestnut and lime, with some younger sycamore, the sections planted between 1834 and 1859 contain Douglas fir, yew, larch and elm. The eastern banks of the White Water are steep and some of the trees here may possibly be successors of primary woodland, but most of Tullyframe Wood has been planted. Beech is dominant and accompanied by ash, sycamore, oak, lime and Scots pine. A similar composition occurs in Greengate Wood, which is pre-1834, whereas the Veetchill and Standing Stone plantations (1834-59) are pure oak.

beginning of the park with mainly deciduous trees scattered through it, in a belt along its eastern margin and in an avenue. By the turn of the century, the park had extended westward and had clumps of predominantly conifer trees – principally Scots pine, larch, silver fir and Austrian pine.

Planting in the eighteenth and nineteenth centuries also took place outside the demesnes in the surrounding

Fig. 8 Threegate Wood, Mourne Park, south county Down. This stand of beech is part of the planting to create a 'natural' landscape; it shows the typical lack of field and ground layers of a beech woodland.

Fig. 9 Ballyedmond, south county Down. The early planting (A) is mainly deciduous and reflects the 'natural' style of landscaping (this is continued in recent planting seen in the foreground). The later nineteenth-century planting (B) in the west of the park is mainly conifers. Note how the band of recent forest planting in the background (on the Cooley peninsula in county Louth) interrupts the slope of the hills.

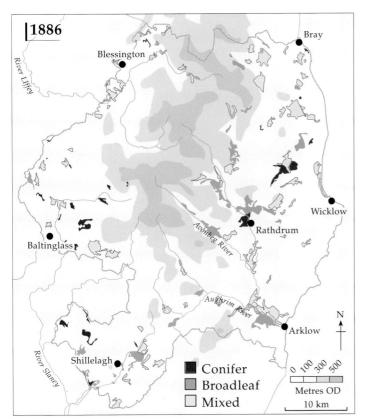

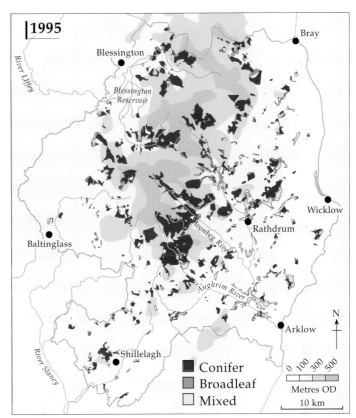

Fig. 10 The spread of forests in county Wicklow, as mapped by Mary Kelly-Quin, from the end of the nineteenth century to the present. Despite clearances from early periods, woodlands survived in the county, fluctuating in size through the centuries. Medieval iron works in Glendalough were supplied with local charcoal and from the seventeenth to the early nineteenth century, wood supply from eastern valleys and Shillelagh and Coolattin in the south-west was sufficient to support a variety of timber-consuming industries, including ironworks and shipbuilding in Arklow. A state forestry school was established at Avondale in 1904 and some of the first state forests were planted in the county. Planting expanded in the early 1920s with the most extensive plantations after 1950. Wicklow today is among the most heavily afforested counties with eighteen per cent of its area under forests, mainly of Sitka spruce. The present distribution of woodland is of small, scattered woods of varied age and composition on the mountain slopes, with new, extensive coniferous plantations in the more elevated and lightly populated central areas. Few plantations, however, extend above 500m. The most striking feature of the two maps is the extent to which forestry has moved decisively to upland areas in the intervening period.

countryside, particularly to enhance the attractiveness of glens, rocky knolls and even archaeological sites. Banagher and Carndaisy Glen, both in county Londonderry, are examples of attractive wooded valleys in which oak dominates but in which there are also beech, sycamore, ash, hazel, elm, sweet chestnut, Norway spruce and Douglas fir amongst others. The picturesque valleys of east county Wicklow, such as the Glen of the Downs, the Devil's Glen and the Dargle Valley, also possess impressive ornamental woods reflecting the presence of numerous major demesnes. Harmonious union of man-made and natural features is the hallmark of the best Irish manner in landscaping, greatly enhancing the aesthetic quality of the countryside.

CONIFEROUS FORESTS

DISTRIBUTION

Around four-fifths of the forest area is in public ownership and over ninety per cent of this is in conifers. The map of coniferous forests is closely comparable with a map of state forests. Except for a few nineteenth and early

twentieth-century plantations, it is only since the late 1980s that conifer planting by private individuals and companies has been significant.

State forests are widely distributed. Most land was acquired through offers by owners and consequently the two outstanding features of the location of state forests are fragmentation and restriction to poor soil. Efficient layout and management of forests under these circumstances has been difficult, limiting the opportunities to consider the visual effects of forest siting.

ORIGIN

Following the Land Acts of the late nineteenth and early twentieth centuries, land came to be owned by the tenants, creating a landscape dominated by small family farms. A fierce attachment to land, which remains strong despite economic problems resulting from a weak agricultural structure, has forced forestry into areas unwanted for agriculture. These mainly peat-covered areas in the uplands, the west and the midlands are often of high scenic value. Even in these agriculturally unfavourable areas, land can

DAPHNE POCHIN-MOULD

Fig. 11 Forestry on the Comeragh Mountains, county Waterford. The planting of marginal hill slopes throws the dark, sharply outlined patches of new forestry into stark visual prominence, an effect clearly seen on the bare flanks of the Comeraghs. This jarring impact on the landscape will be difficult to mollify in the short term.

be unavailable since much is in commonage, joint ownership, joint grazing or turbary rights.

An immediate effect of the Land Acts was a diminution of woodland and forest. Estate owners lost interest in maintaining timber plantations, obtaining capital by selling standing timber. Former tenants also asset-stripped, seeing timber as a source of much-needed capital. In the early 1920s, a woodland total of approximately 100,700 ha was only two-thirds that of eighty years before. Consequently, there were moves to develop forestry but until the late 1940s, in both the Republic and Northern Ireland, forest planting was marked by false starts and indecision and there was neither money nor significant political support for it. This period encompassed both World War I, when further forest destruction took place, and the creation of an independent Irish state, with its insistent emphasis on the maintenance of small farm communities.

RECENT TRENDS IN FORESTRY

FORESTRY IN THE REPUBLIC OF IRELAND

The *White Paper on Economic Recovery* (1949) was a major turning point, not only in planting plans but in moving away from private to state forestry. Any expansion of state forests required an inventory of suitable land. A 1950 plan proposed that forestry should have a two-tier structure – commercial forestry and 'social' forestry, the latter largely in the west. This social aspect, mainly to counter unemployment and emigration, ensured that by 1965 almost half of the annual total planting programme was in the west.

In the 1970s, forestry had become unpopular, at first because of economic recession and later because agriculture prospered under the Common Agricultural Policy (CAP) of the European Community. Alternative enterprises

were not considered. By the 1980s, perceptions were changing; farmers and landowners began to see forestry as economically viable. Additionally, public forestry still had difficulty in obtaining land. These forces led government to consider a change in emphasis from public to private forestry. The major incentive to private forestry was the EC Western Development Programme. This 'Western Package' was initially moderately successful, but through extension and changes to the programme, there were dramatic results. Of particular note were the Compensatory Allowance Schemes from 1986 onwards, whereby farmers who had received livestock headage payments were compensated if they afforested all or part of their land. From 1988, all agricultural land in disadvantaged areas was included rather than only marginal land, disadvantaged areas were expanded, and part-time and retired farmers and farmers' co-operatives were included. The structural problems of agriculture, limitations in milk production by the quota system, and the low returns from traditional farm enterprises all led farmers to consider forestry as a viable option, especially when there was support both for planting and the period of establishment. The state forest enterprise was re-organised in 1989 into a commercial state-owned company (Coillte).

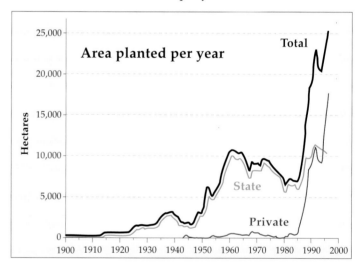

Fig. 12 State and private afforestation levels in the Republic of Ireland, 1900 to the present. State afforestation commenced early in the century but there was no substantial expansion until the 1930s. This was halted during World War II but vigorous afforestation recommenced in the late 1940s. The expansionary trend was checked in the 1960s and 1970s as farm prosperity made land acquisition more difficult and because of government financial constraints. Up to this time, almost all forests were state-owned, but in the 1980s the emphasis shifted to encouragement of private afforestation. Substantial private and public afforestation occurred under the stimulus of substantial funding from the EU. Private planting now greatly exceeds that of the state. Previously confined largely to marginal hill land, forests are now expanding on improved farmland and a rapid increase of the forested area is anticipated in the coming decades. Afforestation in Northern Ireland has been less eventful. The main period of expansion was 1946-1969, and today the main aim of forest policy is the sustainable management of existing forests and steady expansion of tree cover for the timber industry and amenity purposes.

DAPHNE POCHIN-MOULD

Fig. 13 Coniferous plantations on bogland, near Abbeyfeale, county Limerick. Extensive afforestation of both upland and lowland bogs has occurred in recent decades, concentrated mainly in the west. Planting is often patchy and uncoordinated, with negative visual effects.

The 'Forestry Operational Programme 1989-93', approved by the EU in 1990, represented an expansion of the Western Package. By 1993, the annual planting rate of the private sector doubled as compared with 1988 and public sector planting increased by sixty per cent in the same period. Additionally, the programme assisted in improving existing woodlands, reconstituted damaged forests and promoted forest exploitation through access roads. A feature of the programme was species diversification and encouragement for broadleaved planting through higher grants than for conifers. These incentives have continued in the most recent policies, with the ultimate aim that broadleaf planting will reach one-fifth of total planting, to the benefit of both landscape and environment.

These and other recent developments have elicited a considerable expansion of forest cover, but they have been criticised. Despite encouragement to plant broadleaves, the emphasis remains on conifers and on planting areas less favourable for agriculture, which frequently sustain valued environments. Increasing awareness of the ecological value of peatlands may afford protection against excessive planting, but the poorer agricultural lands with less fashionable damp meadows and scrub have valuable habitats too. Conifer plantations are not a traditional element in the Irish landscape; rectangular blocks of sharply pointed trees bear little resemblance to the attractive irregularity and rounded outlines of broadleaves.

The effects of afforestation on streams have also caused concern. High acidity and associated increases in aluminium concentrations are detrimental to salmonid populations; drainage for plantations can change river regimes; trees planted near to rivers can increase shade. These criticisms should be seen in the context of the distribution of recent forestry; the vast majority of private planting has

been in the west with the greatest rates in Mayo, Galway, Donegal, Kerry, Cork and Clare. Taken together with the pattern of state forests, a distinctive Irish landscape quality could be lost, particularly in the west, where vistas of treeless bogs constitute a unique and much loved element.

FORESTRY IN NORTHERN IRELAND

Some early state acquisitions in Ireland were in what is now Northern Ireland; for example, estate woodlands at Ballykelly in county Derry, Knockmany in county Tyrone, and Castlecaldwell in county Fermanagh were acquired between 1910 and 1913. Despite this, when the Northern Ireland Ministry of Agriculture assumed responsibility for forestry in 1923, there were less than 2000 ha of forest: yet throughout the 1923-46 period, the annual planting rate was low. Annual planting rates peaked in the 1960s and early 1970s, following the 1953 Forest Act which implemented a three point policy: to create home-grown timber resources, to provide employment and to encourage private planting. A White Paper in 1970 proposed that 120,000 ha of forest should be planted (90,000 ha in state forest) by 2000 AD, but the annual planting rate has fallen. This results from two inter-related problems. First, as in the Republic of Ireland, land acquisition in large blocks was difficult in a countryside of small family farms. This has led to expensive land acquisition and the random pattern of forests, notably in Fermanagh. Second, the more available hill-land is predominantly in blanket peat where a restricted supply of plant nutrients limits growth. Peat also requires drainage before planting, increasing the risks of windthrow since the spread of shallow root plates is constrained by drains. More recently, as in the Republic, peatland planting has met with environmental opposition.

ROY TOMLINSON

Fig. 14 The Batt estate, south-west Mourne mountains, county Down. Individual trees and groups of conifers have sharp outlines in sympathy with the glaciated landforms. The incomplete cover of rather poorly-grown trees gives a rough texture which parallels the rocky slopes, only thinly covered by drift.

ROY TOMLINSON

ROY TOMLINSON

● Fig. 15 The forest edge at Glenmacnass waterfall, county Wicklow. The geological character is evident through the broken tree cover and the shape and texture of the conifers in this instance conforms with the jagged rocks. Overall, there is an arresting sympathy of tones and textures.

● Fig. 16 Seen from above, the woods in the Rostrevor valley, county Down, enhance the landforms. The woodlands mimic the form of the land, the curves of the valley and the move from incised river to rounded slopes. Tree crowns are rounded and the canopy undulating; tones are varied from the mix of species, especially oaks and beech. The soft greens and browns complement the tones of agricultural land in the valley and heathland on the uppermost slopes.

In future, there will be a general presumption against afforestation of heather moorland, blanket bog and raised bog; undisturbed or cut-over bog capable of natural regeneration also will not be planted. State forestry has been dominated by conifers and particularly by Sitka spruce (three-quarters of new plantings in 1990), with Lodgepole pine on wetter sites.

The annual planting rate for private woodland implied in 1970 has not been achieved; between 1970 and 1986, it was about 112 ha per annum. Grant schemes therefore have been extended; these have given higher grants for planting broadleaves, encouraged rehabilitation and regeneration of existing woodlands, and attempted to interest farmers in tree planting, not merely for conservation, landscape and amenity purposes, but also as part of farm diversification. Thus, although not on the same scale as in the Republic, where there has been more emphasis on productive forestry, there have been similar aims, and private planting has increased sharply since the late 1980s.

The emphasis on broadleaves demonstrates growing awareness that woodlands and forests are a highly visible landscape component. Concern about conifer plantations blanketing uplands has increased as has disquiet about removal of hedges, scrub and small treed areas, as a consequence of attempts to capitalise on the Common Agricultural Policy. CAP surpluses eventually became indefensible but the decline of the small farming communities also had to be prevented – hence the switch from production subsidies to environmental support. The expressed need for woodland conveniently fitted the bill; woods could be extended and managed to meet environmental concerns and also provide some diversification. However, not all of the desirable trends, especially

increased broadleaf planting, are possible in Ireland, where soils and climate are less conducive than in some other parts of the EU.

LANDSCAPE VALUE OF WOODS AND FORESTS

The issue of landscape appreciation is raised by public attachment to broadleaved trees and hostility towards conifers. Modern coniferous plantations, it is argued, smother the land; unity in diversity is replaced by uniformity. However, the generalisation that conifer plantations are detrimental to landscape quality needs to be tempered. On monotonous expanses of blanket bog,

DEPARTMENT OF ARTS, CULTURE AND THE GAELTACHT

● Fig. 17 Killarney woodlands, county Kerry. The woodlands have some sharp boundaries but generally trees lessen in density and height and merge into the land; woodland extends in tongues up streamsides and hollows, emphasising the landforms. The different woodland types, species and density of trees give subtle changes in tone and texture which harmonise with the cover of mountains and lowlands and change in sympathy with the seasons.

conifer plantations may be as attractive as peatland vegetation; whilst vast conifer forests are bland, of unvaried tones and of even height and texture, peatland vegetation too is unvaried, at least from a distance. The abrupt edge effects of forests are their most detrimental feature, but linear plantings occupying only part of a view are also intrusive. Straight edges running directly across or downslope destroy any unity with landforms; there is often a harsh change from heathers and grasses to taller, very dense trees and tones change discordantly from the yellow-greens of the peatland to the solid, dark blue-green of the conifers. Planting over the skyline also intrudes into the general outline of the land, especially if there are different tree heights or fire breaks.

Coniferous plantations can have a positive impact on landscape quality, especially if the trees are not in a continuous blanket and allow the underlying surfaces to show through. Variety in tone and textures can be produced, achieving an overall accord of trees and landforms.

Many remaining broadleaved woodlands have been planted or have survived in steeply sloping valleys and glens. Here the billowing trees, merging textures and tonal variety create some of our most treasured areas, as for example in the Wicklows, the Sperrins and the Mournes.

The Killarney scenery is world renowned and the woodlands play a considerable part in its attractiveness. The deciduous woodland clothes many of the slopes but not in a continuous cover; rather, there are irregular gaps through which the underlying rock may be glimpsed or in which there are treed parklands. The mosses and other epiphytes add to the profusion of the vegetation, stifling noise, and contributing to the humid, calm atmosphere. Oliver Rackham, a major woodland historian, has declared these luxuriant wet carpets to be the Irish equivalent of rain forests, in terms of their astonishing genetic diversity. These woodlands also promote a feeling of well-being which enhances their landscape appeal.

The value of trees and woods was keenly appreciated by the landscape architects who designed parks around the houses of eighteenth- and nineteenth-century landlords. This interest has been re-awakened, though not on such a grand scale, with official attempts to encourage planting around farms for landscape purposes. Most Irish landscapes can absorb some afforestation, providing it is sympathetically planned. An expanding private forest sector could lead to considerable scenic change, and the harmonious integration of many small projects poses explicit challenges for landscape policy and design.

BIBLIOGRAPHY

J. Cruickshank and M. Cruickshank, 'The development of humus-iron podsol profiles, linked by radiocarbon dating and pollen analysis to vegetation history' in *Oikos*, xxxvi (1981), pp 238-53.

DANI, Forest Service, *Afforestation – the DANI statement on environmental policy* (Belfast, 1993).

G. Dunstan, 'Forests in the landscape' in F. Aalen (ed.), *The future of the Irish landscape* (Dublin, 1985), pp 93-153.

K. Edwards, 'The anthropogenic factor in vegetational history' in K. Edwards and W. Warren (ed.), *The quaternary history of Ireland* (London, 1985), pp 187-220 .

E. Farrell, 'Land acquisition for forestry' in J. Blackwell and F. Convery (ed.), *Promise and performance: Irish environmental policies analysed* (Dublin, 1983), pp 156-67.

D. Ferguson and V. Westhoff, 'An account of the flora and vegetation of Derryclare Wood, Connemara (county Galway), Western Ireland' in *Proc. Royal Dutch Acad. of Sci.*, xc (1987), pp 139-72.

Forest Service, *Forestry operational programme 1989-1993* (Dublin, 1991).

D. Gillmor, 'The upsurge in private afforestation in the Republic of Ireland' in *Ir. Geog.*, xxv (1992), pp 89-97.

C. Guyer and C. Edwards, 'The role of farm woodland in Northern Ireland: an appraisal' in *Ir. Geog.*, xxii (1989), pp 78-85.

M. Jones, 'Coppice wood management in the eighteenth century: an example from county Wicklow' in *Irish Forestry*, xliii (1986), pp 15-31.

D. Kelly, 'The native forest vegetation of Killarney, south-west Ireland: an ecological account' in *J. Ecol.*, lxix (1981), pp 437-72.

D. Kelly and E. Kirby, 'Irish native woodlands over limestone' in *J. Life Sci. R. Dublin Soc.*, iii (1982), pp 181-98.

C. Kilpatrick, *Northern Ireland Forest Service: a history* (Belfast, 1987).

E. Kirby and M. O'Connell, 'Shannawoneen Wood, county Galway, Ireland: the woodland and saxicolous communities and the epiphytic flora' in *J. Life Sci. R. Dublin Soc.*, iv (1982), pp 73-96.

J. Larner, *The oakwoods of Killarney* (Dublin, 1992).

E. McCracken, *The Irish woods since Tudor times* (Newton Abbot, 1971).

E. Neeson, *A history of Irish forestry* (Dublin, 1991).

G. O'Sullivan, *Final report CORINE land cover (Ireland) project* (Dublin, 1994).

G. Peterken, *Woodland conservation and management* (London, 1981).

J. Pilcher, 'Application of dendrochronological techniques to the investigation of woodland history' in *Irish Naturalists Journal*, xix (1979), pp 377-80.

J. Pilcher and S. Mac an tSaoir (ed.), *Woods, trees and forests in Ireland* (Dublin, 1995).

O. Rackham, *Ancient woodland: its history, vegetation and uses in England* (London, 1980).

R. Tomlinson, *Tree survey of the Mourne and Slieve Croob AONB* (1986); *Armagh AONB* (1988); *Sperrins and North Derry AONBs* (1989). Reports to Environment Service, Department of the Environment for Northern Ireland.

W. Watts, 'Contemporary accounts of the Killarney woods 1580-1870' in *Ir. Geog.*, xvii (1984), pp 1-13.

FIELDS

Ireland currently possesses a heavily enclosed rural landscape. Eighty per cent of the surface is devoted to agriculture and the farmed land is everywhere divided into fields separated by continuous and permanent enclosures. These enclosures are the most pervasive features of the cultural landscape, allying it with the Atlantic fringe of Europe but distinguishing it from many continental areas where farmland has traditionally been laid out in open-fields which lacked obtrusive divisions.

Sporadic enclosures have long characterised the landscape, varying in their extent from period to period. The ubiquitous spread of enclosed fields did not affect Ireland until the post-Plantation period and was most marked during the eighteenth-century agricultural revolution. Despite the great scale and thorough nature of this recent landscape transformation, environmental constraints and historical inertia have ensured much variety in the shape and size of fields and in the materials and methods used to build field boundaries. Older regional contrasts have persisted in the new enclosure patterns; the individuality of the north is still recognisable as well as differences between the richer east and the poorer west of the country. Often there is intricate variety at local level.

Field boundaries have an estimated total length of 830,000 km and occupy 1.5 per cent of the land area, a higher percentage than that of deciduous forest. The vegetation growing on them influences micro-climates and contributes substantially to the biodiversity of the rural environment. Visually, enclosures dominate the cultural landscape, framing or obscuring the view for those who travel through the countryside. In many areas, the hedged banks, vivid in spring with blossoming furze, hawthorn and blackthorn, are the only features breaking the green monotony of the grassland blanket.

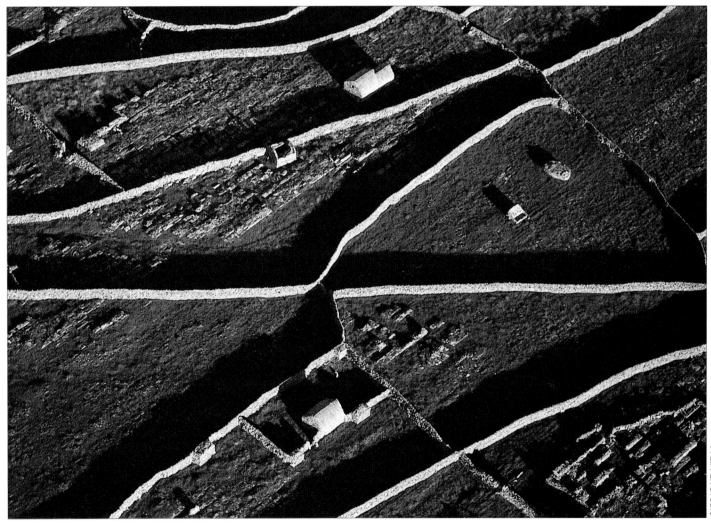

●Fig. 1 Fields on Inishmore, county Galway. Walls are an essential component of the Irish enclosure pattern and vernacular building skills can create strikingly aesthetic effects.

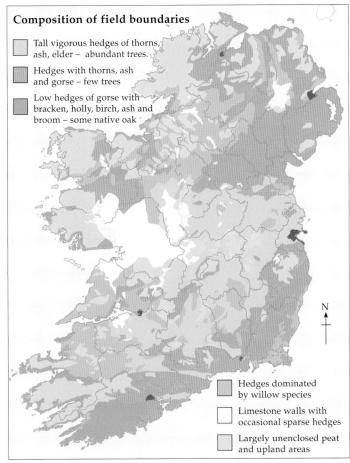

Composition of field boundaries

☐ Tall vigorous hedges of thorns, ash, elder – abundant trees.

☐ Hedges with thorns, ash and gorse – few trees

☐ Low hedges of gorse with bracken, holly, birch, ash and broom – some native oak

☐ Hedges dominated by willow species

☐ Limestone walls with occasional sparse hedges

☐ Largely unenclosed peat and upland areas

Fig. 2 The composition of field boundaries as mapped in 1974 by A. O'Sullivan and J. Moore. The pattern is complex but broad contrasts exist between east and west. The extensive zone of limestone walls to the east of Galway Bay is conspicuous as are the largely unenclosed peat and upland areas of the Atlantic seaboard. This distribution should be compared with that of field patterns (fig. 8).

CHARACTER AND COMPOSITION OF FIELD BOUNDARIES

Planted hedgerows are not widespread or traditional and the commonest type of enclosure on lowland farms is an earthen bank crowned by an untidy quasi-natural growth of vegetation. Many of these 'hedgebanks' are unmanaged and gappy and require some form of fencing or wiring to make them stockproof. Hedge management is most common in the more intensively farmed lowland areas. The composition of bank vegetation varies regionally. On well-drained limestone soils, hawthorn and ash dominate with clumps of hazel; on inferior acid soils, hawthorn and furze are dominant and in damp situations, alder and willow increase. In hill areas and along windswept coasts, the banks are almost bare. The planting of hedgerow trees has been encouraged for several centuries but the earthen banks do not properly support them and their occurrence is sporadic. Dry stone walling is best developed in areas where the drift cover is absent or has a high boulder content. Both stone walls and stone ditches occur; the latter are simply banks of loose stones while the former are narrower and more carefully

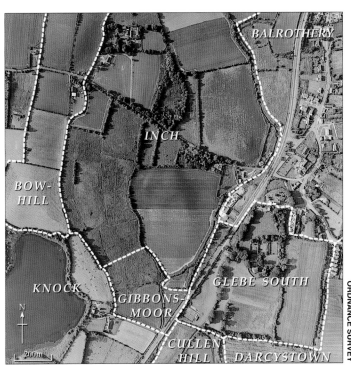

ORDNANCE SURVEY

● Fig. 3 Townlands are the smallest and oldest territorial divisions in rural areas and their boundaries are often associated with old, structurally complex hedges. The irregular curves of the boundaries are also suggestive of pre-eighteenth century origins, in contrast to the field pattern which is essentially modern in appearance with straight-edged enclosures reflecting 'rational' subdivision. In this example from Balrothery, county Dublin, photographed in 1992, the townland boundaries have been picked out.

DAPHNE LEVINGE

Fig. 4 Enclosure and drainage were often simultaneous, complementary operations. In richer areas, the large fields are characteristically enclosed by a combination of drainage ditches and banks, with an unkempt hedge on top. The banks contain a core of stones cleared from the land with a covering layer of sod derived from the flanking ditches. The term 'ditch' is universally applied in Ireland to refer to the field bank as well as the drain.

constructed features of interlocking stones. The nature of the rock and the varied local techniques of construction have led to a diversity of wall types.

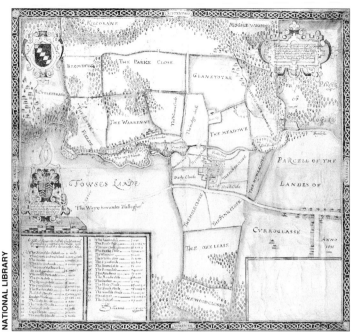

●Fig. 5 Estate cores were the basis of the first systematic planning of field systems. This 1598 map of Sir Walter Raleigh's estate at Mogeely in county Cork shows carefully laid out fields, with resonantly English names.

Field enclosures are multi-purpose, originally built as property boundaries, barriers to stock and shelter belts. The ecological significance of enclosures is now increasingly appreciated. In a closely farmed and lightly wooded countryside, the hedges and banks contribute to biodiversity,

providing the major habitats for wild life (plants, animals, birds and insects) and vital corridors for its movement through the landscape. They are therefore an essential component of the island's ecological infrastructure.

Botanical diversity is generally a guide to the age of well established hedgerows – diversity and age correlate positively. In Ireland, where almost all enclosures are relatively recent, this rule has only limited application and botanic diversity is connected more with local ecology and the intensity of land management.

ORIGIN OF ENCLOSURES

Demarcation of property boundaries, following the establishment of the landlord system in the seventeenth century, provided a basic framework for the widespread formation of fixed regular enclosures in the Irish countryside. In the eighteenth century, when ideas of 'agricultural improvement' and the 'new husbandry' gained momentum, improvement was invariably coupled with enclosure. By the 1770s, when Arthur Young visited Ireland, substantial enclosures, comprising a deep trench and a bank of stone and sods with a hedge on it, had become a feature in the east and a hallmark of *avant garde* improvers.

While enclosures in the modern landscape are predominantly post-medieval, their origins are not everywhere wholly clear. The typical pattern of single dispersed farms is generally envisaged as emerging along with the fields in recent centuries, displacing older nucleated settlement and open-fields, but this picture may be an oversimplification. A surprising persistence of dispersed settlement and enclosed fields is indicated in some places. Abandoned ringforts and adjacent enclosures are preserved in stony western districts, such as the Burren, frequently underly-

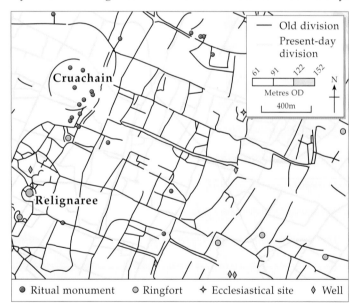

● Ritual monument   ◎ Ringfort   ✦ Ecclesiastical site   ◇ Well

●Fig. 6 Old field divisions around Cruachain, county Roscommon (as mapped by Michael Herity), compared with those of the present day. Suggestive of centralised planning, the grid patterns of ancient fields, bounded by earth and stone banks, are based on long lines up to two kilometres in length laid axially along ridges. The system existed in early medieval times and may have even older roots: it was moribund by the seventeenth and eighteenth centuries but this regular, mainly rectilinear field system could easily have evolved into the present pattern through piecemeal amendments rather than by radical overhaul. Elsewhere, there may well be areas where an evolution of this sort was completed with little or no landlord or other 'improving' influences'.

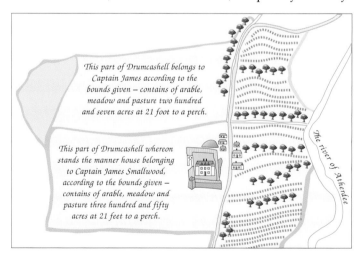

This part of Drumcashell belongs to Captain James according to the bounds given – contains of arable, meadow and pasture two hundred and seven acres at 21 foot to a perch.

This part of Drumcashell whereon stands the manner house belonging to Captain James Smallwood, according to the bounds given – contains of arable, meadow and pasture three hundred and fifty acres at 21 feet to a perch.

●Fig. 7 The manor of Drumcashel in county Louth based on a sketch of 1655 – within a year of its transfer to new Cromwellian owners. The moated manor house lies alongside a motte and cabin cluster. Partially enclosed strips curve down between it and the Ardee river – the obvious survivors of an earlier openfield.

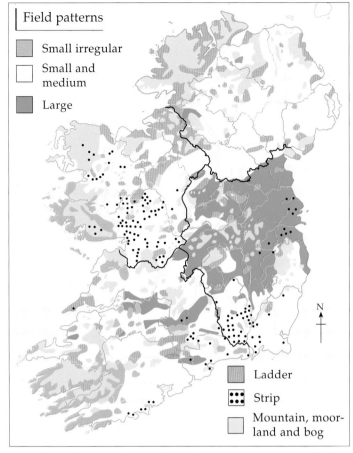

Field patterns

- Small irregular
- Small and medium
- Large

Ladder

Strip

Mountain, moorland and bog

N

Fig. 8 Pierre Flatrès' map of field patterns shows their complex distribution. There is an overall contrast between the Leinster/east Munster pattern of medium and large fields, and the landscape of small fields, including irregular, regular, ladder and strip varieties, in Ulster, Connacht and west Munster.

ing the present-day settlement and field patterns. In the river valleys of south-eastern Ireland, aerial photography has recently revealed extensive crop marks of ringforts and associated enclosures beneath the present well-ordered landscape of large farms and fields. The modern enclosures are generally much more regular than the old, suggesting that they did not evolve from the older system but were directly superimposed on it by improving landowners, without an intervening phase of open-field organisation; had open-fields existed, remnants of the older enclosure pattern could hardly have survived so comprehensively. More significant, an embryonic order is sometimes evident in the old landscapes. Around the Celtic royal site at Cruachain in county Roscommon, for example, grid patterns of elongated rectangular fields, of early medieval or even earlier origin, extend over several townlands; although there was little direct continuity here, the pattern is not deeply divorced from the contemporary one. Modern fields may thus in some localities be the outcome of long, evolutionary processes as well as recent, planned superimposition.

REGIONAL PATTERNS
Leinster

Favoured physically and with a more entrenched estate system, eastern Ireland was ahead of the rest of the country both in the timing and quality of agricultural innovation; here, although there is much local variety, the enclosures are generally larger and older than in the north and west. Eastern farms tend to be bigger and their fields more extensive in area (3-5 ha) and regular in outline. In Leinster, the longest established hedgerows exist; their tall, vigorous growth and diverse species composition reflect their age. Hedges of hawthorn, ash and elder are characteristic, with abundant trees of ash, beech, sycamore, oak and horse chestnut. From the coastal corridor between Dublin and Drogheda, the zone extends west as far as the midland belt of bogs along the Shannon; southwards, it pushes into Kildare, Offaly, Laois, Carlow and Kilkenny, and then on into mid-Munster.

This area of north and west Leinster was heavily settled in the medieval period with manorial villages and open-fields with scattered strip holdings. Around the villages, piecemeal enclosure ensued from the late medieval period and occasional narrow, elongated fields today reflect the

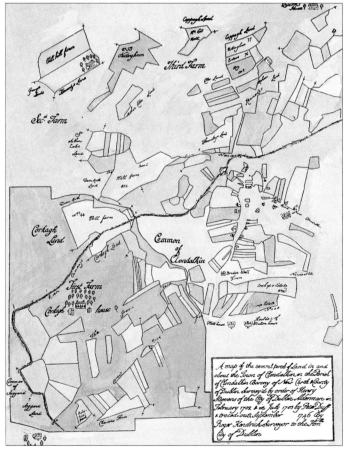

● Fig. 9 The field pattern around Clondalkin, county Dublin, in 1702 was obviously still heavily influenced by the open-field tradition.

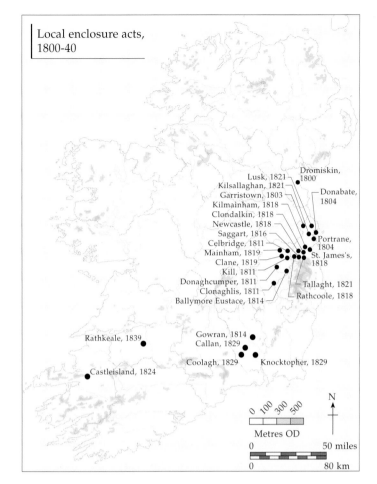

Local enclosure acts, 1800-40

Dromiskin, 1800
Lusk, 1821
Kilsallaghan, 1821
Garristown, 1803
Kilmainham, 1818
Clondalkin, 1818
Donabate, 1804
Newcastle, 1818
Saggart, 1816
Celbridge, 1811
Portrane, 1804
Mainham, 1819
St. James's, 1818
Clane, 1819
Kill, 1811
Donaghcumper, 1811
Tallaght, 1821
Clonaghlis, 1811
Rathcoole, 1818
Ballymore Eustace, 1814

Rathkeale, 1839
Gowran, 1814
Callan, 1829
Coolagh, 1829
Knocktopher, 1829
Castleisland, 1824

0 100 300 500
Metres OD

0   50 miles
0   80 km

Fig. 10 (left) Customary precedents, prominent in the English open-field tradition, were weak in Ireland; landlords had untrammelled authority and no massive parliamentary enclosure movement was necessary. Only a handful of land enclosure acts were passed, mainly in the early nineteenth century and in connection with commons rather than arable land.

old open-field strips. Arable land around the large villages of the Pale, at Dalkey, Swords, Clondalkin, Newcastle Lyons, Crumlin, Ballymore Eustace, Rathcoole and Lusk, for example, was peculiarly resistant to thoroughgoing engrossment. Hedges were simply grown on the old mearings which separated the scattered strip holdings, thus fossilising the medieval lay-out. Elsewhere, little of the medieval system survived the unrest of the late Middle Ages and the traumatic seventeenth-century upheavals; subsequently, the new landlords ruthlessly rationalised the remnants which they perceived as archaic impediments to crop rotation, drainage and enclosure.

In Leinster, the estate system was most firmly established and the numerous demesnes with their ornamental surrounds have left a widespread imprint on the landscape. Some of this old dignity is preserved today in the large stud farms located on former demesnes in Meath, Dublin and Kildare. A distinctive feature of the stud belt is the well maintained fields with neat wooden railings necessary to prevent the horses jumping the hedges.

In the Leinster tillage belt, enclosure proceeded rapidly so that by the mid eighteenth century all land below 150 metres that was not bog was well enclosed. Tillage fields tended to be smaller and their enclosures better maintained than pasture ones, with substantial, stock-proof earthen banks and hawthorn hedges. To improve drainage, these banks often had deep accompanying trenches ('gripes'), notably on the heavy clay lands of north Leinster.

• Fig. 11 In Leinster, landlords were commonly resident. Their demesnes, set within high enclosing walls, contained stately deciduous trees like beech, sycamore and chestnut. They also developed set-piece field patterns in their immediate vicinity, laid out by professional surveyors and landscape gardeners – well exemplified at Narraghmore at county Kildare.

MICHAEL DIGGIN

• Fig. 12 'Striped' farms, the result of the reorganisation of rundale holdings, are characteristic of the Atlantic coastline, as in this example from the Loop Head area of west county Clare.

Fig. 13 Differences between east and west are manifest in the matrix of field boundaries. ● A) The large hedged fields near Stradbally in county Laois are characteristic of the rich lands of eastern Ireland dominated by substantial farms. The regular field outlines and ornamental wooded knoll are legacies of earlier estate organisation. ● B) The intensively settled and stony Aran Islands possess an intricate network of small walled fields developed under acute population pressure. Field patterns are closely adjusted to the slopes and patchy soil cover. The field boundaries traverse the bare limestone bedding planes, generating a geometric lattice. Many fields have no permanent openings – portions are knocked down or rebuilt as required. The walls gain strength by their very flimsiness, which allows the Atlantic gales to pierce rather than flatten them.

In south-east Leinster, especially on the acidic granite and shale stretching through Wicklow and Wexford to south Kilkenny, the decentralising effect of the townland system, environmental pressure towards pastoralism and scarcity of immigrant tenants permitted a less disciplined field pattern to emerge. Medium-sized fields (2-3 ha) are characteristic, enclosed by hedgebanks with hawthorn, ash and furze (gorse). The blaze of furze is a distinctive feature of the south Leinster landscape. As well as an effective barrier and an animal fodder, the furze provided fuel in a largely bog-free region.

Munster

The fields of Munster can be divided into three broad regions. First is the coastal fringe of west Cork, Kerry and Clare. Old, irregular field patterns frequently survive here in poorer areas but more widespread is the characteristic 'Atlantic' pattern of small, reorganised 'striped' farms enclosed by walls or banks enlivened by exotic garden escapees such as fuchsia, buddleia and montbretia. A variant exists on the Namurian flagstone area of west Clare

where the Moher flags create distinctive field walls noted as early as 1688: 'the partitions of land are made by broad stones, like slates, turned up edgeways'. In this cattle country, mountain commonages are still valuable and often demarcated by substantial, lengthy walls crossing the mountain slopes - a pattern especially visible in the stony Burren.

A second region extends from east Waterford through the Blackwater and Lee valleys. Enclosures developed quite early in this old-established tillage zone and substantial hedges are characteristic, dominated by hawthorn, blackthorn and furze (especially evident on the hills). The third region encompasses the Golden Vale of south Tipperary and east Limerick which is an extension of the north Leinster pattern of large farms and fields. Here, the best developed hedgerows with tall, vigorous growth consist of hawthorn, blackthorn and the ubiquitous limestone-loving ash, symbol of the hurling country. In the dairying areas, fields are smaller for purposes of shelter, for keeping grass fresh and to manage meadow land. In high summer, the exuberant growth exudes an overwhelming greenness.

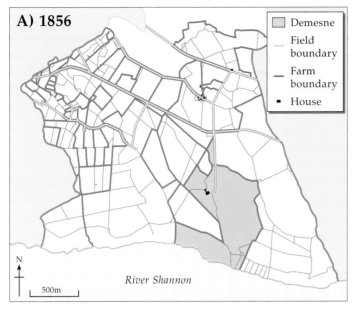

A) 1856

☐	Demesne
—	Field boundary
━	Farm boundary
▪	House

N

500m

River Shannon

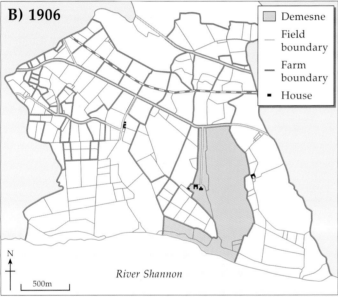

B) 1906

☐	Demesne
—	Field boundary
━	Farm boundary
▪	House

N

500m

River Shannon

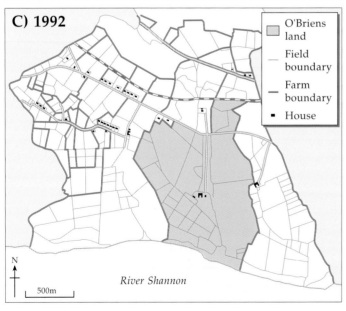

C) 1992

☐	O'Briens land
—	Field boundary
━	Farm boundary
▪	House

N

500m

River Shannon

Connacht

The formation of fields in western Ireland culminated in the nineteenth century when rural population was much greater than today. Their diminutive size reflects the needs of small-scale, subsistence agriculture where the chief implement was the spade. Field shapes vary from regular to highly irregular. Tiny irregular plots, closely adjusted to local topography, generally represent piecemeal, pre-Famine settlement expansion but in some places they may be much older. Considerable reorganisation of western field patterns occurred in the nineteenth and early twentieth centuries, first through landlord interventions and later through the Congested Districts Board and Land Commission, government agencies for land reform and reorganisation. Farm clusters with intermixed holdings were removed. On the lowlands, consolidated holdings were characteristically laid out in blocks with an even spread of farms; on hillsides, new farms were arranged in narrow parallel strips, or 'ladder farms', running down the slopes with the farmsteads arranged in lines along new roads.

On the grazier-dominated limestone lowlands of east Galway, a distinctive pattern of large fields with flimsy, dry-stone walls developed in the eighteenth century suited to extensive cattle grazing. The lightly veneered bedrock afforded plentiful stones which were gradually cleared into cairns or into the walls which partly served as consumption dykes. The walls were typically only one stone thick and head high; despite their apparent flimsiness, they deterred even the most determined cattle, because the loose top stones noisily disengaged when brushed against. These walls, with their lichen-mottled grey stone, dominate the landscape in a great arc east of Galway Bay – challenging hunting country, and home of the celebrated Galway Blazers.

A further region of Connacht enclosure stretched through the wetter, mineral-deficient soils of the drumlinoid

●Fig. 14 This sequence of three maps by Michael Punch shows the evolution of the field and farm system on the Stafford O'Brien estate at Cratloe in south-east Clare between 1856 and 1992. The area is mainly a limestone-based undulating lowland close to the River Shannon, with a narrow rim of 'corcass' lands (flat alluvial meadow with gley soils). A) The 1856 map shows a concentration of small tenant farms on the north-west - a natural basin, with bog and gley soils. The field pattern is very reticulated, with small fields aligned along the slope. Cratloe House and demesne occupy the better soils on a site overlooking the Shannon. B) By 1906, the field pattern is remarkably stable, despite intensive social and economic change in the preceding half century. There is a decreased number of occupiers, a switch towards pastoralism, a decline in the importance of landlordism and a rapid turnover at the level of the smallholders. C) In 1992, the most striking change is the construction of bungalows beaded along the roads: these reflect the influence of Shannon new town on the area. However, the inherited field fabric is still stable, with the only major change being the 'striping' of the 'corcass' lands along the Shannon. The stabilising influence is the dominance of pastoralism which accounts for over ninety-five per cent of land use. Thus the field boundaries here tell a narrative of continuity despite the considerable social and economic transformations.

● Fig 15 Fields in county Leitrim, with Lough Allen in the background. Shaggy hedges of willow, birch and hawthorn sprout undisciplined by human hand, lending a forlorn air to the landscape.

northern third of the province – especially in Leitrim, south Sligo, north Roscommon and parts of east Mayo. This marginal, small farm world has experienced large-scale depopulation and land abandonment. Here, the unkempt hedgerows are colonised mainly by wet-loving species such as willow, alder and birch, which are replaced on the drier slopes by hawthorn and furze.

Ulster

The experience of northern Ireland was comparable to that of the west. At the end of the eighteenth century, only the richer lowlands of mid-Ulster had been enclosed. In the first half of the nineteenth century, comprehensive change occurred under the auspices of 'improving' landlords; farms were dispersed from the old farm clusters and the landscape was enclosed in regular, small to medium fields enclosed by hedged banks. The uniformity of the northern landscape is striking in this respect.

The enclosure movement was belated over the predominantly open-field areas of north and west Ulster, but

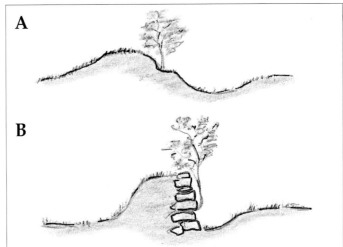

Fig. 16 Two common hedge types in Ulster, shown schematically in cross section. A) Hedge planted in the lip between the trench and the upturned earth forming the bank. B) Hedge planted between field stones on the revetment of an earthen bank. The stone bank was the later form, perhaps spreading from prototypes developed further south and known as 'the Louth ditch'. This in turn had been introduced by the Fosters, the celebrated 'improving' landlords at Collon, copying a south-west Scottish precedent in Galloway. The 'Louth' version improved on the Scottish by incorporating earthen buttressing behind the stone cladding, greatly increasing its stability. In this form, the type was introduced to estates in Ulster, like the Mountjoy and Abercorn, and became especially prominent in Antrim and Down.

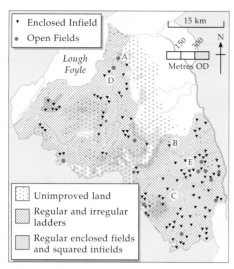

Enclosed Infield
Open Fields

Lough
Foyle

15 km

150 300

Metres OD

N

Unimproved land

Regular and irregular
ladders

Regular enclosed fields
and squared infields

● Fig. 17 Field patterns in county Londonderry 1908.

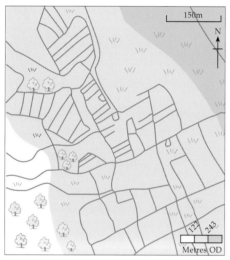

A) Surviving openfield near Bellaghy with unen-closed strips (Ballycarton) and enclosed irregular outfield ladders (Ballymaglin).

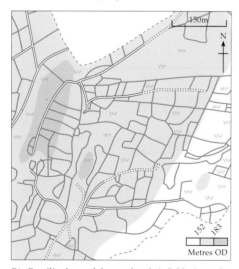

B) Fossilised rundale: enclosed infield, irregular laddered outfield. Small, intensively cultivated arable strips (infield) with loose textured matrix of enclo-sures for rough grazing on unimproved mountain and bog (Halfgayne townland).

FIELD PATTERNS IN COUNTY LONDONDERRY

The research of E. Currie has shown how the field patterns of contemporary county Londonderry have largely emerged out of the reorganisation of earlier rundale networks. Even in 1908, however, some open fields survived, especially on the Vintner's estate at Bellaghy, which remained outside landlord control until the 1870s (A). By the early nineteenth century, landlords began vigorously to reorganise rundale holdings, creating a new pattern of striped ladder farms. These linear farms, despite their ungainly shape, were popular with tenants because they retained the rundale principle of environmental egalitar-ianism, encompassing a range of land use types from lowland arable to rough grazing and bog. In 1817, the Drapers' estate pioneered the new pattern, which was quickly copied by the Fishmongers' and Grocers' estates. It was then adopted by the Mercers and Salters (after the Famine) and by the Skinners and Churchlands (as late as the 1870s). On the very widely distributed hill slopes of the county, notably on the Sperrins, Loughmorne and Slieve Gallion, the ladder farm became dominant by the early twentieth century. It could be initiat-ed by enclosing the cultivated infield, creat-ing a fine mesh of strip fields, while a much coarser matrix of irregular ladder fields partly enclosed the unimproved upland and bog. In this way, a rundale openfield could be fossilised in an incongruous enclosure network (B). More thorough-going rational-isation broke up the clachan into dispersed individual farms (C). Two other field types also existed. In the relatively fertile lower Roe, Faughan and Moyola basins, individ-ual leases were granted in the mid eigh-teenth century, where the adoption of new crops and rotations encouraged the creation of large regular enclosures of 2ha to 4ha in size (D). On the poorer ill-drained basin in east Londonderry, a proto-industrial land-scape of small farms developed, divided into tiny fields of 0.2ha to 0.8ha (E). Remark-ably, these new field patterns were obsolete almost from their completion, due to post-famine population decline which removed population pressure, the main dynamo in reordering enclosure systems.

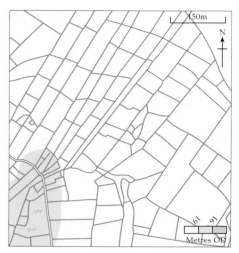

C) Early nineteenth-century reorganisation of rundale. Regular ladder farms on mountain slopes (incorporating rundale principles) with intact fossilised clachan and narrow parallel ladders on infield, and squared outfield (Longfield townland).

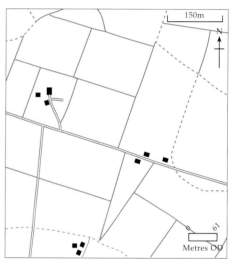

D) Regular enclosed large fields (2ha to 4ha) late eighteenth century (Back townland, near Limavady).

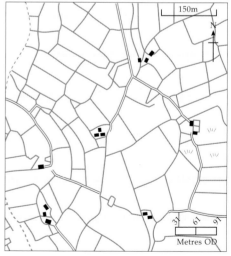

E) Tiny fields (0.2ha to 0.4ha) in an intensively subdivided, small farm, proto-industrial area, with piecemeal enclosure (Curragh townland).

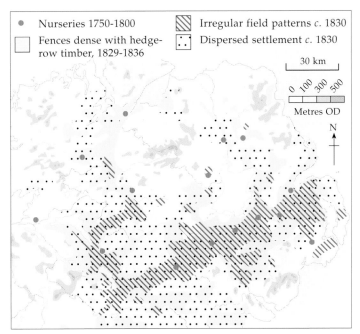

Nurseries 1750-1800

Fences dense with hedge-
row timber, 1829-1836

Irregular field patterns *c.* 1830

Dispersed settlement *c.* 1830

30 km

0 100 300 500

Metres OD

N

Fig. 18   Enclosed fields clustered initially on progressive estates – like Downpatrick (Ward), Hillsborough (Downshire) and Lurgan (Brownlow) – before coalescing into a continuous system on accessible lowlands. Enclosures with irregular field patterns and dispersed settlement first spread along the Lagan valley and then through the Clogher valley to the Erne basin in south county Fermanagh. Two more subdued axes penetrated the Lower Bann and the Foyle basins. As proto-industrialisation intensified, these corridors of early enclosure evolved a denser fieldscape of small enclosures added piecemeal within the master boundaries of townland and leasehold.

●Fig. 19   The most impressive walls in the Irish landscape are those which mark boundaries in open hill areas. Such walls are often up to two metres thick and march over steep terrain, as in this fine example from the Mourne Mountains which defines the Silent Valley reservoir.

accelerated in the nineteenth century when landlords initiated wholesale reorganisation. Two new types of field pattern emerged: regular squares in the lowlands and narrow ladder farms in the uplands of Donegal, the Antrim glens, the Sperrins and the Fews. Field boundaries were either a simple earthen bank or a hedge planted between the stone cladding on one side of an earthen bank.

Enclosure could vary from estate to estate, but the general pattern developed by the mid-nineteenth century has remained intact because of subsequent population decline and a relatively stable land-use pattern. As a cultural phenomenon, the 'protestant hedge', neatly pruned and orderly, is occasionally commented on in Ulster.

Recent Changes in Field Boundaries

In the first half of this century, little change occurred in the basic pattern of enclosed fields, despite an increase in average farm size owing to sustained rural depopulation and ensuing farm amalgamation. Enclosures remained integral to farming systems dependent on manual labour and draft animals.

Since the 1950s, there has been conflict between the increasing specialisation, scale and mechanisation of farming and the small size and sometimes inconvenient shape of traditional fields. The pressure to remove bound-

aries and enlarge fields steadily grew but little change was made until the process was directly supported by government grants and European incentives from the 1960s. Banks and walls were then bulldozed, the stones removed and the earth spread over the field; some were replaced with post and wire fences which occupy little or no productive land and can easily be moved and rearranged for the purpose of strip grazing.

Over recent decades in Ireland, there has been a significant reduction in field boundary length but the precise rate and regional incidence of removal is not accurately known; it is less than in Britain and many parts of Europe where thoroughgoing removal, abruptly transforming the face of whole regions, has usually been associated with highly mechanised arable farming. In Ireland, the overall pastoral bent of farming has been a restraint; boundary removal has been most marked on larger farms and in specialised dairy-

ing and arable areas where the banks and walls have often been replaced by post and wire fences and electric fencing which allow flexible organisation of the land.

Recent CAP reforms aim to reduce overproduction of food through removal of incentives and to promote farming in harmony with the environment; hence there is now renewed interest in conserving field boundaries and even restoring and replanting them. Enclosure removal, like many agricultural activities, is very sensitive to financial inducements but restoration of field boundaries is equally so. However, traditional enclosures are by no means secure; expansion on the edges of rural towns and villages, which has already obliterated many field patterns of historical significance, is likely to continue with destruc-

tive consequences, while uncoordinated expansion of private forestry will submerge field patterns in many rural areas. Nonetheless, enclosures are still a principal component of the Irish rural landscape. They also retain a powerful symbolic charge as jealously guarded property boundaries, as identified in Patrick Kavanagh's poem 'Epic':

> I have lived in important places, times
> When great events were decided, who owned
> That half rood of rack, a no-man's land
> Surrounded by our pitchfork-armed claims.
> I heard the Duffys shouting 'Damn your soul'
> And Old McCabe stripped to the waist, seen
> Step the plot defying blue cast-steel –
> 'Here is the march along these iron stones.'

BIBLIOGRAPHY

F. Aalen, 'The origin of enclosures in eastern Ireland' in N. Stephens and R. Glasscock (ed.), *Irish geographical studies* (Belfast, 1970), pp 209-23.

F. Aalen, *Man and the landscape in Ireland* (London, 1978).

F. Aalen, 'Rural change and rural landscape quality. Experience and planning in Europe and Ireland' in C. Thomas (ed.), *Rural landscapes and communities* (Dublin, 1986), pp 215-44.

R. Buchanan, 'Field systems of Ireland' in A. Baker and R. Butlin (ed.), *Studies of field systems in the British Isles* (London, 1973), pp 580-618.

R. Buchanan, 'Landscape' in J. Cruickshank and D. Wilcock (ed.), *Northern Ireland environment and natural resources* (Belfast, 1982), pp 265-89.

E. Currie, 'Field patterns in county Derry' in *Ulster Folklife*, xxix (1983), pp 70-80.

E. Evans, *Irish folk ways* (London, 1957).

P. Flatrès, *Géographie rurale de la quatre contrées celtiques: Irlande, Galles, Cornwall et Man* (Rennes, 1957).

C. Hegarty and A. Cooper, 'Regional variation of hedge structure and composition in Northern Ireland in relation to management and land use' in *Biology and Environment*, xciv (1994), B, pp 223-36.

D. Jeffrey, M. Jones and J. McAdam (ed.), *Irish grasslands. Their biology and management* (Dublin, 1995).

J. Johnson, 'The development of the rural settlement pattern of Ireland' in *Geografisker Annaler*, xliii (1961), pp 165-73.

E. Kennedy, The effect of government policy and support on field boundaries in the agricultural landscape: a case study, unpublished Ph.D thesis, University of Ulster, 1996.

R. Murray, T. McCann and A. Cooper, *A land classification and landscape ecological study of Northern Ireland*, Report to DOENI (School of Environmental Studies, University of Ulster, 1992).

P. Robinson, 'The spread of hedged enclosure in Ulster' in *Ulster Folklife*, xxiii (1977), pp 159-96.

BUILDINGS

The relatively high proportion of the population which still lives in the countryside, as well as the dispersed pattern of single farms, make buildings a pervasive element of the Irish landscape. In many areas, their visual impact is reinforced by the custom of whitewashing walls, so that buildings stand out sharply against the dominant greens and browns of the background vegetation. Important as visual elements in the landscape, buildings take on added significance as the foci of human activities, as major points of connection between people and places and as expressions of local and regional traditions. The form, materials and construction methods of older buildings illustrate the ecological adaptation of rural society to its varied environments and closely reflect traditional economic and social structures. Newer buildings reflect the rapid pace of recent social change in the countryside, many showing a sharp break with earlier forms and building materials and lacking regional distinctiveness.

Rural buildings serve varied purposes; domestic, agricultural, religious, educational, commercial and industrial. The divisions are not clear cut; houses and agricultural buildings are often linked into farmsteads, shops and houses sometimes occupy the same building, and even churches occasionally have domestic quarters. Houses and agricultural buildings form the most numerous and ubiquitous elements of the rural built environment. Other rural buildings, such as churches, schools, society halls, shops, public houses and factories provide services, amenities and employment for the surrounding population; they have public functions, even though many are domestic in scale and style.

● Fig. 1 Traditional dispersed pattern of small farms, Mourne mountains, county Down.

HOUSES AND AGRICULTURAL BUILDINGS

HOUSES

VERNACULAR TRADITIONS

Until the present century, rural buildings in Ireland and other European countries were regionally varied and deeply traditional. House styles had evolved as adaptations to the local environment and economy, with distinctive forms transmitted as part of a communal tradition. The term 'vernacular architecture' is now widely applied to this broad mass of buildings, in contradistinction to buildings in formal styles which follow national or international fashions and are typically architect-designed and more substantial. Commercial farming, industrialisation and urbanisation have weakened regional traditions and vernacular buildings are rapidly diminishing in absolute and relative importance.

F.H.A. AALEN

WELSH FOLK MUSEUM

Fig. 2 Vernacular house characteristics can be loosely grouped under the headings 'Upland' and 'Lowland'. Some features overlap the regions and considerable relief variation exists within them with reflections in building patterns; the Upland, for example, includes the Scottish and Irish Central Lowlands. In the Upland, early farmhouses are rare; durable houses appeared later than in the Lowland and until *c*. 1700 most rural dwellers lived in hovels of perishable materials. Stone or mud single-storey houses predominated until the mid nineteenth century, with an outer zone of sub-medieval long-houses in Ireland and Scotland. In the Lowland, many late medieval and early modern farmhouses survive. Storeyed houses were common by the mid-seventeenth century, and half-timbered wall construction was widespread, save in northern England and on the Midland oolitic limestone belt.

F.H.A. AALEN

Fig. 3 Single-storey houses of similar, modest proportions with elongated rectangular plans and thatched roofs were common to rural communities in the Upland zone. In the present century, their numbers have been steadily depleted; most markedly in Wales, least in Ireland. The buildings which have replaced them are often a sharp break with traditional forms. Thatch has been widely replaced with corrugated iron, slates and tiles. A) Shetland, Scotland (1970); B) Cardiganshire, Wales (1990); ●C) County Wicklow, Ireland (1970).

●Fig. 4 Built in traditional form and using local building materials, the Irish vernacular house blended easily into the landscape like a natural feature. Near Letterfrack, county Galway.

The vernacular house in Ireland is a modest thatched building, one storey high, with a rectangular plan. The house is rarely more than one room in width and each room opens into the next without a passage or central hall. Entrances and windows are placed on side rather than end walls. Structurally the houses are simple. The roof is supported by the walls and not by internal posts or pillars. Local materials are used to construct the houses; stone or mud for walls, cereal straw or rushes for thatch. Irish houses are thus basically similar to traditional dwellings in Britain and particularly the houses of rural Scotland, parts of Wales and western England.

Irish vernacular buildings utilised simple proportions with an almost classical restraint and were also well integrated into their environment, factors which in combination gave them a notable aesthetic appeal. Åke Campbell, the great Swedish folklife scholar, observed that the vernacular Irish house 'never stands out in bold relief against its background but melts into it even as a tree or a rock. Whenever the old building traditions are faithfully maintained, its features are of a fine simplicity'. While recent developments in Irish housing have been generally inimical to the vernacular tradition, that tradition endures as a rich legacy, still available both as a model and inspiration for future development and as a powerful document recording how the bulk of the Irish people were housed over previous generations.

●Fig. 5 Uniformity of basic house style is still striking in many areas of western Ireland. In this group of houses on Inis Oirr (Inisheer), one of the Aran Islands, the dominant style is the single-storey, three-roomed, gable-ended house found throughout western Ireland. Older houses are thatched, new ones slated. Note also the common orientation of houses. Flat, sloping roofs are common on outhouses on the Aran Islands.

Fig. 6 Traditional western house; single-storey, direct-entry, three-roomed, gable-ended. ● A) Loop Head, county Clare. ● B) Clare Island, county Mayo.

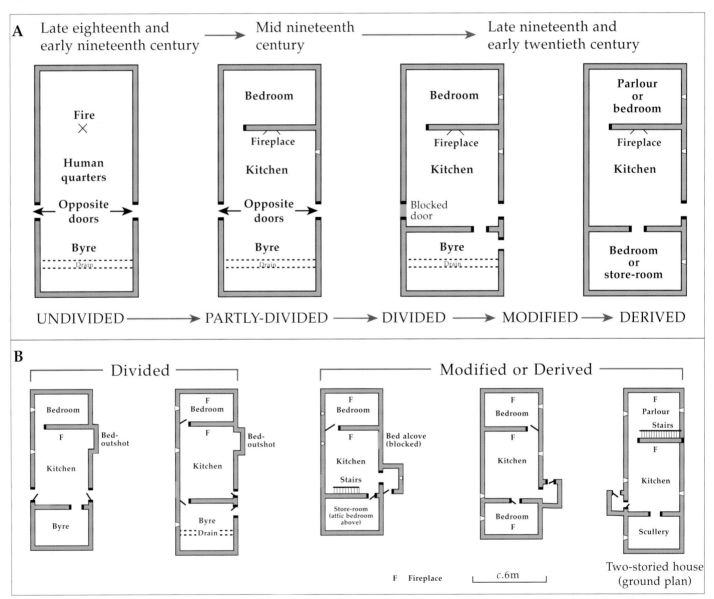

A

Late eighteenth and early nineteenth century ⟶ Mid nineteenth century ⟶ Late nineteenth and early twentieth century

Fire ✕

Human quarters

⟵ Opposite doors ⟶

Byre

Drain

Bedroom

Fireplace

Kitchen

⟵ Opposite doors ⟶

Byre

Drain

Bedroom

Fireplace

Kitchen

Blocked door

Byre

Drain

Parlour or bedroom

Fireplace

Kitchen

Bedroom or store-room

UNDIVIDED ⟶ PARTLY-DIVIDED ⟶ DIVIDED ⟶ MODIFIED ⟶ DERIVED

B

⎯ Divided ⎯

Bedroom
F
Kitchen
Byre
Bed-outshot

F Bedroom
F
Kitchen
Byre
Drain
Bed-outshot

⎯ Modified or Derived ⎯

F Bedroom
F
Kitchen
Stairs
Store-room (attic bedroom above)
Bed alcove (blocked)

F Bedroom
F
Kitchen
Bedroom F

F Parlour
Stairs
F
Kitchen
Scullery

Two-storied house (ground plan)

F   Fireplace   c.6m

Fig. 7 A) Stages of long-house development, north-west Ireland. Increasing internal division of houses reflected new standards of comfort and hygiene and growing concern with privacy and propriety resulting from contacts with urban society. ● B) Ground plans of direct-entry houses, west county Donegal. Variations occur without major violation of a common basic plan developed from the long-house.

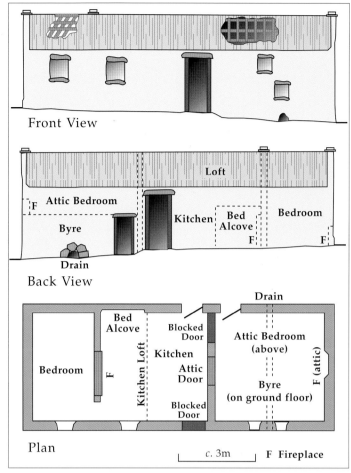

In the left diagram (Fig. 8):

Front View

Back View — Loft, Attic Bedroom, F, Byre, Drain, Kitchen, Bed Alcove, F, Bedroom, F

Plan — Bed Alcove, Blocked Door, Drain, Bedroom, F, Kitchen Loft, Kitchen, Attic Door, Blocked Door, Attic Bedroom (above), Byre (on ground floor), F (attic), *c.* 3m, F Fireplace

• Fig. 8 Deserted long-house, Gola Island, county Donegal. Gola, now depopulated, lies three kilometres off the Donegal coast. Among its deserted dwellings is a number of divided long-houses which were originally unicellular structures.

Regional styles

Contrasts in vernacular styles exist between the poorer, moister parts of the island to the north and west, with numerous uplands, and the east and south, with their richer, accessible lowlands where society, although containing a large body of poor farm labourers, has traditionally been more prosperous and socially stratified.

Western (direct-entry/gable-end hearth) houses Dwellings with exposed gable-ends, and frequently with their hearths on or near the gables, were typical in the west and parts of the north, where stone was the customary walling material. In Donegal, most of Connacht and the peninsulas of western Munster, the typical farmhouse possessed a three-roomed ground plan; the kitchen is central with flanking bedrooms. This house form has developed from archaic structures, termed long-houses or byre-dwellings by ethnologists; widespread in the west until the nineteenth century, they incorporated both byre and dwelling in one compartment. In remote places, such as west Donegal, west Kerry and Connemara, the expulsion of cattle and division

Fig. 9 Rounded ends and hip roofs were found on numerous old houses in west Connacht, but few examples survive and the gable-ended house is now dominant. • A) Achill Island, county Mayo (*c.* 1910). • B) Indreabhán (Inveran), county Galway (1935). C) Rusheeny, county Galway (1949). • D) Carna, county Galway (1980).

ULSTER FOLK AND TRANSPORT MUSEUM

F.H.A. AALEN

Fig. 10 Bed-outshots. • A) A large outshot with small window (Fawney, county Tyrone. • B) Deserted house with small bed-outshot on rear wall, county Mayo.

of the house into different rooms are recent events: oral tradition relates that in some houses the former byre-end has been divided from the kitchen by an internal wall and converted to a bedroom or store-room.

The room beyond the hearth originated as an extension to the house, or, more commonly, by an internal division, perhaps associated with the introduction in the nineteenth century of chimney flues above the open fire which traditionally had lain on the floor at some distance from the

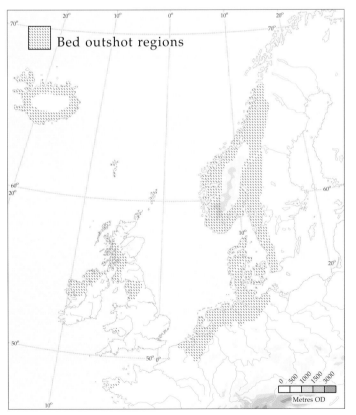

Fig. 11 The bed-outshot tradition in the north Atlantic region. Study of vernacular buildings has been uneven; more evidence may eventually modify this distribution.

gable wall. In older houses, the kitchen characteristically possesses two doors immediately opposite each other and away from the fire, allowing direct entry into the house: this was a useful arrangement for the regulation of draughts and smoke from the turf fire but it was probably also linked to the habit of accommodating livestock and human beings together in the same house. Not all old, three-roomed houses are modified long-houses; the tripartite plan has been perpetuated in many houses not originally built to accommodate livestock and these are best described as derived long-houses.

In some remote places, particularly in west Connacht, there are suggestions that long-houses evolved from archaic structures with oval or circular plans, and extant buildings with rounded ends and hip roofs appear to represent stages in the development. Dome-shaped, stone clocháin may represent the beginning of this evolution.

Older houses often possessed a large alcove or recess near the fire. Sometimes this was merely an intra-mural cavity in the thick side walls, but frequently it forms part of the external structure of the house and is associated with a box-like projection on one of the side walls of the kitchen. These features were used to accommodate a bed but have usually been blocked up or concealed by furniture. Today, the bed-outshot has a clear-cut distribution, occurring widely in the north-west of the country from Galway Bay to north-east Antrim. Bed-outshots once occurred over a wider area to the east but have been progressively confined, along with a variety of other cultural traits, to the remote north-western corner of the country. The bed-outshot was formerly a widespread element of rural building traditions in the north Atlantic region.

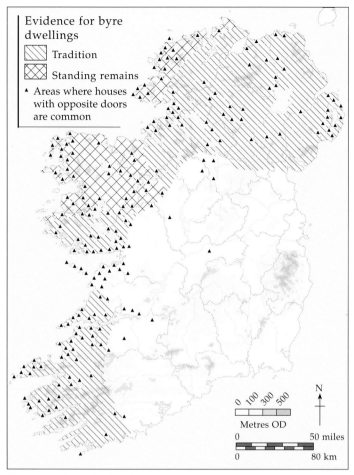

Evidence for byre
dwellings

- Tradition
- Standing remains
- Areas where houses
  with opposite doors
  are common

Metres OD
0 100 300 500

N

0   50 miles
0   80 km

Fig. 12 Evidence for long-houses and areas where houses with opposite doors are common. Note the northern and western distribution.

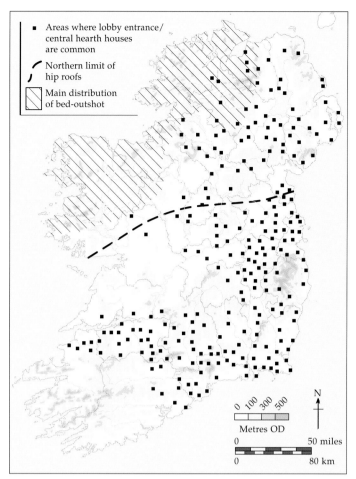

- Areas where lobby entrance/
  central hearth houses
  are common
- Northern limit of
  hip roofs
- Main distribution
  of bed-outshot

Metres OD
0 100 300 500

N

0   50 miles
0   80 km

Fig. 13 Eastern distribution of lobby entrance/central hearth houses, northern limit of hipped roofs, and distribution of the bed-outshot.

Fig. 14 Central hearth/lobby entrance, hipped-roof houses, eastern Ireland. ●A) Beaverstown, county Dublin. A well-maintained, mud-walled house of the classic eastern form. ●B) Kilclone, south county Meath. The original thatch has been covered with corrugated iron, retaining the hip ends. The confusion of electricity and telephone posts and wires is a general characteristic of rural built environment. ●C) Adare, county Limerick. The steeply-pitched roof with hip ends and straw thatch, and the yellow wash on the mud walls are common features in this area.

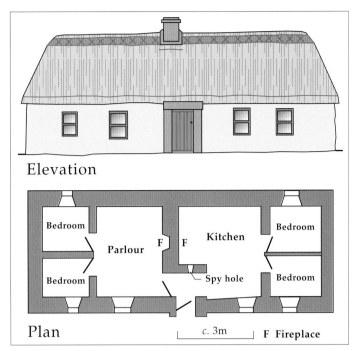

Elevation

Plan   *c.* 3m   F Fireplace

Bedroom / Parlour / F F / Kitchen / Bedroom / Bedroom / Spy hole / Bedroom

• Fig. 15   Elevation and plan of lobby entrance farmhouse, south-east county Wexford.

Eastern (central hearth/lobby entrance) houses   The basic features of eastern houses were the centrally-located hearth, lobby entrance and hipped roof. Walls were made with stone or mud. There is no tradition in eastern houses that animals and humans were accommodated together. Greater emphasis on cultivation in the east may explain the range of functionally specialised farm outbuildings; in the more pastoral economy of the west, people and animals commonly lived under one roof. Juxtaposition of hearth and door at the centre of the eastern house created a lobby entrance, an arrangement clearly ill-suited to the entry and exit of cattle. Lobby-entrance houses have a wide distribution in eastern and central Ireland; they extend westwards

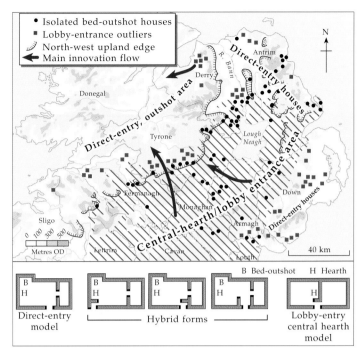

B Bed-outshot   H Hearth

Direct-entry model   Hybrid forms   Lobby-entry central hearth model

Fig. 17 Innovation diffusion on the boundary of the two major Irish house types. A. Gailey and D. McCourt have shown that in the north of Ireland the two main traditional house types occupy complementary areas; direct-entry houses occur in the uplands to the north-west, lobby-entrance houses on the lowlands to the south-east. Roughly along the upland edge, from Enniskillen to Cushendall, the types are separated by a fluid transitional zone. Over centuries, innovations have flowed mainly from the south-east lowlands to the north-west uplands, with the lobby style, associated with English and Scots planters, encroaching on the direct-entry house with bed outshot. Hence, isolated examples of houses with outshots occur well to the south of the present transition zone. Lobby-entrance houses are found outside the main distributional limit, but the upland edge generally retarded the innovation flow and intrusive elements here have sometimes been assimilated into the north-west outshot houses without appreciably altering its basic plan, producing a range of hybrid types. The most significant intrusive feature is the jamb wall, traditionally built at right angles to the hearth wall of lowland houses to separate the fireplace from the front door, but used in new positions in the hybrid houses.

into the lowlands of the Shannon estuary and northwards to the Lough Neagh lowlands, their features often fusing with those of direct entry houses.

• Fig. 16   Rear view of farmstead, Magheraroarty, county Donegal. The domed thatch is typical of the exposed west coast. Often one end of an old house (usually that furthest from the hearth) was given a second-storey and slated. A shallow bed-outshot lies alongside the hearth.

• Fig. 18 Rear view of a western, gable-ended house, Inagh valley, county Galway. The thatch has been replaced by corrugated iron, painted in customary red. The rear wall has only a single small window, near the main hearth of the house.

Building materials and construction methods

Regional variations occur in the methods and materials of construction, roofing, thatching and walling.

Roofs Roof frameworks are usually simple and the main form of roof support is a couple truss resting on the wall heads. In east Ulster, however, roofs were often framed with purlins resting upon the gable walls and have no supporting trusses. Cruck constructions have been recorded mainly in the north of Ireland, particularly in Donegal and Londonderry. Crucks are pairs of curved timbers rising from ground level, meeting at the apex of the house and supporting the weight of the roof. Their distribution may once have been wider, but no examples have yet been discovered in the south and east. Crucks were widely used in vernacular buildings in Wales, Scotland and western England, but not in the south and east of England.

Timber box-framed houses of the kind which flourished in lowland England were built by British settlers in Ulster in the early seventeenth century but otherwise were never numerous in the Irish countryside. They were common in eastern ports, such as Dublin and Drogheda, until the seventeenth century. Timber houses deteriorated quickly in the damp Irish climate and by the nineteenth century had completely vanished from town and country.

Thatching techniques and materials vary from one part of the country to another. In most areas a thin layer of sods or 'scraws' is laid upon and tied to the roof timbers to support the thatch and improve heat insulation. Wheaten straw is the most widely used material for thatch. Northern Leinster, however, preferred oaten straw, and reeds were favoured in some localities of Munster and flax in counties Londonderry, Donegal and Fermanagh. Rushes and tough marram grasses were used in mountainous coastal areas of the north-west and west. The most general method of securing the thatch is by pinning the straw to the scraws

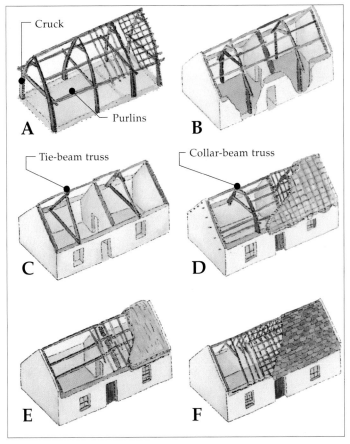

Fig. 20 A classification by Alan Gailey of traditional roof-timbering systems. A) Cruck trusses (continuous blades), through purlins, and over-lying common rafters. B) Cruck trusses (jointed blades) interposed between transverse walls, with through purlins. C) Tie-beam trusses, with through purlins. D) Collar-beam trusses, with through purlins. E) Purlin roof supported on gable and internal transverse wall, with common rafters. F) Common-rafter trusses with ridge piece for slating.

with scollops – pegs made with thin rods of briar and hazel. Along northern and western coasts, presumably in response to the strong winds, the thatched roof is commonly held in place by a rope net tied to pegs in the house walls or to a row of stone weights. Gables may project above the level of the thatch to prevent the wind

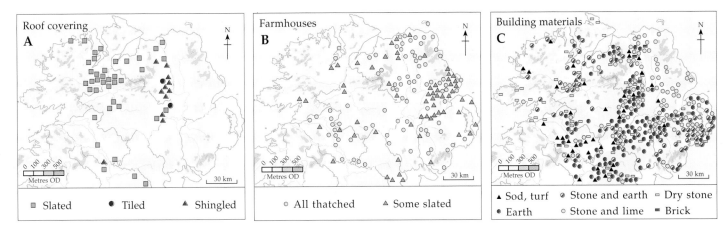

Fig. 19 Rural building and roof materials, Ulster. A) Roof covering other than thatch recorded in early seventeenth-century plantation surveys. B) Farmhouses, by parish, thatched and slated in the 1830s. C) Building materials in the 1830s.

Thatched Houses

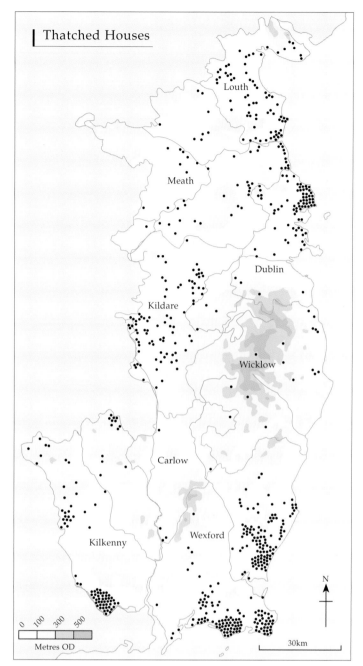

Fig. 21 Thatched roofs, in eastern Ireland, 1990 (as mapped by Michael Higginbotham for the Office of Public Works). Thatched roofs are rapidly disappearing. Thatch is most plentiful in north county Dublin, Kildare and Wexford; it is rare in the Wicklow mountains and county Carlow where stone walling and slated roofs are long established. The clusters in counties Wexford (Kilmore Quay, Blackwater and Lady's Island), Kilkenny (Mooncoin) and Dublin (Rush and Skerries) reflect the continuity of settlement and tenacious building traditions of these areas.

lifting the roof. Alternatively, the thatch is secured to the gable walls by strips of mud or plaster. The distinctive rounded contours of the thatched roofs of county Donegal provide streamlining against Atlantic gales.

The transition from thatch to slate was complex and lengthy, occurring first on superior dwellings in the middle ages. Widespread adoption of slates on vernacular houses

Fig. 22 Roofing materials and construction. ● A) This newly-made thatch has been secured by a rope net tied to pegs in the walls, as is common on the western seaboard. Léitir Fraic, county Galway. ● B) In west county Clare, near Liscannor, the local sandstone flags are used for roofing and for paving.

occurred in the second half of the nineteenth century but in some areas the transition took place more recently. Corrugated iron sheeting is another recent innovation, often concealing earlier thatch. Over wide areas, thatched roofs and thatching skills have now virtually disappeared.

Walling In recent centuries, mass walling has been universal in vernacular buildings. Stone is the most common wall material, although sometimes difficult to recognise owing to external rendering. Packing wedged around roughly-dressed field stones is a widespread walling technique using clay or lime mortar. However, dry stone walling was common in the far west. Good quality ashlar stone-work is rarely encountered in vernacular buildings, except for architectural detailing such as quoins, cornices, lintels and chimney stacks, mainly in estate cottages and in proximity to quarries. Timber and wattle, originally significant building materials, declined in importance as the woodlands

PFEIFFER STUDIO

PFEIFFER STUDIO

F.H.A. AALEN

Fig. 23 Local stone was used in vernacular buildings, but in houses it is often concealed by whitewash or rough harl. Building materials are best displayed in outhouses and deserted dwellings, where the size and type of the stones give the buildings much of their individual character. ● A) The gable of this building in Streamstown Bay, county Galway, is constructed with limestone and granite, using a combination of flat and rounded stones laid roughly in courses. ● B) This stable in Inishowen, county Donegal, is built of roughly-coursed rubble of greenish slate-like local stone. Dry-stone construction is common in the area. The roof slates, from a local quarry, are of a different texture and colour. ● C) The thick gable-end of this deserted house on the western side of the Wicklow hills is built mainly of local granite boulders. Thin flaky slabs from the nearby schist belt on the flank of the main granite mass serve as packing around the roughly-dressed stone.

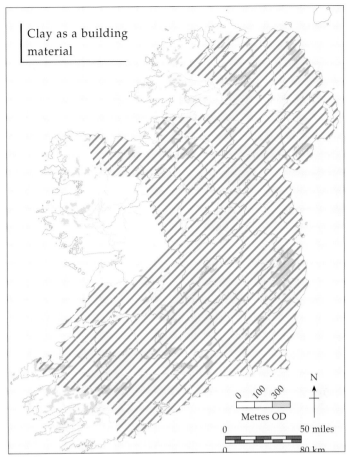

Clay as a building material

Fig. 24 The use of clay as a building material. Until the twentieth century, tempered clay was widely used as a wall-building material in houses and outbuildings, except in three western areas – for the most part stony or boggy tracts where suitable clay could not be found. In many areas, both clay and stone houses are found. Clay-walled houses are particularly numerous and well-constructed in the south-east lowlands of Ireland.

were progressively removed and timber became a scarce commodity for ordinary people, used only in roof construction. In the west, where soils are shallow, it was customary to build in stone as well as in timber; stone became the main material as early as the eighteenth century. In the east, stone houses were less common and, when timber resources dwindled, mud from the thick glacial drift deposits became a popular building material and remained so until industrially produced materials became generally available in the present century. Many thousands of mud-walled houses and barns survive, sometimes difficult to recognise owing to rendering and paint. Walls were made with a mixture of wet clay and rushes built up without any mould or support and trimmed with a spade. Sometimes they rested on basal stone courses. Turf was also used as a building material, especially for temporary farm structures and for shelters for peat cutters. Poor people sometimes built entire houses with turf or used it to build the gables. Bricks were not introduced at vernacular level until the late eighteenth century and not widely used until the late nineteenth century.

F.H.A. AALEN

MAURA SHAFFREY

Fig. 25 Mud-walled buildings. ● A) Decayed, mud-walled house, county Offaly. ● B) This structure in south county Meath was originally a house. The thatched roof has been replaced with corrugated iron while retaining the hipped ends, and the central chimney is still evident.

F.H.A. AALEN

● Fig. 26 House with turf gable, Glencullen, county Dublin, 1960.

DEVELOPED VERNACULAR HOUSES

Substantial two-storeyed houses can be found in the Irish countryside which are clearly elaborations of basic vernacular patterns and retain old ground plans, door and hearth locations. Early examples date from around 1700, but the majority are nineteenth-century dwellings of strong farmers and successful traders and reflect the emergence of a clear social hierarchy within the rural population. Impressive two-storeyed farmhouses were developed on the lobby entrance/central hearth model, especially in counties Meath, Wexford, Kilkenny and Limerick. Some of these retained thatched, hip-ended roofs; others adopted slated, gable-ended roofs. In western areas, development of the direct-entry, long-house tradition produced storeyed houses, retaining opposite doors and a tripartite ground-floor plan.

The improvement of rural housing in the nineteenth and early twentieth centuries was mainly produced by enlarging old houses: owing to difficult economic circumstances

BARRY O'REILLY

BARRY O'REILLY

Fig. 27 Two-storey, central-hearth/lobby entrance, thatched dwelling with mud walls. ● A) Mayglass, county Wexford. This dwelling was built c. 1700, an early date for an Irish farmhouse. ● B) Tullaroan, county Kilkenny. Large, vernacular thatched farmhouse of central hearth derivation (now the Lory Meagher hurling museum).

A

B

PFEIFFER STUDIO

MAURA SHAFFREY

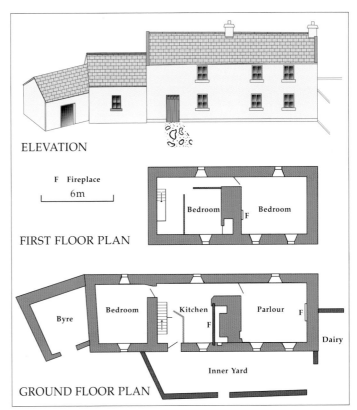

ELEVATION

F Fireplace

6m

FIRST FLOOR PLAN

Bedroom

Bedroom

F

GROUND FLOOR PLAN

Byre

Bedroom

Kitchen

F

Parlour

F

Dairy

Inner Yard

Fig. 30 ● Two-storeyed, direct-entry house (c. 1930). This house developed from a nineteenth-century, single-storeyed, thatched structure. The upper storey retains the ground-floor plan. Slievecorragh, west county Wicklow.

Fig. 28 Linear farmsteads with part of the house raised and slated. ● A) Strabane, county Tyrone. This building has been restored by the National Trust (NI). ● B) Dromore West, near Tubbercurry, county Sligo

and tenacious tradition, this was undertaken piecemeal and hence did not lead to general or sharp departure from vernacular forms. Elongation of houses was often achieved simply by incorporating attached byres and sheds into the house, in which event new outbuildings were constructed, usually separate from the house. However, elongation of houses characteristically one room in width accentuated heating problems, necessitating additional fireplaces and

chimney stacks. An alternative approach was to add an upper storey to single-storey houses. Sometimes only portions of the house were raised, usually an end room. A complete upper storey, however, made a substantial addition to house space with more privacy and rooms for specialised use.

Additions were accompanied by other changes; a slated roof might replace the thatch, doors and windows were more symmetrically arranged. But houses usually remained one room in width and the location of the

A

PFEIFFER STUDIO

B

BARRY O'REILLY

Fig. 29 Traditional single-storey houses of the central-hearth type converted into two-storey dwellings. ● A) Near Knocktopher, county Kilkenny. A first floor was added around the turn of the century, the thatch replaced by slates and the chimney built up in brick. ● B) Ballyragget, county Kilkenny. Gable-ended farmhouse with slated roof. Door and chimney are aligned. The porch is a later addition.

PFEIFFER STUDIO

F.H.A. AALEN

F.H.A. AALEN

Fig. 31 Enlarged, direct-entry houses. ● A) Near Letterkenny, county Donegal. This substantial two-storeyed farmhouse is in the direct-entry tradition with gable-end chimneys. Vernacular influences show in the elongated plan and uneven spacing of windows and doors. ● B) This improved, two-storeyed thatched farmhouse near Tuam, county Galway is built on a direct-entry plan which may reflect long-house antecedents.

PFEIFFER STUDIO

Fig. 33 Nineteenth-century two-storeyed houses, with centrally-located door, symmetrical fenestration and gable-end chimneys. ● A) Blessington, county Wicklow. ● B) Lough Finn, county Donegal.

main chimney and the upper-storey layout were often determined by the vernacular plan of the ground floor while window size remained smaller at the back than at the front.

As the nineteenth century progressed, new two-storeyed and slated houses were increasingly built by ordinary farmers. There are two common types. In the first, the door is located centrally and chimneys are on the gable ends. Usually these houses are elementary in plan, typically with two ground-floor rooms occupying the full width of the house, a central hallway, and two or three bedrooms on the upper storey. However larger, more elaborate versions can be found. The second type of house is hip-ended with centralised chimney stacks on either side of a central hall. Both types, especially the second, adopt features from formal houses, such as large windows and a

● Fig. 32 Evolution of a farmhouse, Castlehaven, Castletownshend, county Cork. The original single-storeyed, two-roomed, thatched house, was first enlarged into a two-storeyed farmhouse and then later extended again.

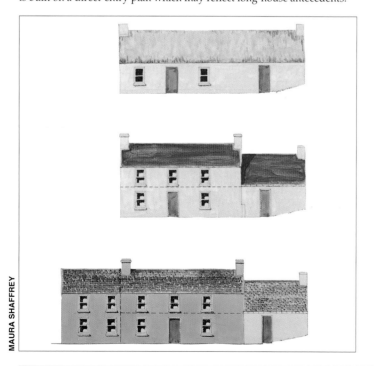

MAURA SHAFFREY

F.H.A. AALEN

F.H.A. AALEN

MAURA SHAFFREY

Fig. 34 Two-storeyed houses, with central hallway, rounded doorway and two centralised chimneys were widely built from the eighteenth century onwards and, in some instances, as late as the 1950s. They usually indicate a farm of more than 40 ha but were often built for traders and professional people including clergy. Although they possess a common basic design, these houses lie on the wide, subtly nuanced frontier between the vernacular and formal, within which stylistic differences carry significant social meaning. Houses at the vernacular end, like the great mass of rural houses, are elementary and are generally referred to simply by the family name of the owner and the townland. Towards the formal end of the spectrum, the houses are grander and have individual names. ● A) Clogheen, county Kildare. In this modest roadside farmhouse, the small windows, subdued arch of the doorway and narrowness of the building suggest the continuing weight of the vernacular tradition. ● B) Woodview, near Portarlington, county Laois. A solid farmhouse built in 1890 on an 80 ha holding. The simplicity is vernacular but the symmetry is formal, as are the large windows and the door. ●C) Near Boyle, county Roscommon. The features of this substantial nineteenth-century dwelling, particularly the quoins and decorative arched entrance, place the building firmly in the formal tradition.

'Georgian' fanlight above the front door; although much diminished, vernacular influences are not entirely eliminated and the houses still tend to conform to the old pattern of being one room in width.

FORMAL ARCHITECTURAL TRADITION

In each locality, house-styles varied with the social status of the occupants. Very large houses rarely have any vernacular flavour, but conform to national and ultimately international standards of taste and design, to canons of formal or 'polite' architecture. Between the great house and the broad mass of vernacular dwellings is a range of well-to-do houses in which formal and vernacular features are fused in varying degree; the influence of formal models is

revealed by their ground plans and their striving after a symmetrical arrangement of doors, windows and chimneys in the facade of the house.

A small number of old, two-storeyed and originally thatched dwellings, with a formal ordering of plan and facade, are found mainly in the lowlands of the south and east and scattered across the north of Ireland. Such houses are associated with larger farms and planter families and probably originated in the seventeenth and early eighteenth centuries. They did not serve as exemplars for any widespread development of storeyed dwellings.

In the late eighteenth and nineteenth centuries, it was common for minor gentry, more prosperous farmers and

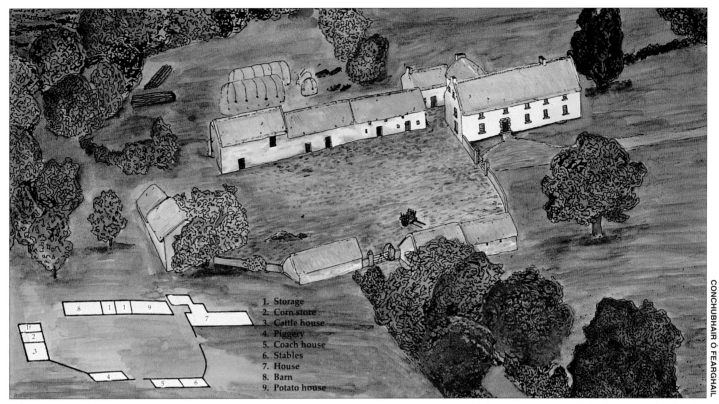

CONCHUBHAIR Ó FEARGHAIL

1. Storage
2. Corn store
3. Cattle house
4. Piggery
5. Coach house
6. Stables
7. House
8. Barn
9. Potato house

● Fig. 35 Large house and farmyard at Newbawn, south-west county Wexford. This complex was built *c*. 1700 by the Catholic Sweetman family who leased the whole townland and were merchants involved in the Newfoundland trade, as well as prosperous big farmers. The house is detached from the farm buildings and transitional in style between formal and vernacular. The large cobbled farmyard is enclosed by outbuildings in the characteristic south-eastern courtyard style – a style probably continental in origin and with medieval precedents in Ireland in moated-site lay-outs.

professional people to replace their old thatched houses with more substantial houses built mainly in formal Georgian style. These houses usually possessed two and sometimes three storeys and slated, hipped roofs; the front door with segmented fanlight is centrally placed in the facade of the house and windows and chimneys are also symmetrically arranged. In the second half of the nineteenth century, when storeyed farmhouses first became numerous and used by ordinary farmers, they were influenced by the larger Georgian houses.

MAURA SHAFFREY

MAURA SHAFFREY

MAURA SHAFFREY

● Fig. 36 Edenballycoggill, near Waringstown, county Down. This Planter's house of *c*. 1700 is very well preserved and has changed little from the original design.

● Fig. 37 Peacefield House, Ballynacor, near Portadown, county Armagh. An elegant mid nineteenth-century farmhouse (top) added to an earlier group of substantial buildings (bottom) located behind the house.

Fig. 38 Houses built in the formal architectural tradition. ●A) Nineteenth-century land-agent's house in sober classical style. Such houses were widely built in the countryside and influenced the architecture of many contemporary and later farmhouses. Kilmainhamwood, county Meath. ●B) Nineteenth-century classical farmhouse, with rear yard and the cylindrical gate posts common to the region. Barrack Crossroads, county Wexford. ●C) A substantial, well-sited, classical three-storey dwelling which served as a farmhouse and as a hotel for passengers on the nearby Mountmellick canal. North-east county Laois.

PUBLIC HOUSING FOR SMALL FARMERS AND LABOURERS: CABINS AND COTTAGES

On large estates, housing for labourers was frequently provided by landlords in the eighteenth and nineteenth centuries, using stone walls and slated roofs. These dwellings, recognisable by their more formal architectural style, were built individually, in pairs and in short terraces, especially in estate towns and villages. However, most rural labourers in the nineteenth century still lived in one or two-roomed dwellings, or cabins, rented from farmers, built of mud or sod and sometimes even lacking doors and windows. Characteristically, cabins were dispersed singly on small plots of potato land, often lying on the edge of commons, moors and bogs.

Little was done to improve labourers' dwellings until the end of the nineteenth century, when the situation was materially transformed by public housing programmes in rural areas. The Labourers' Acts, commencing in 1883, enabled local authorities with state subvention to erect almost 50,000 new cottages for landless labourers by 1921. Building activity was mainly concentrated in the south and east of the country where, owing to the larger farms, labourers were more numerous. Cottage styles varied considerably through time and between localities, but generally they were simple and solid, with masonry or concrete walls and slated roofs, and rather more formal architecturally than private cottages and most farmhouses. Many labourers' cottages, especially early ones, were single or semi-detached and usually scattered along roadsides, each on a 0.2 ha allotment. In the twentieth century, they were sometimes built in terraces in organised schemes; old mud cabins were abandoned and rapidly decayed. Cottage building in rural areas of the South was continued after partition by the Land Commission and County Councils. Thus, Ireland, unlike

Fig. 39 Ballymascanlan, county Louth. A well-designed row of nineteenth-century estate cottages with slated roofs and tall, red-brick chimneys.

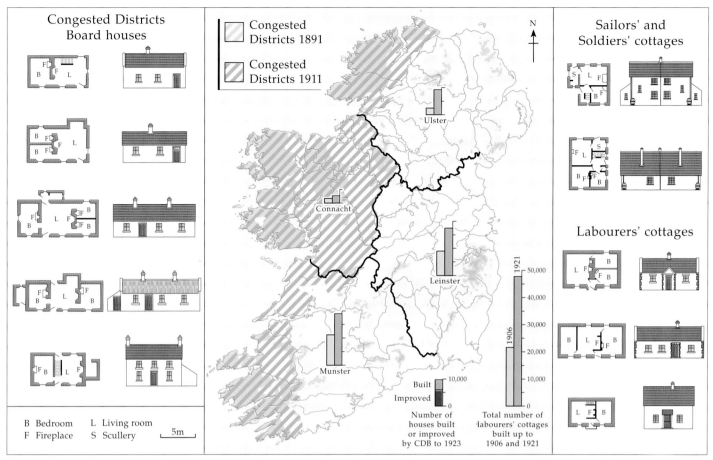

Congested Districts Board houses

Congested Districts 1891

Congested Districts 1911

Sailors' and Soldiers' cottages

Labourers' cottages

B Bedroom   L Living room
F Fireplace   S Scullery

5m

Built
Improved

Number of houses built or improved by CDB to 1923

Total number of labourers' cottages built up to 1906 and 1921

Fig. 40 Rural public housing, *c.* 1880 to *c.* 1921. In the last two decades of the nineteenth century, a coherent national policy for rural housing emerged under the Labourers' Acts and the Congested Districts Board. By 1921, substantial progress had been made towards solving the basic housing problems of low income groups with almost 60,000 houses provided by local authorities. Rural labourers' cottages were most numerous in the south east; they were essentially much-improved versions of traditional dwellings, perpetuating the lobby entrance but replacing the hipped roofs with gables and the thatch with slates. In the north-east of Ireland, where housing conditions were generally better than elsewhere, the local authorities made little use of the new housing legislation. The Congested Districts Board built and improved houses for the impoverished small farmers of western Ireland and perpetuated traditional features such as outshot beds and, sometimes, thatch. Over 4,000 houses were provided for ex-servicemen after World War I. Generally superior to labourers' cottages, they were widely distributed in small groups, many on the edge of landed estates or in the hinterland of major cities.

Britain, is characterised by a long tradition and considerable body of public housing in rural areas. With the introduction of vested ownership in the 1930s, many cottages were improved and enlarged. Alterations have continued

in recent years and the origins of numerous cottages will soon be unrecognisable.

In western Ireland, the labouring class was few and small farmers predominated whose dwellings were as

Fig. 41 ● A) Labourer's cottage with attic bedrooms, county Longford. This was a style widely used by local authorities in south-eastern and central Ireland for several decades after its introduction in the 1880s. It is clearly influenced by the traditional lobby entrance/central hearth house. ● B) Semi-detached, two-storeyed cottages with lean-to scullery, a standard design by the Board of Works for ex-servicemen, 1919-23. Hacketstown, county Carlow.

PFEIFFER STUDIO

• Fig. 42 Long Island, south-west county Cork. Almost all the houses here were rebuilt by the Congested Districts Board, using two standard models – two-storeyed farmhouses and small houses with attic bedrooms. Ruins of discarded, single-storey thatched houses can be seen. Like many off-shore islands, Long Island now has few permanent residents but the houses are occupied by summer visitors. Fastnet rock and lighthouse are in the background.

poor as those of labourers in the east of the country. Between 1891 and 1923, the Congested Districts Board erected or substantially improved over 9,000 farm dwellings, greatly reducing the number of traditional byre-dwellings and almost completely replacing the housing stock in remote western areas and off-shore islands. The Board's houses broadly followed traditional patterns and took account of the social gradations of rural society.

An additional contribution to rural housing was made after World War I, when the British government provided houses for ex-servicemen under the Irish Land (Provision for Sailors and Soldiers) Act of 1919. After partition, the work was undertaken by the Irish Sailors' and Soldiers' Land Trust, which built over 4,000 houses of varied types, but mainly two-storey cottages, semi-detached or in short terraces with front and rear gardens. Many were built in the immediate hinterland of major cities and, like Killester on the northern outskirts of Dublin and Castlereagh outside Belfast, have since been enveloped in suburban growths.

BUNGALOWS: THE NEW VERNACULAR ?

In the present century, traditional dwellings have been largely replaced by new houses and either destroyed or relegated to use as storehouses, garages or byres. New houses, public and private, are of many styles, with the majority flaunting a clear break with older patterns. The most common form of new rural housing is the bungalow, now so dominant as to form virtually a new vernacular. Introduced to Ireland at the end of the nineteenth century, bungalows spread considerably in the inter-war period and proliferated in the major wave of rural house building in the 1970s and 1980s initiated by EC membership and growing prosperity in the farming community. For a large part of the population, increased affluence and use of the car have widened locational choices for residence; many urban workers and retired people, including returned emigrants, have chosen to settle in rural areas, with the bungalow as their favoured dwelling form.

New bungalows are conspicuous and aesthetically controversial elements of the contemporary rural scene, typically lining and facing directly onto main roads, often

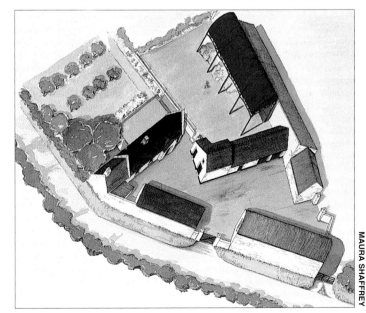

MARGARET O'FLANAGAN

MARGARET O'FLANAGAN

MARGARET O'FLANAGAN

●Fig. 43 Bungalows in Inishowen, county Donegal. A) Modern bungalow built alongside a traditional thatched house, with similar orientation and much the same style and proportions. B) Modern bungalow with front portico, a popular imported design feature. C) Bungalow of the 1980s with a portico and dormer windows, next to a more restrained bungalow in a style used in the inter-war period and not wholly discordant with traditional forms.

AGRICULTURAL BUILDINGS
FARM LAY-OUT

The larger farms in southern and eastern Ireland, with a traditionally greater emphasis on mixed farming, needed a variety of buildings for their closely interrelated farm activities. The farm buildings are frequently grouped around a rectangular yard, with one side formed by the dwelling house, but many farms and especially the smaller ones do not exhibit any distinctive lay-out of buildings.

In the north and west of the country, the older farmsteads commonly constitute a single long range of buildings, with house, stable and byre joined together. Sometimes on the poorest farms, the house stands alone without paddock or garden and accompanied by only a small crude storehouse. The limited development of outbuildings on western farms may well be linked to the pastoral traditions and mild climate but reflects also long-standing use of compact long-houses which accommodated animals and humans under one roof. Detached, functionally specialised buildings have only appeared with the breakdown of the long-house tradition. On many of the older farmsteads in south-western Ireland, the house faces the outbuildings and is separated from them by a laneway sometimes known as the 'street', which connects to the public road.

Barns and other traditional outbuildings on Irish farms are not usually impressive structures; they lack even elementary ornamentation and do not, on the whole, exhibit building techniques of any great antiquity. However, in west Kerry the small stone huts (clocháin), with circular plans and domed roofs (still occasionally used as henhouses or pigsties) perpetuate

on highly visible sites. Many have been designed and built by the occupants but repetition of basic forms reflects the influence of widely-used design manuals. There have been many changes in their dominant style; some bungalows are unassuming and do not contrast sharply with traditional house types, but in most the style, building materials and techniques, siting, landscaping and orientation show little regard for local traditions or sensitive integration into the rural setting. Two-storey houses became increasingly popular in the 1980s, initially mock-Georgian in style but followed by eclectic post-modernism. These latest forms may challenge and replace the bungalow, but future fashion is unpredictable. Without corrective policies, house styles are likely to increase in variety and discordance with the landscape.

MAURA SHAFFREY

●Fig. 44 Farm with an irregular lay-out, Dunmore, county Kilkenny.

an extremely old style of building. Characteristically, the farmers have erected only the most functional of outbuildings. Like the farmhouses, these are rectangular in plan and built with either stone or mud. There is little aesthetically comparable to the spacious and colourful barns of the American countryside, for example, or the distinctive carved timber buildings of Norway and Switzerland. However, the simplicity and directness of agricultural buildings in Ireland and their use of local building materials does connect them naturally to the land, and farmsteads often form pleasing assemblages which nestle comfortably in the landscape.

With the modernisation of agriculture in recent decades, many new farm buildings have been erected,

Fig. 45 Some basic farmyard types. ● A) Lenan Head, county Donegal. In the north and west of the country, farmsteads commonly form a single long range of buildings. ● B) Owning, county Kilkenny. House and outbuildings along three sides of a yard. ● C) Old Conna estate, south county Dublin. This courtyard farmyard has a range of substantial two-storey buildings with characteristic arched doorways and a castellated entrance gate. Elaborate compositions of this scale are confined to larger farms and demesnes.

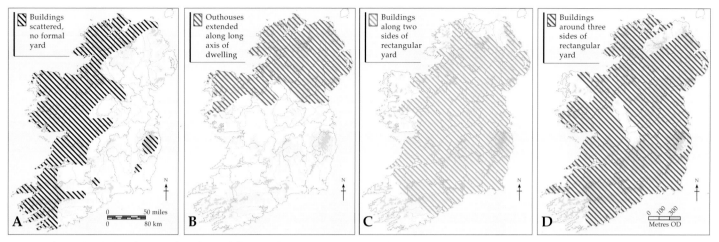

Fig. 46 Generalised distribution of traditional farmyard types. There is considerable overlapping of types. A) Farmyard buildings scattered, no formal yard. B) Farmyard buildings and outhouses extended along the long axis of the dwelling. C) Farmyard buildings around two sides of a rectangular yard. D) Farmyard buildings around three sides of a rectangular yard.

especially in richer eastern areas, modifying traditional patterns of farm lay-out. In particular, there is a tendency towards looser and generally linear arrangements of farm buildings, consistent with increased use of tractors and bulky machinery. The erection of slatted sheds and large metal barns to provide winter shelter for cattle and crop storage has been widespread in recent decades. These structures are usually detached from and dominate the older ranges of buildings and testify to a new attitude to working the land. Farm amalgamation in areas of rural depopulation has led to abandonment or partial use of many farmsteads which frequently become unsightly cattle yards and silage stores, with dilapidated buildings, rusting machinery and decaying vehicles.

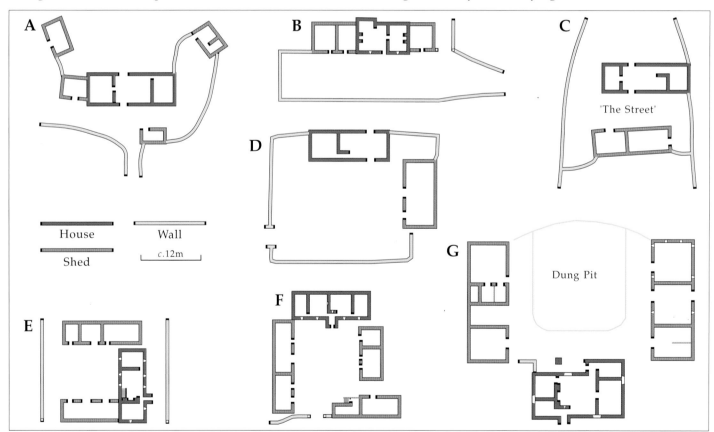

Fig. 47 Traditional farmyard plans. ● A) Irregular farmyard with scattered buildings, Gorumna, county Galway. ● B) Outhouses extended along long axis of dwelling. Glenhull, county Tyrone. ● C) A 'parallel farmstead' with house and buildings separated by a narrow yard or 'street', Bealach Oisín (Ballaghisheen), near Glenbeigh, county Kerry. ○ D) 'Half courtyard' type with buildings along two sides of a rectangular yard, Kilbaha, county Clare. ● E) Buildings along three sides of a rectangular yard, Drishoge, county Dublin. ● F) Buildings forming an almost completely enclosed yard, Castle Otway, near Templederry, county Tipperary. ● G) Improved farm lay-out, c. 1820. The house is detached with front entrance away from the yard. Gosford and Drumbanagher estates, county Armagh.

MAURA SHAFFREY

●Fig. 48 A small farm near Castlebar, county Mayo. The roadside location and compact arrangement of the buildings is characteristic of the west of Ireland. The house is nearest to the road; other buildings include a metal hayshed and a two-storey outhouse, the upper storey used for storage, the lower for animals. There is an improvised air to the lay-out, but the buildings form a pleasant, unassuming ensemble.

MAURA SHAFFREY

●Fig. 49 Typical hayshed, constructed of iron and usually painted in strong colours, most commonly red. Given appropriate siting and colour, these features blend surprisingly well into the landscape.

F.H.A. AALEN

●Fig. 50 Farmstead with large modern sheds and barns near Dunlavin, west county Wicklow. No planning permission is required for these grant-aided developments which have a major impact on the landscape.

RELICS OF THE OLDER AGRARIAN ORDER

An assortment of structures, formerly integrated with rural economic and social life but now virtually obsolescent, are scattered over the countryside. Little understood or valued in a rapidly modernising countryside, they are fast disappearing, owing to destruction or neglect. These structures include corbelled dry-stone clocháin, either curvilinear or rectangular in plan, built as herders' huts, animal shelters, sweat houses, spring and well covers. In earlier times clocháin served as monastic cells, shelters for pilgrims and residences for poor people.

Booleying was the Irish form of the widespread European practice of transhumance or summer movement of herders and animals to mountain pastures at a distance from permanent settlements. Deeply rooted in Irish society, the custom survived, usually in a vestigial form, into recent centuries. Surviving structures on summer milking sites (buaile) are mainly small stone huts. Perishable materials such as timber and wattle or sods were also used on earth or stone foundations but have left few traces.

Derelict lime kilns, corn kilns, kelp kilns, lint kilns (for drying flax), turf shelters, dovecotes, ice houses (partly or wholly subterranean) and soot houses also occur, as well as

MICHAEL DIGGIN

● Fig. 51 Clochán, Great Blasket, county Kerry. Clocháin are dry-stone structures, round or oval in plan both inside and out but sometimes squared inside. A few are rectangular in plan with ridged stone roofs. The structures are built using the corbelling technique – layers of stones laid in circles of ever-decreasing diameter until the chamber can be closed at the top with a single capstone; wall and roof are thus continuous. They are particularly numerous in Kerry, where they are used for varied purposes. A sod cover on the capstones is common.

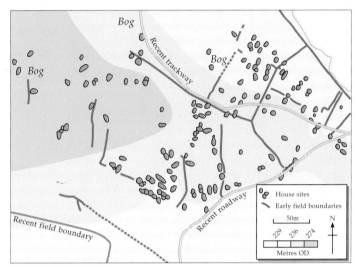

● Fig. 53 Goodland, county Antrim. This remarkable concentration of more than a hundred hut sites lies on the north coast above Murlough Bay, on a rare outcrop of chalk now covered by grassland and blanket bog. After an expansion of farming in the Middle Ages, the area reverted to rough grazing and in the fifteenth and sixteenth centuries was used by transhumant herders who probably erected the huts as seasonal residences. The huts were roughly rectangular, single-roomed and built of sods stripped from the grassland.

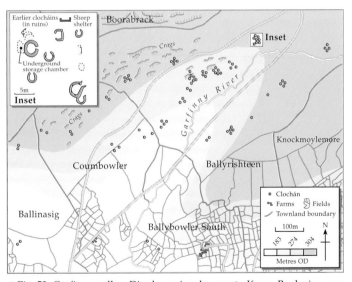

● Fig. 52 Garfinny valley, Dingle peninsula, county Kerry. Booleying was practiced in the mountainous Dingle peninsula until the nineteenth century. Herders sheltered in clocháin with subterranean storage areas.

THERESA MACDONALD

● Fig. 54 Bunowna, Achill, county Mayo. Booleying on the mountainous island of Achill was a vital part of the rural economy and survived well into the present century. Each major settlement had one or more summer villages for herders, in some cases ten kilometers apart. At these sites, the remains are usually small dry-stone huts, oval in plan, with partly corbelled walls and originally thatched. These huts at Bunowna lie in a typical position along the banks of a mountain stream.

● Fig. 55 Painting of a 'buaile' hut on Achill Island, county Mayo, by Francis Walker, 1903. Unlike most landscape painters of the west, Walker captured the authentic customs and impoverished circumstances of rural dwellers at the turn of the century.

Fig. 56 In many parts of Europe in former centuries, pigeons and doves were kept as a useful source of fresh meat, eggs and manure. Dovecotes are not common in Ireland, examples occurring mainly on demesnes and large farms in the south and east and no longer in use. ● A) This substantial dovecote, round in plan with a stone, domed roof is at Kilcooly Abbey, county Tipperary, a twelfth-century Cistercian foundation. ● B) Dovecotes are rare in western Ireland. This ruined structure stands on the farmyard of a large holding (now considerably reduced by the Land Commission) in Carrowbeg, north county Galway. There has been settlement on the site since at least the seventeenth century.

THERESA MACDONALD

● Fig. 57 Soot-houses were simple stone huts, the timber and sod roofs of which were slowly burnt each winter until they collapsed, the ash then being used as fertiliser. Examples are known only from Achill Island, where they were used until the early twentieth century, but almost certainly, soot-houses once had a wider distribution. This example, now destroyed, was in Dooagh townland, Achill Island, county Mayo.

BARRY O'REILLY

BARRY O'REILLY

TH MASON

● Fig. 59 Corn-stands were once common on farms, especially in the east, but most have been destroyed within the last fifty years. They were usually formed with six upright granite pillars (0.6m high) with stone caps, arranged in a circle around a central pillar. Long narrow stones connected the caps to each other and to the centre, providing a platform on which branches were laid and the corn stacked on top for protection from damp and rodents. This example in west county Wicklow was photographed in 1939.

sheep pens and a wide range of abandoned huts, dwellings and enclosures of uncertain age and function. Forges, for the shoeing of horses and making of metal articles for farm and domestic use, were once common in the countryside, usually at crossroads. Since the World War II, forges have ceased to function with the decline of the horse as a means of traction, but the buildings, many with distinctive 'horse-shoe' entrances, survive with new uses.

F.H.A. AALEN

● Fig. 60 Forge at crossroads near Rathangan, county Kildare.

Fig. 58 (left) Lime kilns reduced limestone to a powder by burning; the powder was then spread on the fields as a fertiliser or used in building for mortar or limewash. Until the nineteenth century, many townlands had their own limekiln and especially in hill areas limestone fertiliser played an important role in the reclamation of acid soils. Kilns remained in use until imported guano and artificial manures replaced limestone in the nineteenth century. The structures vary in size and quality. Small round kilns were common in many areas, especially the west. Large rectangular improved types with one or more well-built, arched recesses at the front are plentiful in richer farm areas; they are often associated with the local estate and typically built into the side of a hill close to quarries. ● A) Small round kiln on Inishbofin, county Mayo. ● B) Large, rectangular kiln, Maddockstown, county Kilkenny.

BARRY O'REILLY

F.H.A. AALEN

Fig. 61 Sweat-houses were the Irish equivalent of the Turkish bath or Finnish sauna and the heat treatment they provided was much esteemed by rural people. Most sweat-houses were small, dry-stone structures with low, lintelled doorways. The stone floor was first heated by fires; people then sat inside, naked and sweating profusely, before cooling themselves in a stream or lake. ● A) Sweat-house at Cloghkeating, county Tipperary. ● B) This sweat-house, at Creevaghbaun, county Galway, has a corbelled ridged roof and lies close to a ruined friary and graveyard. Today it is used as a sheep shelter.

PUBLIC BUILDINGS

CHURCHES

While farmhouses are the most numerous rural buildings, churches are generally the most prominent and, save perhaps for houses and buildings on landed estates and a scatter of monasteries, convents, hotels and private schools, also the most substantial. Each parish has a Catholic and a Church of Ireland (Anglican) church; many northern areas have a Presbyterian and Methodist church as well as chapels and meeting houses of other denominations. Churches are characteristically associated with graveyards, church halls, rectories, parochial houses or manses.

Owing to a disrupted religious history and the absence in most areas of traditions of village living, ancient churches in continued use are uncommon in rural Ireland. The strong sense of continuity given to many English and continental villages by an enduring place of worship encapsulating the total history of the community is thus missing. The Irish countryside is rich in ecclesiastical ruins and relics from many periods which poignantly reflect a troubled past.

Most medieval churches are ruinous and often at some distance from modern settlement. The bulk of rural churches are of eighteenth century or later date, although Church of Ireland churches are frequently built on much

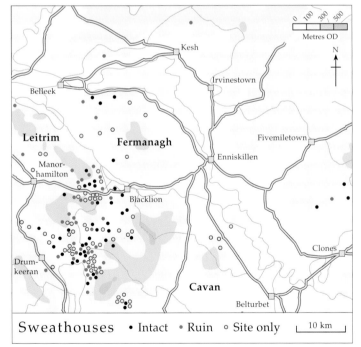

Sweathouses • Intact • Ruin ○ Site only   10 km

● Fig. 62 Use of sweat-houses was once widespread, lingering on in some places into the nineteenth century. Many sweat-houses are known to have been destroyed. Surviving examples are widely distributed but occur chiefly in the northern half of the island with a major concentration in counties Leitrim, Fermanagh and Cavan.

F.H.A. AALEN

● Fig. 63 Ruined medieval church with remnants of an attached residential tower, St James, Coghlinstown, county Kildare. The graveyard is still used and maintained. Many ruined medieval churches are scattered in the countryside. Originally, they were associated with settlements but the Reformation, seventeenth-century religious wars and rural reorganisation under the new estate system led to their abandonment.

F.H.A. AALEN

BRIAN MACDONALD

F.H.A. AALEN

Fig. 64 Church of Ireland churches. ● A) The medieval parish church of St Finians, Newcastle, county Dublin. The strong western tower, virtually a towerhouse, is a characteristic feature of churches in the medieval Pale. The lowest storey of the tower is the entrance lobby to the church; the upper storey was the priest's residence. ● B) St Johns, Clonmore, county Carlow. A nineteenth-century 'tower and hall' building on the site of an ancient monastery. ● C) St Johns, Cloverhill, county Cavan. Situated opposite the entrance to the Saunderson demesne, the church was built in 1856 as part of the estate village.

older sites and sometimes incorporate medieval fabric. In order to serve dispersed farms, churches are often isolated in the countryside, but the Church of Ireland (the Established Church until 1869), which was supported by the gentry, is often in or close to a demesne. Many Catholic churches occur in small settlements or 'chapel villages' which grew around them in the nineteenth century.

In a major operation in the first three decades of the nineteenth century, the Church of Ireland rebuilt half of its churches and erected a similar number of new ones, mainly gothic style churches of the 'tower and hall' variety. A further wave of building occurred after disestablishment in 1869. Today, as congregations shrink and parishes are united, many churches are left to decay, unless converted to secular uses such as dwellings or community and heritage centres.

As the Penal Laws were relaxed towards the end of the eighteenth century, Catholic and Dissenter churches were built in greater number and more substantial form. Their history is one of constant change and the oldest churches

● Fig. 65 Drumkeen Presbyterian church, Aghabog, county Monaghan, built in 1803, with the minister's house attached. The earliest Presbyterian churches, dating from the late eighteenth century, survive mainly in the countryside. They are plain halls, many originally thatched and very similar to their Catholic counterparts. In the nineteenth century, larger hall churches were built with a pilastered, classical facade on one gable.

● Fig. 66 Drumedy Methodist Church, Magheraveely, county Fermanagh. Typical of rural Methodist churches, this mid nineteenth century building is small and plain.

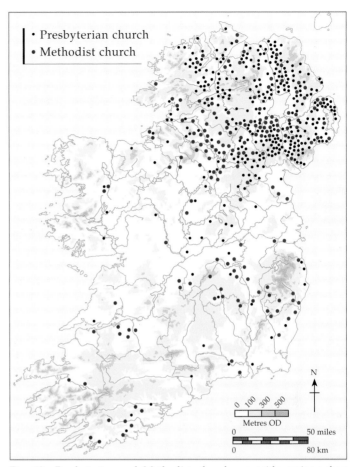

- Presbyterian church
- Methodist church

Fig. 68 Presbyterian and Methodist churches outside major urban centres, *c.* 1910. Presbyterian churches have a clear regional distribution. Presbyterians, associated with Scottish settlement in north-eastern Ireland, form an absolute majority in county Antrim and the north-east of county Down and a majority of the Protestants in many other parts of Ulster, particularly in the rural areas. Methodism made its main impact on Church of Ireland communities. Methodist churches are distributed widely, though with a marked concentration in south Ulster.

survive in poorer, remote districts where there has been less pressure to enlarge or amend. Early Catholic churches were plain in style and modest in scale but from the middle of the nineteenth century foundations were more numerous and buildings larger, initially mainly in Gothic Revival style and subsequently in a variety of styles. In recent decades, there has been experimentation with innovatory designs and indigenous materials. Unlike the shrinking Church of Ireland, Catholic churches and their surroundings have required modernisation through provision of car parks and new graveyards. Modern graveyards, at some distance from the church, are generally more ordered and regimented than older churchyards, lacking their informality and tranquillity.

● Fig. 67 Church buildings are a prominent feature in many rural communities and towns. As rival institutions, Church of Ireland and Catholic churches were often sited on elevated locations within a short distance of each other; by contrast, Presbyterian and Methodist churches are less conspicuous. In Clifden, county Galway, the spire of the Catholic church was apparently designed to overlook that of the Church of Ireland.

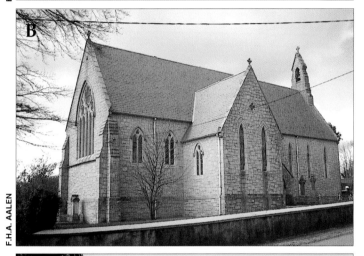

RELIGIOUS SITES AND STRUCTURES

As well as churches, the countryside contains a range of religious structures, including shrines, grottoes, holy wells and small isolated graveyards. Most of these features occur singly, but the holy well and the burial ground are often associated and on some long-established pilgrimage sites there is a cluster of features and 'stations' which may include a holy well, shrines, oratories, beehive huts, cairns and ruined megaliths, as well as natural rocks and trees. Pilgrims customarily make rounds or praying circuits in a clockwise direction from one sacred feature to another.

Shrines are usually small, simple structures located on the roadside; they are not of great antiquity and have a very local significance. Grottoes are larger and more elaborate. They contain statues of the Virgin Mary, are made in both natural and artificial caves and located in church-

Fig. 69 Catholic churches. • A) St Johns, Cratloe, county Clare. An outstanding example of an early T-plan, barn church from the eighteenth century. • B) Church of Our Lady of Mercy, Crosschapel, county Wicklow, built in 1857 in Gothic style in the open countryside. At this period, narrow lancet windows were a standard motif of Irish church design, Protestant or Catholic. • C) Opened in 1982, St Marys, Julianstown, county Meath, reflects post-Vatican II liturgical changes and the move away from hierarchical structures. Constructed at a period when self-conscious modernism dominated architecture, churches of this type reflect a deliberate break with the past and a systematic rejection of the vernacular tradition.

Fig. 70 Religious grottoes. ○ A) Ballinspittle, county Cork. Site of the celebrated 'moving statue' of the 1980s • B) Ballyragget, county Kilkenny.

Fig. 72 Disused burial grounds. These features could date to anywhere between the sixth and nineteenth centuries. ● A) Ballymoyock, county Mayo. This burial place, surrounded by a double, sub-rectangular kerbed wall, lies isolated at the base of Nephin Mountain. ● B) Gormanstown, county Kildare. This site is surrounded by a roughly circular stone wall. In the prosperous eastern countryside, perhaps as a result of eighteenth or nineteenth-century 'improvements', many killeens have well-built enclosures either circular or rectangular in plan.

Fig. 71 Holy wells. ● A) Tober Lugna dedicated to St Lugna, at Leitir near Cadamstown, Slieve Bloom, county Offaly. The holy well which was conserved in 1995 lies in a marshy hollow overhung by sycamore trees, and within view of the medieval parish church of Leitir Lugna. An annual pattern was traditionally held at the well on 27 April, the feast day of the saint. ● B) St Chaois, Kilkee, county Clare.

yards, old quarries and on roadsides. Inspired first by the celebrated Lourdes apparition of 1858, many grottoes were built in Ireland after the Marian year in 1954. There are strong traditions in rural Ireland of visiting and praying at holy wells, each known for curing a particular ailment and associated with sacred trees and venerated stones. Offerings were customarily left at the wells, such as coins or rags torn from the supplicants' garments.

● Fig.73 Roadside shrine, near Swinford, county Mayo.

Some 3,000 wells exist, many now disused and almost forgotten; a number, however, still attract devotees. Many wells have stone covers, sometimes corbelled, or a stone enclosure. The cult of wells has pagan origins but was absorbed readily into the Christian tradition. Most wells are dedicated to saints, especially Patrick and Brigid, and were formerly associated with festivities or 'patterns' on the patron saint's feast day.

Isolated and disused burial grounds, often in ringfort-like enclosures, are widely found in the countryside; they usually contain small unmarked gravestones and some-times the remains of a small oratory or church and an ogham stone. These features perhaps originated as burial grounds for the dispersed farms before improved communications allowed easy access to a churchyard. In recent centuries, they have been used for the burial of unbaptised children and suicides not permitted burial in consecrated ground. A variety of names is given to them: killeen (cillín) is most common in the south-west, lisheen (liosín) in the north-west. The distribution of sites is essentially western but many, especially in the east, have been destroyed by agricultural improvements and land reclamation and the original distribution is therefore difficult to establish.

Fig. 74 National schools. ● A) Kilcullen, county Kildare. Opened in 1925, this school was converted into a community centre in 1995. ● B) Gransha, county Monaghan, opened in 1961.

SCHOOLS, COMMUNITY AND SOCIETY HALLS

Rural schools are numerous, as national education is segregated on a parochial basis with separate Catholic and Protestant schools located near their respective churches. An earlier diversity of country schools was replaced during the nineteenth century by an uniform national pattern. State primary schools are typically single-storey buildings, domestic in scale and built to a standard design of the Board of Works which varied little over many years. In the south, innovations in the decades after Independence included the water tower and pillared playground shelters, but there was no major conceptual break until the 1960s. National schools thus became one of the truly archetypal forms of rural Ireland, perpetuating its plain traditions of building and social life in general.

Many schools originally stood isolated in the country-side in order to serve dispersed farms. Declining rural population and improved transportation since the 1960s have led to the closure of smaller remote schools and centralisation of education in larger villages or towns. Many disused schools in the countryside have been converted to new uses, such as dwellings or community halls.

Several major national organisations, such as the Gaelic Athletic Association (GAA), the Orange Order, the Ancient Order of Hibernians, Muintir na Tíre, Macra na Feirme and the Irish Countrywomen's Association (ICA) have rural origins with numerous local branches and often their own halls, lodges and other facilities. The GAA originated in 1884 with the objective of forming a new national consciousness through native field sports – hurling, Gaelic football and handball. The movement spread rapidly in most rural areas to become Ireland's biggest sporting organisation and its playing fields, dressing rooms and club houses are familiar

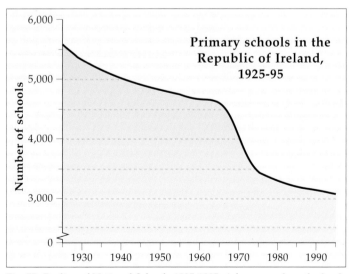

Fig. 75 Decline of National Schools 1925-1995. A large number of schools in the twenty-six counties were closed in the mid-1960s due to a declining rural population and improved transport.

● Fig. 76 Ball Alley, Rathkennan, county Tipperary. This structure re-uses the walls of a former R.I.C. barracks, which in turn may have been an ecclesiastical building. Once immensely popular in rural areas, handball has more recently declined in popularity. Originally, the game was played against a single wall of an existing building; later, three or four-walled alleys became standard, often against or close to old police stations. Ball alleys are one of the very few categories of building unique to Ireland. Handball is now played almost entirely indoors.

● Fig. 77 Orange Hall at Inver near Roslea in county Fermanagh, built in 1868.

features of the countryside. In Ulster, the Orange Order with its multitude of local halls provides a focus for many Protestants. Founded in 1795 in defence of 'Protestant Ascendancy', the order was revived in the 1880s in opposition to Home Rule and its lodges became lively centres of local social life. Muintir na Tíre (founded in 1937) is a major voluntary organisation aiming to further rural community development; initially organised at parochial level, it possesses numerous sports and recreation centres. Foróige (founded in 1944 as Macra na Feirme) encourages educational, cultural and social activities for young people in rural Ireland. The ICA (founded as the United Irishwomen in 1910) has varied objectives and activities, including educational programmes, the encouragement of local crafts and traditions and the co-operative marketing of the produce of its members through a sister organisation, Irish Country Markets.

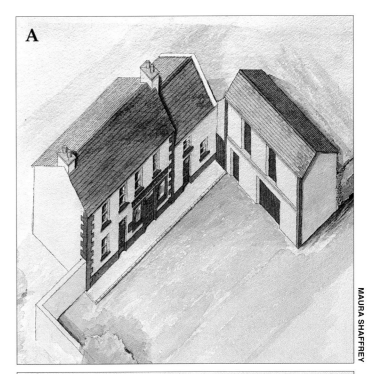

Fig. 78 Country shops. ● A) Shop, public house, general dealer, post office and builders providers combined with dwelling, Carracastle, near Charlestown, county Roscommon. ● B) Dwelling house, pub and shop, near Mullingar, county Westmeath. The simple but attractive front is characteristic of the often high quality of shop design in the late nineteenth and early twentieth century.

RURAL INDUSTRY AND SERVICES

Local pubs and general shops, often combined, are scattered along roads in closely settled rural areas, usually near crossroads or a Catholic church. Some are converted farmhouses and linked to farm buildings, the proprietors living alongside or above the shop. In recent decades, local shops have declined in number; services generally have been concentrated in larger centres of population and draw their custom and labour force from the surrounding countryside. However, large newly-built pubs with extensive car parks have multiplied in rural areas in recent times. Garages and petrol stations are numerous too, since there is a high level of car ownership and commuting has become a

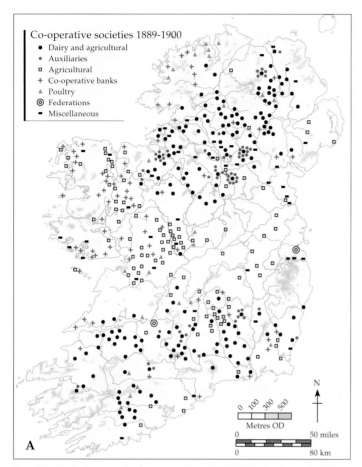

Co-operative societies 1889-1900
- ● Dairy and agricultural
- ● Auxiliaries
- ◻ Agricultural
- + Co-operative banks
- ▲ Poultry
- ◎ Federations
- ▬ Miscellaneous

A

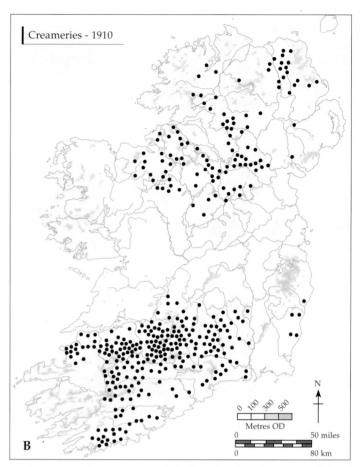

Creameries - 1910

B

Fig. 79 A) Early spread of co-operatives 1889-1900. In the early 1890s, co-operative creameries were successfully introduced in the Golden Vale of Munster, the richest dairying area in Ireland. By 1915, there were 991 co-operative societies organised by the Irish Agricultural Organisation Society with a membership of over 102,000. Geographically the movement spread in an uneven way with major concentrations in the south and north-west. Most progress was made among medium to large farmers in dairying areas. Livestock and meat production, much the major element of Irish agriculture, was almost untouched by the co-operative movement. B) Creameries in Ireland in 1910. The distribution is heavily orientated towards Munster and the hinterland of Cork city, the traditional heartland of Irish dairying. There is also a more subdued zone across the drumlin belt of south Ulster.

A

BRIAN MACDONALD

B

LAKELAND DAIRIES

Fig. 80 Co-operative creameries. ●A) Rural creamery, Butlersbridge, county Cavan. Many early small creameries were of this simple design. The various separators, churns etc. obtained power from a stationary engine driven by a coal or turf-fired steam boiler. ●B) Lakeland Dairies, Tullynahinnera, county Monaghan. Set in the drumlin country of mid-Monaghan, with Lough Egish in the background and a local GAA grounds in the foreground, this rural industrial complex has witnessed several distinct phases of development. Founded in 1902 as Lough Egish Co-op, it became increasingly successful, and larger, in the 1930s and 1940s. It amalgamated with Killashandra Co-op to form Lakeland Dairies in 1991.

NEILL WARNER PHOTOGRAPHY

DEPARTMENT OF ARTS, CULTURE AND THE GAELTACHT

●Fig. 81 Parkmore Industrial Estate, county Galway. Established in 1981, five factories have been completed and opened on the site. The principal occupant is Cardiovascular Healthcare Products.

●Fig. 82 Glendalough Visitor Centre, county Wicklow. Opened in 1987, this well-designed centre was established by the Office of Public Works to meet the needs of visitors to the famous Early Christian monastic site nearby.

major aspect of rural life. There was considerable growth of small industrial enterprises, such as corn and woollen mills, brewing and distilling, in rural areas in the eighteenth and early nineteenth centuries, but they withered with rural depopulation and the growth of urban factory production in the latter half of the nineteenth century, leaving a range of derelict buildings.

Co-operative creameries, established at the end of the nineteenth century, were the earliest major form of modern rural industry and are particularly numerous in the Munster lowlands and in south Ulster where they provided much-needed employment. Normally in modest, plain buildings, many co-operatives have recently closed, as milk processing is increasingly concentrated in larger modern plants. The number of co-operative creameries in the Republic declined from 187 in 1962 to 48 in 1981 and 34 in 1992. Small rural craft industries, pottery, weaving and knitting, have revived in recent decades but not on a scale sufficient to make an appreciable impact on the landscape. Rural recreational activities have directly generated little building activity save for car parks, picnic sites and toilets and, more recently, interpretative centres. Golf courses and their associated facilities, however, are of increasing significance.

Since the 1970s in the Republic, the Industrial Development Authority and Údaras na Gaeltachta have promoted a number of small rural industrial estates in which foreign firms play an important role. Factories are usually modern, purpose-built units. The Local Enterprise Development Unit has had a comparable role in rural industry in Northern Ireland.

BIBLIOGRAPHY

F. Aalen, 'The evolution of the traditional house in western Ireland' in *R.S.A.I.Jn.*, xc (1966), pp 47-58.

F. Aalen, 'The house types of Gola Island, county Donegal' in *Folklife*, viii (1970), pp 32-44.

F. Aalen, 'Vernacular rural dwellings of the Wicklow mountains' in K. Han-nigan and W. Nolan (ed.), *Wicklow. History and society* (Dublin, 1994), pp 581-624.

W. Brenneman and M. Brenneman, *Crossing the circle at the holy wells of Ireland* (Virginia, 1995).

C. Brett, *Buildings of county Antrim* (Belfast, 1996).

Å. Campbell, 'Irish fields and houses – a study of rural culture' in *Béaloideas*, v (1935), pp 57-74.

Å. Campbell, 'Notes on the Irish house' in *Folk-Liv*, i (1937), pp 207-34.

K. Danaher, 'Materials and methods in Irish traditional buildings' in *R.S.A.I.Jn.*, lxxxvii (1957), pp 61-74.

K. Danaher, 'Farmyard forms and their distribution in Ireland' in *Ulster Folklife*, xxvii (1981), pp 63-75.

K. Danaher, *Ireland's traditional houses* (Dublin, 1992).

K. Danaher, 'Traditional forms of the dwelling house in Ireland' in *R.S.A.I.Jn.*, cii (1972), pp 1-36.

E. Evans, *Irish folk ways* (London, 1957).

A. Gailey, 'Vernacular housing' in A. Rowan, *Northwest Ulster* (London, 1979), pp. 87-103.

A. Gailey, *Rural houses of the north of Ireland* (Edinburgh, 1984).

H. Glassie, *Passing the time. Folklore and history of an Ulster community* (Dublin, 1982).

H. Glassie, 'Vernacular architecture and society' in M. Turan (ed.), *Vernacular architecture* (Avebury, 1990), pp 271-84.

D. McCourt, 'The outshot house type and its distribution in county Londonderry' in *Ulster Folklife*, ii (1961), pp 9-18.

D. McCourt, 'Innovation diffusion in Ireland: an historical case study' in *R.I.A.Proc.*, lxxiii (1973), C, pp 1-19.

N. McCullough and V. Mulvin, *A lost tradition. The nature of architecture in Ireland* (Dublin, 1987).

P. Robinson, 'Vernacular housing in Ulster in the seventeenth century' in *Ulster Folklife*, xxv (1979), pp 1-28.

P. Shaffrey and M. Shaffrey, *Irish countryside buildings: everyday architecture in the rural landscape* (Dublin, 1985).

P. Smith, 'The architectural personality of the British Isles' in *Archaeologia Cambrensis*, cxxix (1980), pp 1-36.

TOWNS AND VILLAGES

Small towns and villages are a central component of the history of the island, whose fabric and morphology retain significant traces from the past. Given Ireland's history, urban genesis has been strongly correlated with colonisation, and revolutionary elements in the development of its urban system have overshadowed evolutionary ones – unlike the more stable experience of continental Europe. There have been three pronounced phases of town creation: during the Norman period, in the plantation era of the late sixteenth and early seventeenth centuries, and under landlord influence in the eighteenth century. Yet, the Irish town has also significant indigenous roots, reaching back to the proto-towns of the Early Christian period. The Irish town and village tradition, therefore, is one of continuity as well as change.

No understanding of rural Ireland can be complete without detailed consideration of the influence of towns on its rhythms and structures. Over much of its history, Ireland has been a relatively lightly urbanised society, and the bulk of its population has lived in the country-side. But towns and villages have been vital economic and cultural hubs, profoundly influencing, as well as being influenced by their rural hinterlands.

Rural Ireland is dotted with diminutive towns and villages, many with less than 1,500 inhabitants; few inland towns have a population exceeding 10,000. These numerous settlements function chiefly as service centres for their rural surroundings and have evolved or were planned specifically for that purpose. Fairs and markets periodically brought the country to the town, while rural families have continually replenished its demography. Owing to the general weaknesses of industrial growth, the towns have remained intimately immersed in the countryside. Unless in proximity to major cities, they have had stable or declining populations since the mid-nineteenth century and did not experience sustained pressure for extensive change. In recent decades, however, more accessible towns and villages have revived considerably and are now in a dynamic phase. One consequence has been the stretching of their morphology and erosion of their fabric, especially in response to the overbearing influence of the car in modern society. Moreover, increasing centralisation of schools and other vital services in the larger centres is weakening the fabric of the remoter countryside and intensifying the encroachment of urban influences.

BRIAN REDMOND, ROSCREA

● Fig. 1 Irish towns frequently melt into their surrounding countryside, as in this example of Abbeyleix in county Laois.

NATIONAL LIBRARY OF IRELAND

BILLY COLFER

● Fig. 2 The Vikings conferred the name Weisfiord, the harbour of the mudflats. At times, Wexford resembles a Venetian lido, but the still mirror of its vast surface conceals the shallow, mud-clotted estuary. By 892 AD, Wexford was one of the five principal Viking trading posts in Ireland, which reached from Scandinavia to the Mediterranean. Viking Wexford was a narrow crescent on the waterfront, defined by an earthen rampart and ditch. The Normans subsequently expanded the town and walls. The mid seventeenth-century map (inset) shows the tightly-packed walled town with its crenellated water front.

URBAN GENESIS

The prestigious Early Christian monasteries performed the functions of incipient towns, as early central places with cult, market, educational and political functions. Towns like Kildare, Cashel, Armagh, Glendalough and Kells were significant centres with a broad territorial reach. From their function as oenach (assembly and exchange) sites, the monasteries increasingly acquired market-place functions. By the eleventh century, the major monasteries had well-defined markets, paved streets, artisan quarters and clearly-differentiated sacred and secular sectors. Until the large-scale disruption visited on them by the Vikings, these monastic proto-towns were the economic and cultural hubs of early medieval Ireland.

The initial Viking raids were directed at these obviously wealthy targets but from the ninth century onwards, the Vikings themselves established trading centres, which were subsumed into the far-flung web of long-distance trading ports created by them across Europe, from Dublin to Novgorod. The successful Viking settlements – Dublin,

Wexford, Waterford, Cork, Limerick – were all strategically sited at the head of tidal estuaries. They permanently reorientated the economic and political centre of gravity of the island away from the sequestered midlands towards the more exposed coast, especially the east coast.

THE NORMAN IMPETUS

A further impetus to town foundation in Ireland came with the Normans, who carried with them the innovation of the town charter which conferred urban autonomy in terms of the market and the law within the feudal regime. The importance of the market place and the town wall (a fiscal and administrative as well as a military barrier) physically embodied this new reality in the morphology of the very town itself. The adoption of town charters led to a burst of urban development in Ireland – far in excess of what the economy could actually sustain. Of 270 chartered sites, only 56 developed into functionally significant towns – the great majority in the fertile south-east, where the Norman manorial economy was well entrenched. Outside this zone,

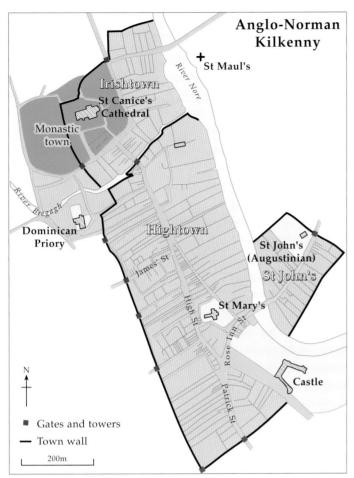

Anglo-Norman Kilkenny

St Maul's

Irishtown

St Canice's Cathedral

Monastic town

Dominican Priory

Hightown

James' St

St John's (Augustinian)

St John's

High St

St Mary's

Rose Inn St

Castle

Patrick St

River Nore

River Bregagh

N

■ Gates and towers
— Town wall

200m

● Fig. 3 When the Normans arrived in the late twelfth century, Kilkenny presented itself as an obvious power base. As well as being a rich ecclesiastical site, it also commanded a fording point on the River Nore in the fertile plain of central Kilkenny. By 1207 Kilkenny had passed to one of the great Norman warlords, William Marshall, who had married Isabella, the daughter of Strongbow, who first conquered Ireland for the Normans. Marshall built an imposing stone castle on a magnificent hilltop site commanding the Nore crossing, a wedge-shaped courtyard with great circular corner towers. On the old monastic site, he built a fine cathedral and the town itself was then planned around a central main street (High Street) axis, linking the castle and the cathedral – the secular and ecclesiastical anchors of medieval power. Kilkenny evolved in the first half of the thirteenth century, and the sheer number and scale of medieval buildings is a powerful reminder of the dynamism and drive of the new colonists who, like the Normans everywhere in Europe, were superb builders and town founders.

sites remained skeletal, or were little more than castellated garrisons. Some Norman towns utilised the pre-existing monastic and Viking centres; others developed under the protective shadow of feudal castles; still others were uncastellated planned towns, anchored on a main street broad enough to accommodate the all-important market.

Geographically, the walled towns exhibit three main features. Firstly, riverine sites dominate. Secondly, the compact distribution sharply delineates the Norman hinterland (80% lie within a quadrangle linking Dundalk, Wexford, Cork and Limerick). Thirdly, the pre-Columban bias towards Britain and the continent heavily weights the distribution. In size, walled towns averaged between six

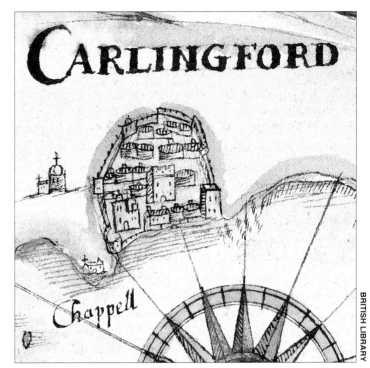

CARLINGFORD

Chappell

BRITISH LIBRARY

● Fig. 4 Carlingford town was essentially founded by the Normans, under the auspices of Hugh de Lacy. The walled town stretching east of the castle was virtually an extended bailey. A tightly packed H-shaped street design was inserted into this narrow site, squeezed in between the mountain and the sea, and anchored on the Market Place, hub of six of the town's streets.

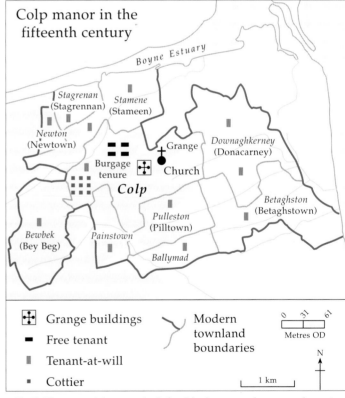

Colp manor in the fifteenth century

Boyne Estuary

Stagrenan (Stagrennan)

Stamene (Stameen)

Newton (Newtown)

Grange

Downaghkerney (Donacarney)

Burgage tenure

Church

Colp

Betaghston (Betaghstown)

Pulleston (Pilltown)

Bewbek (Bey Beg)

Painstown

Ballymad

✠ Grange buildings
━ Free tenant
▮ Tenant-at-will
▪ Cottier

Modern townland boundaries

0   31   61
Metres OD

N

1 km

● Fig 5 The manorial system in Ireland had to struggle constantly against countervailing tendencies, notably the townland matrix, whose centrifugal logic disrupted the centralising force of the manor. In this example of the manor of Colp in Meath in 1408, ten free tenants held the land in separate townlands, denuding the manorial centre.

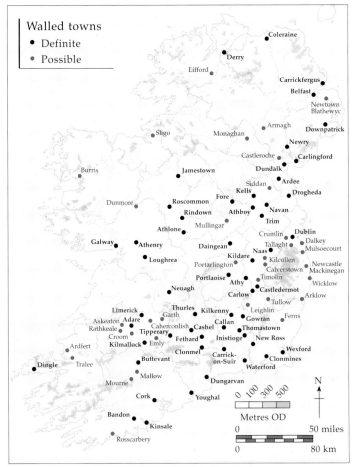

Walled towns
- Definite
- Possible

Fig. 6 The peak in Irish town wall building was between 1285 and 1315, roughly a half-century later than the English-Welsh peak. Initially overwhelmingly coastal, walled towns then fan out along the richer river valleys, especially the Barrow, Nore and Suir, and along the perimeter of the Pale, within the Dublin hinterland. By 1350, a curtain of walled towns ringed the Pale and the south-eastern river valleys, marking the effective limits of the colony. Subsequently, tentative efforts were made to extend walled towns into the marches, but this intrusion was only successfully implemented in the Tudor, Elizabethan and Jacobean periods, when the newly crystallising, multinational British state set out deliberately to subdue its recalcitrant Irish borders.

and fifteen hectares, smaller than English examples, but within the same range as their Welsh equivalents. Kilkenny, New Ross and Drogheda were the three largest towns, which fits well with the trade evidence.

Outside the towns, small manorial villages also developed. These nucleated villages of feudal origin – with their castles, parish churches and manorial mills – should be clearly distinguished from the later clachans – clustered but amorphous agricultural villages, without any visible nucleating agent. The heartland of the manorial villages was in the south-eastern quadrant of the island, which, from the medieval period onwards, was a relatively urbanised, socially stratified, culturally exposed and externally focussed region. Within the Pale and in south Leinster especially, medieval villages developed which closely approximated, albeit in attenuated form, the continental

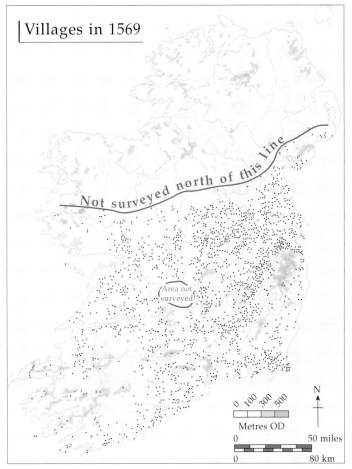

Villages in 1569

Fig. 7 The English military engineer, Robert Lythe, mapped most of Ireland in 1569. This first detailed and accurate survey permitted a tentative nationwide distribution of villages to be plotted by John Andrews. The remarkable concentration in the heavily normanised Pale area is especially noticeable, as is its continuation down the Barrow corridor and into south Wexford. Lythe's villages are presumably the descendants of small manorial villages.

● Fig. 8 Licketstown is one of a number of farm villages to survive in the bend of the Suir in south Kilkenny. The massive ditch and courtyard farmyards bespeak manorial origins in the densely-settled hinterland of Waterford city.

PAT NOLAN

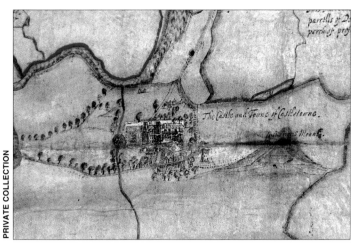

PRIVATE COLLECTION

• Fig. 9 By the late medieval period, the towerhouses anchored agglomerated settlements. These hamlets, crouched under the sheltering castle walls, often had a mill and residual strip fields, reflecting their manorial origins. This seventeenth-century map shows a rare pictorial representation of such a village, Castletown near Dundalk in county Louth.

village prototype – with open fields, greens, parish churches, manorial castles, and other symbols of a strong village solidarity and identity. Nonetheless, many of these villages were still intact, even in shrunken forms, until the early modern period. In 1620, Luke Gernon provides a neat description of them from east Limerick:

> *The villages are distant from each other about 2 miles. In every village is a castle and a church, but bothe in ruyne. The baser cottages are built of underwood, called wattle, and covered some with thatch and some with green sedge, of a round forme and without chimneys, and to my imaginacion resemble so many hives of bees about a country farme.*

DAPHNE POCHIN-MOULD

• Fig. 10 Kiltinan in county Tipperary is one of the best known of Irish deserted villages. Characteristically located within a demesne, its extensive remains feature a clearly recognisable ground plan (low banks and crop marks at centre), adjacent to a church and castle. While the desertion phase is often asserted to be medieval, it is more likely to have been in the seventeenth century.

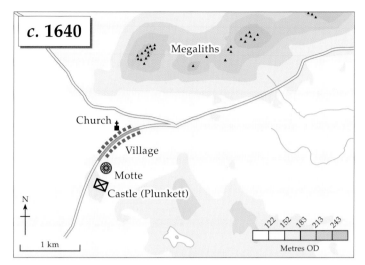

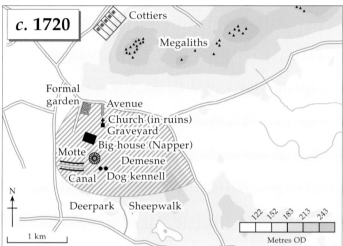

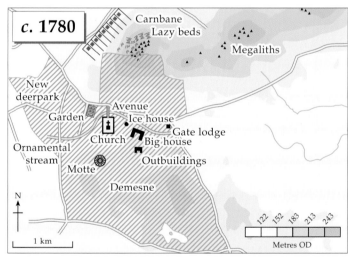

• Fig. 11 The evolution of the settlement pattern at Loughcrew in county Meath encapsulates a common seventeenth-century experience. The long-established village was still intact early in that century, consisting of a cabin cluster under the auspices of the Plunkett castle. By the early eighteenth century, the new landlord family, the Nappers, had radically restructured the landscape, dispersing the villagers to the upper slopes of the Loughcrew hills and dissolving the newly deserted village into their demesne. By the late eighteenth century, the earlier formal demesne with its canals had been remodelled in the 'natural' style, expanding to incorporate the old deerpark and sheepwalk. On the hills, the cottiers' lazy beds were encroaching on the ancient megaliths.

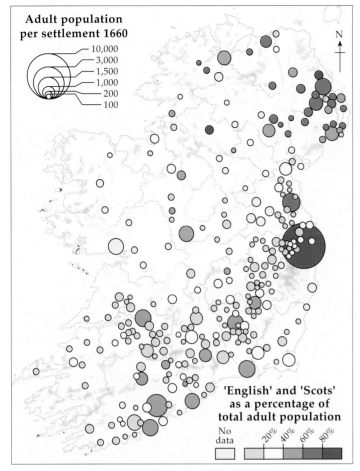

Adult population per settlement 1660

- 10,000
- 3,000
- 1,500
- 1,000
- 200
- 100

N

'English' and 'Scots' as a percentage of total adult population

No data — 20% 40% 60% 80%

Fig. 12 William Smyth's map of the ethnic composition of Irish towns in 1660 clearly delineates a zone of stability within a Dundalk-Ennis-Cork-Waterford quadrangle. The region bears the strongest imprint of the manorial village structure, underpinning later developments. The overwhelmingly non-immigrant composition of the numerous small towns in this zone arcs from the Pale (the anglicised area in the hinterland of Dublin) down through south Leinster/east Munster, where a fusion of Gaelic and Norman culture emerged which was not seriously disrupted in the traumatic seventeenth century. Urban culture was stable, cohesive and resilient, based on commercialised tillage and dairying, and effective participation in the wider Atlantic economy.

THE SEVENTEENTH-CENTURY RUPTURE

The surviving village system was shattered by the cumulative impact of the Reformation, landownership changes and associated economic restructuring and social engineering, especially in the post-Cromwellian period. The twin institutional foci of castle (towerhouse) and parish church were superseded, and a geography of revolutionary transformation implanted a radically new system. The sharpness of the Reformation discontinuity is etched into the Irish countryside. The older parish centres are now evocative ruins, occasionally sentinelled by a graceful round tower, a thriving graveyard and an ivy-rich ruin. Protestant landlords were eager to promote the Anglican church by occupying fresh sites, often as the centrepiece of their gleaming new towns. These upstart neighbours soon displaced their older counterparts, which faded into

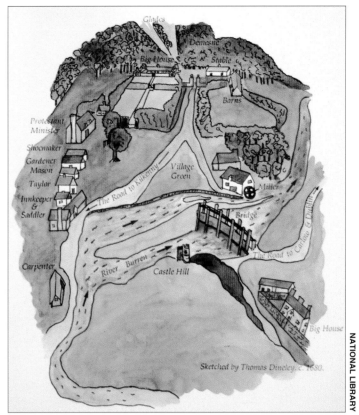

● Fig. 13 Staplestown, county Carlow, as sketched by Thomas Dinely c. 1680. This is a classic seventeenth-century new village, with its diagnostic triangular green, whose apex is the demesne entrance. Around the green are the houses of immigrant Protestant tradesmen, while the bridge, mill and inn reflect infrastructural investment. Almost 400 of these new settlements were established in the seventeenth century, with particular concentrations in Ulster and along the midlands edge of the Pale.

● Fig. 14 Timahoe in county Kildare preserves the triangular green (called a 'diamond' in Ulster) of a seventeenth-century plantation village. It was associated with Quaker settlement.

shabby genteel obsolescence. Consider the relationship between Gort and Kilmacduagh, Enniscorthy and Ferns, and Ballinasloe and Clonfert.

The stripping of the medieval churches, the displacement of the old landowning élite and their dependents, and

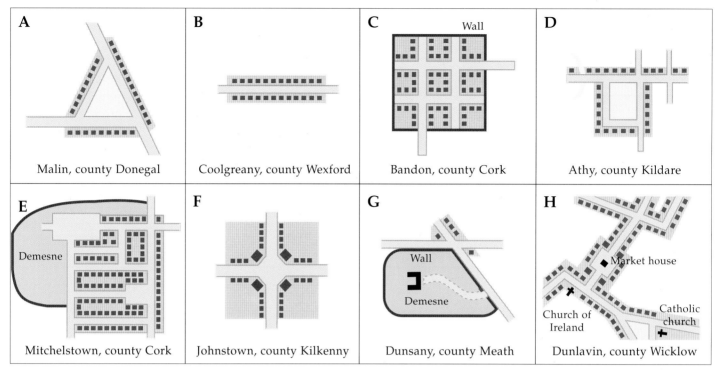

A Malin, county Donegal	**B** Coolgreany, county Wexford	**C** Bandon, county Cork	**D** Athy, county Kildare
E Mitchelstown, county Cork	**F** Johnstown, county Kilkenny	**G** Dunsany, county Meath	**H** Dunlavin, county Wicklow

Fig. 15 Town and village morphology. From the early seventeenth-century green (A), street (B) or more elaborate walled grid (C), the plan evolved to include spacious market squares, from the mid seventeenth century onwards (D). In the eighteenth century, more formal unwalled and elaborate grids became commonplace (E) while by the 1760s, the octagon had become a preferred feature (F). Smaller villages remained strictly allied to their sponsoring demesnes (G). By the mid nineteenth century, a growing institutional sector, including both state and Catholic church buildings, often developed around the fair green, as a counterbalance to the earlier market square/Church of Ireland axis (H).

the new commercialised, pastoralist-oriented agriculture, all truncated older village roots, and culminated in their shrivelling away. The labour-intensive tillage of the old villages now yielded to extensive pastoralism and with that transition came the scattering of the labour force from the villages. This phase of decline, and ultimate desertion, was

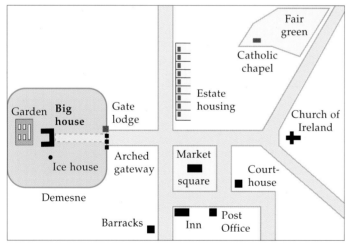

Fig. 16 The typical estate village was constructed with a high degree of architectural unity. The principal focus was the Big House and demesne, but considerable effort was expended in composing a balanced hierarchical layout. The principal components included a market-cum-courthouse (reflecting the linked idea of law and money), and a Church of Ireland church. If present, the Catholic chapel was located on the surreptitious fringes of the town. These elements were deployed within the vocabulary of georgian architecture to create a strongly neo-classical statement, based on principles of rationality and symmetry.

especially evident in the middle of the country (a triangle linking counties Meath, Roscommon and Tipperary), the zone most affected by intensive pastoralisation and its concomitants – privatisation, population displacement and decline, and the narrowing of the social spectrum to a crude dichotomy of graziers and herdsmen. In striking contrast to their European equivalents, the characteristic ruins of parish church and towerhouse are now all that remains of the ripped fabric of many Irish villages; these ruins are typically embedded in their symbolic destroyers, the new seventeenth-century demesnes, which swallowed them whole. Accordingly, many deserted village sites belong, not to the late medieval period, but to the traumatic seventeenth century.

These lost villages are a striking reminder of the volatility of the Irish village tradition. They can be found in two main zones of middle Ireland. The first runs from mid Kilkenny through south Tipperary to Limerick. There are 100 deserted sites in county Tipperary alone. The second zone sprawled across the north midlands from Roscommon to Louth. In one or two pockets, these earlier feudal villages survived the seventeenth-century trauma – famously in the south Kilkenny parish of Mooncoin, along the Dingle peninsula and in Ferrard barony in county Louth.

While one village tradition was being submerged in the traumatic tide of colonisation, the plantation process did

The Tradesmens Houses on The Gran of Dromanna Except the middle building which is an Inn...

● Fig. 17 Lord Grandison was an enthusiastic improver on his west Waterford estate, creating both the linen colony of Villierstown and the green village of Dromana. In 1754, the range of houses on the green belonged to tradesmen, with the exception of an inn. High quality, carefully designed estate housing was a recognised advertisement of responsible landlordism.

initiate a further wave of town and village formation. About 400 new centres were established by plantation grantees and new landlords, as nuclei for their estates, as seedbeds from which settlers could be planted in the surrounding countryside and as commercial, legal and military bastions in a potentially hostile environment. These plantations – in Munster, Ulster, the midlands and the perimeter of the Pale – were in areas which had in the medieval period been marginal, composed primarily of woods and hills. They were now heavily settled (unlike the more developed areas further east), on the back of military subjugation. Towns and villages were the cardinal features of plantation strategy. They fostered infrastructural development (roads, mills, bridges, tanneries, castles) market penetration, the implantation of a central state presence (court house, barracks, gaol), and the nurturing of the established church. The villages were often grouped around a triangular green. In Ulster, the green feature is frequently termed a diamond, but the 'green' villages are found almost universally in Ireland, with their characteristically triangular morphology.

ESTATE TOWNS AND VILLAGES

The Restoration period – a quiet interlude in a stormy century – witnessed a wave of new settlements. This was, in effect, the first generation of estate towns which saw the formation of Blessington, Baltinglass, Newtownforbes, Tulsk, Granard, Hillsborough, Lisburn and a great wave in county Cork – Midleton, Charleville, Castlemartyr, Kanturk, Mitchelstown, Newmarket and Doneraile.

By the early eighteenth century, the definitive conquest of Ireland had finally been implemented – and with it, the possibility of a more expansive and aestheticised urban project. The second quarter of the century saw a sustained rise in rents, as well as the absolute political and economic hegemony of the new landed class. As a result, the period between 1720 and 1740 saw a spate of regularly planned estate villages, formally designed around a wide main street or market square, as at Summerhill, Stradbally, Ballycastle, Ballina, Newtownbarry and Sixmilebridge. The Big House and demesne now replace the earlier castle as

one focal point, with the Protestant church as the other; the village was then poised between these twin peaks of Anglican ascendancy, often with an attractive degree of architectural unity. Lisburn in county Down, quickly rebuilt after a devastating fire in 1706, embodied these new

● Fig. 18 A detail from the *c.* 1740 painting of Stradbally, county Laois, depicts the estate village at the edge of the demesne. Good quality two-storeyed housing fronts the main street which opens onto a market square, complete with arcaded market house. Under the auspices of the Cosbys, Stradbally had been developed as a model village; the impact of Israel Mitchell, a Dublin clothier, was also crucial in developing the textile industry.

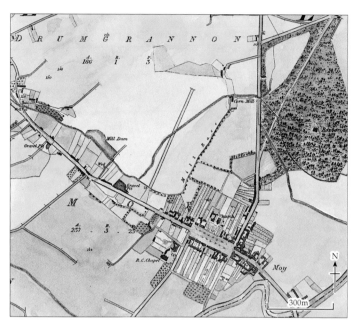

● Fig. 19 Moy, constructed in 1764 on the Tyrone-Armagh border, is a fine example of a well designed small estate town. Allegedly modelled on Marengo in Italy, the centrepiece is an elongated piazza, equally useful as a market and a fair site. The town displays the characteristic Ulster pattern of the Anglican church at the centre, with the Nonconformist and Catholic chapels on the outskirts.

enlightened principles of uniformity. An admiring Thomas Molyneux noted in 1708:

> *If the story of the Phoenix be ever true, sure 'tis in this town. For here you can see one of the beautifullest towns perhaps in the three kingdoms – all brick houses, slated, of one bigness, all new and almost finished, rising from the most terrible rubbish that can be imagined.*

This mid eighteenth-century period also saw an attempt to create linen colonies in new towns south and west of the main Ulster proto-industrial region. Early examples are Manulla (1733) in Mayo, Dunmanway (1740s) and Inishannon (1750s) in Cork, Mountshannon (1740s) in Clare, and Monivea (1750s) in Galway. Later linen villages of the 1760s were Fintona (Tyrone), Emyvale (Monaghan) and Collon (Louth) while Ballymote (Sligo) in the 1770s and Newtown Bellew (Galway) in the 1780s were among the last examples. For landlords, the great attraction of linen was that it was seen as a Protestant industry, that it gave an immense fillip to fairs and markets, that it had a powerful monetising effect, and that it enjoyed considerable government support. As one contemporary observer noted about linen colonies: 'The Protestant religion as well as the linen manufacture would be hereby extended into the Popish parts of Ireland, which would greatly strengthen and promote the Protestant interest.' These linen colonies suffered a high degree of failure – at centres like Creevenully (Roscommon)

Drumersnave and Glenboy (Leitrim), Mullafarry (Mayo) and Grangegeeth (Meath).

The strongest wave of estate village creation came in the 1760s. A series of influences can be traced behind this surge. Rentals had been buoyant since the depressed 1740s, giving landlords more discretionary capital and an awareness that a strong market town accelerated the economic development of their estates. Secondly, the revised road legislation of the 1760s, by strengthening the role of the Grand Jury, provided both the institutional and financial backing to landlords wishing to develop roads. Thirdly, the switch in taste towards informal landscape styles favoured the ready-made 'romanticism' of the Irish countryside, and considerably cheapened the cost of demesne creation or remodelling. Fourthly, the lifting of the ban on live cattle exports in 1759 was a boost to cattle fairs, which were often held in estate villages and strongly supported by 'improving' landlords. Finally, the 1762 reorganisation of the brown linen markets strengthened the autonomy and vitality of small town markets, just as the 1750s bleaching revolution was beginning to concentrate manufacture.

The cumulative impact of these changes had striking social and locational effects on estate villages. It lowered the financial threshold for those keen to develop an estate village, widening the social range of those involved. It also helped to push estate village creation further west, into lands previously considered too poor or too marginal to sustain development. Some developments – Maynooth and Monasterevin in Kildare, Inistioge in Kilkenny, Westport in

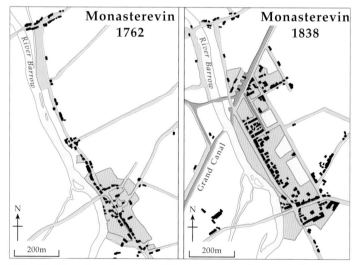

● Fig. 20 Monasterevin, county Kildare, was completely rebuilt between the 1760s and 1780s. When Charles, the sixth Earl inherited in 1758, he commissioned an estate survey by Bernard Scalé, redesigned the main house and demesne, and fundamentally rebuilt the town. The winding narrow street mostly fronted by cabins was straightened and widened; the bridge was resited and the Grand Canal was attracted to the town. A second street was planned parallel to the straightened main street, and a grid of new streets was inserted between them. These streets were flanked by plain but solid Georgian houses.

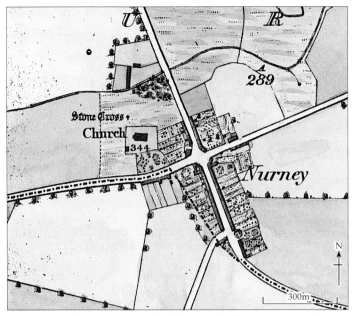

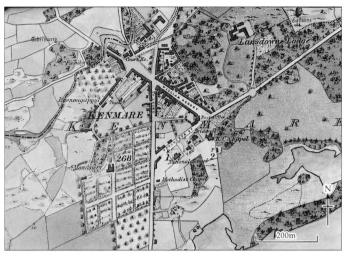

● Fig. 21 Neatly cresting a granite ridge outside Carlow town, and largely built of that fine building stone, Nurney is a miniature estate village financed by the influential Bruen family in the 1790s. The actual implementation of the project was entrusted to Peter Johnson – entrepreneur, miller and builder. The octagonal centrepiece and prominent position of the Protestant church are typical design features.

Mayo, Rathfriland, Hillsborough, Banbridge and Newtownards (Down) – were extensive remodellings of pre-existing settlements. Others, like Moy (1764) on the Armagh-Tyrone border or Hilltown (1766) in Down, were entirely new creations. The octagon became a favoured shape in this period – well displayed at Slane, where an attractive village was built to complement the great mill of the 1760s. Other sites were heavily industrial – as at Blarney, where thirteen mills were developed by the Jefferys around the older castle.

Kenmare was a good example of a 'western' new town. Magnificently located at the interface of mountain, sea and river, on a drowned deep river valley, it had witnessed a failed attempt by the great map-maker, Sir William Petty, to develop a town here in the 1670s. In 1775, William Petty-Fitzmaurice, second Earl of Shelburne, visited his Kerry estate. Shelburne, one of the senior British politicians of his day, was keen to make his Irish estate a showpiece of successful landlordism: 'There is nothing I think of with more pleasure than of laying the foundation of our corner – remote or obscure as it is – making itself known by its industry and order.' He found Neidín to be 'wonderfully calculated for trade' but was horrified to be told (incorrectly) that the name signified 'a nest of thieves' in Irish. He instantly ordered it to be changed to Kenmare and gave instructions as to how to build his prosperous showpiece: 'The town may be begun by laying out two capital streets, fifty feet wide.' Kenmare's success as a

DAPHNE POCHIN-MOULD

● Fig. 22 Kenmare in county Kerry in 1851 (top) and a contemporary view (bottom). The intersecting streets, called Henry and William after members of the landlord family, crossed in an unusual X shape: the top portion of the X served as a triangular Fair Green. The bottom triangle was finished by Shelburne Street, lined subsequently by the town's public buildings and by the entrance to Lansdowne Lodge, the agent's residence completed in 1775. Ten-acre plots were granted to tradesmen willing to move to the town, and a notable catch was George Peet, a Quaker merchant from Killarney, who established a cotton factory in the town. Other buildings followed – a mill, bridewell, market house, butter market, schoolhouse, limekiln, and a handsome inn – the Lansdowne Arms.

town depended especially on the building of two new roads, to Bantry in 1785, and to Killarney in 1823, replacing rough mountain tracks.

A further wave of estate town creation came in the 1780s, when there was a policy of relocating textile industries away from combination-ridden Dublin to greenfield sites in the country, encouraged by hefty government subsidies. New towns so created included Stratford-on-Slaney (Wicklow), Balbriggan (Dublin), Prosperous (Kildare) and Cheekpoint (Waterford). To this generation of new towns also belongs some spectacular failures – the fishing village of Rutland (Donegal) and the supposed Huguenot settlement of New Geneva (Waterford) – of which project the resonant name was the only successful part. But there were some successes – notably Balbriggan,

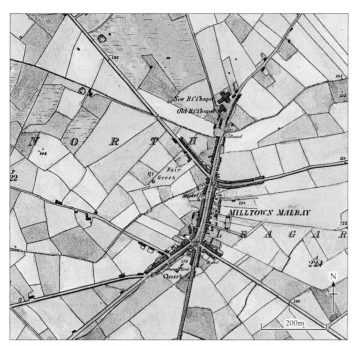

● Fig. 23 Milltown Malbay, county Clare, was one of the new generation of western resort towns which developed from the late eighteenth century onwards, as the vogue for 'taking the waters' deepened.

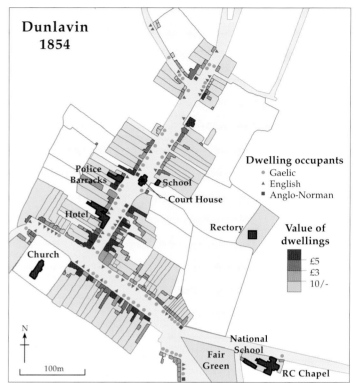

● Fig. 24 Valuation and surnames in Dunlavin, county Wicklow in *c.* 1854, as mapped by Paul Ferguson. The earlier town was centred on a T-shape plan. By the mid nineteenth century, it was lined by highly valued two-storeyed houses, with a strong representation of English surnames. In contrast, the later fair green, with its catholic chapel and national school, had attracted one-storeyed thatched cabins, occupied disproportionately by those with Gaelic surnames. Dunlavin itself occupied a transitional position between the Wicklow Mountains and the plains of Kildare. It had been heavily planted in the seventeenth century, like much of the previously wooded Wicklow fringe. The complex social, ethnic and religious stratification reflects both its historical and geographical situation. The fair green was the scene of a notorious massacre of United Irishmen in 1798, which occasioned the well known song 'Dunlavin Green'.

backboned by Comerford and O'Brien's successful cotton factory. In 1791, it was said that where a few years ago there had only been a few cottages, there were now local tailors, smiths, weavers, butchers, brewers and spinners, all attracted by the factory.

OPENING UP THE WEST

A final phase in estate town foundation was the spectacular intrusion of new landlord settlement into the far west. Examples are Bunbeg, Carrick and Dunfanaghy (Donegal), Louisburgh, Charlestown, Balla, Belmullet and Binghamstown (Mayo), Strokestown (Roscommon), Cahirciveen (Kerry), Kingwilliamstown (Cork), Glin (Limerick), and Clifden and Roundstone (Galway). This pushing west was linked to efforts to remodel rundale systems, and to open up areas only recently settled as a result of population pressure, and with no pre-existing village tradition. Road building was a critical enabling development; witness the web of state-sponsored roads after 1822, notably in Sliabh Luachra, under the auspices of Richard Griffith, of which Kingwilliamstown (now Ballydesmond) was the centrepiece. These new developments reverberated to the furthest reaches of the west of Ireland – expressed by the establishment of new settlements at western road heads, as the market economy spread along the inviting new roads. In the process, these new land-based developments dealt a fatal blow to the older seaborne trade of the west and its multifarious flotilla of small crafts – hookers, púcáns, and gleóiteogí. Their sponsors hoped to spread commerce

(symbolised by the advent of wheeled vehicles in place of the old 'truckle' carts), and the English language: 'leanann an Bearla an tearr' (English follows the roads) as the Irish proverb noted. They also wished to link up the new centres with the state – as in the early warning system of martello towers in case of a French invasion, in the spread of coast-guard stations, which squeezed the lively black economy in smuggled goods, and in the constabulary barracks, which imposed state law and state order in place of the informal moral economy of the prior dispensation.

These western towns were also helped by the advent of a tourist industry. Blocked from the continental Grand Tour by the French Revolution, British travellers and tourists turned instead to their Celtic periphery. This redirection was helped too by the new vogue for 'romantick' scenery and by the rising popularity of the seaside. Throughout the eighteenth century, resort towns had been inland spas, like Lucan, Templeogue, Castleconnell, Mallow and Ballyspellan. Once the vogue for seabathing

NATIONAL GALLERY OF IRELAND

● Fig. 25 Bray, in county Wicklow thrived after the railway reached it in 1854: its prosperity was assured by the railway engineer, William Dargan, who laid out the splendid new esplanade in 1859, boosting the town's resort status, and ensuring that it became a favoured retreat from noisy, dirty Dublin city. So popular did vulgar Bray ('real waves and imitation quality') become that it generated a snobby spinoff in Greystones – deliberately laid out in expensive villas and avoiding guesthouses, hotels and the vulgar ostentation of an esplanade. This painting by Erskine Nichol depicts 'the seafront at Bray' prior to the building of the esplanade.

intensified in the late eighteenth century, new settlements like Tramore (1770s), Portstewart (1792) and Warrenpoint (1790s) developed. A resurgent tourist trade had also been behind the remodelling of Killarney from the 1760s onwards, as it increasingly became a tourist centre of European reputation.

These developments also opened up one of Europe's most remote and dramatic Atlantic coastlines. For example, in west Clare, the Cliffs of Moher became a magnet which galvanised the tourist industry. Inevitably, as west Clare flourished, towns were promoted to tap the trade by local landlords. Milltown Malbay, Ennistymon, Liscannor and Kilrush all belong to this phase. Milltown Malbay, for example, was developed by the Limerick entrepreneur, Thomas Moroney – following on road building and the creation of a Big House. He quickly developed sea bathing boxes, horse races, fairs etc, culminating in the building of the Atlantic Hotel in 1809, with its hot and cold baths, assembly and billiard rooms, livery stables and sixty bedrooms. A commentator observed in 1808: 'A few years ago, there was hardly a house but his own, but now there may be seen in every direction a great number of neat lodges.' Similarly, Ennistymon expanded from three thatched cabins in 1775 to 120 mostly slated houses in 1814. Other settlements sprang up as coaching villages on the new roads – Ashbourne, Enfield, Ballylinan, Roundwood, Ashford, Kilcullen Bridge, Allenwood, New Kildimo, New Pallasgreen.

By the Famine of the 1840s, the impetus behind the foundation of estate villages had finally petered out. The Victorian period saw only cosmetic remodellings – as at Enniskerry – or miniature 'pretty' villages like Ardagh (Longford) or Fenagh (Carlow). Surveying estate towns as a whole, however, it is important not to overstress the role of the landlord in their gestation. Firstly, an energetic middleman or projector frequently lay behind them – as with Israel Mitchell at Stradbally, Peter Bere (Maynooth) and Peter Johnson (Nurney). Secondly, many planned towns were in fact the tortuously slow end product of a long, staggered gestation – partially blocked by the leasing system, partially by the intricate negotiations necessary with local and national interests. Thirdly, many planned towns, especially in the south and east, were cosmetic remodellings of older sites – Ballyragget, Edgeworthstown, Kells and Lismore. In west Ulster, a similar refurbishment occurred in the 1820s and 1830s when the London Companies took a renewed interest in their estates as long-standing middlemen leases fell in. Kilrea, Draperstown and Moneymore were among the towns completely remodelled. Emphasis on the landlord town concept should not blind us to the stability in a substantial segment of the island's town life, more especially evident in those areas which had generated an effective urban system in the medieval period.

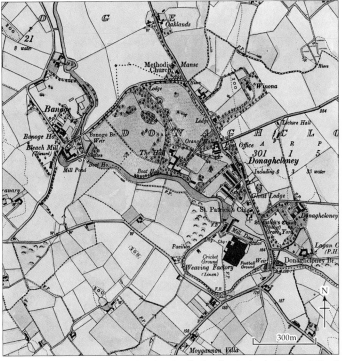

● Fig. 26 Unlike the south of Ireland, which effectively de-industrialised in the nineteenth century, Ulster's linen production permitted a successful industrial economy to develop. Mill villages, like Donaghcloney in county Down, built in the shadow of the great linen factory, were a striking landscape testament to this differential evolution. The cultural particularity predicated partially on this divergence is also reflected in the cricket and soccer grounds, the Orange Hall and Nonconformist chapel – indications of the paternalist Protestantism of the linen industry.

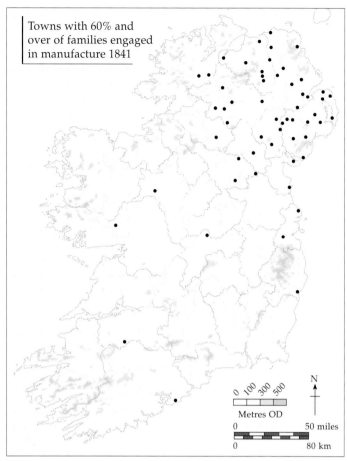

Towns with 60% and over of families engaged in manufacture 1841

Metres OD

Fig. 27 By 1841, only a tiny handful of southern towns had been heavily industrialised, but Ulster, especially Antrim and Down, had a well developed urban industrial base.

POST-FAMINE DEVELOPMENT

Irish towns as a whole entered a recessive phase in the troubled nineteenth century. An American traveller, William Balch, described the principal street in Macroom in 1850: 'On either side are rows of low stone hovels, with thatched roofs, not above seven foot high, looking like a coarse whitewashed wall, perforated with doors and windows, with a row of straw piled on top of it.' In 1841, 66% of the population of Navan were living in squalid one-roomed cabins. A description of Cashel in county Tipperary focussed on the weight of poverty bearing down on the town:

> The suburbs of Cashel – straggling and dirty in the manner of other Irish towns – a legion of cabins of every variety of mud architecture, stretching nearly half a mile towards the next village, like a string of old sticks, clods and other rubbish attached by the urchin to the tail of his kite and with a similar effect viz. to prevent it rising too high in the world.

The second half of the nineteenth century also saw the hey-day of the seaside resort, aided by the railway's ability to link them to urban settlements. Seaside resorts mushroomed within easy access of big cities: Bray near Dublin, Ballycotton and Cobh near Cork, Lahinch, Kilkee and Ballybunion (Limerick), Portrush, Portstewart and Dundrum (Belfast), Greencastle (Derry).

The nineteenth century witnessed the increasing collapse of the colonial underpinnings of many of the urban centres – the triple alliance of the landlord/commercial sector, the military/political nexus, and the established Protestant church. While towns mouldered, the nation-forming class in the countryside – the tenant farmers – saw their interests triumph, as peasant proprietorship was introduced. This copperfastened the strongly rural ethos of the nascent southern Irish state. Only in the north-east was there a zone of industrial and mill villages, where earlier plantation villages had been subsumed into the linen economy in the eighteenth and nineteenth centuries. These villages are especially common in Armagh, Antrim, Down and Tyrone and have done much to maintain the distinctive Ulster ethos. They are Irish outliers of the British industrial village tradition, encompassing company towns like Sion Mills and Bessbrook, and mill villages like Darkley, Milford, Gilford, Drumaness, Ligoniel, Whitehouse, Mossley and Donaghcloney. The Quaker village of Bessbrook in Armagh, established in the 1840s, provided the model for its much more famous equivalent in England – George Cadbury's Bournville. Many were dominated by Presbyterians or non-conformists and the proliferation of the churches of the different sects is a diagnostic feature. Their vitality continued throughout the nineteenth century when landlord-sponsored settlements elsewhere in the island lost their dynamism. Their origins led to strong links between workers and industrialists and a consequent close sectarian solidarity. The industrialisation of these towns revitalised urban Ulster, adding vigorous new impetus to the tradition initiated by the seventeenth-century plantation towns, an impetus which had gradually faltered elsewhere on the island. The political particularism of Ulster in the late nineteenth century may have hinged on this distinctive urban ethos.

The Republic of Ireland maintained its resolutely rural ethos, largely ignoring towns and villages, which were primarily regarded as despicable museum pieces of a colonial past. The draining away of even the scanty residual life in southern towns and villages in the first half of the twentieth century – the Joycean 'paralysis' – invoked some of the sharpest invective of Ireland's cultural commentators in this period – Seán Ó Faoláin, Frank O'Connor, Brinsley MacNamara, Hubert Butler – as they castigated the squalor, decrepitude and numbing stasis of Irish towns.

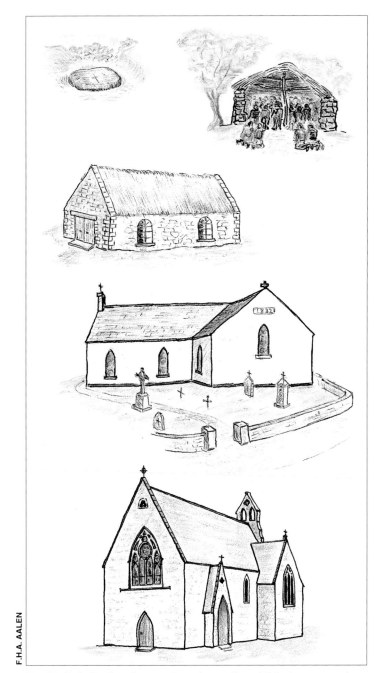

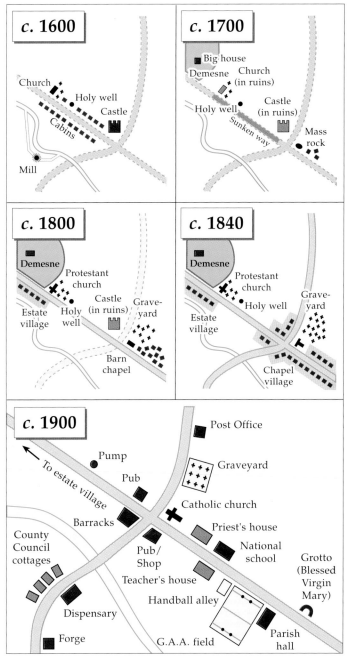

Fig. 28 Catholic chapels went through a well established sequence, from seventeenth-century mass rocks through primitive barn chapels and solid but still restrained T-plan chapels to the assured neo-gothic buildings of the late nineteenth century.

Fig. 29 In the late eighteenth century, based within the redesigned Catholic parish network, newly established chapels at cross-road sites began to accrete small villages around them - often juxtaposed with the abandoned medieval parish centre or the later estate village. By the late nineteenth century, 400 of these humble but striking chapel villages had emerged.

THE CATHOLIC CHURCH

Amidst all this nineteenth-century urban gloom, there was a late blossoming of an unique vein of indigenous village life – the emergence of *c.* 400 chapel villages. Their nuclei were the cores of the newly-constructed Catholic parish system; settlement then accreted around the chapel, generally built on a crossroads, and attracting other functions such as a public house, school, post office, barracks, dispensary and shops. They also quickly gained community allegiance and community-based activities, as in sport and leisure. The quirkiness of the Irish village experience is best summarised in these diffuse, haphazard straggles. Although they were (and are) the most insignificant of places, the importance of these chapel villages lies in their remarkably late emergence – many of them only matured in the twentieth century. This delayed flowering of a new generation of distinctively Irish villages is exceptional in modern Europe and is a striking testimony to both the power of the Catholic church and to the inherent weakness

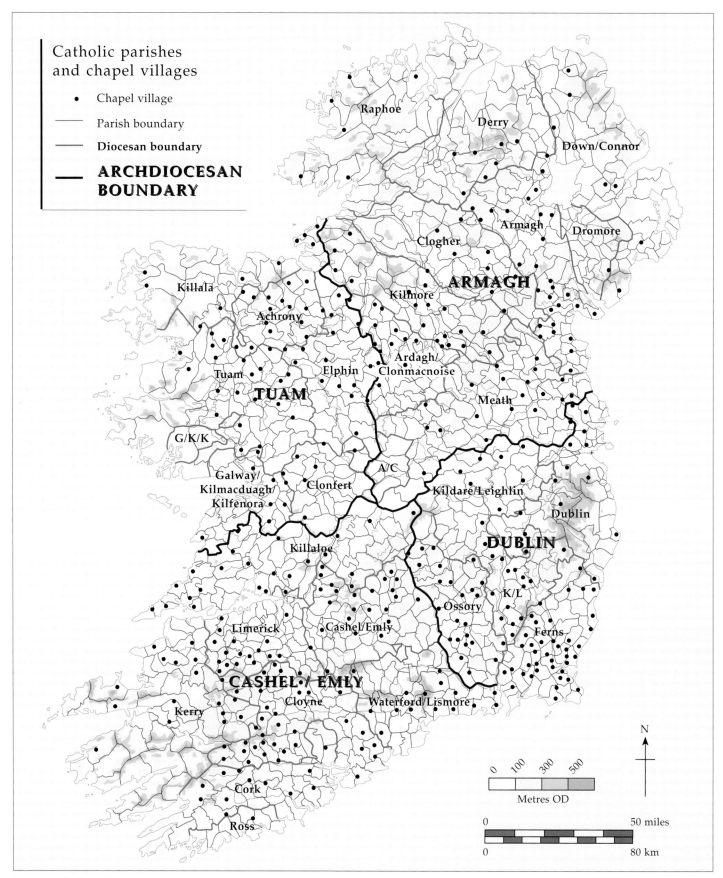

Catholic parishes
and chapel villages

- • Chapel village
- —— Parish boundary
- —— Diocesan boundary
- ━━ **ARCHDIOCESAN
BOUNDARY**

Raphoe

Derry

Down/Connor

Armagh

Dromore

Clogher

Killala

ARMAGH

Achrony

Kilmore

Ardagh/
Clonmacnoise

Elphin

Tuam

TUAM

Meath

G/K/K

A/C

Galway/
Kilmacduagh/
Kilfenora

Clonfert

Kildare/Leighlin

Dublin

Killaloe

DUBLIN

K/L

Ossory

Limerick

Cashel/Emly

Ferns

CASHEL / EMLY

Cloyne

Waterford/Lismore

Kerry

Cork

Ross

N

0   100   300   500
Metres OD

0   50 miles

0   80 km

Fig. 30 In the late eighteenth century and early nineteenth century, the Catholic church had to reorganise its parish system. These units became principal components of social reorganisation in the countryside and chapel villages frequently formed at the parish centres. This map by William J. Smyth depicts the modern parish network.

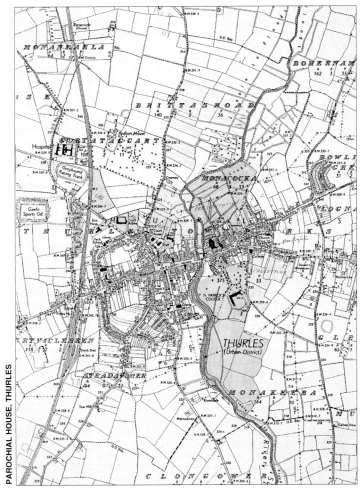

PAROCHIAL HOUSE, THURLES

● Fig. 31 From the 1780s onwards, the Catholic church began its forceful institutional re-emergence. This was often reflected in a distinctive institutional sector in major towns, grouped around the Catholic church and the convents of its teaching orders. At Thurles in county Tipperary, major new components had been added to the town's morphology by 1950, embedding the powerful role of the Catholic church, and reflecting its symbiosis with the state in the provision of educational facilities. Shaded areas highlight lands belonging to the church.

of the older village tradition. The 'urban' experience of many Irish people has been limited to these unpretentious village structures. In county Wexford alone, there are forty such villages, in Limerick thirty, in Tipperary twenty-nine. They are usually linked to the sponsorship role of influential Catholic middlemen, strong farm or mercantile families (just as the Protestant church had previously been sponsored by landlords). These chapel villages and the older estate villages are often found in close and competitive conjunction – for example in county Wicklow, Valleymount and Blessington, Tomacork and Carnew, Curtlestown and Enniskerry, or in county Louth, Castlebellingham and Kilsaran.

The Catholic church also reshaped the morphology of Irish towns, especially in its institutional heartland of south Leinster and east Munster. It was in this zone that revitalised, predominantly Catholic, towns became the hubs of the new natonalist Ireland. These towns – Kilkenny, Thurles, Clonmel, Carlow, Enniscorthy and Mallow – also pioneered the revitalisation of Irish Catholicism and were the seedbeds of the new, aggressive, tridentine church, which was strengthening throughout the nineteenth century. This Catholic/nationalist re-emergence was physically signalled in an unique feature of Irish towns – the growth of a distinctive Catholic institutional sector (consisting of chapels, schools, seminaries, convents etc.), especially in the diocesan centres (e.g. Thurles, Tuam, Carlow, Mullingar, Killarney).

CONCLUSION

Yet, one is still forcibly struck by the overall weakness of town and village traditions in Ireland, and the way in which creative phases so frequently withered away. By 1841, only 14% of the total population lived in centres of 2000+ population. The interplay of a number of forces had weakened urbanism – the rupturing effect of the Reformation, the centrifugal impact of the townland, the dominant family farm system which maintained social networks which transcended or ignored village life, the predominating pastoralism which favoured the intermittent centrality represented by the cattle fair. The porosity of the Irish urban system to rural influences militated against the emergence of a well defined small town or village culture, unlike its English or continental counterparts. Irish towns and villages pulsated instead to the ritual rhythm of the agricultural season.

With the growth of the economy since the 1960s, the towns have revived considerably. But even then, much of the new growth was concentrated in bungalow suburbs festooning the approach roads, and insensitive development, especially for roads and parking, ripped the fabric and destroyed the historic integrity of many of the older centres. In the North, bombing campaigns targeting commercial centres wreaked wholesale destruction. Only in the 1990s has a more focussed approach emerged – helped by increased Irish exposure to urban life elsewhere, by the demands of the tourist industry and by increasing co-operation between heritage specialists and local communities. Most heartening of all, these local communities are increasingly active in preserving the identity and integrity of their towns and villages. Irish towns are now considerably more colourful and cheerful places than they were even a generation ago, and they occupy a more powerful place in the national life and imagination. Their self-confidence and renewal is crucial not just to their own vitality but to that of the Irish rural landscape as a whole.

DAPHNE POCHIN-MOULD

● Fig. 32 In common with other country towns, Abbeyfeale, county Limerick has expanded over the last three decades. This has resulted in untidy sprawling ribbon development, as the town's older Munster Plantation morphology disintegrates under the pressure of change.

BIBLIOGRAPHY

G. Camblin, *The town in Ulster* (Belfast, 1951).

L. Cullen, *Irish towns and villages* (Dublin, 1979).

T. Jones Hughes, 'Village and town in nineteenth-century Ireland' in *Ir. Geog.*, xiv (1981), pp 99-106.

R. Hunter, 'Towns in the Ulster Plantation' in *Studia Hib.*, xi (1971), pp 40-79.

Irish Historic Towns Atlas. Vol. 1: Kildare, Carrickfergus, Bandon, Kells, Mullingar, Athlone (Dublin, 1996).

P. O'Connor, *Exploring Limerick's past. An historical geography of urban development in county and city* (Newcastle West, 1987).

A. Simms and J. Andrews (ed.), *Irish country towns* (Cork, 1994).

A. Simms and J. Andrews (ed.), *More Irish country towns* (Cork, 1995).

A. Simms and P. Fagan, 'Villages in county Dublin: their origins and inheritance' in F. Aalen and K. Whelan (ed.), *Dublin city and county* (Dublin, 1992), pp 79-119.

W. Smyth, 'The dynamic quality of Irish village life – a reassessment' in J. Dewailly and R. Dion (ed.), *Campagnes et littoraux d'Europe* (Lille, 1988), pp 109-13.

A. Thomas, *The walled towns of Ireland*, 2 vols. (Dublin, 1992).

K. Whelan, 'The catholic parish, the catholic chapel and village development in Ireland' in *Ir .Geog.*, xv (1983), pp 1-16.

K. Whelan, 'Town and village in Ireland 1600-1800' in A. Verhoeve and J. Vervloet (ed.), *The transformation of the European rural landscape* (Wageningen, 1992), pp 298-306.

DEMESNES

The demesnes of Ireland occupy a central place in the evolution of the landscape, comprising unique areas of outstanding architectural, archaeological and botanical importance. Defined historically as the lands held by the manor for its own use and occupation, the demesne formerly occupied nearly 6% of the country, as highlighted by the finely engraved stipple on early Ordnance Survey maps. Although dependent upon their surrounding tenanted estates, demesnes evolved as separate social and economic areas, whose distinctive layouts – incorporating farmland, gardens, woods and buildings – still constitute a dominant man-made component of the landscape.

The demesne concept can be traced to the early medieval tenurial system, when a proportion of the manorial lands were set aside 'in demesne' to produce both goods and profits for the estate. The concept survived in Ireland until the break-up of the estate system early in the present century. Although demesnes always retained their primary function as home farms, the process of landscape ornamentation, initially in the formal and later the informal styles, dramatically affected their size and layout during the eighteenth and nineteenth centuries.

Historical continuity is a striking characteristic of Irish demesnes. Many have a medieval nucleus, indicated by the presence of a towerhouse abutting the country house or incorporated into its offices. In other cases, a castle or abbey ruin may be found close by, perhaps adapted as a folly in the landscape park. Indeed, the very nature of eighteenth and nineteenth-century 'natural' parkland provided ideal conditions for the survival of earlier landscape features predating the park's establishment.

●Fig. 1 Stradbally, county Laois, as depicted in a primitive perspective *c.* 1740. It shows a large formal demesne of the kind fasionable in the early eighteenth century. The avenue and bridge in front of the house were laid out in 1714, as was the axial vista to the rear, while the impressive waterworks pre-date 1694. The layout includes tree-lined fields, orchards, flower yards, *bosquets,* ponds and grass *plats.* Most of the charming grottoes, temples and statues were added after 1730. On the skyline may be see the Rock of Dunamase.

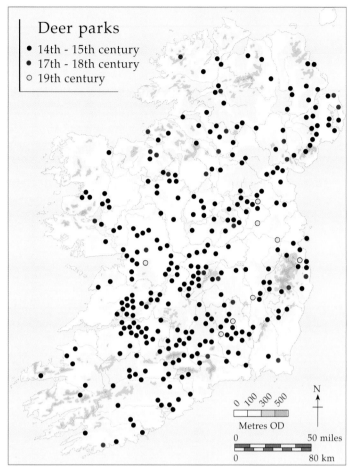

Fig. 2 Medieval and post-medieval deer parks varied considerably in size, but most ranged in area between twenty and one hundred hectares and were invariably located on the demesne perimeter, between one-quarter and one kilometre distant from the manor.

EARLY DEMESNES

The Norman demesnes of the thirteenth century were broadly compatible with their English equivalents. The patchwork of demesne fields, often the only enclosed land in the district, remained a feature of the landscape into the post-medieval period, though manorial economies went into serious decline after the breakdown of central authority in the late fourteenth century.

A distinctive feature of the early demesne was the deer park, quintessential symbol of wealth and prestige. Usually it comprised areas of rough grazing dotted with trees, interspersed with clumps of woodland, and enclosed behind a wooden pale or wall – the former often surmounting a bank with internal fosse. Although some were used for deer hunting – popular until the mid eighteenth century – their main function was the production of venison, a high status food that was reserved for special occasions and much valued in the lean winter months. Fallow deer, first introduced by the Normans, were most popular because of their ability to breed readily and survive on indifferent land.

Despite the considerable costs of their creation and maintenance, many Norman manors east of the Shannon had a deer park, though most, if not all, disappeared with the disturbances of the fourteenth century. A major revival in the seventeenth century was followed by a decline in the later eighteenth century when many were incorporated into the new landscape parks. Renewed interest during the Victorian era was particularly associated with the introduction of exotic species such as sambur and sitka deer.

Deer parks also fulfiled other functions. They provided grazing for cattle and breeding grounds for horses; often they were the location of fish ponds and warrens for smaller game such as pheasant, partridge, hare and rabbit. Rabbits were introduced into Ireland by the Normans and bred in specially constructed enclosures containing groups of long, low pillow mounds, whose former presence may be indicated by placenames with the prefix 'coney'. Their importance to the demesne declined after the mid eighteenth century, though many coastal warrens survived into the nineteenth century to supply the fur market.

Dovecotes, a constant source of fresh meat in the winter, were another fixture of early demesne landscapes. These too were occasionally located in the deer parks, as at Lismore in county Waterford, but more often were erected in a prominent position close to the manor. The medieval columbarium was usually a squat beehive structure; from

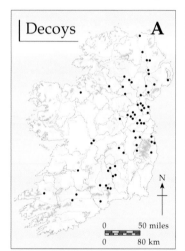

Fig. 3 A) A useful source of food came from trapping wild fowl in decoys. Originating in Holland, these devices were widely used from the 1660s until the 1780s, though a number continued to operate in the nineteenth century. B) Decoy pipe as illustrated by Ralph Payne-Gallwey in 1882. Decoys commonly comprised a shallow pool, usually no more than one hectare in extent, from which radiated curving ditches or 'pipes'. Normally there were four pipes, each with a covering of netting over semi-circular hoops and flanked on one side with overlapping willow screens to hide the decoyman from view. The ducks were enticed into one of these pipes either by bait or by following or 'mobbing' a specially trained dog, as it walked briskly in and out of the screens, until the birds were drawn into the narrow end of the channel and netted. Dense woodland ensured that disturbance was kept to a minimum, while the decoy itself was normally located in a secluded corner of the demesne to encourage the wildfowl to use the ponds as a safe daytime refuge.

the seventeenth century onwards, however, dovecote design became increasingly elaborate. Brick octagonal structures were especially favoured in the eighteenth century, invariably with classical detailing. Frequently, as at Waterston in county Westmeath, they were built as an integral part of the garden or landscape design, though by late georgian times they tended to be designed more as focal features of farmyards.

EARLY GARDENS

High status foods such as meat, fowl and fish formed a central part of the manorial diet during medieval and post-medieval times, but dairy and cereal produce were also important, as were fruit, herbs and vegetables. In the thirteenth century, the principal leguminous crops, notably beans and peas, were grown alongside the cereal crops on the demesne arable, while other vegetables were confined to walled or fenced gardens located close to the manor. The size of these gardens was usually small; even the large monastic gardens were only half a hectare in extent, part of which was generally orchard.

Medieval manorial gardens were clearly similar to those in England with grass or gravel paths, turf benches and raised beds and a range of herbs and vegetables largely restricted to European varieties. The emphasis was on utilitarian plants, but the best gardens must have made a splendid display, especially in the monasteries,

the hubs of a flourishing exchange of seeds and cuttings throughout Europe.

Garden design became increasingly ornamental during the sixteenth century with the introduction of mazes, arbours, topiary and 'knots' (geometric patterns defined by dwarf box, lavender or other suitable perennial plants). An increased availability of exotic plants and a proliferation of gardening texts in the Jacobean period (1603-1625) resulted in Irish demesne gardens becoming larger and more complex. Italian Renaissance ideas, in particular, led to their inclusion as an integral part of the manor house design, with an overall coherence and symmetry. Bowling greens, fountains and statuary were standard features, ornamental ponds became popular and much use was made of terracing, as in the gardens at Lismore Castle, created by the Great Earl of Cork in the 1620s. However, even modest layouts still had to be protected behind palisades, while many of the grandest gardens retained defensive walls, sometimes incorporating turrets and imposing gateways. Not until the relatively settled period following the Restoration of 1660 was it possible for Irish gardens to divest themselves of their need to shelter within fortified enclosures.

GEOMETRIC LANDSCAPES 1660-1750

It was no coincidence that the term landscape, derived from the Dutch *landskip* paintings, came into common

● Fig. 4 Van der Hagen's bird's-eye view of Carton, county Kildare, *c.* 1738, depicts an impressive formal demesne laid out in the 1680s. Its baroque geometry embraced *bosquets,* orchards, kitchen gardens, a bowling green and a canal, with plain grass *plats* bordered by topiary beneath the Palladian house windows. The front court was pierced with iron ballustrading to allow views down the crows-foot avenues of lime.

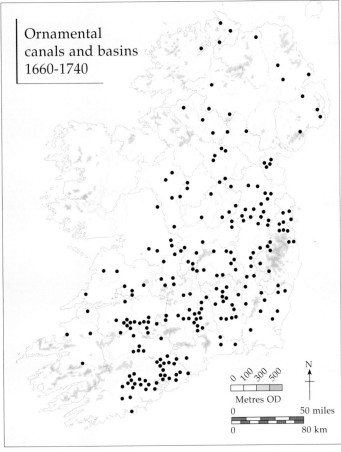

Ornamental canals and basins 1660-1740

0 100 300 500

Metres OD

N

0   50 miles
0   80 km

Fig. 5 (left) Early formal canals and basins 1660-1750. Water ornamentation was a central feature of many layouts. Generally taking the form of linear canals or geometrical basins, these features were arranged axially upon the mansion, incorporating cascades, water stairways and fountains to impart a sense of movement to the design. Most canals ranged from fifty to two hundred metres in length, but some extended to over six hundred metres, despite frequent problems of undulating terrain. Indeed, the excavation, engineering and maintenance of waterworks invariably involved considerable labour commitments, though the majority served a useful function as breeding and holding ponds for fish.

usage during the late seventeenth century. Inspired by ideas from abroad, landowners were now increasingly aware that the countryside around their houses could be 'designed' on a large scale. By reorganising the demesne fields into regular grid-like patterns, and by extending the symmetry of the garden into the landscape through long perspectives, the new unfortified houses of the late Caroline period acquired an imposing setting that reflected their owner's power, status and wealth.

The remarkable popularity of avenues was the most striking characteristic of the period. By the 1730s, almost every house of consequence boasted at least one tree-lined approach, while some had complex avenues radiating across the landscape. Focused on the main facade, and

● Fig. 6 (below) Castle Coole in county Fermanagh, as shown in a reconstruction of the formal layout *c.* 1730 by Stephen Conlin. An avenue and canal are aligned on the house, which overlooks a bowling green, parterre and *bosquet*. On the flanks lie an orchard, a flower yard and haggard. The layout was swept way by the late eighteenth century landscape park.

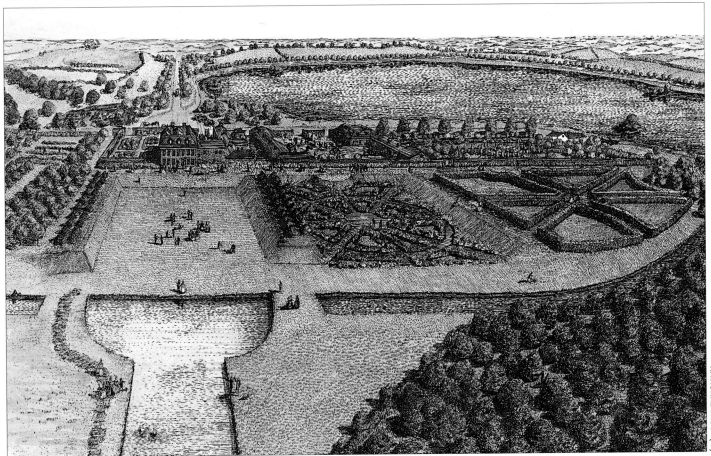

sometimes stretching for miles, these avenues emphasised the centrality of the house in the landscape, whilst demonstrating ownership of all the land over which they passed. The most favoured tree was lime, but elm and chestnut were also frequently used. The trees were usually pruned regularly to reveal straight clean stems and high crowns, whilst along allees or walks they were often trimmed up or 'plashed' to form great walls of greenery.

The upsurge of tree planting during this period was not just confined to avenues. Field boundaries were also lined with trees and woodland blocks were planted in most demesnes, though Irish landowners were slow to appreciate the value of timber production, and the plantations remained small. One popular woodland form, usually found close to the house and flanking the main vista, was the wilderness (*bosquets* in French). Such plantations were dissected by a network of paths and clearings, incorporating clipped hedges, shrubs, ponds and statues. Some *bosquets* were so tamed as to be composed entirely of tall vertical hedges flanking paths laid out in a geometric pattern, often a St Andrew's cross.

Garden elements ranged around the mansion normally included a flower yard, a bowling green, a kitchen garden and orchards. The layout was invariably dominated by a plain grass *plat,* bordered and dissected by gravel paths, while the ground below the main reception rooms was often 'possessed' by a box or flower parterre. Statues, topiary and trees in vases were incorporated into the displays, though from the 1720s their popularity waned as fussy detail became unfashionable. This process of simplification led to the removal of walled courts around the mansion and an opening up of landscape views. It also encouraged an outward migration of garden features into the park, so that temples and other classical structures were built away from the house, crowning hillocks and terminating vistas. Such developments increased the integration of the garden and demesne park, a process later fully realised with the emergence of the landscape park.

LANDSCAPE PARKS 1750-1840

By the mid eighteenth century, a reaction against the tyrannical symmetry of garden and park design led to the adoption of 'naturalised' parklands, whose planting and layout extolled the beauty of the natural world. The new revolutionary style, emanating from England, demanded that flowers, fruit and vegetables be banished to walled gardens away from the house and that formal features, such as parterres, avenues and canals, be swept away and replaced with an idealised conception of 'natural' landscapes. This owed much to the portrayal of idyllic Italian scenery in the

PRIVATE COLLECTION

● Fig. 7 Tollymore Park, at the foot of Slieve Donard in county Down, as depicted by Bernard Scalé in 1777. Serpentine walks curl through planted clumps, and the demesne, designed by Thomas Wright, is trisected by two winding streams, creating a highly fashionable romantic landscape, an effect heightened by the extensive use of gothic details.

paintings of Nicholas Poussin and Claude Lorraine. The ideal was now to surround the mansions with wide expanses of smooth, open turf dotted with clumps of noble trees, secluded from the outside world by plantation belts and perimeter walls. Sunken fences or ha-has permitted uninterrupted prospects of the park from the house, while a diversity of circuit walks and rides orchestrated a succession of pastoral Arcadian scenes, featuring hillocks and winding streams, glinting lakes that mirrored the sky, woodlands that dissolved into sunlit glades, and flocks and herds placidly grazing in the shadow of classical temples and ruins.

From 1760 onwards, the natural style was enthusiastically adopted and had become an ubiquitous feature of the Irish countryside by the end of the century. Even modest houses, such as rectories and town villas, had parkland around them. Though landscape parks continued to be created throughout the nineteenth century, the vast majority were already constructed by the 1840s.

Although the creation of landscape parks involved working with, rather than against nature, their construction was not achieved without considerable effort. Earth had to be moved, hedges grubbed-up, public roads diverted, streams widened, settlements relocated and great numbers of trees planted. Across the country, hundreds of lakes were dug, sometimes re-utilising old canals; in many cases, the mansion itself was rebuilt in a new location to take full advantage of the terrain. While parks were often laid out by their owners in conjunction with the head gardener, professional designers were widely commissioned.

With the emergence of the new 'natural' landscapes, the agricultural and industrial activities associated with

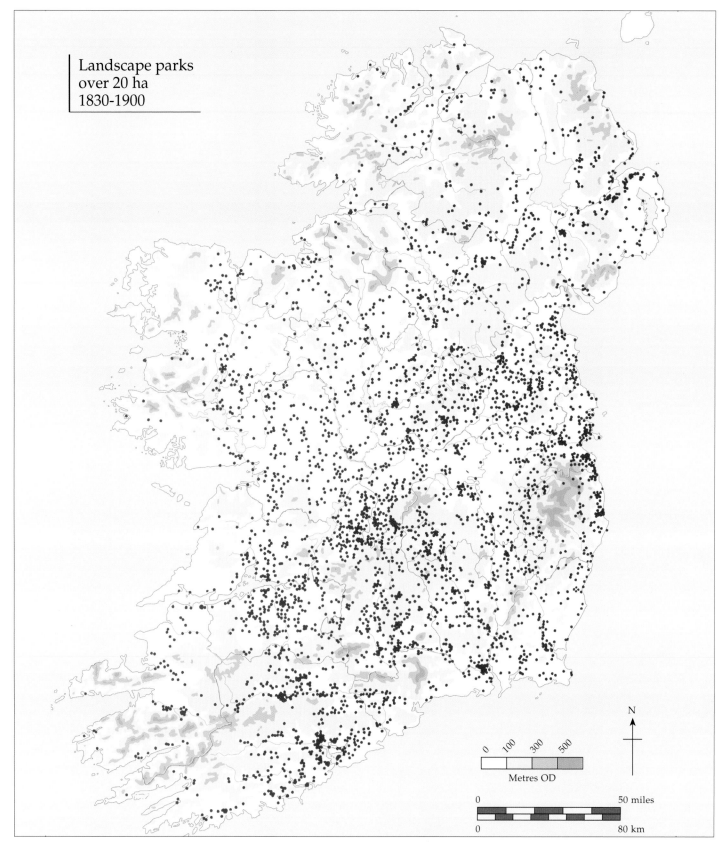

Landscape parks
over 20 ha
1830-1900

Metres OD

N

0   100   300   500

0   50 miles

0   80 km

Fig. 8 Irish landscape parks. Nearly four per cent of the country, or 320,000 ha, was emparked with over 7000 houses featuring associated parks of four hectares or more. Many of the smaller and medium-sized examples were clustered around the urban centres, but in rural areas their distribution reflected the large estates, with fewer parks where small farms flourished. Although ostensibly created as ornamental landscapes, parklands were utilised with profit in mind; the woodland timber was exploited over the medium and longer term, while money was made from the grazing of herds and flocks on the grasslands. Parklands also proved to be superbly suited to the rearing and shooting of game birds, and were ideal for riding and exercising horses.

Fig. 9 A tree-moving machine, as depicted by Henry Steuart in 1828. Patrons demanded that their new parks have an aged appearance from the outset, so great versatility was required in utilising existing trees from woods, avenues and field boundaries, and sometimes in transplanting mature trees with special machines.

the demesne were relocated beyond the parkland perimeter to the tree-lined fields of the home farm. The kitchen gardens, invariably walled enclosures, were isolated away from the house and usually sited near the stable-yard, with its ready supply of manure. According to the importance of the house, these could be anything from 0.2 ha to 2.4 ha in extent and generally contained perimeter and cross paths, a pond, glasshouses and potting sheds. Rectangular plans were standard during the Victorian era, but eighteenth-century walled gardens tended to be more experimental in design, with the frequent adoption of irregular plans to provide as much south-facing walling as possible. Their bounding walls, three and a half to four metres high, were internally lined with bricks to retain the heat of the sun, while shelter belts outside gave added protection from the winds.

A new genre of distinctive estate architecture also emerged, encouraged by a sentimental attitude to rural life and a prevailing utilitarian philosophy. Estate cottages, gate lodges, dairies and hitherto humble farm buildings became worthy of architectural attention, while new model farm buildings were erected, often on the junction between park and home farm. The most abiding image of all parkland buildings continue to be the lodges at the park entrances. These were normally treated in an ornamental manner, in the style of the big house, and announced to the visitor and passer-by the grandeur of the demesne park and the taste of its owner.

The process of parkland construction was facilitated by the abundance of cheap labour during this period and by a need to provide local employment in times of hardship. The gentry had greater wealth at their disposal, due to rising agricultural prices and higher rents, while the new parklands had the attraction of being comparatively cheap to maintain and well suited to the rolling Irish countryside. It was the multi-functional nature of the parks, however, which contributed most to their popularity. The parks also helped to reinforce the social divisions of Irish society by enabling their owners to cushion themselves from the economic realities that sustained them, whilst conveying the comforting notion that the social order was somehow natural, immutable and inevitable.

VICTORIAN AND EDWARDIAN DEMESNES 1840-1914

In the years following the Great Famine of the 1840s, the fortunes of the Irish gentry went into recession. Confronted with drastically reduced rental incomes, hundreds had to sell their inheritance, some of them compulsorily through the Encumbered Estates Court set up in 1849. Shortages of money and labour resulted in new parkland schemes being largely confined to the richer families, while demesne developments were dominated by horticultural and agricultural advances that took place within an existing landscape structure.

The eclipse of the landscape park was accompanied by a popular enthusiasm for plant collecting, sustained by the great influx of seeds, cuttings and rooted plants from abroad and by the improved design and construction of greenhouses. The introduction of numerous exotic tree species led to the creation of pineta and arboreta, while formal avenues were also introduced as a means of displaying new tree varieties. New shrubs were accommodated in magnolia gardens, American gardens and other specially created shrubberies or pleasure grounds. Rose gardens and rock gardens were also developed, together with areas devoted to particular plant themes, such as evergreen or aquatic plants. Formal parterres were reintroduced around the house, sometimes with balustraded terracing, and these were filled with the vast number of new annual and tender plants that were now raised in the heated glasshouses of the walled gardens.

Demesne staff were everywhere curtailed in the 1880s as a result of the agricultural depression and the consequent agrarian troubles. As demesne gardens became less labour-intensive, the concept of the naturalised or 'wild' garden emerged, advocated by the famous Irish horticulturist William Robinson. His philosophy of planting 'perfectly hardy exotics under conditions where they will grow without further care' was well received in Ireland, leading to the creation of bog gardens, rhododendron and

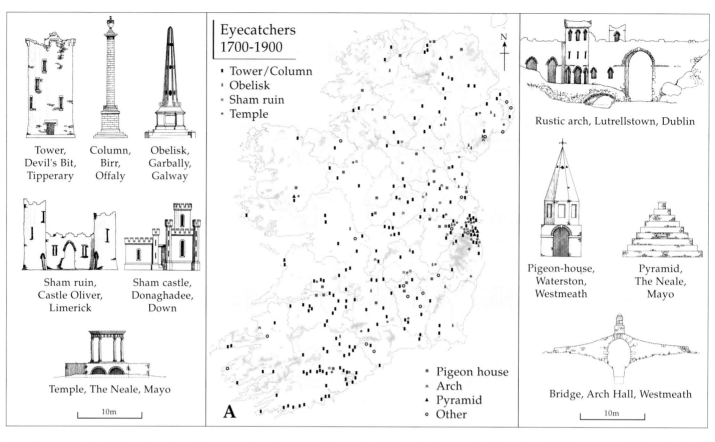

Eyecatchers 1700-1900

- ■ Tower/Column
- ▮ Obelisk
- ▪ Sham ruin
- ▪ Temple

Tower, Devil's Bit, Tipperary

Column, Birr, Offaly

Obelisk, Garbally, Galway

Sham ruin, Castle Oliver, Limerick

Sham castle, Donaghadee, Down

Temple, The Neale, Mayo

10m

- ■ Pigeon house
- ∧ Arch
- ▲ Pyramid
- ○ Other

Rustic arch, Lutrellstown, Dublin

Pigeon-house, Waterston, Westmeath

Pyramid, The Neale, Mayo

Bridge, Arch Hall, Westmeath

10m

A

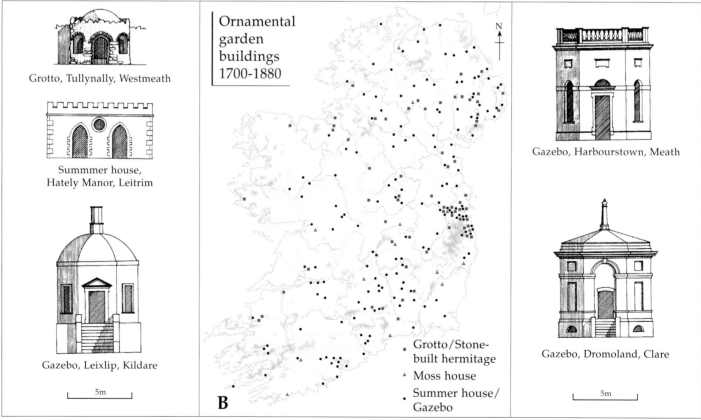

Ornamental garden buildings 1700-1880

Grotto, Tullynally, Westmeath

Summmer house, Hately Manor, Leitrim

Gazebo, Leixlip, Kildare

5m

- ■ Grotto/Stone-built hermitage
- ▲ Moss house
- ▪ Summer house/ Gazebo

Gazebo, Harbourstown, Meath

Gazebo, Dromoland, Clare

5m

B

Fig. 10 A) Demesne park eyecatchers 1700-1900 and B) Ornamental garden buildings 1700-1800. Landscape parks were typically embellished with a range of decorative buildings and eye-catchers. Some were purely whimsical, intended to add interest to their 'natural' surroundings, notably sham ruins, shell houses, grottoes and hermitages; others – temples, gazebos, summer houses and prospect towers – had a more practical value as retreats, tea houses or places to shelter from the weather.

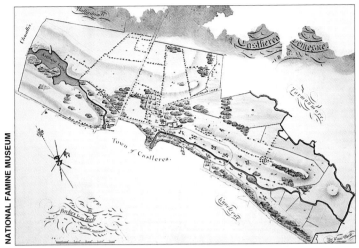

NATIONAL FAMINE MUSEUM

● Fig. 11   Castlerea demesne, county Roscommon in 1826. The fully fledged romantic style of landscaping suited the west of Ireland, with its copious streams and undulating topography.

other woodland gardens, mixed borders, grass paths and the massing of bulbs in grass. The 'Robinsonian' theme was so successful that its legacy survives to this day.

THE DEMESNE IN THE TWENTIETH CENTURY

The process of land redistribution, begun with the Encumbered Estates Act of 1849, was greatly accelerated by a succession of land acts, all of which encouraged tenants to buy out their farms using funds provided by the Treasury. By 1919, five million hectares, or more than half the country, had been affected by these measures. The effects of these sales on demesnes were disastrous, for shorn of rental income from their estates, most had to survive as self-supporting units. Many became neglected and were subsequently sold, often to people interested only in the land; as a result, houses were quickly demolished and the trees unsparingly felled.

The destruction of Ireland's parklands was accelerated considerably by the 1923 Land Act, which empowered the Land Commission to acquire demesne-land through compulsory purchase. Over 120,000 hectares of parkland were subsequently devastated and their lands either subdivided into farmland or blanketed with spruce. Some big

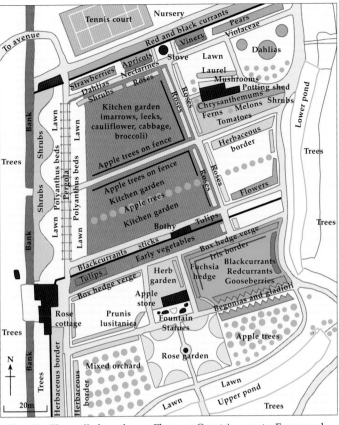

● Fig. 12   The walled garden at Florence Court in county Fermanagh *c.* 1930, typically integrated vegetables, fruit and flowers in a *potager* layout.

houses survived as schools, hospitals, convents, hotels and government buildings, but many more were demolished or became the latest generation of haunting ruins. The sad process of destruction has slowed down considerably since the 1970s, as more people appreciate the demesne's unique importance in the Irish landscape. Many houses and their demesnes receive state support and are open to the public; some now belong to the Office of Public Works and in Northern Ireland a number of magnificent demesnes are owned by the National Trust. However, many pressures still remain, particularly from such sterile developments as housing estates and golf courses. Consequently, the demesnes of Ireland face a mixed future as they struggle to adopt new roles in the evolution of the landscape.

BIBLIOGRAPHY

P. Bowe, 'The Renaissance garden in Ireland' in *Irish Arts Review*, xi (1995), pp 74-81.

J. Dean, *The gate lodges of Ulster* (Belfast, 1994).

R. Desmond, *Dictionary of British and Irish botanists and horticulturists* (London, 1994).

K. Down, 'Colonial society and economy in the High Middle Ages' in A. Cosgrove (ed.), *Medieval Ireland* (Oxford, 1987), pp 439-91.

A. Forbes, 'Tree planting in Ireland during four centuries' in *R.I.A. Proc.*, xli (1933), C, pp 168-99.

J. Howley, *The follies and garden buildings of Ireland* (New Haven, 1993).

K. Lamb and P. Bowe, *A history of gardening in Ireland* (Dublin, 1995).

E. Malins and P. Bowe, *Irish gardens and demesnes from 1830* (London, 1980).

E. Malins and Knight of Glin, *Lost demesnes. Irish landscape gardening 1660-1845* (London, 1976).

E. Nelson, '"This garden to adorn with all varietie". The garden plants of Ireland in the centuries before 1700' in *Moorea*, ix (1990), pp 37-54.

E. Nelson and A. Brady (ed.), *Irish gardening and horticulture* (Dublin, 1979).

R. Payne-Gallwey, *The fowler in Ireland* (Southampton, 1882).

T. Reeves-Smyth, 'The nature of demesnes' in J. Wilson Foster and H. Chesny (ed.), *Nature in Ireland: a scientific and cultural history* (Dublin, forthcoming).

T. Reeves-Smyth, 'Early formal garden and landscape design in Ireland' in P. Pattison (ed.), *There by design: field archaeology in parks and gardens* (London, forthcoming).

T. Williamson, *Polite landscapes* (Baltimore, 1995).

COMMUNICATIONS

Communications are an outstanding feature of Ireland's rural landscape. Some roads date from early times, but a network of roads and lanes, much denser than in most of Europe, developed strongly in the eighteenth and nineteenth centuries to link the diffuse pattern of small single farms, provide access to peat bogs and hill grazing, and serve a population substantially larger than the present. The expansion of roads had profound consequences in pre-industrial Ireland, ending isolation, altering rural settlement patterns and facilitating the erosion of native culture and the process of emigration.

During the same period, and encouraged by central Ireland's low relief, canals were constructed, running in a predominantly east-west direction and serving the ports on the eastern seaboard with produce from an expanding rural hinterland. Unable to compete with the later railways, the canals fell into disuse in the early twentieth century, but have experienced a revival in recent years with the development of waterways for leisure pursuits.

Although relatively underdeveloped, Ireland generated an impressive rail network in the latter half of the nineteenth century. Like the canals, railways were optimistically perceived as instruments of economic development and were extended into remote rural areas to encourage commercial farm production, trade and tourism; in reality, railways facilitated the importation of foreign goods and emigration. With the arrival of motorised road transport after World War II and upgrading of the roads, the railways appeared uncompetitive and a strategy of closure was implemented. Much reduced, the railway system has left a considerable legacy in the Irish rural landscape, including abandoned stations, bridges and embankments.

Thinning of the communications network in the twentieth century, in particular railways and rural roads, has been paralleled by the development of air travel and telecommunications and increasing investment in major roadways and by-passes. As these assume increasing importance, the deterioration of minor roads is likely to accelerate, particularly in the most depopulated regions. It remains to be seen to what extent the technological revolution will alter current trends.

●Fig. 1 Road making in a congested district, county Donegal, *c.* 1900. Ireland has many roads which originated as employment schemes during periods of food shortage. Labour was in plentiful supply and road building was labour intensive; materials for roads and walls were often taken directly from the surrounding fields. In the nineteenth century, roads were regarded by the government as essential to the spread of commercial prosperity and were seen also as instruments of moral improvement, intensifying social contacts and the spread of new ideas into remote areas.

ROADS

Before the twelfth century, the population of Ireland, organised in approximately 150 semi-independent túatha, is unlikely to have much exceeded half a million. The decentralised system and low level of inter-regional trade limited long distance travel; most journeys were short and made on foot or by pack-horse. To facilitate these journeys, a network of paths and tracks evolved from which many contemporary roads are descended. Routes tended to follow the line of least resistance, twisting and turning in order to avoid poorly drained areas and land which was easily overlooked. Bogland was crossed by plank roads (tochair). Today, the earliest routes can be recognised by their convergence on urban centres and religious sites of known early significance. A number of longer, more significant routes did exist: five slíghe radiated from Tara, the symbolic and political capital of pre-Christian Ireland.

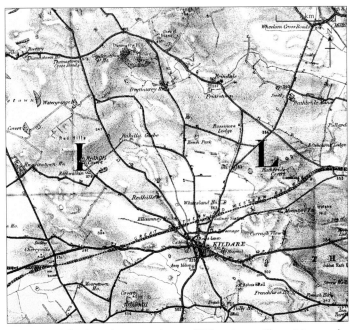

●Fig. 2 Evolved roads converging on Kildare town. The existence of a cathedral, round tower and abbey indicate that Kildare has been a town of importance for a long period; the majority of the roads radiating from the town are presumably of considerable age.

In the late medieval period, trade intensified as towns were founded and market charters granted. Yet, the road system remained neglected and underdeveloped until the end of the sixteenth century. The 1615 Highway Act required that each parish annually appoint two parishioners to act as surveyors and that each farmer send two able-bodied men, a horse team and tools to work on the roads on six days between Easter and summer each year. Administration of this system passed to the counties in 1634. Its impact was limited and seventeenth-century travellers continued to pour scorn on Irish roads.

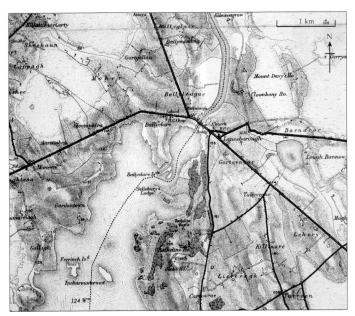

●Fig. 3 Straight-line roads at Lanesborough, county Longford. The ramrod roads radiating from the town contrast with the evolved roads which almost certainly date from an earlier period.

As population increased, as Dublin grew and as the economy became more closely integrated with that of Britain, the rate of road construction and improvement accelerated. The Grand Jury Act of 1765 abolished statutory labour and developed the presentment system whereby an individual wishing to construct or improve a road could submit costed plans for the project to the grand jury of the county. The grand juries were landlord-dominated local authority bodies. If the plans were approved, the individual concerned was ultimately reimbursed the cost of construction. Most roads that came into existence in the eighteenth century were therefore planned in advance. Many can be recognised in the contemporary landscape because they run in straight lines, cutting through the older road pattern with little or no regard for physical features, for example, ill-drained land and hills. Most

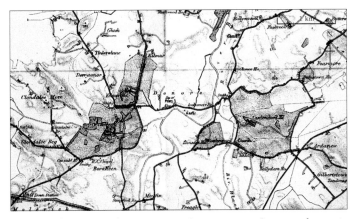

●Fig. 4 The impact of estates on road courses, near Longwood, county Meath. The map shows clearly how roads were routed to pass around rather than through the major demesnes.

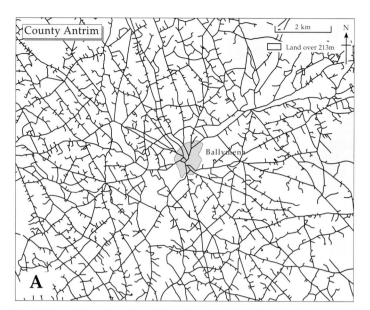

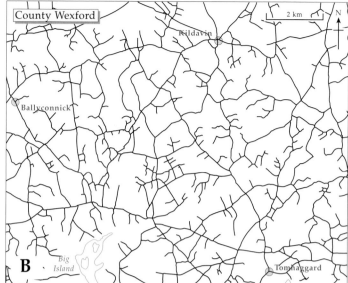

Fig. 5 The pattern of roads and lanes in parts of counties Antrim and Wexford. ● A) The proto-industrial landscape of north-east Ulster contains an exceptionally dense network of roads radiating from the towns in all directions and linked by tie roads at regular intervals; narrow farm lanes connect individual farmsteads to the road network. ● B) In south county Wexford, the scattered farms are connected by a dense network of roads and lanes.

presentment roads were sponsored by local landlords who carefully designed routes to pass close to but around their own demesnes.

Commencing in the eighteenth century, agrarian reorganisation on the larger estates led to the drainage, liming and reclamation of hill areas, the progressive decline of farm clusters and the growing diffusion of independent farmsteads. These changes necessitated the development of a tightly, articulated pattern of access lanes (bóthríní) which remains a feature of the Irish countryside, even though present-day rationalisation is modifying the pattern with many old tracks and lanes becoming disused and overgrown.

Another type of eighteenth-century road was the turnpike which required users to pay fees at tollgates placed at intervals along the route. Profits were then invested in the road. Each turnpike had to be authorised by an act of parliament. The first turnpike in Ireland was created in 1729 when an act was passed to finance the repair of the road from Dublin to Kilcullen by converting it to a turnpike. This was followed by eighty similar schemes involving both the construction of new roads, often along straight alignments, and the financing of improvements on pre-existing roads. In general, Irish turnpike roads were not a success. The relatively dense network of non-turnpike routes ensured that traffic could evade tolls, and disappointing traffic levels meant that most turnpikes generated insufficient revenue to pay for their upkeep.

Fig. 6 Turnpike roads before 1805 as mapped by John Andrews. The new roads focus on the commercialised sector of the country, with the notable exception of the south-east, where transport on the Nore, Suir and Barrow rivers system was still highly competitive.

Mail coaches were introduced in Ireland in 1789 and by an 1805 act of parliament, the Postmaster General was required to survey and map the roads used by the coaches and to suggest improvements. Over 3200 km of route were surveyed between 1805 and 1811; improvements were made and new sections of road built, for example, the

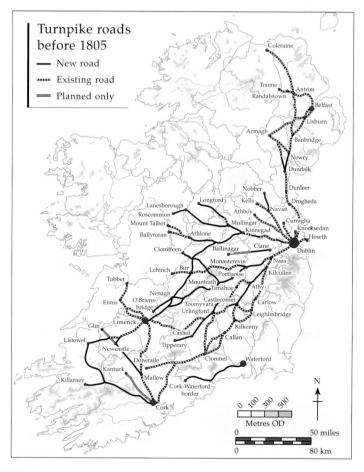

● Fig. 7 The Wicklow military road under construction by Scottish highland soldiers, as painted by T.S. Roberts in 1802. Running through the heart of the mountains, and flanked by impressive barracks, the road was designed to secure a region that had been a stronghold of the United Irishmen, especially Michael Dwyer. Its designer, Alexander Taylor, was later chief post-office engineer, and designed much of the mail coach network.

straight-line route north-westwards from Dublin to Slane. High engineering standards were set in terms of width and gradient. The 1811 mail coach road from Killarney to Tralee had no gradient steeper than one in fifteen; its predecessor, a straight-line route completed in 1759, had gradients as steep as one in eight.

During the seventeenth and eighteenth centuries, Dublin became the dominant node on the Irish road network while Belfast had a regional role only. As a whole, the road system was improved considerably but by 1800, the peripheral areas of the country, and most notably its western extremities, were still poorly served. Roads had not been built in areas where there were few resident landlords, while turnpikes were absent from areas where there was little traffic. A principal reason for the retarded development in the remote areas was that central government declined to become involved directly in the financing and

building of roads, apart from the construction between 1788 and 1796 of a military road (later a turnpike) through county Waterford and the completion in 1804 of a similar road through county Wicklow. Substantial barracks were located along the spectacular Wicklow road which crossed the glen heads to make the mountains more accessible for military purposes.

In 1817, as a result of poverty exacerbated by severe harvest failures and the post-Napoleonic agricultural depression, the government offered loans to support road building projects, in part to create employment in distressed areas. An 1822 act of parliament finally permitted the payment of direct grants from central government funds for road building projects in western and south-western counties, and as a result, many remote settlements were served for the first time, for example, Caherciveen, county Kerry (1822) and Belmullet, county Mayo (1825).

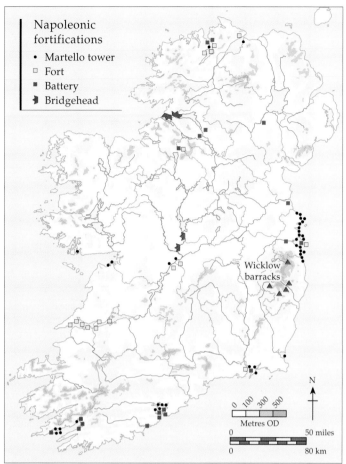

Napoleonic
fortifications
• Martello tower
▫ Fort
▪ Battery
⤙ Bridgehead

Wicklow
barracks

Fig. 8 Influenced by social, military and security problems inside and outside the country, the construction and improvement of roads was accompanied by the completion of numerous buildings relating to security. During the Napoleonic conflict, fortified 'Martello' towers were erected along coasts and major rivers as an early warning system in case of a French invasion. Likely invasion points near major cities were particularly well protected.

The transformation wrought by these roads could be dramatic: Belmullet had only three houses when the first wheeled vehicle arrived in 1823, but ten years later boasted 185 houses, together with corn-stores, shops and hotels. In response to nineteenth-century internal political and agrarian unrest, police barracks were built in most rural districts. Numerous coastguard stations were also erected, mainly in the middle of the century. In 1832, the grants scheme for road construction was handed over to the newly constituted Irish Board of Works which by 1848 was administering 1600 km of road, together with a number of harbours, virtually all of which were in the western counties.

The foregoing sequence of road building and improvements doubled the Irish road mileage suitable for wheeled vehicles between 1700 and 1850. These roads had a number of associated engineering features, most notably bridges of various types. There are currently about 25,000 masonry-arched road bridges of over six foot span in Ireland, virtually all dating from after 1775.

● Fig. 9 Lismore Bridge, county Waterford c.1824, with Lismore Castle in the background.

In response to the enduring problems of the poorest western regions, the Congested Districts Board was created in 1891 to encourage economic development in these areas. The Board supervised the completion of some minor roads

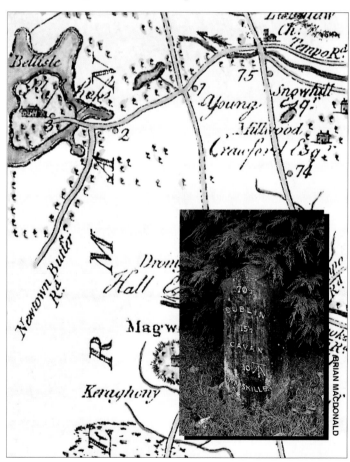

● Fig. 10 Detail of the Dublin/Enniskillen road near Lisnaskea, county Fermanagh, from George Taylor and Andrew Skinner's *Maps of the roads of Ireland*, 1778. The inset shows a surviving milestone on the outskirts of Lisnaskea. The 'crows foot', an Ordnance Survey bench mark, was carved on the stone at a later date.

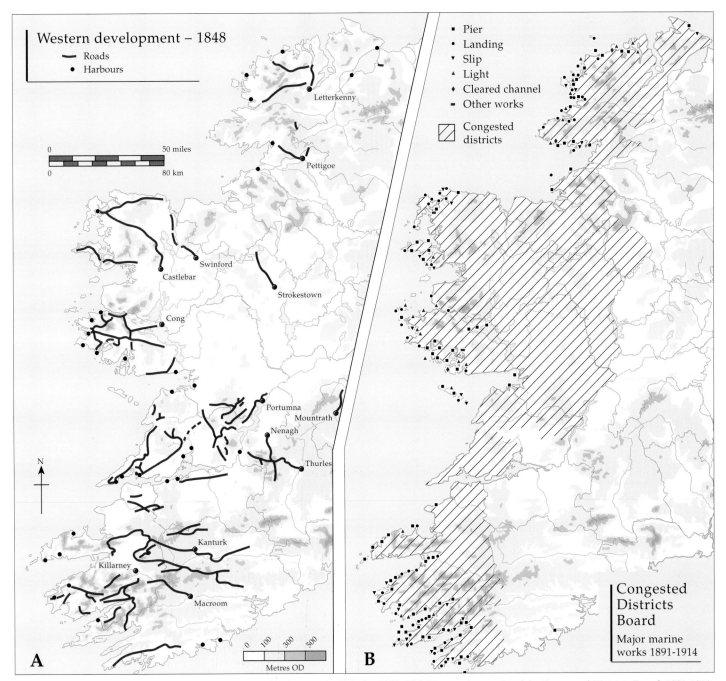

Western development – 1848
Roads
Harbours

0   50 miles
0   80 km

Letterkenny

Pettigoe

Swinford
Castlebar
Cong
Strokestown

Portumna
Mountrath
Nenagh
Thurles

Kanturk
Killarney
Macroom

N

0   100   300   500
Metres OD

A

Pier
Landing
Slip
Light
Cleared channel
Other works

Congested districts

Congested Districts Board

Major marine works 1891-1914

B

Fig. 11 A) Western roads and harbours in operation under the Board of Works, 1848. B) Major marine works of the Congested Districts Board, 1891-1914.

schemes. A lasting landscape impact of the Board's work was the construction of numerous harbours and other marine works to facilitate the fishing industry.

WATERWAYS AND CANALS

Given the varied but often poor quality of roads and the corresponding difficulty and expense of transporting bulky goods, Ireland was easily influenced by the contemporary English craze for the development of waterways and canal building. A 1715 act created commissioners empowered to raise money privately within their counties for such schemes and ultimately to charge tolls. The completed navigations, it was hoped, would simultaneously improve agriculture by draining bogland.

The impact of the 1715 act was limited, as the proposed schemes required substantial sums of money which could not be raised locally. Accordingly, a 1729 act empowered parliament to collect dues on certain luxury goods and to disburse these monies on navigation projects which were placed under the control of four groups of provincial commissioners. This act led to the construction of the Newry Canal and initiation of the Coalisland Canal, both schemes

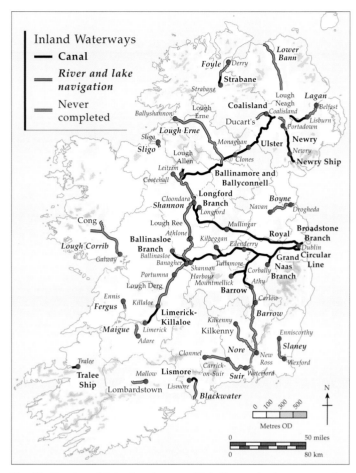

Fig. 12 Canals and inland waterways. Note the emphasis on connecting Dublin with the Rivers Shannon and Barrow.

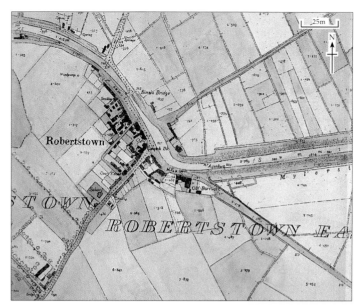

● Fig. 13 Robertstown, county Kildare, is a canal village located on the Grand canal near its junction with the Barrow navigation. With its harbour, hotel and warehouses, it was created to cater for the needs of the canal users.

being particularly encouraged by Dublin interests wishing to provide an outlet to the capital (via the new navigations and by ship from Newry) for what were thought to be considerable coal resources in the Coalisland area of county Tyrone. In 1751, a single Navigation Board was created to oversee the development of inland waterways.

An important contrast between road maintenance and the construction and development of waterways and canals is that central government was responsible for the earliest inland navigations. In 1771-2, an act was passed which enabled private individuals to become involved in such schemes. Given the well publicised profits generated by some English canals, such investments seemed attractive and significant amounts were subscribed. The major canal schemes were initiated during the second half of the eighteenth century. By 1907, there had been a total expenditure of almost five million pounds on the completion and upkeep of 1140 km of inland navigations in Ireland, of which over half had come from private funds.

In Ireland, the main rivers do not correspond to the principal trade routes, which traditionally have been from the interior to the east and south coasts and onwards to

Britain and Europe. The longest river, the Shannon, flows in a south-west direction from county Cavan to reach the sea on the west coast and the Shannon navigation has always been hindered by the presence of falls at Ardnacrusha. Ireland's largest lake, Lough Neagh, is located on the river Bann which flows directly northwards to enter the sea near Coleraine. The cities of Dublin, Belfast and Cork are each located on smaller rivers which have never been navigable upstream for any worthwhile distance.

As might be expected, the system of inland waterways which evolved in Ireland favoured east-west routes linking Dublin and Belfast with the Shannon and serving the midlands en route. Three such waterways were created: the

● Fig. 14 The hotel at Robertstown, erected in 1801 to service the passenger traffic on the canal. Passenger services ceased in 1852 and the hotel was subsequently closed and used as a constabulary barracks.

TERENCE DUNNE

DEPARTMENT OF ARTS, CULTURE AND THE GAELTACHT

● Fig. 15 The Royal Canal from Blackshade Bridge, county Meath. The canal has been raised above the level of the surrounding countryside.

Grand Canal which eventually reached the Shannon in 1805 and also provided a link to the Barrow, the Royal Canal completed in 1817 and the Ballinamore and Ballyconnell Canal completed in 1859 which provided a link from Belfast to the Shannon via the Lagan and Ulster Canals.

Unlike some of their English counterparts, the Irish canals were not a commercial success. This was primarily because they did not tap areas of mineral reserves or reach large industrial centres but rather relied mainly on the transport of bulky agricultural products. While they carried a substantial proportion of the traffic in their corridors in the pre-railway era, the revenues generated were not sufficient to cover costs.

The optimistic belief that canals would transform the Irish countryside and especially the midlands by encouraging industry and agriculture (the latter being associated with drainage schemes) did not prove correct. There were however significant landscape impacts such as the development of canal villages, lock-keepers' houses, warehouses and hotels for overnight passengers, all of which were constructed to a high standard, and thus became an enduring element in the Irish countryside.

RAILWAYS

In 1827, the mailboat to Holyhead commenced running from the harbour at Kingstown (Dun Laoghaire) creating a need for efficient transportation between that port and the capital. A railway was opened from Dublin to Kingstown in 1834, initiating considerable public debate concerning other possible schemes.

In 1836, the United Kingdom government, anxious to see an orderly development of railways in Ireland, appointed a four-man commission, generally referred to as the Drummond Commission after its chairman, to design 'a general system of railways for Ireland'. Its final report was accompanied by a fine series of maps. Those depicting passenger and freight flows are believed to be the first to use lines of varying thickness to depict flows and graduated circles to show urban populations.

The major Irish railway routes had been completed by 1860 when thirty companies were operating a network of 2195 km with 324 locomotives, 867 carriages and 4777 wagons. Although the initial lines were built to various gauges, this was standardised to five feet three inches by act of parliament in 1846. This gauge was wider than that adopted in England, Scotland and Wales and has precluded the use of train ferries on the Irish Sea ever since.

The initial Irish railway routes were built to exceptionally high engineering standards, requiring considerable earthworks, tunnelling, bridges and viaducts. The stations, even in remote places, were generally substantial architectural statements with individual companies favouring particular styles.

The initial Irish railways were financially successful, inevitably leading to numerous suggestions for expansion of the system. Prosperity would allegedly accrue to even the remotest regions if only they could be reached by railway.

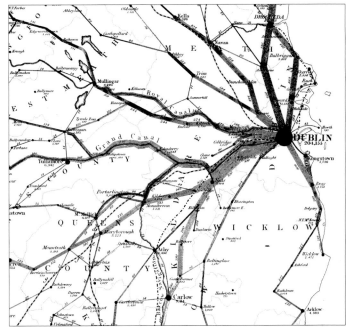

● Fig. 16 Passenger conveyance map (part of) to accompany the 1838 report of the Drummond Commission. Note the importance of the canals as passenger carriers at this time. The routes for the proposed railways are shown; an inland route via Navan and Carrickmacross was suggested for the Dublin to Belfast link, whereas a coastal route via Drogheda was eventually followed.

● Fig. 17 A major engineering work: the Boyne viaduct, Drogheda, county Louth. The construction of the coastal railway route from Dublin to Dundalk and onwards to Belfast was impeded by the valley of the River Boyne at Drogheda. Although the line to Dundalk was completed in 1849, passengers had to be conveyed by road across the Boyne until 1853 when a temporary viaduct came into use. A permanent structure opened in 1855 and was extensively rebuilt in 1932. This painting by Lord Teynham in 1878 shows the Victorian viaduct, a triumph of contemporary engineering.

celebrated West Clare Railway which ran from Ennis to Kilrush and Kilkee, and the Tralee and Dingle Railway in county Kerry, which had the steepest gradient of any line in Ireland. The three foot gauge reduced construction costs. In order to cut costs still further, these routes were frequently built as tramways alongside public roads.

Railways had a significant impact on the economic life of the countryside through which they passed, especially in transporting large volumes of goods and passengers at hitherto unheard of speeds. In the pre-railway age, it could take up to five days to convey bulk goods overland from Galway to Dublin; by 1851, the train took only ten hours. The opening of railways to areas of outstanding natural beauty facilitated the development of tourism on a larger scale than ever before. As early as 1854, the principal railway companies were operating hotels in areas of tourist interest. While their impact was generally positive in an economic sense, the railways had some negative effects, for example, the decline of local industries, which now had to compete with cheaper goods brought in by train, and the stimulation of emigration.

The railways affected pre-existing modes of transport. The major road routes, especially those linking the capital with large towns, were now generally paralleled by railways and, as a result, declined in relative importance. In contrast, the cross-country roads, neglected during the mail coach era, assumed renewed prominence. One indication of this phenomenon was the shrewd decision of Charles Bianconi to revise his famous system of horse-drawn car routes to act as a feeder to the railways using the cross-country roads.

Yet, the economic prospects were unattractive to private developers and hence the extension of lines into such regions was encouraged by a series of acts passed in the 1880s and 1890s which, in effect, gave state assistance to their construction in the same manner as with earlier road building. Thus, the five foot three inch gauge system reached such outposts as Valencia Harbour, county Kerry (1893), Achill, county Mayo (1894) and Clifden, county Galway (1895).

A number of railway routes were constructed to the narrower three foot gauge including two extensive systems in county Donegal, two lines in county Antrim, the

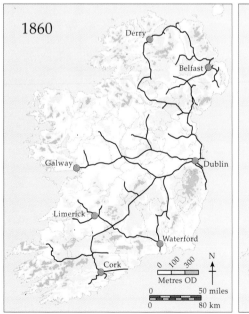

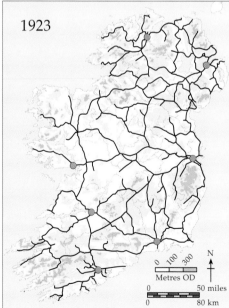

Fig. 18 The growth and decline of the Irish railway network 1860-1983. The early and late systems are remarkably similar.

Railway network

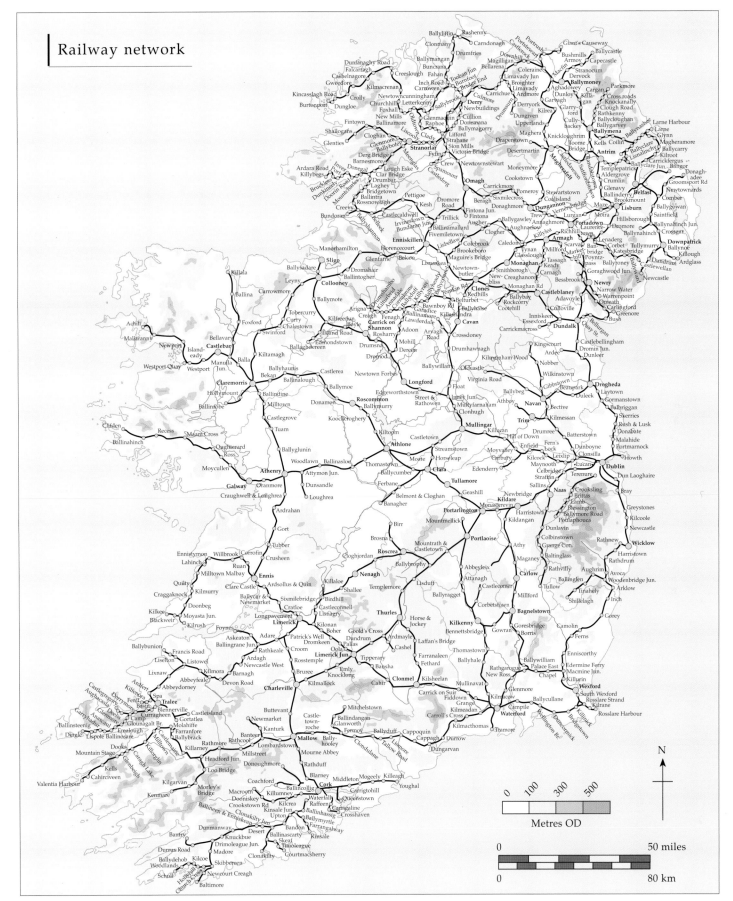

Fig. 19 The railway network at its apogee in 1923. Subsequent closure of railways has affected Ulster most.

● Fig. 20 Killarney emigrants painted by Francis Walker in 1904. The introduction of the railway into Ireland facilitated devastating nineteenth-century population decline and brought cheaper goods from Dublin and England into the country leading to the decline of local industry.

Railways had a dramatic effect on waterway traffic; passenger conveyance virtually ceased when the railways opened and the transport of freight declined sharply. Yet, the main canal systems remained open for goods into the twentieth century.

THE TWENTIETH CENTURY

At the beginning of the twentieth century, with a rapidly declining population base, Ireland was over-provided with transport facilities. A remarkably dense road network comprising routes of various origins had evolved to serve a dispersed, expanding, mainly rural population. This was supplemented by a network of waterways and railways, constructed on the false premise that such transport links on their own would encourage and sustain economic development. During the first half of the twentieth century, the island's transport infrastructure would inevitably be rationalised.

The nature of this rationalisation was strongly influenced by the development of the internal combustion engine and its use in mechanically propelled vehicles. As early as 1909, 3790 motor cars, 3425 motor cycles and 71 heavy motor wagons were licensed to operate in Ireland. The use of such vehicles offered obvious advantages in mobility and flexibility; a dramatic rise in their numbers during the first half of the century dictated that the road system would once again become the primary transport medium.

● Fig. 21 On the Irish narrow gauge near Ballinamore, county Leitrim in 1957. The Irish narrow gauge lines penetrated the very heart of rural Ireland. The Cavan and Leitrim Railway opened from Dromod, county Leitrim to Belturbet, county Cavan in 1887 with a branch from Ballinamore to Arigna, county Roscommon, being added the following year. The latter ran for much of its length alongside the public road. Here a mixed train (passengers and goods) is seen heading westwards from Ballinamore, just two years before closure in 1959.

● Fig. 22 The Ennis road at Bunratty Castle, county Clare. This road scheme is one of those completed in the last twenty-five years thanks largely to contributions from the EU. The impact upon the countryside through which the route passes is obviously considerable; the average width of a four lane motorway excluding the land on either side is 27m as compared to a minimum width of 9.14m which was set for new roads in 1759 and of 12.80m to 15.85m which was set as the width for the new mailcoach roads authorised by parliament in 1792.

While Ireland possessed an extensive road system at the outset of the twentieth century, its quality was generally poor. In order to finance improvements, the Development and Road Improvement Act of 1909 required that mechanically propelled vehicles be taxed, with the proceeds being paid into a road fund for further improvements. Over half a million pounds was paid out by the fund between 1910 and 1922 but this was totally inadequate to effect the necessary works.

During the inter-war period, the administrations in both the Republic and Northern Ireland expended considerable sums on road modernisation. Between 1931 and 1936, for example, 1450 km of road in the Republic were given a surface of tarmacadam, concrete or asphalt; 2805 corners and narrow sections were improved; 365 bridges were replaced; 112 new bridges were constructed, and over 1000 km of new road were brought under the control of the local authorities. By 1950, the main roads had been improved considerably and attention was transferred to the minor roads. Although some of these carried relatively little traffic, virtually all of them were given a tarred surface, in response to the clientelist nature of Irish local

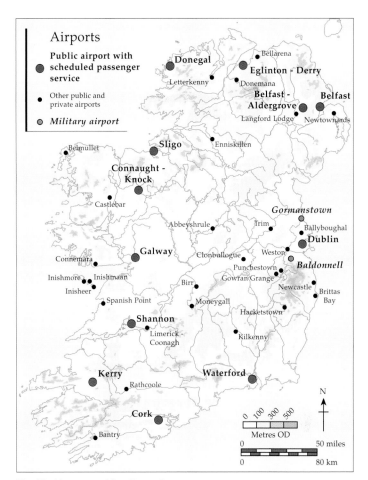

Fig. 23 Airports and landing strips.

● Fig. 24 Connacht Airport near Knock, county Mayo, opened in 1986. This remarkable airport was pioneered by Monsignor James Horan, a local clergyman, who saw it as an infrastructural development essential to the future of the west of Ireland. The runway is built on a bleak bog.

politics. This is a striking example of the dominance of rural values in post-independent Ireland.

The increased personal mobility offered by an ever rising number of privately owned vehicles had a fundamental impact on travel patterns and lifestyles. It also had an impact on the other modes of transport. Waterway traffic declined steadily and, one by one, the various navigations closed. The last freight-carrying barge operated on the Royal Canal in 1951 and on the Grand Canal in 1960; the last section of the Lagan Navigation closed in 1958. Commencing in the late 1920s, closures on the railway system began, generally on a 'last in, first out' principle. A number of routes thus survived for no more than a generation. By 1989, the railway network had shrunk to just 2200 km, a figure which is uncannily similar to that for 1860. The legacy of a once extensive railway network can still be seen in the form of embankments, viaducts, stations and other lineside buildings.

In the middle and later years of the twentieth century, new types of transport and associated developments had pronounced landscape impacts. The emergence of electricity as an ubiquitous power source gave rise to power stations (some using turf for fuel), reservoirs associated with hydroelectric schemes and, perhaps most pervasive of all, a plethora of power lines which bestride the countryside. Air transport necessitated airport construction initially at Dublin, Shannon, Belfast and Cork and more

● Fig. 26 Three generations of transport route near Maynooth, county Kildare. The section of the Royal Canal shown here opened in 1796. The Duke of Leinster was a subscriber to the canal company and at this point a small harbour was built to serve his demesne, the entrance to which is to the left of the photo. In 1845, the canal was acquired by the Midland and Great Western Railway Company which then constructed its railway parallel to the canal; this can be seen to the right. The canal fell into disuse in 1951 but has now been reopened to pleasure craft for part of its length. The road on the left was part of the main Dublin to Galway road until 1994; it has now been replaced as a through route by an 18.5 km bypass to the south which cost IR£62 million, 75% of this coming from the EU.

recently at other locations, notably at Knock in county Mayo, designed to serve the rural population of Connacht.

During the second half of the twentieth century, the number of motor vehicles has continued to rise rapidly. This trend, together with increasing urbanisation, has meant that the largest traffic increases have been within the urban areas and on the main roads between them. Major road improvement schemes have been implemented, including the construction of some completely new sections, for example town bypasses and motorways. These developments occurred sooner in Northern Ireland than in the Republic, and until recently, the road system north of the border was generally perceived as being superior to that in the south. The recent huge influx of EU structural funds has altered this picture, as the Republic has set about modernising its main road system to European standards. At the same time, the intricate network of minor roads, serving a shrinking rural population, has declined in quality; poor maintenance has seen the emergence of pothole candidates in local elections, most notably in the border counties, where cross-border road closures for security reasons have exacerbated the problem of rural accessibility.

Increased leisure time, and a growing emphasis on tourism has led to a renewed interest in the potential of inland waterways and, to a lesser extent, closed railways to

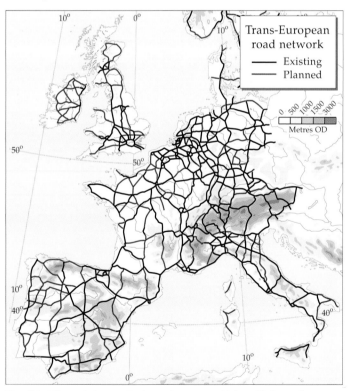

Fig. 25 The existing and planned routes which will form the trans-European road network.

cater for tourist traffic. One of the least successful of the original canal projects, the Ballinamore and Ballyconnell Canal, was re-opened in 1994. In the same year, the Grand Canal, the Barrow Navigation and part of the Royal Canal were open for recreational traffic. Tourist railways have commenced operations in a number of locations. These schemes will undoubtedly proliferate in the years ahead although the availability of EU funds will once again have a crucial bearing on the rate of development. 'Rediscovery' of canals and railways within a leisure context reflects a generally heightened appreciation of heritage.

In the future, the major road and railway routes are likely to be upgraded to become an even more conspicuous feature of the Irish rural landscape. A notable element of recent transport planning has been the emphasis on non-road based transport modes. Thus, in the case of the railways, significant investment is now being made in the main routes, for example that between Dublin and Belfast. It is also likely that rail-based modes, notably light rail transit, will play a greater role in intra-urban transport. Despite these developments, road transport will predominate for the foreseeable future. A key factor determining which projects are implemented in the future will be the level of available European Union (EU) structural funding; finance from this source has become increasingly dominant within the context of transport infrastructure investment in recent years.

While the principal road and railway routes are likely to develop in the years ahead, the overall shrinkage of the communications network is also likely to continue, especially as rural roads are progressively thinned. At present, the rural community could be adequately served by a much reduced road system and rationalisation will undoubtedly gather momentum with the rationalisation of farming, afforestation and the relocation of dwellings to sites adjacent to main roads. Indeed, changes in settlement patterns and communications will be mutually reinforcing: a declining rural population will lead to a decline in the road network which, in its turn, will elicit further rural decline.

The long-term aesthetic, amenity and access consequences of this transport rationalisation may not always be welcomed but the relatively high cost of infrastructure maintenance, in particular of roads, must be borne in mind. Passing these costs on to a reducing rural population is unreasonable; expecting the community as a whole to pay for the upkeep of an unnecessarily elaborate transport network to a relatively high standard could be equally problematic. Although usually discussed in the context of cities, transport issues are clearly at the heart of current social and environmental planning, with wide   implications for the viability of rural communities and the quality of their landscapes

BIBLIOGRAPHY

J. Andrews, 'Road planning in Ireland before the railway age' in *Ir. Geog.*, v (1964), pp 1-6.

J. Andrews, 'The use of half-inch Ordnance Survey maps in Irish historical geography with special reference to road patterns' in *Geographical Viewpoint*, v (1976), pp 20-29.

K. Barbour, 'Rural road lengths and farm-market distances in north-east Ulster' in *Geografiska Annaler*, lix B (1977), pp 14-27.

P. Clarke, *The Royal Canal* (Dublin, 1992).

R. Delaney, *The Grand Canal of Ireland* (Newton Abbot, 1973).

V. Delaney and R. Delaney, *The canals of the south of Ireland* (Newton Abbot, 1966).

O. Doyle and S. Hirsch, *Railways in Ireland 1834-1984* (Dublin, 1983).

H. Fayle, *The narrow gauge railways of Ireland* (London, 1946).

C. Fisher, 'Evolution of the Irish railway system' in *Economic Geography*, xvii (1941), pp. 262-74.

J. Killen and A. Smyth, 'Transportation' in R. Carter and A. Parker (ed.), *Ireland: a contemporary geographical perspective* (London, 1989), pp 271-300.

W. McCutcheon, *The canals of the north of Ireland* (Dawlish, 1965).

K. Nowlan (ed.), *Travel and transport in Ireland* (Dublin, 1973).

P. O'Keeffe, 'The development of Ireland's road network', unpublished paper (Dublin, 1973).

P. O'Keeffe and T. Simington, *Irish stone bridges in history and heritage* (Dublin, 1991).

C. Ó Lochlainn, 'Roadways in ancient Ireland' in J. Ryan (ed.), *Féilscribhinn Éoin MicNéill* (Dublin, 1940), pp 465-74.

MINING, POWER AND WATER

While minerals have been worked in Ireland from the earliest stages of its history, it was mainly during the nineteenth century that mining activity accelerated. Relative to Britain, coal and metal resources were modest and mining activities were consequently scattered, intermittent and economically marginal, undertaken only when market conditions for particular minerals were buoyant. Mineral exploitation was too weak to stimulate the indigenous growth of heavy industry. Industrial regions did not emerge and the landscape generally escaped the clutter and environmental degradation of the Industrial Revolution.

By contrast, quarrying is a major activity with a much greater landscape impact. Gravel, sand and stone occur widely. Since deposits are generally shallow, extensive areas are worked to supply the material for buildings and roads. Because of the high costs of transporting bulky aggregates, quarrying is concentrated close to major urban centres and the impact is especially evident in the immediate hinterlands of Dublin, Belfast and Cork.

Inanimate energy was traditionally generated mainly by water, supplemented by wind. It was required chiefly for the processing of local agricultural produce, including corn milling, brewing, distilling and linen production. Small-scale industry flourished in the eighteenth and early nineteenth centuries, attracted to rivers and streams in the countryside. Few of these enterprises survived into the present century. Given the dearth of fossil energy, water has continued to be a significant power resource, although wind has growing potential. Large reservoirs for water supply and electricity generation have been built in upland areas near major cities. In the twentieth century, electricity has permitted a wide dispersal of modern 'foot-loose' industries, facilitating the retention of the dispersed rural settlement pattern.

Fig. 1 The building of Ardnacrusha power station on the Shannon between 1925 and 1929 was the flagship civil engineering enterprise of the Irish Free State. Seán Keating's exuberant painting, *Night's candles are burnt out*, captures the excitement and intense pride which surrounded the project.

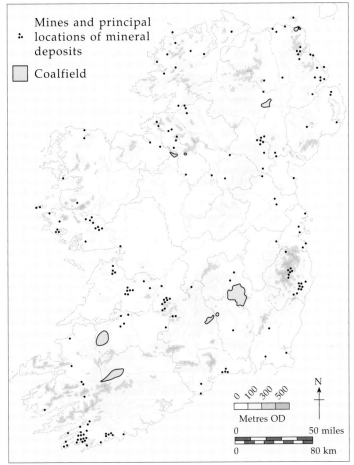

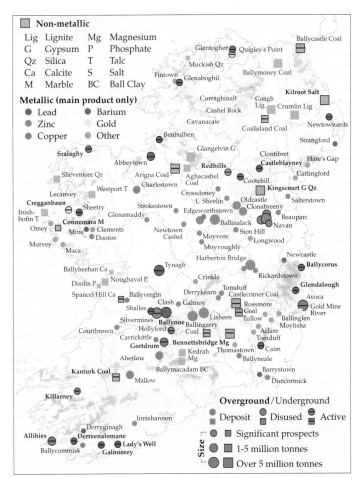

Fig 2. Principal locations of minerals of economic importance, metallifer-ous mines and coalfields, 1922. The map shows localities where mines, excluding individual coal mines, had been opened at various times, and places where minerals of economic importance had been found in signifi-cant quantity. Mineral occurrences and mines are widely scattered but large empty areas occur, especially in the lowlands of central Ireland and east Connacht, and there is a distinct grouping of minerals and mines in certain districts. In the south-west, a wide diffusion of copper ores and barytes occur, mainly associated with Devonian rocks; west Tipperary and east Clare contain lead, copper and zinc deposits; in south-east Wicklow, the metamorphic aureole possesses copper, iron, lead and zinc.

Fig 3 Metalliferous mines, 1994. While the more important mineral deposits are shown, not all the workings are in continous production. A major trend of recent decades has been the discovery and exploitation of large deposits of heavy metals in the Central Lowlands, for example the lead and zinc mines at Tynagh (county Galway) and at Navan (county Meath) which is one of the greatest discoveries of its type in the world. Major developments (lead, zinc) are now underway at Galmoy in county Kilkenny and Lisheen in county Tipperary. In the west of Ireland, gold is a current source of interest, located in rocks which underlie areas of great natural beauty and tourist appeal. Opencast mining of lignite deposits is a potential threat to the landscape around Lough Neagh.

MINING AND QUARRYING

Mining

Copper, lead, zinc, iron, coal and bauxite are among the diverse minerals found in Ireland. The major metalliferous belt lies along the flanks of the Leinster granite, where ore bodies of copper, iron, lead and zinc occur. Mining in Ireland, traditionally dispersed and intermittent, declined sharply at the end of the nineteenth century, leaving only a scatter of decayed installations, often in desolate hilly areas. Mining has revived since the 1960s as new prospect-ing methods have discovered valuable heavy metals in the central lowlands.

Copper mining has a venerable history in Ireland. Indeed, prehistoric copper workings at Ross island, county Kerry, and Allihies, in west Cork, are among the oldest in north-west Europe. Copper continued to be sporadically

exploited in later periods. The Napoleonic wars led to an expansion of Irish copper mining in several places, but the mines were generally small and short-lived except at Allihies where ore was produced on a regular basis from 1812 to 1884. After 1885, production went into precipitous decline due to the importation of cheaper American ores. Scattered tip heaps and abandoned settlement are the main relics.

The commonest lead ore was galena (lead sulphide), often found with iron, copper and zinc ore. Most Irish lead ores were also silver bearing. By the end of the thirteenth century, lead and silver were already mined by royal patent at Knockaunderrig (Silvermines) in county Tipperary. In the nineteenth century, the principal lead mines were in counties Tipperary (Silvermines), Wicklow (Luganure, Glendalough, Glenmalure), Clare (Ballyhickey,

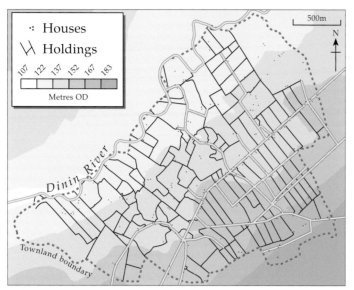

Fig. 4 Mining was dispersed and spasmodic, with violently fluctuating output. Resulting landscape modification was generally superficial. Only modest employment was provided, including both local people and skilled immigrants such as Welsh lead miners and Durham coal miners. In Moneenroe on the Castlecomer plateau, the Wandesforde family created a planned mining/small farming community, whose settlement is depicted on this illustration based on an 1812 estate map.

Kilbrickan) and Down (Conlig, Newtownards); major smelters were located at Ballycorus in county Dublin and Cornamucklagh in county Monaghan. Zinc gained in importance with the development of galvanising in the mid-nineteenth century, whereby it was coated on corrugated iron and steel plates. The main zinc ores, calamine and zinc blende (sphalerite), were both raised at Silvermines between 1859-1874.

Iron pyrites and copper pyrites are significant sulphur sources, the key component of gunpowder and of sulphuric acid – a crucial substance in the manufacture of textile bleaches and dyes. In 1840, there was an interruption in the sulphur trade with Sicily (the primary European source of sulphur), leading to the development of the abundant iron pyrites in the Avoca mineral belt in county Wicklow. However, these mines were largely abandoned in the 1880s. Barytes became important during the second half of the nineteenth century for various industrial purposes. The main Irish mines were in the Bantry district, county Cork, where activity began in the 1840s and output was for a time the greatest in the United Kingdom. Bauxite is the chief source of aluminium. Production in the United Kingdom was long limited to county Antrim (with occasional supplies from county Londonderry) where mining began in the 1870s and continued until the inter-war period.

From prehistoric times, iron was obtained from bog ore (hydrated ferric or iron oxide) extracted from bogs and lakes. Easily reduced in primitive smelters, it was exten-

sively used in the Middle Ages. From the seventeenth century, larger mining and smelting operations were developed. Siderites – coal measure iron ores – were mined around Lough Allen in county Leitrim, while bedded haematites and limonites were exploited at Dysert (county Laois) and in counties Down and Tyrone. Before the introduction of coke in the eighteenth century, charcoal was universally used as a fuel for blast furnaces: iron works depended on supplies of readily available wood and were sited in proximity to woodland. As Irish woodlands dwindled, the rural iron industry died. The Industrial Revolution in iron and steel manufacture in England, based on the substitution of coal for charcoal as fuel, did not take place in Ireland. Irish coal resources were meagre and difficult to work; from the late eighteenth century onwards, iron manufacture concentrated in Irish ports, where ores, bar iron and fuel could be easily imported. Little iron was mined in Ireland during the nineteenth century. The major centre was in the Vale of Avoca in county Wicklow where iron and copper mining have left a considerable landscape imprint.

Irish coal deposits are in carboniferous strata broadly similar to those of England, Scotland and Wales. However, whereas the coal measures of Britain were well preserved, their Irish equivalents were seriously eroded; twisted and contorted by geological movements, they were difficult and expensive to mine. The Castlecomer and Slieve Ardagh plateaux in counties Kilkenny and Tipperary contain the most significant Irish coalfield,

Fig. 5 The remains of mining from many periods are found throughout west Cork. The most productive mines were near Allihies at the western tip of the Caha peninsula where copper and lead were worked in the nineteenth century. No water power was available and steam-driven machinery was used; 1000 workers were employed. Scattered tip heaps are the main legacy. There is also evidence here of prehistoric mining. Exploitation was renewed on a small scale in the 1950s.

producing anthracite over several centuries. A distinctive community of miner farmers was established at Castlecomer on the extensive Wandesforde estate in the 1770s. Only in this district has coal working had appreciable effects on the landscape, mainly abandoned adit mines, tips and colliery settlement. Small scattered pits also occur on the Munster coalfield to the south of the Shannon estuary, at Arigna in county Roscommon and around Ballycastle in county Antrim.

Ireland's coal deposits were worked from the seventeenth century onwards, arousing increasing interest from about the middle of the eighteenth century. Mining technology was archaic and ultimately wasteful until the introduction of English colliers from the Durham coalfields to Castlecomer in the 1820s. Deeper mines were sunk, worked by steam-powered pumps and winding gear (already in use at many Irish metal mines). However, Irish pits were poorly served by transit facilities; as late as the 1920s, very few had proper railway feeder lines, confining coal consumption to within a narrow radius of the mines. In the present century, coalmining has experienced near-terminal decline and most workings have been closed.

After Independence, there was renewed interest in Irish ore deposits, but mining was negligible until government tax exemptions facilitated prospecting and mining activity by multi-national companies between 1956-1974. A large lead and zinc mine was worked at Avoca in county Wicklow between 1958 and 1962, but it was not until advanced prospecting techniques were applied in the early 1960s that substantial new ore bodies were identified, mainly in the central lowlands. Most lie near the surface and can be extracted by opencast methods. In 1961, a rich lead-zinc-copper-silver deposit was discovered at Tynagh in eastern Galway which was worked first by opencast and later by underground methods until 1980. Other mines worked around the same time included Gortdrum (copper-silver, 1967-1975) and Silvermines (lead-zinc, 1968-1982), both in county Tipperary. The lead-zinc deposit discovered near Navan, county Meath in 1970, and worked since 1977, is one of the greatest discoveries of its type in the world with the largest mine currently worked in Ireland (Outokumpo Zinc – formerly Tara Mines). The above ground works here are well screened by trees and there are high levels of general environmental protection, including the revegetating of tailing ponds. Development is imminent at other sites, such as the lead/zinc ores at Galmoy and Lisheen in county Kilkenny, and there are major possibilities for gold mining in the west and north of the country, including areas of high landscape value such as Mayo and Wicklow.

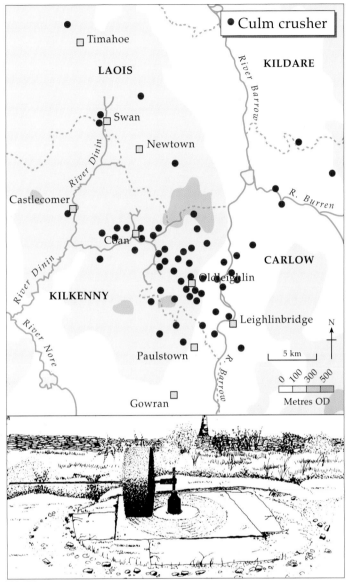

Fig. 6 Culm crushers in the Barrow valley. Culm was the fine dust (slack) derived from the anthracite mined in the Castlecomer coalfield, and widely used as a cheap domestic fuel. The culm was very difficult to burn unless mixed with yellow clay and compressed into 'culm balls' or 'bombstones'. This mixing was most effectively performed by a culm crusher – a large granite grinding stone drawn by a horse, rotating over a flagstone bed on which the culm and yellow clay were spread. Of 58 identified examples, the vast majority are in the Castlecomer – Old Leighlin area. They date largely from the late nineteenth century.

Quarrying: Stone, Clay, Gravel and Sand

Irish building stones mirror the geology of their immediate environs. With the exception of Wicklow and many of the Ulster counties, good quality carboniferous limestone was freely available throughout Ireland and there is usually a belt of past or presently active quarries around each major town. Burnt (calcined) limestone was also a useful fertiliser, as well as the principal component of render and mortar (before the widespread adoption of Portland cement). It was also utilised in the production of bleaching powder and of soda for common salt, in tanning, and in the

223

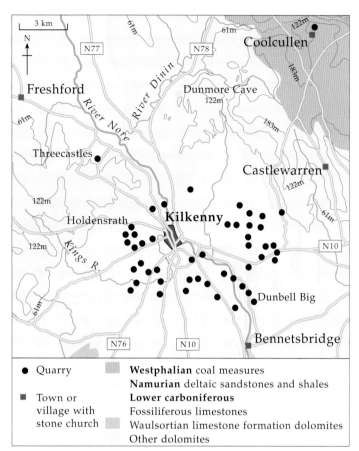

● Fig. 9 Now abandoned, this large barytes mine and its associated installations and tailings ponds nearby at Silvermines, county Limerick, are a prodigious scar on the landscape. No remedial action was undertaken to infill or reclaim the open pit which is now accumulating water. The suggested use of this pit for large-scale rubbish dumping has alarmed local inhabitants. Vegetating would improve the level areas and stabilise the slopes, and screening by trees would be desirable.

Fig 7 Quarries around Kilkenny city. Kilkenny was a key centre in medieval Ireland with many substantial buildings, including a major cathedral and castle. The main building material was Kilkenny limestone, won from numerous quarries in the rural hinterland. Its blue colour imparts a distinctive character to the city's architecture.

purification of town gas. Black marbles were quarried in Kilkenny and Galway while decorative red marbles were extracted in county Cork (Little Island, Fermoy) and near Adare in county Limerick. Sandstone ('brownstone') was also extensively quarried throughout Ireland. Apart from more obvious uses such as in buildings and road construction, sandstone was also used in millstone manufacture. Conglomerate sandstones were generally preferred for this purpose and during the nineteenth century large millstone

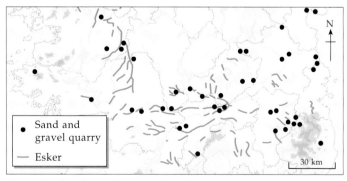

Fig. 8 Sand and gravel quarries (1994) are conspicuous along the main esker ridges of the Midlands and south-east Connacht. The map shows quarries in continuous operation. New quarries and pits are constantly being opened and existing ones closed, sometimes temporarily.

quarries were in operation at Drumdowney, county Kilkenny and in counties Cork and Galway. Sandstone flags, such as the famous Shankill flags of Kilkenny, were also in demand for flooring and road construction.

Granite from the Dublin and Wicklow mountains was to the architecture of Dublin what limestone was to the towns of Cork and Limerick. The streets of Dublin were granite-flagged and the stone also underpinned the city's bridges and quaysides. Polished granite was manufactured at Bessbrook (Armagh), at Carnsore (Wexford) and Arklow (Wicklow). Extensive slate quarries were established near Killaloe, county Clare and on Valencia Island in the early decades of the nineteenth century. Valencia slate was used in the roofing of the English houses of parliament and of Waterloo and Charing Cross railway stations in London.

Irish clays have been used in making pottery for millennia and in the manufacture of architectural brick for at least four centuries. Brickfields were established on many estuaries (particularly those near ports) during the eighteenth century, to facilitate ease of transportation by lighter or skiff. The finished product was often poorly fired brick, only suitable for external use if plastered over. With the introduction of improved kilns after 1850, good quality brick became more widely available, such as that manufactured at Haypark in Belfast and at Youghal, Belvelly and Ballinphellic in county Cork. The discovery of kaolin (china clay) on the Bloomfield estate in Fermanagh led to the establishment of the Belleek Pottery in 1858. Other industrial-scale potteries operated in the Youghal district of county Cork and at Mountmellick, county Laois. The Ulster

CRH PLC

Fig. 10 Stone quarry at Belgard on the fringe of Dublin city. Thin drift gives ready access to the underlying limestone. The insatiable demand for building materials has created a conspicuous ring of quarries around cities.

Fire Clay Works in Coalisland, county Tyrone was the only notable attempt to manufacture items such as flooring tiles and sewer pipes from the fire clay often found in association with coal seams.

Sand was quarried and taken from beaches for general building purposes, for use as fertiliser, in iron foundries and for glass manufacturing. Gravel was quarried principally for road-metalling, but from the late nineteenth century it was more extensively employed as aggregate for making concrete.

With the widespread introduction of concrete blocks and the use of mass concrete in building construction, demand for cut stone in twentieth-century Ireland has dwindled. The vast bulk of Ireland's gravestones are now constructed of garish imported stone from Italy and China. Most quarried stone is nowadays crushed into aggregate or fertiliser. Glacial meltwaters have deposited vast quantities of natural aggregate throughout Ireland, most of which is extensively quarried wherever and whenever practicable. However, the principal quarries are now situated near larger cities. Stone quarries at Belgard, Feltrim and Huntstown in county Dublin and sand and gravel quarries in county Wicklow supply the city of Dublin, while an enormous limestone quarrying operation at Carrigtwohill and sand and gravel pits at Garryhesta in county Cork supply Cork's needs. There is also an impressive line of quarries along the Eiscir Riada between Dublin and Galway. Gypsum is quarried at Kingscourt, county Cavan, barytes at Ballynoe, county Tipperary.

POWER GENERATION
Wind Power

Windmill development   Wind was first harnessed on a large scale to grind corn. Windmills appeared in northwest Europe in the twelfth century AD, the earliest recorded Irish example being at Kilscanlan, near Old Ross in county Wexford, in 1281. These early windmills were post-mills, so-called because the mill's wooden body was supported on a vertical post around which it pivoted to face the sails into the wind.

Over succeeding centuries, postmills were superseded by stone-built tower mills in which the body remained stationary, while the cap and sails turned to the wind. All surviving Irish windmills are of this type, the oldest examples dating to the early eighteenth century. Erected by the local landlord, these mills operated under a system known as milling soke; tenants were obliged to have their grain (mostly oats) ground at the mills, paying a toll (generally a proportion of the meal) for the privilege.

Identical in design to those found along Britain's western seaboard, these windmills comprise rubble-stone cylindrical towers, three to four and a half metres in internal diameter and six to seven and a half metres high. Their power output was little more than five to ten kilowatts, sufficient at best to drive two sets of millstones.

Between 1770 and 1815, cereal cultivation intensified throughout Ireland and substantial capital was invested in the erection of windmills. In contrast to their simple predecessors, these windmills exhibit considerable architectural and technological sophistication. Tapered in profile, they were typically five to eight metres in diameter and stood over ten metres high. Some were very large indeed, measuring up to nine metres in internal diameter and over thirty metres high. Apart from creating the additional storage space necessary for merchant milling, such heights enabled the installation of large diameter sails, the enhanced power of which could then drive up to four sets of millstones.

Wind power versus water power   All else being equal, water power was preferred to wind power on account of its reliability, storability (in mill-ponds) and easy regulation (by means of sluice gates). As well as being inoperable on very calm or gale days, wind power is impossible to store and difficult to harness and control. Sails were prone to destruction in gales and expensive to maintain. Their speed could only be regulated by altering the area of sail canvas catching the wind, and the cap had to be periodically rotated as the wind changed direction. The consequent dominance of water power is well illustrated in

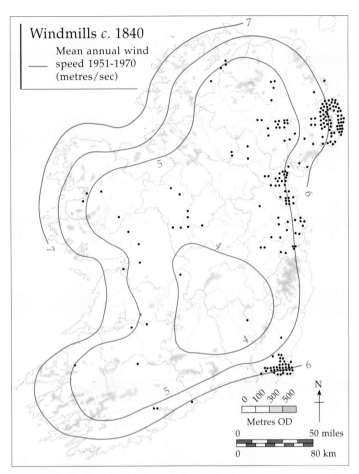

Windmills *c.* 1840

Mean annual wind
—— speed 1951-1970
(metres/sec)

Metres OD

0   50 miles

0   80 km

Fig. 11 Windmills *c.* 1840. The majority are in the eastern cereal-growing areas with their limited water power; striking concentrations occur on coastal promontories with strong winds, especially in east Down and south Wexford.

county Kilkenny; whereas some 180 watermills were in use there during the nineteenth century, only a single windmill is recorded.

Windmill distribution   With the publication of the nation-wide Ordnance Survey six-inch maps in the 1830s and 1840s, the distribution of Irish windmills becomes apparent. Many windmills were already disused, due to the unprofitability of cereal milling after the Napoleonic wars ended in 1815. Nevertheless, almost 250 windmills are recorded. The vast majority were situated along the eastern seaboard, where extensive cereal growing and high population densities created the greatest demand for milling capacity.

Watermills were usually employed to meet this demand. However, many watercourses along the east coast have restricted catchments and are prone to drying up, rendering their mills inactive for part of the year. In the Ards peninsula, for example, many watermills operated for less than half the year. Fortunately, this paucity of water was matched by an abundance of wind which

Fig. 12 Tacumshin mill, county Wexford. Built in the 1840s, and now preserved by the Office of Public Works, its thatched cap and tailpole were once common features in Irish windmills.

achieves its highest speed along the coastal strip. The combination of poor water, good wind and heavy tillage is particularly evident in the eastern halves of counties Down and Wexford, and here the concentration of windmills is highest.

Windmill demise   The later 1800s saw the inception of large, port-based flour mills in Belfast, Cork, Dublin, Limerick and Waterford. Increasing importation of foreign grain, the introduction of roller mill technology and the use of steam engines ensured that traditional cornmills, and windmills in particular, could not compete. Ballycopeland windmill on the Ards peninsula, said to be the last working Irish example, stopped around 1915.

Capless shells are still prominent hilltop features along the east coast, although many windmills are remembered only in placenames. Two have been preserved by the state;

● Fig. 13 Blennerville windmill, county Kerry. Erected in 1800 to grind wheat, it is now restored to full working order.

MICHAEL DIGGIN

Fig. 14 Slievenahanagan wind farm in county Antrim. On wind farms, turbines are normally arranged in rows on hills or other exposed sites. Most installations in use today have ten towers, producing a total of 5MW. Transmission lines and access roads are also needed. Noise and visual intrusion, the main negative factors, can be mitigated with careful siting, avoidance of bright colours and use of matt gel to reduce the impact of light catching the blades and structure.

Ballycopeland in county Down, and Tacumshin in county Wexford. Both mills are now tourist attractions, as are the mills at Blennerville, county Kerry, and Elphin in county Roscommon which have recently been restored to working order. Traditional working windmills would have been a rare sight in the later 1800s but wind powered devices nevertheless continued to be used for land drainage and pumping well water to dwelling houses. However, the increasing use of oil, diesel and petrol engines from the 1920s onwards caused a dramatic decline in their use and today only a handful remain at work.

Recent developments Interest in wind-generated electricity revived in the 1970s as a consequence of the leap in oil prices. Ireland ranked fourth out of the then nine EC member states in terms of its wind energy potential. The ESB set up a combined wind and diesel project on Clear Island off the Cork coast in 1985. This supplied over half the island's energy, greatly reducing dependence on imported fuels. A similar system, utilising three 33kW turbines, was also set up on Rathlin Island by the Northern Ireland Electricity Service (NIES) in 1992.

In 1990, the NIES commissioned a 300kW turbine on Slievenahanagan, near Clough Mills, county Antrim, to feed electricity into the grid. It is typical of the modern generation of turbines which have evolved from American prototypes over the past fifty years. Unlike turbines of the previous decade, these are more powerful and considerably more reliable.

Despite the success of these experiments, there was little incentive to utilise wind on a large-scale on account of the vast over-capacity of existing power stations. Until recently,

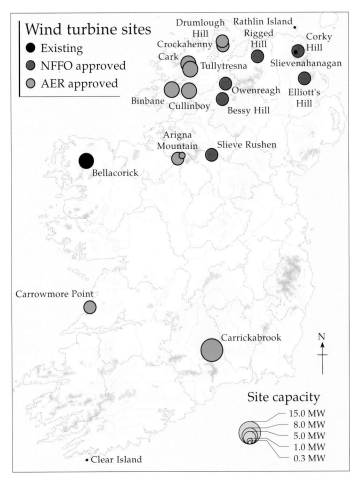

Fig. 15 Existing wind turbines, and locations of approved AER and NFFO schemes. Turbines are located in some of the windiest places in Ireland.

Bellacorick, county Mayo, boasted the Republic's only wind farm. This was set up by a private consortium in 1992 near an existing peat-fired station. Operated by Bord na Móna, it comprises twenty one wind turbines with a combined output of 6.5MW which is fed into the ESB grid.

Future prospects Renewable energy sources are generally viewed in terms of reducing dependence on imported, environmentally unfriendly and increasingly expensive fossil-fuels. Whilst this will remain so, a fresh dimension has been added to the environmental debate in recent years, as European governments are now encouraging the use of alternative energy sources in an effort to stem pollution from power station emissions. To this end, the Alternative Energy Requirement (AER) and Non-Fossil Fuel Obligation (NFFO) were introduced in 1994 by the respective governments of the Republic and Northern Ireland. Attention has again turned to wind power, and the development of wind 'farms'. Used as a substitute for fossil fuels, a single turbine of the size of that at Slievenahanagan can reduce carbon-dioxide emissions by upwards of 700 tonnes per year. Of the target set by alternative energy

schemes, almost half is anticipated to come from wind and less than ten per cent from water. By early 1995, sixteen wind farm operators had been contracted to generate electricity for their respective grids, and the wind power target should be comfortably exceeded. Wind power has three advantages over hydro power: the resource is infinitely greater, many more sites are available to harness it, and much more power can be tapped at each location simply by adding more windmills. As regards the environmental impact of wind turbines, noise is generally not a problem except at very close range. Concern has been expressed over the visual obtrusiveness of turbines on the skyline, but this can be mitigated by careful site selection. Offshore developments, which will eventually ensue, should lessen this problem considerably. Although water has played a more significant role than wind in supplying the country's energy needs over the past 1500 years, this situation looks set to be reversed in the future.

Water Power

Irish watermill development   Early Irish manuscripts imply that water-powered mills were in use by the mid first millennium. Conclusive evidence is available in the form of tree-ring dated timbers unearthed in peat bogs. Early mills utilised horizontal waterwheels, although the more powerful and efficient vertical wheel eventually

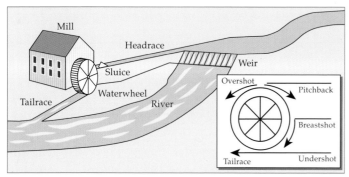

Fig. 16 The operating principle of a water mill, and types of waterwheel. To harness the water, weirs were erected across rivers to divert some of their flow along a headrace to the waterwheel. Most Irish wheels had a series of 'buckets' around their circumferences, each being filled in turn by the oncoming water. In this way, the weight of the water turned the wheel. Depending on where the water feeds into the buckets, such wheels are known as overshot, pitchback or breastshot. At the bottom of its rotation, the water emptied from the buckets and returned to the river via the tailrace. The water's potential energy was thus transformed into kinetic energy, this rotative motion being transmitted to the machinery through a series of gears and shafts. The power of the wheel is a function of the flow of water as well as the height through which it falls whilst in the buckets. The head, typically two to five metres, is determined by the length of the headrace and natural gradient of the river. Millwrights understood intimately the relationship between head and flow, and designed their wheels according to the power required, the topography and the water regime prevailing at a particular site. In upstream situations, large-diameter overshot, pitchback or high breastshot wheels were usually employed, the high head compensating for the relatively low flow. In downriver locations, the flow of water was generally adequate for the purpose at hand, and so breastshot wheels sufficed. Typical power outputs range from 10 to 50 kW.

superseded them. By the nineteenth century, many thousands were at work throughout the country; while most were used for corn and flour milling, other applications

Fig. 17 Annalong mill, county Down, is a typical early nineteenth-century Irish corn mill, with an external breastshot waterwheel. An oil engine was added in the early 1900s to compensate for a reduction in the water supply; the two black cylinders are cooling tanks for the engine. The mill has been recently restored to full working order.

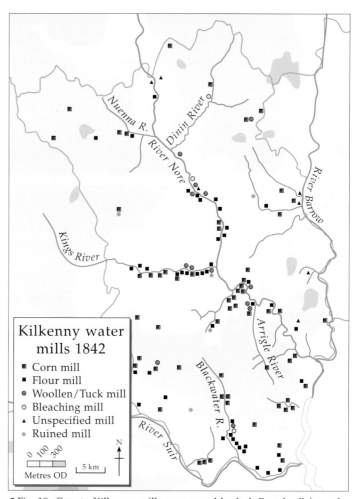

● Fig. 18 County Kilkenny mills as mapped by Jack Burtchaell from the first edition Ordnance Survey maps in 1842. The Kings River valley was an early cradle of milling innovation in the mid eighteenth century. The variety of mill types is also noticeable.

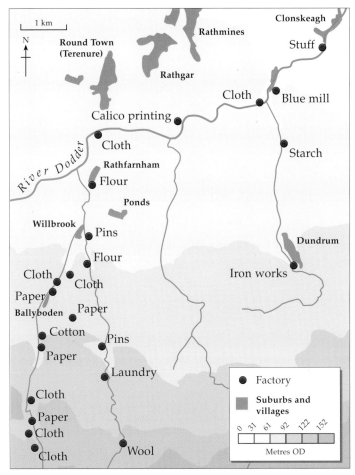

Fig. 19 Industries in the south Dublin valleys in 1837 as mapped by T.W. Freeman. The swift-flowing Dodder and its tributaries powered a seam of early industrialisation between the northern flank of the Wicklow mountains and the southern edge of the city of Dublin.

included stone crushing, threshing, sawing, pumping, and the manufacture of textiles, paper, agricultural tools, beer and whiskey.

Principles of operation   Most mills were located not on the rivers themselves but on specially created adjacent water channels (races). These substantial engineering works are frequently discernible long after the actual building has disappeared. Where possible, mills were located beside natural waterfalls and rapids in order to minimise the length of the head-race. However, where the river bed had a gentle gradient, a headrace of several kilometres in length might be required to create an adequate head. The power abstracted by the wheel is a function of this head and the flow of water; the latter is determined by the river regime at its point of abstraction. Where water was in short supply (not uncommon in summer), a mill pond was utilised to store it overnight, ensuring an adequate flow for a reasonable period the next day. Adjoining river catchments were 'captured' by diverting their water along specially dug channels into the headrace.

Fig. 20 The largest complex of watermills in Ireland is at Ballincollig, county Cork. Spread along 2.5km of the River Lee, over thirty mills manufactured gunpowder during the nineteenth century. Two massive headraces fed the mills. These were wide enough to enable the use of punts for safely moving dangerous materials about the site. The masonry blast walls separated pairs of incorporating mills, fed from the tree-lined canal to their left. One mill has recently been restored to working order.

The wider context   Mills worked independently of one another, but where they shared the same headrace, a degree of co-operation between the owners was obviously required (but not necessarily obtained!). Regional specialisation sometimes occurred. During the late eighteenth and early nineteenth centuries, for example, numerous paper mills were in operation along the Dodder, south of Dublin, and on the Six Mile Water, west of Belfast. In both instances, there was access to a plentiful rag supply, from which the paper was made, and readily accessible markets for the finished product.

Ulster is well known for linen, mainly produced in a multitude of mills in the Lagan and Bann valleys from the mid eighteenth century onwards. Many mill owners also built houses for their workers, and villages are commonly found next to spinning mills and weaving factories, both of

Fig. 21 Edenderry, county Down. This typical nineteenth-century mill village focused on a weaving factory (bottom left) established on the River Lagan in 1860s.

● Fig. 23 Turlough Hill pumped storage scheme, county Wicklow. Unique in Ireland, this scheme involved the creation of an artificial reservoir on the summit of Turlough Hill, 300m above Lough Nahanagan; the power station is buried in the mountainside between them. The two lakes are linked by a vast underground pipe, containing four reversible turbines. At night, the turbines are reversed and use excess electricity generated by conventional power stations to raise water from the lower to upper lake. At times of peak demand, this water is released back into the lower one, so driving the turbines and feeding electricity into the grid. Although more energy is actually consumed than delivered, Turlough Hill plays a key role in the ESB supply network for three reasons. First, it eliminates the need to erect conventional power stations in order to meet peak demand. Second, it enables existing power stations to operate continuously at their optimal output levels. Third, the water contained in the upper reservoir can be tapped almost instantaneously to meet unexpected short-term surges in demand, such as at half-time during World Cup matches.

which require a high labour input. Pioneering mill villages include Bessbrook (county Armagh), Sion Mills (county Tyrone), and Portlaw (county Waterford), all founded in the mid nineteenth century by Quaker entrepreneurs. Many retain their original one-storey terraces and distinctive layouts to this day.

▪ Fig. 22 Ardnacrusha power station, near Limerick, built by Siemens of Germany in the 1920s. The massive project involved the damming of the Shannon at O'Briens Bridge, and the excavation of a 12 km headrace to Ardnacrusha. Lough Derg, upstream of the weir, acted as a giant storage reservoir, smoothing out fluctuations in supply.

Water turbines and hydro-electricity   By the mid nineteenth century, the dynamics of water power were well understood, and the use of cast-iron was commonplace. Improved wheels such as those devised by Poncelet and Fairbairn made their appearance. Water turbines also developed at this time. Compact, easier to maintain and more efficient, they enabled water-powered sites to remain viable in the face of competition from steam-powered mills elsewhere.

It was in the production of electricity that turbines had their most lasting impact. Electric tramways were installed at the Giant's Causeway between 1883-6 and at Bessbrook in 1885. In 1891, Carlow and Galway were the first Irish towns to be lit by hydro-electricity. During the early 1900s, many towns and villages throughout the country adopted similar schemes to light their streets and houses, the turbines invariably being set up in existing mills. However, whilst cost-effective, such undertakings were of limited output and therefore restricted to local use. All this was changed in the 1920s, with the setting up of the Electricity Supply Board (ESB), and the construction of a 86MW hydro-electricity power station at Ardnacrusha, near Limerick. The station began operation in 1929, and cities and towns throughout the Free State were linked to the supply during the 1930s.

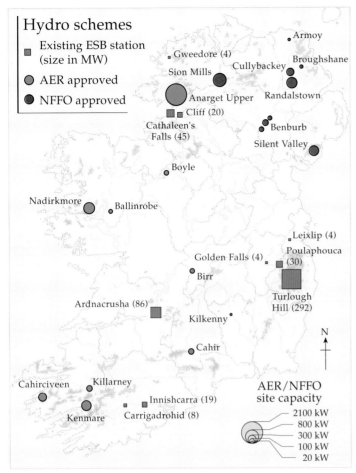

Hydro schemes

■ Existing ESB station (size in MW)

● AER approved

● NFFO approved

Armoy

Gweedore (4)

Broughshane

Sion Mills

Cullybackey

Anarget Upper

Randalstown

Cliff (20)

Cathaleen's Falls (45)

Benburb

Silent Valley

Boyle

Nadirkmore

Ballinrobe

Leixlip (4)

Golden Falls (4)

Poulaphouca (30)

Birr

Turlough Hill (292)

Ardnacrusha (86)

Kilkenny

N

Cahir

AER/NFFO site capacity

Cahirciveen   Killarney

Innishcarra (19)

Kenmare   Carrigadrohid (8)

2100 kW
800 kW
300 kW
100 kW
20 kW

Fig. 24 AER and NFFO hydro schemes approved by the ESB and NIE (Northern Ireland Electricity). In practice, operators sign contracts to generate and supply electricity to the grid. In the first round of submissions in 1994/95, nineteen contracts were awarded under these schemes; most will be operational by the end of the decade.

Powered by the Ardnacrusha scheme, the ESB was able to embark on its Rural Electrification Scheme in 1946. By the mid-1960s, almost every house in the Republic had been electrified, transforming living standards, and greatly boosting the efficiency of agriculture and industry; the scheme generated an immense network of power lines and pylons, with wires and electricity poles shadowing every Irish road. Other hydro-electric schemes followed in the 1950s, notably on the Lee and Liffey, and brought the total hydro capacity to 220MW. At Inniscarra, Leixlip and Poulaphouca, the reservoirs supplying the turbines are also tapped for drinking water.

Recent developments   With the ever increasing demand for electricity since the 1960s, the limitations of hydro power have again become manifest. As with traditional mills, the flow and fall of the river place an upper ceiling on the output of existing stations, whilst the commissioning of new sites is not cost-effective because of high capital costs. Accordingly, peat, coal, oil and gas-fired power

stations have come to the fore and now supply well over ninety per cent of Ireland's energy requirements.

In 1973, the ESB opened a 292MW pumped storage station at Turlough Hill in the Wicklow Mountains. Completion of this scheme more than doubled the existing generating capacity of the ESB's hydro stations, bringing it to 512MW. Since the 1980s, there has also been a revival in small-scale hydro generation, particularly amongst owners of defunct watermills. Given that the construction of weirs and races can account for half their total cost, it is obviously very cost-effective to refurbish existing waterworks rather than build anew. Although such schemes typically produce less than 20kW, they are ideal for the generation of electricity for space heating. Eighty-five were in operation by the early 1980s, and there are almost five hundred further potential sites.

Future potential   The objective of the AER and NFFO programmes is to create additional generating capacity from renewables, of which 5MW will be from water. As hydro schemes proliferate, so the issue of their environmental impact will come inescapably to the fore. Anglers have voiced particular concern over high water abstraction and low compensation flows over weirs. Yet, given Ireland's abundance of rainfall, water power cannot but continue to play a part in 'greening' the environment.

WATER SUPPLY

Evolution   Piped water supplies are now taken for granted, but prior to the nineteenth century, town and countryside relied on direct supplies from nearby rivers, springs, wells and lakes. Town sources proved increasingly susceptible to pollution by sewage and industrial waste, and epidemics of waterborne diseases, such as typhus and cholera, were commonplace. To alleviate the situation, artesian wells were dug, wells capped and hand-operated pumps and fountains were installed. But post-Famine urbanisation and industrialisation and the advent of domestic plumbing, sanitation and sewage disposal placed a severe strain on these resources. The provision of purpose-built reservoirs by local authorities in the second half of the nineteenth century rectified the situation. Subsequent efforts have focused on meeting the unrelenting demand of proliferating urban consumers and on extending mains supplies to rural dwellers.

Water pollution long afflicted densely populated rural areas but most farms and villages obtained adequate water supplies locally with no treatment apart from rudimentary filtration. In some counties, less than one-fifth of rural households were served by piped public supplies as late as

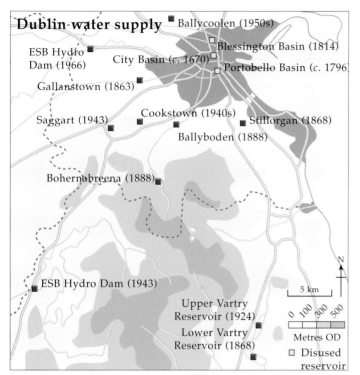

Dublin water supply — Ballycoolen (1950s)

ESB Hydro Dam (1966)
City Basin (c. 1670) — Blessington Basin (1814)
Gallanstown (1863) — Portobello Basin (c. 1796)
Saggart (1943) — Cookstown (1940s) — Stillorgan (1868)
Ballyboden (1888)
Bohernabreena (1888)
ESB Hydro Dam (1943)
5 km
Upper Vartry Reservoir (1924)
0 100 300 500
Lower Vartry Reservoir (1868)
Metres OD
□ Disused reservoir

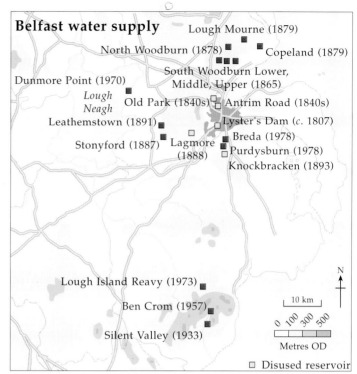

Belfast water supply — Lough Mourne (1879)
North Woodburn (1878) — Copeland (1879)
Dunmore Point (1970)
South Woodburn Lower, Middle, Upper (1865)
Lough Neagh — Old Park (1840s) — Antrim Road (1840s)
Leathemstown (1891) — Lyster's Dam (c. 1807)
Stonyford (1887) — Lagmore (1888) — Breda (1978)
Purdysburn (1978)
Knockbracken (1893)
Lough Island Reavy (1973)
N
10 km
Ben Crom (1957)
0 100 300 500
Silent Valley (1933)
Metres OD
□ Disused reservoir

• Fig. 25 Dublin waterworks. Big cities are voracious consumers of their hinterland's resources, not least in the provision of water.

• Fig. 26 Belfast waterworks. The provision of a clean, reliable water supply was a major concern of rapid urban growth in the Victorian period.

1960. This situation has been transformed over the last three decades with the development of district water supplies throughout the country. Rural electrification also enabled people to pump water directly from their wells into the house. Such amenities were essential for the retention of families in rural areas.

Unlike drier parts of Europe, water supply has never heavily influenced rural settlement patterns. The ready availability of water permitted the widespread dispersion of rural settlement. It has also minimised the need for elaborate irrigation works or water storage tanks, although the latter may be found on the dry Burren and Aran islands.

Reservoirs Reservoirs have considerable landscape impacts; agricultural and peat resources are often submerged as well as settlements and archaeological sites. The new water bodies provide significant scenic and recreational resources. Upland areas near major cities, such as the Wicklow and Mourne mountains, are especially favoured for reservoirs for four reasons. First, they are sparsely populated, so resettlement and land purchase costs are minimised. Second, cultivation is generally marginal, so there is little risk of contamination from agricultural activities. Third, these areas are invariably wetter than the lowlands, particularly in summer when water may be scarce. Lastly, being at a much greater height than the areas supplied, the water flows under gravity to the service reservoir without expensive pumping.

Fig. 27 Blessington Reservoir. Formed in the late 1930s to enlarge Dublin's water supply and generate electricity, the Blessington reservoir drowned 2600 ha of land in west Wicklow and is among the largest man-made lakes in Europe. Seventy-six houses, a graveyard and a holy well were submerged. The lake is now a major amenity, its scenic attractiveness enhanced by the irregular shoreline, over 20 km in length.

Water for major centres Medieval Dublin depended on the Poddle river for drinking water, augmented by the Dodder. The city's explosive eighteenth-century development forced the Corporation to augment supplies by tapping the Grand and Royal Canals. By mid nineteenth century, the limitations of the supplies – inadequate flows, low pressure, increasing pollution – were obvious. To alleviate the situation, Dublin Corporation instigated the Vartry waterworks in 1861. This entailed the impounding

Fig. 28 Water pumps and towers are distinctive features of the country-side. A) Water pumps, like this one near Tuam in county Galway, were once familiar features of rural roads, installed by landlords or by the Local Authorities in association with labourers' cottages. There is a welcome tendency to preserve and reuse surviving examples. ● B) This reinforced-concrete water tower was erected by Donaghadee Urban District Council in 1914. By raising the level of the water in this way it is brought to a usable pressure. Such towers became a familiar feature of the skyline of many towns and villages.

of the Vartry river by an earthen dam near Roundwood in the Wicklow mountains. Capacity was later increased with the building of a second, higher dam and electricity was generated by the flow between dams. The township of Rathmines and Rathgar opened its own reservoir at Bohernabreena on the Dodder headwaters in 1888. In the 1930s, the ESB constructed the Poulaphouca reservoir on the Liffey headwaters to generate electricity and this also provided water for an expanding capital city. The most recent development has been the tapping of the Liffey at Leixlip in the 1960s.

Belfast was initially supplied with water from the Farset river. With the rapid nineteenth-century growth of the city, several small purpose-built reservoirs were provided but demand for water far outstripped the supply and in 1923 work began on the massive Mourne scheme. This entailed construction of an earthen dam, the largest in Ulster, on the headwaters of the Kilkeel river in what was subsequently called the Silent Valley. In 1952, the supply was augmented

by a diversion of the Annalong river and in 1957 by the construction of the Ben Crom reservoir. Several other small reservoirs also exist in the Mournes, notably Lough Island Reavy and Spelga. In the 1970s, a proposal for another Mourne reservoir was rejected on environmental grounds. With ever increasing demand for water in the Greater Belfast area, attention therefore turned to Lough Neagh, the largest freshwater lake in Britain and Ireland. This source has now been tapped and will supply the bulk of Belfast's future water requirements.

In general, with suitable upland sites for new reservoirs becoming increasingly difficult to find, attention is again turning to natural lakes and rivers, as was the case with early water supplies. Dundalk, for example, has abandoned its nineteenth-century reservoirs in favour of Lough Muckno, although expensive pumping is now required along with extensive chemical treatment to comply with EU requirements. Such developments could limit the landscape impacts of future water supply schemes.

BIBLIOGRAPHY

D. Bishopp, *Irish mineral resources* (Dublin, 1943).

G. Bowie, Watermills, windmills and stationary steam engines in Ireland, with special reference to problems of conservation, unpublished Ph.D, Queen's University, Belfast, 1975.

G. Cole, *Memoir and map of localities of minerals of economic importance and metalliferous mines in Ireland* (Dublin, 1922).

Commission of enquiry into the resources and industries of Ireland. Memoir on the coalfields of Ireland, 2 vols. (Dublin, 1921).

D. Cowman and T. Reilly, *The abandoned mines of west Carbery: promoters, adventurers and miners* (Dublin, 1988).

Department of Economic Development, N. Ireland, *Prospects for renewable energy in northern Ireland* (Belfast, 1993).

Department of Energy, *Small-scale hydro-electricity potential of Ireland* (Dublin, 1985).

H. Gribbon, *The history of water power in Ulster* (Newton Abbot, 1969).

G. Kinahan, 'Economic geology of Ireland' in *Jnl. Geological Soc. Ire.*, viii (1889), pp 371-476.

M. Manning and M. McDowell, *Electricity supply in Ireland: the history of the E.S.B.* (Dublin, 1984).

W. McCutcheon, *The industrial archaeology of Northern Ireland* (Belfast, 1980).

National Economic and Social Council, *Irish energy policy* (Dublin, 1983).

W. O'Brien, *Mount Gabriel: bronze age mining in Ireland* (Galway, 1994).

C. Rynne, 'The introduction of the vertical watermill into Ireland: some recent archaeological evidence' in *Medieval Archaeology*, xxxiii (1989), pp 21-31.

M. Shiel, *The quiet revolution; the electrification of rural Ireland* (Dublin, 1984).

R. Watson, 'Wind energy' in J. Feehan (ed.), *Environment and development in Ireland* (Dublin, 1992), pp 202-7.

Fieldscape in county Louth

THE CHALLENGE

OF

CHANGE

THE CHALLENGE
OF
CHANGE

CONTEMPORARY CHALLENGE

The landscapes of Europe have been rapidly transformed in recent decades by economic and social forces, notably mechanised farming and forestry. A marked reduction of their scenic, historic and environmental appeal has replaced regional distinctiveness by sterile standardisation. Unique landscapes, each rich in superimposed patterns stretching back to prehistory and testaments to distinctive cultural formations, are being eradicated at precisely the time when post-industrial societies seek more varied environments and are increasingly sensitive about the survival of their cultural identity in a centralising Europe. Rapid landscape changes are also seen as a symptom of ecological malaise, an unravelling of local ecological coherence which impairs the long-term sustainability of the rural economy. In response, there has been an upsurge of interest in landscape conservation and management, an interest more regional than national, or, as the Swedish geographer Staffan Helmfrid has it, 'less concerned with hegemony than with hearth and home'. Beneath the superficial surface of standardisation, the pulse of place still beats strongly and may increasingly be a potent force in environmental planning. Ireland urgently requires an effective landscape policy developed through sustained interaction between local communities and central government.

● Fig. 1 This large aluminium plant (Aughinis Alumina) on the Shannon estuary in county Limerick is sited alongside sheltered deep water for the import of bulky raw materials. The plant is a dramatic visual intrusion on the coastal landscape. Ireland's reliance on imported industrial raw materials has intensified development pressures on the coasts, especially at estuarine sites, where population, fishing and tourist destinations are already markedly concentrated. As timber processing plants and agri-industries multiply, comparable pressures will be experienced widely in the countryside, increasing the urgent necessity for landscape conservation and pollution controls.

CONTEMPORARY AND FUTURE CHANGE IN THE LANDSCAPE

THE FORCES OF CHANGE IN EUROPE

In farm landscapes, the most potent transforming force has been agricultural intensification through advanced technology, a trend encouraged by national and European policies. While bringing benefits in cheap abundant food, this has resulted in monotonous landscapes, machine rather than man-made, commonplace and artificial. Biological diversity, long-term ecological viability, farming jobs and farm holdings have all been diminished as a direct result.

Depopulation, especially in remote and mountainous areas, has promoted the abandonment of productive land, initiating a vicious downward spiral of social and economic services. Centralising policies aimed solely at economic efficiency and economy also leach vital rural services, such as schools and post offices, and intensify depopulation. In these declining peripheral areas, landscape quality remains high, providing a basis for recreation and tourism which often replaces farming as the economic mainstay. Ill-conceived tourism and recreational activity can lead to attrition of landscape and cultural quality. Hence the emphasis on 'protected areas' in these peripheral regions and the frantic search for bogus substitutes in which heritage is cheapened by the creation of 'experiences', packaged for mass consumption and rife with self-inflicted ethnic stereotyping to attract the fickle tourist.

In contrast to the countryside, cities, towns and urbanised transportation corridors have relentlessly expanded their population and area. Their many-faceted influences affect commuter settlements, recreational facilities, urban building styles, motorways and power lines in their hinterlands. Centralisation of commerce, industry and government in major urban centres encourages cultural standardisation while reducing the ability of rural people

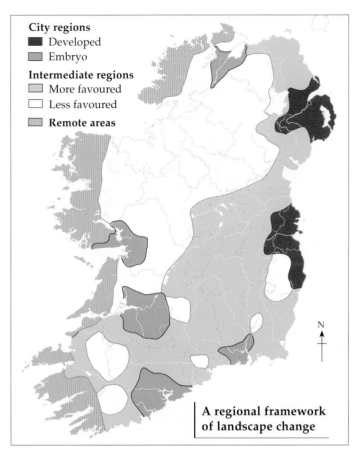

City regions
■ Developed
■ Embryo

Intermediate regions
□ More favoured
□ Less favoured

■ Remote areas

N

A regional framework of landscape change

Fig. 3 The nature of landscape change varies substantially in different types of region, ranging from strong urban encroachment in city hinterlands to rapidly evolving agricultural land use in intermediate areas and depopulation, tourism development, land abandonment and afforestation in remote areas.

to determine their own life styles or to counteract the government policies which debilitate them.

Clearly, these forces have an uneven impact and three broad categories of region are recognisable within most countries. First are city regions where urban and rural interests are intertwined and conflicting. Here, economic activity constantly converts agricultural to residential and commercial usages. The built environment may expand at a pace which surrounding rural communities cannot absorb and with a scale and style of development which swamps rural character. In the absence of physical planning policies, the rural/urban boundary is irremediably blurred. Agricultural production eventually ceases and the rural areas become gentrified by urbanites. The second are remote or sparsely populated areas, such as the Atlantic peripheries, which have suffered sustained depopulation, economic decline and loss of essential services. The total collapse of rural society precipitates a reversion to wilderness or deliberate afforestation. Few economic prospects remain for such regions under current conditions. Tourist developments are at best a local palliative. Third are the intermediate areas between urban cores and peripheries.

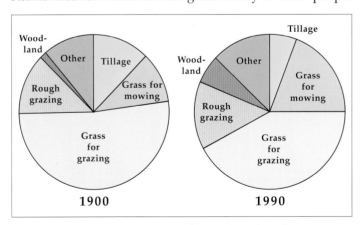

Tillage
Wood-land
Other
Tillage
Rough grazing
Grass for mowing
Grass for grazing

1900

Tillage
Wood-land
Other
Grass for mowing
Rough grazing
Grass for grazing

1990

Fig. 2 Land use in Ireland, 1900 and 1990. Grass for either grazing or mowing has remained the dominant use. Tillage has shrunk and forestry expanded but the overall pattern of use is stable and this has encouraged landscape continuity.

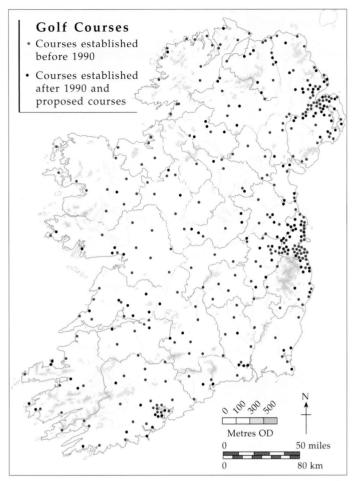

Golf Courses

• Courses established before 1990

• Courses established after 1990 and proposed courses

Fig. 4 Widespread and increasing in number, golf courses are among the strongest recreational influences on the rural landscape, especially in the hinterland of Dublin, Belfast and Cork.

Farming remains a dominant activity and landscape change derives primarily from within farming itself. These areas are therefore especially vulnerable to rapid changes in land use and farm structure. Extensive areas of this volatile 'middle ground' exist in Ireland. Future landscape fortunes here are likely to be varied, a blend of new forests, 'wildscape' and 'islands' of intensive farming; tourist attractions are limited and industrial possibilities modest. These three distinct types of region thus present different sets of problems and any national landscape policy needs to be calibrated accordingly.

RECENT LANDSCAPE CHANGES IN IRELAND

In Ireland, landscape shifts have been relatively restrained, more incremental than abrupt. This partly explains the low profile of landscape issues and the subdued concern for landscape protection. Throughout the present century, an impressive stability has reigned in agricultural land use, with permanent grassland and livestock enterprises as predominant features. This pattern was conducive to landscape continuity, with most change a gradual continuation

of trends initiated in the previous century. Forestry, for example, has increased, but from a very low base-line; woodland is still modest by European standards although its landscape imprint has been considerable and at times controversial. Cut-over bogs have generally been replaced not by redesigned landscapes but by degraded forms of the older bogs or by coniferous plantations.

Since the 1950s, landscape transformation has quickened, but in response to increasing intensity of grassland farming and rising living standards in rural areas, rather than to shifts in basic land use. Changes in the style, scale and siting of rural buildings have been conspicuous, as well as rationalisation of the layout of farmyards, fields and other rural infrastructure. Change has inevitably involved the creation of new features and the removal of old ones; land improvement schemes have inflicted widespread archaeological destruction, while drainage and reclamation projects and agricultural pollution have damaged vulnerable wildlife habitats, aquatic and terrestrial.

ENVISAGING THE FUTURE

Further profound landscape changes are imminent in Ireland and throughout western Europe. Increasing farm productivity will permit food needs to be met from ever smaller areas of land with reduced labour. Future agricultural production will be industrial in character, concentrated where soil, topography and communications are most favourable, and dominated by large agro-businesses. Over the next few decades, the farm population will rapidly contract and the surplus farmland will go to other uses, especially to forests and recreation. This is in strong contrast to most other parts of the world.

After decades of subsidy and price stability, EU and national policies are now forcing agriculture to be more

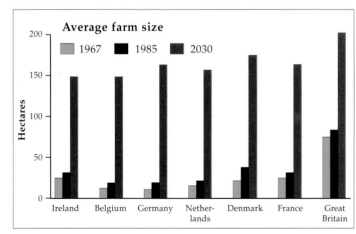

Fig. 5 H. Mentink's extrapolations indicate that average farm size will have changed dramatically in Ireland and the neighbouring countries by 2030. Accelerating enlargement of holdings will have major effects on the visual landscape.

market orientated, which will intensify instability in land use, promoting sharp shifts in landscape character. At the same time, there has been a welcome trend away from production subsidies to environmental concerns, integrating rural conservation with social and economic development. However, in this scenario of continuous evolution powered by relentless market forces allied to technological innovations, environmental policies may amount to little more than cosmetic damage limitation. The foresight and energy of indigenous intervention and conservation action at regional and local levels will then be crucial: flexible responses attuned to local needs are absolutely critical.

Apocalyptic generalisations about the prospects for land use and landscape are unhelpful. Intensified change is imminent but strong elements of continuity will remain. Individual trends and their interactions will vary between core and periphery and in response to local environmental conditions. In core areas, intensive agriculture will compete with conservation and recreation. Centralisation will prevail with the attendant weakening and perhaps terminal decline of the rural fabric in remoter areas. The disturbing possibility then looms of acquisition and control of the countryside by large institutions or agencies for extensive activities such as forestry, recreation or conservation, with resulting standardisation of the landscape and restricted public access.

RURAL COMMUNITIES AND THEIR LANDSCAPES

Cultural landscapes can hardly be conserved while the rural cultures that sustain them are decaying. Safeguarding the landscape entails equal concern for the well-being of the rural community. The European Council for the Preservation of the Village and Small Town (ECOVAST) and other bodies have eloquently voiced the vital need to establish a balanced and mutual support between them. Rural socio-economic development is entirely consistent with respect for landscape quality. Effective landscape management cannot be a purist pursuit dictated by aesthetic or preservationist values to the neglect of other essential interests; it needs to be embedded harmoniously in wider environmental, economic and social policies. Owing to its restrained economic development, Ireland and the European periphery in general have preserved a higher quality environment than the European core. Moreover, principal growth sectors in Ireland, such as agriculture, tourism and forestry, are intimately dependent on the maintenance of this environmental advantage. The central challenge is to promote growth consistent with environmental quality, to simultaneously utilise and protect the landscape for sustainable development.

F.H.A. AALEN

● Fig. 6 Tyrrellspass, county Westmeath. This village was laid out in a crescent around a green in the late eighteenth century. The original plan and coherence of the settlement have been preserved and owing to recent community efforts the buildings now exhibit a high maintenance standard.

In recent decades, many developments have been inimical to local landscape and culture but there are some encouraging trends. Inspired from various sources, a new vision has emerged of a renewed, sustainable, multipurpose countryside, where food and raw material production is no longer paramount but sensibly integrated with social development, landscape and wildlife conservation, and public access to and enjoyment of rural amenities. Reinforcing this vision, there has been a renewed respect for the countryside and an enhanced appreciation for the vernacular, the traditional and the locally distinctive. There is evidence of this in tourist destinations and in the dramatic rise of local history and community development groups. Within the last decade, Ireland has experienced this strongly, and the influences will be far-reaching. These trends can help evolve a modern way of life in rural areas which understands and respects heritage, enriching rather than diminishing it.

A PHILOSOPHY OF LANDSCAPE POLICY

Ireland now faces an unprecedented challenge but also an opportunity to initiate landscape management geared to the new millennium, policies which enhance the visual, historic and environmental qualities of the inherited landscape, and nurture its regional distinctiveness. Traditionally, regional landscape identity resulted largely from the necessity for rural communities to adapt to their local environment. Now that traditional limitations have been decisively and irrevocably breached, landscape coherence and identity becomes emphatically a question of conscious

local building materials and methods and developing the essentials of traditional building forms. Practical application of these guidelines requires attentive study of the authentic character of the landscape and of the appropriate methods of working in and with it. Present attempts to mimic local style and tradition are often shallow; insertions into the rural landscape should be made with the same informed consideration and sensitivity now customary when amending a piece of outstanding architecture.

CHANGE IN MAJOR LANDSCAPE COMPONENTS

In order to retain landscape quality, it is essential to identify and understand damaging contemporary trends in different landscape components and to develop strategies which counter their adverse impacts.

BUILDINGS

The massive wave of new buildings in the countryside is the most conspicuous element in recent change; their style and siting have provoked sustained controversy and the issue remains politically sensitive. Without rapid resolution of this intractable problem, landscape quality will be irrevocably impaired, inflicting irreversible long-term damage.

Common problems are found throughout the island, but are more acute in the Republic where a great rebuilding got underway in the 1960s as rural living standards rapidly rose and urban influences and commuters penetrated ever more deeply into the countryside. The 1960s was the decade when architectural taste was most hostile to tradition; while Georgian Dublin was being ravaged, a less heralded but even more damaging attrition gained momentum in the Irish countryside. Standardised urban designs were widely and unimaginatively used. Older buildings,

CHRISTOPHER HILL

● Fig. 7 Celebrated in mythology and heroic literature, Navan Fort (Eamain Macha) in county Armagh is an enclosed site of 7.2 ha on a low but commanding eminence, which perhaps served ceremonial rather than defensive purposes. Owing to its location and restrained design, the new visitor centre (middle foreground) by McAdam Design (1993) does not intrude on the extensive open site. Encroaching quarrying and farming have disfigured the surrounding landscape.

design rather than necessity. A design philosophy is therefore required which has historical continuity as its touchstone and conveys a sense of local distinctiveness and evolving tradition. This philosophy should nourish valued regional identities while facilitating desirable socio-economic developments. Landscape conservation is inescapably intertwined with broader development goals; the landscape's beauty is a major economic and social resource in itself and important historic and aesthetic elements, such as deciduous woodland and enclosures, often coincide with functional features of land use and ecology. An enduring link thus exists between the well-being of a region and the beauty of its landscape.

While striving for a renewed, sustainable and multi-purpose countryside, all necessary innovations should be attentive to the landscape and harmonised with existing features – working with the grain of field and farm patterns, respecting the layout of historic settlements, using

MAURA SHAFFREY

● Fig. 8 This roadside dwelling, near Trim, county Meath, retains the hipped, thatched roof, central chimney and whitewashed walls characteristic of the region; it clearly demonstrates the attractiveness of vernacular houses when they are carefully maintained along with their outbuildings.

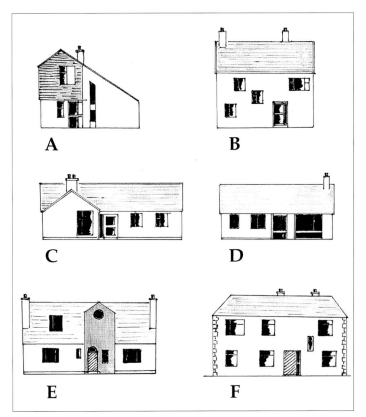

Fig. 9 Examples of rural house designs propagated by official bodies and architects and widely used in the 1970s and 1980s. A, B and C were designed specifically for farmers and published by An Foras Talúntais in 1973; D is a plan in a Department of Environment brochure of 1972; E and F appeared in *Buildings of reality* (1987). There is little evidence of serious involvement with traditional values in any of these ugly designs.

● Fig. 10 Assertive dwellings of this scale end eccentric design show scant regard for their rural setting and have an adverse impact on it. This example is from county Monaghan.

especially those in the vernacular idiom, were hastily discarded, starting with the dwelling houses and quickly embracing farm buildings, many of which lapsed into squalid dereliction. There was little attempt to preserve or adapt old buildings or to develop new forms in sympathy with the countryside. This rebuilding surge, hostile or oblivious to the existing tradition, also entailed wholesale relocation to conspicuous roadside locations. Thus, it is not only their alien style but the sheer number and blatant exposure of these new buildings which has heightened their intrusive profile in the countryside. A vital component of local distinctiveness has been peremptorily cast aside, rupturing any sense of an evolving architectural tradition, blurring the difference between town and country and degrading the visual identity of rural Ireland. Some progress has been made with the conservation of rural houses in Northern Ireland but in many areas little of the vernacular now survives. The official policy of concentrating rural development in selected centres proved ineffective, and scattered housing has spread along roadsides to the detriment of the landscape.

Under pressure from hostile commentary, the stated policy of most local authorities in the Republic is to curtail dispersed buildings, prevent ribbon development and maintain the aesthetic calibre of the landscape. However, long-standing structural weaknesses in the planning system, notably its susceptibility to political pressure, have ensured that these guidelines are only feebly implemented. Rural communities, eternally suspicious of authoritarian or elitist external edicts, have never willingly acquiesced in the principles of land use or building controls, arguing instead that local people should not be subject to planning restrictions in their choice of housing sites and styles. There is a deepening conflict between that local autonomy and the wider national goal of a well-managed landscape, increasingly seen as of vital strategic significance for economic and environmental reasons.

How can a sensitive rural housing policy be developed throughout the island? It cannot be imposed externally: only when rural communities themselves accept the need for appropriate approaches can housing policy deliver the desired results. Rural communities need to be persuaded that informed building and landscape decisions are in their own best interests, not something foisted on them to their detriment by uncaring outsiders. Only when that perception becomes widespread will the siting and design of buildings respect variations in the landscape and vernacular building traditions. It is therefore necessary to stress constantly that such policies will confer long-run economic and environmental advantages on rural societies, while enhancing their inherited identities. It is equally necessary to emphasise that such sympathetic solutions do not incur additional costs. Stringent guidelines and resolute implementation of them by local authorities can only be successful when they chime in with informed local pride and long-term interests, as well as making an appeal to the rural pocket through financial incentives for good design. If this

GRAFTON ARCHITECTS

●Fig. 11 This new house in Doolin in county Clare (designed by Grafton Architects) echoes the traditional narrow, gable-ended, two-storeyed houses of the region. The stone field walls anchor the building successfully in the regional landscape.

BILLY COLFER

●Fig. 13 In this successful Local Authority estate at Fethard, county Wexford, the houses are strongly reminiscent of the vernacular farmhouses and cottages of the region. The white pillars at the entrance echo the traditional gate posts of local farms and neatly frame the medieval ruin.

consciousness-raising was systematically targeted, good building practices would root themselves throughout the countryside, not just in tightly controlled designated areas, or in once-off developments.

With this enhanced consciousness in place, and given a supportive rather than adversarial architectural and planning regime, it should be possible to develop contemporary rural housing which retains a respect for regional coherence, enhancing the evolving tradition of the Irish countryside. This can be achieved by reviving and developing older building traditions, responding to local styles without merely mechanically reproducing them, and using the language and scale of older buildings with an informed imagination, disciplined by an awareness of the history and authentic character of the surrounding landscape. Outside towns and villages, houses should generally be single-storey with long, low shapes, their internal lay-out

and external features, such as doors, windows and chimneys, reflecting regional and local patterns. Two-storeyed houses would be acceptable in many eastern areas where they are rooted in both the vernacular and classical tradition. Buildings everywhere should be restrained in their ornamentation, avoid elaborate mixtures of materials, and express an organic link with their surroundings by using local building materials as far as possible. The dormant skills of local craftsmen – masons, thatchers, carpenters – should be reactivated as widely as possible.

Buildings and their outdoor space should be planned and designed together not merely to produce an attractive garden but in order to blend into the surrounding landscape. Existing trees and hedges should be retained as far as possible and respect shown for the field boundary pattern. The pre-eminence of the road engineers, with their emphasis on sight lines and wide entrances, should

A

MAURA SHAFFREY

B

MAURA SHAFFREY

●Fig. 12 This simple but attractive house, near Cobh in county Cork, has been extended at the rear into an L-shape, without altering the original, vernacular character of the building. This is the simplest effective strategy for conserving the local flavour of houses.

be challenged, in an effort to integrate new houses more harmoniously into the existing fieldscape. The same local stone should be used for both buildings and boundaries, although fences are appropriate where there is no local tradition of walling or hedging. Rock outcrops should not be concealed. On bare sites, native trees should be planted and, where possible, linked with the surrounding woodland.

New rural building should be concentrated in villages; this preserves the countryside, allows public services (water, sewers and electricity) to be provided more cheaply and strengthens the basis of village communities. There should be a strong presumption against expansion by a ribbon of bungalows or other suburban styles. New building on the edge of settlements should be congruent with the scale, proportions and materials of the existing buildings and arranged around cul-de-sac roads or with informal layouts reminiscent of traditional settlements.

In the open countryside, new buildings should be considered only if they are sited and designed in strict accordance with planning policies. Ribbon developments effectively suburbanise the countryside, are expensive to service and create a proliferation of vehicular accesses onto main roads. In particular, rural buildings should respect their landscape context and not be visually prominent; they should not, for example, block scenic views or break the skyline as seen from main roads.

In order to dilute the deleterious impact of the numerous new and mediocre buildings, the surviving stock of vernacular buildings should be attentively preserved. Comprehensive inventories, as carried out in towns by An Foras Forbartha and the Ulster Heritage Society, should be extended to rural areas and embrace used and derelict traditional buildings. These would allow accurate assessment of the local building stock. Thatch should not be lazily assumed to be the only hallmark of the vernacular; two-storeyed slated houses are equally genuine parts of the vernacular heritage, as deserving of attention as the trademark thatched ones. There should be a sympathetic response to proposals for sensitive re-use, conversion and rehabilitation of traditional buildings which are structurally sound, and active discouragement of conversions which destroy traditional character.

Farm buildings as well as houses require attention. The older outbuildings on Irish farms are elementary functional structures, sometimes aesthetically satisfying but generally architecturally unimpressive. Many are now terminally obsolete. Some might serve to accommodate small rural manufacturing, service or tourist facilities; for the majority, there may be no realistic prospect of long-term viability.

● Fig. 14 There is a gradual renewal of interest in local building styles and materials, evident in the construction of this new barrel-pier gate and wall in Portersgate townland, county Wexford. The trend needs to be encouraged by supportive public policies.

Concern must therefore focus on the new farm buildings which are much larger, and whose materials, colour and texture are alien to the local landscape. With specialist advice on detail, design, colour, siting and surroundings, a positive contribution can be made to the landscape. However, ungainly farm buildings, although among the most obtrusive elements in the landscape, are usually subject to minimal planning. Their growing scale and constant replacement in response to volatile agricultural policies makes any consistent control formidably difficult.

Although the quantity of rural buildings diminishes with population decline, their variety increases in response to rural diversification. Farms will steadily decrease in number, but tourism facilities, second homes, heritage centres, recreational facilities, timber processing plants and high tech factories, for example, will multiply. Some of these new activities are heritage based and can readily adjust to a vernacular idiom; others are novel developments, especially in industry and manufacturing, with a pressing requirement for innovative architectural solutions, marrying tradition and modernity harmoniously. Industrial forms are technical extensions of the city and are too often rudely inserted in the rural landscape. Nevertheless, except in highly scenic areas, there are no good reasons why industries should be timidly concealed by using, for example, screens of trees or artificial mounds. A positive alliance of industry and countryside is required, not a guilty complicity. It is more important that confident design connections are made with the surroundings. Industries should contribute to their host landscape through commitment to its ecological diversity and an enriched cultural environment, maintaining the history of the land while adapting it to modern purposes.

Recent housing change in Kilclone, county Meath

The rich pasturelands of south Meath have witnessed a stable pattern of occupation and settlement. A series of significant phases from the past two centuries can be identified in the legacy of buildings still in use today. These are well illustrated in the Kilclone district of south Meath, approximately twelve kilometres west of Dublin. Housing change since the 1970s has markedly transformed the area's landscape.

PATRICK DUFFY

Fig. A Killeany House, a large farmstead with two-storeyed house set back from the main road.

FIVE PRINCIPAL HOUSE TYPES

The large farmstead is a residence on some fifty or more hectares. Characterised by its relationship with the townland, it is often called the 'townland farm'; frequently the house is called after the townland, as with Staffordstown House, but more often than not it flaunts an eccentricity of names such as Black Hall or Dolly's Grove. It is also characterised by resilience – many farms having been occupied by the same family for several generations. Traditionally, these farms have been in pasture, fattening large herds of bullocks for the English market and the farmers here were known as graziers. Today, many are involved in the bloodstock industry.

Large farms are in well-appointed settings, frequently at the end of a tree-lined avenue, surrounded by mature trees and possessing substantial outbuildings. The houses mirror the formal architecture and setting of the mansions of the nineteenth-century landlord class, with whom the grazier families frequently mixed, and many continue as places apart from the local community.

Small houses for labourers and farm-workers were associated with the large farmsteads. Though the labour requirements on pasture farms were comparatively small, workers were needed, including cattle drovers and herders. They lived in small two or three-roomed thatched houses, built in the vernacular tradition with mud walls and hipped roofs. Most of the thatch has been roofed over with red-painted corrugated iron. In many cases, this class of occupier has been rehoused in local authority housing of various styles since the late nineteenth century: there are, for example, two houses built by the Poor Law Union, some cottages built before the advent of the County Council in the early 1890s, and a selection of council cottages built at various stages since the 1930s.

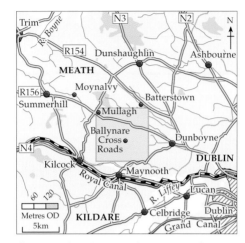

● *Fig. B The Kilclone study area in south county Meath is within commuting distance of Dublin city.*

There is also a scatter of nineteenth-century **small farmhouses or cottages** built in vernacular style, with mud walls and hipped roofs. A couple survive with galvanised iron roofs to the present; most are derelict.

Between the late 1930s and the early 1960s, the **Land Commission** programme of resettlement of small farmers from congested areas in the west of Ireland was aimed especially at large farm regions like south Meath, where the aim was to break up the large grazier holdings

MAURA SHAFFREY

Fig. C A County Council cottage built in 1938.

Fig. D A Land Commission farmhouse.

estates. Houses were grouped for social reasons at crossroads or along new Land Commission lanes. Frequently, attempts were made to locate migrants together from the same districts in the west of Ireland. The houses and out-offices were in simple designs which changed from period to period; two-storeyed or single-storeyed tiled houses with pebble-dashed exteriors and small farmyard buildings, generally with asbestos roofs.

Houses built mainly since 1970. A spate of new housing in the 1970s and 1980s was closely linked with the Land Commission farms, and directly related to the area's accessibility to Dublin. By then, these small farms were no longer viable units. Firstly, the offspring of the farmers began to commute to work in Dublin. In many cases, they built houses on the family farms, where low-cost sites were available. Secondly, as the area became

Fig. F A small farmhouse with the central hearth and hipped roof characteristic of eastern Ireland. Corrugated iron has replaced the thatched roof.

and replace them with a small farm, tillage economy. Farms or estates that were underused, or let on a long-term basis, were taken over by the state and sold to migrants from the west. Each migrant was given a small plot of land ranging from 10 ha in the late 1930s to 18 ha in the 1960s, together with a house, outbuildings and some livestock. The farms were carved out of the earlier

incorporated into the Dublin hinterland, newcomers arrived in search of house sites. Many small farms were then engaging in capitalisation programmes, investing especially in dairying following EEC membership, and the sale of 0.2 ha sites was a convenient way of obtaining capital. At the peak period, two roods of land could be sold for £11-12,000. Especially during the period 1973-1977 when a local man, James Tully, was minister for Local Government, Meath County Council adopted a relaxed attitude to rural housing. As a result, large-scale ribbon development occurred along the roads and lanes of south Meath. The houses were predominantly bungalows, adhering to standard floor areas and exhibiting a motley of styles from popular house pattern books, notably those of the Meath-based architect, Jack Fitzsimon, in **Bungalow Bliss.**

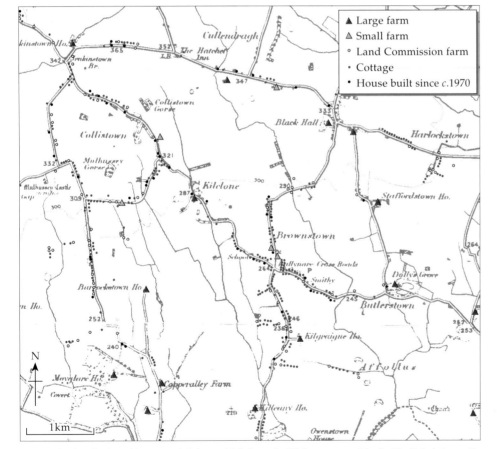

Fig. E The distribution of houses and their spatial linkages in Kilclone, county Meath. The links between the Land Commission farms and new bungalows are obvious; the gaps in the pattern reflect surviving large farms which were not involved in selling sites for housing

Legend:
- ▲ Large farm
- △ Small farm
- ∘ Land Commission farm
- · Cottage
- • House built since c.1970

Fig. G Recently constructed roadside bungalows.

FORESTS

Until the 1980s, the great bulk of forested land, north and south, was state owned and almost entirely coniferous. To avoid conflict with farming interests, it was restricted largely to scattered upland and bogland sites of minimal agricultural value. Recent incentives offered by the changing agricultural policies of the EU have spawned a surge of private forestry and, in the Republic, the semi-privatisation of the state forest sector which now runs on a narrowed, commercial basis. In Northern Ireland, the Forest Service (NI), whose remit is to provide multi-purpose forestry, still controls state forests and regulates private forestry. Modern private afforestation is similar to state activity in being predominantly coniferous, even though extra financial inducements are available to encourage the use of broadleaf trees.

To sustain a competitive timber processing industry, the Republic plans to more than double the current area under trees (from 8% to 17%) by the year 2030. This is still less than half of the current EU average and planting will be unevenly spread; the north-west could have twice the national average, while fertile eastern Ireland, excluding Wicklow, will continue to have low levels. In Northern Ireland, growth targets are more modest; private planting has increased but the emphasis on productive forestry is less than in the Republic.

Judiciously introduced and managed, forestry can bring multiple benefits to rural society, producing timber, jobs, recreational amenities, wildlife habitats and, not least, attractive landscapes. In Ireland, however, the successful incorporation of forestry as a major component of integrated rural development has had only limited application. Given a high level of farmer involvement, as in other European countries, forestry could make a material contribution to diversified and balanced rural development. But Irish forestry has been a state monopoly; there is no tradition of farm forestry and indeed there is often hostility to it among farmers who perceive it as an intrusive, competitive and alien land use. Where farmers have become involved, it is solely as an investment. The establishment and management of forests on their land is invariably carried out by companies. This corporate forestry has negative consequences for the fabric of rural society, leading to resource ownership in non-local hands and to the threat of multi-national control. In many areas, isolated rural dwellers are powerless to resist encirclement and eventual entombment in gloomy conifer forests.

Forestry undoubtedly brings abrupt, massive and long-lasting changes to the countryside but many Irish landscapes, both upland and lowland, can accommodate

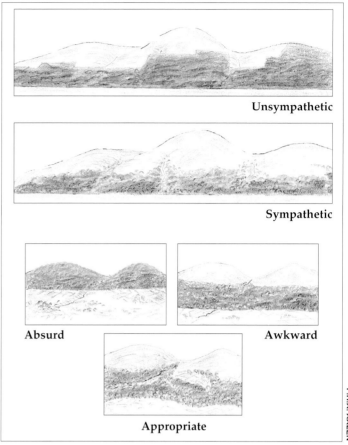

F.H.A. AALEN

Fig. 15 Visual integration of forests into the upland landscape. The contrast of texture and colour of plantations with open hill slopes gives a strong visual impact. Boundaries which follow the straight or geometric shapes of old enclosures or property boundaries appear markedly unsympathetic to the flowing landforms and the skyline. An irregular upper boundary is more compatible, rising in hollows and falling in convexities and not extending to the skyline. A fringe of scattered trees creates a natural transition to the hill surroundings. A solid blanket of trees obscures or truncates the details of the terrain. Small unplanted areas allow visibility of attractive features such as old settlement, water courses and cliffs, and contribute to landscape diversity.

afforestation, provided it is sympathetically introduced. Indeed, forestry has a proven capacity for absorbing visitors and recreational facilities and mollifying the visual impact of infrastructure, mines and quarries. Forests should fit the landscape, enhancing natural features. This positive potential has not always been released and there have been serious failings in forestry design and management. State forests are often visually obtrusive in areas of highly valued upland scenery. Where forests are extensive, the monotonous monoculture and concealment of the local terrain have been criticised; where they are fragmented, the harsh dark edges and geometric grids of the forests have been condemned as alien to the flowing topography of the open hills.

Being uncongenial to native plants and animals which are adapted to deciduous woodland, the coniferous forest is of limited conservation value. Renewed interest in the

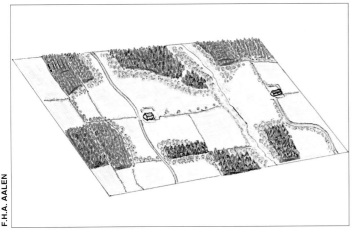

F.H.A. AALEN

Fig. 16 The lowlands in coming decades could be reduced to a mere chequerboard of single-species plantations, damaging to landscape continuity and coherence. Careful management will be required to retain continuous tracts of farmland with intervisible farmsteads. Forest should not overwhelm features such as townland boundaries or ancient enclosures, and open vistas should be preserved within the forests. Deciduous belts with natural uneven edges would conceal the dour coniferous tracts, especially along roadsides and river valleys. Linking with the pattern of hedgerows, deciduous belts could act as vital ecological corridors through the landscape.

planting of more broadleaved species, and the creation of open spaces and structural diversity in the forests could improve landscape and forest ecology by providing a mosaic of habitats. Recent official guidelines in the Republic emphasise that unplanted areas should be planned to form a diverse, interlocking pattern which accentuates natural features, provides for visual and ecological diversity and forms recreation areas and viewing points. This is a welcome and eagerly anticipated objective.

With privatisation, some shift of forests to the lowlands had been expected but the package of schemes remains more attractive on poorer land and much expansion is attracted to the edges of the existing upland forest; planting is sensitive to external influences and the future distribution is difficult to predict owing to ever-changing policy. Using better lowland soils would permit increased diversity of tree species but will also require more careful insertion of woodland within the complex fabric of the human landscape. If smaller woodland patches are fitted into the lowland pattern of fields and hedges, a fragmented, chequered pattern could result which, on aesthetic and ecological grounds, might benefit from connecting hedgerows and groups of trees.

Throughout Ireland, forestry activities are mostly exempted from the planning control process. In the Republic, official environmental guidelines have been published for grant-aided forestry projects but they are not always observed. The views of Local Authorities are taken into account by the Forest Service only when forestry development is proposed in areas of landscape or amenity

importance identified in county development plans. Environmental Impact Assessments (EIAs) and planning permission are required for planting of over 200 ha, a high threshold which excludes the vast majority of projects. More important, there is no provision for dealing with contiguous developments which together may amount to much more than 200 ha. In Northern Ireland, with its stronger emphasis on multiple-use forestry, the environmental consequences of planting receive greater attention. For example, extensive areas in AONBs and ESAs are to be left unplanted and in designated areas EIAs are required for planting on sites of over 100 ha.

Some expansion of forests was long foreseen but the sudden surge of incentive-led private planting was unexpected. The landscape implications are profound. Forestry is now developing fast in the Republic but in a piecemeal fashion, without the guidance of any overall land use or landscape strategy. A more strategic approach to afforestation would be to use Indicative Forest Strategies (IFS) which identify the least and the most suitable land for planting; these can minimise land-use conflicts, enabling land managers to plan ahead confidently.

AEROFILMS

●Fig. 17 Croagh Patrick, county Mayo, a majestic, isolated mountain (765m) developed on a quartzitic ridge, overlooks the small farm landscape of the shores and partly submerged drumlins of Clew Bay. This is Ireland's most holy mountain, St Patrick's choice of a desert retreat and still a place of pilgrimage. Coniferous plantations have introduced incongruous regular outlines on the flowing topography. Uses of the mountain, recreational, religious and economic (grazing, forestry and, in the future, possibly mining) require sensitive, co-ordinated management.

FIELD PATTERNS

Whilst the *bocage* landscapes of Brittany and Normandy have been seriously disrupted, the scale of change in Ireland has been tempered and the enclosed fields, despite modification by various factors, remain essentially intact. The spread of forests has submerged field patterns in hill areas and urban growth has obliterated them on the edge of lowland towns, but the major removal of enclosures has resulted from intensified farming and the introduction of large farm machinery since the 1950s. This has been strongly influenced by grant aid. Removal is concentrated in areas with a significant level of arable farming, such as south Kildare, north Carlow and east Down. Elsewhere, field enlargement is localised and associated with large mechanised farms, irrespective of whether they are devoted to tillage or grazing.

Current EU efforts to encourage environmentally-friendly farming have renewed interest in conserving and even restoring field boundaries. No wholesale eradication of boundaries for reasons of farm efficiency thus seems imminent but piecemeal, patchy change is likely. However, as farming becomes increasingly confined to the most productive areas, considerable landscape reorganisation could occur, with field sizes likely to increase and permanent boundaries to disappear.

Representative fossil field patterns from the Neolithic to the modern period merit careful preservation; in many cases, they are the sole sources of knowledge about agricultural development and landscape history. Efforts should also be made to preserve field boundaries of historic, wildlife or aesthetic significance, including townland and demesne boundaries and head dykes in hill areas. Good farming and the retention of valued boundaries can be reconciled, providing there is local understanding of the significance of field patterns.

ARCHAEOLOGY

The abundance of archaeological sites is integral to the appearance of the Irish landscape and to an understanding of its history. Recent survey and fuller recognition of low-visibility sites have led to a welcome realisation of the wealth of archaeological features, especially in uplands, in raised bogs, and in productive farmland. Post-medieval archaeology remains underdeveloped and little attention has been given to Plantation sites, to vernacular houses or to the massive post-famine settlement desertion.

Archaeology is a threatened and diminishing resource owing to afforestation, bog exploitation and more intensive farming activities which take little account of low-visibility sites. Deep ploughing and the development of

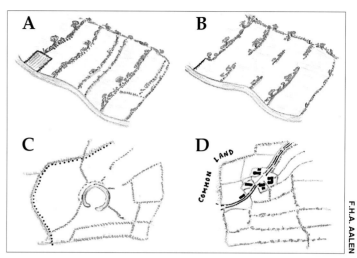

F.H.A. AALEN

Fig. 18 Working with the historic grain of fields and farms. A) Long, narrow fields have often evolved directly from medieval open-fields and retain the original curvature of plough strips. Where possible, this historic pattern should be preserved. B) The inconvenience for heavy machinery could be overcome by making gaps in the field boundaries rather than entirely removing them. Dense, diverse hedgerows are likely to be the oldest and special efforts are needed to preserve them. C) The main landscape features here are the ditched ringfort and its radiating fields and the strongly defined townland boundary. Modern farm management has been facilitated by breaching the field boundaries without loss of this historic pattern. Good shelter for animals is provided in and around the ringfort. D) In this locality, the major historic landscape elements which merit preservation are the old farm cluster and the narrow curved fields to the north-east which are relics of older open-field organisation, the lane linking the settlement and the common land, and the contrast between the area of stone walls and the hedged fields.

tree roots inflict severe damage and the destruction of architectural heritage by upland forestry has been considerable. The incentives to plant on better land present more intractable problems. Most lowland archaeology is not visible on the ground but appears as ephemeral crop-marks. The extensive area of permanent grassland in Irish lowlands limits the capacity of aerial photography to detect sites, and unheeded destruction from afforestation is therefore inevitable.

The identification and protection of archaeologically-rich countryside could be beneficial; here, destructive activities such as forestry or land clearance would be discouraged or cautiously introduced and intensive survey initiated where new planting seemed imminent. Certain landscapes, such as the Bend of the Boyne in county Meath, Lough Gur and environs in county Limerick, the Aran Islands in county Galway and the Knocknarea/Carrowmore district in county Sligo, possess an assemblage of associated monuments which provide exceptional evidence of earlier socio-cultural patterning. They are an invaluable framework for the study of past human communities and their relationship with the landscape, and thus merit special protection as 'historic landscapes'. The emphasis in archaeological protection needs to shift decisively from site to area-based designation.

Field boundaries and landscape change

In recent decades, farm modernisation has led to the removal of hedgebanks, hedgerows and stone walls and an enlargement of fields. Some boundaries were replaced by wire and moveable electric fencing; nevertheless, there has been a net reduction of boundary length. While less than in England, the rate of enclosure removal has been largely unknown. A study by Eilis Kennedy between 1990 and 1992 on a sample of 320 farms in selected counties in the north and south of Ireland showed that removal or alteration of traditional field boundaries had occurred on over 80% of the farms since the 1930s. The process accelerated in the 1970s in response to grant incentives for agricultural modernisation and was most influential on larger farms. Increase of field size was greater in the south owing to the larger proportion of big farms and the higher level of agricultural support from the EEC. Between 1930 and 1990, field size in the north increased from 1.0 to 1.4 ha and in the south from 1.5 to 2.4 ha. In the 1990s, grants have been available throughout Ireland for maintenance and replacement of field boundaries and have led to some limited restoration of the traditional landscape.

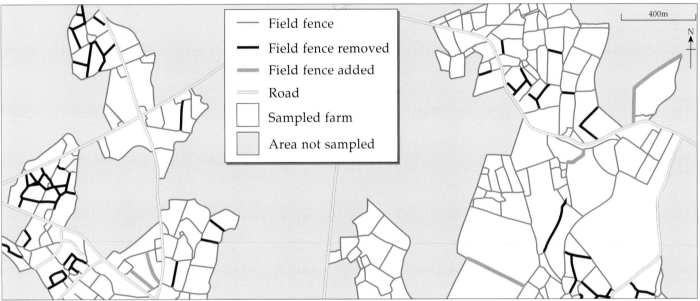

● Fig. A This sample of farms is taken from OS 1:10,560 sheet 34, near Ennis, county Clare. The most marked changes occurred in clusters of small fields. On some holdings no change has taken place, and there has been some recent restoration of boundaries.

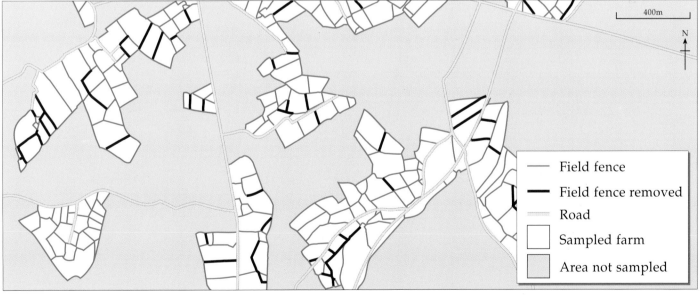

● Fig. B This sample of farms is taken from OS 1:10,560 sheet 41, near Magherafelt, county Londonderry. The amount of enclosure removal on the northern farms is comparable with that in the south but it is more uniformly distributed and the replacement of boundaries is less.

The destruction of antiquities: an aerial view

The landscape is a dynamic entity which provides a rich record of both past and present activities. Over time, new components are added to the landscape, whilst older features are modified or destroyed. The fragments from the past are not only of academic significance, but also add considerable interest and variety to the modern landscape.

In the twentieth century, the pace of landscape change has accelerated, and many archaeological features have been levelled through agricultural activity. The various editions of the Ordnance Survey maps provide the opportunity to monitor these patterns of destruction. The prehistoric and historic components embedded within the modern landscape are a fragile resource, often jeopardised by agricultural intensification and land improvement, quarrying, new housing schemes, the installation of gas pipelines and road developments.

●Fig. A (below) One earthwork survives in the modern landscape at Connahy, county Kilkenny, but an adjacent enclosure, recorded from the air as a cropmark image, had been levelled before 1839. Variations in land use history have influenced the survival of field monuments and landscape evidence at the local and regional level. Distribution maps of archaeological sites based on Ordnance Survey maps need therefore to be treated with some caution.

●Fig. B Shanrath, south county Kildare. The earthwork enclosure of the 'Sean Ráth' or 'old fort' recorded on the Ordnance Survey maps of 1908 and 1939 (inset) was destroyed at ground level. Paradoxically, the cropmark image provides a more detailed record of the original character of the monument, including the well-defined souterrain in the interior. Although many field monuments have been levelled, new components of the archaeological record are also being discovered – by chance, through field survey and by aerial reconnaissance.

● Fig. C (right) Cropmark images of archaeological sites provide a valuable addition to the archaeological record in the fertile, arable regions of Ireland but they are vulnerable features. Dispersed housing has encroached on one segment of this triple ditched cropmark enclosure near Leighlinbridge, county Carlow, destroying the underlying archaeological deposits. Limited resources restrict the archaeological exploration of sites threatened by landscape change, including both 'upstanding' field monuments and the fragile 'hidden' features revealed as cropmarks.

● Fig. D (below) Quarrying has seriously affected the landscape setting of this earthwork enclosure near Ardfinnan, county Tipperary. Although the monument has survived, important archaeological and palaeo-ecological deposits within the old land surfaces surrounding the site may well have been destroyed. Ideally the conservation of antiquities in the countryside should extend beyond the narrow confines of the monuments themselves and incorporate a broader zone of environmental protection.

GILLIAN BARRETT

GILLIAN BARRETT

LANDSCAPE CHANGE IN THE DINGLE PENINSULA, COUNTY KERRY

The repercussions of agricultural change on landscape character and archaeological resources are not restricted to the fertile, arable zones of Ireland. Land improvement schemes and the rationalisation of field systems are widespread throughout the country. From the air, the extent and implications of these changes can be monitored and specific monuments and landscapes placed at risk can be identified and assessed. The townland of Glanfahan in county Kerry illustrates some of the conflicts between modern farming practice and the conservation of historic landscapes. The townland is located at the south-west tip of the Dingle peninsula, and extends from the summit of Mount Eagle down through steep hillsides to cliffs overlooking Dingle Bay. The small farms dispersed on the lower hill slopes are surrounded by a high density of archaeological field monuments within an area of supreme natural beauty. The remains provide an unparalleled record of Early Irish and later domestic architecture and land divisions and have been a constant object of antiquarian interest. Their destruction is a major archaeological tragedy.

CUCAP

Fig. F In 1964, aerial photographs of Glanfahan by Keith St Joseph recorded a largely unchanged, multi-period landscape. The stone forts or cashels which functioned as farmsteads in the Early Christian period remain fossilised in the landscape, surrounded by a scatter of clocháin or corbelled stone huts, and set within an intricate network of small land divisions. The ringforts depicted are: Cathair na gConchúrach (foreground), Cathair na Máirtíneach (centre) and Cathair Bheag na Máirtíneach (background).

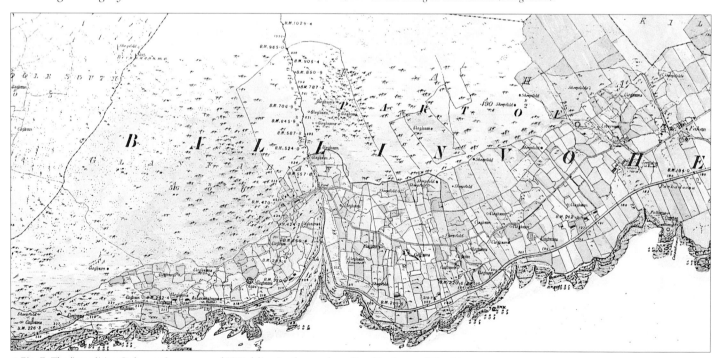

● Fig. E The first edition Ordnance Survey map of 1841 delineates the complex cultural landscape of Glanfahan.

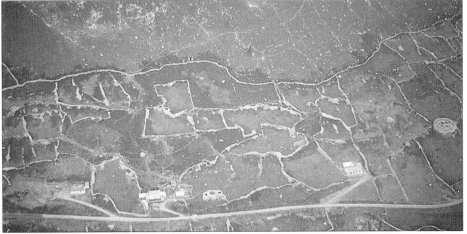

Fig. G (left) An aerial view of 1990 reveals a landscape at risk. The complex mosaic of dry stone walls has been reorganised and rationalised. In the vicinity of Cathair na Máirtíneach (centre), approximately forty small land divisions have been cleared to form one large field. Material from the old field boundaries have been swept downhill, forming the large pile of stones south of the coast road. The character of the landscape and the context of an important sequence of archaeological sites have been substantially modified. Cathair na Máirtíneach, restored by the Office of Public Works in 1984, now forms an 'island of survival' within this enlarged field unit, its surrounding landscape setting destroyed.

Fig. H Cathair na Máirtíneach in 1964. The aerial view documents the multi-layered landscape which once surrounded Cathair na Máirtíneach (foreground) and Cathair na gConchúrach (background). Some field boundaries have been cleared and the green roadway which once linked the townlands of Fahan and Glanfahan has been truncated.

Fig. I (left) West of the Glanfahan river, Cathair Mhurfaí and a sequence of clocháin are located within a system of field boundaries largely unchanged since the nineteenth century. Zones of survival such as these with their varied chronological horizons, combined with a rich and varied flora and fauna, are increasingly rare in a rapidly changing countryside and deserve active management and protection.

GILLIAN BARRETT

GILLIAN BARRETT

CUCAP

BOGS

While forests are expanding, bogs are a diminishing land-scape component. In the Republic, the boglands have an important role in national energy plans and at present production levels will last only four decades or so. As well as creating distinctive upland and lowland landscapes, bogs contribute to the stability and general well-being of the environment, conserving biodiversity, providing clean water and preventing flooding. They are valued too for their archaeological remains and their remarkable archival record of climate and vegetation history. Their diminution therefore has wide implications.

The rapid loss of peatland has varied causes. In the lowlands, it results from drainage schemes, large-scale mechanical harvesting and small-scale private cuttings. Mountain peatlands have also been widely damaged in recent years by overgrazing, repeated burning and private cutting. Use of the cut-away areas will be a major determinant of landscape character, especially in the extensive raised bogs of the Central Lowlands. In the Republic, the bulk of cut-away will be converted to coniferous forest and grassland, with about one-third reverting to wetland. Some tracts that lie below the regional water-table might be flooded for amenity and recreational purposes. However, the productive potential of cut-away varies over short distances: each bog is unique and requires individual decisions as to future use.

Ireland remains unique in western Europe in having a complete range of bog types which are of international importance and there is now a strengthening interest in bog conservation. Many of the conserved sites are also nature reserves. Conservation policies are, however, too modest to have an appropriate effect on overall land-scape character.

DEMESNES

Although abandoned and forlorn, demesnes are still a principal component of the landscape and present a formidable problem for landscape conservation. Some of the great houses are now used as educational or religious institutions, hotels and country clubs, museums and research centres. Historic houses are a valuable tourism resource but their upkeep is costly and the vast majority have been abandoned and are in ruin.

From a landscape viewpoint, the parkland surroundings are more important than the houses. Their disappearance would leave innumerable holes in the landscape; the nodes around which it was so comprehensively structured would be lost and many features of the countryside rendered unintelligible. No long-term solution to this

● Fig. 19 The extensive demesne at Mount Juliet on the banks of the Nore, county Kilkenny, was developed in the late eighteenth century by the Earl of Carrick. In the 1980s, it was converted into a golf course designed by Jack Nicklaus and the mansion is used as a country club and hotel.

problem is apparent. Only if the state or local authorities, heritage/amenity organisations, or wealthy institutions or individuals acquire the demesnes for recreational, amenity or conservation purposes is there a likelihood of their preservation reasonably intact. Carefully planned conversion to golf courses or forest parks, for example, can allow the retention of original features. Clearly, only a fraction of the demesnes can be saved in these ways. However, where complete preservation is impracticable, valuable scenic elements, such as trees, avenues, water courses and the perimeter wall should be retained as far as possible and integrated into the surrounding land-scape. There is scope here for the application of imaginative landscape architecture.

● Fig. 20 Historic houses and demesnes are considerable tourist attractions. The splendid surroundings of Rockingham House overlooking Lough Key in county Roscommon have been successfully converted by the Office of Public Works into a forest park for public use.

MANAGEMENT OF THE LANDSCAPE

At present in Ireland, we have a designation policy rather than a landscape policy, a concern with sites rather than landscapes, with elements rather than wholes. The chief strategy has been to establish enclaves encompassing valued resources and to safeguard them by limiting human use. Landscape is treated as a series of discrete elements to be planned in isolation; the outcome is a fragmented and confused perspective, inimical to the landscape which is holistic and requires broad strategic approaches. Nowadays, whole landscapes are the issue, not sites. The tired protective policies applied to special areas need urgent complementing by others which address the realities of constant unpredictable change on a nationwide scale. The radically changed objective must be accompanied by a fundamental shift in approach.

PROTECTIVE POLICIES

Existing conservation policies in the countryside are heavily concerned with the protection of individual features, not with the landscape as a unified whole. Negative protection is the dominant mode rather than proactive management, in an ever-changing countryside, of the landscape's overall character, cultural associations and visual appearance. At present, three main types of protective policy exist.

THE PROTECTION OF VALUED AREAS AND SITES

This activity is undertaken mainly by local authorities and central government agencies – the Department of Environment in Northern Ireland and the National Parks and Wildlife Service and National Monuments and

● Fig. 1 While the dramatic mountain and lake areas of Ireland are justifiably famous, the extensive farmed lowlands, shown here in county Limerick, are more characteristic and possess a special beauty and historic interest which is often undervalued. Through millennia of human activity, these landscapes have been moulded into harmonious, integrated wholes. Conservation requires a matching strategic vision and must decisively broaden its present emphasis on the protection of sites and intimate details to an informed involvement with the broad sweep of the evolving landscape. The integrity of the landscape cannot be guaranteed by restrictions and controls. Change is inescapable but there must be insistence on a better kind of progress guided by education and inducements so as to enhance the cherished qualities of the landscape. Without this, Ireland's precarious beauty will perish.

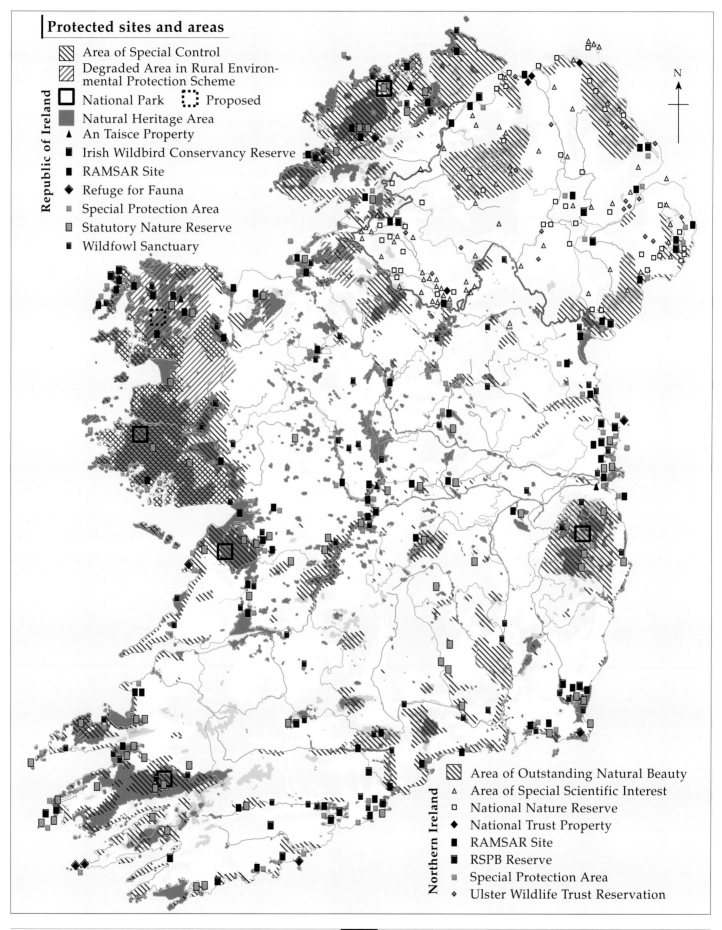

Protected sites and areas

Republic of Ireland

Area of Special Control

Degraded Area in Rural Environmental Protection Scheme

National Park ⬜ Proposed

Natural Heritage Area

▲ An Taisce Property

■ Irish Wildbird Conservancy Reserve

■ RAMSAR Site

◆ Refuge for Fauna

■ Special Protection Area

■ Statutory Nature Reserve

■ Wildfowl Sanctuary

Northern Ireland

Area of Outstanding Natural Beauty

△ Area of Special Scientific Interest

⬜ National Nature Reserve

◆ National Trust Property

■ RAMSAR Site

■ RSPB Reserve

■ Special Protection Area

◆ Ulster Wildlife Trust Reservation

Historic Properties and Waterways under the Department of Arts, Culture and the Gaeltacht in the Republic. In both jurisdictions, conservation strategy includes the designation, management and in some cases acquisition of important sites as well as the enforcement of national, EU and international laws and conventions concerned with species, habitat and landscape protection, such as Biogenetic Reserves (Council of Europe) and Biosphere Reserves (UNESCO).

Policies have accumulated piecemeal as the product of different concerns and there is a wide array of designations. Protection is afforded to wild life and plants, ancient monuments and areas of scientific interest such as semi-natural woodland, bogs, sand dunes, karst and freshwater lakes. These sites are generally small and scattered and the level of protection is low. The Republic of Ireland has the smallest area devoted to nature protection of any European country and less than 1% is in protective ownership. The most extensive conservation sites are the Natural Heritage Areas (NHAs), which have evolved from the earlier Areas of Scientific Interest (ASI) designation. They are nationally significant ecosystems, protected species locations and natural history sites covering circa 5% of the country. They have as yet no formal legal status but it is proposed to give them statutory protection.

There are five national parks in the Republic (Killarney in county Kerry; Connemara in county Galway; Glenveagh in county Donegal; the Burren in county Clare; Wicklow, in county Wicklow) containing mainly scenic mountain and hill areas in the west and covering 32,000 ha or 0.5% of the country. Unlike national parks in England and Wales, they are in state ownership. Within them, nature conservation as well as public use and appreciation are basic objectives; where conservation and public access come into conflict, conservation takes precedence. National parks are expanding slowly but are unlikely to occupy more than 1% of the territory in the foreseeable future. Protected areas of this sort, although scientific and social assets, cannot provide models for the flexible guided management required in the wider landscape, where economic land-use, public access and conservation must be fused.

Northern Ireland, in common with Scotland but unlike the Republic, England and Wales, has no national parks. It designates Areas of Outstanding Natural Beauty (AONBs) in recognition of their amenity and scientific value. These cover approximately 20% of the territory and include the Mourne Mountains and the Glens of Antrim. They aim to protect and enhance valued landscape features through stricter planning controls and to promote their enjoyment by the public, especially through improved access. Designation does not affect land ownership or occupation, unlike the national parks in the Republic.

Although the protection of designated sites should be expanded, it does not constitute a landscape policy; on the contrary, it reflects an eclectic involvement with elements rather than wholes. The proliferation of designations encourages a compartmentalised mentality which increasingly disaggregates the landscape, treating it as a series of disparate parts rather than as an intricate unified system of interacting elements.

ENVIRONMENTAL IMPACT STATEMENTS

Large-scale industrial and other developments are now required by law to prepare Environmental Impact Statements (EIS) which include their landscape effects. The visual obtrusiveness of a new development is among the topics which must be considered, as well as its combined effects on landscape character. The inclusion of landscape in EIS is a useful but limited step; it provides a means of checking the worst excesses but cannot counter the insidious cumulative effect of numerous small projects. EIS are no substitute for landscape policy and cannot be effective unless they operate against the background of agreed long-term principles and policies.

PHYSICAL PLANNING

As opposed to nature conservation, designation measures for landscape protection can be taken at local government level. County development plans frequently distinguish areas of landscape quality where stricter planning controls are applied. Only in these circumstances do we find the wide spatial perspective necessary to effective landscape management. Achievements, however, have been modest. In the Republic and Northern Ireland, the powers of physical planning in rural areas have always been severely limited by the exemption of most farming and forestry activities. In the Republic, there has been a recurrent failure to implement official policies because of inadequate planning resources and limited public support. Given the intense localism and clientelism of

Fig. 2 (left) Distribution of protected sites and areas as compiled by Ute Bohnsack and the Office of Public Works (NHAs). The concentrations on mountains, coasts and midland bogs reflect the concerns of ecologists and botanists with relatively 'natural' areas. Fewer sites occur on the deeply humanised landscapes of the south and east and the drumlin belt is poorly represented. There is a confusing array of overlapping designations, statutory and non-statutory. An excess of 'environmental labelling' reflects a fragmented understanding of the landscape and impedes its effective management. Local authority plans in the Republic distinguish areas of valued landscape where stricter planning controls are exercised. These are collectively known as Areas of Special Control (ASC). There is a decided emphasis on mountains, lakes and western coastal areas. Northern Ireland designates Areas of Outstanding Natural Beauty (AONB) which have a comparable role and are mainly peripheral mountain areas.

Irish politics and loopholes in the planning legislation itself, individual interests have persistently triumphed over wider concerns and some authorities contravene their own development plans. Under the Republic's planning legislation, a Special Amenity Area Order (SAAO) can give legal protection to landscapes and sensitive ecosystems. The designation has only been used around Dublin in the Liffey Valley, Bull Island in Dublin Bay and the Howth peninsula. It is complex and politically problematic, and cannot be seen as a comprehensive solution to general landscape management.

Local development plans already provide a useful and publicly accountable means for making choices about the desired environment and for shaping the future landscape. Planners were involved in land use and landscape policies decades before the contemporary enthusiasm for landscape management and environmental sustainability. They tried to control and place conditions on individual development proposals; some of their objectives were met but overall landscape quality has deteriorated. The planning system alone apparently cannot achieve wide environmental objectives because individual controls are not sufficient to regulate cumulative effects and cannot suppress market forces. This languishing system must now be revived and re-equipped to meet modern environmental challenges. However, the most enlightened and energetic local planning endeavour will be stultified without supportive national policies and integration with the policies of other agencies influencing environmental issues.

A NEW APPROACH TO LANDSCAPE MANAGEMENT

The protected approach is dependent on central authority and top-down planning, interventionist and professional. It is too costly to apply to the major part of the nation's landscapes with its thousands of independent farmers largely exempted from planning control; landscapes cannot be monitored by battalions of public sector conservationists. A shift is therefore required from regulatory planning to guided management. The planners' role will remain important but countryside management aimed at farmers and other land managers is increasingly seen as a vital complement to planning. Such management involves positive action on the ground to care for the countryside, either directly through farmers, or indirectly, through public bodies who influence work through advice, grants and regulation. The potential for guided development, as distinct from regulatory or punitive planning, is now considerable owing to the interest among farmers in conservation which, for the first time, attracts significant money through CAP payments to agri-environmental

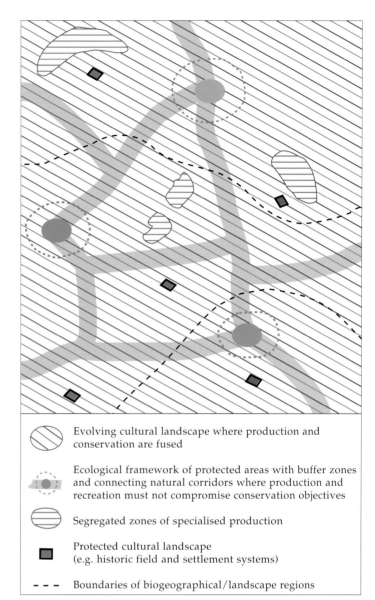

Evolving cultural landscape where production and conservation are fused

Ecological framework of protected areas with buffer zones and connecting natural corridors where production and recreation must not compromise conservation objectives

Segregated zones of specialised production

Protected cultural landscape (e.g. historic field and settlement systems)

- - - Boundaries of biogeographical/landscape regions

Fig. 3 Schematic structure of the future landscape. Restraints on food production and the increasing confinement of farming to the most productive areas open up large possibilities for conservation, recreation and amenity on the surplus land. The main challenge for landscape management is in the wider countryside where environmentally safe farming must function along with and sustain wild life, amenity and beauty. Whilst polarisation of use may develop on highly productive land, the overall aim is not to segregate production and conservation but to fuse them and inject landscape quality into all land uses. An evolving rather than a pickled landscape is envisaged. A system of interconnected protected areas will be supportive of this primary objective but not the major element of landscape strategy.

schemes. It may be possible now to perform the environmental alchemy of converting farmers into countryside managers through education and financial inducements. Large payments for set-aside, for example, mean that farmers will be asked to manage surplus land in a more environmentally supportive manner. Dragooning and compulsion may then not be required.

A growing level of local involvement in the preparation of agri-environment measures (and wider agricultural policies) is essential if they are to reflect diverse conditions and are to be developed for environmental rather than solely agricultural purposes. The Rural Environment Protection Scheme (REPS) in the Republic, for example, is a national scheme open to any farmer and administered by the Department of Agriculture. A basic aim is to combine efficient food production with the retention of traditional landscape features. Participants comply with a set of environmental prescriptions and a central feature is that an agri-environment plan for the management of the farm, identifying its main environmental features, is drawn up by an approved agency. The scheme can thus be adapted to local conditions at the individual farm level. Local authorities, local residents (most of whom nowadays are not farmers or landholders) and rural interest groups are not currently involved although their participation would introduce a much needed bottom-up element.

Agri-environmental schemes, while increasing in number and resourcing, remain at individual farm level; accordingly, their uptake is largely voluntary and they are run by competing agencies: the resulting series of *ad hoc* improvements on individual farms cannot produce a coherent landscape. By mid 1996, less than 20,000 farmers had joined the REPS scheme. Frameworks are needed at a higher spatial level, for example on a townland or parish basis. Integrated Rural Development or LEADER Programme areas could provide useful frames within which to explore wider management issues. Landscape identity is most often evident at this larger scale and understanding of its visual structure, ecological coherence and historical development requires a matching strategic vision. The involvement of local communities in the management of their landscapes, including the setting of long-term objectives and guidelines, is a relatively unexplored area but experimentation is underway in various European countries which may serve as a guide for Irish initiatives. The sense of place and local identity remains high in Ireland, but it needs to be more securely anchored to the local landscape.

Useful approaches to large-scale landscape planning and management are thus emerging but they have not yet been drawn together anywhere into an effective integrated system. The following principles are strongly commended for successful landscape management and as a basis for national landscape policies to which the government should be encouraged to make a firm commitment.

It is absolutely necessary to encourage greater public awareness of the significance of landscapes. Landscapes and changes within them require greater study, control and management at national, regional and, most crucially, local levels. Local communities should be educated, motivated and aided to safeguard their landscape heritage. They should study, record and monitor their landscape, identifying its economic, social, cultural and ecological values and defining its overall character and the appropriate design for new developments to enhance diversity and distinctiveness. Landscape history should be included in the training of architects, agriculturists, foresters, engineers and planners, and other disciplines relevant to landscape management. Landscape should be treated as an environmental resource in the planning process. There should, however, be acceptance of the inevitability of landscape change and understanding of its causes and consequences. A distinctive landscape coherently defines natural and cultural processes and is therefore an appropriate scale for studying the interactions between people and their environment. It is also a suitable framework for environmental policy and management. There should be effective machinery to protect special landscapes as laboratories for the study of ecological processes, as precious historical and cultural assets, and as natural diaries of a community's evolution.

BIBLIOGRAPHY

F. Aalen, *The future of the Irish rural landscape* (Dublin, 1978).
F. Aalen, 'Rural change and rural landscape quality' in C. Thomas (ed.), *Rural landscapes and communities* (Dublin, 1986), pp 215-44.
F. Aalen (ed.), *Landscape study and management* (Dublin, 1996).
Bord Fáilte, *Building sensitively in Ireland's landscapes* (Dublin, 1988).
D. Cabot (ed.), *The state of the environment* (Dublin, 1985).
Council for the Protection of Rural England, *Local influence* (London, 1995).
Department of Arts, Culture and the Gaeltacht, *Strengthening the protection of the architectural heritage* (Dublin, 1996).
ECOVAST, *A strategy for rural Europe* (Brussels, 1995).
Environmental Protection Agency, *Advice notes on current practice* (Dublin, 1995).
J. Feehan (ed.), *Environment and development in Ireland* (Dublin, 1992).
J. Fitzsimmons, *Bungalow bashing* (Kells, 1990).
C. Foley, *Farming and the historic landscape* (Belfast, 1992).
An Foras Talúntais, *Farm buildings and the environment* (Dublin, 1987).
D. Hickie, *Evaluation of environmental designations in Ireland* (Dublin, 1996).

D. Hogan and A. Philips (ed.), *Seeking a partnership towards managing Ireland's uplands* (Dublin, 1996).
[H. Hossack], *Buildings at risk, 3 vols* (Belfast, 1993-1996).
J. Meeus, M. Wijermans and M. Vroom (ed.), 'Agricultural landscapes in Europe and their transformation' in *Landscape and urban planning*, xviii (1990), pp 289-352.
J. Meldon and C. Skehan, *Tourism and the landscape: landscape management by consensus* (Dublin, 1996).
Netherlands Scientific Council for Government Policy, *Grounds for choices. Four perspectives for the rural areas of the EC* (The Hague, 1992).
T. O'Regan (ed.), *Irish landscape forum '95* (Cork, 1996).
Royal Society for the Protection of Birds, An Taisce and Irish Wildbird Conservancy, *Ireland's forested future* (Dublin, 1995).
D. Stanners and P. Boureau (ed.), *Europe's environment. The Dobris assessment* (Copenhagen, 1995).
G. Stout and M. Keane, *Farming and the ancient countryside* (Dublin, 1996).

Croagh Patrick, county Mayo

REGIONAL

CASE

STUDIES

REGIONAL CASE STUDIES

THE HOOK, COUNTY WEXFORD

Because of its peninsular character, the Hook has always been considered an isolated area; yet its association with two estuaries, especially Waterford Harbour, has given the Hook strategic importance, particularly evident in the medieval period. Remoteness by land and accessibility by sea have had a marked impact on the development of landscape and settlement, contributing to cultural identity and continuity. Two major periods of colonisation and change in landownership in the twelfth and sixteenth centuries led to a three-tiered society made up of Irish, Old English and New English. By the mid-nineteenth century, the baronies of Shelburne, Forth and Bargy had a higher density of Old English family names than anywhere else in Ireland. Similarly, the high ratio of placenames with cultural elements is the product of this distinctive settlement history. Because of the secluded, cul-de-sac nature of the area, older landscape and cultural features have frequently survived the intrusive forces of change: the resultant landscape and society are remarkable palimpsests of complex origin.

© JOHN IRONSIDE

Fig. 1 This view, taken from 3,000m looking towards the north-east, dramatically illustrates the peninsular, rock-bound topography of Hook Head, its threat to shipping emphasised by the imposing medieval lighthouse. The regular estate field-system of Loftus Hall in the middle-distance contrasts sharply with the small fields and fragmented holdings associated with the farmhouse cluster of Churchtown in the left foreground. In the right foreground, the townland of Slade replicates the contrasting field patterns. The manorial village of Slade, with its towerhouse, developed at the only natural landing-place on the peninsula, beside a small bay sheltered from the prevailing south-westerly winds. In the far distance, the promontory of Baginbun and the island of Bannow, both associated with the arrival of the Normans in Ireland, are visible.

GEOLOGY AND SOILS

The tapering promontory of Hook Head, located in the barony of Shelburne in the south-western corner of Wexford, forms the eastern boundary of the great estuary known as Waterford Harbour. Although the name refers specifically to the headland, a larger triangular district, situated between the estuary and Bannow Bay, is more generally regarded as the Hook area.

This district, approximately 15 km by 15 km, narrows from a broad base in the north to the point of Hook in the south. It is physically a part of the south Wexford lowland plain. For the most part, it lies under 60m in elevation, except for some low hills to the north between Ramsgrange and Campile. Principal streams enter the sea at Tintern, Poulfur, Fethard, Duncannon and Campile.

The bedrock consists of three types of sedimentary rock: shale and slate lie to the north while south of these a band of old red sandstone runs across the peninsula from Broomhill to Carnivan. The point of Hook itself consists of rich, fossil-bearing carboniferous limestone. About two million years ago, climatic fluctuations introduced warm periods during which sea-levels were higher than at present. Evidence for this can be seen at Wood village, near Fethard-on-Sea, where there is a fine example of a raised beach.

The soils of the Hook were formed from the level till blanket deposited by a glacier which advanced from the Irish midlands, carrying with it granite boulders from the Blackstairs Mountains. However, by comparing the geological and soil maps, it is obvious that the nature of the soils is also influenced by the underlying bedrock. Most soils are moderately well to imperfectly drained and, with proper management, are suitable for a wide range of crops.

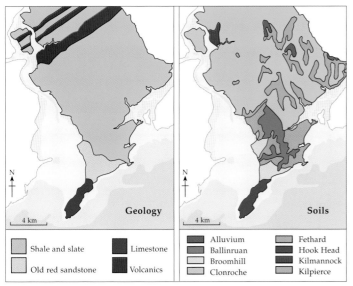

Fig. 2 Geology and soil series of the Hook.

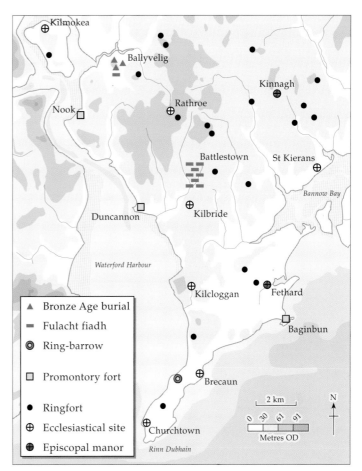

Fig. 3 Prehistoric and Early Christian sites and monuments in the Hook.

PREHISTORIC AND EARLY CHRISTIAN PERIODS

Despite its apparently advantageous coastal location, no evidence has yet emerged to indicate mesolithic or neolithic settlement activity in the Hook. The Bronze Age, however, is represented by a number of sites with a northern concentration. A cist burial and two urn burials have been found in Ballyvelig where there is also a Bronze Age cooking place, or fulacht fiadh. The grouping of fulachta fiadh is a recurrent feature; at Battlestown, for example, there is a cluster of eight.

Evidence of Iron Age settlement in Wexford is still meagre; the principal sites are all situated in the Hook where three promontory forts have been identified. Extensive ramparts survive at Nook and Baginbun, but at Duncannon, which has been fortified repeatedly, only the Celtic name survives. These sites indicate the emergence of an Iron Age society in the locality about 200 BC and an awareness of the strategic significance of the headland.

The landscape provides more substantial indications of settlement during the Early Christian period, including twenty ringforts, the defended farmsteads of the time. While these are now found mostly to the north of the

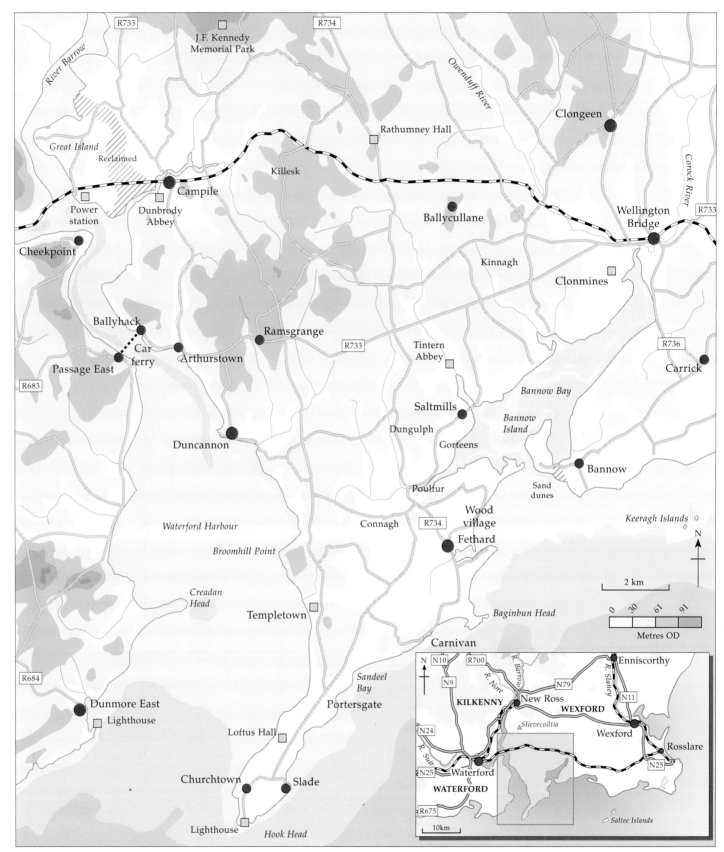

Fig. 4 The Hook area. In addition to cultural features, the region contains natural features of high scientific interest, with six sites designated as Natural Heritage Areas (NHAs). Hook Head is internationally rated for its outstanding landscape, geology and bird life; Baginbun Head, with its sea cliffs and bird life, is an area of landscape importance, as is the saltmarsh of Fethard, with its rare plants and the glacial features at nearby Wood village. The sand dunes and saltmarshes of Bannow Bay are of international significance for bird and plant life while Tintern Abbey is of zoological importance because of its breeding bats and is also an area of notable landscape importance.

BILLY COLFER

Fig. 5 Kilmokea monastic site. The circular enclosure, including part of the double rampart, survives in the landscape. The church at the centre may have been encircled by a smaller enclosure. Remains of a horizontal mill discovered near the church were dated to the Early Christian period. In spite of the impressive nature of this monastery, no references to it have been identified in historical sources. Adjacent to the enclosure is a medieval moated site.

region, their survival elsewhere may have been affected by the impact of medieval settlement.

The principal Early Christian monastic site was at Kilmokea on Great Island, formerly an island in the River Barrow but now joined to the mainland by late nineteenth-century land reclamation. Four other sites, also believed to have Early Christian origins, were of minor significance. There is a bullaun stone in the remains of a church at St Kierans on the shore of Bannow Bay, associated with the saint of that name. Three Welsh monks of the same family are said to have been responsible for fifth-century foundations on the point of Hook: Alloc at Kilcloggan, Dubhan at Churchtown and Brecaun on the cliffs at Portersgate. Dubhan's monastery gave its name to the promontory which was known as Rinn Dubhain until the late middle ages when it was incorrectly anglicised as Hook Head. The medieval parish church at Churchtown incorporates elements of an Early Christian structure, including traces of antae. Pre-Norman episcopal manors at Kinnagh and Fethard added another dimension to ecclesiastical influence in the area.

THE NORMAN PERIOD

South-west Wexford was directly involved in the initial phases of Norman activity in Ireland. Following the first landing at Bannow Island in 1169 and the capture of the Norse town of Wexford, Diarmuid Mac Murchada granted extensive lands to Hervey de Montmorency, including the barony of Shelburne in which the Hook is located. Montmorency organised his new estates according to the laws of the feudal system. He established his headquarters

on what is now Great Island. For a time, this was known as Hervey's Island and his lands were referred to as the Manor of the Island. The remains of a large ringwork site on Great Island may represent Hervey's original *caput*. Hervey's principal contribution to the settlement of the area was the granting of a large estate for the foundation of a Cistercian abbey at Dunbrody. A survey carried out by the Cistercians in the 1170s describes the land as waste and infertile and the natives as wild and ferocious.

A number of factors led to almost all of the land in the Hook area being granted to ecclesiastical interests. The bishop of Ferns already had two manors here at Fethard and at Kinnagh, where the surviving circular church site indicates a pre-Norman origin. During his visit to Ireland in 1172, Henry II granted the Hook peninsula to the Knights Templars, south of a line from Duncannon to Carnivan. This was a security measure to protect the strategically important Waterford Harbour: the Knights Hospitallers were installed at Ballyhack where their fifteenth-century towerhouse (now a national monument) dominated the waterway and the lucrative ferry crossing. As a result of a vow made at sea when in danger of shipwreck, William Marshal founded another Cistercian monastery, in unusual proximity to Dunbrody, on the shore of Bannow Bay. Here monks from Tintern Abbey in

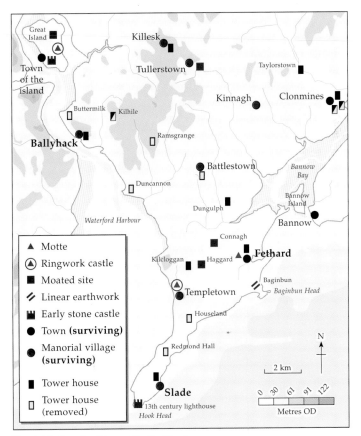

Fig. 6 Medieval settlement in the Hook area.

Shropshire established a monastery which became known as Tintern de Voto (of the Vow).

The Normans utilised pre-existing territorial divisions in the process of infeudation. Of twenty placenames listed in the charter to Dunbrody, eight can be identified with modern townlands. Two others, Campile and Taghmon, also refer to surviving settlement features. Similarly, the Tintern charter lists four identifiable modern placenames. A close link between manorial and parochial development in medieval Ireland has been well established and evidence from charters and monastic extents makes it possible to produce an accurate map of the extensive medieval church lands in the Hook area. The remaining land was distributed to lay tenants, some of them located in a shallow corridor between the lands of Dunbrody and Tintern, possibly in an attempt to create a buffer zone between them.

As the Normans were operating in a frontier situation, defence was a critical consideration. The extensive linear earthworks at Baginbun, constructed in 1170 by Raymond le Gros, were described in 1189 by Gerald of Wales. At Fethard, the remains of a small motte-and-bailey castle survive alongside the medieval parish church and later stone castle, while a mound at Templetown may be the site of the Templars' early ringwork castle. Three rectangular moated sites (defended farmsteads associated with a secondary phase of settlement), located on the knights' fees of Tullerstown and Connagh and at Haggard on the Templars' manor of Kilcloggan, have been removed from the landscape. The outline of a larger moated site can still be identified as part of the field pattern on Great Island. No defensive earthworks have been identified on the lands of the Cistercian abbeys. There was an early thirteenth-century stone castle on Great Island, and the Tower of Hook, built on the tip of the headland as a navigation aid, dates from the same period. In the fifteenth century when towerhouses were built as a response to the Irish revival,

DEPARTMENT OF ARTS, CULTURE AND THE GAELTACHT

Fig. 7 Tintern Abbey was established by William Marshal *c.* 1200, beside an inlet where a stream flows into Bannow Bay. It was colonised by Cistercian monks from Tintern Major in Wales. Following its dissolution *c.* 1540, the abbey and its lands passed to the Colclough family who occupied it for four centuries. In converting the ecclesiastical structures into a domestic dwelling, they levelled the claustral and conventual buildings. Recent excavations have uncovered the cloister arcade and south aisle.

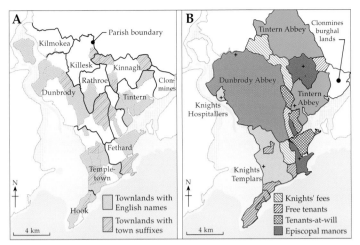

Fig. 8 Following the arrival of the Normans, most of the land in the barony of Shelburne was granted to the church. The remainder was held by lay tenants, either by knight's service or for rent. Because of the tithing system, the medieval parochial organisation developed out of the land division structure.

their distribution corresponded to the land divisions which had been established more than two centuries earlier. The exceptions were at Ramsgrange and Battlestown, on the lands of Dunbrody Abbey, which may have been in the hands of lay tenants by then.

Manorial organisation was accompanied by the development of nucleated settlement including chartered towns and manorial villages. The Town of the Island was established by de Montmorency; Clonmines, at the head of Bannow Bay, by Marshal, and Fethard by the bishop of

Ferns. By the sixteenth century, the Town of the Island and Clonmines had ceased to function, presumably due to the accelerating economic superiority of New Ross. Only Fethard survives as a settlement, partly due to its revival as an estate village in the eighteenth century. The exact site of the Town of the Island has not been established but extensive remains of stone buildings at Clonmines, including the parish church, an Augustinian priory, a fortified church, two towerhouses and a fortified hall, indicate the substantial nature of this town until its demise, probably in the sixteenth century. Manorial villages, based on a church, a castle and sometimes a mill, developed on some manors, particularly on knights' fees and on the lands of the military orders. Of the seven recorded, Ballyhack and Slade survive as settlements in the modern landscape. Clonmines, where the surviving buildings combine with a spectacular location to create an evocative atmosphere, has been described as the finest Irish example of a deserted medieval borough.

The townland system, regarded as having emerged late in the Early Christian period, is the most pervasive survival from that era. Of 82 townlands, slightly more than half have Irish names. Townlands with English names form a pattern related to Norman settlement. The lands of Dunbrody Abbey and the Knights Templars contain a core of English placenames while those in the knight's fee of Tullerstown were almost completely anglicised. Names on

BRITISH LIBRARY

Fig. 9 This dramatic aerial perspective of Hook Head, attributed to Thomas Phillips c. 1690, shows the thirteenth-century crenellated light-tower with a lamp, erected in the 1670s, on its summit. The number of ships in Waterford Harbour emphasises its importance as a trade route. Landscape features include the castle and an early pier at Slade, Redmond Hall, and the promontories of Baginbun and Duncannon in the distance. Four men in a small fishing boat are shown near the rocks in the left foreground.

BILLY COLFER

Fig. 10 Clonmines. The extensive survival of stone buildings in a spectacular setting makes this site one of the finest examples of a deserted medieval borough in Ireland. Key: A) Towerhouse; B) Augustinian priory; C) Fortified building; D) Towerhouse; E) Fortified church; F) Parish church.

the lands of Tintern Abbey remained Irish to a greater degree. Irish placenames form definite groupings, indicating that the Irish population remained strongest in peripheral locations on the various land-grants. The distribution of ringforts reinforces this point. They are almost completely absent from the heartland of the Dunbrody and Templar estates, perhaps due to a policy of removal on some church lands. Nine townland names contain a personal name followed by the suffix 'town', an element diagnostic of Norman settlement. Six (Galgystown, Lewistown, Battlestown, Drillistown, Tullerstown and Templetown) can be related through documentary sources to the original Anglo-Norman landholders. Other names refer to activity associated with a particular townland. These include two Granges; two Haggards; two Saltmills, where the Cistercians harnessed the sea to generate power; a Ramsgrange; a

Lambstown; a Haytown and a Milltown. Four names, Redmond (now Loftus) Hall, Houseland, Portersgate and Stonehouse, indicate the former existence of specific settlement features. Three names (Broomhill, Castleworkhouse and Ramstown) are of later origin.

The landholding system was considerably influenced by soil quality. In a number of instances, property divisions and soil-type boundaries were almost coincidental. The medieval parish of Hook, occupied by free tenants of the manor of Kilcloggan, provides the most striking example, as it coincided almost exactly with the Hook Head soil series which has a wide use range. Fethard parish also corresponded quite closely to the Fethard series which has a limited use range. The estate of Dunbrody Abbey and the knights' fees of Tullerstown and Killesk were located on the Clonroche series, which is easily tilled with a wide use

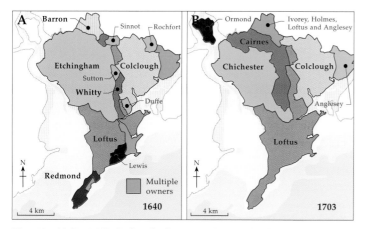

Fig. 11 A) By 1640, Loftus had acquired more land in the parish of Fethard and the townlands of Ballygowny and Baylestown in the former knight's fee of Tullerstown. The Colclough lands were enlarged by the addition of the episcopal manor of Kinnagh. The Barrons – or FitzGeralds – retained the fee of Killesk and Lewis and had exchanged Lewistown for the townlands of Great Graigue and Lambstown. Remaining land was held by new proprietors, with multiple owners in the parishes of Fethard and Clonmines. B) By 1703, Loftus had increased his holding, acquiring the lands of the town of Fethard, Redmond of the Hall, Lewis of Great Graigue and Whitty of Dungulph. A grant of six townlands to William Cairnes had reduced the Etchingham holding but these were subsequently recovered.

range. The lands of Tintern Abbey, allocated later than the rest, had a mixture of the versatile Clonroche series and the more limited Kilpierce series. Townlands with English names tend to be located on the best soils. These observations suggest that, as in the country as a whole, soil quality was taken into account in the allocation of land in the Hook area during the twelfth and thirteenth centuries.

The Development of the Estate System

The structure of the estate system in south-west Wexford was predetermined by extensive land grants given to the church by the Normans. At the dissolution of the monasteries c. 1540, this land reverted to the crown and thus became available for re-granting. The individual monastic estates were passed intact to individuals loyal to the crown; as Protestants, these added a new element to the rich social mix of the area. At the end of the sixteenth century, another dimension was introduced with the construction of an impressive military fort at Duncannon. Built to control access to Waterford Harbour in the event of the arrival of the Spanish Armada, the fort emphasised, yet again, the strategic nature of the estuary in an European context.

The new landlords on the former monastic lands were Colclough at Tintern, Etchingham at Dunbrody and Loftus at Templetown. Some tenants on the manor of Templetown remained in possession of their lands, however, principally Redmond of the Hall and Lewis of Lewistown. When landholding c. 1640 is mapped from the Civil Survey, the situation remains relatively unchanged. As most of the land in

the area was already held by Protestant landlords, the confiscations which followed the Cromwellian campaign concentrated on the small estates held by the Old English Catholic families which were then added to the Loftus estate in particular.

At the end of the seventeenth century, this process consolidated an estate system in south-west Wexford which would have major social and political influence for more than two centuries, as well as profound landscape implications. The new proprietors' first priority was to modernise their estates. The Colcloughs adapted the Cistercian church at Tintern as a residence which they were to occupy for four centuries. At Dunbrody, the Etchinghams (later Chichester and Templemore) lived in a Tudor house which they built over the south transept of the abbey. After the acquisition of the Redmond lands, the Loftus family made Redmond Hall their principal residence. An account written in 1684 by Robert Leigh gives an insight into the changes initiated by the new landlords:

> The parish belongs at present to Henry Loftus Esq. who has repaired the old Mancon House there, and added other considerable buildings of lime and stone thereunto, and enclosed his gardens with high stone walls to preserve some fruit trees newly planted there, and dwells in that house now. It was formerly called 'Redmond's Hall' from ye old proprietor; it is now called Loftus Hall. Mr. Loftus is now building a key for fishing boats, on the east side of the peninsula neere a place called ye Slade.

The walls and gardens built by Loftus, including a large deerpark with impressive late seventeenth-century piers, still survive at Hook Head. They evolved into an estate landscape with large regular fields, surrounded by walls constructed of local limestone.

The importance of the sea to the estate economy, both for fishing and trade, was shown by the construction of piers at St Kierans by Colclough, at Fethard and Slade by Loftus and at Duncannon, Ballyhack and Arthurstown by Chichester. Local stone was exploited on the Loftus estate. At Harrylock, on the cliffs at Templetown, mill-stones and a range of other objects were cut from the old red sandstone. Extensive quarrying and burning of limestone took place. From the many limekilns which dot the peninsula, burnt limestone was used for building purposes and also spread on the land; a field called Limekiln Park is recorded in an estate survey of 1771. Limestone rock was also transported by boat to Fethard, St Kierans, Tintern and other locations, where the kilns in which it was then burned still stand. A rock on the cliffs at Slade where limestone was quarried is still known as Carraigahoy, from the Irish

Fig. 12 The Hook in 1591. This chart of Waterford Harbour was prepared by Francis Jobson in the aftermath of the Spanish Armada. It shows the defensive works at Waterford, Passage and Duncannon and depicts prominent man-made landscape features, particularly medieval churches and castles, landmarks and navigational aids to shipping.

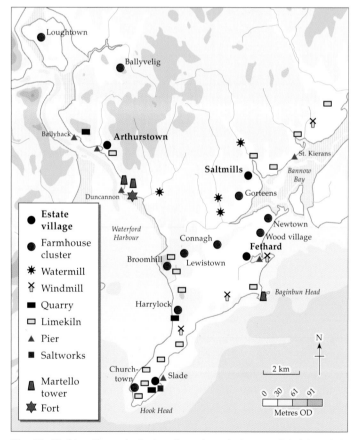

Fig. 13 Eighteenth- and nineteenth-century features, related to estate development and the exploitation of natural resources of both land and sea, survive in the landscape.

Carraig an Aith (Limekiln Rock), indicating that Irish was spoken in the Hook early in the nineteenth century. This is corroborated by the census of 1871 which recorded seventy-eight Irish speakers in the barony of Shelburne.

Late in the seventeenth century, Loftus leased the townland of Slade to his wife's brother-in-law, William Mansell, from the Gower peninsula in Wales. Mansell developed Slade, formerly a cluster of cabins around the Laffan tower-house, as a miniature estate village. He improved the harbour and established a salt works, possibly to capitalise on the expanding Newfoundland trade. The venture would appear to have been short lived, although the remains of the factory, known as the Salthouse, still survive. Like a number of other buildings in the village, it was constructed of limestone, with a distinctive corbelled roof, reflecting the

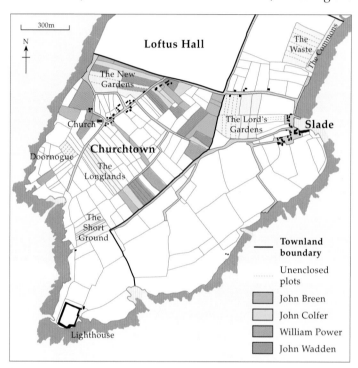

Fig. 14 A detailed account of landholding is given in the Loftus estate maps compiled in 1872. In Slade, two open-fields were held by a number of tenants. 'The Waste' contained 3.7 ha (nine acres) and was held in unenclosed strips by eight tenants. 'The Lord's Gardens' contained 7.4 ha and was held by fifteen tenants. These fields are still held in substantially the same manner. The townland of Churchtown contained 88 ha which was shared by twenty-eight tenants, some of them holding less than 0.4 ha. The lands of four of the principal tenants are shown here, illustrating the dispersed nature of the holdings. John Breen held just over 6.4 ha in seven lots; John Colfer held 3.7 ha in six lots; John Wadden held 5.2 ha in eight lots and William Power held 6.8 ha in seven lots. A field called 'The New Gardens' was held in ten unenclosed lots by nine tenants, and a comparison of the estate map with the 1924 ordnance map indicates that other holdings were unenclosed also. At present, as well as 'The New Gardens', there are two other open-fields in Churchtown; 'The Short Ground' has five strips and five owners and 'Doornogue' has seven quarters and two owners. It has been established that the medieval system of land tenure survived into the nineteenth century in parts of county Dublin. Similarly at Slade and Churchtown, the modern pattern of land-holding, with long narrow strips, dispersed holdings and open-fields, may have originated in the manorial three-field system of land tenure.

Slade : the development of a fishing village 1450 to 1850

1450

BILLY COLFER

Fig. 15 The name Slade is of topographic origin, derived from the Gaelic word Slád, *meaning a glen. This is an accurate description of the locality as the village is situated in a small valley through which the sole stream on the peninsula flows into an inlet. This bay is the only natural landing place in the Hook as it is sheltered from the prevailing south-westerly winds and has sandy beaches where boats can be brought ashore. The townland of Slade was held by the Laffans, an Irish family, as tenants of the manor of Kilcloggan. Slade village, with its fifteenth-century towerhouse, was located just to the south of the inlet, possibly to avail of the protection it afforded and to take advantage of the natural harbour. Adjoining land, which is still laid out in large fields, was retained by the principal tenant; the land to the north of the inlet, where there are unenclosed strips and small fields, was held by the labourers and sub-tenants.*

Fig. 16 Shortly after the construction of the towerhouse, probably in the late fifteenth century, a defended hall was added to the east. As the Laffans held only 81 ha, other revenue, perhaps from fishing and smuggling, would have been required to construct such an elaborate dwelling. Although there must have been an earlier pier, the first recorded quay was constructed in 1684 by Henry Loftus, the new landlord. This was probably the still surviving 'ould quay' built to the north of the inlet. At the end of the seventeenth century, William Mansell, related by marriage to Henry Loftus, acquired the townland. Mansell developed Slade as a tiny estate village, building a substantial house for his family and comfortable dwellings for his tenants. He also set up a saltworks, housed in unusual corbelled stone buildings, some of which survive. As part of the development, he constructed a new pier to the east, to form a safer, enclosed harbour.

1750

BILLY COLFER

1850

BILLY COLFER

Fig. 17 By the end of the eighteenth century, the lands of Slade were leased to the Breens, a Catholic merchant family of Taghmon. The saltworks had been abandoned and the east pier was in a ruinous condition. The population of c. 200 was concentrated in cabins to the south of the castle and in a row of houses to the west of the harbour. The castle, occupied by a number of families, had been developed as a 'tenement', with an outside stairs added to the east wall giving separate access to the first floor. At the onset of the Great Famine, an act 'to encourage the sea fisheries of Ireland' led to the construction of a new pier on the site of the old one, with an approach road and slipway. Later, two walls were constructed across the harbour creating an 'inside' dock for greater protection in stormy weather. At present, eight of the fourteen houses in Slade are used as holiday homes. The harbour is used by eight local fishermen and by pleasure craft during the summer season.

Fig. 18 The seventeenth-century piers which marked the entrance to the deer park of Loftus Hall and to the Hook proper.

scarcity of timber and the ready availability of stone on the peninsula. Maps prepared for the Loftus estate in 1771 show farm patterns, and even field names in some cases, substantially the same as at present.

Fethard had been developed as an estate town by Loftus although it lost its borough status at the Act of Union. Early in the nineteenth century, the old village of Tintern was removed and a new estate village was built at Saltmills on the Colclough estate. About the same time, the village of Arthurstown, named after Arthur Chichester, was being constructed, with a new quay, on the Dunbrody lands.

Although the three estates in south-west Wexford were among the most powerful in the county (Dunbrody, for example, was one of thirteen valued at more than £5,000 in 1876), they contained some of the finest examples of archaic agrarian landscapes to be found in south Leinster. These were the farmhouse clusters, without a church or other institutional buildings, associated with unconsolidated holdings sometimes consisting of scattered parcels of land in open-fields. The Shelburne examples can be seen as an extension of the south Kilkenny grouping which is regarded as the heartland of this type of settlement. The clusters, located in Old English baronies, appear to be deep-rooted, containing communities where traditional values and practices thrived. Some of them were of significant size; for example, Broomhill had 143 occupants living in 21 houses in 1841. Today, only one house remains occupied and the cluster has disintegrated. The isolated nature of the peninsula may have contributed to the survival of these clusters, as they are concentrated on the Loftus lands in the more remote part of the area.

Slade and Churchtown, the southernmost townlands on the peninsula, contain remnants of dispersed holdings, some in large open-fields. In medieval times, Churchtown was part of the lands of Redmond of the Hall and Slade was held by the Laffan family, both as tenants of the manor of Kilcloggan. Churchtown's population of 158 people, living in 29 houses in 1841, is now reduced to 41. At present, the marked contrast in field size and pattern distinguishes quite clearly between the land held by the principal tenant and the area occupied by sub-tenants and workers. Churchtown, possibly because of its exposed location, was occupied by the servile element on the manor of Redmond (later Loftus) Hall. The 1771 survey recorded that Churchtown was in the hands of His Lordship's labourers. Four large open-fields with unenclosed strip-holdings still survive in the two townlands. The strips, known as 'quarters', are separated by narrow lengths of uncultivated ground called 'bones' (from the Irish *bona*, a boundary).

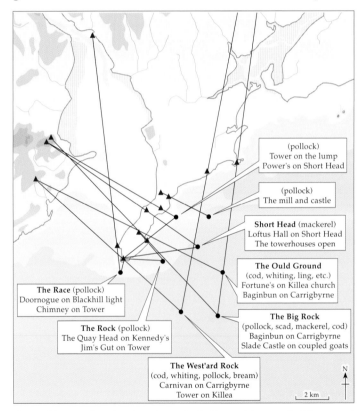

Fig. 19 The sea played a pivotal part in the lives of the people. Men rowed long distances in small boats to set lobster-pots made from willow saplings and to fish the 'marks' which enabled them to identify good fishing areas on the sea-bed. By using features on land as co-ordinates to locate these 'marks', a complex system had been developed for identifying and exploiting the underwater landscape. However, the introduction of modern navigational technology has caused this traditional method to become almost obsolete. Mackerel and pollock, caught from the rocks with lures of goat-hair and goat-skin (known as a 'torgan') during the autumn months by those who did not have boats, were salted and dried for winter consumption. At low tide, the sea-shore was also a source of food, providing barnachs and piothans (limpets and periwinkles) as well as crabs. The sea-shore yielded another type of harvest early in the summer when seaweed ('woar') was collected for use as a fertiliser.

THE MODERN LANDSCAPE

By the beginning of the nineteenth century, the present settlement pattern and agrarian landscape was substantially in place. The international significance of the estuary and peninsula was further underlined during the Napoleonic Wars when three Martello towers were constructed, two at Duncannon and one at Baginbun. In the aftermath of the 1798 Rebellion, a straight military road (still called 'the new line') was constructed, connecting Duncannon Fort with Wexford town. This road improved access to the Hook area quite considerably as it involved the bridging of the Owenduff and Corock rivers at the head of Bannow Bay. It later led, with the arrival of the railway at the turn of the century, to the emergence of Wellington Bridge as a new focal point.

In the course of the nineteenth century, a number of settlement developments centred on the construction of both Church of Ireland and Catholic churches. The medieval parish centres were largely abandoned and new parochial structures were put in place. Churches were built at Saltmills on the Colclough estate and at Clonsharragh on the Templemore estate. By contrast, however, the old centres were retained on the Loftus estate, initially by the construction of a new church at Templetown, incorporating the medieval church tower, and later in the century by the restoration of the medieval parish church at Fethard which still serves as a place of worship. As the Penal Laws were relaxed, the building of Catholic churches gathered momentum. Templetown was again chosen as the location for an early barn church and

similar buildings were erected at Poulfur, St Leonards and Ballycullane. During the 1840s, a church was built at Ramsgrange to the design of the renowned architect Augustus Welby Pugin, followed by a convent for the nuns of the Order of St Louis and a monastery for the Christian Brothers. At the end of the century, new churches were erected at Duncannon and Templetown, replacing earlier structures. The contrast between the locations of Poulfur church, hidden in an isolated wooded hollow at a time when the Penal Laws were still on the statute books, and Templetown church, built high on a hill a century later, makes an eloquent comment on intervening social and landscape changes. The introduction of education legislation resulted in the building of national schools in close proximity to the Catholic churches. At Ramsgrange and Ballycullane, other developments, attracted by the church and school, led to the emergence of a characteristic new type of settlement, referred to as a chapel village.

In the period from 1880 to 1920, former tenants were assisted to become owner occupiers. On the Loftus estate, the lands and large mansion, rebuilt in the 1870s, were sold in 1913. The Colclough family remained on until 1959 when the surviving estate was sold to the Land Commission; the abbey, at present being conserved by the Office of Public Works, was handed over to the state. The Templemores, descendants of the Tudor Etchinghams, still occupy part of the Dunbrody lands, and represent the surviving remnants of an estate system whose origins lie in twelfth-century Norman land grants.

The collapse of the estate system affected the area in a number of ways. Many jobs which the estates had provided were lost. This had major social implications, leading to hardship and emigration, a trend already established due to the involvement of the area in the Newfoundland fisheries during the eighteenth and nineteenth centuries. The population of Hook Head has fallen from 526 in 1841 to 132 in 1995. The economy continues to be based on mixed farming, with some fishing and trade in the coastal villages.

The traditional Hook house, constructed of local stone, had two ground-floor rooms, lit by two front windows, with central fire and doorway, sometimes protected by a small porch. Two gable windows lit low loft bedrooms under a slated roof. The early local authority, or 'Land League', labourers' cottages in the district were of similar design but higher, giving more head room on the first floor. Some houses had mud walls and thatched roofs but slate was preferred on this windswept peninsula. Houses on larger farms were typically two-storeyed, slated, stone structures, lit by front windows on both floors. However, there were also smaller, single-storeyed farmhouses, occasionally

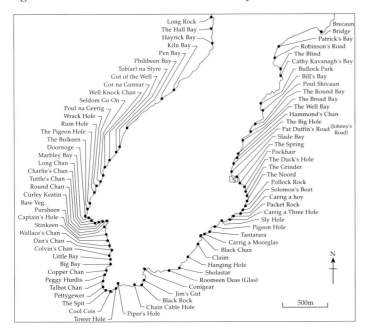

Fig. 20 The former economic and cultural significance of the coast is highlighted by the richness and diversity of its placenames, especially around the point of Hook itself.

BILLY COLFER

Fig. 21 Ballyhack originated as a typical church-and-castle manorial village, on lands granted to the Knights Hospitallers by William Marshal early in the thirteenth century. The Hospitallers were installed to protect Marshal's interests and to provide security on the strategic waterway. Always an important crossing point, Ballyhack is now linked with Passage in county Waterford by a modern car-ferry.

thatched. Traditional farmyards were usually of the courtyard type, consisting of a cobbled, rectangular space surrounded by farm buildings. The farmhouse gable and the outhouses on one side of the yard were located on the roadside boundary in some cases. The gate was hung on solid cylindrical stone piers with conical tops which are still a feature of the south Wexford area. In most instances where improvements have been carried out, the original farmhouse has been upgraded and the courtyard complexes have usually disintegrated, being superseded by buildings suitable to modern agricultural practices.

Construction of the Rosslare-Waterford railway along the northern perimeter of the Hook, with stations at Campile, Ballycullane and Wellington Bridge, strengthened communication with other communities. The significance of the railway for the farming community was highlighted by the establishment of the Shelburne Co-operative at Campile in 1919 and by the setting-up of a sugar-beet depot at Wellington Bridge. For many people, however, the railway had a different significance: it made the trip to the emigrant ship, and a new life, quicker and easier.

The situation at the end of the twentieth century has changed in a number of basic ways for people living in the Hook area. In the 1950s, rural electrification and a public water scheme introduced basic lifestyle improvements with profound long-term implications, including the abandonment of numerous wells and springs which had provided water and social contact for many centuries. Demographic and economic factors have been responsible for the closure of the Garda barracks at Fethard in the 1970s

and the post office at Slade in the 1980s. The small national schools at Loftus Hall and Templetown were closed in the 1960s and amalgamated with a large central school at Poulfur. The Church of Ireland community in Fethard has seen the closure of its national school and the loss of a full-time rector. However, the establishment of a second-level community school at Ramsgrange in the 1970s was of major significance. An increase in private transport, communications and education has removed many barriers as well as developing an awareness of the region's numerous attractions. People are still leaving to find employment, but workers also commute to surrounding towns, aided by the introduction in 1982 of a modern car-ferry plying between Ballyhack and Passage.

Farming has become more intensive, leading to specialisation on individual farms, with some land reclamation and removal of field boundaries. Inshore fishing has also expanded in the fishing villages of Fethard, Slade, Ballyhack and particularly Duncannon. Expanding markets and an increase in the number and size of well-equipped boats have led to increased catches, resulting in a depletion of stocks, particularly of lobster and salmon. However, fishermen are still operating from harbours with limited facilities developed during the last century. The 1990s have seen the introduction of mariculture to Bannow Bay where oysters and mussels are being farmed. With the exception of the traditional activities of agriculture and fishing, there has been no significant employment-generating development, apart from the construction in the 1960s of an oil-fired power station on Great Island.

Because of its maritime location, the Hook has been a popular holiday destination for several centuries. This is illustrated by two advertisements which appeared in *Finn's Leinster Journal* in 1782:

> *To be let during the season, a good house between Loftus Hall and Fethard, within musket shot of a remarkably good strand for bathing.*

> *To be let during the season, or for a longer term if required, two neat lodges in Slade, furnished or unfurnished. N.B. A butcher and baker are engaged to attend twice a week, and a dairyman resides on the spot.*

Writing about Fethard in 1837, Lewis commented:

> *There are numerous comfortable farmhouses and bathing lodges in the parish which is frequented for the benefit of sea-bathing.*

Tourists are attracted to the Hook area, and particularly to the main centres of Fethard-on-Sea and Duncannon, by the many quiet beaches and the scenic peninsular location. The rocky coastline and varied sea-life make Hook Head an ideal destination for scuba-diving clubs in the south-east. Other water sports are catered for by the Outdoor Education Centre established at Shielbaggan in the 1970s. The rocks from Slade to the point of Hook, which at one time provided the locals with a precious supply of fish, are now used extensively by angling clubs and sport fishermen. An undesirable aspect of this has been the numbering of the rocks with paint to facilitate the organisation of angling competitions.

In recent years, tourist interests have reappraised the rich cultural landscape of south-west Wexford as a resource to be exploited in the heritage tourism market, particularly the many monuments and settlement features surviving from the medieval period. Of thirteen national monuments in Wexford, five are located in the south-west; the Cistercian abbeys of Dunbrody and Tintern, Rathumney Hall and the castles of Slade and Ballyhack. Two other

BILLY COLFER

Fig. 23 The vernacular architectural style of any area is developed and sustained by the widespread use of common design features. If the vernacular language is applied to new developments, modern buildings, in the Hook and elsewhere, can blend harmoniously with the traditional landscape, as is demonstrated by this example at Slade, constructed in 1992. Building materials, and the scale, proportions and layout of the buildings echo older traditions.

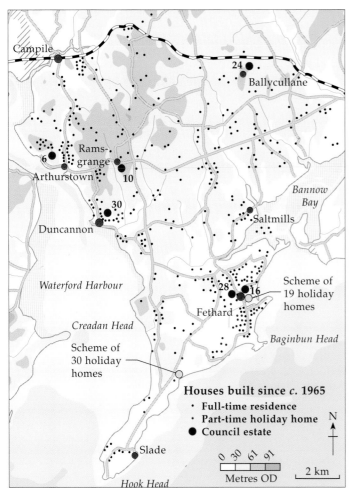

Fig. 22 Houses built in the Hook area since 1965. During the past thirty years, 512 houses have been built in the area. Of these, sixty-five (12.5%) are holiday homes, concentrated mostly in the vicinity of Fethard-on-Sea. A further thirty holiday cottages were recently constructed at Sandeel Bay. Council estates have been located at Fethard, Duncannon, Ballyhack, Ballycullane and Ramsgrange. Few new houses have been constructed on the sensitive landscape of Hook Head.

sites at Duncannon Fort and Fethard Castle are being developed by community groups. Despite their major importance, the remains of Clonmines, at the head of Bannow Bay, have not received any official recognition or status. The possibility of opening up the thirteenth-century tower of Hook as a tourist attraction, subsequent to the automation of the lighthouse in 1996, is currently being considered. If the challenge of conserving, interpreting and presenting these and other heritage features can be responded to with care and imagination, they could become an important ingredient in the economic and social structure of the Hook area. The lack of development in the district can be considered an advantage as it presents an opportunity for a sensitive, restrained approach, respecting the integrity and requirements of both monuments and society. In the Hook, as elsewhere, these monuments exist, not in isolation, but in relation to each other and to the environment. If the interpretation of these heritage features can be presented in a cohesive way, it will lead to a more profound appreciation of the complex origins of the modern landscape.

The impact of relatively restrained tourist activity, originating in the 1960s, has not been excessively intrusive. There are three quite unobtrusive caravan parks, a holiday chalet complex and schemes of well designed holiday homes at Fethard-on-Sea, the main tourism centre, and at Sandeel Bay. Duncannon also has a caravan park beside its blue flag beach and a complex of self-catering apartments. A fifth caravan park is situated overlooking the sea at Houseland. Another scheme of thirty holiday homes has been built in 1995 beside Sandeel Bay on the east coast of the peninsula. A considerable number of houses have been built as holiday homes, particularly in the vicinity of Fethard. Recently there has been a welcome tendency towards restoration, perhaps due to stricter planning requirements for new houses as well as an appreciation of the aesthetic qualities of vernacular buildings. On the point of Hook, ten traditional houses have been restored as holiday accommodation and at least ten other derelict sites would benefit from similar treatment.

During the past thirty years, there has been a marked increase in the construction of dwellings in the district. The County Council, abandoning its previous policy of erecting isolated cottages, has located public housing schemes at Fethard, Duncannon and Ballyhack. The evidence of new private housing is pervasive throughout the area, with concentrations at Duncannon, Fethard and Arthurstown. While sufficient care has not always been taken to design houses in relation to their environment and traditional building practices, most new dwellings, with a few ugly exceptions, blend reasonably well with the landscape. Relatively few new houses have been built on the sensitive point of Hook which is correctly subject to stringent planning requirements.

CONCLUSION

Since the medieval colonisation and organisation of south-west Wexford, settlement and landscape patterns have not been disrupted to any great extent. Isolation and stability allowed traditional practices and values to resist estate development and outside influences: although the region is now much more open and accessible, no significant modern changes have yet been imposed on the cultural and physical landscape of the Hook area. This continuity, combined with the local topography, has created a landscape with a distinctive character. This applies in particular to the narrow, rock-bound point of Hook where the flat, treeless landscape emphasises the prominence of the Tower of Hook, Slade Castle and Loftus Hall. Stone walls and large fields recall estate development and organisation. The estate entrance, still referred to as 'the piers of Portersgate', was also the symbolic limit of the Hook peninsula and people from beyond that point were referred to as 'outsiders' by the natives who preferred to stay inside the 'piers' as far as possible, their sense of identity reinforced by the self-contained nature of the headland. The small fields of Slade and Churchtown, created by repeated subdivision, point to the pressure put on available land by a rising population. Subsequent emigration reduced the community to a quarter of its former level and left a melancholy legacy of ruined houses, still known poignantly by the names of the former occupants.

The distinctive personality of the Hook can be attributed to the many historic influences concentrated in a compact, well-defined landscape. This combination creates a space, dominated by sea, sky and the elements, with a unique quality which is appreciated, subliminally at least, by the inhabitants and by the many visitors who are attracted by the ancient lighthouse, winter storms and peninsular location.

BIBLIOGRAPHY

T. Barry, *The archaeology of medieval Ireland* (London, 1987).

E. St John Brooks (ed.), *Knights' fees in counties Wexford, Carlow and Kilkenny* (Dublin, 1950).

B. Colfer, *The promontory of Hook* (Wexford, 1978).

B. Colfer, 'Anglo-Norman settlement in county Wexford' in K. Whelan (ed.), *Wexford: history and society* (Dublin 1987), pp 65-101.

B. Colfer, *Historic Hook Head* (Slade, 1992).

E. Culleton, *Early man in county Wexford* (Dublin, 1984).

A. Gwynn and R. Hadcock, *Medieval religious houses: Ireland* (London, 1970).

P. Hore, *History of the town and county of Wexford*, 6 vols. (London, 1900-1911).

J. Hurley, *The south Wexford coast* (Kilmore, 1994).

S. Pierce, *Dunbrody Abbey* (Arthurstown, 1994).

R. Simington (ed.), *The Civil Survey, A.D. 1654-56, county of Wexford* (Dublin, 1953).

G. Stout, 'Wexford in prehistory 5000 BC to 300 AD' in Whelan (ed.), *Wexford*, pp 1-39.

K. Whelan (ed.), *Tintern Abbey, county Wexford* (Saltmills, 1993).

N. White (ed.), *Extents of Irish monastic possessions 1540-41* (Dublin, 1943).

THE LECALE PENINSULA, COUNTY DOWN

Lecale peninsula is a wedge-shaped lowland, of 180 km², located on the low-lying south-east coast of county Down, 32 km south of Belfast. To the east and south, it is bounded by the Irish Sea, to the north by Strangford Lough, and to the west by a broad belt of marshes, once the tidal estuaries of the Quoile and Blackstaff rivers. Their converging courses made Lecale virtually an island. The ancient name of the peninsula was Magh-Inis, the insular plain; among older inhabitants, it is still known as 'Isle-Lecale'. Insularity, fertile soil and coastal location on the north-eastern margin of the Irish Sea have shaped the area's distinctive history, providing a secure base and livelihood to native and sea-borne colonist alike. The landscape carries the imprint of five millennia of habitation, with a particularly rich legacy from the medieval Normans and the improving landlords of the eighteenth century.

THE PHYSICAL LANDSCAPE

As elsewhere in county Down, the Lecale bedrock consists of silurian slates or shales, outcropping as jagged reefs and subdued cliffs along the rocky eastern shore. Inland, this surface is remarkably uniform, rarely rising above 60m except in the north-east, where Slieve Patrick and Castlemahon Mountain reach heights of 125m and 128m respectively. These two summits are miniature mountains: their bare rock and shallow soils blaze with golden gorse in spring and early summer. From these high points, a low ridge runs south-west, its alignment following the trend-line of Caledonian folding in the silurian strata: it may be caused by later igneous intrusions, similar to those which form the Newry granites to the south-west.

Glaciation diversified this monotonous silurian landscape, mantling the rock surface with thick deposits of boulder-clay, deepening valleys and eventually creating

•Fig. 1 This view from Rathmullan looks towards Dundrum Bay over the fertile farmlands of Lecale. Just beyond the church spire in the middle distance, a medieval motte indicates the attraction of this region to the Normans.

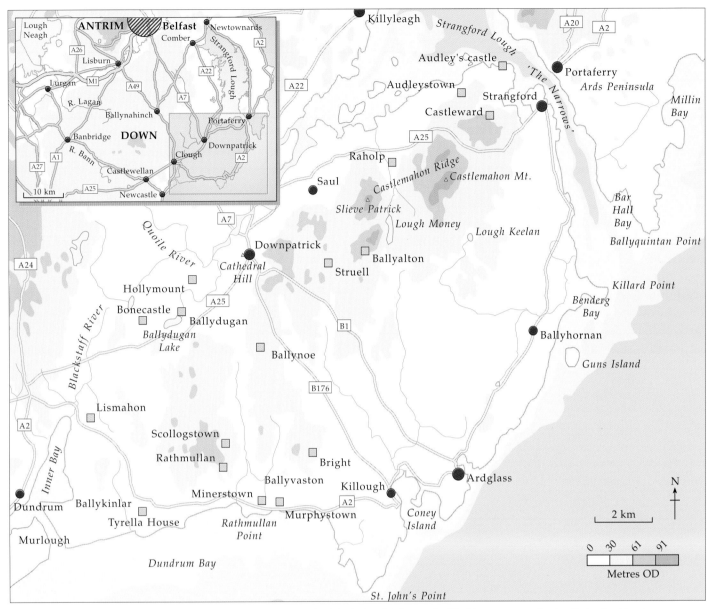

Fig. 2 The Lecale lowland in south-east Down was practically an island ('Isle-Lecale') for much of its history, preserving its distinctive identity.

the inland sea which made Lecale an island in post-glacial times. To the north and west of the Castlemahon ridge, the glacial drift has been moulded into drumlins, steep-sided in the Quoile and Blackstaff marshes, and in the distinctive islands of Strangford Lough; to the south and east, they are lower and more subdued, and almost non-existent along the Irish Sea coast.

Glacial action was also responsible for the two north-south valleys which strike across the grain of the Caledonian folding. The deep trench which forms the narrow entrance to Strangford Lough is the most notice-able. The second valley lies to the west of Castlemahon Mountain; its northern end is occupied by Lough Money, its southern widens into an extensive marshland, under-lain by sand or marine clays, entering the Irish Sea

through land-locked Killough Bay. This valley may well be an overflow channel from an enlarged Strangford Lough of glacial times, its broad trench now occupied by shrunken, sluggish streams.

Post-glacial changes in sea level have also left their mark upon the coast, notably in the raised beaches at Ardglass Harbour and Killard Point, and in the shallow caves cut into the boulder clay on both sides of Killough Bay. This rocky eastern coast has many creeks and inlets, fringed by fine sandy beaches at Ballyhornan and Benderg, and with good natural harbours at Strangford, Ardglass and Killough. Coastal diversity here sharply contrasts with the gently-shelving shoreline of Dundrum Bay, whose sandy beaches are interspersed with patches of shingle and boulders. Here, glacial deposition has created a low

R.H. BUCHANAN

Fig. 3 Drumlin topography is exceptionally well developed on the lowlands around Bonecastle, wedged between the Quoile river and Dundrum Bay.

R.H. BUCHANAN

Fig. 4 'The Narrows', at the entrance to Strangford Lough from the Irish Sea. This view looks north from Bar Hall Bay in the Ards peninsula, with Strangford village and the demesne of Castleward visible in Lecale.

shoreline 16 km in length, from St John's Point in the east to the foot of the Mourne Mountains at Newcastle in the west. The only break occurs between the sand-dune systems of Ballykinlar and Dundrum, where the Blackstaff river enters the Irish Sea through Dundrum's inner bay. Now an insignificant stream, the Blackstaff was a broad river in immediate post-glacial times, its estuary stretching far inland and linking eastward to the Quoile to form a shallow inland sea. At that time, Lecale really was an island: as late as the sixteenth century, the Quoile and Blackstaff estuaries were still tidal, with consequences described by an English soldier, Sir Thomas Cusack, who came here in 1552:

> *The next country to the same eastward is Lacaille. . . which is a handsome plain and champaign country of ten miles long and five miles breadth, without any wood growing thereon. The sea doth ebb and flow round that country so as in full water no man may enter therein upon dry land – but in one way which is less than two miles in length.*

Prehistoric Occupation

The tidal reaches of the Quoile and Blackstaff rivers with their extensive mudflats and estuarine marshes are rich habitats for wildlife, which provided a secure, year-long food supply for the mesolithic people who first colonised Ireland. Their artefacts and middens are found at several sites around the Lough shores, whence there was easy access to a plentiful supply of fish and other marine life. Apart from stray finds, notably a stone club found at St John's Point, no settlement sites have yet been identified within Lecale. In contrast, evidence of neolithic occupation is much more common, from summer campsites in the

sand-dunes at Murlough on Dundrum Bay, to rock scribings and megaliths, of which the two outstanding examples are the court-cairns at Ballyalton and Audleystown. These major sites are located on the shallow, well-drained and fertile soils of north-east Lecale, which, with a lighter forest cover, were well-suited to neolithic farming. Audleystown, like the similar cairn at Millin Bay nearby in the Ards, is located near the sea, and it is tempting to see this site as a landfall for immigrants from across the Irish Sea. Grave goods found at these two excavated sites, and polished stone axes from the factory at Tievebulliagh in county

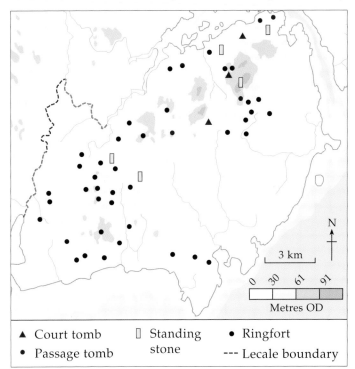

| ▲ Court tomb | ▯ Standing stone | ● Ringfort |
| ● Passage tomb | | --- Lecale boundary |

Fig. 5 The distribution of ancient monuments in Lecale suggests that early farmers preferred freely draining slopes with easily worked shallow soils to the heavier lowland clays.

R.H. BUCHANAN

Fig. 6 Loughmoney portal tomb in the parish of Saul is one of the distinctive archaeological sites of Lecale.

Antrim, recovered on Downpatrick's Cathedral Hill, point to the benefits of this coastal location for seaborne travel and trade, a continuing feature of its later history. The stone circle at Ballynoe was also constructed in the late Neolithic, a type of monument not common in Ulster, and in this case resembling monuments in Cumbria.

Ballynoe was still in use when knowledge of bronze-making came to Ireland; Bronze Age people built houses, circular in plan, on the Quoile shore near what is now Church Street in Downpatrick. This is the earliest habitation site known in Lecale, though similar settlements may yet be identified in the north-eastern hills, where Bronze Age round-cairns are found near the neolithic megaliths. The most significant find from this period is the gold hoard from the graveyard on the Cathedral Hill in 1954, a further indication of the attraction of the drumlin islands for early settlement. Excavations of the low earthwork which encircles the Cathedral Hill suggested that this was a hill-fort of late Bronze Age date, defended by an elaborate system of timber ramparts and deep ditches, repaired and strengthened over a long period. More recent work, downslope of the earlier excavation, found no evidence of these prehistoric defenses but instead Early Christian and medieval structures, artifacts and burials. Undoubtedly, the Cathedral Hill and the earthwork on the adjoining drumlin (known locally as 'The Mount') became the most important settlements in Lecale from the Early Christian period, as the political capital of the local ruling family, and the monastery traditionally associated with St Patrick.

EARLY CHRISTIAN AND NORMAN PERIODS

Patrick's association with Lecale is remembered in several places, but especially at the monastic sites of Raholp and Saul, near the mouth of the River Slaney where the saint reputedly landed and where he established his first church. Nearby are the holy wells and bath complex at Struell,

where a major pattern was held until the late eighteenth century; the only surviving ecclesiastical building from this period is the little church at St John's Point, dated to the late tenth/early eleventh century. Secular settlements are represented by ringforts, which are less common here than in the adjoining districts of mainland county Down. Their absence may indicate a low population density, but this seems unlikely, given the good quality soil and long-established rural communities; indeed, the *Annals of the Four Masters* states quite explicitly 'Magh Inis in Ulidia was cleared of wood'. A more likely explanation is that ringforts were not the only forms of settlement, and that many farmers lived in unenclosed farmsteads which have left no visible trace in the present landscape.

Lecale's insularity, its many creeks and natural harbours, and its location on the north-western corner of the Irish Sea made the peninsula attractive as a landfall and refuge for the missionaries, scholars and craftsmen who travelled widely along the western seaways in the service of the early church. These same qualities also drew Vikings to its shores, although their legacy is now only apparent in placenames such as Strangford and Gun's island, rather than in settlements. The Normans, pushing north from Dublin in 1177, left a more durable legacy. They established ports at Ardglass and probably at Strangford; built the walled town of Downpatrick which became the principal urban centre; and established mottes, one on each of their newly formed manors. These were occasionally erected on top of existing ringforts, as at Rathmullan, a symbol of the replacement of native land-holder by Norman lord. Lecale quickly became the core of the

NOEL C. MITCHEL

Fig. 7 The Cathedral Hill in Downpatrick is traditionally considered to be the burial place of St Patrick and the site of the monastic church, built initially by St Malachy, and subsequently occupied by de Courcy's Benedictine Abbey. In this photograph, 'The Mount' is to the left – a possible tribal centre of the first millennium AD, later partially incorporated into a motte and bailey. Beyond lies the River Quoile.

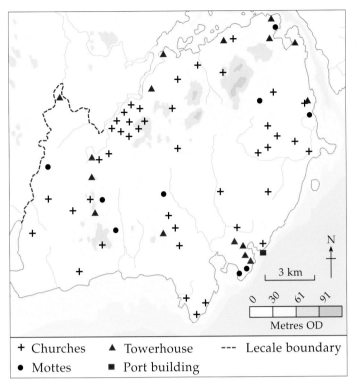

C.F.S. NEWMAN

Fig. 9 Audley's castle is a fifteenth-century towerhouse which retains the name of an earlier owner, John Audley. The attached bawn is now reduced virtually to its foundations. The towerhouse was built on an elevated site overlooking a sheltered bay at the entrance to Strangford Lough, north of Strangford village.

Key:

+ Churches   ▲ Towerhouse   --- Lecale boundary

● Mottes   ■ Port building

Fig. 8 Medieval sites, in contrast to prehistoric settlement, show a greater preference for the fertile lowlands, capable of sustaining arable production.

Norman colony in Ulster, a bridge-head for expansion north into Antrim, and a refuge, safe behind the encircling marshes, when Norman political power waned irretrievably in the fourteenth and fifteenth centuries.

The characteristic settlements of the Norman colonisation of Ireland can be found in Lecale. However, with the exception of simple rectangular keeps built on the mottes at Clough and Greencastle, no major stone castle was built. The nearest was at Dundrum, a strongly-fortified military castle held by the Crown, commanding the land-entry to Lecale across the Blackstaff river and the inner bay. Timber-frame hall dwellings may have been built on the Lecale manors: one was excavated at Lismahon in 1958, on property held by Christ Church in Dublin. With the less settled political conditions of the fifteenth century, stone-built towerhouses were constructed on nearly every manor in Lecale: today, they form the largest concentration of this settlement type in Ulster. Ardglass, for example, has several towerhouses within the compass of the medieval town, and a fine range of defended warehouses on its quay, a visible reminder of the extensive trade carried out by wealthy local merchants with ports in Ireland, northern England and the Isle of Man, and with continental Europe. Abbeys built by the Normans and staffed by monks from north-west England survive at Inch and at Downpatrick, where the cathedral stands on the site of the Benedictine Abbey and incorporates some of its fabric.

NEW LANDOWNERS

Following the Dissolution, the extensive lands of the rich Abbey of Down passed eventually into the hands of the Cromwells, a west-of-England family who became landowners of Downpatrick. In the aftermath of the 1641 rebellion, the Old English landowners, descendants of the Normans, lost their estates, the exception being the manors of Ardglass and Strangford, the property of the well-connected Earls of Kildare. By the end of the seventeenth century, a new generation of English landowners had taken possession of Lecale, the most prominent being the Southwells, inheritors through marriage of the Manor of Down; and the Wards, a Cheshire family who came to Ireland in the service of the Elizabethan army. In their wake came immigrants from Britain, families like Carson and Napier from Scotland and Press, Seeds and Swail from England. Their descendants still live here, forming small congregations of Presbyterians and Anglicans. However, there was no formal plantation in Lecale: the Old English and Irish farming families remained on their ancestral lands and this conferred a continuity on Lecale which was rare elsewhere in Ulster.

As a result, Lecale was little affected by the political unrest and civil strife that recurred at intervals during the seventeenth century. By the early 1700s, it embarked on unprecedented economic development under the leadership of the Southwells and the Wards, families which produced several notable improvers and entrepreneurs. Downpatrick was largely rebuilt, extended and provided with several major public buildings, of which the Southwell Charity, opened in 1733, is an outstanding example. In 1745, Edward Southwell erected flood-gates across the Quoile, inaugurating drainage schemes and

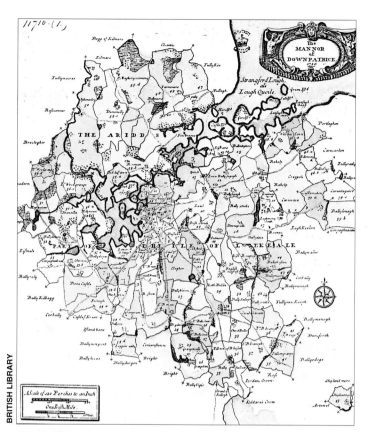

Fig. 10 This early map of the manor of Downpatrick in 1710 shows a well settled area, laid out in townlands, with many clachans. It also shows clearly the quasi-insular nature of 'The Isle of Lecale' – known in Irish as Magh-Inis, the insular plain.

Fig. 11 Killough was planned and developed by its landlords, the Wards, in the early eighteenth century. This view shows the main axis, Castle Street, laid out parallel to the shoreline on the shallow but sheltered bay. To the right is the Church of Ireland, facing the tree-lined square; to the left is the harbour, with its warehouse-lined quay. The Shiel's almshouses are the buildings in the trees behind the town and beyond is Dundrum Bay.

reclaiming an extensive area of former tidal marshes. Both he and his successors stimulated husbandry on their estates, encouraging hedged enclosures on farms through the provision of longer leases. The Ward property, extending from Castleward demesne in the north to the shores of Dundrum Bay, profited from the business acumen and management skills of Michael Ward, Judge of the King's Bench in Dublin and a notable agricultural improver. He planned and developed a new town at Killough in the l730s and 1740s, building the harbour and quays, warehouses, mills and a salt pan, and traded with Britain, using his own vessels. He promoted the use of locally available marl as a fertiliser among his tenants, and by skillfully lobbying for the provision of government subsidies for Irish-grown wheat, he established a profitable new arable economy based on the export of wheat and barley to Dublin and to the ports of north-west England.

The many water and wind mills still visible on the Ward estate, the fine houses built by local merchants and shipowners in Killough and Downpatrick, and the many comfortable farmhouses are testimony to the agricultural prosperity which benefited farmer and landowner alike and which lasted until the end of the Napoleonic wars in 1815. With the subsequent collapse of the lucrative grain

trade, Killough entered a long period of decline as a port but Ardglass revived under its first resident owner, a Scotsman, William Ogilvie, who acquired the derelict medieval port following his marriage to Emily, Dowager Duchess of Leicester and Countess of Kildare. Ogilvie rebuilt the harbour, added quays and new streets and promoted new businesses, laying the foundations of a fishing industry which by the end of the nineteenth century had made Ardglass the premier herring port in the northern Irish Sea.

Few estate maps survive to document the transformation which occurred in the eighteenth century. An urban survey of 1710 shows Downpatrick at the beginning of its

Fig. 12 Downpatrick is the 'capital' of Lecale. The main thoroughfare of the medieval town, English Street, runs from the centre towards the cathedral, high on its wooded hill above the marshes. English Street has several fine eighteenth-century houses, the Southwell school and almshouses, the county court house and gaol. At the town centre, with its nineteenth-century assembly rooms, two nineteenth-century streets, Market Street and Church Street, run to the left and right of the photograph respectively. Irish Street, the old road to Dublin, and Scotch Street are in the foreground.

Fig. 13 Ardglass, the main port of Lecale in the medieval period with defended warehouses and towerhouses, revived in the nineteenth century to become an important fishing port. This photograph shows Ardglass Castle, three towerhouses, King's Castle (a nineteenth-century conversion of a former towerhouse) and the medieval church of St Nicholas.

expansion under the Southwells, and a small-scale estate map from 1729 indicates the form and pattern of settlement. Judging from these documents, leases and a 1768 survey of the parish of Bright on the Ardglass estate, the rural landscape of Lecale closely resembled the current one, with its hedged fields, farmsteads and close-knit pattern of roads and laneways. The principal difference is that many farmsteads were then grouped in small clusters, known locally as 'towns', but termed clachans in the geographical literature. Across much of northern and western Ireland, clachans were associated with open-field farming by groups of related families holding and working land in common, but it is by no means certain that this was the case in eighteenth-century Lecale: documentary proof is lacking. In two locations, however, at Ballyvaston on Dundrum Bay and Sheeplands near Ardglass, open-fields survived into the twentieth century, with the farmers holding a joint lease and living in clachans.

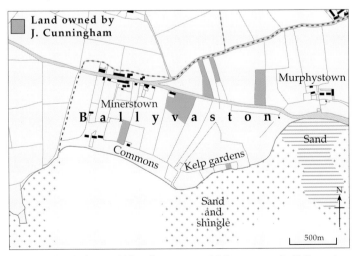

Fig. 14 The clachans of Murphystown and Minerstown, in Ballyvaston townland, with their open-field systems which survived into the twentieth century.

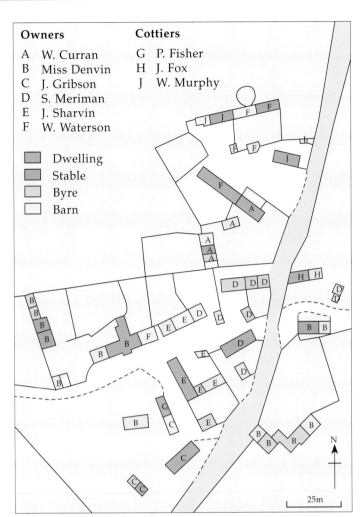

Fig. 15 The clachan of Scollogstown – a tightly packed cluster of dwellings inhabited by farmers and cottiers in 1834 – is typical of a tillage area.

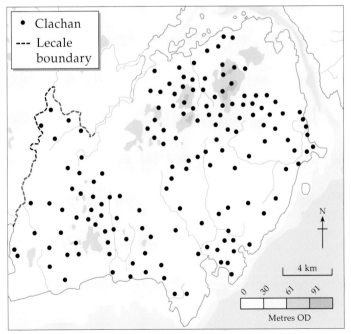

Fig. 16 In 1834, the first edition Ordnance Survey maps allow the distribution of clachans in Lecale to be mapped. They were the dominant settlement form over large areas of the barony.

R.H. BUCHANAN

Fig. 17 A corbelled pig sty at Murphystown – one of only two pig sties ever listed as historic monuments.

POPULATION DECLINE AND LANDSCAPE CHANGE

Many of the clachans depicted on the 1729 estate map had increased in size by 1834 when the first edition of the Ordnance Survey was published; others had contracted, sometimes to a single farmstead. This trend became more pronounced as population fell from its 1841 peak of 25,723 to its 'lowest level of 10,800 in 1937. This steady decline followed the loss of agriculture and textile employment, an economic decline of greater consequence than the Great Famine, from whose consequences Lecale was well cushioned. The landscape legacy of this decline is still visible, in ruined dwellings, overgrown fields and spade ridges faintly etched on hillsides which have long since been abandoned to pasture. But there have also been many improvements. With the transition from tenancy to owner occupancy following the Land Acts of the late nineteenth century, many farmsteads were 'raised', from one storey to two, the new houses resplendent with 'Bangor-blue' slate roofs, sash windows, and chimneys of yellow brick, brought by rail to local builders.

The prosperity of farming after World War II, boosted by membership of the EEC, has encouraged a great rebuilding in the second half of the twentieth century, with larger holdings, new techniques and improved technology. The outbuildings of a single farm now sprawl across as large an area as the clachan sites which some of them occupy. While fewer jobs are available on the farm, cars make it possible to commute to Downpatrick or Belfast, and many farmers' children prefer to build new houses near their parental homes rather than live in the town or city. Public housing has also contributed a new element to the settlement pattern, initially as farm labourers' cottages located near their employers' farm, built under the 1883 Act. After World War II, housing provided by local councils and the Northern Ireland Housing

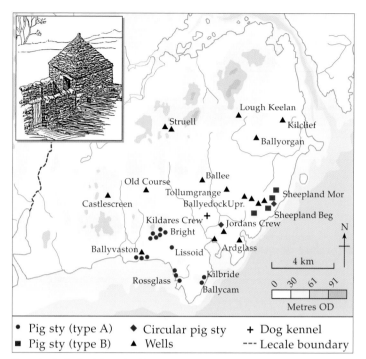

Fig. 18 Corbelled farm buildings, built mostly in the late eighteenth and early nineteenth centuries, are distinctive to Lecale. The inset shows one of the many corbelled structures in Bright townland.

Executive were grouped in clusters of ten or more dwellings, similar in size to the clachans of earlier times, but unlike them planned in regular alignments along roads where services were available.

CONSERVING LANDSCAPE AND ENVIRONMENT

Five thousand years of human habitation have left many marks upon the Lecale landscape: the prehistoric megalithic tombs and stone circles, the Early Christian churches and ringforts, the Norman mottes, towerhouses and abbeys. These relict features are mostly scheduled for protection under legislation and many are maintained by the state agency, the Historic Monuments and Buildings Branch of the Department of the Environment for Northern Ireland. The Branch sets high standards for the maintenance of monuments in its care, while its professional officers added greatly to knowledge of the district's prehistory during the 1950s and 1960s , through excavation undertaken as part of the pioneering archaeological survey of county Down.

Preservation of historic buildings is also undertaken by a non-governmental body, the National Trust for Places of Historic Interest or Natural Beauty. In 1953, following the death of the sixth Viscount Bangor, for example, the eighteenth-century mansion and demesne of Castleward, ancestral home of the Wards, one of Lecale's most influential families, came under the Trust's control. Its furnishings, paintings and memorabilia form an invaluable microcosm of Lecale's more recent history. The farmyard preserves a

ALAN JOHNSTON

Fig. 19 Castleward on the edge of Strangford Bay was the ancestral residence of the Wards, Elizabethan settlers who became the major landowners in Lecale. An early seventeenth-century towerhouse survives along with the eighteenth-century mansion. This photograph shows the back entrance to Castleward, at high tide.

working cornmill and sawmill, as well as the towerhouse residence of the first Wards to settle here at the end of the sixteenth century.

Other historic elements survive in the present landscape more by accident than by design. The abrupt agricultural transformation through new farming techniques and technologies has had a major impact, not least through ditch and hedgerow removal and field enlargement. Yet much of the past remains intact, for this modernisation has taken place largely within the inherited framework of fields and property boundaries. For example, open field strips still survive at Ballyvaston, though no longer in multiple ownership; in the Demesne of Down, the field pattern laid out by the Southwells early in the eighteenth century is still visible, despite suburban encroachment from Downpatrick; at Bright, a newly designed golf course sits within a field pattern which has changed little from that depicted on a survey of 1768. Older farm-buildings have survived less well, because they no longer meet modern needs and standards. They have been replaced by wide-span sheds whose ungainly size and industrial materials bear more resemblance to miniature factories than traditional farm yards. Two examples of Lecale's most distinctive farm-buildings have been preserved, the small stone-built corbelled roof pigsties which were unique to the peninsula.

In the countryside, few vernacular dwellings survived the major attempts by state bodies to improve housing standards and the increasing prosperity of the rural community since World War II. No examples of the distinctive local stapple thatch technique now survive in lived-in dwellings, and the urban-styled bungalow is ubiquitous. Planning legislation may have inhibited new

building, especially along the coast, designated as an Area of Outstanding Natural Beauty, but it has not been notably restrained elsewhere. As a settlement form, the clachan has all but disintegrated, and new settlement displays a linear pattern, individual houses strung like beads along roads, especially where water mains have been laid. The coastal villages have experienced significant growth in the post-war period, Ardglass in particular having several suburban accretions of public and private housing along its main approaches. The statutory listing of historic buildings and private houses has contributed to the preservation of individual properties in Killough and Strangford, and in English and Irish Streets in Downpatrick. Urban conservation areas (statutory designations intended to preserve historic streetscapes) have worked tolerably well in the villages, although schemes intended to enhance their amenities and visual appearance have been implemented only slowly. The historic core of Downpatrick is also a conservation area, and English Street in particular has benefited from work on its public buildings, the Southwell School, Cathedral, County Court House, the old gaol (now the Down County Museum), and several notable private dwellings. But not all the historic townscape has been preserved: a new road, scheduled to begin in 1996, will largely destroy the medieval pattern of street and building lots of Lower Scotch and Saul Streets, just outside the medieval walls.

Conservation of the natural environment has been more successful under existing legislation and the rich natural habitats of the peninsula are protected under a

ALAN JOHNSTON

Fig. 20 Ballydugan Mill. Arable farming has long traditions on the dry coastal lowlands of county Down. In the eighteenth century, Down was one of the main 'corn counties' whose produce was exported to Dublin and to north-west England. This imposing, six-storey flour mill was built at Ballydugan near Downpatrick in 1792 to grind wheat grown in the Lecale district. The mill was driven by water from Ballydugan lake and by a steam engine with a brick stack. Abandoned for many years, the impressive building is currently under renovation.

DOWN COUNTY MUSEUM

ALAN JOHNSTON

Fig. 21 The late eighteenth-century county gaol in Downpatrick has been restored and now houses the County Museum.

Fig. 22 Farmland in northern Lecale. In the background are drowned drumlins in the Quoile estuary. Strangford Lough is of international significance for its wildlife, especially breeding seabirds, summer migrants and wintering wildfowl. Strangford is only the second Marine Nature Reserve to be designated within the United Kingdom.

variety of designations. The foreshore, several bays and islands on Strangford Lough have been protected since 1966 by the National Trust under its wildfowl scheme. Since then, various steps have been taken to ensure the conservation of the Lough's wintering wildfowl and summer migrants, as well as the salt marsh vegetation and unique marine life. Various sections of the Lough shore are designated as Areas of Special Scientific Interest and Nature Reserves, culminating in 1995 with the designation of a Marine Nature Reserve covering the Lough, and its immediate approaches from Killard and Ballyquinton Points. Other nature reserves include the beaches and banks at Killard, with their rich flora; the sand-dune systems at Murlough, owned by the National

Trust and just outside the peninsula on Dundrum inner bay; the woodlands at Hollymount on the edge of the Quoile marshes; and the Quoile Pondage, created following the erection of a tidal barrage at Castle Island in 1957. The slow desalination of this former tidal estuary and marshland afforded a welcome opportunity to study the plant succession from salt-tolerant to fresh-water species, creating new habitats for wildfowl. The barrage and related drainage schemes finally terminated Lecale's status as a tidal island, the main feature of its natural environment which has had such a profound influence on its human history and landscape.

BIBLIOGRAPHY

R. Buchanan, 'Corbelled structures in Lecale, county Down' in *Ulster Journal of Archaeology*, xix (1956), pp 92-113.

R. Buchanan, The barony of Lecale: a study in regional personality, unpublished PhD thesis, The Queen's University of Belfast, 1958.

R. Buchanan, 'Stapple thatch' in *Ulster Folklife*, iii (1957), pp 19-28.

R. Buchanan, 'Common fields and enclosure: an eighteenth-century example from county Down' in *Ulster Folklife*, xv-xvi (1970), pp 99-117.

J. Frey (ed.), *Lecale: a study in local history* (Belfast, 1970).

E. Green, *The industrial archaeology of county Down* (Belfast, 1963).

W. Harris, *The ancient and present state of the county of Down* (Dublin, 1744).

E. Jope (ed.), *An archaeological survey of county Down* (Belfast, 1966).

T. McNeill, *Anglo-Norman Ulster* (Edinburgh, 1980).

J. Mallory and T. McNeill, *The archaeology of Ulster* (Belfast, 1991).

E. Parkinson, *The city of Downe* (Belfast, 1928).

V. Proudfoot, Settlement and economy in county Down from the late Bronze Age to the Anglo-Norman invasion, unpublished PhD thesis, The Queen's University of Belfast, 1957.

J. Stevenson, *Two centuries of life in county Down* (Belfast, 1920).

THE BURREN, COUNTY CLARE

The Burren plateau of north-west county Clare is the finest example of a karstic landscape in Ireland, with a full assemblage of the curious landforms and subterranean drainage systems that characterise such limestone terrains. However, the internationally recognised significance of the Burren owes more to its remarkable flora and rich archaeological heritage. The area preserves a complex record of human interaction with the karstic environment from prehistory onwards. From the perspective of their inhabitants, karstic environments throughout the world are characterised by common problems – a lack of water and soil resources, a difficult and fragmented topography – which tend to elicit similar cultural responses.

The sharp edges to the Burren reinforce its distinctive character – the Atlantic to the west, the damp Namurian landscapes to the south, and the Galway lowlands to the north and east. Although often described as a natural landscape, the Burren has been profoundly influenced by human activities. Early farmers, for example, removed the natural woodland cover, thus inducing soil erosion and enlarging the exposure of the underlying limestone. Human impact on the landscape has fluctuated with changing land use and settlement intensity. Contemporary pressures on the environment are particularly severe; despite a contracting population, land reclamation and tourism developments threaten this unique landscape.

Fig. 1 In this recent satellite image, the extensive areas of bare rocks or of patchy soil cover (red on the image) that characterise the Burren are very apparent. To the east of the Burren proper, the low-lying terrain between Kinvarra, Gort and Corofin also exhibit large areas of rock. The major fracture (joint) trends in the limestone rock orientated from north to south can be seen on the uplands. Further east and south, the obvious 'grain' of the topography, north north-east to south south-west and then east to west, is a reflection of the orientation of deposits laid down by glacial ice which moved across this area from the north-east 25,000 to 17,000 years ago.

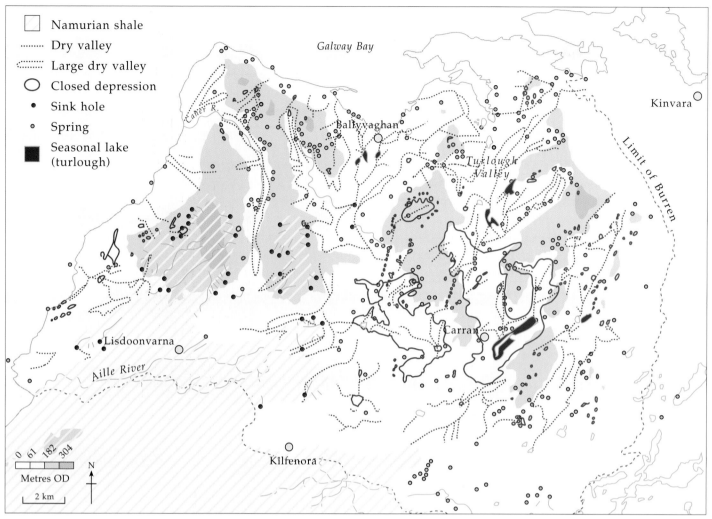

Namurian shale
.... Dry valley
.... Large dry valley
◯ Closed depression
• Sink hole
◦ Spring
■ Seasonal lake (turlough)

Galway Bay

Kinvara

Caher R.

Ballyvaghan

Turlough Valley

Limit of Burren

Lisdoonvarna

Carran

Aille River

0 61 182 304
Metres OD
N
2 km

Kilfenora

Fig. 2 Geology and landforms. The Burren is developed in the uppermost 500m of the Carboniferous strata. The younger shales and sandstones which overlie them in west Clare project into the limestone plateau (Slieve Elva and Knockauns mountains) or form islands of boggy, acid shale country surrounded by the freely draining alkaline limestone (Poulacapple Hill). The karst geology also creates distinctive landforms, including dolines and poljes.

THE GEOLOGICAL BASIS OF THE LANDSCAPE

The Burren is bounded to the west and north by the Atlantic Ocean and Galway Bay respectively. Its southern edge may be defined geologically as the southern extremity of the limestone outcrop where it passes beneath younger rocks of Namurian age. This approximates to a line from Corofin through Kilfenora and Lisdoonvarna to the coast at Doolin. An arbitrary eastern limit to the Burren might be the foot of the scarp at *c.* 60m altitude which extends from Corranroo Bay in the north to Kilnaboy in the south-east. Thus defined, the region encompasses 360 km² and forms a gently inclined plateau at 200-300m in the north and 100-150m in the south, bounded by steep scarps on all but the southern flank. Only isolated summit areas exceed 300m, peaking in the shale-capped Slieve Elva at 345m. A further 200 km² of lowland to the east of the plateau bears many resemblances to the upland Burren in geology, hydrology and ecology whilst the Aran islands are essentially a western extension of the main Burren.

DAVID DREW

Fig. 3 The northern escarpment of the Burren to the east of Ballyvaghan. The great expanses of bare rock and the relatively smooth slopes are the result of intense erosion of loose rocks and other debris by glacial ice which crossed Galway Bay (background) and then over-rode the Burren plateau. Parallel to the direction of ice movement, the effects of glacial erosion have emphasised pre-existing landforms such as the cliffs and terraces and, in the centre of the photograph, the col that separates the two mountains.

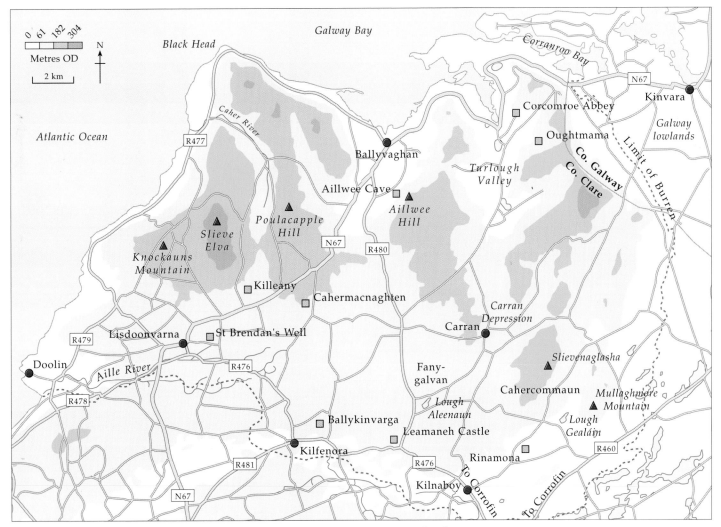

Fig. 4 The Burren, county Clare, showing relief, settlements and other locations mentioned in the text.

While rocks form the skeleton of any landscape, the very bones are visible in the Burren. At least 60% of the area is bare rock or rocky pasture. Accordingly, structural differences in the limestone are often manifested in particular landforms or other landscape features. For example, the hills overlooking Galway Bay rise in dramatic tiers of cliffs and terraces where horizontal lines of weakness in the rock have been exploited by erosive groundwaters and the loosened rock has been subsequently scraped away by glaciers. Below these terraces, massive, unfractured limestones form smooth slopes: above them, the limestones have crumbled more readily, allowing a shallow soil cover to develop – the winterage pastures of the Burren. These uppermost limestones of the plateau are interbedded with thin chert layers – a siliceous rock which does not dissolve in water and prevents rainwater percolating downwards through the limestone fissures. Numerous small springs occur where these chert bands outcrop, the water sinking underground again within a short distance: these provide the only sources of water for stock on the otherwise waterless karst.

In the south-eastern Burren, the rocks have been folded and fractured by earth movements and each distortion of the strata is reflected in the landscape: the single folds (monoclines) near Rinamona form asymmetric valleys while symmetrical folds are exposed at Mullaghmore.

The effects of the ice ages on the Burren were mainly erosive, removing the upper layers of partly weathered rock and deepening valleys and hollows, particularly where they paralleled the direction of ice movement – from the north-east during the final glaciation. However, glacial deposits were laid down in the larger valleys and hollows, facilitating the development of deeper soils. These now form green islands of agriculture such as the Ballyvaghan and Turlough valleys in the northern Burren and the Carron depression in the central plateau.

THE LANDFORMS

The landscape of the Burren seems a stony chaos to the casual observer; the ubiquitous river valleys of Ireland with their attendant slopes are largely absent, despite

ORDNANCE SURVEY

Fig. 5 Mullaghmore mountain in the extreme south-east of the Burren. Here, the limestones have been distorted by earth movements into a series of folds and the topography faithfully reflects the underlying rock structures. Mullaghmore is developed in a downfold (syncline). At the foot of the mountain is Lough Gealáin – part turlough and part permanent lake. In dry weather the lake contracts to a small, water-filled hollow some 14m deep as in the photograph. In wet conditions, however, the lake is filled by water from springs and extends over the surrounding lighter coloured grassland.

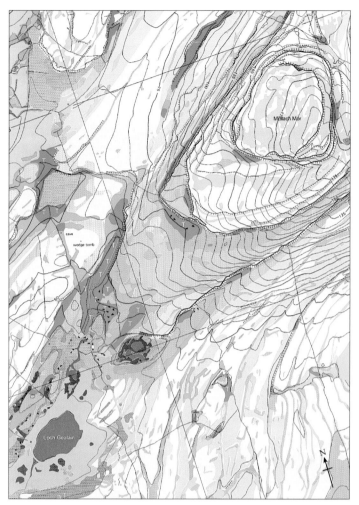

Fig. 6 A habitat map of Mullaghmore by R. Moles and I. Travers showing the area depicted in the preceding illustration. Lough Gealáin is apparent on both with its minimum and maximum extent. The extreme range of environments encompassed within this small area includes the vegetationless areas (white and grey) of bare rock, sward (yellow and light green), and reed and sedge dominated wetlands (brown) around the lough. The markedly strip-like form of some of the vegetation types (orientated north north-east to south south-west) is a reflection of the accumulation of soil and of shelter in the series of parallel trenches formed by folding. Small enclosed depressions (dolines) similarly form vegetational 'islands' amidst the pavements. The line of tall scrub and trees (dark green) which crosses the lowland and then runs over the western shoulder of Mullaghmore is unusual in its orientation. This is because the linear declivity in which the richer vegetation is established occupies a broad mineral vein with the north/south orientation typical of such veins in the Burren.

annual rainfall of more than 1500mm. Instead of forming rivers, the rain is soaked down by countless fissures: such fragments of valleys, or more commonly gorges, that do exist have no streams and seem to lead nowhere. Only at the junction of the limestones and the impermeable shale rocks, around Slieve Elva, for example, are there valleys containing streams. Where these streams cross from the shales to the limestones, they disappear underground at swallow holes, emerging from springs such as those at Killeany and St Brendan's Well near Lisdoonvarna. Away from the limestone, the rain water has dissolved the rock to form enclosed basins which act as funnels, directing the water into the subterranean drainage systems. Some of these basins are a few metres in depth and width, but others, for example the enclosed depression (*polje*) in which the settlement of Carron is located, are several square kilometres in extent and tens of metres in depth. The river systems of the Burren lie underground, channelled in the cave systems that carry water to the springs. Ancient subterranean streamways, now fossil, such as Aillwee cave near Ballyvaghan, may be preserved when the water excavates new routes through the rock.

The limestone also has a landscape in miniature etched into exposed slabs of rock. The bare surfaces (pavements)

are fretted with hollows and channels where acidic rainwater has selectively dissolved the rock. An extreme example of these micro landforms occurs on the coast in the zone between high and low tide. Here the limestone has been dissolved into a myriad of small pits, each with its own flora and fauna, which mimic the morphology of the macro landscape.

THE BURREN FLORA

From above, the upland Burren appears to be largely composed of bare rock. This bare world disappears under a closer scrutiny, for cloistered in the rock fissures, an exotic

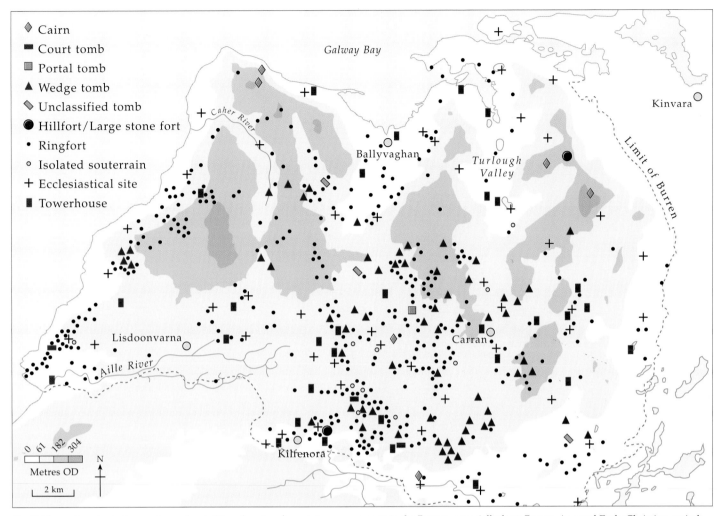

◆ Cairn
▬ Court tomb
▢ Portal tomb
▲ Wedge tomb
◇ Unclassified tomb
● Hillfort/Large stone fort
• Ringfort
○ Isolated souterrain
+ Ecclesiastical site
▮ Towerhouse

Galway Bay

Caher River

Kinvara ○

Ballyvaghan

Turlough Valley

Limit of Burren

Lisdoonvarna ○

Carran

Aille River

0 61 182 304
Metres OD
N
2 km

Kilfenora

Fig. 7 The archaeological map shows the striking density of surviving monuments in the Burren, especially from Bronze Age and Early Christian periods.

vegetation flourishes, nourished by the limestone and sheltered from the incessant Atlantic winds. At ground level, the barren limestone is only one element in a mosaic of environments with varying types and thicknesses of soil, varied flora and distinctive microclimates. Owing to its coastal location and mild winters, vegetation is thicker than on the limestone pavements of the English Pennines. Apart from soils developed on glacial materials, the characteristic Burren soils are rendzinas – dark, thin, largely organic soils which are bound by plant roots into a single carpet.

The remarkable juxtaposition of flora characteristic of Arctic-alpine, Mediterranean and Mediterranean mountain regions is well known. However, a tree cover may have existed over a considerable part of the Burren in prehistoric times, perhaps destroyed by early farmers. In the post-Famine period and particularly in recent decades, decreased agricultural pressure has allowed shrubs (hazel and blackthorn) to invade many areas that were previously rocky pasture or limestone pavement. There is a notable absence of plants, such as gorse and bracken, which are widespread elsewhere on the acid soils of Ireland.

The distinctive Burren flora ceases abruptly around Lisdoonvarna where the Namurian shales produce heavy damp soil and the vegetation is rushy, with peat accumulations in ill-drained depressions. Much of this area has been recently planted with coniferous forests, heightening the contrast with the Burren limestones.

THE CULTURAL LANDSCAPE

The Burren – the 'rocky place' – is a world of stone – stone walls, stone cottages, stone fields, stone monuments. It possesses perhaps the highest density of field monuments of any upland area in Ireland, encompassing a record of human settlement on the plateau since neolithic times. Most uplands discouraged close human settlement but the Burren has manifestly been an attractive environment for farmers until recent times. On the thicker valley soils, changing agricultural practices have destroyed the record of what went before but on the plateau, stone structures have been preserved to give a palimpsest of cultural landscapes.

The remarkable concentration of human constructions in what is currently a region with a very limited resource

DAPHNE POCHIN-MOULD

Fig. 8 The stone fort of Ballykinvarga near Kilfenora. The large fort of prehistoric or early historic period age dominates the photograph but also preserved are myriad other enclosures large and small and smaller cahers, all of unknown age. Only the relatively modern straight stone wall has any function in the present day agricultural economy.

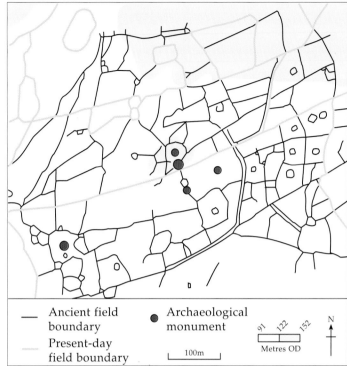

Fig. 9 Ancient field divisions in Fanygalvan townland, three kilometres south-west of Carron village in the Burren, county Clare as mapped by Christine Grant. The pattern is made up of mound walls, low grass-grown forms perhaps 2000 years old. These walls focus on groups of small, roughly circular enclosures and cairns, the settlement nodes from which the field system presumably grew. Linear features, trending east to west, may be later attempts to rationalise the system. The present-day divisions shown on the Ordnance Survey map are much larger than the old, although boundaries do coincide over small stretches.

base occurs in part because these features span at least 6000 years of occupancy. Only a proportion was in use at any given time. In many cases, precise dating of the period when particular field monuments were constructed and used is all but impossible. Reasonably definite ages can be assigned to funerary monuments and major settlement sites. The portal and wedge tombs are from the Neolithic and Bronze Ages while the large forts or cahers, such as Ballykinvarga and Cahercommaun, range in date from the Iron Age to the beginning of medieval times. The plateau also preserves a high density of stone-built circular enclosures of indeterminate age often linked to small fields. These various monuments show a marked concentration in the south-central part of the Burren plateau, in contrast to monuments of medieval and later times, such as Corcomroe monastery and Leamaneh towerhouse, which

are located in the more fertile valleys or in areas peripheral to the main karstic plateau. It remains unclear whether this is a real distinction in responses to past environments or is simply a function of differential preservation.

The Burren was only very lightly touched by landlordism, and the region had few newcomers. Accordingly, the old use of the high Burren for grazing continued, with the hill pastures being carefully managed by skilled herdsmen. The distinctive tapering townlands, running upslope, point to the pre-eminence of upland grazing. Burren cattle always had a reputation for being healthy, sturdy animals, easy to fatten once they were transferred to lush pastures. There was always demand for Burren cattle and so the cowman rather than the ploughman was king in this region.

The Burren developed an unusual variant of the transhumance tradition. Elsewhere in Ireland, cattle were moved onto the mountain pastures in spring, and returned to the lowland in autumn. On the Burren, cattle were moved to the uplands for the winter months. The permeable limestone remains dry even in wet western winters, thus eliminating the danger of cattle contracting diseases and parasites, like the liver fluke, which lurk in wet pastures. The bare rock also minimises excessive poaching,

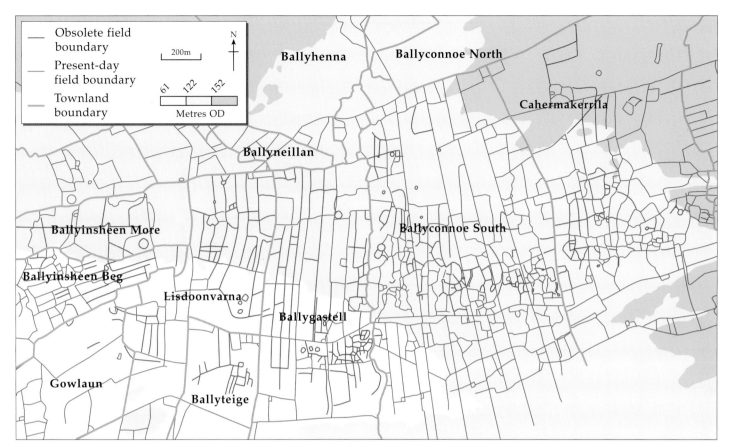

Obsolete field
boundary

Present-day
field boundary

Townland
boundary

200m

N

61 122 152

Metres OD

Ballyhenna

Ballyconnoe North

Cahermakerrila

Ballyneillan

Ballyinsheen More

Ballyconnoe South

Ballyinsheen Beg

Lisdoonvarna

Ballygastell

Gowlaun

Ballyteige

Fig. 10 The Burren field pattern is in places a remarkable palimpsest, with irregular prehistoric and medieval patterns discernible under a more modern imprint of linear boundaries created by landlords and the Congested Districts Board. The earlier boundaries are being progressively removed.

to which wet clay lands are susceptible. The growing season is surprisingly long, due to maritime influences and the infrequency of frosts. The expanse of bare rock also acts like a giant storage heater over the winter period, slowly emitting heat which it has earlier absorbed. Thus, vegetation grows freely in the sheltered grykes and a persistent beast finds fodder ensconced in the nooks and crannies. Because of the limestone base, the vegetation is rich in calcium, ensuring that Burren cattle are healthy. In spring, the cattle return from the uplands and many are sold in the adjoining towns of Gort, Kilfenora, Ennistymon and Milltown Malbay. The dominance of this system has one unusual repercussion: the farmhouses of the area are surprisingly devoid of outbuildings as no overwintering facilities are necessary. The strong demand for Burren cattle has assured that the local farmers are quite 'snug', to use a local term. Thus, there is a settled, solid look to their neat farmhouses, which exhibit the tidiness characteristic of dry limestone areas.

North-west Clare, in common with most of Ireland, experienced a population boom in the pre-Famine period. By 1841, the Burren area was heavily settled, with the precious pockets of glacial drift being ruthlessly exploited to support small potato gardens. The meagre supplies of

AEROFILMS

Fig. 11 Cahermacnaghten and the adjacent farmhouse capture the continuity of the Burren's pastoral tradition. The caher was strengthened in the late middle ages and the Ó Duibhdabhoirenn's had a school of Irish Law here in the late seventeenth century. Traces of fields and huts are discernible on the surrounding land.

Fig. 12 The southern slopes of Slievenaglasha, south-east of Carron in the centre of the Burren. Despite the patchy nature of the soil and vegetation, extensive plateau areas comprise the 'winterage' pastures for cattle. The difficult, broken terrain provides relatively rich grazing and these uplands appear to have been settled since prehistoric times as is evidenced by the high density of field monuments. Cahercommaun, perched on a cliff edge with its three concentric walls, is comparable to Dún Aengus on Aran and is the most elaborate of the many stone forts of the Burren.

turf in the Burren were augmented by supplies distributed from Connemara. Seaweed was used extensively as a fertiliser and great floating piles were constructed and ingeniously used as a raft (called a 'climeen') to bring them to the requisite spot. This seaweed was mixed with sand to produce a soil base, which was then laid directly on the limestone. Only in this painstaking way could the Burren support a large population. The drift-lined valleys sustained the heaviest population – over 160 per km^2 – a density it shared only with the coastal margins of the far western peninsulas. Yet, none of these regions shed population so severely as the Burren did in the post-Famine period.

Away from the better lowlands, many field walls are obsolete and ruined. Their relation to intact boundaries and

Fig. 13 An expanse of bare limestone near Lough Aleenaun in the south-central Burren. Such limestone 'pavements' result when glaciers scrape away all the loose rocks and soil from horizontal massive limestone strata. Fissures (joints) in the rock have been enlarged subsequently by rainwater, dissolving the limestone.

Fig. 14 Limestone pavement seen at ground level. Vegetation has colonised the enlarged fissures and other solution hollows on the rock surface. The limestone pavement is an ephemeral feature of the Burren landscape. The bare rock will crumble allowing a complete cover of soil and eventually plants.

to the profusion of archaeological and historical sites is not always clear. There is no convincing relationship with megaliths but the old fields frequently abut raths, cahers and circular huts. Distinct types of boundary and field patterns of varying size and shape are identifiable but, with few exceptions, they are difficult to date relatively or absolutely. Boundaries include single-stone walls (one stone wide), which are constructed in different ways and have a wide distribution; double walls (with a core of rubble and larger stones on either side) which are found mainly in the lowlands; earth banks, confined to badly

Fig. 15 A large early monastic settlement at Oughtmama located at the boundary between the thick, glacially derived soils on the floor of the broad Turlough valley and the rocky, steep valley slopes – two strongly contrasting environments. A series of large springs emerges from the limestone at this point to form a stream which then sinks underground within a few metres. The presence of springs in an otherwise waterless region was almost inevitably an important determinant of the location of this and many other Burren settlements.

DAVID DREW

ORDNANCE SURVEY

Fig. 16 The summit area of Aillwee Hill to the south-east of Ballyvaghan is pitted with enclosed basins (dolines) that are typical of karst regions worldwide. The dolines range in size from a few metres in width and depth to complicated landforms such as the one in the centre of this photograph in which hollows are nested within hollows. On the Burren, such dolines often contain thicker and more fertile soils than the surrounding plateau and they are commonly the location for springs. In recent years, access roads for farmers' use have been built to these formerly remote locations as is shown here.

Fig. 17 Even the most barren areas of the Burren show abundant evidence for prolonged human occupancy, unlike many other upland regions. Cathair Dhúin Irghuis lies near Black Head. While some of the surrounding enclosures may be associated with the caher, others have no obvious rationale in the present environment. Only the conspicuous townland boundary wall is still maintained.

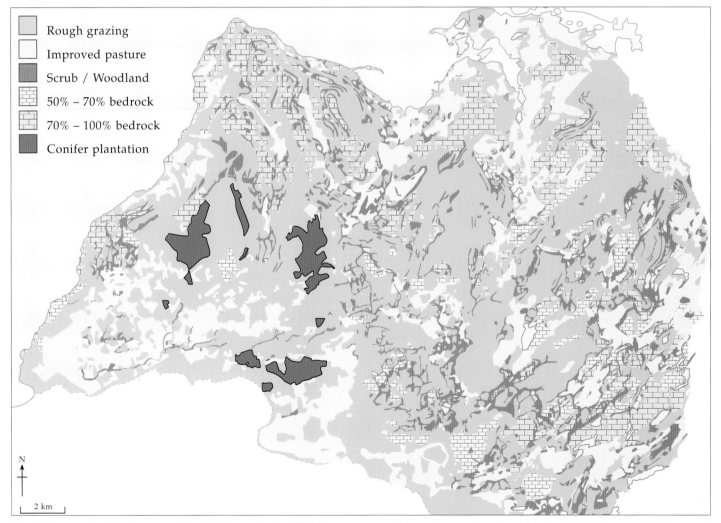

Rough grazing

Improved pasture

Scrub / Woodland

50% – 70% bedrock

70% – 100% bedrock

Conifer plantation

N

2 km

Fig. 18 The mosaic of land uses typical of the Burren in the 1990s. The map shows the dominance of rough grazing in the high Burren, and of improved pasture around the Burren fringes and valleys.

Fig. 19 Recent land use changes in the Burren using modern machinery, fertilisers and pasture seeding have created uniform grassland from areas previously occupied by hazel scrub, rough grazing or limestone pavement. The drastic nature of this imposed change in environment in the Burren is shown by these photographs depicting an area prior to (A) and during (B) reclamation.

drained, wet grasslands; tumble walls (linear heaps of stone that were originally single walls); slab walls formed of upended limestone flags sometimes fixed into the grykes; and mound walls, which are low, vegetation-covered boundaries believed to be the oldest type and perhaps associated with the wedge-tomb builders.

Field patterns are varied but the two main types are irregular and often curvilinear, or regular with straight boundaries in strip or block arrangements. All are subdivided into small, medium or large plots. Most field lay-outs are formed with a mixture of boundary types. In some lowland areas, probably in response to the strengthening of commercial husbandry in the eighteenth century, regular fields displaced irregular, while large regular forms in time replaced smaller regular forms. In poorer areas, irregular fields are still preserved in various stages of decay. Small varieties are often attached to and presumably contemporary with cahers; the large irregular fields are probably associated with an early modern phase of extensive pastoral holdings after the Plantations but before the onset of strong commercial forces and marked pre-famine population growth. Thomas Molyneux in 1709 commented on the absence of field divisions in the Burren save for 'a few old enclosures of stone'. By the early nineteenth century, extensive areas, particularly the better soils, were subdivided by a variety of field patterns.

THE BURREN TODAY

Burren farms are predominantly small, averaging 16-20 ha, and traditionally have been in rough pasture, supporting sheep and cattle. Sheltered north-south trending valleys, for example around Ballyvaghan, have rich grasslands and larger holdings. The Burren is now thinly populated relative to surrounding regions but a century ago it was more closely settled, especially in the valleys. The abandonment of the Burren and the peripherality of its settlement has been marked in post-famine times; population fell from 4000 to 2500 between 1900 and 1991, and deserted farmsteads are very numerous. Instead of being a focus for human activity, the Burren has become a centrifugal area in settlement terms with only marginal settlements such as Ballyvaghan, Lisdoonvarna and Corofin maintaining or increasing their populations.

Since prehistory, land use in the Burren has been in considerable part a consequence of agricultural activities and the 'natural' Burren of the present day simply reflects the current pressure being exerted on the land. For example, areas of limestone pavement may have halved in post-famine times whilst the area occupied by scrub may have doubled. However, changes in agricultural practice driven by European policies from the early 1970s onwards have led to drastic and irreversible changes in land use. Land reclamation has converted more than 4% of the Burren from rocky pasture, pavement or scrub land into large fields of seeded pasture, often used for silage production and no different in appearance or ecology to any area of lowland Ireland. Almost all the natural flora is confined to patches surrounded by unvegetated limestone or rubble fields. These patches are inexorably shrinking and successful conservation requires the stabilisation of their size. Ecological diversity is one of the great attractions of the Burren – its gentians and orchids, its otters and pine martens, its wheatears and stonechats, its pearl-bordered fritillaries – a remarkable profusion that is now under

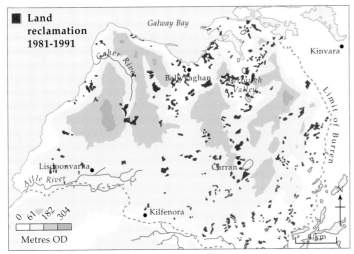

Fig. 20 Intensive land reclamation is increasingly a problem on the sensitive Burren limestones.

intense pressure. The recent wholesale loss of geological and ecological diversity and of archaeological monuments does not augur well for the future of the Burren as a repository of such a wealth of natural and cultural features.

The sulphur and iron springs at Lisdoonvarna were the basis of a Victorian tourist trade in the Burren, but tourist and recreational enterprises are now being encouraged as an alternative to declining agriculture. The Aillwee Cave development is a major initiative which attracts over 100,000 visitors annually and brings considerable economic benefit to nearby Ballyvaghan. These new activities depend largely on the distinctive karstic landscape and the varied botanic and historic resources. Without careful planning and management, they also threaten them. Traffic is generated which the old, narrow roads cannot absorb while indiscriminate road improvements may impair landscape character. New buildings are particularly awkward in this open, treeless landscape. They require

Fig. 21 Areas of limestone pavement and boulder-strewn rough grazing are punctuated by large tracts of hazel scrub and zones of recently and intensively reclaimed land.

Fig. 22 Aillwee Caves visitor centre, near Ballyvaghan. Designed by A. and D. Wejchert in 1979, this building is an example of environmentally sensitive design, carefully integrated into its vulnerable surroundings.

careful siting and designs, appropriate to the building traditions of the region.

Increasingly, the inescapable problems of water supply and effluent disposal are apparent in a landscape where surface supplies are scarce and ground water pollution is already serious, owing to use of silage and other cattle feeds. The feeding of silage can bring excessive nutrients into the traditional winterages with change from a species-rich flora to monotonous grasses as well as polluting ground water. Heritage and agri-tourism, pony trekking, hillwalking and other outdoor pursuits, now actively encouraged as year-round pursuits on the dry surfaces, accentuate these pressures.

Effective landscape management at a regional scale is a long way off but essential ingredients are beginning to emerge. Properly implemented, REPS (Rural Environmental Protection Scheme) clearly has considerable potential in this vulnerable environment. Much of the

High Burren and foothills has merited designation as NHAs (Natural Heritage Areas) which enhances the level of REPS payments. Participation precludes damaging farm activities such as land reclamation and improvements, rock removal and infilling, and the use of fertilisers and herbicides. Sustainable stocking levels are made obligatory as is the avoidance of bare rock pavements for animal feeding sites. Close monitoring of these developments could help to evolve sustainable farming systems, an indispensable component of any strategy for rural development in this exceptional and ecologically sensitive landscape. The situation is now precarious; without coherent policies, landscape and general environmental quality will rapidly deteriorate. Remedial action requires a new harmony between farming, tourism and the landscape, involving the collaboration of a wide range of public and private interests. Above all, local communities need to become actively involved in sustaining their magnificent landscape, admirably described in John Betjeman's poem 'Ireland with Emily':

> Stony seaboard, far and foreign,
> Stony hills poured over space,
> Stony outcrop of the Burren,
> Stones in every fertile place,
> Little fields with boulders dotted,
> Grey-stone shoulders saffron spotted...

BIBLIOGRAPHY

A. Darcy and J. Hayward, *The natural history of the Burren* (London, 1992).

G. Cunningham, *Burren journey* (Limerick, 1978).

G. Cunningham, *Burren journey west* (Limerick, 1980).

D. Drew, 'Landforms of the Burren, county Clare' in *Geographical Viewpoint*, iv (1975), pp 21-38.

D. Drew, 'The hydrology of the Burren' in *Ir. Geog.*, xxiii (1990), pp 69-89.

D. Drew and E. Magee, 'Environmental implications of land reclamation in the Burren, county Clare' in *Ir. Geog.*, xxvii (1995), pp 81-96.

T. Finch, *Soils of county Clare* (Dublin, 1971).

P. Halton, 'Tourism usage issues in the Burren, county Clare' in *Ir. Geog.*, xxvi (1993), pp 158-69.

D. Jeffrey, M. Jones and J. McAdam, 'The management of Burren grasslands' in D. Jeffrey (ed.), *Irish grasslands. Their biology and management* (Dublin, 1995), pp 267-75.

L. Jelicic and M. O'Connell, 'History of vegetation and land use from 3200 BP to the present day in the northwest Burren, a karstic region of Ireland' in *Vegetational History and Archaeobotany*, i (1992), pp 119-40.

C. Nelson and W. Walsh, *The Burren* (Aberystwyth, 1991).

J. O'Connell and A. Korff (ed.), *The book of the Burren* (Galway, 1991).

M. O'Connell, (ed.), *The Burren, county Clare* (Dublin, 1994).

E. Plunkett Dillon, The field boundaries of the Burren county Clare. Unpublished PhD thesis, Trinity College Dublin, 1986.

C. Self, *Caves of county Clare* (Castle Cary, 1981).

D. Webb and M. Scannell, *Flora of Connemara and the Burren* (Cambridge, 1983).

T. Robinson, *The Burren. A map of the uplands of north-west Clare* (Galway, 1977).

THE BEND OF THE BOYNE, COUNTY MEATH

East of Slane in county Meath, the Boyne river loops dramatically southwards. This begins the famous Bend of the Boyne, which encompasses the impressive passage tomb cemeteries of Knowth, Dowth and Newgrange, burial grounds of the societies that first farmed this fertile valley. During subsequent millennia, the area's remarkable history has left an enduring physical and symbolic impression on the landscape, punctuated with such events as the coming of Christianity, the arrival of the Cistercian 'white monks', the Battle of the Boyne, famine and emigration, and cultural tourism in the twentieth century. There is an accumulated time depth in this rural landscape but it is not fossilised; it is a composite creation in continuous evolution, now increasingly driven by the twin dictates of farming and tourism. Today, it is recognised as a world heritage zone by UNESCO and has been earmarked as Ireland's first archaeological park because of its outstanding cultural legacy. The establishment of the park presents an unique opportunity to explore the broader cultural history of the area and to trace the gradual evolution of its prized landscape. This can best be achieved by concentrating on the well-preserved cultural components and by placing them in their temporal and spatial contexts. By freezing the frame at particular epochs, the physical inheritance can elucidate the many societies who have made the Boyne valley their home over the last five millennia.

ORDNANCE SURVEY

Fig. 1 Low-level, vertical aerial coverage shows the core area of the proposed archaeological park within the Bend of the Boyne in 1991. The 'bend' respects a geological obstruction in the course of the Boyne, downriver from the village of Slane in county Meath. Here, the river abruptly changes direction and runs southwards below an elevated ridge. Subsequently, the river flows parallel to the ridge for some distance until it twists northwards through a glacial gorge, eventually assuming its eastward course to the Irish Sea. This bend cradles a region which has been to the forefront of settlement history for more than five thousand years.

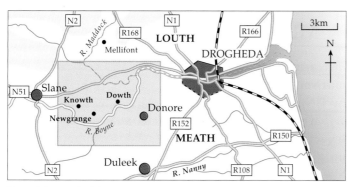

Fig. 2 The Bend of the Boyne in its regional setting.

Fig. 3 (right) The Bend of the Boyne was formed 12,000 years ago. As ice retreated to the north-west, the river incised itself into a glacial plain, its course dictated by a fault line in the underlying rock. North of the river is an elongated ridge of carboniferous shale with a mantle of glacial till giving rise to a grey brown podsolic soil. On the south side of the river, a steep gravel escarpment – which terminates in Donore Hill – is covered by heavy gley soils and cut by a glacial gorge running south-west from the Boyne.

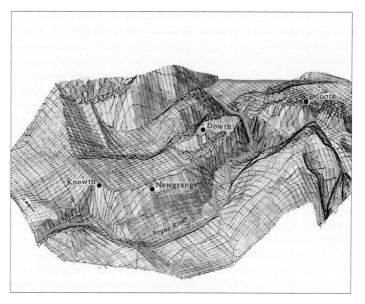

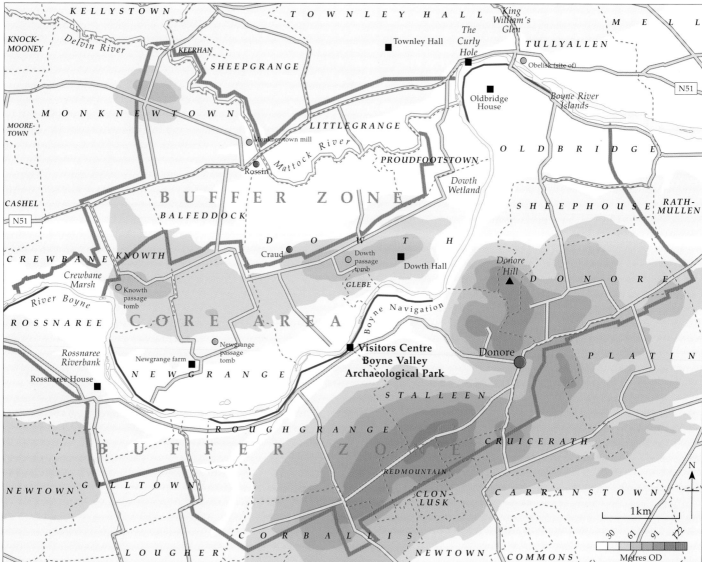

Fig. 4 The Bend of the Boyne. The proposed Boyne Valley Archaeological Park measures 8 km by 6 km, comprising a core area of 780 ha surrounded by a buffer zone of 3300 ha. These zones will be subject to strict planning controls. In addition to the rich cultural component, there are four Natural Heritage Areas within the park area: Crewbane marsh, Rossnaree riverbank, Dowth wetland and the Boyne islands.

THE FIRST FARMERS

The oldest surviving monuments in the valley are the great passage tombs, their round, kerbed mounds dominating the ridge and south-facing terraces which run between the rivers Boyne and Mattock. These megalithic tombs were built by neolithic farming communities from 3260 BC to 3080 BC. With evidence of up to forty identified tombs distributed throughout the Bend of the Boyne, a sense of order and formality is still retained in their arrangement on the landscape. They appear in clusters or cemeteries built on the most prominent knolls, with the smaller tombs deployed around the larger sites; a circular pattern exists at Knowth, a linear one at Newgrange, and a dispersed one at Dowth. Their densest concentration is around the main mound at Knowth at the western edge of the ridge. This mound contains two opposing passages and the finest collection of megalithic art in western Europe. The circular arrangement at Knowth is all the more intriguing because some of the smaller tombs actually preceded the main mound.

As these monuments were designed to be seen, their conspicuous position on the ridge indicates considerable clearance of the native forest in their environs, a fact confirmed by archaeological excavation. The Knowth and Newgrange tombs were built on open farmland cleared during the five centuries preceding their construction. The first farming communities arrived around 3700 BC, moving into a heavily forested valley of oak and elm on the higher ground, flanked by hazel with birch and alder in the valley bottom. Red deer and hare were among the few large mammals roaming these woodlands, but there was an abundance of salmon and trout in the river. Pollen and seed analysis from Knowth and Newgrange shows that a

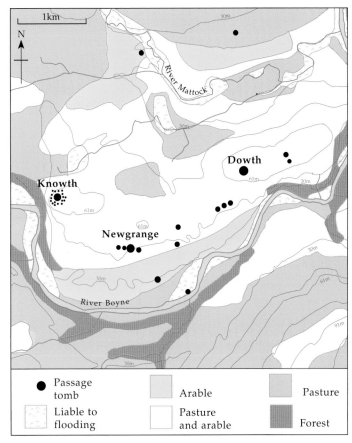

Fig. 6 A probable pattern of neolithic land use in the vicinity of the passage tomb cemeteries has been reconstructed by Gabriel Cooney combining the evidence of excavation with the geomorphology, geology and the modern soil pattern. The soil in the main cemetery area is a grey brown podsolic suitable for pasture and tillage. The upper terrace below Newgrange is a deep, well-drained soil more suited to cereal cultivation, while the lower terrace was probably used for pasture because of the danger of flooding. Heavy gley soils in the valley of the River Mattock were also likely areas of cattle rearing.

mixed pastoral and tillage economy was practised by these pioneering groups. The making of fields was an integral part of this activity, probably using bramble and crab apple as hedging material. Domesticated cattle and sheep were also introduced. The steadily growing population lived in simple, rectangular timber houses, which were eventually enclosed within large palisaded enclosures. These centuries of successful agricultural activity provided a strong economic basis for the rich Boyne valley culture that was eventually to thrive in this fertile tract.

A RITUAL LANDSCAPE IN THE LATE NEOLITHIC/EARLY BRONZE AGE

From as early as 2855 BC, there was a renewed phase of monument building in the Bend of the Boyne as the environs of the larger passage tombs once again became a focus for intense ritual activity. Large enclosures were constructed from stone, timber and earth for great assemblies. At key periods in the solar calendar, fires were set and deep

Fig. 5 Knowth is located on the western edge of a ridge above the Boyne. The orientation of the small tombs in the Knowth cemetery faced towards the ridge top containing the main mound. Extensive excavation has revealed continued re-use of this site from the Neolithic through to the medieval period.

Fig. 7 The main passage tomb at Newgrange straddles the most prominent ridge above the north bank of the Boyne. Here, the builders skilfully positioned the tomb entrance to permit the sun to enter through the roof box above it, illuminating the inner chamber on the morning of the winter solstice, the shortest day of the year. The facade of white quartz has been a subject of much controversy since its construction in the 1970s when the site was developed for tourism purposes.

pits were dug to receive votive offerings of burnt animals, especially pig. The stones of the outer circle at Newgrange were erected at this time, possibly to mark special sunrise positions by shadows cast on the elaborately decorated entrance stone of the passage tomb. Labour input into the construction of these mainly open enclosures was immense and on a par with the earlier tombs, though the burial practices of this time were much simpler. Remains of the dead have been discovered in stone boxes or cists, occasionally marked by a stone, as at Monknewtown and Oldbridge, or simply inserted as cremations into the earlier tombs, as at Knowth.

This renewal of activity is linked to the arrival of a new population group from Britain identified by their distinctive pottery styles. The 'Beaker' folk forged a strong economic base from the rich farmland along the Boyne in which they practised mixed farming. There is faunal evidence for cattle, sheep, goats, pigs, dogs and horses and

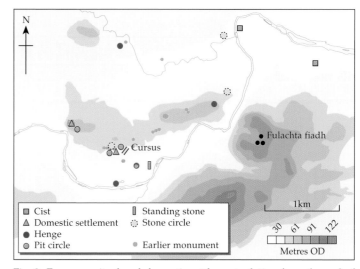

Fig. 8 Funerary, ritual and domestic settlements dating from the end of the Neolithic and beginning of the Bronze Age have been found in close proximity to the earlier passage tombs. This passage tomb heartland continued to be a major focus for ritual activity.

macroscopic confirmation of barley seeds, indicating grain cultivation. The recognition of vetch, a legume, in the Beaker levels at Knowth suggests that crop rotation was taking place. This community may also have had limited knowledge of metallurgy. There are copper resources in the immediate area and a bronze axe with metal-workers' tools were found at the Newgrange excavations.

The large concentration of earthen embanked enclosures (henges) in the region is the most notable legacy from the period, constituting the most remarkable group outside Britain. There is a close spatial relationship between these henges and the passage tombs in the Boyne. A tomb lies just east of the henge at Monknewtown and another tomb has actually been incorporated into the monument on a

Fig. 9 Twelve standing stones of a great circle of stones surround the base of the earlier passage tomb at Newgrange. A computer simulation of the movement of the sun for the period c. 2000 BC has demonstrated that these stones throw shadows on the decorated entrance stone of Newgrange during such key times in the year as the winter and summer solstices and equinoxes, thus suggesting their use as a ritual calendar.

GILLIAN BARRETT

Fig. 10 The ploughed-out remains of a still impressive henge monument at the edge of the Boyne below Newgrange passage tomb cemetery and a second henge on a terrace enclosing a small passage tomb. The 'Boyne type' henges have their own regional characteristics. With broad, flat-topped banks, they are circular to oval in shape with a domed or hollowed profile (depending on whether material for the bank was scarped from the centre or the perimeter of the interior). Diameters exceed one hundred metres. The henges are inward looking, and usually have only one entrance, orientated towards the east or west/south-west.

terrace south of Newgrange, as is also evident in its timber version, the pit circle on the ridge east of Newgrange. This can best be explained as a desire to locate ritual activities in an area of established ritual significance.

This spate of early Bronze Age innovation was followed by a period of virtual inactivity in the Bend of the Boyne from 1800 BC to the first century AD, leaving little tangible landscape impact. The valley was apparently deserted with much of the land reverting to secondary woodland and scrub. At Red Bog, north of the Bend of the Boyne, a pollen core shows that arable cultivation virtually disappeared during this period. The most tantalising indication of a human presence in the area during the later Bronze Age is the recent discovery of cooking sites (fulachta fiadh) in a natural basin high above the south bank of the Boyne at Sheephouse, indicating the presence of a small community around 1400 BC. While there are some late Bronze Age finds from Newgrange, the mounds there and at Knowth had collapsed to cover over all traces of earlier Neolithic and Beaker settlement. The entrance at Newgrange remained hidden for a thousand years.

LANDSCAPE AND LEGEND IN THE IRON AGE

Early in the first millennium AD, the Boyne cemeteries attracted renewed interest and Newgrange became a place of religious significance in the Celtic world. According to the tenth-century *Dindshencas*, the Síd in Bréga was the dwelling place of the Celtic god Dagda. From the first to the late fourth century AD, pilgrims deposited Roman coins and gold ornaments in front of the main tomb at Newgrange. The ford of Brow situated just below the passage tomb was a strategic crossing over the Boyne on the Slíghe Midluachra, a key route between Tara and Ulster. An early text (*The wars of Fergus and Concobhar*) describes conflict between Ulster and Tara around the first century AD and outlines a route from Tara to Ulster via Sídh Elcmar, Brugh Meic an Oigh (at the ford of Newgrange), Dubhros (Rossnaree), and Sliabh Bregha near Mellifont. The ford below Newgrange was still identified as the ford of Brow on eighteenth-century Caldwell estate maps and the placename is retained in the names Breo House and Breo Park today. In Tudor and Stuart records, Brows weir was located in this area. The term Brú na Bóinne is now commonly used to describe this whole sweep of territory, but in early documents it refers only to a very localised area around the important ford.

The kings of Tara were allegedly buried at Brú from the time of Conchubair mac Nessa until the coming of St Patrick and Christianity. Excavations at Newgrange produced no evidence to substantiate these claims. However,

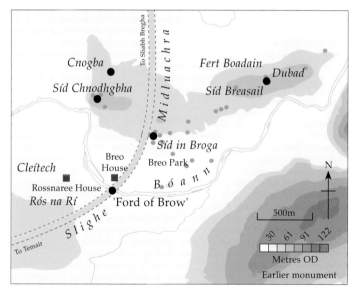

Fig. 11 Mythology in the landscape. Placename evidence substantiated by early documentary sources indicates that the fording point south of Newgrange known as the 'ford of Brow' (below present day Breo House) was an important Boyne crossing in the Iron Age on a key route between Tara and Ulster. To the north is Síd Chnodhgbha or the other-world dwelling of Knowth; west is Rossnaree House, on the site of the House of Cleítech, an early residence of the kings of Tara; east is Fert Boadain, the grave of Boadan at Dubad (Dowth); and to the south is Bóann or the Boyne.

a large number of extended inhumations of Iron Age date accompanied by blue glass beads and dice were revealed at Knowth. At this time, the main passage tomb mound was transformed into a well protected site by the digging of defensive ditches with a causeway in the south-east. The final attempt to bury a king of Tara at the Brú is told in the story of the death of King Cormac MacAirt in the third century AD and preserved in a twelfth-century version *Senchas na Relec*. The tradition is also enshrined in the local placename of Rossnaree (the wood of the king). According to tradition, Cormac died at the house of Cleítech after a salmon bone stuck in his throat. He told his people not to bury him at Brú but his servants were determined to bring him to the place where the kings of Tara had always been buried. However, the Boyne river swelled up three times, preventing the bier from crossing: it was then carried down to an area called Ros na Rí (Rossnaree). The house of Cleítech is described as an early residence of the kings of Tara, lying near a ford above the Boyne and the Brú, and close to Rossnaree and Knowth on the south bank of the river, with a glen to the south and a grave to the north-east. The topographical detail concerning Cleítech would place it on the plateau where Rossnaree House stands today.

The Boyne is also the location for one of the best known tales from Irish mythology. Fionn inadvertently acquired his wisdom from the river's bradán feasa (salmon of knowledge). The association between the Boyne and (virtually) miraculous salmon remains. The 'curly hole' is a popular location for salmon fishing which has made a near total recovery from the drainage works undertaken on this river in the early 1970s. Although there is little tangible evidence from the Iron Age in the Bend of the Boyne, these evocative tales draw a significant number of 'new age' visitors attracted not to the archaeologist's mounds but by the sacred sites of a pagan era.

EARLY CHRISTIAN EXPANSION

In a field below Knowth where the ground falls away steeply to the Boyne, a most imposing fortification stands at the edge of a deep ravine, taking full advantage of this natural defence. Its deep enclosing fosse and inner rampart provide shelter for the cattle that today now graze its flanks. This unusually large ringfort holds a commanding sway over the countryside to the north-west and to the south and may have helped to defend the ancient territory of Bréga over a thousand years ago. On the immediate western horizon is the hill of Slane where tradition recounts that St Patrick lit a Paschal fire in 432 AD, igniting the flame of Christianity in this country. The name Slane

DEPARTMENT OF ARTS, CULTURE AND THE GAELTACHT

Fig. 12 Colour vertical photographs taken in 1991 revealed traces of buried enclosures appearing as crop marks in tillage fields. This site, south of the Boyne in the townland of Gilltown, is a levelled ringfort with an annex adjoining its northern section.

itself derives from the dynasty of Síl nAed Sláine, kings of northern Bréga in the ninth and tenth centuries whose residence at Knowth gave them the title 'Rí Cnogba'.

During the reign of the Síl nAed Sláine, the Bend of the Boyne experienced an upsurge in activity and considerable population growth. Settlements dating from this period are still traceable in the fields north and south of the river and such townland names as Cashel and Donore indicate even greater expansion of the farmed area. The ringforts at Knowth and Newgrange, the latter on a low ridge just north of the passage tomb, are the remains of the largest enclosed farmsteads. In general, local ringforts are single-banked with artificially raised interiors, an adaptation to a low lying landscape. In the cultivated fields south of the river, many of these enclosed settlements have been levelled, such as at Gilltown and Lougher, appearing only as distinct vegetation marks at very dry times of the year.

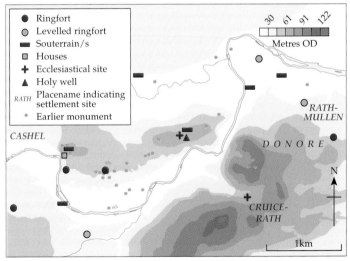

Fig. 13 Early Christian sites in the Bend of the Boyne.

Fig. 14 Slane Hill was the religious centre for the Síl nAed Sláine dynasty, kings of northern Bréga in the ninth and tenth centuries who resided at Knowth. Slane is of paramount importance to the history of the Irish church for it was here that St Patrick reputedly lit the paschal fire in defiance of the order from the pagan high king at Tara. Today the hill of Slane is capped by the impressive remains of a medieval parish church and Franciscan College founded in 1512 by Christopher Fleming, Lord of Slane.

The excavations around the passage tomb at Knowth have provided considerable evidence for nucleated unenclosed settlement in the Early Christian period. From the eighth century, the tombs became the focus for an extensive unprotected settlement consisting of houses and nine souterrains. This concentration of underground passages is unusual in Ireland and once more highlights the exceptional significance of this area throughout the ages. The inhabitants at Knowth practised a mixed agriculture dominated by cattle rearing with sheep and pigs of lesser importance. Wheat and oats, ground on rotary querns, also featured in their diet. More typical isolated souterrains are numerous in this area with occurrences at Oldbridge, Rossnaree and Sheephouse on the south side of the river, and Dowth on the north. Unenclosed settlement with associated souterrains may have developed as an alternative to ringfort occupation; indeed, settlements which resorted to souterrains as their sole means of defence could indicate a population of tillage farmers.

This agricultural community was rich enough to attract the attention of raiding Vikings. The *Annals of the Four Masters* records a fleet of Norsemen on the Boyne at Linn Rois (Rossnaree) in 841 and the pillaging of the souterrains at Knowth and Dowth in 863. Particularly noteworthy is that Early Christian architects actually copied passage tomb design in their corbelled structures and incorporated the burial chambers at Knowth and Dowth into the later

structures in an ingenious way. Souterrains with corbelled beehive chambers are a distinct feature of north county Dublin, Meath and south Louth, the ancient territory of north Bréga.

Slane was the main religious centre of the Síl nAed Sláine and on the hill is an Early Christian house-shaped shrine associated with St Erc (d. 512-514) whom Patrick had made bishop of Slane. The burning of a round tower at Slane by the 'Foreigners' in 948 indicates a substantial monastery. There were smaller ecclesiastical foundations in the Bend of the Boyne at Dowth and possibly Staleen. The Annals of Ulster from 1012 contain an intriguing reference to the slaying of Oengus, airchinnech (monastic manager) of Sláine by the airchinnech of Dubad (Dowth). The Four Masters also list the church at Dowth amongst those burnt in 1170 by Diarmait MacMurchada. Further documentary evidence for an early foundation at Dowth is found in a twelfth-century missal from there. Yet, the only landscape trace for this early foundation is the holy well near the later medieval church at Dowth. The medieval parish church presumably replaced the Early Christian foundation. A slab-lined burial was discovered south of the river at Staleen in the mid 1930s. The body was extended east-west in a form consistent with Early Christian practice and may indicate another ecclesiastical centre.

MOULDING THE MEDIEVAL LANDSCAPE

The Cistercian monks were firmly established in the Bend of the Boyne before the coming of the Normans and represent the arrival of a new style of European monasticism and land management. The house at Mellifont, on the banks of the Mattock, was founded in 1142; by the time the Normans arrived in 1169, there were already twelve Cistercian houses in Ireland affiliated to it. In their customary way, the Cistercians divided their larger estates on the Boyne into outlying farms (granges) including Newgrange, Sheepgrange, Roughgrange and Littlegrange, all worked directly by lay brothers. Each grange had its own farm buildings. In Ireland, buildings associated with these early granges are scarce, but an insight into their arrangement is given in directions sent by Stephen of Lexington to the Cistercians in Jerpoint, county Kilkenny in 1228. He advised that buildings should not be erected in the centre or precinct of the granges, but rather along the sides in a circle on account of thieves and that barns and animal sheds should be the only buildings. There was a grange at Knowth from at least 1185. This medieval farm is possibly represented by a group of low-lying enclosures north of the passage tomb cemetery at Knowth in fields which border a stream that runs into the Mattock. They are centred on a

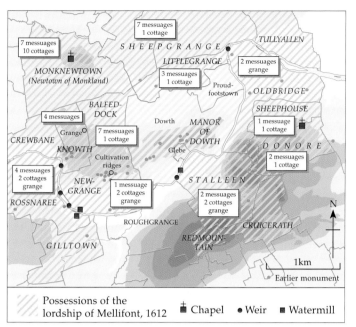

Possessions of the lordship of Mellifont, 1612 ✚ Chapel • Weir ■ Watermill

Fig. 15 The Norman manor of Dowth, associated with the Netterville family from the thirteenth century, was surrounded on all sides by Cistercian farms. This map shows the extent of the lands of Mellifont Abbey within the Bend of the Boyne when granted to Sir Gerald Moore in 1612. The number of messuages (dwelling houses with out-offices and land) at Monknewtown, Sheepgrange and Balfeddock indicate villages at these locations in the early seventeenth century.

pear-shaped enclosure with an attached series of fields. Excavations on top of the mound at Knowth revealed a mortared wall enclosing a rectangular area with two houses. The walls were well finished with shaped sandstone blocks and a number of the structural stones were dressed, indicating a building of some status. The windows were divided into panels by a lattice of lead and glazed. Amongst the finds were tiles bearing the name 'Maria' and a font. This building must have been an oratory associated

Fig. 16 This aerial view of the Boyne below Newgrange shows the remains of a mill race, all that survives of Broe mill first established by Cistercian monks in the twelfth century.

with the grange. An entry in Bishop Doppings' Visitation Book of 1682-1685 indicates that there was still a church at Knowth in the late seventeenth century.

Monastic granges were centres of intense agriculture, including grain cultivation and cattle and sheep rearing. Sheep were a valuable commodity, linked to the woollen export industry which the Cistercians developed. The townlands of Sheepgrange and Sheephouse were likely locations for these extensive sheep farms. There were sizeable exports of grain from this area to England in the thirteenth century, indicating a substantial area under tillage. Excavation has uncovered ridge and furrow south-east of Newgrange and this was extensive, to judge from the presence of medieval plough pebbles (inserted into wooden ploughs as an anti-wear device) in the fields at Balfeddock, Knowth, Townley Hall and Donore. At Knowth, plough pebbles were found with thirteenth-century potsherds.

The Cistercians played a key role in developing the milling and fishing resources of the Boyne. Mills and millponds are specified in twelfth-century charters confirming lands to the Mellifont house. These were probably vertical-wheeled mills. In 1539, the monks' mills were located at Staleen and Rossnaree, where there are still vernacular-style watermills, and at Browe's mill on the Boyne at Newgrange. A mill at Broe also appears on a Caldwell estate map from 1760, but only the mill race is visible on the ground today.

The Boyne fisheries above the tide-way included three valuable salmon weirs at Rossnaree, Knowth and Staleen and these were amongst the possessions of the Mellifont monks confirmed in a charter of 1203. At the dissolution of the monastery in 1539, it owned fishing weirs at Oldbridge, Rathmullen, Newgrange, Knockcommon and Rossnaree. Two methods of fishing are given prominence in the sources: weirs and nets. A fishing weir is an obstruction wholly or partially across a river channel, working on the basis of a constant flow of water in one direction. Salmon and other fish were caught on their way upstream in cribs or traps and eels were caught while migrating downstream in the autumn. The weirs were formed of post-and-wattle barriers or stone walls. The fish were taken out from a pool within an enclosure or trapped in a 'coghill' net. The weirs at Oldbridge and Rossnaree are virtually the same as those erected by the monks in medieval times. The fishing weirs at Newgrange and Staleen have not been used recently for salmon but the weir at Staleen has been used as an eel trap. Netting for salmon was another method of fishing practised on the Boyne in medieval times. The fish were surrounded and pulled out onto a flat hauling ground. The boat used in this form of

DEPARTMENT OF ARTS, CULTURE AND THE GAELTACHT

PRIVATE COLLECTION

Fig. 17 This painting, by Joseph Tudor, *c.* 1746, shows fishermen drag-netting on the Boyne at Oldbridge. This method of fishing was traditional on the Boyne, perhaps the most important river for salmon in the country during the medieval period. The Boyne salmon is short for its size, deep shouldered and shaped like a bow. Strong as a horse, it is never out of season. It is featured in traditional stories relating to Fionn MacCumhaill who was attacked by Boyne fishermen. Amongst the traditional 'buadha' or prescriptions of the High King of Ireland for a life without misfortune was the fish of the Boyne. The obelisk in the painting was built in 1736 to commemorate the Battle of the Boyne. It was blown up in 1923.

fishing at Oldbridge was the Boyne currach, a broad, oval-shaped craft covered in hide. In 1539, the income of Mellifont Abbey included an annual rent arising from sixteen of these fishing currachs at Oldbridge.

Although the Cistercian granges dominated the medieval landscape within the Bend of the Boyne, some secular settlement was present. The passage tomb at Dowth was used as the site of a De Lacy motte castle. Dowth was part of the eastern Liberty of Meath, granted to Hugh De Lacy in 1172 and sub-infeudated to the Netterville family. A manorial extent for the manor from 1253 shows that it then incorporated five ploughlands (*c.* 592ha). There were nine fee farm tenants on the manor (six English and three Irish) of whom the English had holdings

ALBERT KAHN COLLECTION

Fig. 18 Currachs are small boats made of wickerwork covered with watertight material. The elongated, sea-going currachs are rowed; the oval river craft were paddled. Dug-outs were normally used on most inland waters, the currachs in only a few places, such as the Shannon, Erne and Boyne rivers. The Boyne currach possessed an oval wickerwork frame of hazel wands with a covering of ox-hide. Light and manoeuvreable, the craft was well adapted to the drift-net salmon fisheries on the Boyne pools, where it continued in use until the present century. This photograph dates from 1913.

Fig. 19 In the early stages of the Norman advance into the eastern Liberty of Meath, the prehistoric passage tomb at Dowth was re-used as a motte. A manorial village developed close by, focused around the surviving parish church and manor house visible in the south-east corner of this photograph.

ranging from 9 ha to two ploughlands (*c.* 2.4 ha). There was one English and one Irish free tenant. The only other tenants on this small manor were a number of cottiers whose labour service had been commuted.

Clear evidence survives of this medieval manor – the parish church and manor house, a fifteenth-century tower house with a sunken way leading up to it and associated earthworks which run north/south across the field between the passage grave and church. At the northern end of the large field enclosing the manor today, there are spade-dug cultivation ridges in three irregularly shaped fields which are earlier than the modern field pattern and also predate the Dowth to Newgrange road. The Netterville grant was a smaller one, the larger ones in the Boyne area going to such families as the Flemings in Slane where there is a motte. For a short time, Knowth was included in the land of the Norman knight Richard Fleming who fortified it in 1176 as an aid to holding his recently acquired lands around Slane.

THE SEVENTEENTH-CENTURY LANDSCAPE:
A MILITARY PERSPECTIVE

Should visitors approach the Boyne on the road from Donore village to Oldbridge, they pass a thatched cottage with a mural entitled 'Battle of the Boyne 1690'. On 1 July 1690, King William of Orange defeated James II, securing the English throne for the protestant succession. The main battle took place along the Bend of the Boyne and signposts draw attention to such landmarks as a 'Jacobite camp' on

the hill of Donore, on the southern 'catholic side' of the river, and King William's Glen on the northern 'protestant side' opposite Oldbridge which is located on a strategic pass, fordable at low tide. As a political symbol, the impact of this battle was profound and it is commemorated to the present day. Yet the evidence on the ground is negligible; the most significant remains are the entrenchments near Tullyallen. However, by following the stages of this battle on the ground, the local terrain can be seen with the eye of a military strategist, identifying the hills, glens and passes that could have provided natural defence and military advantage at any stage in the area's history.

Amongst the many accounts of the Battle of the Boyne, George Story's *Impartial History* (1693) is particularly enlightening, with its accompanying topographical maps of the battlefield and the surrounding countryside. On the north bank of the river, his map shows a church and a village on Donore Hill. Today, the ruins of this church stand isolated on the hill; in 1690, thousands of Jacobite troops sought the cover of its walls during the attacks by William of Orange and the Enniskilleners. From Donore Hill, the

B

Fig. 20 Many local traditions relate to the Battle of the Boyne. A) Patrick Sarsfield was brought to this miller's house along King William's Glen. B) During the battle, bread was baked for the men in the oven of this miller's house at Staleen.

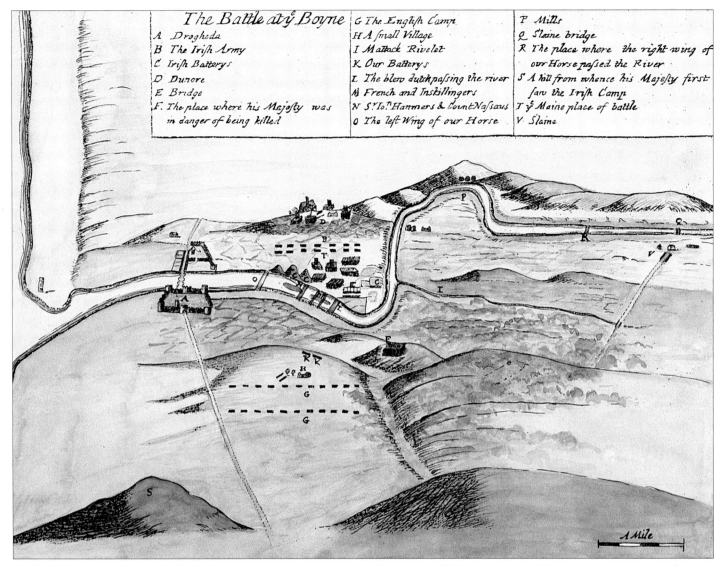

The Battle at y Boyne

A Drogheda
B The Irish Army
C Irish Batterys
D Dunore
E Bridge
F The place where his Majesty was in danger of being killed

G The English Camp
H A small Village
I Mattock Rivolet
K Our Batterys
L The blew dutch passing the river
M French and Inskillingers
N S.r Io.n Hanmers & Count Nassaus
O The left Wing of our Horse

P Mills
Q Slaine bridge
R The place where the right wing of our Horse passed the River
S A hill from whence his Majesty first saw the Irish Camp
T y.e Maine place of battle
V Slaine

A Mile

Fig. 21 This reconstruction of the Battle of the Boyne is primarily based on Story's map of 1693 with some additional detail recounted in other eye-witness accounts. The reconstruction is drawn from the 'protestant' perspective, looking south with north at the bottom of the map.

ground falls away gradually towards Oldbridge, ideal terrain for cavalry charges during the battle. Eye witness accounts describe ploughed fields, enclosed by stone walls and fences. Clustered around a church, there were half a dozen houses at Oldbridge, of which two had yards walled in on each side of a road. These were set amongst corn-fields, meadows and gardens. The construction of a canal a century later and the creation of a demesne associated with the Coddington family removed all trace of this village.

Opposite Oldbridge, Story's map shows a deep valley with narrow defiles that run down to the river's edge. This is the ravine known today as King William's Glen. The north bank of the river along this section was heavily wooded westwards to the 'hamlet' of Monknewtown, just as it is today. This provided good cover for Schomberg and his troops moving to outflank the Jacobite army, by using the ford at Rossnaree where there were stone houses.

Included in Story's map is the village of Slane and the town of Drogheda. Linking roads and field enclosures are hinted at. A cluster of mills is shown on the south bank of the river at Rossnaree. The Civil Survey for county Meath in 1654 lists mills at Rossnaree, Staleen, Redmountain, Roughgrange and Newgrange, indicating a strong corn-growing area. In general, the detail west of Oldbridge is minimal on the map. The passage tombs are not marked nor the manor of Dowth which in 1654 contained a castle, stone house, stable, cornmill, tuckmill and various outbuildings. The Civil Survey mentions farm houses at Balfeddock, Kellystown and Knowth and battle accounts describe deserted crofts at Staleen. In landscape terms, this evidence points towards the gradual enclosure of the larger field systems of the Cistercian granges and open fields associated with the medieval manor.

LANDLORD, LABOURER AND LANDSCAPE

The transformation of the landscape commencing with the dissolution of Mellifont was copperfastened with the Williamite victory at the Boyne. A strife-free century ensued during which the current enclosed landscape of farm, field and demesne was established. Thompson's *Statistical Survey of County Meath* (1802) provides a broad insight into the life of the farming community in the Boyne valley at the beginning of the nineteenth century. This survey deals with farming practices, the nature of land ownership and the general state of rural housing in county Meath. At this time, half of the barony of Slane was under tillage and half under grazing, which is reflected in the presence today of both ploughmen's and herds' houses in the Bend of the Boyne. The area around Drogheda was particularly good for red wheat, producing large quantities of rye for boiling and seed with a good deal of oats and barley. The Boyne navigation built in the mid eighteenth century had greatly encouraged corn growing and milling in this area. In presenting a breakdown of the main classes of rural society, Thompson identified a close link between house type and holding size, ranging from the elegant

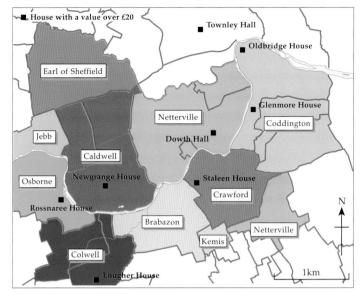

Fig. 23 The main landowners and mansions in the Bend of the Boyne in the mid nineteenth century.

mansion of the nobleman's seat to the mud-walled house of the cottier on a half acre of potato ground.

Griffith's Valuation of 1850 offers further insights into the social structure and standards of housing in the Bend of the

GERALDINE STOUT

Fig. 22 A lock-keeper's house at Staleen.

NATIONAL GALLERY OF IRELAND

Fig. 24 Andrew Caldwell of Newgrange painted by Gilbert Stuart in 1776 and completed by Robert Woodburn in 1795. Stuart was an American artist famous for his portraits of George Washington. The patronage of such an established painter is evidence of both the wealth and aesthetic awareness of at least one local landlord.

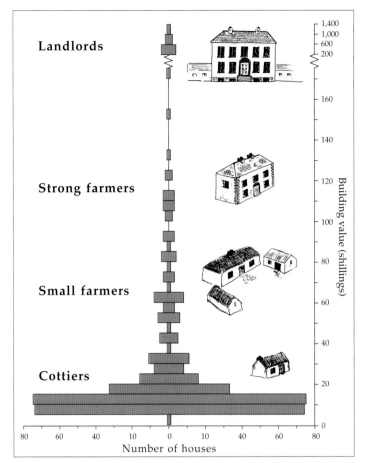

Fig. 25 Valuation figures for housing in the Bend of the Boyne in the mid nineteenth century. A pyramidal structure appears with a broad base and a narrow top, reflecting an entrenched hierarchical society.

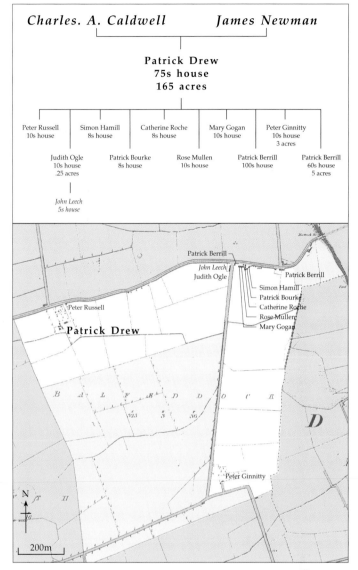

Fig. 26 The land and sub-tenants of middleman-farmer Patrick Drew in the townland of Balfeddock in 1850. Drew leased 165 acres (67 ha) from two landlords and sublet houses and a small portion of this land to ten tenants. One of these sub-tenants, Judith Ogle, leased a cabin to a further tenant.

Boyne in the mid nineteenth century. It presents valuation figures for the houses, buildings and land of the 285 households, leaseholders to the dozen large estates in the area. This was clearly an hierarchical society, with house valuations as low as five shillings and as high as sixty-five pounds.

There is also a strong correlation between house type and land holding size. At the bottom of the scale are landless labourers and cottiers who comprised 76% of the total population, followed by small farmers (holding *c.* 30 ha) at 9%, strong farmers (holding *c.* 60 ha) at 6% and the landlords' and entrepreneurs' seats at 9%. A close examination of the leasing structure in Balfeddock shows that the main holdings were sub-let by a local middleman. The landless labourers and cottiers had house valuations of £1 and under and lived in single-storey, mud-walled cottages. This housing was dispersed throughout the area with some clusters as at the now deserted nineteenth-century hamlet at Craud, and at Balfeddock, now 'Rossin'. The Ordnance Survey letters of the first half of the nineteenth century speak of a village of thatched houses at Craud; the only legacy today is a lane with low earthworks adjoining the remains of house foundations. Small farmers with land-

holdings of 20 ha to 40 ha had house valuations ranging from 25 shillings to £5; they lived mainly in single or two-storey vernacular farmhouses with outbuildings often organised to form a front yard. In the Bend of the Boyne, vernacular-style buildings were confined to the smaller farmers, cottiers and landless labourers. Strong farmers with 40 ha to 80 ha holdings tended to have architecturally-designed houses in a formal style. Their fine residences have survived into the twentieth century and are a prominent feature of the countryside. At the top of the social pyramid was an easily recognisable class of housing, the country mansions with their demesnes. These were the residences of owner-occupiers, landlords who held the land in fee. Oldbridge House, residence of the Coddington family, had the highest valuation (£65) in the Bend of the

GERALDINE STOUT

Fig. 27 A 'big house' at Oldbridge (built *c.* 1750, extended *c.* 1832), associated with the Coddington family, with a £65 valuation in 1850.

GERALDINE STOUT

Fig. 29 Small farmer's house at Monknewtown, with a 50 shilling valuation in 1850.

GERALDINE STOUT

Fig. 28 Strong farmer's house at Rossnaree, with a 130 shilling valuation in 1850.

GERALDINE STOUT

Fig. 30 Landless labourers' houses at Staleen, with a 10 shilling valuation in 1850.

Boyne; it was followed by Dowth Hall, the residence of Richard Gradwell. Of the nineteenth-century building stock, only the more substantial housing has survived in the contemporary landscape. The once typical vernacular-style housing is a rarity, demanding immediate attention by the conservation lobby.

THE CONTEMPORARY LANDSCAPE

Farming is still the major land use in the Bend of the Boyne. The area has a mixture of both large and small farms with 58% of the holdings below 20 ha and 10% over 60 ha. Many of the smaller holdings derived from the Land Commission settling migrant families from Mayo in the late 1930s and 1940s. The size of these farms has proved inadequate in the present farming climate and many are currently held in conacre and used for drystock. The larger farms practise intensive dairying, dry stock and tillage. In the last forty years, there has been significant re-structuring. The setting for the Boyne monuments is being gradually transformed

Fig. 31 Lithograph of Monknewtown mills in 1856. The mill at Monknewtown had a valuation of £134 in 1850, making it the single most valuable premises in the Bend of the Boyne. More than £7000 had been spent in the building of this complex. However by 1856, the area under grain had contracted dramatically and the mills at Monknewtown were for sale as an Encumbered Estate. The disused milling complex survives as an impressive ruin.

GERALDINE STOUT

Fig. 32 A Land Commission house at Newgrange built in the 1930s. This is one of a number in the Bend of the Boyne built to house migrant families from county Mayo in the late 1930s and 1940s.

as removal of field boundaries and construction of larger farm buildings create a new agricultural landscape. These changes have largely resulted from farm development schemes operated by the Department of Agriculture through the provision of grant aid. The impact of these schemes on the Boyne valley highlights the need to consider contemporary agricultural practices in any realistic programme of landscape conservation.

Since 1950, there have been three principal farm development schemes available to farmers in the Boyne valley. These were aimed directly at improving the structure of farms in order to increase agricultural production. One-fifth of the land within the Bend of the Boyne has undergone grant-aided reclamation between 1950 and 1990 and 7% of the field boundaries were removed. Development works consisted mainly of drainage improvement which involved re-conditioning of watercourses, culvert construction, demolition of banks and clearing ditches of

N

1km

Proposed Boyne Valley Archaeological Park

Reclaimed field

■ Grant-aided building/s

＼ Field fence

Field fence removed between 1950-1990

Fig. 33 The impact of farm development schemes in the Bend of the Boyne, 1950-1990. One-fifth of land in this archaeologically sensitive area underwent reclamation. In addition, state grants facilitated the removal of 7% of hedgerows. Grant-aided farm buildings include loose-houses, silos, dungsteads, cubicle houses and slatted houses.

vegetation. However, the construction of industrial-scale buildings rather than hedgerow removal has made the greatest visual impact. The introduction of the Farm Modernisation Scheme initiated a farm building boom in the Bend of the Boyne. In contrast to earlier reclamation, larger land holders obtained this funding. These conspicuous industrial-scale farm buildings have had a profound effect on the visual quality of the Bend of the Boyne in terms of design, colour and materials. There is rarely any effort to screen them from view and the ordered composition associated with older farms is lacking. The new buildings appear as awkward appendages to the old farmyard which is often left derelict. Buildings have gradually accumulated with the introduction of each new scheme, without any design principle other than accessibility. The end result is an untidy sprawl.

LANDSCAPE CONSERVATION

While public-funded farm development schemes have changed the face of the countryside in the Bend of the Boyne, there have been no special planning arrangements to take account of their environmental impact. Planning permission is not needed for field drainage and, until recently, agricultural structures were exempted from

DEPARTMENT OF ARTS, CULTURE AND THE GAELTACHT

Fig. 36 Considerable modernisation has taken place on this farm at Newgrange over the last three decades. Originally, it was an elegantly landscaped farm with a triangular yard formed by fine stone outbuildings. By 1964, the farm had been extensively modernised. Further changes occurred prior to 1991 when loose houses, silos and yards were constructed with the assistance of EU funding. Newgrange, the farm nearest to the most visited monument within the Bend of the Boyne, is now open to the public, introducing visitors to the workings of a modern farm.

planning constraints. Another vexing problem has arisen with the ever increasing number of visitors to the area which, at peak times, creates huge traffic congestion. Between 1969 and 1994, visitor numbers at Newgrange passage tomb soared five-fold, from 30,437 to 143,927. In 1987, the government announced its intention to create an archaeological park in the Bend of the Boyne, focused around the tombs of Knowth, Dowth and Newgrange. Its objectives are to ensure the preservation of the archaeological remains in the valley and their setting, to cater for the obvious tourist potential of the area by providing facilities for visitors, and to facilitate archaeological research. Landscape conservation of such an extensive fertile lowland is unique in Ireland where attention has been biased towards upland and marginal areas.

The Bend of the Boyne is demonstrably a dynamic rural landscape, whose fertile soils and south-facing slopes have provided a stable economic base for the many societies who have farmed this valley for at least five thousand years. Future development should be closely monitored to assess its effects on this conservation zone; regulation will be needed to mitigate damage and at the same time permit legitimate and necessary farming practices. While there was an obvious difficulty in managing a heritage landscape so influenced by the Common Agricultural Policy, the EU has more recently recognised the pivotal role farmers have in safeguarding the countryside. The Rural Environmental Protection Scheme (REPS) emphasises the need to keep farmers on the land in order to maintain

ORDNANCE SURVEY

Fig. 35 The impact of industrial-scale farming is shown in this photograph of recent field clearance and a large pig fattening unit – catering for over 3000 pigs.

traditional landscapes. Farmers, as environmental managers, need to be carefully advised by conservation, agricultural and planning authorities if deterioration is to be avoided and the area's visual quality guaranteed.

The twentieth-century landscape is a composite creation which has evolved over thousands of years. The proposed establishment of this conservation zone presents an unique opportunity to investigate the broader cultural history of the region, utilising the Boyne landscape to narrate the story of the various societies who have lived in the area. While the visitor centre's main focus will inevitably be the passage tomb cemeteries, interpretation and future research should incorporate wider aspects of the rich cultural and natural heritage in the Bend of the Boyne. Like the painstaking excavators of Knowth and Newgrange, we must continue to peel back this wonderful landscape layer by layer in order to evaluate its complex historic and pre-historic components.

BIBLIOGRAPHY

F. Byrne, 'Historical note on Cnogba (Knowth)' in G. Eogan, 'Excavations at Knowth' in *R.I.A.Proc.*, lxvi (1968), C, pp 383-400.

G. Cooney, 'The place of megalithic tomb cemeteries in Ireland' in *Antiquity*, lxiv (1990), pp 741-53.

G. Cooney, 'Irish neolithic landscapes and landuse systems: the implications of field systems' in *Rural History*, ii (1991), pp 123-9.

Fr Colmcille, *The story of Mellifont* (Dublin, 1958).

P. Ellis, *The Boyne water* (Belfast, 1976).

G. Eogan, *Knowth and the passage-tombs of Ireland* (London, 1986).

G. Eogan, 'Prehistoric and early historic culture change at Brugh na Bóinne' in *R.I.A.Proc.*, xci (1991), C, pp 105-32.

G. Eogan and H. Roche, 'A Grooved Ware wooden structure at Knowth, Boyne valley, Ireland', in *Antiquity*, lxviii (1994), pp 322-30.

T. Finch, *Soil survey of county Meath* (Dublin, 1983).

H. Hickey, *I send my love along the Boyne* (Dublin, 1960).

A. Ireland, 'Caldwell estate' in *Journal of the Old Drogheda Society*, vi (1989), pp 59-64.

A. MacCabe, 'The glacial stratigraphy of Meath and Louth' in *R.I.A.Proc.*, lxxiii (1973), B, pp 356-77.

G. Mitchell, 'The landscape' in G. Eogan, *Excavations at Knowth* (Dublin, 1984), pp 9-11.

C. O'Kelly, *Illustrated guide to Newgrange and the other Boyne monuments* (Wexford, 1978).

M. O'Kelly, *Newgrange: archaeology, art and legend* (London, 1982).

M. O'Kelly, R. Cleary and D. Lehane, *Newgrange, county Meath, Ireland: the Late Neolithic/Beaker period settlement* (Oxford, 1983).

M. O'Kelly and C. O'Kelly, 'The tumulus of Dowth, county Meath' in *R.I.A.Proc.*, lxxxiii (1983), C, pp 135-90.

C. Mount, 'Aspects of ritual deposition in the Late Neolithic and Beaker periods at Newgrange, county Meath' in *Proceedings of the Prehistoric Society*, lx (1994), pp 433-43.

A. O'Neill, National Archaeological Park: Boyne valley (unpublished consultancy report, 1989).

S. Ó Ríordain and G. Daniel, *Newgrange and the Bend of the Boyne* (London, 1964).

G. Story, *An impartial history of the wars of Ireland* . . . (London, 1693).

G. Stout, 'Embanked enclosures of the Boyne region' in *R.I.A.Proc.*, xci (1991), C, pp 245-84.

G. Stout, 'Grant-aided change in the Boyne Valley Archaeological Park: agricultural grants 1950-1990' in *Ir. Geog.*, xxvi (1993), pp 79-88.

D. Sweetman, 'An earthen enclosure at Monknewtown, Slane, county Meath' in *R.I.A.Proc.*, lxxvi (1976), C, pp 25-72.

D. Sweetman, 'A Late Neolithic/Early Bronze Age pit circle at Newgrange, county Meath' in *R.I.A.Proc.*, lxxxv (1985), C, pp 195-221.

R. Thompson, *Statistical survey of county Meath* (Dublin, 1802).

C. Trench, *Slane* (Dublin, 1976).

L. Van Wijngaarden-Bakker, 'The animal remains from the Beaker settlement at Newgrange, county Meath: first report' in *R.I.A.Proc.*, lxxiv (1974), C, pp 313-83.

L. Van Wijngaarden-Bakker, 'The animal remains from the Beaker settlement at Newgrange, county Meath: final report' in *R.I.A.Proc.*, lxxxvi (1986), C, pp 17-111.

W. Wilde, *The beauties of the Boyne and its tributary the Blackwater* (Dublin, 1849).

THE RING OF GULLION, COUNTY ARMAGH

The interpenetration of mountains, hills and lowlands underlies major landscape contrasts in Northern Ireland. In the eastern borderlands of Ulster and Leinster, igneous intrusions have formed four distinctive mountain masses: the Mournes, Slieve Croob, the Carlingford peninsula and Slieve Gullion. Of these, Slieve Gullion and its remarkably complete ringdyke is the smallest but also the most compact and coherent. As in the other mountain areas, geological background, broken topography and altitudinal zonation of climate, soil and vegetation have led to patterns of settlement history and land use distinct from and more intricate than those of the surrounding lowlands.

Ice erosion strongly affected the relief and soil cover of the mountains: their drift-free slopes overlook territory thickly blanketed by drumlinised drift. Population pressure and energetic land improvement in the eighteenth and nineteenth centuries extended settlement to the limits of workable soil and today the upper boundary of close settlement and improved land corresponds broadly with the extent of drift, reaching up to 305m and even higher in places. The boundary of improved land is a striking feature of Slieve Gullion's human landscape. Above it, moorland, bog and forest dominate, while below, the land is covered by small farms and an intricate network of fields. Owing to a traditional fusion of intensive agriculture with industrial activities, the area has relatively high population densities despite prolonged emigration.

The individuality and outstanding scenic qualities of Slieve Gullion, its surrounding farmland and ring of hills were officially recognised in 1991 when it was designated an Area of Outstanding Natural Beauty.

Fig. 1 Looking north-west to Camlough Mountain and Ballymacdermot Mountain from Slieve Gullion.

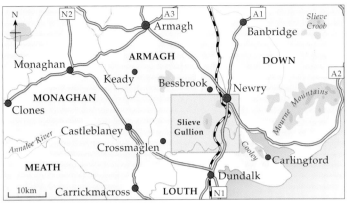

Fig. 2 Regional setting of the Ring of Gullion.

VOLCANIC ORIGINS

The contemporary landscape of the Ring of Gullion is superimposed on the remains of a huge volcanic complex which erupted around sixty million years ago in the Tertiary period. The 'Ring' is a circular volcanic dyke (ringdyke) about 11 km in diameter which surrounds Slieve Gullion; because of its hard granitic rocks, the dyke forms a striking ring of steep and craggy hills 230m to 300m high and including Sturgan Mountain, Slievenacappel, Mullaghbane Mountain, Slievebrack, Croslieve, Tievecrom, Slievebolea, Feede Mountain, Anglesey Mountain, Flagstaff, Fathom Mountain and Camlough Mountain. In the middle of this ring squats Slieve Gullion itself; higher, broader and totally dominating the landscape – a mountain hulk built up by layer upon layer of intruded volcanic rocks. Between the mountain and its ring lie lowlands of varying width, from a narrow valley at Lislea to a broad plain at Killeen. Adjacent to Slieve Gullion, a second ringdyke complex appears in the Carlingford peninsula and comparable features are also found in western Scotland.

In subsequent epochs, the landscape was worn down by wind, water and ice to create the familiar landforms of mountain, valley and lake. The last Ice Age had a dramatic

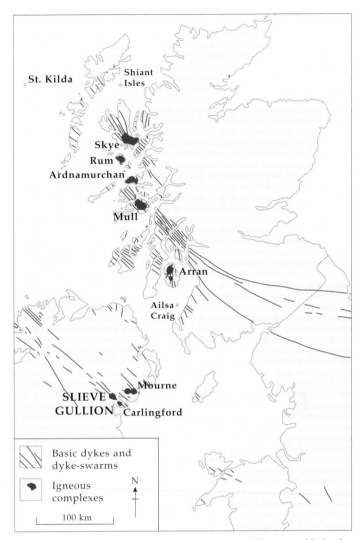

Fig. 4 Tertiary igneous complexes and dyke swarms of Britain and Ireland.

effect which, in combination with the geology, has greatly influenced the evolution of the cultural landscape. During this glaciation, an ice cap built up over the north of Ireland: glaciers flowing outwards from this cap crossed the Ring of Gullion from north-west to south-east. The moving ice

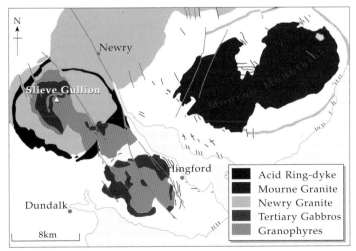

Acid Ring-dyke
Mourne Granite
Newry Granite
Tertiary Gabbros
Granophyres

Fig. 3 Igneous complexes in the region of Slieve Gullion.

ENVIRONMENT AND HERITAGE SERVICE

Fig. 5 The volcanic cone of Slieve Gullion from the west.

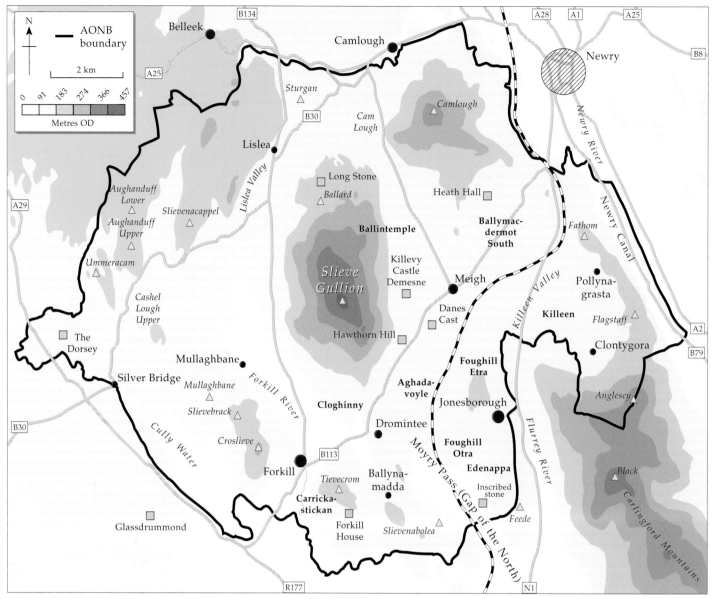

N

AONB boundary

2 km

0 91 183 274 366 457

Metres OD

Belleek

Camlough

B134

A28 A1 A25

Newry

B8

A25

Sturgan

Cam Lough

Camlough

B30

Lislea

Long Stone

Ballard

Heath Hall

Lislea Valley

Aughanduff Lower

Slievenacappel

Ballintemple

Ballymac-dermot South

Fathom

A29

Aughanduff Upper

Slieve Gullion

Killevy Castle Demesne

Meigh

Pollyna-grasta

Ummeracam

Danes Cast

Killeen Valley

Killeen

Flagstaff

A2

Cashel Lough Upper

Hawthorn Hill

Clontygora

B79

The Dorsey

Foughill Etra

Mullaghbane

Aghada-voyle

Jonesborough

Anglesey

Silver Bridge

Mullaghbane

Forkill River

Cloghinny

Flurrey River

B30

Slievebrack

Cully Water

Croslieve

Dromintee

B113

Foughill Otra

Edenappa

Inscribed stone

Black

Carlingford Mountains

Forkill

Tievecrom

Ballyna-madda

Moyry Pass (Gap of the North)

Feede

Carricka-stickan

Slievenabolea

Glassdrummond

Forkill House

R177

N1

Fig. 6 The Ring of Gullion, county Armagh, designated an Area of Outstanding Natural Beauty, lies north of the border with the Republic of Ireland.

picked out any weaknesses in the underlying rocks. Thus, the hard rocks of the ringdyke and Slieve Gullion were scoured bare of soil and in many places gaps and small hollows were excavated. In contrast, the surrounding softer rocks were more easily worn away and valleys deepened. The main ice streams passed to the east along the line of the Newry river, and to either side of Slieve Gullion, developing the Camlough and Forkill valleys. On the valley floors, the glaciers deposited streamlined ridges of boulder clay. One such rounded ridge forms a 'tail' in the wake of Slieve Gullion on which the village of Dromintee is sited.

The ice sheets eventually melted away some 12,000 years ago. The ringdyke had been breached in many places and these gaps were to become the major routeways through the area. Lakes formed as the depressions filled with water and small rivers squeezed uncertainly

Fig. 7 Mullaghbane Mountain. The ringdyke hills, covered by moorland and rough grazing, rise abruptly from surrounding agricultural lowlands.

ENVIRONMENT AND HERITAGE SERVICE

Fig. 8 Ladder farms run up the gradual slopes of Slieve Gullion but higher fields have recently been partly colonised by bracken and gorse and planted with conifers.

through the muddle of glacial deposits which littered the valley floors.

Although the vegetation history of this area has not been studied in detail, we can assume that plant colonisation followed the pattern elsewhere in the north and midlands of Ireland. By the time the first humans arrived in Ireland about 10,000 years ago, the primeval woodland was well established. Juniper, willow, birch, hazel and pine were prevalent on the rocky hillsides while alder, oak, ash and elm occurred on the glacial deposits in the valleys. At the same time, bog moss accumulated in the waterlogged valley bottoms, building up to form thick peat deposits and spreading into some of the small lake basins. At Cashel Lough Upper, the tree stumps in shallow water around the

Fig. 9 Cam Lough is the largest of the numerous water bodies in the area and probably the best example of a glacial ribbon lake in Northern Ireland. It lies in a steep and narrow trough separating Camlough Mountain from Slieve Gullion. The water level was raised by an embankment built in the late nineteenth century but the lough retains much of its natural character. As a multi-purpose water resource, wildlife habitat and landscape feature, and increasingly popular for a variety of recreational activities, the lough requires an integrated management strategy.

lough shores are remnants of a forest drowned by a rising water table around this time. The forest may have thinned out on the steeper slopes and mountain tops, giving way to a juniper heath with heather, bilberry and gorse.

ARCHAEOLOGICAL RECORD

Mesolithic sites are known from the nearby coast at Dundalk Bay and it is likely that early hunters and gatherers travelled through the Ring of Gullion in search of food. The first certain evidence of human occupation comes from the Neolithic period about 5000 years ago when farming communities initiated woodland clearance for grazing and cultivation. A substantial population would have been required to build the twenty or so large megalithic tombs which are known in the area.

Three types of tombs are well represented. The King's Ring at Clontygora and the tomb at Ballymacdermot are some of the best examples of court tombs in the north of Ireland. The Hag's Chair at Ballykeel is a fine portal tomb. The most celebrated Irish passage tombs are found in the Boyne valley 48 km to the south; the passage-grave cairn on the south slope of Slieve Gullion, although more modest, is dramatically sited, commanding extensive views over parts of Ulster and Leinster.

Excavations at several of these burial sites have discovered human remains, pottery and stone tools. Some sites continued to be used for over a thousand years, probably

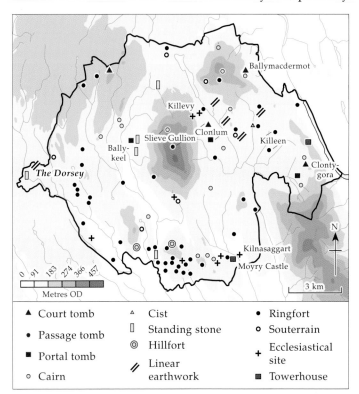

Fig. 10 Archaeological sites and monuments in the Slieve Gullion area. Named sites are historical monuments in state care.

ENVIRONMENT AND HERITAGE SERVICE

Fig. 11 The court tomb at Ballymacdermot is characteristically sited on elevated ground near the present-day limits of improved land.

serving not only as burial places but as focal points for the local communities. The concentration of these monuments in the area may reflect the availability of suitable stone, the resilience of such massive monuments and the continuing local tradition which enveloped them in a protective aura of respect.

Metal working arrived in the area about 4000 years ago and the changing culture is reflected in a move from large communal tombs to individual burials in small pits or stone cists. A round cairn containing two cists survives on the northern summit of Slieve Gullion. A few standing stones, such as the Long Stone at Ballard, may also date from the Bronze Age.

The earliest Irish sagas are thought to relate to events associated with Gaelic chiefs during the Iron Age (about 250 BC to 400 AD) and the Dorsey 'enclosure', which lies

ENVIRONMENT AND HERITAGE SERVICE

Fig. 12 Portal tomb, Ballykeel. This monument, reconstructed after excavation in 1965, stands at the southern end of a rectangular cairn.

ENVIRONMENT AND HERITAGE SERVICE

Fig. 13 North cairn on the summit of Slieve Gullion. Two Bronze Age cists found in the cairn may have been deposited as secondary burials.

Fig. 14 The Dorsey. This linear earthwork, comprising a bank and ditch, was built as a defensive feature in the Iron Age.

on the western edge of the Ring of Gullion, dates to this period. The Dorsey consists of the remains of two, roughly parallel, massive earthen bank and ditch ramparts over 1.6 km long which lie astride an ancient road to Emain Macha (Navan Fort, near Armagh), the ancient capital of Ulster. Recent evidence gives the earthwork a date of about 100 BC, contemporary with a major phase of development at Emain Macha and so supporting the tradition that the Dorsey was then a fortified 'gateway' of Ulster. Fragments of another similar earthwork, known locally as The Dane's Cast, survive at Aghayalloge, near Meigh.

Routeways continued to have a significant influence on settlement in the Ring of Gullion during the Early Christian period (fifth to twelfth centuries AD). Slíghe Midluachra, the ancient road from Tara to Dunseverick, passed through the Gap of the North at Moyry. Close to the road are two early religious sites, Kilnasaggart and Killevy. The pillar stone at Kilnasaggart, marking the site of a cemetery, can be dated to about 700 AD. Killevy is the site of one of Ireland's most important early convents, founded by St Monenna (or Bline) in the fifth century. Although plundered by the Vikings, the foundation continued here for a thousand years.

The rural economy prospered during this period and there are many surviving raths and cashels. Several raths are grouped on the boulder clay hills of the south and south-west slopes of the Ring near Forkill, Carrickastickan

and Tievecrom. Cashels are usually found on rockier substrates, for example at Lisbanemore and Lisdoo in Killeen townland.

During the medieval period, the Ring of Gullion assumed a strategic position on the northern edge of the English 'Pale', straddling the land routes to strongholds at Newry, Downpatrick and Carrickfergus. Much of the land was clothed by either thick woods or bog, in marked contrast to the predominantly arable farms established on the Norman lowlands of county Louth. The Ring of Gullion was traversed with difficulty, not least because of the independence of the indigenous population and their resistance to intrusive forces.

Knowledge of the appearance of the countryside during these early stages of human settlement is limited and the evidence is subject to varied interpretations. The density of surviving neolithic tombs and of Early Christian farmsteads suggests that during these periods there were well-developed farming communities and significant areas of land must have been brought into use for crops and livestock grazing. The more limited evidence of settlement in the intervening periods and in the subsequent medieval period perhaps indicates phases of agricultural retreat in this area.

THE MAKING OF THE MODERN LANDSCAPE

At the outset of the seventeenth century, this region was considered by the English to be a 'wild' area, with extensive woodland, treacherous bogs, rocky passes and lawless

Fig. 15 Kilnasaggart pillar stone with Slieve Gullion in the distance. Over two metres high, this is the earliest datable cross-inscribed stone in Ireland.

Fig. 16 Moyry Castle is a square, three-storey tower with musket loops. It was built on a hill commanding the Gap of the North.

inhabitants. In 1600, Lord Mountjoy secured the Moyry Pass, or Gap of the North, for the English and established Moyry Castle on a small but strategic hill overlooking the Pass. The castle was built for a garrison of twelve men armed with muskets.

As the Plantation of Ulster progressed during the seventeenth century, south Armagh was slowly drawn into the wider market economy. Pockets of English and Scottish settlers eventually established themselves on newly founded estates like those of Thomas Ball at Glassdrummond and Richard Jackson at Forkill. Population growth and an influx of Irish settlers from the north and east led to expansion of settlement into the wooded hills and bogs, facilitated by cultivation of the potato. Social and economic links were forged with the linen manufacturing triangle of Ulster, Slieve Gullion lying at the southern limit of the linen country.

During the eighteenth century, influential estate owners established new fairs and markets at Jonesborough, Forkill, Belleek and Camlough. A focus for the local economy, these were linked to one another and the nearby towns of Newry and Dundalk by a spreading network of new roads. These routeways were critical to the development of the area, enabling the transport of raw materials like lime and peat, agricultural products (oats, barley and potatoes) and linen. Transporting limestone into the hill areas, burning it in kilns and applying it to the acid soils was a prerequisite of intensive settlement along with drainage and enclosure. Robert Stephenson wrote in 1795 that 'the business of carrying limestone into all the recesses of the mountains is incessantly practis ed and in return bringing turf down to the bleach yards around the city of Armagh'. Roads thus gave impetus to agricultural improvements and, naturally, to roadside and

crossroads settlements and became a fundamental structural component of the landscape.

Less important for the local economy of the Ring of Gullion but crucial to wider regional development was the opening of the Newry Canal in 1742 and the Great Northern Railway a century later in 1852. The canal brought a commercial and industrial boom to Newry and its immediate hinterland, leading the way in the industrial revolution of Ulster. The later railway almost marked an end to this period as Belfast assumed pre-eminence in the economy of the North. Proximity to the industrial and port complexes of Newry, Bessbrook and Dundalk added an extra dimension to the local economy, providing a market for agricultural goods and seasonal employment for labourers – often 'across the water' in England. This additional income helped to support a growing rural population and the local landlords benefited from commercial interests, using the gains to embellish their estates.

Surging population and subdivision of small farms in the eighteenth century were supported by intensive cultivation, combined with the domestic linen industry and employment in neighbouring towns. By the early nineteenth century, the area was among the most heavily settled parts of Ireland with population densities exceeding

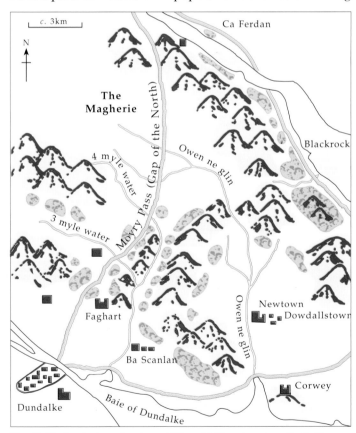

Fig. 17 Carlingford peninsula and Slieve Gullion, based on Bartlett's map of c. 1600. The emphasis is on the importance of the Moyry Pass. The map also suggests the wooded character of some of the hill areas.

150 to the square kilometre. Moreover, the landscape was totally transformed. Bogs had been drained, woods cleared, mountain slopes brought into cultivation, fields enclosed in rectangular strips and farmhouses built close to the roads. Only in a few locations did the irregular clusters of farms, known as clachans (or locally as 'streets'), continue to develop, for example, at Clontygora, Ballynamadda and Pollynagrasta. The large houses of the landlords set within wooded estates, parkland and gardens at Heath Hall, Killevy and Forkill were new landscape features. Victorian civil engineering – the railway, the Newry Ship Canal and the enlargement of Camlough Lake to provide water for linen mills in Bessbrook – also had a lasting impact on the landscape.

The Famine which struck in the period 1846-50 initiated a dramatic decline in the rural population, a trend which has only recently been reversed. In the Famine years, the population of townlands such as Edenappa, Foughill Etra and Foughill Otra, fell by over a third due to death and emigration. The ruins of farmhouses, abandoned fields, derelict walls and overgrown lanes are monuments to this vanished generation. For a combination of reasons, including the land reforms of the late nineteenth century, the estates fell into decline and only fragments, such as the

Fig. 18 Killevy demesne with its ornamental woodlands and an adjacent area to the north of reformed, elongated ladder farms in Ballintemple townland.

Fig. 20 Killevy demesne. Although now neglected, the large castellated house and its surrounding wooded parkland and large fields are prominent features in the present-day landscape.

Fig. 19 The long narrow holdings running down the slope show up in the farmed landscape in Ballintemple townland.

Fig. 21 Nineteenth-century gate lodge, Hawthorn Hill (a listed building). Here, as on many estates, the gate lodge has outlived the great house.

estate buildings and walled garden of Hawthorn Hill (now part of Slieve Gullion Forest Park), survive intact today.

CONTEMPORARY LANDSCAPE

The natural resources of the Ring of Gullion have been used to the full. Woods have been felled and the timber exported, peat has been dug and burnt in generations of hearths, stone has been quarried, water has been channelled into mills and soils have been cultivated. And yet, despite this progressive exploitation, the countryside maintains a rich diversity of natural habitats and historical heritage.

The more productive farmland of the Ring of Gullion has been improved progressively over the last few hundred years. The best agricultural soils are those of the glacial deposits which form low rounded ridges astride the ringdyke hills. In these areas, farmland is neatly divided into strips of rectangular fields, each strip originally worked as one farm. The arrangement is suggestive of eighteenth-century estate planning. Typically, the roads run along the crest of the ridges and the strips are orientated at right-angles, running down into the intervening boggy hollow. The farmhouse is sited near the road. Thus, each farm had access to a variety of land for crops, grazing and turbary. Fields in the Slieve Gullion area are enclosed by combinations of banks, stone walls and hedges in varying proportions. Stone walls are a particular feature around Aghadavoyle and Clontygora but hedges are more typical elsewhere. Traditional gate posts are substantial, whitewashed stone pillars, either cylindrical or square with domed or conical caps.

As in other hill areas of Ulster, gable-ended, direct-entry type houses are general. Many have been enlarged piecemeal within the last century or so, with rooms added to

Fig. 23 Elongated farmhouse, whitewashed and partly two-storeyed. Part of the rich store of vernacular architecture within the AONB.

older structures or a new storey built over part or whole of the house. Farm dwellings and outbuildings are customarily whitewashed. Deeply traditional features such as the bed-outshot, now largely confined to the north-western part of Ireland, are found in a few of the older houses.

Dispersed rural settlement is the dominant traditional pattern in the area. This has, however, been changing, with new roadside dwellings, overwhelmingly bungalows, built to replace older, sub-standard houses which are often situated down lanes. The materials and designs used for new buildings often show little affinity with older houses, and the treatment of adjoining gardens and boundaries contrasts markedly with surrounding fields, walls and hedges. Sited in more prominent positions, the intrusive wave of buildings is one of the greatest threats to the outstanding landscape quality. However, some older houses have been successfully modernised and renovated without losing their traditional character.

In the past, most farms would have grown some crops of oats and potatoes, but grassland and cattle now predominate. Half of all farm businesses are classified as 'mainly beef cattle' but sheep have become more important in recent years due to EU subsidies. The farms are minuscule; even after many years of rationalisation, the average holding is only 15 ha. Three-quarters of farm businesses are not considered viable as a full-time operation. The grassland has seen many years of intensive cropping and manuring and as a result very few fields retain a natural diversity of plants. Species-rich grasslands with marsh and butterfly orchids are restricted to a few damp meadows.

Fig. 22 Typical cylindrical gate posts and wrought iron gates, near Forkill.

Fig. 24 Cluster of traditional whitewashed farmhouses and buildings at the foot of Slieve Gullion.

The mountain slopes adjoining the lowlands provide evidence of earlier phases of agricultural expansion. Sometimes, small irregular fields have been created within the confines of rocky slopes and crags above the present limit of farming and are usually associated with old spade-dug cultivation ridges ('lazy beds') formed in the early nineteenth century for potato growing. Elsewhere, on more even ground, narrow strips of 'ladder farms' run up the slopes. Cleared stones have been built into the thick field walls or piled neatly nearby in small cairns. There may be remains of a small farmhouse or cabin, and often a small stand of sycamore trees and a few forlorn thorn bushes. Tracks lead through the fields to the upper unenclosed slopes but much of this marginal land has now reverted to bracken and gorse and is grazed extensively by cattle and sheep.

The native woodland cover is fragmentary and almost entirely of secondary origin – either planted or naturally regenerating scrub. On the steep slopes of valleys and hillsides, there are small native woods of hazel and ash, with sycamore, oak, rowan and willow. Lowland bogs which have been drained and cut-over for peat are rapidly colonised by willow, birch and alder scrub. The most mature woods are those which were planted on the old estates, notably at Killevy Castle, Hawthorn Hill and Forkill. In these woods, beech and oak are common.

Farm land use and livestock, Ring of Gullion, 1990

Livestock	Numbers	Land Use	Holdings (ha)
Cattle and calves	17,604	Crops	137
Sheep and lambs	23,487	Grass < 5 years old	2,046
Goats	281	Grass > 5 years old	5,873
Horses	57	Rough grazing	1,978
Pigs	2,249	Woods	36
Poultry	12,268	Other land	177
		Total area of holdings	10,247

Beneath the trees, the ground flora includes plants which are suited to the generally acidic soil conditions – bilberry, bracken and brambles.

Commercial forestry is a major land use affecting 6% of the area in the Ring of Gullion. The forests have been planted within the last thirty years, comprising mainly conifers – Sitka spruce, lodgepole pine, Japanese larch and Scots pine. The variety of species, often planted in irregular blocks, with areas of unplanted hillside and pre-existing broadleaved trees, combine to produce attractive landscape features and sites for forest recreation. These forests are probably the greatest single landscape change in this century.

Apart from woodland, the other main natural habitats in the Ring of Gullion are heathland, bog and wetland. The craggy hills, with thin acidic soils overlying granitic rocks, have an extensive cover of heathland which makes up one-tenth of the land area. Slieve Gullion is by far the largest area of moorland, dominated by ling heather with scattered bilberry. The lower hills of the ringdyke, such as Mullaghbane Mountain, Ummeracam and Ballard, have a greater diversity of habitats and plants. These glacially scoured hills have a ridge and basin topography. Dry heaths with ling, bell heather and western gorse are characteristic of the better drained, shallow peaty soils of the ridges and slopes. Cross-leaved heath becomes more typical on poorly drained peaty soils, where it forms a wet heath community with deer grass, bog asphodel and cotton grass. Sedges and bog mosses are typical of the basins and the margins of small lakes. Where heathland has been severely disturbed by heavy grazing or repeated burning, bracken, bramble and gorse tend to be invasive. The bogs of the valley bottoms have been greatly disturbed by centuries of turf cutting, drainage and reclamation. The fragments which survive contain mixtures of fen, bog and woodland scrub.

CONSERVATION

The evolution of the cultural landscape is a dynamic process, but current rates of change are quicker and, owing to modern technology, the impacts greater than ever before. Among diverse developments in the Slieve Gullion area are new road alignments; agricultural improvements; hedge and wall removal; building of large new houses, schools and workshops; and emplacement of new infrastructure and border observation posts.

The pace and extent of development are a cause for concern because they directly affect the most valued characteristics of the Ring of Gullion's landscape, heritage and wildlife. Proposed changes clearly must have regard to the

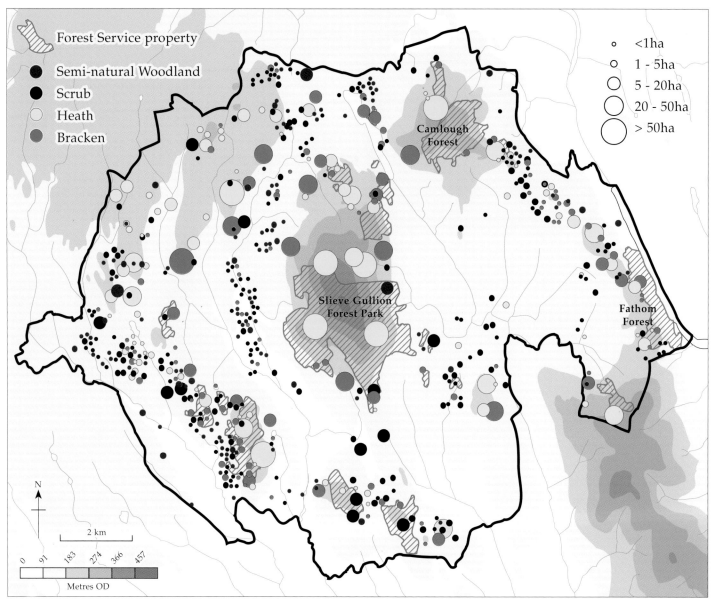

Fig. 25 The ringdyke and Slieve Gullion have a clear influence on the distribution pattern of Forest Service property, woodland, scrub, heath and bracken.

Fig. 26 Modern forestry plantation, Camlough forest, Slieve Gullion. Some of the most dramatic landscapes and panoramic viewpoints in the Ring of Gullion are found here.

Fig. 27 Heath and bog, Slieve Gullion. The abandoned cut-away bog in the foreground contains deep pools, banks of bilberry and heather and a regenerating cover of birch and willow scrub.

Fig. 28 Cattle graze the furze-covered slopes of Slieve Gullion. The ringdyke hills are visible in the distance.

Fig. 30 Folk Museum, Mullaghbane. The thatched farmhouse and buildings, cylindrical gate posts and whitewashed walls make an attractive ensemble.

widest range of economic, social and environmental considerations. Too often, short term economic expediency is the driving force in landscape change, with scant regard for longer term social and environmental costs.

One step towards readdressing this balance has been the designation of the Ring of Gullion as an Area of Outstanding Natural Beauty (AONB) in 1991. This AONB was the fourth to be designated in Northern Ireland under the Nature Conservation and Amenity Lands (NI) Order, 1985. In international terms, an AONB is a Category V Protected Landscape (IUCN, 1987). Within an AONB, the legislation permits the Department of the Environment (NI) to formulate proposals for: conserving or enhancing the natural beauty or amenities of the area; conserving wildlife,

historic objects or natural phenomena within it; promoting its enjoyment by the public and providing or maintaining public access to it.

As part of this process, the Department published a 'Guide to Designation' which contains a policy statement and an action plan for the conservation of landscapes, wildlife and heritage. The topics covered include farming, tourism, buildings and monuments, public access, roads and nature conservation. Policies and proposals for action were developed in full consultation with local community groups, the Newry and Mourne District Council and all the government departments and agencies involved. Following designation, an environmental interpretation and education centre has been established in the old courtyard buildings in Slieve Gullion Forest Park. The centre is managed by a community-based company and conservation work in the AONB is co-ordinated by a Countryside Officer. The Ring of Gullion was also designated an Environmentally Sensitive Area (ESA) in 1994. The ESA designation is a voluntary scheme which provides financial

Fig. 29 Mullaghbane. Strip and ladder farms run across the drift-covered portion of the ringdyke in the foreground.

Fig. 31 Ballymacdermot South shows a characteristic variety of enclosure methods, including dry stone walls, banks and hedges.

encouragement for farmers to adopt farming practices which maintain and enhance the landscape, wildlife and heritage of their land holding.

There are also special measures to safeguard historic monuments and buildings in the Ring of Gullion. Twelve of the best preserved and most important sites are in state care. Enjoyment and appreciation of these sites is encouraged through the provision of public access and explanatory notices. A further 23 sites, in private ownership, are protected as Scheduled Ancient Monuments. Most of the buildings of historical interest – farms, mills, and old estate buildings – are also in private ownership but there is an ongoing programme to protect these buildings by Listing. However, despite these measures, it is clear that the landscape will be best conserved through promoting respect for the local heritage and providing advice on how best to maintain buildings and monuments.

As yet the area is poorly served by nature conservation designations. Only one site – the Slieve Gullion Forest Nature Reserve – is specifically conserved for wildlife and yet there are many sites of local interest and some wetland, lowland heath and geological sites may be of regional or national importance. Survey and scientific evaluation of these areas is in progress and it is likely that Areas of Special Scientific Interest (ASSIs) will be declared.

Promising steps have thus been taken to protect landscape quality in this area. The AONB designation, however, merely provides a framework in which various aspects of conservation and the promotion of public enjoyment of the countryside may be co-ordinated. Planning authorities are still constrained and powers are absent in respect of much countryside change. There is a range of complex problems and pressures to be faced. As elsewhere, the future of farming and land use is uncertain; changes could come quickly and unpredictably both on the enclosed lower areas and the open uplands in response to changing government policy objectives and declining levels of farm subsidy. Woodlands have been adversely affected by livestock grazing, litter dumping and invasion by sycamore: the existing woods, along with hedges and trees, require care and management. The search for new sources of employment is likely to intensify, with small-scale activities springing up sporadically. Exploitation of the considerable landscape and heritage resources in order to encourage recreational and tourism activities will almost certainly be one significant avenue of development. Conservation and development will require careful reconciliation. The siting and design of new houses and other buildings also require sensitive attention in this densely settled, upland area as the character of the community changes and the traditional dependence on farming declines. Finally, although useful co-ordinating structures are now in place, effective landscape conservation will only be achieved through the full and sustained commitment of individual landowners, local community groups and the responsible authorities.

BIBLIOGRAPHY

T. Canavan, *Frontier town: an illustrated history of Newry* (Belfast, 1989).

C. Coote, *Statistical survey of the county of Armagh* (Dublin, 1804).

W. Crawford, 'The reshaping of the borderlands 1700-1840' in R. Gillespie and H. O'Sullivan (ed.), *The borderlands* (Belfast, 1989), pp 93-06.

DANI, *Environmentally sensitive areas in Northern Ireland* (Belfast, 1990).

DOENI, *Historic monuments of Northern Ireland: an introduction and guide* (Belfast, 1987).

DOENI, 'The Iron Age gates of Ulster? The Dorsey, county Armagh' in *Pieces of the past* (Belfast, 1988).

DOENI, *Ring of Gullion AONB – Guide to designation* (Belfast, 1991).

J. Donaldson, *A historical and statistical account of the barony of Upper Fews in the county of Armagh 1838* (Dundalk, 1923).

R. Gillespie, 'The transformation of the borderlands 1600-1700' in Gillespie and O'Sullivan, *Borderlands*, pp 75-92.

V. Hall, 'Ancient agricultural activity at Slieve Gullion, county Armagh: the palynological and documentary evidence' in *R.I.A.Proc.*, xc (1990), C, pp 123-34.

IUCN, *Protected landscapes: the UK experience* (Manchester, 1987).

W. McCutcheon, 'Transport 1820-1914' in L. Kennedy and P. Ollerenshaw (ed.), *An economic history of Ulster 1820-1939* (Manchester, 1985).

M. Murphy, *At Slieve Gullion's foot* (Dundalk, 1940).

J. Pilcher, 'History of vegetation in north-east Ireland' in P. Hackney (ed.) *Stewart and Corry's flora of the north-east of Ireland* (Belfast, 1992).

A. Smith and J. Pilcher, 'Pollen analysis and radiocarbon dating of deposits at Slieve Gullion passage grave, county Armagh' in *Ulster Jn. Archaeology*, xxxv (1972), pp 17-21.

R. Stephenson, Report on south Armagh in 1795, P.R.O.N.I., D. 562/1270.

A. Stott, 'From land use survey to policy implementation: the designation of AONBs in Northern Ireland' in A. Cooper and P. Wilson (ed.), *Managing land use change* (Dublin, 1992).

D. Sutherland (ed.), *Igneous rocks of the British Isles* (London, 1940), pp 405-10.

R. Tomlinson, M. Butcher and S. Kerr, South Armagh tree survey, unpublished report for DOENI, 1987.

A. Whittow, *Geology and scenery in Ireland* (London, 1975).

H. Wilson, *Regional geology of Northern Ireland* (London, 1972).

CONNEMARA, COUNTY GALWAY

Connemara, an unofficial and variously defined region, occupies the southerly portion of west Connacht between Galway Bay and the deeply dissected highland borders of counties Galway and Mayo. The region can be divided into two contrasting zones roughly separated by the Oughterard-Clifden road. To the south, the landscape is low lying and festooned by bog patches and peaty lakes. To the north, the land rises abruptly and includes major mountain ranges. Much of Connemara, even the low-lying portions, is devoid of soil and the ancient, intensely glaciated rock surfaces are generally barren and rugged. The region's inhospitable physical character is accentuated by high rainfall and exposure to Atlantic winds which, near the sea, virtually eliminate tree growth, although scrub is characteristic of many coastal areas and islands.

Like much of the Atlantic seaboard, settlement here is markedly coastal and the interior is desolate. Sustained post-famine emigration and population decline have left a deep impress on society and landscape, sharpening the long-standing contrast between littoral and interior. In recent decades, extensive house building has created what are virtually coastal suburbs, banal and crowded.

Much of the wild, awesome beauty of Connemara lies in its natural features. The human influence on the landscape can be underestimated, partly because the physical evidence of settlement between early prehistory and very recent centuries is so slender. Research in various disciplines, however, has shown that the long-term human impact on vegetation, drainage and soils has been profound and landscapes widely regarded as 'natural' are the outcome of earlier land use.

MICHAEL DIGGIN

Fig. 1 In the foreground is the harbour of Roundstone village, constructed by Alexander Nimmo in the 1820s. The narrow, closely settled coastal fringe of Connemara can be seen, contrasting with the desolate interior of bog-strewn, granitic lowland backed by the Twelve Bens or 'Pins', a cluster of quartzite peaks with summit levels at approximately 610m.

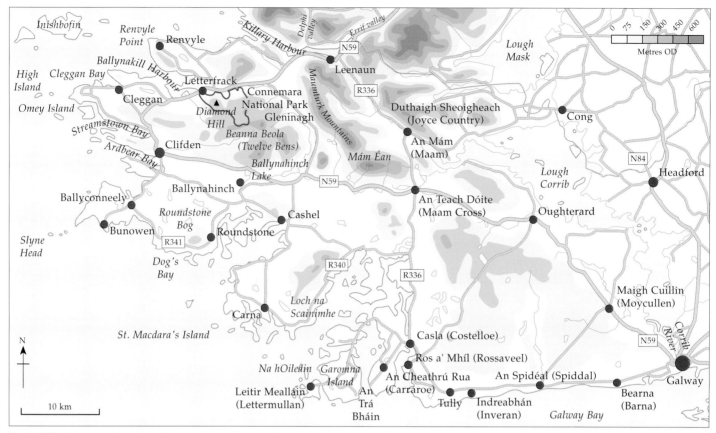

Fig. 2 Relief, routes and major settlements in west county Galway.

DEFINITIONS

A popular view of Connemara as forever wrapped in the mists of nostalgia, 'soft days' and poitín fumes can afford one useful hint before it is dismissed as ungeographical. In defining a region, to delimit it precisely is not always a clarification; exact boundaries can obscure the essence of a topographic entity. Since Connemara does not have a statutory existence, and since the logic of vague or 'fuzzy' sets has now been made academically respectable, the conventional location map is here supplemented with one showing the definiteness or indefiniteness of my feelings that various areas belong to Connemara – a preliminary and reductive representation to which more research into other people's opinions on the matter would add many finer shadings. Three levels of Connemaricity are identified:

Indubitably Connemara This is the old barony of Ballynahinch, erected in the 1580s when Elizabethan statesmen were reconcieving the west; it corresponds to medieval Conmaicne Mara, the territory of the Conmaicne of the Sea (whence the name Connemara).

Arguably Connemara The Gaeltacht of Conamara Theas (South Connemara) overlaps the above at Carna in the west, and its eastern end is drowned in the suburbs of Galway. Oughterard thinks of itself as the Gateway to Connemara. The Joyce Country is

also largely Irish-speaking, and prefers to distinguish itself from Connemara proper, but a well known sheep farmer of that locality is undoubtedly the 'Queen of Connemara'.

Fancifully Connemara The man leaning over the parapet of the bridge at Galway, watching the salmon fighting up the Corrib river, thinks that everything west of him is Connemara. Guidebooks to Connemara tend to wander into the Cong area and even up the Delphi valley into the mountains of south-west Mayo.

This vagueness of focus allows treatment of such units, both bigger and smaller than any of these gradations of Connemara, as are called forth by various contexts.

PHYSICAL BACKGROUND

Most nineteenth-century references, notably Daniel O'Connell's oration at his monster Repeal meeting in Clifden in 1843, repeat the folk-etymological derivation of 'Connemara' from 'cuan na mara', bad Irish for 'the bays of the sea'. The perception that Connemara is littoral as well as montane is sound; the bays penetrate deep and bring human settlement into the mountain wildernesses. Killary Harbour, a sixteen kilometre long fiord, is just one of the fault-controlled, glacially deepened valleys transecting the

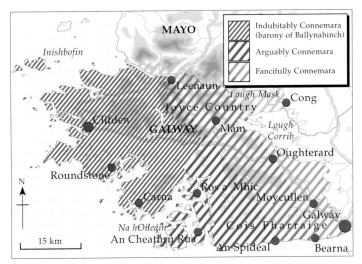

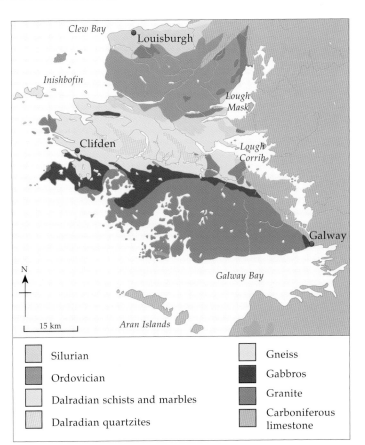

Fig. 3 Three levels of 'Connemaricity': indubitable, arguable, fanciful.

600-800m massif straddling the Galway-Mayo border. The geology is igneous and metamorphic, and heavily glaciated: along the Galway Bay shore, granite, denuded and moulded into the hummocky terrain known as 'cnoc and lochán', invaded by tentacular sea-inlets; to the north, Caledonian folded metasediments eroded into quartzite peaks; and in between, an east-west band of schists and gneiss, including strands of marble, worn down into a plain with long finger-lakes and a few isolated drumlins. The contrast between this tough old precambrian and ordovician geology and the carboniferous limestone plains east of Galway city is decisive; it is difficult to think of the soft landscape developed on the limestone where it extends for a few miles west of Lough Corrib as being in Connemara. But the area that distinguishes itself from limestone-land in this way is virtually the whole cape between Galway Bay and Clew Bay: ordovician and silurian north of the Killary and for a few miles south of it, then dalradian metasediments and gneiss, with a southern rim of the 400-million-year-old granite. The slopes and skirts of this Atlantic coastal region are as wet as anywhere in Ireland except perhaps the Reeks in Kerry; blanket bog covers, or covered, virtually all.

MESOLITHIC TO EARLY CHRISTIAN

While the hunter-gatherers of the Mesolithic have left abundant traces in the Corrib river area near Galway, evidence for their presence further west is confined so far to a few worked flakes found near Oughterard. However, a pebble hammer axe from Omey Island may be mesolithic, and some of the shell middens exposed in the wind-wasted dunes around the west and south coasts look promising. The earliest settled landscape of relevance is the north-western coastal fringe from Clifden to Leenaun, where, with the help of the fossil pollen record, one can picture the

Fig. 4 The geology of west Connacht between Clew Bay and Galway Bay is dominated by very ancient igneous and metamorphic rocks which form scattered mountain ranges separated by lowland corridors; major relief features are related to rock character, especially resistance to denuding forces. Carboniferous limestone underlies the lowlands of east Connacht.

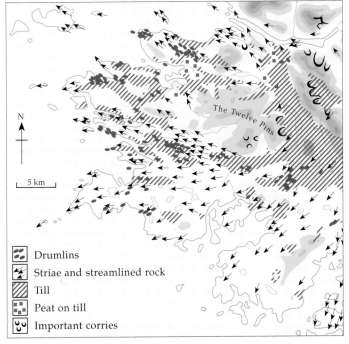

Fig. 5 Glacial features of Connemara. The region was severely glaciated. Eroding ice deepened the valleys, formed impressive corries and scoured the rock surfaces. The effects of glacial deposition are limited. Isolated drumlins and erratics occur, but even in the lowlands, little drift was deposited and even this was later covered by blanket bog.

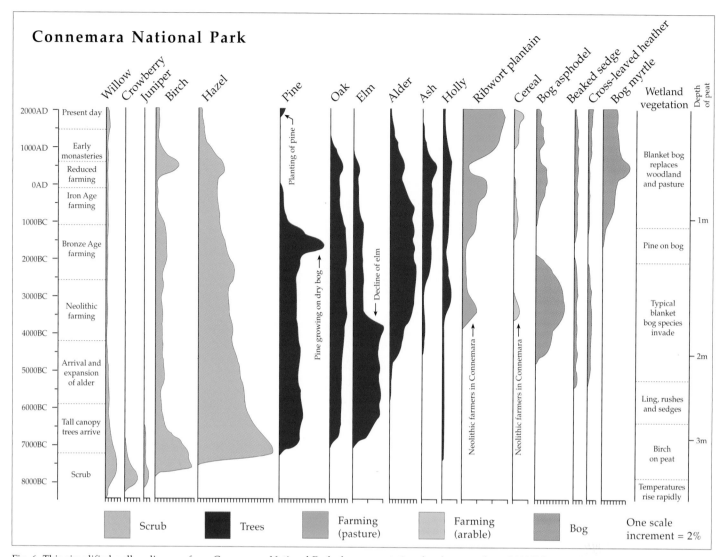

Connemara National Park

Willow · Crowberry · Juniper · Birch · Hazel · Pine · Oak · Elm · Alder · Ash · Holly · Ribwort plantain · Cereal · Bog asphodel · Beaked sedge · Cross-leaved heather · Bog myrtle · Wetland vegetation · Depth of peat

Scrub	Trees
Farming (pasture)	Farming (arable)
Bog	One scale increment = 2%

Fig. 6 This simplified pollen diagram from Connemara National Park shows vegetation development from 9000 BC to modern times. Early scrub vegetation gave way to tall canopy trees around the middle of the eighth millennium and the area was eventually dominated by woodland with lake basins and valley bottoms progressively overgrown by bog. Shortly after 4000 BC, neolithic peoples initiated major changes in the environment, creating large clearances in the forest cover. Forests were replaced by heathy grasslands, but around 1200 BC, blanket bog spread more widely and submerged farmland and settlements. Some revival of settlement occurred in Early Christian times associated with the foundation of monasteries along the coast, but treeless blanket bog and lakes remained dominant features of the landscape to the present day.

TIM ROBINSON

first small clearings being made in a primeval forest of oak, hazel, alder and holly. Around Lough Sheeauns near the head of Cleggan Bay, for instance, the record of neolithic (wheat) cultivation at *c.* 3880 BC is as early as any in Ireland. Virtually total clearance of forest there, and its replacement by pasture, with still only a little cereal farming, follows after that date. Stone field-walls exhumed by recent turf-cutting, although not as extensive and regular as those of the Céide Fields of north Mayo, also

Fig. 7 Ancient mounds or 'middens', containing layers of shells which have been opened and their contents used as human food, frequently occur in sandhills and other recent deposits along the coasts of Ireland. This midden is wasting away with erosion of the dunes at Doonlaughan on the western coast of Connemara. Similar sites nearby have been dated to about 2000 BC, in the early Bronze Age, but it is probable that traces of neolithic occupation can be found here too. The mesolithic coastline has been drowned, but sand dunes at a higher level, on Omey Island, have provided possible evidence of a mesolithic presence.

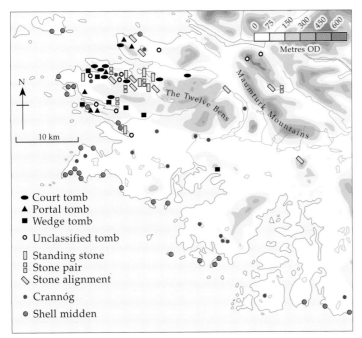

Fig. 8 Prehistoric sites in Connemara. Striking concentrations of megalithic tombs, standing stones and stone alignments occur on the northwestern peninsulas. Elsewhere, prehistoric monuments are sparse.

indicate that this ultra-western province was fertile and populous. But, in Sheeauns at least, this phase of intensive agriculture only lasted a hundred and fifty years, after which the forest closed in again and was undisturbed until the Bronze Age.

While this favoured corner of Connemara is part of a wider neolithic and Bronze Age scene stretching north and east around the Sheefry Hills and Croagh Patrick to Westport, it is distinguished within that area by an exceptional clustering of monuments from either period. The concentration of neolithic tombs around the heads of the long bays of Streamstown, Cleggan and Ballynakill suggests at first glance that these pioneer farmers penetrated the area

by boat, an idea in harmony with a traditional theory of their immigration up the Atlantic coast from Brittany. However these bays owe their existence to glacial wearing of the east-west bands of the weaker metasediments, and so their settings offer good soils derived from marble; the local Neolithic, if it was not an indigenous development, could equally well have been drawn to these crumbs of edaphic comfort from further east, via the strings of lakes and streams. Also, among the mixture of wedge, court and portal tombs here, equally impressive examples that do not fit into this standard classification are numerous enough to reinforce the suggestion of localism.

Michael Gibbons, whose fieldwork has brought much of its archaeology to notice in the last decade, sees this same area as a Bronze Age ritual landscape. On several of the drumlin-tops are standing stones, some of milky-white quartz, many of them intervisible. Near Renvyle, an impressive row of three granite boulders and three slabs of schist are aligned with a nick in the mountain profile to the south-west in which the sun goes down at the winter solstice. A few such monuments have also been recently found further east in the Maumturk valleys, and at Gleninagh the meaningful bearing of a stone alignment is spectacularly pointed out by the midwinter sun as it sets at two o'clock in a high pass of the Twelve Bens. Many of these megaliths are coming to light through turf cutting, having been drowned by the bog that started to expand out of the valley bottoms from the Bronze Age onwards. By burning forest and overworking the soil, farmers of the late Bronze Age unleashed this dull force that would eventually wipe their profound symbolism off the hills.

The Iron Age is puzzlingly difficult to bring into focus in Connemara. A few very effaced promontory forts in Inishbofin and on the mainland at Renvyle Point and Fahy

Fig. 9 An early neolithic court tomb by Cleggan Bay. Studies of pollen preserved in lake sediments a mile to the east show that the area was settled about 4100 BC.

Fig. 10 At a quarter past two in the afternoon, the midwinter sun sets between two peaks of the Twelve Bens, as seen from the Bronze Age stone alignment in Gleninagh.

DEPARTMENT OF ARTS, CULTURE AND THE GAELTACHT

Fig. 11 Peat cutting, Connemara. In this treeless landscape, the peat cover has, over centuries, been extensively cut for fuel, often down to the underlying rock. Cutting continues and the bogs are scarred by a multitude of banks, old and new. Humans were implicated in the early spread of the bogs as well as in their recent depletion. Charcoal particles produced by deliberate, frequent firing of the vegetation cover in prehistoric times accounts for the dark basal peat. Pine stumps occur at or near the base of most bogs, the product of periodic expansion of pine onto the peat during phases of drier climate.

west of Clifden may date from this period, but there is nothing to compare with the great cashels of Aran or Clare, nor does palynology indicate any activity to compare with the heydays of the Neolithic and the Bronze Age. The reason for the 'Late Iron Age Lull', the apparent near-absence of population towards the beginning of the Christian era, is an enigma Connemara shares with much of the rest of the country. However, about twenty-five crannóga are now known from the treeless blanket bogs of the lowlands, and many other overgrown lake-islets would bear examination. These habitation sites are natural islands or shoals that have been built up, revetted and ramparted with stone. Scottish parallels suggest a rather earlier date for these than for the more usual type of wooden crannóg;

TIM ROBINSON

Fig. 12 A droughty summer reveals traces of the circular outline of a crannóg in Ballinafad Lake near Ballynahinch.

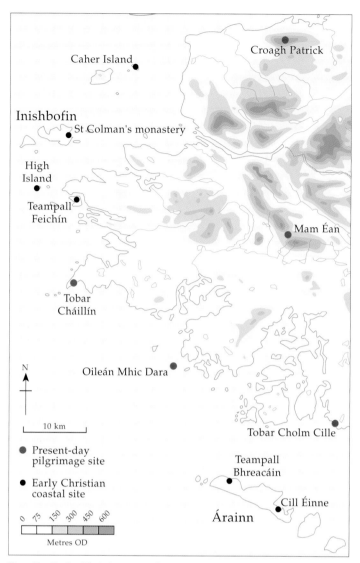

Fig. 13 Early Christian coastal sites and present-day pilgrimage sites. Many of the coastal and island sites may have been associated with medieval, maritime pilgrimages.

perhaps then Iron Age Connemara is already the land of two hundred lakes. In Loch Scaineamh near Carna is one of the best island-cashels of Ireland, and the towerhouse of Ballynahinch (Baile na hInse, the settlement of the island), which was later to become central to Connemara's history, is said to be based on an older crannóg.

Connemara does not have the countless little raths of the rest of Galway or Clare. Secular settlement in Early Christian times seems to have been largely unenclosed, and has left its mark in the shape of hut sites, hearths and mountainous shell middens in dunes and machair areas all around the coastline. Ecclesiastically, Early Christian Connemara is a segment of that extraordinary rosary of island and coastal hermitages the length of the Atlantic coast from the Skelligs to Tory and, perhaps one should add, onwards to the Scottish Isles. A traditional maritime pilgrimage may have linked many of these holy places,

R. SCOTT

Fig. 14 Oileán Mhic Dara, St Mac Dara's Island. This remarkable oratory stands on the site of an early monastery founded by a sixth-century saint named Mac Dara and is still a place of pilgrimage. Mass is celebrated here on the saint's day, 16 July. Built entirely of stone, the building has the steeply pitched roof (restored in 1975) characteristic of early Irish building as well as antae or stone prolongations of the side walls beyond the gables, probably in imitation of the crucks of primitive wooden churches.

for transport and trade, for fish and for seaweed to improve the land. The one inland castle – and it is only 5 km as the salmon swims from the head of one of the long bays of the south – is Ballynahinch, built on a crannóg which perhaps had been a stronghold of the now dispossessed Ó Cadhla chiefs of Conmaicne Mara.

During the centuries of growth of the walled town of Galway from its Norman origin, and of its commercial connections with the Atlantic fringe of Renaissance Europe, Iar-Chonnacht remained a refuge of the old clan life. In 1585, Elizabeth's Lord Deputy in Ireland drew up the *Composition of Connaught*, under the terms of which 'the Country of the O'Fflahertyes called Eyre-Conaght' was divided into four baronies: Moycullen, just west of Galway town; Ballynahinch beyond it; Ross, which is the Joyce Country in the north-east, so called because it was settled by the Welsh-Norman Joyces under the protection of the O'Flahertys; and the Isles of Aran. The only O'Flaherty chieftain to sign this deed was the one most neighbourly to Galway; he had been knighted and at least nominally granted the whole of the mainland territory of the O'Flahertys although he was not the Taoiseach of the clan. But the more western chieftains were not to be so easily inveigled into the feudal system; they held aloof, still the 'Ferocious O'Flahertys' against whom the Galwegians prayed for God's protection. As late as 1698 an English traveller, John Dunton, described Iar-Chonnacht as 'a wild mountainous country in which the old barbarities of the Irish are so many and so common, that until I came hither, I looked for Ireland in itself to no purpose.' Dunton actually visited an O'Flaherty chief, and found

reaching its peak of popularity in the eleventh and twelfth centuries. Today, of the four important pilgrimages of Connemara, three are marine: St Colm Cille's well (and the stone boat on which he sailed across from the Aran Islands) near Indreabhán in the south; St Macdara's Island with its beautiful stone oratory, where mass is celebrated and traditional boats are raced on his feastday; St Cáillín's well on the rocky slopes above a wild shore near Slyne Head, visited by hundreds of local people in November but scarcely known outside this south-western corner of Connemara. (The fourth is in the mountain pass of Mám Éan, where, just as on Croagh Patrick, Christianity has usurped the Celtic feast of Lughnasa.)

MEDIEVAL AND MODERN CONNEMARA

Politically and militarily, from the Norman invasion to that of Cromwell, Connemara has to be identified with Iar-Chonnacht or West Connacht. Originally this denomination included the O'Flaherty territories from Kilmaine in south Mayo to Dunkellin, around the head of Galway Bay, but after the advance of the Norman de Burgos in the mid-thirteenth century, it refers only to the area in which the O'Flahertys took refuge, moated off from the rest of Ireland by Lough Corrib and Killary Harbour. Their late fifteenth-century towerhouses stand around the periphery of the region, foreshadowing the pattern of settlement we inherit today and indicating their dependence on the sea

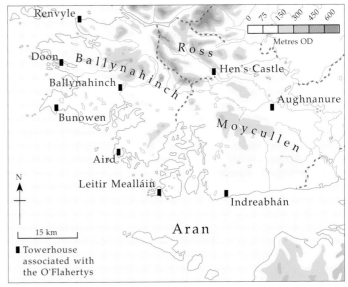

Fig. 15 Towerhouses associated with the O'Flahertys. These late medieval fortified residences belonged to the most powerful ruling clan to the west of Galway city. They are mainly coastal, foreshadowing the modern pattern of settlement.

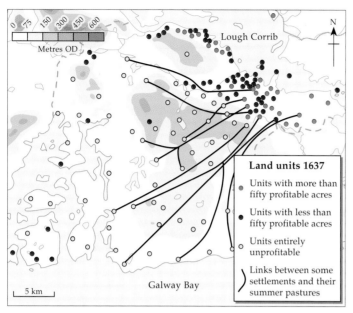

Fig. 16 The territory of Gnó Mór, Moycullen barony, county Galway, showing permanent settlements on the rich limestone lowlands around Lough Corrib and their booleys or summer pastures on the marginal land to the west in 1637. Later, many of the temporary summer grazings were permanently settled.

him not in his 'mansion by the sea' but at a buaile, a summer pasturage in the interior, sharing a large temporary cabin of wattle plastered with cowdung and clay, with a lusty company of his relatives and dependants, including their priest. This custom of transhumance (buailíocht, hence 'booleying'), the ancient Celtic partition of the year into a Bealtaine-to-Samhain summer spent with the cattle in the hills and a Samhain-to-Bealtaine winter by the sea, was still widespread in the region until late in the last century, and the traces of little booley huts still show on the mountainsides.

Although they retained the ancient ways, the O'Flahertys had lost their power a generation before Dunton's visit. Having been active in the Rebellion of 1641, they were expropriated by the victorious Parliamentarians and their territories parceled out, some of it to the financial backers and functionaries of the Cromwellian regime (most of whom took one look at their new properties and sold on as soon as possible), and the rest to Catholic landowners transplanted from Meath and the better parts of Galway. Among the latter were representatives of two of the merchant families known as the Tribes of Galway: the D'Arcys, who were granted a large tract of nethermost Connemara, and the Martins, who by astute manoeuvring through the following Vicar-of-Bray period, put together the biggest fee-simple estate in either Britain or Ireland.

In fact by the time peace returned, after the definitive victory of King William, so much of the land beyond Galway city belonged to the Martins that Connemara

became virtually synonymous with the Martin Estate; many nineteenth-century accounts quote Thomas Moore:

> O place me where Dick Martin rules
> The houseless wilds of Connemara.

This 'houseless' aspect of Connemara, adversely commented upon by several nineteenth-century travellers, was a delusion due to the fact that the tourist route, from Galway to Ballynahinch and later on to the new town of Clifden, led them through the desolate interior, whereas the Connemara fisherman-farmer was an amphibious creature whose clustered dwellings clung barnacle-like to the shoreline. The existence of teeming villages like An Trá Bháin on the island of Gorumna would have scarcely been known to the outside world, though the land agent would have had a sharp eye on it, and the lament 'Amhrán na Trá Báine' is one of the classics of traditional song.

Especially along the south coast, ramifying inlets and disseminated archipelagos provide an extraordinary high ratio of shoreline to land area. It was primarily the abundant 'yellow-weed' (Ascophyllum) of these sheltered shallow shores that fed the poor sour pastures and potato plots. In the eighteenth and nineteenth centuries, vast amounts of seaweed were also burned to ash in little kilns on the seashore for sale as kelp to representatives of a Glasgow firm (kelp was an important source of alkalies for the Industrial Revolution, and later of iodine). Sand was essential too for improving the soil. Here and there are beaches of so-called 'coral', lime-rich fragments of Lithothamnium seaweed, and tracts of 'machair' or muirbheach as it is called locally; cattle suffering from the 'cripple' due to chronically damp and rushy pasturage could be brought to recover on these calcarious swards, the land around the unique Foraminifera-based sand of Dog's Bay near Roundstone being especially highly regarded for this quality.

At the other, inland, limit of cultivation was the bog, equally vital to survival, providing an inexhaustible lebensraum to be nibbled at by land reclamation, as well as summer pasturage and the only fuel in this treeless land. During the last century, the hillocks of the coastal areas were stripped back to the granite as peat that had been two or three metres deep was dug for turf; the bays swarmed with sailboats carrying it to the turfless limestone-lands of Aran and the Burren, and to Galway city.

The field system that developed as a communal ecological adaptation to these two boundary conditions of life, the sea and the bog, looks on a map like a natural infusion of the coastline's exuberant angularity into the monotonous continuities of the hillsides: countless irregular hummocky plots (that became smaller and smaller as the huge population growth forced repeated subdivision); a close network of walls built from the stones the glaciers had scattered so abundantly, loosely built so as to temper the gales to stock and crop; a maze of narrow twisting boreens branching off the wider lanes linking the loosely clustered settlement to its seaweed-shore and its turbary and (to a very secondary degree) the neighbouring settlements. Under the 'rundale' system so deplored by contemporary commentators, each household had a scattered selection of these plots, comprising a little of every sort of land from the best to the worst, and could graze a certain agreed number of cattle, sheep, geese, etc., on the commonage, the hinterland of bog and heath. A crazy system in the eyes of up-to-date thinkers, necessitating endless trailing to and fro and an inefficient fragmentation of the tenant's effort: in fact, had it not been sucked dry by rents and driven into its eventually fatal complicity with the potato, rundale was a good ecological jigsaw-puzzle interlock between that rapidly multiplying population and the narrow strip of habitable complexity between sea and bog.

The contrast between the high London-society profile of the famous 'Humanity Dick' Martin, and his feudal lifestyle when at Ballynahinch, protected from duns and

Fig. 18 Roundstone Bog, seen from the top of Errisbeg hill near Roundstone. This complex mosaic of lake and bog is a wintering-ground for Greenland white-fronted geese, and famous for its rare plants, including heathers of Iberian affinity.

process-servers by his devoted tenantry, attracted the romantics of that century, but the gospellers of agricultural improvement found little to commend on the Martin estate. Connemara had been famous for its small hardy horses, but injudicious breeding had led to a decline in

Fig. 17 South-west Connemara. With deep inlets and many islands and reefs, the coast is a fractal of unusually high dimensionality. Settlement is largely coastal and extends onto the islands and islets, some of which are connected to the mainland by sandy tombolos and are accessible only at low tide. The numerous lakes of Roundstone Bog are a striking feature lying like fragments of a pane of glass flung down and shattered.

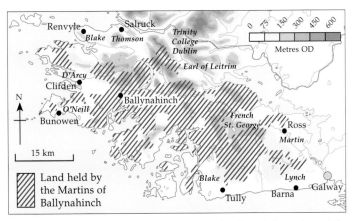

Fig. 19 The estates of the Martins of Ballynahinch and the major neighbouring landlords in the nineteenth century. The Martin estate of over half a million acres (2000 km²) was the most extensive in Ireland, much of it unimproved and difficult of access.

their reputation, and in the Martin stables the agriculturalist Hely Dutton noted 'some stallions that were sufficient to destroy the breed of any country, especially Cunnamara; before he introduced such horses, he should have shewed his tenants how to provide food for their progeny.' A Mr Chisterholm, 'a very celebrated irrigator from England', had prepared over 8 ha of watered meadow for the Martins at Ballynahinch, but Dutton found that after a few years and an expenditure of £700 it had been neglected – another bad example to the tenantry. In general, the hand of improvement had hardly been stretched more than a few hundred metres from their mansion by Ballynahinch Lake, and the smallholders and labourers got on with their own lives, neither assisted to raise themselves nor on the other hand rackrented or harassed by evictions, as they were, for instance, on the estate of the much-hated 'improving' landlords, the Blakes of Tully.

Fig. 20 Clifden Castle, built by John D'Arcy in about 1815. This fine Gothic mansion, one of Connemara's treasures and a potential tourist attraction, has been neglected to the point of ruination because of the subdivision of the demesne for grazing.

Fig. 21 A pack-horse bridge five kilometres east of Ballynahinch, on the old bridle path through the Martin estate from Oughterard, predating the Galway to Clifden road laid out by Nimmo. When his friend the Prince Regent boasted of the great drive at Windsor, Dick Martin retorted that his drive was forty miles long.

West of the Martins, the D'Arcys were much more enterprising. At the height of the boom years of the Napoleonic wars, they built themselves a Gothic mansion and began the development of the town of Clifden. In the depression that came with peace, progress was slow; much of the harbour was government-funded relief work during the near-famine of 1822. The quays were still unfinished in 1829, but the *Fishery Report* of that year states that some good stores had been built on them, and merchant vessels were discharging iron, pitch, ropes, earthenware, etc., and taking away fish, corn, kelp and marble. Despite several episodes of 'distress' due to failure of the potato crop and the decline in agricultural prices, these were forward-looking times in Connemara. Reporting progress to Dublin Castle in 1831, John D'Arcy boasted:

> Fifteen years ago it [Connemara] was inhabited by a race of people, wild as the mountains, whose principal occupation was smuggling. About that time I undertook the difficult task of improving the land and civilising the people, for which purpose I commenced building the town of Clifden on the Bay of Ardbear, and I have so far succeeded that it already consists of three hundred houses, slated, two and three stories high, contains a population of two thousand souls, and returns a revenue to the Crown of between five and six hundred pounds a year.

In 1818, Thomas Martin obtained a presentment for a road to link the new town to Galway, replacing the ancient pack-horse trail winding through the bogs of Martin-land; again, after many delays, and largely as a relief work in years of distress, this road was completed about 1835. The engineer who laid out the road network of Connemara, as

TIM ROBINSON

Fig. 22 The eloquent skyline of a deserted settlement at Aill na Caillí, just north of Roundstone.

well as the harbours at Cleggan, Clifden, Roundstone and Ros a' Mhíl, was the great Alexander Nimmo. (In 1814 Nimmo had reported on the economic potential of the bogs of Connemara; fortunately, his elaborate scheme for reclaiming them, by a system of canals serving both to drain them and to bring in copious bargeloads of crushed limestone, was never implemented). Nimmo himself leased land from the Martins by his harbour at Roundstone and sublet it in small plots for houses to be built on, so bringing into existence a neat Scottish-looking herring-fishing village, which flourished for some years and then fell into decline.

All this faltering development was stricken dead by the Great Famine of 1845-8. Roofless villages, traces of potato ridges running high up the sides of deserted valleys, nondescript little boulders marking nameless graves on the seashore, and, far away across the ocean, the monument to

DEPARTMENT OF ARTS, CULTURE AND THE GAELTACHT

Fig. 23 These abandoned potato ridges, or lazy beds, in north-west Connemara reflect the heavy depletion and abandonment of land as well as the decline in subsistence cultivation. Lazy beds often extend under and hence predate the field walls and banks.

the fever-victims on Grosse Isle in the St Lawrence river, suggest a little of the sufferings of Connemara. The big estates, already weakened by generation of *folie de grandeur* and now left rentless, were finally bankrupted by famine relief rates and went on sale through the Encumbered Estates Court. The D'Arcys' land and castle were acquired by their mortgagees, the Eyres of London and Bath. In the south-west corner of Connemara, the Geoghegan or O'Neill estate and mansion at Bunowen were sold off to various parties, some of whom had capital to invest in improvement. (The Doohulla river near Ballyconneely thus became one of the first salmon fisheries to be scientifically developed, by the famous Ramsbottom of Yorkshire). The Martin estate, though, was found to be so untouched by enterprise, and so pauperised by famine, that it remained unsold for twenty years, during which time its mortgagees, the Law Life Insurance Company of London, vigorously swept it clear of superfluous humanity.

It is one of the strangest of the contradictions of this contradictory region that humanity has in fact clung onto it with such tenacity and to such effect that (the negative aspect) in the 1890s Connemara was a natural fief of the Congested Districts Board (CDB), and (two indications of the positive) that the treasuries of folklore and song recorded from the parish of Carna in the 1930s and more recently are practically bottomless, and that even today Conamara Theas and Dúthaigh Sheoigheach, the Joyce Country, are, with the Aran Islands, strongholds of spoken Irish.

For the CDB, this rundown rundale, uphill-and-downdale landscape, crazed with thousands of miles of walls and millennial right-of-way disputes, was to be rationalised by the buying-out of landlords, the breaking-up of the huddled bailte in which everyone was, in the expressive Irish phrase, comharsa bhéal dorais, literally a doorway-neighbour, and the resettling of the former tenants in soundly slate-roofed cottages each in its own stripe of land. On the other hand, for the folklorists and the artists and, increasingly importantly, the tourists, Connemara was a toyland of picturesque archaicisms, and its skeletonised terrain was 'unspoiled countryside'. Much of the present day problematic of 'What is to be done about Connemara?' and 'What are we who live here to do, in this waterlogged and timelogged land?' can be situated in this gap between socio-economic and cultural or aesthetic evaluations. A brief ramble through its perplexities will show how short we are of answers.

CONCERNS OF THE PRESENT AND FUTURE

Mass emigration, the CDB's land-reformation, and recent decades of political clientelism under which every planning

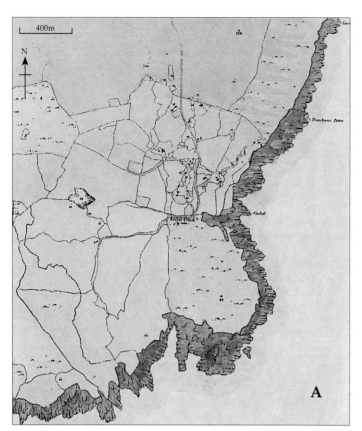
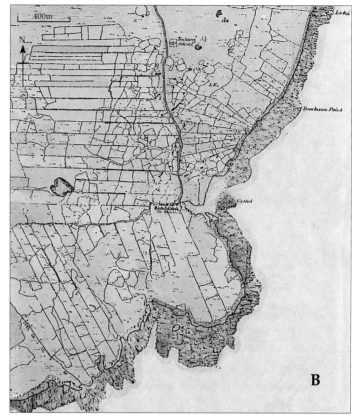

Fig. 24 An Trá Bháin on the south-western coast of Gorumna Island. A) In the early 1840s, the settlement here was a sprawling cluster of small farms, without any institutions. The surrounding farmland was divided into irregular stone-walled fields which, close to the farms, were divided into small, scattered and unenclosed plots (not shown on the map). Around the enclosed area lay extensive tracts of bog and lake. B) Early in the present century, the farmland was 'striped', i.e. enclosed in long, narrow divisions, although many old, irregular boundaries survived. The form of the settlement itself is little changed, the school being the main innovation.

application was an opportunity to oblige a voter, have weakened the distinction between settlement and its natural setting. The thin scattering of cottages along both mainroad and sideroad, which must have been lonely for a generation or two, has come to seem desirable now that the car and TV reinforce new ideals of privacy. There is no politically sustainable argument against letting the spaces between the cottages be occupied by new dwellings; house sites are already too expensive for local people, especially young couples, and planning restrictions are felt as oppressive by small farmers: they find that their one disposable asset, a site with a view, can neither be sold nor built on for their offsprings' use because of something called 'scenic amenity' or technicalities about septic tanks in areas of shallow soils. So, despite the planning authorities' attempts to rein it in, there is a steady increase of one-off bungalows, many of them second homes. In the season, this leads to a lively swallow-like to-and-fro of holiday-home owners, many of whom have been coming here for decades and constitute a mobile web of conviviality. But less and less do these prosperous visitors leave money in the village shops; their freezers are stocked from the supermarkets of Dublin and Galway. Then suddenly, with the first rainy week of

autumn, they are gone, and in many areas more than half the houses are empty. In the villages too, the conversion of old houses, coastguard stations and derelict stores into blocks of holiday apartments means a rather traumatic seasonal alternation between frenzy and stagnancy in the streets.

This hundred-day-summer cannot sustain many worthwhile jobs in itself, and is difficult to extend, given the logistics and weather-pattern of Connemara. For many, tourism offers a supplement to the income of a small farm – but that basic income has become more and more artificial, demeaningly dependent on grants, some of them for the production of goods no longer needful. Sheep have been the mainstay of western upland farming for centuries, and prices, after being derisory for some years, are now recovering with the expansion of the European Union. Overstocking was part of the problem; many people who never had sheep before found them worthwhile for the headage payments alone, and some farmers are receiving tens of thousands of pounds a year to support vast flocks of miserable animals that are eating the mountainsides bare. The short-term fixes proposed are the division and fencing of commonage, and the use of fertiliser sprayed by helicopter. In the longer term, headage payments are leading to a

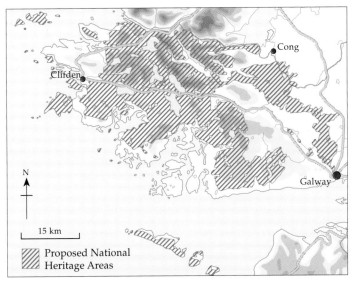

Fig. 25 Extent of National Heritage Areas (within county Galway). The bulk of the area is covered by this new designation which replaces the Areas of Scientific Interest (ASI). The designation covers a wide range of natural and semi-natural habitats, but very little of it is in protective ownership and all other sites are exposed to destruction and damage from landowners.

degree of erosion that may take centuries to make good; already huge areas are trodden to a black slime in winter. Many farmers recognise the problem, but, according to a local agricultural expert, 'They couldn't be expected to reduce numbers unless they were properly compensated.' I am reluctant to believe that the Connemara farmer is so indifferent to everything – the beauty of his countryside, his children's livelihood, the sufferings of his stock – beyond the capacity of his pocket.

But if and when the headage payments dry up and are only partially replaced by the system of subsidies proposed in the Rural Environment Protection Scheme, will there be a renewed move to afforest the bogs and hillsides? A few years ago just when Coillte, the State forestry body, was

ceasing to expand into this area, having belatedly realised that western blanket bog grows trees that spring up like rushes and are blown down before their timber is worth harvesting, grants and tax exemptions and minimal planning controls suddenly made private forestry financially attractive. But straight away this new enthusiasm fell foul of the designation of large tracts as Areas of Scientific Interest, within which such EU-funded grants were not available. The constitutionality of the ASI system was successfully challenged in the courts by a group of Clifden businessmen who had been frustrated by it in their scheme for an airport on Roundstone Bog, and is now being replaced by a more open but probably toothless system of designation of National Heritage Areas. A dire result of these controversies is the existence in Connemara of a small but influential anti-environmentalist backlash; environmentalists are accused of wanting to turn the place into a reservation for wildlife and a few quaint old countryfolk. Simultaneously there is an increasing awareness of the need to conserve the quality that draws the tourists to Connemara. Because of the row over Clifden Airport, visitors now ask to be directed to Roundstone Bog, and this tract of lake-flecked lowland blanket bog, without parallel anywhere nearer than the Outer Hebrides, has for the first time an existence in local consciousness as an entity, rather than as so many separate grazing and turbary rights. But with their renown, the question of the fragility of such wonderful places immediately arises. The National Park, holding a large north-western sector of the Twelve Bens, preaches the value of wilderness to humans – but has had to ask visitors not to climb the jewel in its crown, Diamond Hill, because they are beating a wide muddy path to its summit.

What is needed, more than generalised conservation measures that are immediately at loggerheads with local

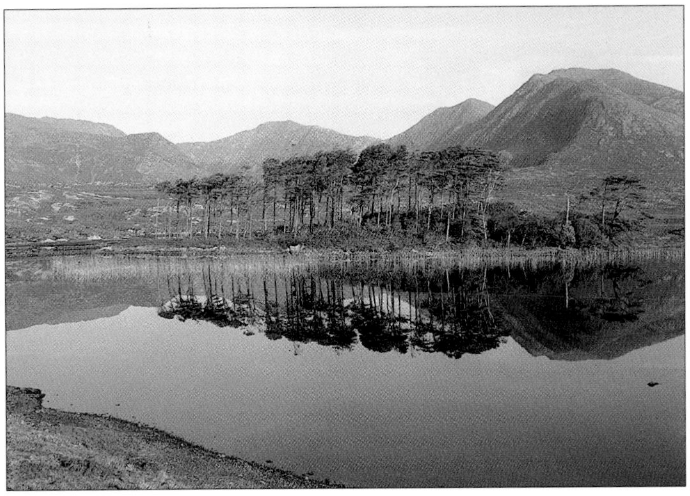

Fig. 26 Derryclare Lough. Natural woodland is confined to lake islands which are inaccessible to cattle. The Twelve Bens (described by Somerville and Ross as 'the far off struggle of Connemara') form the backdrop.

Fig. 27 An isolated farm above Kylemore Lough with traces of abandoned fields on the steep mountain slope to the rear. Settlement desertion of this type is common in interior Connemara.

Fig. 28 Fish farms floating in Connemara's scenic fjord, Killary Harbour.

economic interests, is open, detailed, locally-informed but disinterested planning – a recipe for Utopia! Consider the following actual and potential conflicts in land- and water-use. The run-off from eroded sheep-walks and the silt and chemicals washing down feeder streams from forestry operations are inimical to the wild salmon fisheries which are, or should be, a prime asset of the tourist industry. The seatrout have been virtually wiped out in recent years, probably by a combination of causes including the above as well as the presence of sealice-infested salmon-cages in the bays which the seaward-bound fish have to negotiate. But salmon farming is now a most important source of income in the historically poverty-stricken south of Connemara, and if it is curtailed many jobs will be lost, both directly and indirectly. The interests of the inland fisheries and the fish farms could be adjusted by fallowing or resiting of the cages – but there is also a deep division in Connemara between areas now dependent on finfish rearing, and those

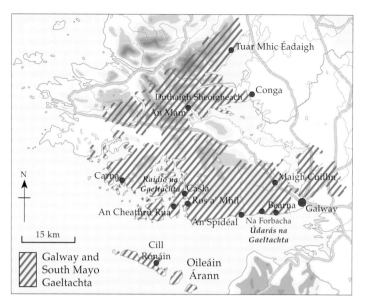

Fig. 30 Remoteness, a subsistence economy and the paucity of towns and demesnes have helped to preserve the Irish language and with it something of the traditional way of life. The closely settled coastal fringe includes one of the largest surviving areas of Irish speech, with An Spidéal as the main centre.

that have invested their effort in shellfish farming, since it is feared that the chemicals used to control sealice threaten the spat of oysters, mussels and scallops. And those bed-and-breakfast owners and hoteliers who live off the charm of Connemara are not happy to see either of these types of small-industrial developments proliferating in its severely beautiful lakes and bays.

A result of nineteenth-century emigration is that Connemara now has important centres of gravity overseas and especially in the United States, remorselessly drawing away its young. This attraction is not solely due to economic necessity; a better educated and TV-informed generation looks to Boston, New York, New Orleans or Australia for more exciting chapters in its *bildungsroman* than 'going

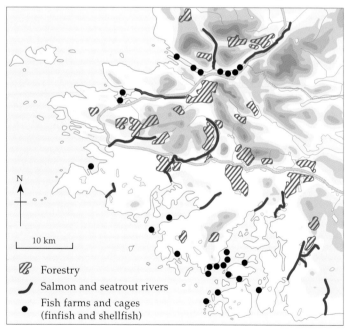

Fig. 29 Forestry, salmon and seatrout rivers and fish farms.

Fig. 31 The annual Maam Cross horse fair, at the end of October. The breeding of Connemara ponies is an important business around Clifden, Cashel and Roundstone.

on the buildings' of London like their fathers. So communities wane, schools are reduced from three teachers to two to one, and then to none. Where schools in Irish-speaking areas are amalgamated with ones in non-Irish speaking areas, the Gaeltacht is undermined. Emigration, unemployment, environmental and cultural loss – a baffling concatenation of ills.

In certain lights, certain moods, Connemara looks sick. Here, a quarry is spreading like a festering sore; there, another hillside has come out in a rash of deep ploughing for forestry; a favourite boreen has its hedgerows ripped out and replaced by barbed wire and a calf-shed the size of a small factory. A village development committee proposes that a road be widened, a verge sprayed with weedkiller, a green field turned into a carpark; everywhere, nature stamped down in favour of convenience. Perhaps the generation now doing ecology projects and commercial studies in school will in time bring a new intelligence to its cure; otherwise – best resign yourself to the inevitable so that you can enjoy what's left of it, for Connemara is dying.

But one's mood recovers on thinking about some current efforts at renewal. Organisations like Connemara West at Letterfrack and Muintearas Na hOileáin in the south are intertwining the strands of economics, culture and environment; a new countryside wisdom could grow out of such communal self-development. The Clifden Community Art Week brings artists of national and international standing to a purely local celebration. Psychologically, one of the most important initiatives of recent decades in Connemara has been the revival of the traditional workboats, the Galway hooker and its smaller relations, the gleoiteóg and púcán, with their tarred wooden hulls and tannin-brown sails. When their career of turf-carrying and fishing had lapsed, they were left to rot in muddy creeks, until a few enthusiasts dragged some of them out and restored them; now these lovely craft are flaunting themselves at regattas, and the old skills of building and sailing them and writing songs about them are highly regarded once again. These regattas welcome visitors, but they are organised by local communities as occasions for their own delight, at which past and present can drink to each other with mutual respect.

In our future of worldwide interactive complexity, it is impossible to predict what will become of Connemara. A

Fig. 32 Traditional wooden-hulled workboats in the Roundstone regatta.

R. SCOTT

return to nature, with a residual negative-farming presence supported by grants for setting aside land and reducing stock, policed by eyes in the sky (already our ever-resourceful farmers are painting boulders white to fool the sheep-counting satellite!); a new transhumance of emigrants wintering in Florida and flocking back to service the visitors; bailte beaga of tele-cottages strung on the Internet; waiting lists for the experience of solitude? But Connemara's simultaneous and mutually contradictory weathers will still stride across the landscape, gesticulating like shepherds after trespassing sheep; the moody Atlantic light will still present the Twelve Bens as a succession of instants each worthy of eternity. What makes the matter of Connemara of passionate importance to the world is, finally, its beauty. Everyone, not just the artist and ecologist, has to bow to the transcendent value of Connemara, if only as a refuge from a noisy, messy stage of civilisation. One summer evening, coming from Galway on the bus – and surely there is a point on that road where a sudden

lifting of the heart, in defiance of all logics fuzzy or stark, unarguably fixes the beginning of Connemara! – the gossiping shoppers and the foreign tourists rhapsodising over the sky-coloured mountains and mountainous skies fell quiet, and we rolled on in hushed silence, past lakeful after lakeful of sunset, as if through the sequence of a lofty ceremony over which our driver presided with his accustomed friendly seriousness. If any individual may figure in a celebration of rural Ireland, it should be such a country bus driver as Michael Geoghegan of Connemara, who threads through every loop of his network in the course of the weekly schedule, knows every regular traveller, and on wild winter nights waits with the headlights shining outside an isolated cottage while the old fellow with a pint or two in him safely dismounts, crosses the road and fumbles his way up to his front door. On this occasion as we got out of the bus at Roundstone, we said to Michael something about the exceptional splendour of the journey, and he replied: 'I know, that's why I didn't turn on the old radio.'

BIBLIOGRAPHY

A. Bleasdale and M. Sheehy-Skeffington, 'The influence of agricultural practices on plant communities in Connemara' in J. Feehan (ed.), *Environment and development in Ireland* (Dublin, 1991), pp 331-6.

M. Cawley and E. Scannláin, 'North-west Connemara: processes and patterns of landscape change during the nineteenth century' in T. Collins (ed.), *Decoding the landscape* (Galway, 1994), pp 99-113.

Fourth report of the commissioners on the bogs in Ireland (London, 1814), appendix 12.

M. Gibbons, J. Higgins and M. O'Connell, 'The island habitation sites of Connemara, county Galway: observations on the archaeology and palaeoenvironmental context of the island cashel and crannóg sites of west Connemara' in V. Buckley (ed.), *Crannógs* (Oxford, forthcoming).

P. Gosling (comp.), *Archaeological inventory of county Galway. Volume 1: west Galway* (Dublin, 1993).

J. Graham, 'Rural society in Connacht, 1600-1640' in N. Stephens and R. Glasscock (ed.), *Irish geographical studies* (Belfast, 1970), pp 192-208.

P. Harbison, *Pilgrimage in Ireland; the monuments and the people* (London, 1991).

J. Hely Dutton, *Statistical and agricultural survey of the county of Galway* (Dublin, 1824).

C. Huang and M. O'Connell, 'Recent land-use history in eastern Connemara: a palaeoecological case study at Ballydoo Lough, Connemara, county Galway' in J. Feehan (ed.), *Environment and development in Ireland* (Dublin, 1991), pp 318-30.

B. Kosko, *Fuzzy thinking: the new science of fuzzy logic* (London, 1994).

S. Lynam, *Humanity Dick Martin, 'King of Connemara', 1754-1834* (Dublin, 1989).

'Mr. Nimmo's Coast Survey', *First Report of the commissioners of enquiry into the state of the Irish fisheries* (Dublin, 1836), appendix.

National Archives, *State of the Country Papers*, 1831/126, J. D'Arcy (Clifden Castle) to E.G. Stanley (Dublin Castle), 18 January 1831.

M. O'Connell and W. Warren (ed.), *Connemara* (Dublin, 1994).

M. O'Connell, *Connemara vegetation and land use since the last ice age* (Dublin, 1994).

R. O'Flaherty, *A chorographical description of west or H-Iar Connaught, written 1684*, ed. J. Hardiman (Dublin, 1846, facsimile repr. Galway, 1978).

T. Robinson (ed.), *Connemara after the famine. Journal of a survey of the Martin estate by Thomas Colville Scott 1853* (Dublin, 1995).

T. Robinson, *Setting foot on the shores of Connemara* (Dublin, 1996).

Tenth Fishery Report (London, 1829), appendix.

K. Villiers-Tuthill, *History of Clifden 1810-1860* (Clifden, 1981).

D. Webb and M. Scannell, *Flora of Connemara and the Burren* (Cambridge, 1983).

T. Whilde, *The natural history of Connemara* (London, 1994).

N. Wilkins, *Ponds, parcs and passes; aquaculture in Victorian Ireland* (Sandycove, 1989).

APPENDIX: FIGURE SOURCES AND ATTRIBUTIONS

Unless specifically attributed, all the maps and diagrams in this volume are based on research by the individual contributors. The abbreviations listed here are used for sources that occur frequently; other sources are given in full.

C.D.B.	Congested Districts Board
C.U.C.A.P.	Cambridge University Committee on Aerial Photography
Ir. Geog.	*Irish Geography*
N.A.I.	National Archives Ireland
N.L.I.	National Library of Ireland
O.P.W.	Office of Public Works
O.S.	Ordnance Survey of Ireland
P.R.O.N.I.	Public Records Office, Northern Ireland
R.I.A. Proc.	*Proceedings of the Royal Irish Academy*
R.S.A.I. Jn.	*Journal of the Royal Society of Antiquaries of Ireland*
SMR	Sites and Monuments Records, Dublin and Belfast.
T.C.D.	Trinity College Dublin
U.C.D.	University College Dublin
Ulster Jn. Arch.	*Ulster Journal of Archaeology*

Ordnance Survey maps are used by permission of the Government, Permit No. 6395. Unless otherwise stated, O.S. maps are 1:10,560 (six inches to one mile) sheets.

THE MAKING OF THE IRISH LANDSCAPE
Photo: Liam Lyons. Deserted settlement, county Galway.

The Irish rural landscape: synthesis of habitat and history, pp 4-30.
Fig. 5 Based on Geological Survey, Ordnance Survey and other sources.
Fig. 6 Based on D. Jones 'Shaping the land: the geomorphological background' in S. Woodell (ed.), *The English landscape* (Oxford,1985), p.11; B. Andersen and H. Borns, *The ice age* (Oslo, 1994), pp 81, 91.
Fig. 9 Based on *Atlas of Ireland* (Dublin, 1979), pp 18, 19, 21.
Fig. 12 Based on J. Johnson, *The human geography of Ireland* (Chichester, 1994), p. 7.
Fig. 18 After F. Synge, in T. Freeman, 'The Castleblaney district, county Monaghan' in *Ir. Geog.*, i (1949), p. 107.
Fig. 27 Based on F. Aalen, *Man and the landscape in Ireland* (London, 1978), p. 25; *Atlas of Ireland*, pp 30-3.
Fig. 29 Based on F. Mitchell, *The Irish landscape* (London, 1976), p. 187.
Fig. 30 Unpublished map by T. Jones Hughes based on *Townland Index of Ireland* (Dublin, 1901).
Fig. 31 Commissioners for Bogs 1809-13, Map Library, T.C.D.
Fig. 32 Based on M. Gardiner in *Atlas of Ireland* (Dublin, 1979), p. 28 and Johnson, *Human geography of Ireland*, p. 21.
Fig. 33 Based on D. Gillmor, *A systematic geography of Ireland* (Dublin, 1971), p. 101 and Johnson, *Human geography of Ireland*, p. 37.
Fig. 34 Based on R. Hammond, *The peatlands of Ireland* (Dublin, 1979) and Mitchell, *The Irish landscape*, pp 112, 186.
Fig. 35 Based on H. Arbman, *The Vikings* (London, 1961), pp 76-7; E. Bowen, *Saints, seaways and settlements* (Cardiff, 1977), p. 23; G. Daniel, *The megalithic builders of western Europe* (London, 1963), pp 26, 97; R. Lebeau, *Les grands types de structures agraires dans le monde* (Paris, 1969); T. Powell, *The Celts* (London, 1959), pp 99, 175.

Fig. 38 Unpublished map by K. Whelan based on *Townland index of Ireland* (Dublin, 1901).
Fig. 42 After W. Smyth 'Society and settlement in seventeenth century Ireland: the evidence of the 1669 census' in W. Smyth and K. Whelan (ed.), *Common ground* (Cork, 1988), p. 61.
Fig. 44 After W. Smyth in Smyth and Whelan (ed.), *Common ground*, p. 74.
Fig. 48. Commissioners for Bogs, Map Library, T.C.D.
Fig. 49. After Johnson, *Human geography of Ireland*, p. 27.
Fig. 50. After Johnson, *Human geography of Ireland*, p. 41.

Early Landscapes: from Prehistory to Plantation, pp 31-66.
Fig.2 After P. Woodman, 'Problems in the colonisation of Ireland' in *Ulster Jn. Arch.*, xlix (1986), pp 9, 14.
Fig. 3 After P. Woodman, *Excavations at Mount Sandel 1973-1977* (Belfast, 1985), p. 165.
Fig. 4 After Woodman, *Mount Sandel*, p. 160.
Fig. 5 After M. O'Kelly, *Early Ireland: an introduction to Irish prehistory* (Cambridge, 1989), p. 129.
Fig. 6 After S. Ó Nualláin, *Survey of the megalithic tombs of Ireland, V: County Sligo* (Dublin, 1989), fig. 84.
Fig. 9 After Ó Nualláin, *Megalithic tombs: Sligo*, fig. 84.
Fig. 11 After G. Eogan, *Knowth and the passage-tombs of Ireland* (London, 1986), p. 91.
Fig. 12 After E. Shee-Twohig, *Megalithic art of western Europe* (Oxford, 1981), p. 12.
Fig. 13 After G. Burenhault, *The Carrowmore excavations: excavation season 1980* (Stockholm, 1984), opposite p. 6.
Fig. 15 After C. Doherty, Palaeological investigations of a peat profile adjoining a Bronze Age passage grave at Seefin, county Wicklow, unpublished BSc thesis (University College Dublin, 1991), p. 46.
Fig. 16 After S. Caulfield's illustration in the Céide Fields Visitor Centre.
Fig. 17 Based on J. Waddell, *Irish Bronze Age burials* (Galway, 1990), p. 36; (with additional material from Sites and Monuments Records).

Fig. 18 After Ó Nualláin, *Megalithic tombs: Sligo* (Dublin, 1989), fig. 84.
Fig. 20 G. Stout, 'The embanked enclosures of the Boyne region' in *R.I.A. Proc.*, xci (1991), C, p. 282.
Fig. 23A After A. Burl, *The stone circles of the British Isles* (London, 1976), p. 9.
Fig. 24B After S. Ó Nualláin, 'The stone circle complex of Cork and Kerry' in *R.S.A.I. Jn.*, cv (1975), pp 119.
Fig. 25 After G. Stout, 'Wicklow's prehistoric landscape' in K. Hannigan and W. Nolan (ed.), *Wicklow. History and society* (Dublin, 1994), p. 9.
Fig. 27 After B. Raftery, 'Irish hillforts' in C. Thomas (ed.), *The Iron Age in the Irish Sea province* (London, 1972), p. 41; (with additional material from SMR); G. Eogan, *Hoards of the Irish Later Bronze Age* (Dublin, 1983), p. 218.
Fig. 30 After B. Raftery, *Pagan Celtic Ireland: the enigma of the Irish Iron Age* (London, 1994), p. 227; B. Raftery, *The La Tène in Ireland* (Dublin, 1984), p. 360.
Fig. 32 After J. Mallory and T. McNeill, *The archaeology of Ulster* (Belfast, 1991), p. 119.
Fig. 33 From C. Lynn, 'Navan Fort' in S. Moscati (ed.), *The Celts* (Milan, 1991), p. 611.
Fig. 34 After SMR and R. Lamb, *Iron Age promontory forts in the British Isles* (Oxford, 1980), p. 5.
Fig. 35 O.S., aerial photograph 8-0081 (1991).
Fig. 36 After R. Macalister, *Corpus inscriptionum insulum Celticarum*, 2 vols (Dublin, 1945-49).
Fig. 39 After M. O'Connell, 'Vegetational and environmental changes in Ireland during the later Holocene' in M. O'Connell (ed.), *The post-glacial period (10,000-0 B.P.): fresh perspectives* (Galway, 1991), p. 26.
Fig. 40 After L. Black, Early Christian settlement in the Braid and Upper Glenarm valleys, unpublished BA thesis (Queen's University of Belfast, 1994), p.15.
Fig. 41 Based on SMR. This map shows all sites which have been positively identified as ringforts and 'enclosures' which are ringforts in the vast majority of cases.
Fig. 42 After R. Warner, 'The archaeology of early historic Irish kingship' in S. Driscoll and M. Nieke (ed.), *Power and politics in early medieval Britain and Ireland* (Edinburgh, 1988), p. 66.

Fig. 46 M. Stout, 'Ringforts in the south-west midlands of Ireland' in *R.I.A. Proc.*, xci (1991), C, p. 237.

Fig. 47 Based on SMR.

Fig. 48 Based on SMR.

Fig. 51 Based on Ordnance Survey, *Monastic Ireland* (second ed., Dublin, 1979); L. Swan, 'Enclosed ecclesiastical sites and their relevance to settlement patterns of the first millennium A.D.' in T. Reeves-Smyth and F. Hamond (ed.), *Landscape archaeology* (Oxford, 1983), p. 275; P. Harbison, *The high crosses of Ireland: an iconographical and photographic survey*, 3 vols. (Bonn, 1992), i, p. 441; L. Barrow, *The round towers· of Ireland* (Dublin, 1979), endpapers (round towers).

Fig. 53 After L. Swan, 'The Early Christian ecclesiastical sites of county Westmeath' in J. Bradley (ed.), *Settlement and society in medieval Ireland* (Kilkenny, 1988), p. 7.

Fig. 55 Based on F. Byrne, 'The Irish abroad *c. 590-c.* 1240' in T. Moody, F. Martin and F. Byrne (ed.), *A new history of Ireland: vol. ix; maps genealogies, lists* (Oxford, 1984), p. 17.

Fig. 56 After C. Norton and D. Park, *Cistercian art and architecture in the British Isles* (Cambridge, 1986), pp xviii-xix.

Fig. 58 Based on SMR and R. Glasscock, 'Moated sites and deserted boroughs and villages: two neglected aspects of Anglo-Norman settlement in Ireland' in N. Stephens and R. Glasscock (ed.), *Irish geographical studies* (Belfast, 1970), p. 169.

Fig. 63 Based on Ordnance Survey, *Monastic Ireland* (second ed., Dublin, 1979) (Augustinians); P. Conlan, *Franciscan Ireland* (Dublin, 1988), pp 6, 20, 34 (Franciscans).

Fig. 67 Based on SMR.

Fig. 68 After A. Simms, 'Newcastle as a medieval settlement' in P. O'Sullivan (ed.), *Newcastle Lyons – a parish of the pale* (Dublin, 1986), p. 21.

Fig. 71 After R. Loeber, *The geography and practice of English colonisation in Ireland 1534-1609* (Athlone, 1991), map 6.

Fig. 72 J. Andrews, 'Plantation' in T. Barry (ed.), *Irish settlement history* (London, forthcoming).

The modern landscape: from plantation to present, pp. 67-103.

Fig. 1 By kind permission of the British Library.

Fig. 3 Based on an unpublished map by Jack Burtchaell utilising S. Pender (ed.) *A census of Ireland circa 1659* (Dublin 1939).

Fig. 4 O.S. one-inch map, county Louth, 1857.

Fig. 6 Manuscripts Dept., T.C.D. MS. 1209/82.

Fig. 7 'A mapp of sever. lands, tenements and denominations in the Barony of Foarth and county of Wexford being parte and parcell of the real estate of Henry Edwardes esq... 27 March AD 1729' by Jas Turner, Edwards papers, N.A.I.

Fig. 10 Van Keulenboech chart, c. 1708, N.L.I. (Colour Neg. 16095), 16/B/23/25.

Fig. 11 Thomas Dinely, 'Milking a Cow', N.L.I. MS. 392.

Fig. 12 David Dickson, An economic history of the Cork region in the eighteenth century, unpublished Ph.D. thesis (T.C.D. 1977), p. 319.

Fig. 13 C. Ó Gráda, *A new economic history of Ireland 1780-1939* (Oxford,1994), p. 37.

Fig. 15 C.U.C.A.P., BDT 58.

Fig. 16 Ó Gráda, *Economic History*, p. 38.

Fig. 17 Flour bounties: *Jnl of the Irish House of Commons*, 1760, appendix; Mills: *Jnl of the Irish House of Commons*, 1795, appendix; Malt: *Jnl of the Irish House of Commons*, 1797, appendix.

Fig. 19 Barony map of Kells, county Kilkenny *c.* 1817 by David Aher and Hill Clements, Kilkenny Historical and Archaeological Society, Kilkenny; J. Andrews, 'David Aher and Hill Clements' map of county Kilkenny 1812-24' in W. Nolan and K. Whelan (ed.), *Kilkenny. History and Society* (Dublin, 1990), pp. 437-63.

Fig. 20 Arthur Young, *A Tour of Ireland* (Dublin 1780).

Fig. 21 O.S. first edition, county Wexford, 1841, Sheet 4.

Fig. 22 'A map of the townland of Ballykealey in the county of Carlow 1787' by Francis Mathews, N.L.I., 15-B-6 (11).

Fig. 23 T. Jones Hughes, 'The large farm in nineteenth-century Ireland' in A. Gailey and D. Ó hÓgáin (ed.), *Gold under the furze* (Dublin 1992), pp 93-100.

Fig. 24 P.R.O.N.I., D 1462/2.

Fig. 25 P.R.O.N.I., T 1340.

Fig. 27 O.S. first edition, county Down, 1841, Sheet 27.

Fig. 28 W. McCutcheon, *The industrial archaeology of Northern Ireland* (Belfast, 1980), between pp 292-3; O.S. first edition, Donegal 1833-6, Leitrim 1836, Cavan 1835-6, Monaghan 1835 and Louth 1835.

Fig. 29 J. Andrews, 'Land and people c. 1780' in *A new history of Ireland*, iv (Oxford, 1986), p. 250; W. Crawford, *The handloom weavers and the Ulster linen industry* (Belfast, 1994), p. 5.

Fig. 30 'Spinning and reeling with the clock reel and boiling the yarn' by William Hincks, 1783. Ulster Folk and Transport Museum, TR 76/7.

Fig. 31 After D. McCourt, 'The dynamic quality of Irish rural settlement' in R. Buchanan, *Man and his habitat* (London, 1971), pp 126-64.

Fig. 32 J. Graham, 'Transhumance in Ireland' in *Advancement of Science,* xxxvii (1953), p. 75.

Fig. 34 O.S. first edition, county Mayo, 1838, sheet 24.

Fig. 36 Land Judge's map of Brockey, the estate of the trustees of William King (decd), [c.1890], in possession of F.H.A. Aalen.

Fig. 37 'The kelp gatherers' by Samuel Lover, c. 1830, Dept. of Irish Folklore, U.C.D.

Fig. 38 M. O Donnell, 'Settlement and society in the barony of East Inishowen, 1850' in W. Nolan, L. Ronayne and M. Dunleavy (ed.), *Donegal. History and Society*, (Dublin, 1995), p. 536.

Fig. 39 J. Andrews, 'The struggle for Ireland's public commons' in P. O' Flanagan, P. Ferguson and K. Whelan (ed.), *Rural Ireland 1600-1900* (Cork, 1987), p. 15.

Fig. 40 E. Evans, *Ireland and the Atlantic Heritage. Selected Writings*, (Dublin, 1996), p. 201.

Fig. 41 'The village of Dugort, Achill Island' in J. Howard, *The island of saints or Ireland in 1855* (London, 1855).

Fig. 42 O.S. first edition, county Kildare, 1838, sheet 9.

Fig. 43 A. Bourke, 'The visitation of God?' The potato and the Great Irish Famine (Dublin, 1993), p. 21.

Fig. 44 T. Freeman, *Pre-Famine Ireland*, (Manchester, 1957). Composite of regional maps pp 169, 177, 184, 212, 220, 226, 251, 255, 265, 277, 291, 297, 302.

Fig. 45 Ó Gráda, *Economic history* , p. 39.

Fig. 46 'The discovery of the potato blight in Ireland' by Daniel Mc Donald, 1847, Dept of Irish Folklore, U.C.D.

Fig. 47 *Seventh report of Relief Commissioners* (London, 1847), supplementary appendix.

Fig. 48 W. Smyth 'Landholding changes, kinship networks and class transformation in rural Ireland: a case study of county Tipperary' in *Ir. Geog*, xvi (1983), pp 16-35.

Fig. 49 Design for farm offices to be erected at Newstone, county Meath, by J. Symes, 1852, O.P.W papers, N.L.I. See R. Lohan, *Guide to the archives of the Office of Public Works* (Dublin, 1994), p. 251.

Fig. 50 Based on table in C. Ó Gráda, *Ireland before and after the Famine* (Manchester, 1988), p. 147.

Fig. 51 Lawrence Collection, N. L. I.

Fig. 52 (a) 1822: T. O' Neill, 'Clare and Irish poverty' in *Studia Hib.*, xiv (1974), pp 7-28; (b) 1848: C. Kinealy, *This great calamity. The Irish Famine 1845-52* (Dublin, 1994), p.176; (c) 1891: Relief of Distress Papers, Box 33, N.A.I.; (d) C.D.B., *A new history of Ireland*, vol. ix, p. 74.

Fig. 53 Photographic section, N.L.I.

Fig. 54 Land Judge's map of Clare Island, the estate of Isomena Mc Donnell [c.1895], Land Commission papers, N.A.I.; C.D.B. map of Clare Island, August 1897, N.L.I.

Fig. 55 C.U.C.A.P., ALN-78.

Fig. 56 O.S. first edition, county Mayo, 1838, sheet 99; second edition, 1893.

Fig. 57 Wynne photographic collection, N.L.I.

Fig. 59 M. Landers and K. Whelan, 'Golden. The evolution of a landscape and a community' in *Baile* (1979), pp 11-19.

Fig. 60 *Dublin Opinion,* October 1950, p. 110.

Fig. 61 *Dublin Opinion,* September 1949, p. 275.

Fig. 62 Asahi Chemical Industry (Ireland) Ltd., Killala, Ballina, county Mayo.

Fig. 63 Based on a map by J. Lee, An Foras Talúntais, *c.* 1980.

Fig. 64 Based on A. Horner, 'Dividing Ireland into geographical regions' in *Geographical Viewpoint*, xxi (1993), p. 11.

COMPONENTS OF THE IRISH LANDSCAPE

Photo: O.P.W. Clonmacnoise, county Offaly.

Bogs , pp 106-21.

Fig. 2 Based on Wildlife Service, O.P.W. 'Former and present extent of raised bogs' (Dublin,1989), and *Ireland peatland map*, National Soil Survey, An Foras Talúntais (Dublin, 1978).

Fig. 3 Estate map, Birr Castle, county Offaly.

Fig. 4 Commissioners for Bogs, Map Library, T.C.D.

Fig. 5 Geological Survey of Ireland, Ordnance Survey one-inch sheet 117 (Dublin, 1901).

Fig. 7 *Illustrated London News*, 28 September, 1850, p. 264. The Illustrated London News Picture Library, London.

The great bog of Ardee

Fig. A After F. Mitchell and B. Tuite, *The great bog of Ardee* (Dundalk, 1992), p. 20.

Fig. B Mitchell and Tuite, p. 28.

Fig. C Mitchell and Tuite, p. 27.

Fig. D Mitchell and Tuite, pp 74, 83-4

Fig. F Mitchell and Tuite, p. 30.

Fig. 25 O.S. aerial photograph, 10-4855 (I993).

Forests and Woodlands, pp 122-33.

Fig. 1 Manuscripts Dept., T.C.D., MS 1209(9).

Fig. 2 Based on O. Rackham, 'Ancient woodland and hedges in England' in S. Woodell (ed.), *The English Landscape* (Oxford, 1985), p. 75.

Fig. 3 Based on the Land Cover (Ireland) Programme database compiled by visual analysis of LANDSAT. The map is derived from the CORINE TM images of May 1989-90. The minimum unit size delimited is 25ha, so that small woodland patches which have survived in difficult terrain or those planted by landowners under woodland planting schemes are excluded. Use of reflectance data also excludes conifers newly planted on peatland. The saplings are too small to affect the overall reflectance of the site; rather, this results from the dominant vegetation cover between the saplings. New plantations therefore are not distinguishable from their peatland surroundings. Mixed woodlands are also difficult to map from satellite reflectance data; some may have been included in the broadleaved category and are therefore absent from the map, whereas others perhaps should have been included in the broadleaved woodland. The areas involved, however, are likely to be small.

Fig. 4 After Office of Public Works, *Killarney National Park* (1990).

Fig. 10 Based on Mary Kelly-Quinn, 'The evolution of forestry in county Wicklow from prehistory to present' in K. Hannigan and W. Nolan (ed.), *Wicklow. History and society* (Dublin, 1994), pp 848, 850.

Fig. 12 After Forest Ecosystem Research Group, U.C.D.

Fields, pp 134-44.

Fig. 2 After *Atlas of Ireland* (Dublin, 1979), p. 47.

Fig. 3 O.S. aerial photo, OS8-9287.

Fig. 5 'A topographical lineament of all such enclosed lands as are holden by Henry Pyne esq. from the Right Honourable Sir Walte Raley' [by John White?], 1598, N.L.I. MS 22,028.

Fig. 6 Based on M. Herity, 'A survey of the royal site of Cruachain in Connacht' in *R.S.A.I. Jn.,* cxviii (1988), pp 70-71.

Fig. 7 After J. O' Loan, 'Land reclamation in Drom-iskin, county Louth' in *Dept. of Agriculture Jnl.*, liv (1957-8), p. 7.

Fig. 8 After *Atlas of Ireland*, p. 46. The distribution of field patterns is based on a map in Pierre Flatrès' *Géographie rurale de quatre contrées celtiques. Irelande, Galles, Cornwall and Man* (Rennes, 1957), with minor revision by F. Aalen.

Fig. 9 'A map of the several parcels of land in and about the town of Clondalkin surveyed in February 1702 and July 1703 by Peter Duff and traced out September 1746 by Roger Kendrick', Roger Caldwell collection, EC2553, Box 3782, Land Commission papers, N.A.I.

Fig. 10 After J. Andrews, 'The struggle for Ireland's public commons' in P. O' Flanagan, P. Ferguson and K. Whelan (ed.), *Rural Ireland 1600-1900* (Cork, 1987), p. 12.

Fig. 11 O.S. first edition, county Kildare, 1837-38, sheet 32.

Fig. 14 After M. Punch, People and landscape in south-east Clare, unpublished BA thesis (T.C.D, 1993), pp 64-9.

Fig. 16 Based on P. Robinson, 'The spread of hedged enclosures in Ulster' in *Ulster Folklife*, xxiii (1977), p. 65.

Fig. 17 After E. Currie, 'Field patterns in county Derry' in *Ulster Folklife*, xxix (1983), pp 70-80.

Fig. 18 After Robinson, 'Hedged enclosures', pp 61, 63.

Buildings, pp 145-79.

Fig. 2 Based on P. Smith 'Architectural personality of the British Isles' in *Archaeologia Cambrensis*, cxxix (1980), pp 20-21, and F. Aalen 'The vernacular architecture of the British Isles' in *Yearbook,* Association of Pacific Coast Geographers (1973), p. 28.

Fig. 6 Based on F. Aalen, 'The house types of Gola Island, county Donegal' in *Folklife*, viii (1970), pp 32-45.

Fig. 10 Based on G. Meirion-Jones, 'The bed-outshot in Brittany' in *Ulster Folklife*, xxv (1979), p. 31.

Figs. 12/13 Based on K. Danaher in *Atlas of Ireland* (Dublin, 1979), p. 91 and 'The combined byre and dwelling in Ireland' in *Folklife*, ii (1964), pp 58-75.

Fig. 15 After K. Danaher, 'Traditional forms of the dwelling house in Ireland' in *R.S.A.I. Jn.*, cii, 1 (1972), p. 87.

Fig. 17 Based on D. McCourt, 'Innovation diffusion in Ireland: an historical case study' in *R.I.A. Proc.*, cxxiii, (1973), C, p.11, and A. Gailey, *Rural houses of the north of Ireland* (Edinburgh, 1984), p.182.

Fig. 19 Based on P. Robinson, 'Vernacular housing in Ulster in the seventeenth century' in *Ulster Folklife*, xxv (1979), p.15, and A. Gailey, 'The housing of the rural poor in nineteenth-century Ulster' in *Ulster Folklife*, xxii (1976), p. 46.

Fig. 20 After Gailey, *Rural houses of the north of Ireland*, p. 73.

Fig. 21 Based on unpublished material collected by Michael Higginbotham for the O.P.W.

Fig. 24 Based on K. Danaher, 'Materials and methods in Irish traditional buildings' in *R.S.A.I. Jn.*, lxxxvii (1957), pp 61-74 and 'Some distribution patterns in Irish folk life' in *Bealoideas*, xxv (1957), p.115.

Fig. 35 Reconstruction by C. O Fearghail and K. Whelan, watercoloured by Sabhdh McElveen.

Fig. 40 Based on F. Aalen, 'Public housing in Ireland, 1880-1921' in *Planning Perspective*, ii (1987), pp 178, 180, 183; 'The rehousing of rural labourers in Ireland under the Labourers' (Ireland) Acts, 1883-1919' in *Jnl. of Historical Geography*, xii (1986), p. 301, and 'Homes for Irish heroes' in *Town Planning Review*, lix (1988), pp 305-23.

Fig. 46 Based on K. Danaher, 'Irish farmyard types' in *Studia Ethnographia Upsaliensia*, xi (1956), pp 6-15, and 'Farmyard forms and their distribution in Ireland' in *Ulster Folklife*, xxvii (1981), pp 65, 67, 69, 71.

Fig. 47 After N. McCullough and V. Mulvin, *A lost tradition* (Dublin, 1987), p. 71, and Danaher, 'Farmyard forms' (1981) pp 65, 67, 73.

Fig. 52 After F. Aalen, 'Clochans as transhumance dwellings in the Dingle peninsula, county Kerry' in *R.S.A.I. Jn.*, xciv, 1 (1964), p. 42.

Fig. 53 H. Case *et al.* 'Land use in Goodland town-land, county Antrim, from neolithic times until today' *R.S.A.I. Jn.* xcix, 1 (1969), p. 41.

Fig. 55 From *Ireland painted by Francis Walker and described by Frank Mathew* (London, 1905).

Towns and Villages, pp 180-96.

Fig. 2 [Inset map of Wexford *c.* 1660], N.L.I.

Fig. 3 After J. Bradley, 'The early development of the medieval town of Kilkenny' in W. Nolan and K. Whelan (ed.), *Kilkenny. History and society* (Dublin, 1990), p. 69.

Fig. 4 By kind permission of the British Library. Part of collection entitled 'The state of Fortes in Ireland as they were in the yeare 1624', Add. MS. 24200.

Fig. 5 After A. Simms, 'Continuity and change: settlement and society in medieval Ireland *c.* 500 - 1500' in W. Nolan (ed.), *The shaping of Ireland* (Cork, 1986), p. 56.

Fig. 6 From A. Thomas, *The walled towns of Ireland* (Dublin, 1992), i, p.182.

Fig. 7 Unpublished map by J. Andrews, based on a conflated version of Robert Lythe's map of Ireland 1569.

Fig. 12 W. Smyth, 'Society and settlement in seventeenth-century Ireland' in W. Smyth and K. Whelan (ed.), *Common ground* (Cork, 1987), p. 78.

Fig. 13 Thomas Dinely *c.* 1680, 'A town in Ireland', N.L.I. MS 392. Coloured by Sadhbh McElveen.

Fig. 17 A plan of Dromana, the seat of the Right Honourable John, Earl of Grandison. By Henry Jones, 31 July 1754. Irish Architectural Archive 94/73.

Fig. 18 A detail from painting of Stradbally, *c.* 1740. Private Collection.

Fig. 19 O.S. first edition, county Tyrone, 1834, sheet 62.

Fig. 20 Based on A. Horner, in F. Aalen, E. Colhoun, D. Gillmor and A. Horner (ed.), *County Kildare. A geographical background for planning* (Dublin, 1970), ii, pp 45-54.

Fig. 21 O.S. first edition, county Carlow, 1839, sheet 12.

Fig. 22 O.S. first edition, county Kerry, 1841, sheet 93.

Fig. 23 O.S. first edition, county Clare, 1840, sheet 30.

Fig. 24 Unpublished map by P. Ferguson, based on O.S. first edition, county Wicklow, 1838-39, sheet 15, and on *Griffith's Valuation*, 1850.

Fig. 25 National Gallery of Ireland.

Fig. 26 O.S. second edition, county Antrim, revised 1903-16, sheet 20.

Fig. 27 Based on *Census of Ireland*, 1841.

Fig. 30 Unpublished map by W. Smyth. (Cartography by Michael Murphy, Dept of Geography, University College, Cork); chapel villages by K. Whelan, A geography of society and culture in Ireland since 1800, unpublished PhD thesis, National University of Ireland, 1980.

Fig. 31 Map of ecclesiastical property in Thurles, parochial house, Thurles, county Tipperary.

Demesnes, pp 197-205.

Fig. 2 Based on first edition O.S. maps.

Fig. 3 Based on first edition O.S. maps; decoy pipe as illustrated by R. Payne-Gallwey, *The wild fowler in Ireland* (1882).

Fig. 4 Johann Van der Hagen's view of Carton *c.* 1730. Private collection.

Fig. 5 Based on first edition O.S. maps.

Fig. 6 Drawing by Stephen Conlin/National Trust (NI). Coloured by Sadhbh McElveen.

Fig. 7 'A survey of Tollymore Park in the county of Down, the seat of the Right Hon-ble James, Earl of Clanbrasill' by Bernard Scale, 1777. Private collection.

Fig. 8 Based on first edition O.S. maps.

Fig. 9 From H. Steuart, *The planter's guide* (Edinburgh, 1828).

Fig. 10 Based on first edition O.S. maps. Examples of buildings from J. Howley, *The follies and garden buildings of Ireland* (New Haven and London, 1993), pp 17, 20, 28, 35, 41, 46, 59, 102, 109, 121, 133, 142, 172, 186, 211.

Fig. 11 J. Longfield, 'A book of maps of the estates of Henry Baron Mount Sandford in the county of Roscommon' 1826, National Famine Museum, Strokestown, county Roscommon.

Communications, pp 206-19.

Fig. 1 Ulster Museum.

Fig. 2 O.S. 1:63,360 (one inch to one mile), 1904, sheet 119.

Fig. 3 O.S. 1:63,360, 1904, sheet 88.

Fig. 4 O.S. 1:63,360, 1902, sheet 100.

Fig. 5 Redrawn from: K. Barbour, 'Rural road lengths and farm-market distances in north-east Ulster', *Geografiska Annaler*, lix B, (1977), p. 16; O.S. 1:126,720 (one-half inch to one mile), sheet 23.

Fig. 6 Redrawn from J. Andrews, 'Road planning in Ireland before the railway age', *Ir.Geog.*, v, (1964), p. 23.

Fig. 8 P. Kerrigan, *Castles and Fortifications in Ireland 1485-1985* (Cork, 1995), p. 155.

Fig. 9 Reproduced in P. O'Keeffe and T. Simmington, *Irish stone bridges. History and heritage* (Dublin,1991), p. 253.

Fig. 10 George Taylor and Andrew Skinner, *Maps of the roads of Ireland* (Dublin,1778).

Fig. 11a) Redrawn from Andrews, 'Road planning in Ireland', p. 28.

Fig. 11b) Redrawn from T. Moody, F. Martin and F. Byrne (ed.), *A new history of Ireland*, ix (Oxford, 1984), p. 75.

Fig. 12 Redrawn from V. Delany and D. Delany, *The canals of the south of Ireland* (Newton Abbot, 1966), p. 12.

Fig. 13 O.S. first edition, county Kildare, 1838, sheet 13.

Fig. 16 *Atlas to accompany the second report of the Railway Commissioners* (London, 1838).

Fig. 18 Redrawn from O.Doyle and S. Hirsch, *Railways in Ireland 1834-1984* (Dublin, 1983), pp 28, 90-91, 107.

Fig. 19 Reproduced in Doyle and Hirsch, *Railways in Ireland*, pp 90-91.

Fig. 20 From a tour book on Ireland published in 1907.

Fig. 21 N. Spinks, *Ir. Railway Rec. Soc. Jn.*, xviii (1993), p. 81.

Fig. 23 Source: *A.B.C. World Airways Guide*, (Dunstable, 1994).

Fig. 25 Based on *Proposal for a Council of Europe Parliament decision on Community guidelines for the development of the Trans-European Transport Network* (Luxembourg, 1994).

Mining, power and water, pp 220-33.

Fig. 1 'Night's candles are burnt out' by Sean Keating, commissioned by the Electricity Supply Board. Courtesy of Oldham Art Gallery.

Fig. 2 Based on G. Cole, *Memoir of the Geological Survey of Ireland*, (Dublin, 1922), endpapers.

Fig. 3 After map of 'Mineral Deposits of Ireland', CSA Computing and Geological Survey(Dublin, 1994).

Fig. 4 After W. Nolan, *Fassadinin. Land, settlement and society in south-east Ireland 1600-1850* (Dublin, 1979), p.119.

Fig. 6 M. Conry, *Culm crushers and grinding stones in the Barrow valley and Castlecomer plateau* (Kilkenny, 1990).

Fig. 7 After D. Tietzsch-Tyler, *Building stones of St Canice's Cathedral, Kilkenny* (Dublin, 1994).

Fig. 8 Based on Geological Survey, *Directory of active quarries, pits and mines in Ireland* (Dublin, 1994).

Fig. 11 Based on O.S. first edition maps, 1830s and 1840s.

Fig. 15 Based on data from Electricity Supply Board and Northern Ireland Electricity Service.

Fig. 18 Based on O.S. first edition, county Kilkenny, 1842.

Fig. 19 After T. Freeman, *Pre-Famine Ireland* (Manchester, 1957), p. 166.

Fig. 24 Based on data provided by ESB and NIES.

CHALLENGE OF CHANGE
Photo: Michael Diggin. Fieldscape in county Louth.

Contemporary challenge pp 236-54.
Fig. 2   After A. Fenton and D. Gillmor (ed.), *Rural land use on the Atlantic periphery* (Dublin, 1994), p. 60.
Fig. 3   Based on A. Horner, 'Dividing Ireland into geographical regions' in *Geographical Viewpoint*, xxi (1993), p. 11.
Fig. 4   Unpublished map by A. Horner.
Fig. 5   After H. Mentink, 'Long-term developments in European agriculture and their visual impact on the landscape' in *Landscape and urban planning*, xviii (1990), p. 205.
   Recent housing change in Kilclone, county Meath
   Fig. E   Drawn on O.S. black and white 1:63,360 (one inch to one mile) map.
Fig. 25   After E. Kennedy, The effect of government policy and support on field boundaries in the agricultural landscape: A case study. PhD Thesis, University of Ulster, Coleraine, 1995.
   The destruction of antiquities
   Fig. E   O.S., county Kerry, 1841, sheet 52.
   Fig. F   C.U.C.A.P., AJW-67.
   Fig. H   C.U.C.A.P., AJW-70.

Management of the landscape, pp 255-259.
Fig. 2   Compiled by Üte Bohnsack; information on NHAs provided by O.P.W. New sites and changing designations create a fluid, complicated situation.

REGIONAL CASE STUDIES
Photo: Liam Lyons. Croagh Patrick, county Mayo.

The Hook, county Wexford, pp 262-276.
Fig. 9   Hook Head 1690, by kind permission of the British Library, K.TOP.LV.43.
Fig. 12   Manuscripts Dept., T.C.D., MS 1209/64.
Lecale, county Down, pp 277-86.
Fig. 10   Manor of Down, By kind permission of the British Library, Map 11710 (1).
Fig. 15   O.S., county Down, 1834, sheets 44/45.
Fig. 16   O.S., county Down, 1834. sheets 44/45.

The Burren, county Clare, pp 287-298.
Fig. 2   Based on an unpublished map by Barbara Yeates.
Fig. 6   After R. Moles and I. Travers, and O.P.W., 1981.
Fig. 7   Based J. O'Connell and A. Korff (ed.) *The book of the Burren* (Galway, 1991), pp 65, 79, 114, 125.
Fig. 9   After C. Grant, in *Archaeology Ireland*, ix (1995), p. 31.
Fig. 10   Unpublished map by F. Aalen, based on aerial photos and field work.
Fig. 18   After D. Drew and E. Magee, 'Environmental implications of land reclamation in the Burren' in *Ir. Geog.*, xxvii (1994), p. 86.
Fig. 20   Drew and Magee (1994), p. 87.

The Bend of the Boyne, county Meath, p. 299-315.
Fig. 1   O. S., composite aerial photograph.
Fig. 4   Digital terrain model produced by Gearóid Ó Riain using Arc-Info software and hand coloured by Sadhbh McElveen. Vertical scale greatly exaggerated.
Fig. 6   After G. Cooney, 'Irish Neolithic landscapes and land use systems: the implications of field systems' in *Rural History*, ii (1991), p. 131.
Fig. 11   Based partially on E. Hickey, 'The house of Cleítech' in *Ríocht na Midhe*, iii (1965), pp 181-5.
Fig. 23   Based on *Griffith's valuation for county Meath*, 1850.
Fig. 25   Based on *Griffith's valuation*. House illustra-

tions by F. Aalen.
Fig. 26   Based on *Griffith's valuation*. Map extract from O.S. third edition sheet 19.
Fig. 31   M. Lyons, *Illustated encumbered estates: Ireland 1850-1905* (Whitegate, Clare, 1993), p. 168.
Fig. 34   After G. Stout, 'Grant-aided change in the Boyne Valley Archaeological Park: agricultural grants 1950-1990' in *Ir. Geog.*, xxvi (1993), p. 85.
Fig. 35   O. S., aerial photograph 8-1078 (1991).

The Ring of Gullion, county Armagh, pp 316-28.
Fig. 2   Based on DOENI, *Ring of Gullion area of outstanding natural beauty – Guide to designation* (Belfast, 1991), p. 7.
Fig. 3   Based on H. Wilson, *Regional Geology of Northern Ireland* (HMSO, Belfast,1972), pp 68-70.
Fig. 4   Based on *Igneous Case Study* (Open University, 1976), p. 8.
Fig. 10   Based on SMR.
Fig. 17   Based on a redrawing by J. Andrews of J. Barthelet's map in *Ulster and other Irish maps, c. 1600* (Dublin, 1964), p.
Fig. 18   O.S. first edition, county Armagh, 1835.
Fig. 25   DOENI, *Ring of Gullion*, p. 13.

Connemara, county Galway, pp 331-44.
Fig. 5   Based on A. Orme, 'Drumlins and the Weich-sel glaciation of Connemara' in *Ir. Geog.* v (1967), p. 265.
Fig. 6   After M. O'Connell, *Connemara vegetation and land use since the last ice-age* (Dublin, 1994), pp 18-19.
Fig. 16   After J. Graham, 'Rural society in Connacht 1600-1640' in N. Stephens and R. Glasscock (ed.) *Irish geographical studies* (Belfast, 1970), p. 197.
Fig. 17   T. Robinson, *Connemara, a one-inch map, Pt 2* (Roundstone: Folding Landscapes, 1990).
Fig. 24   O.S., county Galway, first and second editions, sheet 90.

PLACENAME INDEX